Developments in Intelligent Agent Technologies and Multi-Agent Systems:
Concepts and Applications

Goran Trajkovski
Algoco eLearning Consulting, USA & Virginia International University, USA

INFORMATION SCIENCE REFERENCE
Hershey · New York

Director of Editorial Content: Kristin Klinger
Director of Book Publications: Julia Mosemann
Acquisitions Editor: Lindsay Johnston
Development Editor: Myla Harty
Publishing Assistant: Julia Mosemann & Keith Glazewski
Typesetter: Keith Glazewski
Production Editor: Jamie Snavely
Cover Design: Lisa Tosheff

Published in the United States of America by
      Information Science Reference (an imprint of IGI Global)
      701 E. Chocolate Avenue
      Hershey PA 17033
      Tel: 717-533-8845
      Fax: 717-533-8661
      E-mail: cust@igi-global.com
      Web site: http://www.igi-global.com

Copyright © 2011 by IGI Global. All rights reserved. No part of this publication may be reproduced, stored or distributed in any form or by any means, electronic or mechanical, including photocopying, without written permission from the publisher. Product or company names used in this set are for identification purposes only. Inclusion of the names of the products or companies does not indicate a claim of ownership by IGI Global of the trademark or registered trademark.

Library of Congress Cataloging-in-Publication Data

Developments in intelligent agent technologies and multi-agent systems :
concepts and applications / Goran Trajkovski, editor.
      p. cm.
  Includes bibliographical references and index.
  Summary: "This book discusses research on emerging technologies and systems
based on agent and multi-agent paradigms across various fields of science,
engineering and technology, offering a collection that covers conceptual
frameworks, case studies, and analysis"-- Provided by publisher.
  ISBN 978-1-60960-171-3 (hardcover) -- ISBN 978-1-60960-173-7 (ebook) 1.
Intelligent agents (Computer software) 2. Multiagent systems. I. Trajkovski,
Goran, 1972-
  QA76.76.I58D48 2011
  006.3--dc22
                        2010045847

British Cataloguing in Publication Data
A Cataloguing in Publication record for this book is available from the British Library.

All work contributed to this book is new, previously-unpublished material. The views expressed in this book are those of the authors, but not necessarily of the publisher.

Table of Contents

Section 1
Concepts and Challenges

Section 2
Emergencies

Detailed Table of Contents

Section 1
Concepts and Challenges

Chapter 1

Gus Koehler, University of Southern California, USA

Agent-based computer simulations use agents on landscapes to investigate epidemics, social phenomena, decision making, supply networks, the behavior of biological systems, and physical and chemical processes, among other things. This essay examines how agents and landscapes are oriented in time and this orientation's relevance to observing and interpreting findings. I argue that the proposed temporal deepening of how simulations are constructed involving interaction of multiple temporalities (itself a kind of temporality) could lead to the unexpected triggering of cascades of secondary emergences. Such cascades may already be there but going unobserved. Buddhist cosmology is briefly used as a contrast with current simulation temporal orientations to illuminate key points. Katherine Hayles's work on media, my theoretical work on time-ecologies and heterochrony, and J. T. Fraser's theory of the nested hierarchy of time and associated causalities are used to explore these issues.

Chapter 2

Adam J. Conover, Towson University, USA
Robert J. Hammell, Towson University, USA

This work reflects the results of continuing research into "temporally autonomous" multi-agent interaction. Many traditional approaches to modeling multi-agent systems involve synchronizing all agent activity in simulated environments to a single "universal" clock. In other words, agent behavior is regulated by a global timer where all agents act and interact deterministically in time. However, if the objective of any such simulation is to model the behavior of real-world entities, this discrete timing mechanism yields an artificially constrained representation of actual physical agent interaction. In addition to the behavioral autonomy normally associated with agents, simulated agents must also have temporal autonomy in order to interact realistically. Intercommunication should occur without global coordination or synchronization. To this end, a specialized simulation framework is developed. Several simulations are conducted from which data are gathered and we subsequently demonstrate that manipulation of the timing variable amongst interacting agents affects the emergent behaviors of agent populations.

Gergely Palla, Hungarian Academy of Sciences, Hungary
Tamás Vicsek, Hungarian Academy of Sciences, Hungary & Eötvös University, Hungary

Our focus is on the general statistical features of the time evolution of communities (also called as modules, clusters or cohesive groups) in large social networks. These structural sub-units can correspond to highly connected circles of friends, families, or professional cliques, which are subject to constant change due to the intense fluctuations in the activity and communication patterns of people. The communities can grow by recruiting new members, or contract by loosing members; two (or more) groups may merge into a single community, while a large enough social group can split into several smaller ones; new communities are born and old ones may disappear. According to our results, the time evolution of social groups containing only a few members and larger communities, e.g., institutions show significant differences.

António Jorge Filipe Fonseca, ISCTE, Portugal

Several informational complexity measures rely on the notion of stochastic process in order to extract hidden structural properties behind the apparent randomness of information sources. Following an equivalence approach between dynamic relation evolution within a social network and a generic stochastic process two dynamic measures of network complexity are proposed.

Filippo Passerini, Humboldt-University, Germany
Simone Severini, University College London, UK

We introduce a novel entropic notion with the purpose of quantifying disorder/uncertainty in networks. This is based on the Laplacian and it is exactly the von Neumann entropy of certain quantum mechanical states. It is remarkable that the von Neumann entropy depends on spectral properties and it can be computed efficiently. The analytical results described here and the numerical computations lead us to conclude that the von Neumann entropy increases under edge addition, increases with the regularity properties of the network and with the number of its connected components. The notion opens the perspective of a wide interface between quantum information theory and the study of complex networks at the statistical level.

Section 2
Emergencies

Chapter 6

Stéphane Airiau, University of Amsterdam, The Netherlands
Lin Padgham, RMIT University, Australia
Sebastian Sardina, RMIT University, Australia
Sandip Sen, University of Tulsa, USA

Belief, Desire, and Intentions (BDI) agents are well suited for complex applications with (soft) real-time reasoning and control requirements. BDI agents are adaptive in the sense that they can quickly reason and react to asynchronous events and act accordingly. However, BDI agents lack learning capabilities to modify their behavior when failures occur frequently. We discuss the use of past experience to improve the agent's behavior. More precisely, we use past experience to improve the context conditions of the plans contained in the plan library, initially set by a BDI programmer. First, we consider a deterministic and fully observable environment and we discuss how to modify the BDI agent to prevent re-occurrence of failures, which is not a trivial task. Then, we discuss how we can use decision trees to improve the agent's behavior in a non-deterministic environment.

Chapter 7

Marek Grzes, University of Waterloo, Canada
Daniel Kudenko, University of York, UK

A crucial trade-off is involved in the design process when function approximation is used in reinforcement learning. Ideally the chosen representation should allow representing as closely as possible an approximation of the value function. However, the more expressive the representation the more training data is needed because the space of candidate hypotheses is larger. A less expressive representation has a smaller hypotheses space and a good candidate can be found faster. The core idea of this chapter is the use of a mixed resolution function approximation, that is, the use of a less expressive function approximation to provide useful guidance during learning, and the use of a more expressive function approximation to obtain a final result of high quality. A major question is how to combine the two representations. Two approaches are proposed and evaluated empirically: the use of two resolutions in one function approximation, and a more sophisticated algorithm with the application of reward shaping.

Chapter 8

Andrea Kulakov, University of Sts Cyril and Methodius, Macedonia
Joona Laukkanen, The American University of Paris, France
Blerim Mustafa, University of Sts Cyril and Methodius, Macedonia
Georgi Stojanov, The American University of Paris, France

Open-ended learning is regarded as the ultimate milestone, especially in intelligent robotics. Preferably it should be unsupervised and it is by its nature inductive. In this chapter we want to give an overview of attempts to use Inductive Logic Programming (ILP) as a machine learning technique in the context of embodied autonomous agents. Relatively few such attempts exist altogether and the main goal in reviewing several of them was to find a thorough understanding of the difficulties that the application of ILP has in general and especially in this area. The second goal was to review any possible directions for overcoming these obstacles standing on the way of more widespread use of ILP in this context of embodied autonomous agents. Whilst the most serious problems, the mismatch between ILP and the large datasets encountered with embodied autonomous agents seem difficult to overcome we also found interesting research actively pursuing to alleviate these problems.

Chapter 9

    Goran Trajkovski, Algoco eLearning Consulting, USA
    Georgi Stojanov, The American University in Paris, France
    Samuel Collins, Towson University, USA
    Vladimir Eidelman, Columbia University, USA
    Chris Harman, Swarthmore College, USA
    Giovanni Vincenti, Gruppo Vincenti, S.r.l., Italy

Fuzzy algebraic structures are a useful and flexible tool for modeling cognitive agents and their societies. In this chapter we propose a fuzzy algebraic framework where the valuating sets are other than the unit interval (lattices, partially ordered sets or relational structures) . This provides for a flexible organization of the information gathered by the agent (via interactions with the environment and/or other agents) and enables its selected use when different drives are active. Agents (Petitagé, ANNA, POPSICLE and Izbushka) , which are instantiations of our model, are also given in order to illustrate the use of this framework, as well as its possible extensions.

Chapter 10

    James Braman, Towson University, USA

Designing computer interfaces and other technologies that interact with users in adaptive ways that attempt to emulate their natural styles of learning is generally difficult. As technology has become common in our daily interactions, adaptive interfaces are key in helping users in many situations. In this chapter the preliminary investigation with the intelligent agent Izbuhska is discussed, along with how it can be used to collect various data from users in an attempt to understand how they perceive the program and "learn" while interacting. Izbushka as a tool will help to generate new ways of understanding and conceptualizing interaction by presenting users with a "zero-context" environment. Izbushka presents users with a unique interface in an attempt to study user interactions that lack traditional metaphors or ontological grounding typical in many computer interfaces. The Izbushka agent is our first step towards filtering our preconceived metaphorical ideas in order to generate new understanding of human-computer interaction.

Chapter 11

Partha Mukherjee, University of Tulsa, USA
Sandip Sen, University of Tulsa, USA
Stéphane Airiau, University of Amsterdam, The Netherlands

Effective norms can significantly enhance performance of individual agents and agent societies. Previous researches have studied social learning of self-enforcing behavioral norms from interaction experiences. In this model, individual agents repeatedly interact with other agents in the society over instances of a given scenario. Each interaction is framed as a stage game. An agent learns its policy to play the game over repeated interactions with multiple agents. We term this mode of learning social learning, which is distinct from an agent learning from repeated interactions against the same player. We are particularly interested in situations where multiple action combinations yield the same optimal payoff. The key research question is to find out if the entire population learns to converge to a consistent norm. While previous research assume agents have no prior biases to any of its actions, in real-life agents may have pre-formed biases or preferences which may hinder or even preclude norm emergence. We study the success and speed of norm emergence when different subsets of the population have different initial biases. In particular we characterize the relative speed of norm emergence under varying biases and the success of majority/minority groups in enforcing their biases on the rest of the population given different bias strengths

Chapter 12

Christopher Goldspink, Incept Labs, Australia

This chapter documents the findings of research into the governance mechanisms within the distributed on-line community known as Wikipedia. It focuses in particular on the role of normative mechanisms in achieving social self-regulation. A brief history of the Wikipedia is provided. This concentrates on the debate about governance and also considers characteristics of the wiki technology which can be expected to influence governance processes. The empirical findings are then presented. These focus on how Wikipedians use linguistic cues to influence one another on a sample of discussion pages drawn from both controversial and featured articles. Through this analysis a tentative account is provided of the agent-level cognitive mechanisms which appear necessary to explain the apparent behavioural coordination. The findings are to be used as a foundation for the simulation of 'normative' behaviour. The account identifies some of the challenges that need to be addressed in such an attempt including a mismatch between the case findings and assumptions used in past attempts to simulate normative behaviour.

Section 3
Applications

Chapter 13

Ying Guo, CSIRO ICT Centre, Australia
Rongxin Li, CSIRO ICT Centre, Australia

In order to cope with the unpredictability of the energy market and provide rapid response when supply is strained by demand, an emerging technology, called energy demand management, enables appliances to manage and defer their electricity consumption when price soars. Initial experiments with our multi-agent, power load management simulator, showed a marked reduction in energy consumption when price-based constraints were imposed on the system. However, these results also revealed an unforeseen, negative effect: that reducing consumption for a bounded time interval decreases system stability. The reason is that price-driven control synchronizes the energy consumption of individual agents. Hence price, alone, is an insufficient measure to define global goals in a power load management system. In this chapter we explore the effectiveness of a multi-objective, system-level goal which combines both price and system stability. We apply the commonly known reinforcement learning framework, enabling the energy distribution system to be both cost saving and stable. We test the robustness of our algorithm by applying it to two separate systems, one with indirect feedback and one with direct feedback from local load agents. Results show that our method is not only adaptive to multiple systems, but is also able to find the optimal balance between both system stability and energy cost.

Chapter 14

With this chapter we intend to demonstrate the potential practical use of intelligent agents as autonomous financial traders. We propose an architecture to be utilized in the creation of this type of agents, consisting of an ensemble of classification and regression models, a case-based reasoning system and an expert system. This architecture was used to implement six intelligent agents, each being responsible for trading one of the following currency pairs with a 6-hour timeframe: CHF/JPY, EUR/CHF, EUR/JPY, EUR/USD, USD/CHF and USD/JPY. These agents simulated trades during an out-of-sample period going from February of 2007 till July of 2010, having all achieved an acceptable performance. However, their strategies resulted in relatively high drawdowns, and much of their profit disappeared once the trading costs were factored into the trading simulation. In order to overcome these problems, we integrated the agents in a multi-agent system, in which agents communicate their decisions to each other before sending the market orders, and work together to eliminate redundant trades. This system averaged out the returns of the agents, thus eliminating much of the risk associated with their individual trading strategies, and also originated considerable savings in trading expenses. Our results seem to vindicate the usefulness of the proposed trading agent architecture, and also demonstrate that there is indeed a place for intelligent agents in financial markets.

The chapter presents an empirically oriented investigation on the dynamics of a specific case of a multi-agents system, the stock market. It demonstrates that S&P500 market space can be described using the geometrical and topological characteristics of its dynamics. The authors proposed to measure the coefficient R, an index providing information on the evolution of a manifold describing the dynamics of the market. It indicates the moments of perturbations, proving that the dynamics is driven by shocks and by a structural change. This dynamics has a characteristic dimension, which also allows for a description of its evolution. The consequent description of the market as a network of stocks is useful for the identification of patterns that emerge from multi-agent interaction, and defines our research, as it is derived from a system of measure and it is part of the logic of a defined mathematics.

While real world economies may be shaky, economies in virtual worlds keep growing as sites such as Second Life become more and more mainstream. Research firm Gartner Media estimates that by 2011, 80% of internet users worldwide will be using Second Life (Gartner, 2007). This growing popularity has real world financial implications. On a typical day, Second Life members spend close to $1.5 million on virtual items and virtual real estate transactions (Alter, 2008), and some residents generate six-figure incomes in real world dollars (Hemp, 2006). Second Life is still in an early stage of development, and there are many financial and legal regulatory issues to be resolved. But with these challenges come opportunities; Second Life may be the impetus for a new accounting platform that may bring different practices together and provide new growth opportunities that financial communities have been looking for in the virtual world.

In this article, a study on informal communication network formation in a university environment is presented. The teacher communication network is analyzed through community detection techniques. It is evident that informal communication is an important process that traverses the vertical hierarchical structure of departments and courses in a university environment. A multi-agent model of the case study is presented here, showing the implications of using real data as training sets for multi-agent-based simulations. The influence of the "social neighborhood," as a mechanism to create assortative networks of contacts without full knowledge of the network, is discussed. It is shown that the radius of this social neighborhood has an effect on the outcome of the network structure and that in a university's case this distance is relatively small.

This qualitative case study investigated how the integration of a Problem-Based Learning (PBL) curriculum in an online MBA program impacted the learner experience. The learner experience included three stances as created by Savin-Baden (2000). The stances were personal, pedagogical and interactional. The overarching theme was to examine the experiences of eight learners all in different BPL courses and at different stages in an online MBA program (the beginning, the middle and at the end of the program). The primary research question was: How does problem-based learning (PBL) in online MBA courses impact the learner experience? Purposeful sampling, specifically multiple variation sampling was chosen. The data was collected in accordance with Yin's (2003) five key components derived from documentation, archival records and interviews. The variety of data collection methods served to triangulate sources corroborating findings and offsetting the pitfalls of any one given method. Data analysis consisted of the constant comparison method using NVivo7 as the primary data management tool. Key findings correlated with the Savin-Baden (2000) study revealing how the stances were interdependent upon one another

Chapter 19

Towards Learning 'Self' and Emotional Knowledge in Social and Cultural Human-Agent

Wan Ching Ho, University of Hertfordshire, UK
Kerstin Dautenhahn, University of Hertfordshire, UK
Meiyii Lim, Heriot-Watt University, UK
Sibylle Enz, Otto-Friedrich-Universitaet Bamberg, Germany
Carsten Zoll, Otto-Friedrich-Universitaet Bamberg, Germany
Scott Watson, University of Hertfordshire, UK

This chapter presents research towards the development of a virtual learning environment (VLE) inhabited by intelligent virtual agents (IVAs) and modelling a scenario of inter-cultural interactions. The ultimate aim of this VLE is to allow users to reflect upon and learn about intercultural communication and collaboration. Rather than predefining the interactions among the virtual agents and scripting the possible interactions afforded by this environment, the authors pursue a bottom-up approach whereby inter-cultural communication emerges from interactions with and among autonomous agents. The intelligent virtual agents that are inhabiting this environment are expected to be able to broaden their knowledge about the world and other agents, which may be of different cultural backgrounds, through interactions. This work is part of a collaborative effort within a European research project called eCIR-CUS. Specifically, this chapter focuses on our continuing research concerned with emotional knowledge learning in autobiographic social agents. For the background section of this chapter, we introduce how humans represent emotional concepts in semantic memory and why empathy is essential in the learning process. In the main body of the chapter, the authors discuss how autobiographic memory can facilitate agents' cultural learning. Finally, as the first step towards this goal, they illustrate key modules in the agent architecture and specify the "minimum requirements" for the inclusion of computational autobiographic memory in the design of an agent architecture. In a psychologically inspired view, these requirements can allow emotional knowledge to emerge from agents' social and empathic interactions.

Preface

This book is a compilation of the articles published in the four issues of the first volume of the *International Journal of Agent Technologies and Systems (IJATS)*. (Trajkovski, IJATS, 2009). It showcases multiple (personal) researchers' journeys coming from many directions and traditional disciplines and backgrounds, to help advance the emerging science of Agent Technologies and Systems.

Anything surrounding us could serve as a motivation for a study or exercise in agents or multi-agent systems. That is what I, as well as many of my colleagues find fascinating about what we do. For example, if you have an infant or own a pet, you are probably fascinated when watching them learn new environments and interact with them and other agents in these environments. The motivations in my personal research at its early days, for example, came from being intrigued in watching infant explore of an environment and watching humans interact with their pets. I became fascinated by the emergent behaviors in agents and their societies, regardless whether they are artificial or biological, homogenous or heterogeneous. How people think, make decisions, communicate, and imitate each other are questions that have always been challenging to me. Everyone else that researches these areas, I believe, has their personal story from where the passion for studying this emergent cross/interdisciplinary area stems.

This was the motivation to establish the *International Journal of Agent Technologies and Systems in* 2009.

THE INTERNATIONAL JOURNAL OF AGENT TECHNOLOGIES AND SYSTEMS

In this section we will review the founding principles behind *International Journal of Agent Technologies and Systems* that have been shared with the scientific community in the wide campaign of soliciting contributions.

International Journal of Agent Technologies and Systems publishes original contributions in the areas of theories of agency and multiagent systems. It covers conceptual frameworks, case studies, empirical analysis, analytical and simulation models of agent anthropologies and sociologies, and their application. It covers topics that include the following general areas:

- Conceptual agent frameworks
  - Agent development environments
  - Agent models and architectures
  - Representation of agents and representation in agents

- ◦ Modeling other agents and self
- ◦ Developmental and cognitive agents
- ◦ Knowledge management and ontologies
- Simulations and constructions of agents
  - ◦ Agent-based modeling and simulation
  - ◦ Tools and cases
  - ◦ Agent-based social simulations
  - ◦ Emergent behavior in agents and agent societies
  - ◦ Multi robot systems
  - ◦ Robot teams
- Multiagent systems
  - ◦ Learning in multi-agent systems
  - ◦ Social and organizational structure in agent societies
  - ◦ Inter-agent interaction
  - ◦ Agent languages
  - ◦ Information propagation and exchange in multi-agent systems
  - ◦ Artificial social systems
  - ◦ Homogenous and heterogeneous agent societies
  - ◦ Colonies and swarm intelligence
- Applications
  - ◦ Human-agent interaction
  - ◦ Interface agents
  - ◦ Virtual humans
  - ◦ Software and pervasive agents
  - ◦ Agent-based data mining
  - ◦ Agent-oriented software engineering
  - ◦ Agents in electronic business and virtual organizations
  - ◦ Ethical and legal issues pertaining to agency and multi-agent systems.

Naturally the topics are not intended to act as requirements but rather as examples of acceptable topics that are of interest to *IJATS*. This volume illustrates a diverse range of questions that were taken upon in the first volume of the journal.

IJATS AS AN AGENT IN THE EMERGENCE OF A NEW SCIENCE

The area of Agent Technologies and Systems is an emerging field of study, and, arguably, does not yet have a mainstream core that the majority of researchers agree on, or build their research on. All efforts are unique in the sense that they explore and unite knowledge from different other disciplines in contributing to what has been an exciting emergent new field and discipline. Journals, such as *IJATS*, and volumes such as this one, are themselves acting as *agents* itself in building the bona fide science of Agent Technologies and Systems.

IJATS, in my subjective opinion, hit its goals from its very first issue. It was set to increase awareness and interest in agent research, encourage collaboration and give a representative overview of the current state of research in this area. It aims at bringing together not only scientists from different areas of computer science, but also researchers from different fields studying similar concepts. The journal now serves as an inclusive forum for discussion on ongoing or completed work in both theoretical and practical issues of intelligent agent technologies and multi-agent systems. It focuses on all aspects of agents and multi-agent systems, with a particular emphasis on how to modify established learning techniques and/or create new learning paradigms to address the many challenges presented by complex real-world problems. *IJATS* was created this journal to disseminate and discuss high quality research results on emerging technologies and successful systems based on the agent and multiagent paradigms, with a comprehensive coverage and understanding of the implications of these paradigms from and to various fields of science, engineering, and technology. It is an interdisciplinary journal that brings together researchers from academia, industry, and the government in discussing conceptual and implementation issues in using the agent approach in solving real life problems. It also acts as a medium of communication among those researchers and practitioners with interest in exploring the benefits of the concepts, simulations, constructions, and applications of theories of agency beyond disciplinary boundaries. It is an open forum for exchange of ideas, so that neither of us reinvents the wheel. Often times the solutions we are looking for has be found in a different discipline in a different context.

THE (EMERGED) STRUCTURE OF THIS BOOK

Deciding the order of the articles in an issue of the journal can sometime be tricky in a discipline that is just emerging and stabilizing. Putting 19 articles together in a book is a significantly more complicated task. The order of the chapters needs to tell a consistent story with a logical flow.

Our *Handbook of Agent-Based Societies: Social and Cultural Interaction* (Trajkovski & Collins, Handbook of Research on Agent-Based Societies: Social and Cultural Interactions, 2009) is the natural prequel of this book. This Handbook was organized in three sections: *Initial States, Emergencies,* and *Second-Order Emergencies.* The first section, *Initial States* contains the chapters that refer to the foundation concepts that are treated with models in the other sections. The second section, *Emergencies*, contains models of artificial societies where the agents interact in the environment and phenomena emerge, but unlike in the chapters in Section 3, *Second Order Emergencies*, the agents do not change their behaviors based on these emergencies. (Trajkovski & Collins, Towards More Lively Machines, 2009) This creates a platform for classification of research in this area.

In this book, we continue the same tradition from the *Handbook*, while taking into consideration the papers that were present in *IJATS* in its first year. The following three (loosely distinct) sections of the book emerged: *Concepts and Challenges, Emergencies,* and *Applications.* Naturally, there are no clear-cut topical boundaries, and chapters could easily migrate between sections, or be reordered.

SECTION 1: CONCEPTS AND CHALLENGES

As Bragin states in his review (Bragin, 2009) of the *Handbook of Agent-Based Societies: Social and Cultural Interaction* (Trajkovski & Collins, Handbook of Research on Agent-Based Societies: Social and Cultural Interactions, 2009):

"Agent-Based Modeling is generally held to be the core methodology of human complex systems science. Although it is possible to express any ABM in mathematical terms (see (Erdi, 2008), § 9.1.3 for an example of how this has been done with one of the Sugarscape models of Epstein and Axtell) there are a number of reasons why ABM approaches are fundamentally more useful, practical and provide greater explanatory insight for social scientists than do mathematical and statistical models (see (Macy & Willer, 2002) and (Gilbert, 2008)). Nevertheless, the agent-based modeler must be as rigorous as the mathematician or statistician: "agent-based models have to be complete, consistent, and unambiguous if they are to be capable of being executed on a computer" (Gilbert 2008)."

It is exactly with these challenges that we open the book with. The first chapter investigates the notion and nature of time in ABS, and stresses how important time considerations are in being able to interpret results from simulations. Koehler's chapter "*Attending to Temporal Assumptions May Enrich Autonomous Agent Computer Simulations*" (Koehler, 2009) is a study that transcends computer science and philosophical ontology. It examines how agents and environments are oriented in time and this orientation's relevance to observing and interpreting emergent phenomena. This study emphasizes the problems in interpreting computer simulated results of agent societies, and the difficulties in deciphering what exactly those digital simulations show when investigating an essentially analog phenomena in a world evolving in time. The essay begins with the observation of the NetLogo platform, a programmable simulation computing environment. (Wilensky, 2009) and the temporal assumptions in common computer stimulations. These discussions have long been a topic in the studies of non-linear systems, sensitive to initial conditions, where generally the concept of chaos was studied at length. Koehler digs deep into the J.T. Fraser's the hierarchical theory of time (Frasier, 1998) that distinguishes between five types of temporality. He argues that the proposed temporal deepening of how simulations are constructed involving interaction of multiple temporalities could lead to the unexpected triggering of an avalanche of unexpected phenomena. The article raises important questions on the validity of the conclusions we get out of stimulation explorations, juxtaposed to philosophical (and other) concepts and understandings of time.

The following chapter expands the Game of Life by experimentation of the timing in the simulations, and more. In their paper "*Temporally Autonomous Agent Interaction,*" Conover and Hammell (Conover & Hammell, Agent Interaction via Message-Based Belief Communication, 2009) reflect into the concept of "temporally autonomous" multi-agent interaction. This paper builds upon the problems with discrete simulations. Namely, in most simulations, agent behavior is regulated by a global timer where all agents act and interact deterministically in time. The authors argue that this discrete timing mechanism yields an artificial reflection of actual physical agent interaction. To this end, a specialized simulation framework is developed, several simulations are then conducted from which data are gathered and it is subsequently demonstrated that manipulation of the timing variable amongst interacting agents affects the emergent behaviors of agent populations. The observations of agents interacting "passively," (Conover & Trajkovski, Effects of temporary asynchronous interaction on simple multiagent behavior, 2007) are now observed in simple "active interactions." The authors observe that the timing of the agent interaction influence the emergent behaviors in the system. The Game of Life (Gardner, 1970) is the starting point of this elaborate investigation. Agents in the society share three beliefs (RED, BLUE and GREEN) with associated belief levels. The dominant belief is shared with the neighbors (if the two highest belief levels are equal, a random belief is broadcasted to the neighbors). While it would be interesting to observe how political beliefs may spread in a society, this study's also emphasizes the sensitivity of simulations to decisions on temporality of the programmers.

The dynamics in social networks is the focus of Palla et al. (Palla, Viscek, & Barabási, 2009), in their paper titled "*Statistical Properties of Social Group Evolution.*" It investigates social networks, as highly connected circles of friends, colleagues, or family members that grow, shrink, merge, split, appear, or disappear over time. Statistical investigations have been made possible by the explosion of the social networks online, and the databases of captured data that enable their study. This is a move away from the earlier quantitative studies that were usually based on qualitative data analysis from typically about a dozen interviewees. The strengths of the links in the network can be objectively measured via aggregating the number of e-mails, phone calls, post etc between two individuals in a network. This study uses the Clique Percolation Method (CPM) (Palla, Derényi, Farkas, & Vicsek, 2005) to study the dynamics of communities. Results indicate a significant difference between smaller circles and institutions. Small communities appear to be stable if a few strong relationships persist, which does not hold for institutions. All members of the institution might change and the institution may still exist. The authors show that the knowledge of the time commitment to a community can predict its lifetime. As such, it gives a new insight in the differences between small and large multiagent systems.

In his chapter titled "*Two Informal Complexity Measures in Social Networks and Agent Communities,*" Fonseca looks at the network dynamics, (Fonseca, 2009) but from the Information Theory perspective. He looks into measures: Entropy Density and Excess Entropy over the stochastic relational changing. In practice estimates can only be obtained, but nevertheless, they can be used to draw conclusions. The mechanics of the measure computation is illustrated in an artificial social network of agents where there is one coordinator for each task, an agent performs a part of the task and there is a directory facilitator. The coordinator communicates with the agents contributing to the that it is responsible for at fixed intervals, the agent communicates with the coordinator to adjust its goal, and the directory facilitator randomly exchanges messages with very agent at the agents' request in order to facilitate the communication in the system. Fonseca studies the agent's social predictability and the commitment to the community as characteristics of the society members.

Neumann entropy was defined in von Neumann's work on quantum mechanics (Von Neumann, 1955), and today it is an important tool in quantum Information Theory. In their chapter "*Quantifying Disorder in Networks: The von Neumann Entropy,*" (Passerini & Severini, 2009), the authors study the Von Neumann entropy of graphs, thus transcending the fields of quantum Information Theory and Complex Networks. This marriage happens at a statistical level. Two theorems are stated and proven, and a wealth of directions for further work stated. The article proposes a new way of quantifying disorder/entropy in social networks. The results indicate that Von Neumann entropy increases with the regularity properties of the network and with the number of its connected components.

SECTION 2: EMERGENCIES

In this section we ordered the chapters with respect to the order of the emergencies they treat, from first-order to second-order emergencies. (Trajkovski & Collins, Towards More Lively Machines, 2009) This section is a collection of models that attempt to solve agency problems, and come from researchers with a variety of different backgrounds. Some attempt to solve problems that traditional Artificial Intelligence (AI) had left open; others look at societies in a brand new light.

Belief-Desire-Intention (BDI) agents (Bratman, Israel, & Pollack, 1988) are artificial agents that are capable of simple adaptations to behaviors, encoded in their hierarchical plans. These plans are indexed by goals. Execution relies on the context sensitive expansion of goals, and therefore choices and planning happens on multiple levels of abstractions. The choices the agent makes are in direct response to the current status of the environment; should the effort fail due to changes in the environment, a backtracking mechanisms is put in action. In their chapter "*Enhancing the Adaptation of BDI Agents Using Learning Techniques*," Airiau et al. (Airiau, Padgham, Sardina, & Sen, 2009) outline standard BDI approach in programming of agents, and propose enhancements to account for some of its shortfalls. The major drawback of the BDI (and really most of the traditional AI approaches) is that the coder would need to spoon-feed the machine with pairs of plans and contexts for those plans. As a proposed solution to overcome this issue the authors propose looking into the agent's history to improve the context conditions for the plans as the agents sojourns in the given environment. The open questions are related to figuring out what to do when a plan does not exist? The authors performs experiments in so called non-deterministic environment, but then what would happen if the agent experiences perceptual aliasing, when two locally distinct places in the environment look the same to the agent? This approach is a hybrid of merging the rather typical efforts to resolve the challenges of the traditional AI approaches to agency problems and the post-AI Agents Science.

The practicality of using Reinforcement Learning (RL) in agents presents us with the challenge of computationally heavy functions that the agent need to manipulate with quickly. The more complex the environment is to be learned is, the training set gets larger. In the training process, a value function is fitted, that serves as a measure of "how good" it is for the agent to execute a particular action while in a given state. From an engineering perspective, approximations are the next best thing to using the actual value functions, in finding a good candidate faster. The approximations are finer or coarser (or more or less expressive) based on the size of the tiles (or how fine the tessellation is) of the rank of the function. In their paper titled "*Reward Shaping and Mixed Resolution Function Approximation*," (Grzec & Kudenko, Reinforcement Learning with Reward Shaping and Mixed resolution Fubction Approximation, 2009) Grzec and Kudenko attempt to propose a hybrid approach that uses approximations to provide useful guidance of the agent, and then towards the end a more expressive approximation to get a high-quality final result. Three approaches are investigated: a combination of less and more expressive representations of one value function representation, use a less expressive function to learn the potential for reward shaping, and then use it to shape the reward of learning with a desired resolution, and a hybrid approach of the two – use less expressive approximation for the learning potential, and using it to guide learning, which combines a less and more expressive function approximation at the ground level. The paper is rich in experimental results from a mountain car (Sutton & Barto, 1998), car parking (Cichosz, 1996) and boat navigation (Jouffle, 1998) from one to another bank of the river, that are used for benchmarking purposes, and expose the mixed method as superior.

Effective open-ended learning is what cognitive robotics strives to achieve. Open-ended learning is not task specific, and should preferably be unsupervised, which makes it inherently inductive in nature. The chapter "*Inductive Logic Programming and Embodied Agents: Possibilities and Limitations*" by Kulakov et al. (Kulakov, Lukkanen, Mustafa, & Stojanov, 2009) overviews innovative attempts to use Inductive Logic Programming (ILP) as a machine learning technique in the context of embodied autonomous agents, and highlights novel efforts in bridging the problems between the large datasets and ILP in these agents. Artificial curiosity mechanisms drive the agents to learn. The paper overviews ILP, and explores its potential use in robotics by proposing solutions to overcome some of the ILP shortcomings. Four general issues are discussed: overcoming difficulties by oversimplifying the environment, dealing with uncertainty, dealing with high dimensionality and noise, and discussing the scalability issue. While the merger of cognitive robotics with ILP may seem promising, some questions still remain open. Further directions of the investigation are seen in infusing probabilistic tools, layers of abstraction and work on the issue of scalability, as the environmental stimuli generates overwhelming amount of data that needs managed. Innovative heuristics may also be needed.

In the next chapter titled *"Cognitive Robotics and Multiagency in a Fuzzy Modeling Framework"* (Trajkovski, Stojanov, Collins, Eidelman, Harman, & Vincenti, 2009) we present a general fuzzy-logic based framework for cognitive robotics modeling. The modeling uses lattice, poset and relational structured valued fuzzy relational and algebraic structures that are applied in various capacities in cognitive agent. Five related but distinct case studies in agency and multiagency are presented. The agent(s) is (are) brought in an unknown environment and motivated to explore using inborn schemes, which represent a sequence of actions they can perform. Based on the success of an action, and the perception of the environment while the action is performed, the agent builds perception-action pairs that are the inner representation of the environment that the agent uses to diminish pain in the new environment, by using what it had learned to anticipate the success of its next move towards getting to the place that can satisfy its active drive(s).The agent Petitagé is the base of all studies, and multiple metrics on its behavior in an unknown environment have been gathered via a simulation in the PYRO (Python Robotics) simulation environment for a single agent and in a multiagent setting. ANNA (Artificial Neural Network Agent) learns the environment using neural networks, and performs comparably to Petitagé. In order to be able to calibrate the simulations on robotic agents, data from human subjects have been harvested using POP-SICLE (Patterns in Orientation: Pattern-Aided Simulation Interactive Context Learning Experiment), and the Izbushka experimental setup.

To calibrate simulations of multiagent environments it is necessary to be able to have enough data from the agents that are being modeled. The Izbushka experiment is discussed in detail in the chapter *"Interactions in Context-Zero: Towards Conceptual Adaptation through the Izbushka Agent"* (Braman, 2009). It investigates human behavior in context of varying side. This experiments aims to understand how human agents learn in a Petitagé-like environment. Izbushka is an agent in itself that monitors the success of the human that interacts with it, and based on the observations presents the human subject with the environment, which is dynamically changing. Both qualitative and quantitative data is collected from the subjects and analyzed. As such Izbushka, even on its own is a bona fide autonomous intelligent agent that couples with the human agent thus forming a heterogeneous multiagent system. The repercussions of this study are far-reaching in the efforts to achieve true virtual personal assistants that learn from and about the user, which is basically the underlying idea of the Web 3.0 hype and hope.

Through interaction in multiagent societies, societal norms emerge and propagate between the population. In the essay on emergence of social norms, *"Norm Emergence with Biased Agents,"* Mukherjee et al. (Mukherjee, Sen, & Airiau, 2009) observe phenomena in a multi-agent simulation where the agent are randomly paired and interact with each other privately. Each agent is learning from the agents they are paired with over time. The simulations in the study were carried in three types of populations: with same initial bias, in a population where initially 50% of the population shares a bias that is opposite than the initial bias of the other half, and an initial population where the opposing norms are unevenly distributed. The society is homogenous and uses the WoLF-PHC (Win or Learn Fast – Policy Hill Climbing) algorithm for learning norms. (Bowling & Veloso, 2002) While this algorithm converges in a two person, 2 actions game against an opponent in a Nash equilibrium, it is not known if that would be the case with social learning. The experiment is modeled after the game of traffic where drivers arrive at intersections simultaneously. In these societies the norms emerge via a bottom-up process that depends on direct individual experiences, and not on gossip or observations. These interactions happen with random strangers in the society that were originally biased. One notable observation is that norms converge faster when there the majority is larger. This study opens the doors for many related simulations with varying parameters, such as the population size, varying population size, number of original biases, expanding the social learning to include observations and gossip, and many more.

A case study in norm dynamics is the presented in the following chapter. Distributed online communities have been experiencing wide acceptance and use. Goldspink's paper "*Governance Mechanisms in Web 2.0: The Case of Wikipedia*" (Goldspink, 2009) focuses on the Wikipedia community, and investigates how social self-regulation is achieved via normative mechanisms. It is an empirical study of norm innovation in this system. Although novel users are typically surprised when they encounter Wikipedia, and may expect that such an open collaborative system is not likely to produce credible encyclopedic entries, reality check witnesses to the contrary, despite the nonexistence of the typical editorial checks and balances involved in a classical encyclopedic project. (Giles, 2005) The question examined here is how social communication influences the behaviors of others in open systems, and particularly the processes that enable self-regulation, whether the findings are consistent with existing theories, and what alternative hypotheses can be drawn based on this case study. In Wikipedia, much alike any other wiki, there are two main activities: editing and conversations about editing. This article studied discussion pages on selected controversial articles in Wikipedia. Although the norms that emerged could be seen all over the place, in Wikipedia order appears to have emerged. Due to the open contribution and the participation of anonymous volunteers, the neutral style of communication is prevalent. The communication style and emerged norm do not appear to have a lot to do with the content of the articles being edited. The paper states other hypotheses as well that challenge some existing theories. Although this institution is based on voluntary participation, and there is no product involved, as in e-commerce sites, for example, it represents a solid kick-off to a sizable study of social norm innovation in open institutions.

SECTION 3: APPLICATIONS

Multiagent technologies and systems provide a range of tools that are increasingly being used to solve real-world problems. This section consists of a collection of chapters that emphasize how models and approaches from this discipline can give valuable insight into challenges that range from energy consumptions and crises in the stock markets, to distance education.

The energy utilization system is a dynamic one, and experiences steep ups and downs in usage in the traditional manner. In their paper "*A Multi-Agent Machine Learning Framework for Intelligent Energy Demand Management*," Guo et al. (Guo, Zeman, & Li, 2009) discuss an agent technology application for energy demand management, where appliances are individual agents that can defer their energy consumption if there is a need on the power system for them so to do. High demand of electricity equals higher price for this utility. When the energy demand is high, agents collaborate in a multiagent environment and defer the energy consumptions by appliances when the energy price peaks. The study simulates the Australian power brokerage system. It highest priority is the stability of the power system, so the system has two goals – maintain that stability and optimizing the cost. A cap function is defined to denote the capped energy consumption, and its behavior observed in a multi-agent simulation. The energy broker is dually rewarded (using the two goals) to accommodate the attentive plans for energy consumptions of the individual agents. Two simulations are presented, one featuring the feedback of the group agents (aggregation of feedback from individual agents/appliances), and one without, showing consistent improvement when the two goals are used in the reward functions. It turns out that price itself is not a reward function enough to keep this system stable, and avoid peaks in usage of power.

In their paper "*A Step-By-Step Implementation of a Multi-Agent Currency Trading System*," Barbosa and Belo (Barbosa & Belo, 2009) present the details of a successful software agent that trades US and Japanese currency (denoted by USD and JPY respectively) on the Foreign Exchange Market (Forex). The agent uses prediction and mitigates risk. Taking into account the broking fees, the system over 17 months generated a return of about 50%. The system is based on simple trending principles that have proved successful in the trading of the USD/JPY currency pair in a 6 hours timeframe. This is an encouraging agent, but as the authors indicate, it would be a mistake to use it life just yet on the stock exchange, as a successful trading is based on trading a diversified portfolio. And, for a diversified trading activities, more and different other agents - implementing a diversified range of trading techniques - will need to be developed.

Araúho and Louça, in the paper titled "*Modeling Multi-Agent Systems as a Network: A Methaphoric Exploration of the Unexpected*," explore the S&P500 stock market over the years. (Araújo & Louça, 2009) The S&P 500 index have been monitoring 5000 large-cap common stocks in the United States since 1957. Using mathematical approaches, namely geometrical and topological characterizations (with the appropriate metrics), the paper shows how the stocks have been clustering and re-clustering over the years, forming clusters in the network of stocks. Case studies of "rough" and "smooth" periods of the market are shown. The authors construct a coefficient that quantifies the distribution and intensity of the correlations among stocks in the market over a decade. This coefficient clearly marks the crises on the market in 2001-2002, and in 2008.

Romero (Romero, 2009), in the chapter "*Accounting Implications in Virtual Worlds*," discusses the emerging economies of the virtual world of Second Life. As its popularity is growing, so are its real world financial implications, as members spend a lot on virtual items and virtual real estate transactions, and some residents generate hefty incomes in real world dollars. Second Life (Linden Research) is still in an early stage of development, and there are many financial and legal regulatory issues to be resolved. But with these challenges come opportunities; Second Life may be the impetus for a new accounting platform that may bring different practices together and provide new growth opportunities that financial communities have been looking for in the virtual world. The emerging economies are phenomena worth monitoring in this real-world online multiagent system.

CIUCEU (Comunicação Infromal entre Utilizadores de Correio Electrónico Universitário – Informal Communication between Users of a University E-mail System) is a model developed using MASON (Multi-Agent Simulator of Neighborhoods), (Luke, Balan, Sullivan, Panait, Cioffi-Revilla, & Paus) and is the focal point of the Rodrigues' research presented in the chapter titled "*Multi-Agent-Based Simulation of University Email Communities.*" (Rodrigues, 2009) It models the informal communication via e-mail at his affiliate institution. The data from communication between teachers, students, and employees of the institution, over a short period of 62 days was observed. The simulation shows that even this period provided sufficient data to capture the latent structure of the network. The observation of the clique percolation, for example, reveals that vertical hierarchies are very loose and communication transcends departments. Cluster algorithms have been applied to gather conclusions on the groupings of the users. The research also emphasizes the need for careful consideration of the setup of the simulation, and making a balance between a totally open system and some rules (introduced from the real data) in order to gather insights that would be interpretable.

Welzant's study of a specific student experience in an online system of distance education, titled *"Impact on Learner Experience: A Qualitative Case Study Exploring Online MBA Problem-Based Learning Courses,"* (Welzant, 2009) concludes that there is a significant need for problem-based learning (PBL) in online courseware. In agent terms, students prefer learning based on new environments and via exploration. The various communication methods used in the distance education arena today enable agent interaction and collaboration when solving problems they are faced with PBL challenges.

Ho et al., (Ho, Enz, Dautenthahn, Zoll, Lim, & Watson, 2009), in their chapter titled *"Towards Learning 'Self' and Emotional Knowledge in Social and Cultural Human-Agent Interactions,"* present research towards the development of a virtual learning environment inhabited by intelligent virtual agents and modeling a scenario of inter-cultural interactions. This is a part of the research of a team focused on emotional knowledge learning in autobiographic social agents, and aims to promote intercultural empathy. The ultimate aim of this environment is to allow users to reflect upon and learn about intercultural communication and collaboration. Rather than predefining the interactions among the virtual agents and scripting the possible interactions afforded by this environment, the authors pursue a bottom-up approach whereby inter-cultural communication emerges from interactions with and among autonomous agents. The intelligent virtual agents that inhabit this environment are expected to be able to broaden their knowledge about the world and other agents, which may be of different cultural backgrounds, through interactions.

REFERENCES

Airiau, S., Padgham, L., Sardina, S., & Sen, S. (2009). Enchancing the Adaptation of BDI Agents Using Learning Techniques. (G. Trajkovski, Ed.) *IJATS, 1* (2), 1-18.

Araújo, T., & Louça, F. (2009). Modeling Multi-Agent Systems as a Network: A Methaphoric Exploration of the Unexpected. (G. Trajkovski, Ed.) *IJATS, 1* (4), 17-29.

Barbosa, R. P., & Belo, O. (2009). A Step-by-Step Implementation of a Hybrid USD/JPY Trading Agent. (G. Trajkovski, Ed.) *IJATS, 1* (2), 19-35.

Bowling, M. H., & Veloso, M. M. (2002). Multiagent Learning Using a Variable Learning Rate. *Artificial Intelligence, 136* (2), 215-250.

Bragin, J. (2009, October). *Review of the "Handbook of Research on Agent -Based Societies: Social and Cultural Interactions"*. Retrieved June 6, 2010, from Journal od Artificial Societies and Social Simulation: http://jasss.soc.surrey.ac.uk/12/4/reviews/bragin.html

Braman, J. (2009). Designing Izbushka: Investigating Interactions in Context Zero Environments. *IJATS, 1* (1), 74-95.

Bratman, M. E., Israel, D. J., & Pollack, M. E. (1988). Plans and Resource-Bounded Practical Reasoning. *Computational Intelligence, 4* (4), 349-355.

Cichosz, P. (1996). Truncated tempporal Diffeernces with Function Approximations: Successful Examples using CMAC. *Proceedings of the 13th European Symposium on Cybernetics and Systems reseraach.*

Conover, A. J., & Hammell, R. J. (2009). Agent Interaction via Message-Based Belief Communication. (G. Trajkovski, Ed.) *IJATS*, *1* (3), 1-28.

Conover, A. J., & Trajkovski, G. (2007). Effects of temporary asynchronous interaction on simple multiagent behavior. *Emergent agents and socialities; Social and organizational aspects of intelligence. fs-07-04*, pp. 34-41. Menlo Park: The American Association for Artificial Intelligence.

Erdi, P. (2008). *Complexity Explained.* Berlin & Heidelberg: Springer-Verlag.

Fonseca, A. J. (2009). Two Informal Complexity Measures in Social Networks and Agent Communities. (G. Trajkovski, Ed.) *IJATS*, *1* (4), 58-67.

Frasier, J. (1998). From Chaos to Conflict. In J. Frasier, M. P. Soulsby, & A. Argyros, *Time, Order, Chaos.* Madison, Conn: International University Press.

Gardner, M. (1970, October). Mathematical Games: The fantastic combinations of John Conway's new solitaire game "life". *Scientific American*, pp. 120-123.

Gilbert, N. (2008). *Agent-Based Models.* London: SAGE Publications.

Giles, J. (2005, February 2). Internet encyclopaedias go head to head. *Nature*, *438* (7070), p. 890.

Goldspink, C. (2009). Social Self-Regulation in Computer Mediated Communities: The Case of Wikipedia. (G. Trajkovski, Ed.) *IJATS*, *1* (1), 19-33.

Grzec, M., & Kudenko, D. (2009). Reinforcement Learning with Reward Shaping and Mixed resolution Fubction Approximation. (G. Trajkovski, Ed.) *IJATS*, *1* (2), 36-54.

Grzec, M., & Kudenko, D. (2009). Reinforcement Learning with Reward Shaping and Mixed resolution Function Approximation. (G. Trajkovski, Ed.) *IJATS*, *1* (2), 36-54.

Guo, Y., Zeman, A., & Li, R. (2009). A reinforcement learning Approach to Setting Multi-Objective Goals for Energy Demand Management. (G. Trajkovski, Ed.) *IJATS*, *1* (2), 55-70.

Ho, W. C., Enz, S., Dautenthahn, K., Zoll, C., Lim, M., & Watson, S. (2009). Towards Learning 'Self' and Emotional Knowledge. (G. Trajkovski, Ed.) *IJATS*, *1* (3), 51-78.

Jouffle, L. (1998). Fuzzy Inference System Learning by Reinforcement learning. *IEE Transactions of Systems, Man, and Cybernethics, Part C: Applications and Reviews*, *28* (3), 338-355.

Koehler, G. (2009). Attending to Temporal Assumptions May Enrich Autonomous Agent Computer Simulations. (G. Trajkovski, Ed.) *IJATS*, *1* (1), 1-18.

Kulakov, A., Lukkanen, J., Mustafa, B., & Stojanov, G. (2009). Inductive Logic Programming and Embodied Agents. (G. Trajkovski, Ed.) *IJATS*, *1* (1), 34-49.

Linden Research. (n.d.). *What is Second Life*. Retrieved June 5, 2010, from Second Life: http://secondlife.com/whatis/

Luke, S., Balan, G. C., Sullivan, K., Panait, L., Cioffi-Revilla, C., & Paus, S. (n.d.). *MASON*. Retrieved June 2, 2010, from http://cs.gmu.edu/~eclab/projects/mason/

Macy, M. W., & Willer, R. (2002). From Factors to Actors: Computational Sociology and Agent-Based Modeling. *Annual Review of Sociology, 28*, 143-166.

Mukherjee, P., Sen, S., & Airiau, S. (2009). Norm Emergence with Biased Agents. (G. Trajkovski, Ed.) *IJATS, 1* (2), 71-83.

Palla, G., Derényi, I., Farkas, I., & Vicsek, T. (2005). Uncovering the Overlapping Community Structure of Complex Networks in Nature and Society. *Nature, 435*, 814-818.

Palla, G., Viscek, T., & Barabási, A.-L. (2009). Statistical Properties of Community Dynamics in Large Social Networks. (G. Trajkovski, Ed.) *IJATS, 1* (4), 1-16.

Passerini, F., & Severini, S. (2009). Quantifying Complexity in Networks: The von Neumann Entropy. (G. Trajkovski, Ed.) *IJATS, 1* (4), 58-67.

Rodrigues, D. (2009). CIUCEU: Multi-Agent-Based Simulation of University Email Communities. (G. Trajkovski, Ed.) *IJATS, 1* (4), 30-48.

Romero, J. A. (2009). Virtual Worlds and the Implication for Accountants: The Case of Second Life. (G. Trajkovski, Ed.) *IJATS, 1* (3), 45-50.

Sutton, R. S., & Barto, A. G. (1998). *Reinforcement Learning: An Introduction.* Cambridhe: MIT Press.

Trajkovski, G. (Ed.). (2009). *International Journal of Agent Technologies and Systems, 1.* Hershey, PA, USA: IGI Publishing.

Trajkovski, G., & Collins, S. G. (Eds.). (2009). *Handbook of Research on Agent-Based Societies: Social and Cultural Interactions.* Hershey, PA, USA: Information Science Reference.

Trajkovski, G., & Collins, S. G. (2009). Towards More Lively Machines. In G. Trajkovski, & S. G. Collins (Eds.), *Handbook of Research on Agent-Based Societies: Social and Cultural Interactions* (pp. xvii-xxii). Hershey, PA, USA: Information Science reference.

Trajkovski, G., Stojanov, G., Collins, S., Eidelman, V., Harman, C., & Vincenti, G. (2009). Cognitive Robotics and Multiagency in a Fuzzy Modelling Framework. (G. Trajkovski, Ed.) *IJATS, 1* (1), 50-73.

Von Neumann, J. (1955). *Mathematische Grundlagen der Quantenmechanik (Mathematical Foundations of Quantum Mechanics).* Berlin: Springer.

Welzant, J. H. (2009). Impact on learner experience: a qualitative case study exploring online MBA problem-based learning courses. (G. Trajkovski, Ed.) *IJATS, 1* (3), 29-44.

Wilensky, U. (2009, December 20). *NetLogo 4.1 User Manual.* Retrieved June 2, 2010, from NetLogo: http://ccl.northwestern.edu/netlogo/docs/

Acknowledgment

As the Editor-in-Chief of *IJATS* and editor of this volume, I would like to thank all the contributors, the associate and guest editors, and the editorial review board of the Journal for their impressive hard work. Colleagues that wrote book reviews further enhanced the diversity of the scope of the Journal. This whole team of people made the process of putting together each issue of the journal a seamless and a very enjoyable experience. IGI Global has further made my job easier by providing timely and superb assistance to my every need. I am looking forward to compiling the sequel to this volume, based on the second volume of *IJATS*.

Goran Trajkovski
Editor

Section 1
Concepts and Challenges

Chapter 1
Attending to Temporal Assumptions May Enrich Autonomous Agent Computer Simulations

Gus Koehler
University of Southern California, USA

ABSTRACT

Agent-based computer simulations use agents on landscapes to investigate epidemics, social phenomena, decision making, supply networks, the behavior of biological systems, and physical and chemical processes, among other things. This essay examines how agents and landscapes are oriented in time and this orientation's relevance to observing and interpreting findings. I argue that the proposed temporal deepening of how simulations are constructed involving interaction of multiple temporalities (itself a kind of temporality) could lead to the unexpected triggering of cascades of secondary emergences. Such cascades may already be there but going unobserved. Buddhist cosmology is briefly used as a contrast with current simulation temporal orientations to illuminate key points. Katherine Hayles's work on media, my theoretical work on time-ecologies and heterochrony, and J. T. Fraser's theory of the nested hierarchy of time and associated causalities are used to explore these issues.

INTRODUCTION

In an earlier paper, "Computer Simulation as Hidden Time-Ecologies," NetLogo is used to show how a limited concept of temporality affects NetLogo's simulations (Koehler, in press). Here we will look more closely at how a limited temporal perspective of the programmer/ experimenter raises problems with understanding exactly what the simulation is showing. As noted by Wilensky (1999):

[NetLogo] is a programmable modeling environment for simulating natural and social phenomena. NetLogo claims to be particularly well suited for modeling complex systems developing over time. Modelers can give instructions to hundreds or thousands of independent "agents" all operating concurrently. This makes it possible to explore the connection between the micro-level behavior

DOI: 10.4018/978-1-60960-171-3.ch001

Copyright © 2011, IGI Global. Copying or distributing in print or electronic forms without written permission of IGI Global is prohibited.

of individuals and the macro-level patterns that emerge from the interaction of many individuals.

NetLogo is used to simulate emergent phenomena involved in AIDS epidemics, altruistic acts, ethnocentrism, chemical and physical processes, earth sciences, segregation, art, mathematical problems, and ant activity without any variations in temporal concepts.

Rehearsing the general theoretical argument, I start with the point that in a digital computer, the simulation creation instructions are "in the form of COMMAND (ADDRESS) where the address is an exact (either absolute or relative) memory location, a process that translates informally into "DO THIS with what you find HERE and go THERE with the result." Everything depends not only on precise instructions, but on HERE, THERE, and WHEN being exactly defined." (Dyson, 2005). With these instructions, a simulation as ones and zeroes in a machine is established without a one-on-one referent in the real world. There are no actors playing out ethnic community relations for example, only digits. The instantiation of these temporal relationships in computer based media—hardware, program, computer processing, and visualization—suggests that analysis of each is necessary to understand the temporal assumptions of a simulation as it is constructed, how temporality is incorporated and limited by its operation, and how media shapes interpretations of the results by the temporally instantiated experimenter. For example, artistic control for interactive evolution of images and animation is important for 2D images seen in a simulation. Attractive and expressive mutation types and genotype transforms are sometime introduced as a way to make genotypes more receptive to mutation. For evolving animation, tree alignments of evolutionary sequences may be introduced. The result is an intervention that provides greater control and expressive power over space-time as governed by the artistic eye of the programmer and experimenter.

I will hold that simulation representations and the technologies producing them are inextricably intertwined. (This discussion draws heavily from Hayles, 1999, 2002, and 2005). Further, the form of the representational artifact always affects what the semiotic components mean, be they "turtles" or "landscapes" on a computer screen. For example, much current analysis of simulations does not account for the signifying components that reveal the simulation process, its manipulation and interpretation such as sound, animation, motion, visualization, and software functionality, among other factors. Efforts are underway to design avatars—a more sophisticated turtle—to appear more trustworthy and to interact more gracefully, suggesting that the information conveyed is more reliable, which isn't necessarily so (Donath, 2007). Such design considerations are also relevant to simulation control panels and data visualization methods (Chen, 2004). These become significant issues as agent simulations and virtual worlds are used for scientific social research (Bainbridge, 2007).

The NetLogo world is constructed by programming interactions among three interrelated types of agents, all controlled by a computer "timer"— the when—with a resolution in milliseconds or so depending on the underlying Java Virtual Machine. The first, an "agent"—one semiotic component—appears to move (actually different pixels light up) according to programmed rules over the second called "patches" or a landscape, another semiotic component. Agents can be designated as "breeds" of agents such as foxes, chickens, and grass that interact in set ways. The third agent—a third and complex semiotic component—is an "observer" which "hovers" over the unfolding agent-landscape and uses the clock to demark agent and landscape activities. "[All three] are beings that can follow instructions. Each... can carry out its own activity, all simultaneously." (Dyson, 2005). Agents execute commands asynchronously but are programmed to "wait" for the others to complete their commands before going on. Groups of agents (foxes and chickens for example) are started randomly every time the program is initiated so as not to favor one agent or segment of the landscape over another. Landscapes may have a preferential point such as a pile of grass for a chicken agent, but its constituent patches may be set or evolve according to some rule.

NetLogo exclusively uses three temporalities to simulate five very different realms. The five realms are mathematical formulae, and physical, biological, psychological, and social processes. The first of three NetLogo temporalities is the computer's "timer," which regulates all three agents. The second is that of programmer-observer who controls the number of variables and generates and interprets results. The third is asynchronous and random agent programmed control strategies across the entire NetLogo "world" at whatever level. These often simple programs and rules lead to the emergence of very complex patterns at various scales.

A Simulation's Space-Time Relational Structures are Complex

Like conventional reality, a simulation's space-time structure involves relational structures within an agent and between agents, the landscape (often parts of the landscape), and an observer that together create events that comprise a simulation's "reality" and history. Each interaction is an instantiated feedback loop with its own temporal and other characteristics among these various elements.

Understanding these relationships in both the conventional world and that of the simulation involves a study of "place," in the sense of "to place" or topos. Agents, landscape, and the internal computer observer are "placed" in relationship to each other by a program and machine operations in virtual reality and then viewed on an electronic screen usually involving pixels, sweep times, etc., another "place." Such time-space

nested placements involves defining "continuity," "connectivity," and "orientability" from element to element (Reichenbach, 1956). As such, they create a simulation of Being in the conventional world and constitute one type of Being itself. It is an arena of circumscribed relationships involving both proximity and envelopment to and by other agents and landscapes. Such simulation arenas can be "wild" and becoming-ever-different (Merleau-Ponty, 1968) which involves the continuous introduction of some degree of novelty, of intuition or, as physics would have it, of some type of noise (pink, brown, black, etc).. As continuous reflexivity through various types of feedback, they can create dynamic hierarchies of emergent behaviors (Hayles, 2005).

Proximity and envelopment, including continuity, connectivity, and orientability, together express the time-space dimension of depth or thickness produced by landscape-agent-observer interactions leading to a move in their apparent location. They may even be acted through, much like a filter. Observed changes in pixel patterns reveal the process to the eye involving issues of proximity and envelopment as well. This activity semiotically reveals the simulation's computation.

By attending to proximity and envelopment, we must be careful not to move away from dynamical event processes, replacing them with a static, placed *thing*. Such a move abstracts and spatializes time even as it instrumentalizes it: "it subjugates the contingency and volatility of time by reconstituting it as external to phenomena as a finitude and regularity; it becomes a technique of measurement embodied in economic axioms and algebraic laws." (Kwinter, 2002, p. 4). Rather, time is expressed in both conventional and simulation reality as an event involving continuous placement—that is motion—of proximity and envelopment, of local instantiation in multiple temporal realms as we have hinted at.

For example, if we occupy a place as a "point" on a sheet of paper in two dimensional space—Abbott's Flatland (Stewart, 2001)—and the paper is crumpled, we would not be able to see the wrinkles and their effect on orientability, envelopment, and other factors because these dimensions extend into a third dimension of space that affects movement in our "flat" world. A new possibility for movement—one or more new dimensions—is embedded by the wrinkles in the earlier two. When we try to change our posture and proximity in relation to other points by moving from one area to another in our two-dimensional space we would feel a mysterious, unseen "force" whenever we came to a wrinkle; it would be a mysterious envelopment that would change local two-dimensional proximity in unexpected ways. This wrinkle changes the geometry of our local posture in our two dimensional world making it impossible to move in straight lines under specific *local* conditions (Wertheim, 1999) For Riemann this led to the conclusion that gravity was "caused by the crumpling of our three-dimensional universe in the unseen fourth dimension." (Kaku, 1994). (For a visualization of the problem see the hypercube model at http://www.mathcs.sjsu.edu/faculty/rucker/).

Such spatial and temporal dimensions can be locally large and extended or small and curled up (the term local varies with scale). This is important because, as we will see, each of the five temporalities that define our cosmology extends itself differently, suggesting limits to its influence and complex interactions with other temporalities and their space. Some spatial and probably temporal dimensions are small—point and tendril-like—while others are large and extended with ripples, suggesting a very complex "rolling up." For example, Abbott's flatlander would have a difficult time discovering if she lived spatially on a sphere if the sphere was very large (Stewart, 2001).

The problem of measuring different time dimensions is even more difficult. Varying *space* dimensions (four or more), have been explored using projections and shadows (Banchoff, 1966). For physics, there is only one dimension of time, which is rolled up or extended in as many as 10

space dimensions (Greene, 1999). Kaluza, by adding an additional fifth spatial dimension (still one time dimension) was able to unify Einstein's general relativity theory and Maxwell's electromagnetic theory. Again, why can't we see all five of Kaluza's dimensions? This is because three are extended and one is tightly curled up much like Riemann's wrinkles. In either case it is the particular deformation of the topology of the spatial fabric of the local universe in which all forces that determine how objects—and agents—are instantiated.

The instantiation of placement, proximity, envelopment and the other factors identified above occupy local space-time in both conventional and simulation arenas. Their manner of instantiation is complex, involving multiple nested scales. For example, we may be trying to simulate a complex adaptive system's dynamics with emergent temporal properties involving psychological, governmental, social, or economic relationships that influence the development and growth of each. This is done by triggering emergent processes and structures as they continuously co-evolve because of differing causalities out of differing pasts into differing futures in geographic and virtual space presents (Holland, 1995). It may be helpful to envision this as analogous to a cymatic pattern of sand that Jenny created using sound; in this case, we are looking at the structuration of agent relationships in an extended temporally varying space (Jenny, 2001). I will call the temporal structure of such a natural complex system a *time-ecology*, whose operation will be central to my examination of simulation temporality.

Temporal Aspects of Time-Ecologies

I have argued that a natural time-ecology *is* multiply emergent spatial-time pattern(s) formed by a five-temporal-nested heterochronic event (Koehler, 2001, 2003). It is the dynamical form of this heterochronic process. Time is the local relationship(s) of placed processes and rates that regulate flows in the multidimensional space of a time ecology. A single local point may have one or many temporalities (a desert has one; a man walking on a desert is two, a man thinking about a lizard as he walks in the desert is three, and so forth). Each of the five temporalities unfolds according to its own causalities with different rates of complexification producing different forms. Again, and as will be suggested shortly, these forms *are* time (Fraser, 1999).

Landscapes and agents are themselves a kind of turbulence, an ordered field (attractor basin of some kind) with flows and eddies in space defined by morphodynamic rules. Nothing has an independent existence outside of these configurations; all is oscillation as orderly heterochronically combining event streams.

A time-ecology can be decomposed into component systems with boundaries defined according to their number and rate of interaction (Simon, 2005). This is not to say that fewer interactions or lower frequencies are unimportant; sensitivity to initial conditions is dependent on such relationships and is one causal factor leading to emergence. It is just *this* collection—perhaps even a limited number—of heterochronic flows between temporally based causalities that maintains a time-ecology.

In a natural time-ecology, an agent is defined by its varying time independent relational state, its placement as *continuity, connectivity*, and *orientability*, as heterochrony (Koehler, 2001, 2003). A *state* which we typically observe is an instantaneous statement of heterochronic frequencies, as of internal processes of the form being generated.

Ecological layers are interdependent in such a way as to constrain the range of morphodynamic rules of emergent structures from the top down or induce emergent structures from the bottom up. Present, past, and future have no necessary directionality in such hierarchies if all five temporal levels are involved.

Change is continuous in a time-ecology, involving varying temporal causalities across linked temporal dimensions (*developmental, phenomenological, social*, and *clock* are examples of temporal dimensions). Change varies according to its time dimension and velocity-cone propagation characteristics (Koehler, 2004). (For example, backward causation is possible in what Fraser calls nootemporality since we can indeed choose what we remember). It may be that the nested temporally based local causalities of different time-ecology layers may account for new emergent properties.

Novel time-ecology emergents can be seen according Tooley (1997) as,

[S]omething new coming into being with each instance of some level or pattern of lower level constituents.... [A]n ontological emergent would be a temporal emergent the first time an instance appeared. [Emergence presupposes levels.]... [T]he nature of levels remains that of ontological inclusiveness: higher levels include lower levels as constituents.... Any causal consequence of a higher level of organization will affect lower, constituent patterned levels. Causal emergence implies downward and upward causation. This causal theory of temporal order and direction in relationships produces a contingent absolute space being space-time points that stand in causal relations to one another. This makes it possible for an event that is not causally related to any other [local] events to have, nevertheless, spatial-temporal location.... [I]f the direction of time is given by the direction of causation, and space-time points themselves stand in causal relations, then time is, as one naturally thinks of it as being, an all-pervasive feature of the world [and of a time-ecology].

This is supported in work by Hanson and Crutchfield (1997). (This feature of CAs is discussed at greater length in Richardson, 1975). They have shown that through the application of different filters (what they call "mechanical transducers") a hierarchy of quasi-particles emerge from the fundamental cellular automata (CA) substrate, each potentially with its own temporal characteristics. So, although only "cells" are included in the basic definition of CAs, a hierarchy of quasi-particles emerges from the recursive application of the nonlinear local rules. Furthermore, these quasi-particles interact with each other, implying the existence of causal processes that are "above" the level of the application of the rules. The various temporalities that are being proposed here may act similarly The work by Jenny (2001) shows such emergence. Clearly, cellular automata are far more than simple pattern generators in that they give rise to new rules at higher orders. By looking more closely at how these orders are temporally organized, we gain additional insight into emergence.

Time, the Familiar Simulation Stranger: Why Simulations are Incomplete

So far, we have been proceeding as though we know what time is. The theologian and philosopher St. Augustine nicely summarized our dilemma. "What is time? If no one asks me, I know but if I wanted to explain it to the one who asks me, I plainly do not know." (Fraser, 1975). Going farther, we find the dilemma is much deeper. On the other hand, people with the same information generally agree, at least at a superficial level, on the time order of events—even if they don't agree on their duration, tempo, rhythm, and other characteristics—suggesting some sort of a unique and, to some degree, single observer-independent succession, and even duration of events. Unfortunately, this view is inconsistent with the psychological and neuropsychological literature (Antonia, 2002). Apparently, consciousness requires an ongoing brain-based (very local) sense of time, melding past, present, and future together, creating a flow that is individually unique (Lloyd, 2002).

Lloyd's work supports Husserl's view that individuals formulate unique conscious perceptions that are in constant temporal flux. Port and Van Gelder assert that cognition is a time-based dynamical system and not discrete-event based even if it involves multiple agents on a large landscape like NetLogo, which is the current orthodoxy used by most agent-simulation researchers (Port & Van Gelder, 1995; Parunak & Van Dyke, 2003).

We begin to see the dilemma for time and simulation placements in four critical areas: (1) the levels and basic concept of time; (2) the temporal state of the agent, (3) landscape event states in regards to their local placement, proximity, tempo, and envelopment—that is the particular local rolling-up of space-time dimensions—and (4) the resulting local direction of the flow of time for the agent, for the landscape, and for their interactions.

First, returning to the NetLogo example, simulations time is background dependent. That is, the measurement of the duration of an event in NetLogo is defined by the intervals of the computer's clock. Taking after Newton, "absolute, true and mathematical time, of itself, and from its own nature, flows equitably across the arena without relation to anything external." (Callender & Edney, 2001). Agents, landscapes, and the observer are placed in this flow. Absolute or mathematical time—Newton's pure time—is the sole concept of time used to grow, show, and develop all simulations. Even so, and as Newton has pointed out, time should not be confused with its sensible measuring method. So what is a simulation's, its agent's, and its landscape's temporality if it is not the flow of the "measuring" clock? Even more important, what vantage point do we stand on that permits us to know this "flowing"?

In contrast to background-dependent time, background-independent or relational time emerges from changes occurring between two agents or agents and their landscape. Time is instantiated in a relationship, in its mode of causality: it is found only there. As such, time is demarked by agent or landscape placement as a condition of growth, proximity, and envelopment in flows of relationships with varying durations. For our purposes, time is taken to be background independent, as a complex flow of interactions that, following an emergent rule tied to their scale of interaction, continuously structurates the placement of form, be it an agent or landscape or observer. (Here we are following Bohm's suggestion, 1980, that we try to use verbs to describe the continuous process of changes and organization). I will hold with Michon (1999) that time is local and relational in that an agent and its networks do not live in background-dependent space-time. The flow of their patterned relational structures constitutes multiple local streams coming together *as* space-time (John, 1999). As Bickhard and Campbell (n.d). suggest, these flows create a placement of a type of forms as they come together according to local conditions: "[Agents], flames, waves, vortexes—none are supervening on underlying constituents. They are more like knots or twists in the flow. Nothing persists other than the organization [pattern] of the knot itself. They are topological entities [a metapattern of continuous flows], not substantive entities."

Each of these contrasting concepts of time— time as background dependent or as background independent—produce serious difficulties with describing where in time an event, particularly a simulated one, is located and explaining what casual laws govern it. This is significant for how we conceptualize agents, their interactions, their virtual landscapes, the observer's role, and what the progress from one computer screen scan to the next as a causal pattern of relational temporal events may mean.

Virtual space is an electronically constructed space-time visualized according to various electronic requirements constrained by a particular human visual, auditory, temporal, and tactile sensorium. Cultural icons and other semiotics— including a "living" agent—reveal multimedia patterns of information, "a consensual hallucination experienced. . . as lines of light ranged in the nonspace of the mind, clusters and constellations of data." (Gibson, 2004). This display is "seen" by

the "virtually trained eye" as a world of its own (Hayles, 1999, 2005). Here information, occupying virtual space, is perceived to be free to create diverse spatial-time patterns—but really only one as constrained by the computer's clock and the observer biological time and limited imagination. Clearly, difficult explanatory problems are also raised.

Time Ecology Levels Increase Temporal Causal Complexity

J. T. Fraser's hierarchical theory of time recognizes five stable, hierarchically nested temporal levels in nature with five different forms of causation (Fraser, 1998). Each integrative level subsumes the functions and structures of a level or levels beneath it. Each adds additional degrees of freedom to its predecessor. Each has its own characteristic causality, also nested. Starting from the most complex, the five levels and their forms of causation (Fraser, 1998, 2000) are:

1. **Nootemporality:** The temporal reality of human mind or noetic intentionality. Its level-specific causation is "noetic intentionally in the service of symbolic causes" and is reversible through feedback loops that redefine earlier essential contexts.

2. **Biotemporality:** The temporal reality of living organisms. Its characteristic distinction is the biological ability to distinguish past and future relative to its own organization. Its level-specific causality is "intentionality in the service of biological needs." "In sum: organic intentionality and its corollary, freedom of choice, came about with biogenesis. It cannot be identified in the inanimate world" (Fraser, 2000). For biotemporality, there is, "no von Neumann address matrix, just a molecular soup, and the instructions say simply "DO THIS with the next copy of THAT which comes along." The results are far more robust. There is no unforgiving

Figure 1. Three principal temporalities and associated causalities with examples (with apologies to JT Fraser)

	Time is:	Propagation in Space is:	Past-Present Future Relationship Is:	Causality is:
Nootemporal	Local Chunking	Networks via Local or Extended Hubs and Nodes	Pst-pres-pres -pst-fut-pst-pst pst... (continuous redefining)	Complex
Biotemporal	Bounded Developmental /Growth	Local Reproductive Networks	Unidirectional Morpho-dynamics	Unidirectional Interactive/ Natural Selection
Eootemporal	Now-less flow	Inverse Square Law and diffusion	Unidirectional	Deterministic

central address authority, and no unforgiving central clock. This ability to take general, organized advantage of local, haphazard processes is exactly the ability that (so far) has distinguished information processing in living organisms from information process-ing by digital computers." (Dyson, 2005).

3. **Eotemporality:** The universe of large-scale matter. Its time is the physicist's *t*. Causality is deterministic, making possible predictions and retrodictions.

4. **Prototemporality:** The time of elementary objects. It is undirected and discontinuous. Its level-specific causality is probability where predictions and retrodictions can only be stochastic.

5. **Atemporality:** The mode of time charac-teristic of a black hole. There is no mode of causation because it is a level of absolute chaos or pure becoming. There is no "now" and "then," no "here" and "there"—all are discontinuities.

The three most significant layers of time and their characteristics for simulation are summarized in Figure 1. How time is defined, its manner of propagation, past-present-future, and causality are all very different. They cannot be subsumed under a single temporal concept.

Fraser's well accepted work raises very serious questions about social simulations. For starters, we can see that physics' *t* or eotemporality is not appropriate for either nootemporality nor biotem-porality, but is nested in both. This suggests that each agent positioned on its landscape, and the landscape itself for that matter, is positioned dif-ferently based on where it is relative to these nested processes—maturation, for example. As such, each local placement would exhibit quite different nested forms of time and causality. Similarly, the proximity, envelopment, orientation, temporal progression, velocity cones, and other key factors. These difficulties raise questions about how these temporal levels are causally tied together as local-background-independent time-influencing event processes unique to one level while constraining others perhaps at other levels. A contemporary example is the rate at which new technologies like nanotechnology are unfolding, the rate of loss of technically competent workers to deal with it due to aging, and government's rate of creating and evolving training systems for the new Latino workforce. (Time Structures has prepared multiple studies on this issue which are available on our web site, www.TimeStructures. Com,)

Generally, programmers are typically inter-ested in simulating the heterochronic flows in agents and landscape of three nested types of time: nootemporal time, agent time as biotemporal, and eotemporal or physics' time. Agent time as noological and biological, recognizes that everything, be it social (nations, communities, roads, IT, air transport, fashion, styles of consumption, etc). or social constructs, goes through developmental cycles with a beginning, middle, and end. These processes can be accelerated only up to a point without fundamentally restructuring the biotemporal and nootemporal aspects of the agent itself. For example, agent time may include aging, human migration, and related factors which if accelerated lead to different behaviors and have implications other local agents and landscape. Human agents not only develop and grow, but also have characteristic temporal noetic intentionality accompanying each stage. For example, older people are not in the same temporal reality as younger people, which creates practical synchronization problems (Hancock, 2002, p. 135). Disruption of agent time leading to the agent's fundamental restructuring of its nootemporality (bifurcation point, particularly if it is at the edge of chaos) could be a response if a noetically rooted chaotic or catastrophic future horizon like a natural disaster (eotemporality temporality) is seen to be approaching.

Nootemporal time is discrete and punctuated. Nootemporally, one thinks about the past, present, or future but not all at the same time or in any order relative to the arbitrary point of taking action in the present. There is a "space" between these temporal reorientations; consciousness involves time-space chunking (Lawrence, 2003, Chapter 5; and Lloyd, 2002). This suggests that the direction of causality in nootemporality is highly complex indeed. For example, if we mark a present event and then mark the following causally connected event such a mark can emerge noetically in the past or in the future—in the past because we are constantly reinventing it (Reichenbach, 1958). The past is embedded in the present as noted by Lloyd's findings or extends into a created, approaching future which then changes the present. (There is

an extensive empirical literature on nootemporal time for individual's work vs. family time, in organizations, recall of past events, and other contexts that can be used to inform agent-based simulations. Examples include: Farmer and Seers, 2004; Klein, 2004; Flaherty & Seipp-Williams, 2005; Jarvis, 2005; Carrasco & Mayordomo, 2005; Westenholz, 2006; Elchardus & Smits, 2006; and Branas-Garza, Espinosa-Fernandez, & Serrano-del-Rosal, 2007).

For current simulations, it would be difficult to place biotemporal or nootemporal elements in an ordered temporal context by level and as extended in geographic space unless their particular modes of temporally based causality are properly linked. This weakness makes it difficult to specify how independent and dependent temporal variables are heterochronically embedded in the process.

The problem is deepened by the adoption of Newtonian or eotemporal time as the sole time for extended simulation landscapes. This reduction to a single abstract time dimension seems to ignore not only other temporal levels and causality with their accompanying measurement methods but also temporal qualitative or subjective values (this is a "good time" or "these are bad times") that may be tied to a particular patch on a landscape but not to another. We are not denying that clock time permits multiple events at different scales across an extended geographic and historical space to be tied together, only noting that an inadequate specification of temporal independent levels and variables provides an inadequate specification of key casual factors. This is particularly so for agent-based biotemporal variables associated with development and growth, and with noetic intentionality. The notion that a particular time-ecology's local present is the result of the heterochronic interaction of various quite different temporalities and causalities in varying space settings, including biological processes, as well as of the semiotic characteristics carried forward by cultural artifacts of whatever size, in multiple temporal realms, appears to have been overlooked in current simulations.

The local landscape space-time that agents are instantiated in is not the same in all directions (proximity, etc)., especially not from an agent's local relational perspective. For example, certain Indian pilgrimages involve vast numbers of people walking across the surface of the earth in coordination with the movement of objects in the heavens. As a time-ecology, local time involves the biotemporal ecology and the local ecology, both of them as a local human-dominated corridor, and as more extensive geo-ecosystems, nootemporal, eotemporal, and additional dimensions. All of these factors have their own long-term cycles and synchronicities. The timing of these pilgrimage festivals is established by a calendar built upon the movement of the sun and the phases of the moon. For example, the catchment area of the pilgrimage to Pandharpur, India, includes 28 routes of palkhis (palanquins in which the silver replicas of feet of saints are carried). Some 100,000 pilgrims walk along these routes to Pandharpur, reaching it on sukla ekadasi, the eleventh day of the waxing moon of Asadha. The stopping times along the routes are precisely set by the motion of the moon along the elliptic. Owing to the changing speed of the moon in its elliptical orbit, pilgrims must change their walking speed. Simultaneously, aspects of the landscape that are significant to a biotemporal agent, availability of grass and local foods, are evolving both independently of and dependently on the agent (Nowak & Sigmund, 2004). Clearly, any point on a landscape involves multiple evolving long- and short-term temporalities similar to those of the agent moving across it.

Janelle, and others, working at the biological and social level, explore what this nesting of temporalities means in terms of nootemporal characteristics of human populations and metropolitan spatial development and movement (Foresight for Transport, 2001). Janelle finds that travel times between two fixed points considered in two different periods can show either convergence or divergence. There is considerable variation in convergence and divergence between places that are even adjacent to one another. For example the time it takes to travel from an inner city ghetto, compared with moving from an affluent neighborhood to downtown, varies considerably because of transport opportunities.

Thus, the local temporal geometric form is severely restricted by the equations defining the topological structure of agent/landscape's respective five dimensional space-times. It is even unclear how these temporalities interact in the continuous forming of an agent on a landscape. An instantiated, unique agent and/or landscape may rotate its topological form continuously from one of five space-time dimensions to another and back as practices create qualitatively different event streams (Stewart, 2001). Each dimension, depending on its characteristics, is in turn undergoing its own variations in frequency and amplitude.

Unique rates of Agent Temporal Progress and Rhythm regulate Proximity to and envelopment with a Landscape and Other Agents Producing Complex Orientability, Connectivity, and Continuity

Temporal progression is the dimension of process and motion which describes, among other things, the "how" of movement or flow of the present into the future, the past into the present, the present itself (Victoria, 1997; Koehler-Jones, 2003). The question here is "how" each is moved into the future and out of the past relative to its placement and proximity—its continuity, connectivity, and orientability—to other agents and the landscape.

Tempo and rhythm describe the speed and nature of this "how" in motion. Tempo refers to the pace of activity. With respect to future events, tempo includes both the rate at which the future approaches and the speed of onset of specific events. (With respect to past events, it is how fast they fade away). Tempo also involves relativism of related flows or independence of flow. The dimension of tempo then, covers "fastness" and

Figure 2. Temporal orientation and perspective vary by individual

Differing pasts:		*Differing Futures:*
Experiences		Expectations
Expectations		Control
Rate of movement into the present	*Differing* :	Depth
Rate of vanishing into the past	Narrow or wide Rate of movement into the past	Rate of movement into future
Near or far		How the past is brought forward
Density	Rate of movement into the future Density	Density

Source: Victoria Koehler-Jones, 1999.

whether that "fastness" has independence for the actor.

Rhythm refers to the regular recurrence of certain features of time. It asks whether time moves in "pulsating" or periodic cycles, whether its motion is smooth, or whether it is irregular and unpredictable. It may be that within a rhythmic system change occurs gradually or in sharp disjunctive motions, bringing unexpected novelty. Is the rhythm or the cadence within the rhythm smooth, choppy, disjunctive, etc.?

Both the temporal perspective and temporal progression "move" time in different ways (Figure 2). From a temporally background-independent viewpoint, they establish dynamical relationships with the past and future that inform what and where the local present is, and thus agent placement and envelopment. Each agent's local rules are contextualized by the temporal-signature. Such principles must be incorporated into a simulation seeking to show nootemporal activities produce a particular outcome.

Agent Local Time Emerges from Multiple, Differing Temporal Velocity Cones

A "velocity cone" refers to the velocity at which any event's causal process propagates, including

that of the Temporal Signature (Reichenbach, 1958). At maximum speed, an event of a particular temporal type can only propagate a specific distance either into the future or from the past at a temporally limited rate with the distance narrowing the closer it comes to the immediate present. The velocity cone can depict all events that can be reached by a particular eotemporal, biological, or nootemporal signal traveling into the future, or coming from the past (Kaufmann, 1973; Smolin, 2001). This suggests that an agent's placement is very local indeed in that its varying temporal characteristics and temporal signature propagate at varying rates creating varying time-dependent backgrounds. Obviously, this applies to the continuous structuration via the heterochrony of morphogenesis of the organism itself from fertilization to death.

The propagation of spatial-temporal events using various media reveal the motion—ordered, chaotic, etc.—of a landscape and its agent's multiple "velocity-cones." This spatial-temporal limitation defines and delimits an agent and the influence that various events propagating at different speed can causally have on its structuration rate(s), depending in turn on linkages to velocity cones of resources, energy, and information (Parunak, Van Dyke, & Brueckner, 2001). Here the focus is on the continuous heterochronic flow of a "wave front" as it is received at different rates by agents and networks organizing a landscape. Instantaneous, parallel reordering of agents is not the same.

Our discussion of an agent's temporal levels suggests that there are three fundamental velocity cones: that of biotemporality or allometric velocities; that of physics time or eotemporality; and that of nootemporal or noetic velocities. Propagation of ordered relational motion is distinct in these temporalities and is not instantaneous as in a computer simulation. Further, individual heterochronic flows vary in their timing: some are continuous and some punctuated; some are cyclical; some proceed out of the past; some approach from the future as projections and emergent properties, etc. Structuration of local agent is maintained by synchronization, entrainment, etc., of such varying heterochronic rates (Winfree, 1980).

Large-scale spatio-temporal phenomena are significant for simulations. Pipes and various surfaces such as political jurisdictions extend beyond a single node's velocity cones to remote portions of the landscape or to other agents (Tyler, 1995). Large portions of a landscape can be influenced by overlapping surfaces that change local time. Simultaneity can occur at multiple local points beyond the extent of any one agent's velocity cone via pipes like the internet or other electronic communication traveling at the speed of light, but the signal can only be processed as placement, envelopment, etc., of information at the rate it can be transduced and interpreted by biological and noetic systems. Agent life-worlds are the dynamic extensions and entrainments of their temporal signatures upon such locally extended surfaces.

We know from the agent's time-signature that the past recedes and the future approaches at different rates for different agents. It does so in a relatively straightforward clear, more complicated, or complex—even chaotic—way. Thus, a social world is a dynamical world because "what facts

there are depends upon what time it is." (Tooley, 1997).

At any one point, time-space causality may vary considerably, being the result of multiple local heterochronic agent-landscape-pipe past-present-linkages, each with its own dynamical pacing, temporal perspective, and temporal progression, all embedded in biotemporality. The result is complex action where local relationships indicate temporal priority between two events by identifying the direction of causation via the direction of local time determining proximity, orientability, continuity, and ultimately connectivity. Again, we are looking at this as a multilayered heterochronic flow of events that structurate agents and landscapes.

For example, temporal/spatial geographic analysis, using Geographical Information Systems and other computer-based tools, depict dynamic relationships with extending or contracting temporal social patterns. This represents a kind of geographic space/time plasticity in, of, and between social entities at all scales, be they cities or their social-culture groups (Janelle, 2002; Koehler, 2003b). Multiple parallel nested temporal processes, including nootemporally differing pasts, presents and futures, interpenetrate, feeding forward and backward at different points across the multiple layers of this geographic time-ecology. Temporally the local relationship of agent-landscape events that are accessible to the agent vary in their duration, in their scheduling (time and sequence in the network), and by their own unique temporal characteristics (Janelle, 2002).

Difficulties with Determining Temporal Causality

Parunak, Van Dyke, and Brueckner (2001) point out:

Input and output of the various Agents are coupled to elements of state, but the environment does not distinguish which elements of state are so coupled.

That distinction depends on the agents that exist at any moment and the capabilities of their sensors and effectors. The lack of a distinguished input and output means that the environment, unlike an agent, is unbounded. The fact that an environment, like an agent, has state and process means that putting a boundary and associated input and output values around an environment (and its associated agents) yields a higher-level agent.

A number of temporal issues emerge. Is the environment in fact unbounded and without temporality, or is it locally temporally textured? Is the boundary really that of the observer and the electronics of the computer? The momentary local activity of an agent suggests a local temporal connection with the environment, a kind of boundary. All of the agent structuration and local interactions are immersed in this complex periodicity. While it changes, it shapes how chemical, biological, nootemporal, and other reactions take place. More exactly, what is the effect of this suboscillatory field on these instantiated processes? (Jenny, 2001; Winfree, 1980). What can be said of this boundary making and closing process? Is this "higher level agent" consistent with the boundaries being simulated or is it an imposition of an unrelated space-time? What is the cause of its placement, orientability, etc.? Finally, a simulation often involves a very large number of runs. How are these to be reinterpreted from the scale of the electronic clock to the scale of subjective, history-interfering nootemporal world? It would seem that boundaries create causal contexts by selecting how the local becomes the "general."

More to the point, when an effort is being made to observe transitions of a large number of complex agents, understanding their behavior requires the determination of the actual landscape of transitional structures and possible intermediaries between one agent state and another. For example, the interaction of various temporalities may resemble the hidden "wrinkle" that distorts flatland behaviors. Only when the time scale of simulation and observation is appropriate can such hidden intermediaries like those suggested by Hanson & Crutchfield at a hidden scale be observed and identified. Such intermediaries may occur from the interaction among multiple time domains requiring complex programming and quantitative or qualitative visualization instrumentation. Generally, the time scales incorporated into a simulation's time-ecology and their heterochronic interactions dictate the validity of the theoretical approach and what simulation approximations are appropriate. Those incorporated time scales also dictate which elements of state can be coupled to others or even the movement of various states around a landscape. Each bears on continuous placement, proximity, envelopment, continuity, connectivity, and orientability as the simulation proceeds. Each of these factors increases the complexity of explanation by making it necessary to deal with concerted (or concurrent) versus consecutive step dynamics across multiple orientations and layers of continuous structuration (Baum, Yang, & Zewail, 2007). Such a complex system may give rise to unexpected temporalities in dimensions that are not accessed with existing instrumentation. This approach gives a wider meaning to complex systems' being sensitive to initial space-time conditions—conditions that may be hidden. (For a useful discussion of causality issues, see Kellert, 1993).

An Example of a Different Time-Ecology: Buddhist Time

It is the interaction between the creation of "digital creatures living in computers" and human consciousness that necessitates new strategies for making, reading, and interpreting programs as texts, how these texts are instantiated in different computer-based media, and the assistance that literary and cultural theory provides for interpreting scientific research (Hayles, 2005). Hayles call this *materiality*, "an emergent property created through dynamic interactions between physical characteristics and signifying strategies. Materiality thus marks a junction between physical reality and human intention." (Hayles, 2005). It also marks the juncture between the mathematical world of the simulation and the narrative one of programming. A brief discussion of Buddhist time shows how materiality might differ from a different time perspective in how the behavior of an agent is defined, in the state of the observer, and in how their materiality comes together.

The Buddhist perspective holds that *multiple* conventional discrete instants make up our experience of time. (For a discussion of the Buddhist concept of instants see Satkari, 1991; Gupta 1991; Prasad, J., 1991; and Stcherbatsky, 1991). There are, 6,400,099,188 such instants in a day. Thus, instants or moments are quantum-like, rather than a continuous unbroken flowing (Katagiri, 2007). Buddhism holds that a durational instant cannot be *a present* in *a* past or *a* future. There is only a four dimensional conventional or local present instant. (For a similar view see Inada, 1991).

The time we call spring blossoms has an existence called flowers. The flowers, in turn, express the time called spring. This is not existence within time; existence itself is time." (Goodhew & Loy, 2002). Time is instantiated in the local relationship "flower-spring." Time's instants result from continuous and changing relationships that are strictly local yet "are" time. "'Being-time' means that time itself is being... and all being is time.... If time merely flies away, you would be separated from time [including the observer from the simulation]. The reason you do not clearly understand being-time is that you think of time as only passing. (Tanahashi, 1985, pp. 76-80).

The materiality of the placement and interpretation of an agent on a Buddhist landscape would involve determining which layer (conventional or ultimate) is appropriate and how much interpenetration there might be even as the observer-simulation is time. Proximity would vary by layer too, one being immediate, the other simultaneous across all time and aspects of the landscape. Time as being, as placement on the ultimate and conventional planes, also suggests a difference in envelopment. Velocity cones are very different as well. Issues of causality would be very difficult to work out.

Agent Simulation Temporal Issues Present Significant Problems

I have argued that the proposed temporal deepening of how simulations are constructed involving interaction of multiple temporalities (itself a kind of temporality) could lead to the unexpected triggering of cascades of secondary emergences. Such cascades may already be there but going unobserved. The proposed perspective—even that of being time—may stimulate the creation of more interesting simulations, and more interesting research results. It also suggests that the "materiality" of the simulation includes the observer in very interesting ways, highly conditioning what is "seen" and how it is interpreted.

Fraser, the time expert, states, "It is not possible to make predictions about the conduct of a human group, acting in the service of concrete or symbolic causes, without allowing for [temporal,] noetic and biological intentionalities, as well as the deterministic, probabilistic and chaotic contributions." (Fraser, 1998). This warning, when combined with our analysis of how simulations are constructed and interpreted, expands on the list of complex temporal challenges to complex system autonomous agent simulations:

- Placement, the temporal signature, and velocity cones and all that they involve suggest that landscapes and agents are much more complex than they are currently depicted, including potential unknown levels and intermediaries at unexpected temporalities.

- The heterochrony of agents and landscapes suggest that it could be difficult to trace the causes of structuration at any level, particularly if critical intermediary processes go undetected. New filters and methods of visualizing agent process and intermediaries as they occur may be necessary.

- Temporally complex agents and landscapes may interact across temporal levels that differ locally and via pipes to other local portions or levels of the time-ecology. This produces a 3-D to 5-D "spaghetti-like" connectivity leading to a very complex causality.

- The Feigenbaum Map traces the various forms of causality and its associated temporality leading from formal unpredictability, to self-similarity or emergence of patterns, ending with the intentional noetic creation of additional patterns in complex systems (Fraser, 1998). Such an approach could lay the foundation for determining the role that time plays in emergence (Koehler, 1996).

- The programmer generates the system and in turn, trhough acts of interpretation and visualization, becomes the system. This sort of reflexivity confuses and entangles the boundaries of the system, qualifying in unconsidered ways what the autonomous agent simulation is doing and showing as it evolves along with the programmer.

ACKNOWLEDGMENT

This essay falls between computer science and ontology. Temporal concepts are clearly related to concepts that define a domain and that generate ways of thinking about that domain. Philosophical ontology is also relevant as seen in my attempts to define the five levels of time as background independent. Such formal computer and philo-sophical ontology discussions are beyond the scope of this article.

REFERENCES

Antonia, D. Remembering when. (2002). *Scientific American, 66*, September.

Bainbridge, W. (2007). The scientific research potential of virtual worlds. *Science, 317*, 473. doi:10.1126/science.1146930

Banchoff, T. (1966). *Beyond the third dimension.* New York: Scientific American Library.

Baum, P., Yang, D.-S., & Zewail, A. (2007). 4D visualization of transitional structures in phase transitions by electron diffraction. *Science, 318*, 788–792. doi:10.1126/science.1147724

Bickhard, M., & Campbell, D. (n.d). Emergence: www.lehigh.edu/~mhb0/emergence.html. Retrieved February 18, 1999.

Bohm, D. (1980). *Wholeness and the implicate order.* New York: Routledge & Kegan Paul.

Branas-Garza, P., Espinosa-Fernandez, L., & Serrano-del-Rosal, R. (2007). Effects of gender and age on retrospective time judgements. *Time & Society, 16*, 1. doi:10.1177/0961463X07074104

Callender, C., & Edney, R. (2001). *Introducing time.* Santa Cruz, CA: Aerial Press.

Carrasco, C., & Mayordomo, M. (2005). Beyond employment: Working time, living time. *Time & Society, 14*, 231–259. doi:10.1177/0961463X05055195

Chen, C. (2004). *Information visualization: Beyond the horizon.* London: Springer.

Donath, J. (2007). Virtually trustworthy. *Science, 317*, 53. doi:10.1126/science.1142770

Dyson, G. (2005).Turing's cathedral: A visit to Google on the occasion of the 60th anniversary of John von Neumann's proposal for a digital computer: http://www.edge.org/3rd_culture/dyson05/dyson05_index.html.

Elchardus, M., & Smits, W. (2006). The persistence of the standardized life cycle. *Time & Society, 15,* 303–326. doi:10.1177/0961463X06066944

Farmer, S., & Seers, A. (2004). Time enough to work: Employee motivation and entrainment in the workplace. *Time & Society, 13,* 213. doi:10.1177/0961463X04044574

Flaherty, M., & Seipp-Williams, L. (2005). Socio-temporal rhythms in e-mail: A case study. *Time & Society, 14,* 1. doi:10.1177/0961463X05049949

Foresight for Transport. (2001). A Foresight exercise to help forward thinking in transport and sectoral integration. European Community. Funded by the European Community under the "Competitive and Sustainable Growth" Programme: http://www.iccr-international.org/foresight/.

Fraser, J. T. (1975). *Of time, passion and knowledge.* Princeton, NJ: Princeton University Press.

Fraser, J. T. (1998). *From chaos to conflict.* In Fraser, Soulsby, & Argyros.

Fraser, J. T. (1999). Appendix B, Complexity and its Measure. In *Time, conflict, and human values.* Chicago: University of Illinois Press.

Fraser, J. T. (2000). Human freedom. *KronoScope, 2*(2), 223–247.

Fraser, J. T., Soulsby, M., & Argyros, A. (Eds.). (1998). *Time, order and chaos: The study of time IX.* Madison, CT: International Universities Press.

Gibson, W. (2004). Neuromancer. In Nayar, P. (Ed.), *Virtual Worlds.* New Delhi: Sage.

Goodhew, L., & Loy, D. (2002). Momo, dogen, and the comodification of time. *KronoScope, 2*(1). doi:10.1163/15685240260186817

Greene, B. (1999). *The elegant universe.* New York: W.W. Norton.

Gupta, R. (1991). The Buddhist Doctrine of Momentariness and its Presuppositions. In Prasad, H. (1991).

Hancock, P. (2002). The time of your life: One thousand moons. *KronoScope, 2*(2). doi:10.1163/156852402320900715

Hanson, J. E., & Crutchfield, J. P. (1997). Computational mechanics of cellular automata: an example. *Physica D. Nonlinear Phenomena, 103,* 169–189. doi:10.1016/S0167-2789(96)00259-X

Hayles, N. K. (1999). *How we became posthuman.* Chicago, IL: University of Chicago Press.

Hayles, N. K. (2002). *Writing machines.* Cambridge, MA: MIT Press.

Hayles, N. K. (2005). *My mother was a computer.* Chicago, IL: University of Chicago Press.

Holland, J. (1995). *Hidden order. Redwood City, CA.* Redwood City: Addison-Wesley.

Inada, K. (1991). Time and temporality – A Buddhist approach. In Prasad, H. (1991).

Janelle, D. G. (2002). Embedding time in accessibility analysis. CSISS Workshop on Accessibility in Time and Space. The Ohio State University, 22 July 2002: http://www.csiss.org/aboutus/presentations/files/janelle_etaa.pdf.

Jarvis, H. (2005). Moving to London time: Household co-ordination and the infrastructure of everyday life. *Time & Society, 14,* 1. doi:10.1177/0961463X05050302

Jenny, H. (2001). *Cymatics: a study of wave phenomena and vibration.* Newmarket, NH: MACROmedia.

Kaku, M. (1994). *Hyperspace: A scientific odyssey through parallel universes, time warps, and the tenth dimension.* New York: Oxford University Press.

Katagiri, D. (2007). *Each moment is the universe: Zen and the way of being time*. Boston: Shambala Press.

Kaufmann, W. (1973). *Relativity and cosmology*. New York: Harper and Row.

Kellert, S. (1993). *In the wake of chaos*. Chicago, IL: University of Chicago Press.

Klein, O. (2004). Social perception of time and high speed trains. *Time & Society*, *13*, 213. doi:10.1177/0961463X04043504

Koehler, G. (1996) *The Feigenbaum diagram: A metapattern for the social construction of time*, a paper presented at the Sixth Annual International Conference of the Society for Chaos Theory in the Psychology and the Life Science, June 25-28, 1996, University of California, Berkeley.

Koehler, G. (2001). A framework for visualizing the chronocomplexity of politically regulated time-ecologies. A paper prepared for the International Society for the Study of Time Conference, Gargonza, Italy, and for the Society for Chaos Theory in Psychology and the Life Science Conference, Madison, Wisconsin.

Koehler, G. (2003a). Time, complex systems, and public policy: A theoretical foundation for adaptive policy making. *Nonlinear Dynamics Psychology and Life Sciences*, *7*, 1. doi:10.1023/A:1020418210366

Koehler, G. (2003b). EU transport foresight planning: Comments on how chronocomplexity limits such strategic planning efforts. A paper presented at the Society for Chaos Theory in Psychology and Life Sciences, 12th Annual Conference, Portland State University, Portland, Oregon.

Koehler, G. (2004). Sorting out the temporal confusion of computer simulations. International Society for the Study of Time, Conference, Cambridge, England, August.

Koehler, G. (in press). Computer simulations as hidden time-ecologies. In Vrobel, S., Rossler, O. E., & Marks-Tarlow, T. (Eds.), *Simultaneity: Temporal Structures and Observer Perspectives*. Singapore: World Scientific.

Koehler-Jones, V. (2003). The Temporal signature of small manufacturers. Unpublished draft report available from www.timestructures.com.

Kwinter, S. (2002). *Architectures of time*. Cambridge, Mass.: MIT Press.

Lawrence, W. (2002). *Dynamical cognitive science*. Boston, MA: MIT Press.

Lloyd, D. (2002). Functional fMRI and the study of human consciousness. *Journal of Cognitive Neuroscience*, *14*, 818–831. doi:10.1162/089892902760191027

Merleau-Ponty, M. (1968). *Lingis, Alphonso, trans. The visible and the invisible*. Evanston, IL: Northwestern University.

Michon, J. (1999). Models of local time. Paper presented at the XIth International Conference of the European Society for Cognitive Psychology, Ghent, Belgium, September 1-4.

Mookerjee, S. (1991). The Buddhist doctrine of flux (the nature of existence). In Prasad, H. (1991).

Nowak, M., & Sigmund, K. (2004). Evolutionary Dynamics of Biological Games. *Science*, *303*, 793–799. doi:10.1126/science.1093411

Parunak, H., & Van Dyke, H. (1977) "Go to the Ant": Engineering principles from natural multi-agent systems. In *Annals of Operations Research*, Special Issue on Artificial Intelligence and Management Science, 75, 69-101.

Parunak, H., Van Dyke, H., & Brueckner, S. (2001). Entropy and self-organization in multi-agent systems. Paper presented to Agents'01, May 28-June 1, 2001, Montreal Quebec, Canada.

Port, R., & Van Gelder, T. (1995). *Mind as motion: Explorations in the dynamics of cognition.* Cambridge, MA: MIT Press.

Prasad, H. (1991). *Essays on time in Buddhism.* Delhi: Sri Satguru Publications.

Prasad, J. Discussion of the Buddhist doctrine of momentariness and subjective idealism in the Nyaya-stras. In Prasad, H. (1991).

Reichenbach, H. (1956). *The direction of time.* New York, NY: Dover.

Reichenbach, H. (1958). *The philosophy of space and time.* New York, NY: Dover.

Richardson, K. (1975). The Hegemony of the Physical Sciences: An Exploration in Complexity Thinking. *Futures, 37,* 615–653. doi:10.1016/j.futures.2004.11.008

Simon, H. (2005). Foreword. In *Callebaut, W. & Rasskin-Gutman, D. Modularity: Understanding the development and evolution of natural complex systems.* Boston: MIT Press.

Smolin, L. (2001). *Three roads to quantum gravity.* New York, NY: Basic Books.

Stcherbatsky, T. The theory of instantaneous being. In Prasad, H. (1991).

Stewart, I. (2001). *Flatterland.* Cambridge: Perseus.

Tanahashi, K. (1985). *Moon in a dewdrop: Writings of Zen master Dogen.* San Francisco: North Point.

Tooley, M. (1997). *Time, tense and causation.* Oxford: Clarendon Press.

Tyler, V. (1995). *Metapatterns: Across space, time, and mind.* New York, NY: Columbia University Press.

Victoria, E. (1997). The Use of temporal constructs as a model for understanding perceptions of environmental hazards. Dissertation, Department of Sociology, University of Nevada, Las Vegas.

Wertheim, M. (1999). *The pearly gates: A history of space from Dante to the Internet.* New York: Norton.

Westenholz, A. (2006). Identity, time, and work. *Time & Society, 15,* 1. doi:10.1177/0961463X06061349

Wilensky, U. (1999). NetLogo 3.1.2 User Manual: http://ccl.northwestern.edu/netlogo/. Center for Connected Learning and Computer-Based Modeling, Northwestern University, Evanston, IL.

Winfree, A. (1980). *The geometry of biological time.* New York: Springer-Verlag.

This work was previously published in International Journal of Agent Technologies and Systems (IJATS), edited by Goran Trajkovski, pp. 1-18, copyright 2009 by IGI Publishing (an imprint of IGI Global).

Chapter 2
Temporally Autonomous Agent Interaction

Adam J. Conover
Towson University, USA

Robert J. Hammell
Towson University, USA

ABSTRACT

This work reflects the results of continuing research into "temporally autonomous" multi-agent interaction. Many traditional approaches to modeling multi-agent systems involve synchronizing all agent activity in simulated environments to a single "universal" clock. In other words, agent behavior is regulated by a global timer where all agents act and interact deterministically in time. However, if the objective of any such simulation is to model the behavior of real-world entities, this discrete timing mechanism yields an artificially constrained representation of actual physical agent interaction. In addition to the behavioral autonomy normally associated with agents, simulated agents must also have temporal autonomy in order to interact realistically. Intercommunication should occur without global coordination or synchronization. To this end, a specialized simulation framework is developed. Several simulations are conducted from which data are gathered and we subsequently demonstrate that manipulation of the timing variable amongst interacting agents affects the emergent behaviors of agent populations.

INTRODUCTION

In this paper, previous simulations (Conover & Trajkovski, 2007; Conover, 2008b) involving *passively interacting* temporally autonomous agents are expanded to accommodate *active* agents which directly communicate — albeit in a primitive manner. Throughout the sections of this paper,

several agent activation models are explored. In each model, agents exchange "beliefs" via simple messages which are reflective of an agent's internal state. Loosely speaking, it is the goal of any given agent to "convince" neighboring agents to adopt the given agents currently held belief (internal state). Though agents may take on many states during a simulation, each agent communicates only its currently active state only with its spatially embedded neighbors.

DOI: 10.4018/978-1-60960-171-3.ch002

Copyright © 2011, IGI Global. Copying or distributing in print or electronic forms without written permission of IGI Global is prohibited.

The first model to be discussed is divided into two distinct subtypes. The first subtype, discussed in the next section, is a direct extension our previously studied "Conway" *Game of Life* models (Conover, 2008a; Conover 2008b); but agents respond to events generated by neighbors rather than vivificating[1] autonomously. The second subtype, discussed in the third section, is a completely new model based upon *temporally variant* belief interaction. We have found that both subtypes display interesting and unique behavioral characteristics.

MESSAGE ACTIVATION MODEL

In this mode, each agent begins in a random Boolean state conforming to the basic "Conway" life/death (active/inactive) *Game of Life* rules (Gardner, 1970). As with the threaded model discussed in previous work (Conover, 2008a), the agents behave autonomously within a global mean vivification delay time d_m of 500ms with delay variances d_v chosen to produce d_v / d_m ratios r_{vm} ranging from 0.0 to 2.0[2]. However, instead of agents simply examining their neighborhood at intervals which are independent of the environment, the agents trigger the vivification of their neighbors by sending event messages. To maintain temporal autonomy, each agent periodically queries an internal message queue (once per vivification cycle) for the presence of pending notifications received from other agents. The agent adopts a new state from the *statistical mode* derived from the queued messages as well as its current state. If an agent is inactive, it cannot become active until it receives a notification from an active neighbor. Only active agents are capable of sending messages to other agents. When any given agent vivificates, it determines the state of its own environment and sends notifications to all neighbors, if it becomes or remains active. An agent will only send one message to each of its neigh-

boring agents once per vivification cycle regardless of how many messages are in the queue. Once the vivification cycle completes (all neighbors have been notified), the sending agent clears its message queue and again awaits new messages from neighboring agents.

The primary focus of this section is an exploration of the average population density of active agents and average age of the agents as a given trial progresses. However, in this section, the number of messages received by each agent between vivifications is considered. A summary of the data gathered in the first set of message based activation trials is shown in Table 1, ordered by r_{vm}. Other values include the average population density pd_{avg}, the population's average age age_{avg}, the average number of messages received per agent mgs_{avg}, and the standard deviations σ_{pd}, σ_{age}, σ_{msg}, of data in each sample set grouped by r_{vm}.

Figure 1 shows the data pertaining Message Activation Ratios as they relate to population densities of each agent population. Specifically, population age and density versus r_{vm} are both illustrated in Figures 1a and 1b. Figure 1c shows the average number of messages received per agent per vivification. The lighter line in each of these is a simple cubic regression plot. One curiosity depicted in these graphs is the absence of the smooth curves generated by the models examined in the "passive models" described in previous research (Conover, 2008a; Conover 2008b).

A few points of interest are immediately apparent in this data: First and foremost is that the average number of messages received and the average population age curves are nearly identical in shape. This is mirrored by the similarity of the respective standard deviations (shown with the data in Table 1). The standard deviations were computed individually for each set of five trials for each r_{vm}. A close examination of this table

Table 1. This table shows the results of 45 individual Message Activation trials — five for each given r_{vm}, averaged together — sorted by age_{avg}

r_{vm}	age_{avg}	pd_{avg}	msg_{avg}	σ_{pd}	σ_{age}	σ_{msg}
0.15	4.44	40.7%	35.5	0.00055	0.030	0.217
0.25	4.54	40.9%	36.3	0.00045	0.024	0.217
0.50	4.72	41.1%	37.8	0.00055	0.031	0.278
0.75	5.14	41.5%	41.1	0.00045	0.059	0.464
1.00	5.33	41.7%	42.6	0.00055	0.019	0.167
1.25	6.00	42.0%	48.1	0.00045	0.061	0.501
1.50	6.17	42.1%	49.3	0.00045	0.066	0.534
1.75	7.02	42.3%	56.2	0.00045	0.103	0.850
2.00	7.12	42.4%	56.9	0.00110	0.137	1.163

Figure 1. Boolean Message Driven Agent Results: Graphs of the statistical information gathered for the experiments conducted this section: (a) Average Ages for each Variance Ratio r_{vm}; (b) Average Population for each Variance Ratio r_{vm}; Average Messages Exchanged for each Variance Ratio r_{vm}

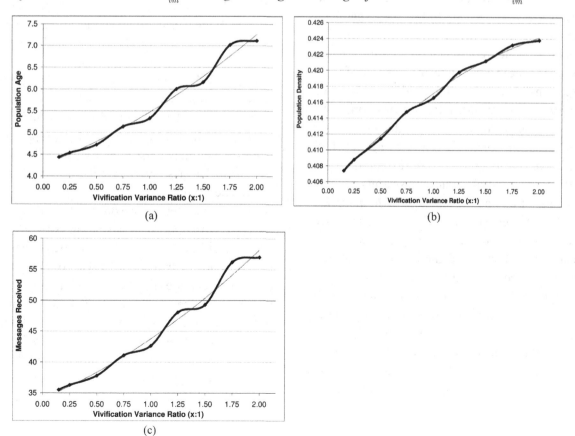

reveals a small empirical correlation between σ_{age} and σ_{msg} and age_{avg} and msg_{avg}. As was seen in earlier work, higher deviations from mean tend to produce longer lived agents.

INTRODUCTION TO THE AGENT SOCIETY

In the *Message Driven* architecture, each agent actively attempts to influence its neighbors "beliefs" by promulgating belief messages to all adjacent agents upon vivification. For the purposes of this discussion, a "belief" will be defined as an agent state brought upon by interaction with the environment and neighboring agents. The actual manifestation of these states will be discussed below.

Though formal models of agent belief interaction have been studied by others (Cantwell, 2005; Pasquier & Chaib-draa, 2003; Deffuant, Neau, Amblard, & Weisbuch, 2001), the experiments conducted here require only a very simplistic model of belief representation. In a similar spirit to work done in dynamic team formation of agents (Gaston & desJardins, 2005) and "Naming Games in Spatially-Embedded Random Networks" (Lu, Korniss, & Szymanski, 2006), this research examines agent clustering driven by agent beliefs. However, the focus here is on an exploration of the effects of temporal variance in swarms of agents capable of interacting purely asynchronously.

Every agent participates in a primary active belief which is directly conveyed to each of its spatially embedded neighbors via "belief messages". Agents send and receive messages corresponding to some belief and may adopt a new belief based upon "peer-pressure" from neighboring agents. As agents receive messages, they modify their own active belief in accordance with the messages received from other agents. This introduces a feedback system (Schilling, 2006),

in which agent state at time $t + \Delta t$ may be indirectly affected by its actions at time t.

Loosely speaking, the goal of any individual is to convince its neighbors to adopt its belief. At any given time, each agent possesses a single belief about its environment. Messages generated by any given agent directly correspond to the active belief and will potentially affect the beliefs of other agents in the immediate neighborhood, which in turn will continue to affect others even farther away. This also introduces feedback into the system, since any agent propagating a message will eventually be affected by its own actions at a later point in time. Ultimately, a clustering of agents with the same "beliefs" can be seen, but whose populations are driven primarily by the "temporal variability" of the actual interactions.

In this simulation, there are three distinct message types, each of which corresponds to one of three agent beliefs. An agent belief is represented by a unique primary color; RED, GREEN, or BLUE. Each belief represents an arbitrary perception of the world. For example, an agent may believe that the "the world is BLUE" and attempt to convince neighboring agents of this belief by emitting BLUE messages. Any agent's active belief is represented by the color of the agent (and optional textual label) in the simulation environment. This offers the ability to visually represent agents which may exist in a "transitional" state as a blend of these primary colors, making the agent's belief state easily recognizable.

The experimental reason for having three message types represented by color is two-fold. First, physical entities are rarely restricted to two simple states or population types, so there was a desire to capture the effects of more than two competing forces within a population. Second, the ability to clearly visualize the behavior of the system in real-time was also desirable. To foster intuitive visualization as the simulation unfolded in real-time, three beliefs was an ideal number. Given that three primary colors may be easily blended into a single color, it can then be easily seen which "beliefs" are actively competing. A similar technique was used by Lu and Korniss when visualizing "naming game" simulations where colors represent words learned by agents (Lu et al., 2006).

As agents communicate, their internal state is visually represented by a blending of the colors corresponding to the actual beliefs. Though any agent may be in a "fuzzy" belief state at any given moment, the belief that is communicated is always discrete. If an agent has been exposed to multiple RED, GREEN, and BLUE messages, it will exist in a state that blends these beliefs, but will always communicate the discrete belief most closely represented. In other words, all messages sent by an agent carry equal weight.

In the "Agent Society" model, the vivification process is similar to that of the "Threaded Selection" and "Message Activation" models described earlier. As in those models, each agent is triggered into vivification by an agent specific timer operating within an agent specific thread. However, in this model, agents are always "listening" for messages from neighbors. As an agent sits otherwise idle, receiving messages from neighboring agents, the sum of number of messages of each type is maintained. Only upon vivification do the agents respond to the received messages, adopt a new state and forward a new message on to its neighbors based on the newly adopted state. The method used to determine the most appropriate message associated with a belief is based on color values themselves. The messages are blended into a single color in 24-bit RGB color-space and the message generation algorithm is derived from the following rules applied in order:

1. If there exists an RGB color component that exceeds all others, the message corresponding to the dominant color component is chosen.
2. If any two RGB color values are equal (with the third type having a lesser value), a random

message type corresponding to one of the two equal values is chosen.
3. If all three RGB color component values are equal, a message type is chosen at random.

Figure 2 is a series of three screen-shots taken from a running simulation. Each agent is displayed as a cell labeled with a single letter corresponding to the fundamental belief and a color representing the agent's belief state. Snapshots of a progressing simulation can be seen in Figures 2a-2c. The first image shows the starting state of a simulation with all agents in one of three random states. The second image is further along in a simulation where clustering of beliefs begins to take place. Finally, the last image shows the near complete clustering of beliefs. The general pattern that emerges from unregulated "Agent Society" simulations is that small groups tend to form very quickly, which slowly give way to monolithic homogeneous groups. These homogeneous regions will be regarded as areas of "belief agreement". The phenomena is illustrated in Figure 2 and is described in greater detail below, where it will shown that belief populations can be sustained via manipulation of agent's temporal variability.

All simulations described in the remainder of this research took place on a 50×50 grid. This grid-size was chosen because it was noticed that smaller grids tended to be less "stable" for visualization purposes, since smaller absolute populations tended to die out or dominate very quickly. This is consistent with the discoveries may by Baray (Baray, 1998). Larger grid sizes produced the same trends, but tended to be too computationally expensive. Though the *general* behavior the agents is independent of the world size, the rate at which "belief agreement" is reached is much faster in smaller worlds. This makes intuitive sense, since there are simply fewer agents involved. As a general rule, in the simulations conducted, the clusters of "belief agreement" were reduced to single homogeneous regions very early in the simulation process. Generally, within

Figure 2. Message Propagation Collage: Three snapshots of the clustering of agent types throughout the world: (a) Starting Configuration; (b) Clusters Forming; (c) Homogeneous Clusters Formed

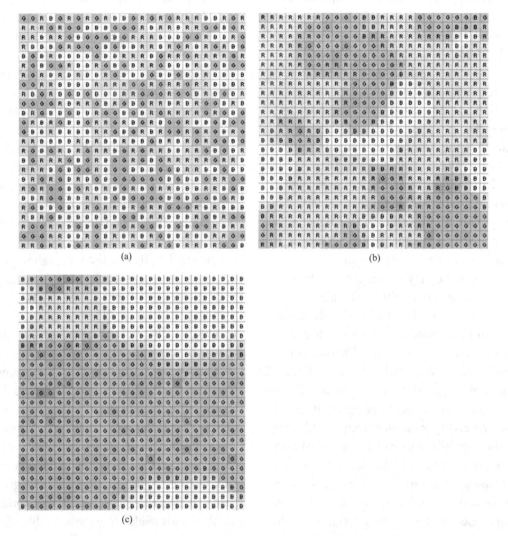

(a)   (b)

(c)

1000–2000 statistical snapshots (less than 10% of the trial progress) there existed no more than one discrete cluster per belief, though the shapes of these clusters would continue to morph until extinction or trial completion.

Occasionally, configurations arise where competition *seemingly* "stabilizes" for an extended duration. This apparent stabilization may last several thousand agent generations and occurs when a nearly equal number of agents of two given types are lined up along a "belief boundary". An illustration of this effect is shown in Figure

3. However, in all trials conducted where these scenarios arose, the population with the greatest number of participating agents ultimately survived. A plot of the populations versus time for the trial snapshots shown in Figure 3 may is seen later in Figure 5. Given the discrete nature of the two-dimensional grid on which all agents exist, any isolated group A which is surrounded by a competing group B will be at a disadvantage. For example, a group of agents A on a discrete grid which approximate a disk will have a perimeter approximating πr^2 agents whereas the enclosing

Figure 3. Population Stability: This figure illustrates a nearly stable configuration which results from boundary of nearly equal number of agents at a population boundary

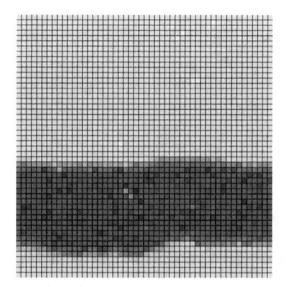

circle of agents B would be comprised of approximately $\pi(r+1)^2$ agents (where r is the discrete radius of A). With a linear boundary, this effect is mitigated and the competition is limited to the "strength" of the beliefs manifested by the number of agents participating in the respective beliefs.

The corollary of this phenomenon is that small groups will be consumed relatively quickly due to being "outnumbered" at their "belief boundaries". If smaller groups are naturally consumed by larger groups due to their lower resiliency to influence, and larger groups demonstrate greater resilience to alteration, than worlds will invariably degenerate into large homogeneous groups. In other words, given randomly driven belief cluttering, certain smaller clusters are more likely to exist in situations where they are partially (or mostly) surrounded by agents of competing beliefs. More simply, larger groups have a greater probability of survival than smaller ones, so over the course of a long trial, the smaller groups will inevitably dissolve. Even the methods of popula-

tion stabilization discussed in subsequent sections do not entirely mitigate this effect. Again, this is largely due to the issues described in the previous paragraph where population clusters, which are *surrounded* by competing populations, will be at a natural disadvantage when attempting to propagate beliefs to competing agents.

Given the random initial starting conditions of the simulations, the random timing variability of interaction, and the randomized order in which neighbors are sent messages, it would be very difficult to predict the nature of the belief clusters moments after the beginning of a trial. However, it should be noted that it becomes easier to predict the resulting state of any simulation as it progress due to the "self organization" which is exhibited. Again, this is a natural extension of fact that large populations tend exhibit greater stability than smaller populations, affording the larger populations time to merge into larger groups, further enhancing their own stability.

Natural Population Progressions

The first trial using "belief" based message communication involves allowing the agents to freely interact while employing the same d_v and r_{vm}. In all of the *Agent Society* simulations conducted[3], each cell was populated with an agent possessing a random RED, GREEN, or BLUE belief. The probability of any agent adopting a given belief was exactly 1/3 and all agents possess a variance ratio of 1.0 with a mean vivification time of 500ms. The trials involving a "natural progression" were run until one homogeneous population remained, at which point the simulation was terminated. It should be noted that the actual number of snapshots taken is not considered relevant in these trials. Since the focus here is on the general behavior of the system (independent of trial duration), the time axis in subsequent graphs depict the percentage of progress through a given simulation.

Figure 4. Agent Society – Natural Progression 1: Figure 4a illustrates a trial run until only one agent population survived. Figure 4b zooms in on just the first 20% of the trial

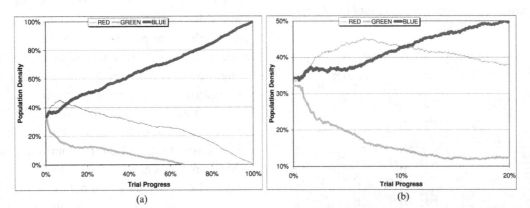

(a)   (b)

Figure 4 depicts a typical trial starting with a randomized population. Typically, in these simulations a single belief will quickly dominate the population. Though it is not always the belief with the greatest number of initial participants that becomes dominant, a greater initial population produces a greater probability that a given belief will dominate. As shown in Figure 4a, once the BLUE agents gain a strong majority, BLUE quickly dominates the population, with RED and GREEN decaying at nearly even rates. A closer inspection of the initial moments of the trial in Figure 4b shows that RED had the initial "momentum", yet BLUE was able to overtake RED by about 10% through the trial. In total, this trial consists of 2556 snapshots. The trial began with a randomly generated RED population of 837, GREEN population of 805, and BLUE population of 858.

Empirical evidence gathered over multiple trials shows no clear pattern which can be used to predict which belief will dominate at the outset. However, in ten trials of this type conducted, any belief which had established dominance by approximately the 25% point in a trial was invariably the sole surviving agent type at the conclusion of the simulation. This phenomenon is independent of the initial starting conditions. Observation suggests that the number of discrete population groups is the primary determining factor for the long-term survival of group. In other words, if population **A** has more members than population **B**, but **A** is separated into a larger number of smaller discrete clusters (each containing fewer agents) than **B**, the **B** population will generally overwhelm the **A** population. This phenomena should be viewed as a corollary the "Population Stability" phenomena discussed 8.

Figure 5 illustrates the data from a trial where the agents of one belief were almost immediately absorbed by the others. The trial began with a randomly generated RED population of 834, GREEN population of 833, and BLUE population of 833. As previously noted, depending of the configuration of the clustering of agent populations, beliefs may compete for an extended period or become extinct very quickly. In this trial, both phenomena can be observed. The BLUE population — which began the simulation with numbers comparable to RED and GREEN — survived little more than 0.5% of the trial, as illustrated in Figure 5b. On the other hand, Figure 5a shows the more drawn out competition between RED and GREEN. Though GREEN ultimately became extinct, distinct surges of growth can be seen at around the 25% and 50% progress points. This is appears to be a byproduct of the dynamically changing topology (shape) of the "belief clusters" as any given simu-

Figure 5. Agent Society – Natural Progression 2: Figure 5a illustrates a trial run very similar to the one shown in Figure 4a. However, in this trial the BLUE agents were almost immediately overwhelmed by RED and GREEN. Figure 5b zooms in on the life-cycle of BLUE

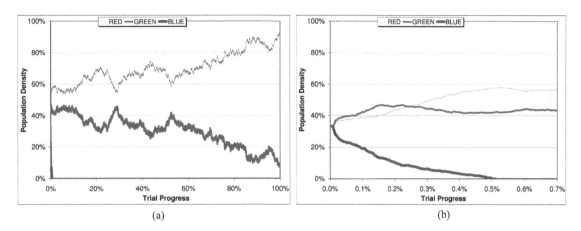

(a)   (b)

lation progresses. Early in a simulation, discrete belief clusters may also merge together causing brief spikes in apparent growth, but if an overall population remains smaller than a competing population, the lesser populated belief will most probabilistically be overwhelmed.

Manual Modulation of Temporal Variability

Though the simulation engine allows for beliefs and message types to carry distinct weights, in experiments outlined here, all beliefs and messages carry the same weight. In other words, the "popularity" of a belief is based solely upon the number of messages exchanged within the environment and not any properties inherent in the beliefs themselves. The only aspect of the simulation varied during the course of an experiment is the allowable timing variances of each of the three primary message types. In the trials conducted in this section, the timing variation is always manually controlled. The most striking — and readily observable — phenomenon is the somewhat non-intuitive effect that timing variance has on population density; the lower the timing variance (i.e., the closer the variability is to zero),

the more likely a certain belief is to survive. The messages being passed with the *least* amount of timing variation are the messages *most* likely to influence the beliefs of the recipients.

In previous sections, it was established that variations in r_{vm} yielded predictable effects on the population dynamics of simple interacting agents. In this section the effects of r_{vm} and groups of competing agents are explored. To this end, beliefs b, where $b \in \{RED, GREEN, BLUE\}$, are assigned unique r_{vm}^{b} values which represent the inherent timing variance ratios of the agents associated with that particular belief. All agents participating in a given belief adopt the prescribed vivification properties of the belief itself. When an agent adopts a new belief b, its d_v (and hence r_{vm}) will be updated to match the current r_{vm}. For example, an agent participating in a GREEN belief might announce that belief with very regular vivifications; while an agent with a RED belief may announce that belief with an extreme timing variation. The population density of the agents participating in any given belief at any given time will be denoted as pd^{b} where $b \in \{RED, GREEN, BLUE\}$. A subset of data gathered from a sample trial of this simulation

Figure 6. Manually Modulated Agent Populations: A set of plots which depict population response to manual r_{vm}^{RED} manipulation. The heavier lines indicate the relative population of each of the three belief types and the light lines represent the manual modification of r_{vm}^{b} over time: (a) Population vs. Time; (b) Red variance vs. Time and Population; (c) Green variance vs. Time and Population; (d) Blue variance vs. Time and Population

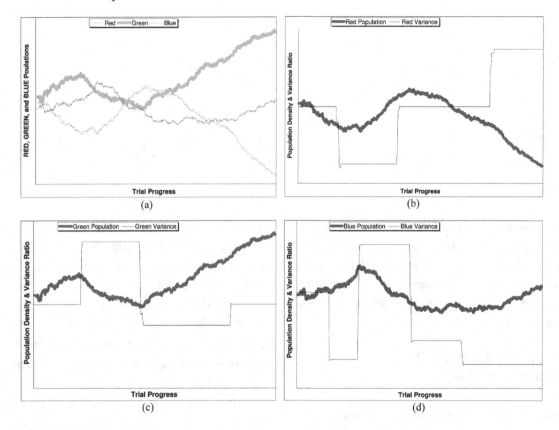

type is shown in Figure 6 which is divided up in four distinct sub-figures as described below.

Figure 6a shows a plot of the *relative* population densities for the three message types from the beginning of a trial to an arbitrary point in time within the trial. In this plot, the relative number of agents participating in a given belief versus time is represented. Figures 6b through 6d require a bit more detailed explanation. The heavier solid line in each of the three figures corresponds to one of the lines in Figure 6a and the lighter broken line represents the d_v of all the agents of a particular belief. As this particular simulation ran, the r_{vm}^{b} values were manually

manipulated, directly affecting the global populations of agents with given beliefs over time. The r_{vm}^{b} alterations shown in these figures were in response to real-time observation of the unfolding trial.

For example, the plot of the GREEN belief variance (Figure 6c) depicts the total population agents participating in the "GREEN" belief and the corresponding r_{vm}^{GREEN} value over time. The values of r_{vm}^{GREEN} were manually altered over time via the dedicated GUI interface controls, thereby influencing the overall population behavior. The higher the thin/broken line on the graph, the greater the variance of vivification at that time.

The "GREEN" plot clearly illustrates the population of agents participating in the belief changing inversely with the variance level. The "RED" belief plot (Figure 6b) is also interesting to observe since the same effects can be seen, but the population density changes lag slightly behind the changes in r_{vm}^{RED}. The "BLUE" belief exhibits this phenomenon as well, though only one of the variance changes produce a clearly discernible response with an immediate change in population; the other responses are more subtly visible. Common to Figures 6b–6d are consistent decreases in pd^b which follow increases in r_{vm}^b and increases in pd^b which follow decreases in r_{vm}^b. Using Figure 6b as an example, when r_{vm}^b is adjusted down, pd^{RED} then increases. When r_{vm}^b is adjusted up, pd^{RED} then decreases.

A SOCIETY OF AGENTS

In the final set of simulations, *automated* temporal variability was added. This means that as any given trial progresses, the r_{vm}^b values are automatically altered based upon the current state of the environment in attempt to reach and maintain a target "belief ratio" $\mathcal{B}_b$ of a given belief. As before, $b \in \{RED, GREEN, BLUE\}$. The increments by which any given r_{vm}^b may be adjusted is defined as Δr_{vm}^b and has been set to 0.01 (1%) for all of the following trials. In other words, changes in r_{vm}^b are done at $\pm .01$ increments.

In this version of the "Agent Society" model, the global statistics calculator (which is activated once per world "snapshot") is responsible for adjusting the r_{vm}^b with every snapshot. This is the only simulation type where there is any form of "communication" between the agents and the simulation framework. The rationale for this is simply to verify the hypothesis that the manipulation of vivification ratios can support a population indefinitely. Of course, given the probabilistic nature of the simulations, the validity of the hypothesis is limited to the finite duration of any given trial. However, extrapolation of the results gained in this section serve to support the theory that vivification variance can be adjusted in a manner which supports continuously stable population numbers of agents participating in any given belief. Once this hypothesis has been validated, a mechanism which gives agents awareness of their own population numbers will be explored.

Modulated Variability in the Agent Society

The trials presented in Figure 7 and Figure 8 were each run to 32,000 snapshots where snapshots occurred at an approximate rate of $3 \times d_m$. For added confirmation of the behavior observed here, several trials were run for longer periods; one for approximately 100,000 snapshots and two for approximately 320,000 snapshots. In each case, the results were consistent with the results presented below. In each of the trials described in this section, target "belief population ratios" were chosen somewhat arbitrarily; they were simply chosen in a manner which would make possible an empirical observation of the data in real-time. The general algorithm for automating r_{vm}^b is as follows:

1. Agents continuously vivificate per the rules previously discussed, sending and receiving messages.
2. With each statistical snapshot, the following takes place:
   (a) The total number of agents participating in each belief is calculated.
   (b) Any agent below its target population threshold has its corresponding r_{vm}^b decreased by Δr_{vm}^b.

Figure 7. Agent Society – Regulated Progression: This figure illustrates the first trial in which the population densities are regulated by automated manipulation of communication timing variance. Initial target populations were set to RED = 25%, GREEN = 50%, and BLUE = 25%: (a) A Complete Trial with Automated r_{vm}^b Modulation where GREEN Becomes the Dominant Belief; (b) A magnification of the first 10% of Figure 7a; (c) A magnification of the first .5% of Figure 7a to better illustrate the initial conditions; (d) A magnification of the GREEN population (Figure 7a) once "stability" was achieved at around 20% trial progress

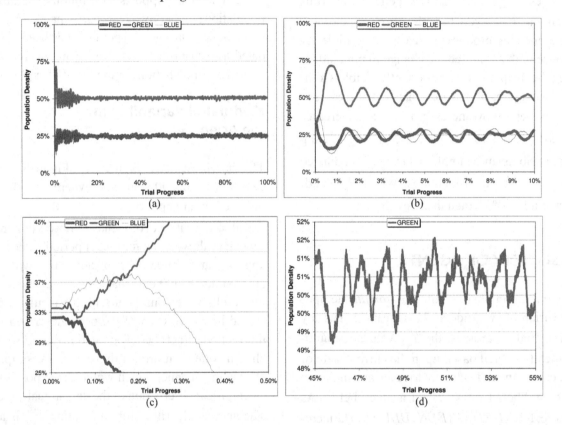

(c) Any agent above its target population threshold has its corresponding r_{vm}^b increased by Δr_{vm}^b.

Before examining the specific details of r_{vm}^b modulation, the core population behavior is explored. The trial depicted in Figure 7 began with a randomly generated RED population of 807, GREEN population of 839, and BLUE population of 854. In the initial moments of the trial, an oscillation can be clearly seen. This is more vividly depicted in Figure 7b, which is further magnified in Figure 7c. Though this oscillation appears periodic at the beginning of the trial, any periodicity becomes much less discernible once the various beliefs begin to "settle" near their target ratios. Figure 7d magnifies a section of the middle of the trial, focusing exclusively on the GREEN belief. This figure illustrates the chaotic fluctuations in agent population, even when "stability" has otherwise been obtained relative to the populations of agents participating in a given belief.

Figure 8. Automatically Modulated Agent Populations: These graphs depict the general behavior of the distinct agent populations as a result of automated modulation of the r_{vm}^b values for each b

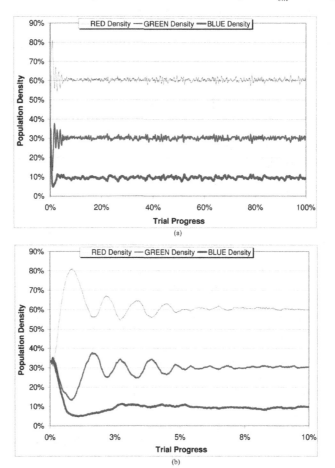

(a)

(b)

Details of Automated Modulation

Finally, the mechanism of automated vivification variance ratio and its relationship to population stability is examined in detail. Though more than ten simulations of this type were conducted (with differing population variance ratios), only one will be discussed here do to the highly consistent behavior observed in all trials. All trials exhibited the same general behavior, independent of the target population ratios. Though discussed in more detail later, Table 3 statistically summarizes the data collected from the trials actually conducted. The following trial began with a RED population of 833, GREEN population of 834, and BLUE

population of 833. As discussed at the beginning of this section, the r_{vm}^b values for each belief are adjusted with each statistical snapshot of the agent environment. As with all previous trials, the statistical snapshot frequency is three times the d_m.

In this last set of trials — depicted in Figure 8 and further explored in Figure 9 — the actual r_{vm}^b values are shown along with the population densities with respect to time. As is typical of all simulations of this type, a distinct pattern of "damped oscillation" occurs as the populations begin to quickly stabilize. This effect can be seen in Figure 8a, which shows a trial in its entirety. Figure 8b better illustrates this initial oscillation

Figure 9. Automatically Modulated Agent Populations in Detail: These graphs reflect the populations of the distinct agent populations as a result of automatically modulating the r_{vm}^b values for each b: (a) RED; (b) RED Zoom; (c) GREEN; (d) GREEN Zoom; (e) BLUE; (f) BLUE Zoom

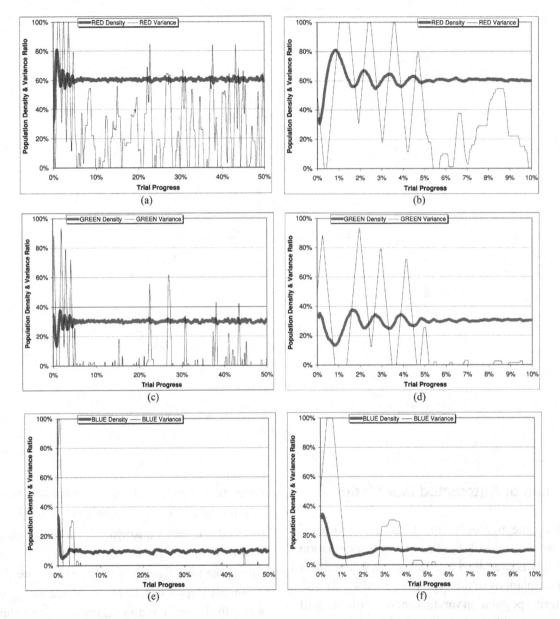

phenomenon by focusing on the first 10% of the trial. Once the distinct populations stabilize, only minor fluctuations occur for the remainder of the simulation, showing that relative stability is achieved. However, it should be noted that — due to the probabilistic nature of the simulation — there were several trials which resulted in at least one belief collapsing before the completion of the trial. These cases will be discussed in more detail below.

In the previous section, it was established that increasing vivification variance ratio r_{vm}^b for any given agent population decreased its overall stability and made the population more prone to "takeover" by neighboring, more stable populations. By allowing r_{vm}^{b} to dynamically respond to the global environment, population stability is achievable. However, when plotting the values of r_{vm}^{b} over time, two unique patterns are revealed. First, as the populations stabilize, the frequency and magnitude of r_{vm}^{b} fluctuations are diminished. Second, the lower the target belief population density relative to other beliefs, the less fluctuation in r_{vm}^{b}.

Both of these phenomena can be seen in the sub-figures of Figure 9. This figure is limited to the first 50% of the trial simply to allow for better visualization, as plotting the entire trial compresses an excessive amount of detail, while revealing little useful information. Additionally, the lighter lines in the sub-figures — which represent the dynamic r_{vm}^{b} values — should be viewed as 0 – 100% of the maximum allowable r_{vm}, which is 2.0:1. In other words, 100% r_{vm}^{RED} would indicate that the r_{vm} of the RED belief is 100% of its maximum value, which is 2.0. A value of 50% would represent a r_{vm} of 1.0, etc.

Figures 9a, 9c, and 9e show the belief population density and r_{vm}^{b} with respect to time for each b. All three population types stabilize quickly, but each r_{vm}^{b} exhibits unique behavior. BLUE, with a target population ratio of 10% exhibits a large r_{vm}^{BLUE} spike at the very beginning of the trial but stabilizes quickly. GREEN, with a target population ratio of 30% exhibits several large r_{vm}^{GREEN} spikes at the very beginning of the trial, but then exhibits several smaller spikes later in the trial. RED, with the largest target population ratio of 60%, exhibits large r_{vm}^{RED} spikes throughout the trial. Figures 9b, 9d, and 9f illustrate magnified sections of Figures 9a, 9c, and 9e respectively. Though only one trial has been graphically depicted here, a more complete summary of individual trial results is presented in Table 2.

To conclude the discussion of automatically adjusted vivification variance ratios, the correlations ρ between the various data attributes listed in Table 2 are examined. In Table 3, the dependant variable $\mathcal{B}_{b}$ is correlated with both pd_{avg}^{b} and μr_{vm}^{b}. Additionally, pd_{avg}^{b} is correlated against μr_{vm}^{b}. This latter correlation was done to see if μr_{vm}^{b} correlated better with the initial target population ratio $\mathcal{B}_{b}$, or the actual population average pd_{avg}^{b}. As would be expected, pd_{avg}^{b} had a slightly better correlation to μr_{vm}^{b} than did $\mathcal{B}_{b}$. This is expected because pd_{avg}^{b} and μr_{vm}^{b} are both based on the *actual* behavior of the agents within the simulation. Whereas $\mathcal{B}_{b}$ is simply a target which the agents attempt to achieve. However, this difference is very slight. All correlations are accompanied by a Pearson's product-moment coefficient calculated by *Microsoft Excel*.

More interesting is the apparently higher correlations achieved when *all* trials are considered — and not just the ones where all beliefs survived. Upon closer inspection this behavior appears reasonable, since after one population dies off, the "dead" population density pd_{avg}^{b} has a perfect correlation to the vivification variance ratio r_{vm}^{b}, since neither undergoes any further changes. Additionally, there is less "competition" between the remaining populations, giving them a stronger correlation to their own r_{vm}^{b} than they would otherwise have with more competition. This is due to the lower frequency of r_{vm}^{b} changes when only two belief populations compete.

It should be emphasized that the Pearson's product-moment coefficient (ρ) is really just a measure of a linear degree of mapping between the values of one data-set to the values of another data-set. Since there is limited variation in the $\mathcal{B}_{b}$ values, and limited data are available (for an accurate correlation), the information pre-

Table 2. Agent Society Statistical Data: This table is a sampling of the data gathered from the auto-matic modulated r_{vm}^{b} trials. The symbols in the table heading are as follows; $\mathcal{B}_{b}$ is the target belief ratio, pd_{avg}^{b} is the actual average population density of a given belief, and μr_{vm}^{b} is average vivification vari-ance ratio for a given belief. In each case $b \in \{RED, GREEN, BLUE\}$. The rows below the single solid hori-zontal line in the table are from trials in which at least one belief became extinct before the completion of the trial (32,000 snapshots)

$\mathcal{B}_{RED}$	$\mathcal{B}_{GREEN}$	$\mathcal{B}_{BLUE}$	pd_{avg}^{RED}	pd_{avg}^{GREEN}	pd_{avg}^{BLUE}	μr_{vm}^{RED}	μr_{vm}^{GREEN}	μr_{vm}^{BLUE}
0.10	0.30	0.60	0.0956	0.2996	0.6040	0.0135	0.0501	0.2614
0.10	0.40	0.50	0.1016	0.3972	0.5008	0.0004	0.0009	0.0042
0.20	0.30	0.50	0.1956	0.2960	0.5076	0.1066	0.1290	0.5041
0.20	0.30	0.50	0.1968	0.2992	0.5036	0.0240	0.0399	0.1476
0.20	0.30	0.50	0.1964	0.2988	0.5040	0.0147	0.0313	0.1290
0.20	0.30	0.50	0.1960	0.3028	0.5008	0.0245	0.0296	0.0575
0.20	0.30	0.50	0.2000	0.2996	0.4996	0.0316	0.0302	0.0278
0.20	0.30	0.50	0.1992	0.2980	0.5020	0.0310	0.0361	0.0607
0.20	0.30	0.50	0.1968	0.2984	0.5040	0.0496	0.0727	0.3044
0.20	0.30	0.50	0.1968	0.2988	0.5036	0.0381	0.0538	0.1684
0.20	0.30	0.50	0.1988	0.2984	0.5024	0.0248	0.0329	0.0599
0.20	0.40	0.40	0.1972	0.4032	0.3992	0.0446	0.1928	0.0668
0.25	0.25	0.50	0.2488	0.2496	0.5012	0.0122	0.0111	0.0188
0.25	0.25	0.50	0.2476	0.2480	0.5036	0.0289	0.0339	0.1292
0.25	0.25	0.50	0.2492	0.2468	0.5032	0.0858	0.0749	0.2092
0.33	0.34	0.33	0.3280	0.3380	0.3332	0.0129	0.0181	0.0579
0.35	0.35	0.35	0.3520	0.3216	0.3256	0.0481	0.0019	0.0039
0.35	0.35	0.35	0.3424	0.3280	0.3288	0.0068	0.0038	0.0079
0.15	0.25	0.60	0.0020	0.2568	0.7408	0.0089	0.8598	0.9915
0.20	0.30	0.50	0.1604	0.2416	0.4072	0.0297	0.0340	0.0952
0.20	0.30	0.50	0.0012	0.3100	0.6880	0.0057	0.8737	0.9946
0.20	0.30	0.50	0.0004	0.3084	0.6904	0.0041	0.8725	0.9961

sented in Table 3 serves as only a guide to gen-eral behavior of the model.

Shown in Figure 10 is a graph of μr_{vm}^{RED}, μr_{vm}^{GREEN}, and μr_{vm}^{BLUE} from Table 2 where $\mathcal{B}_{RED} = 20\%$, $\mathcal{B}_{GREEN} = 30\%$, and $\mathcal{B}_{BLUE} = 50\%$.

Table 3. Correlations for Agent Society Statistical Data: A table of correlations for the data shown in Table 2. In this table, X and Y represent the data-sets being compared, and $\rho_{x,y}^{b}$ represents the Pearson's product-moment coefficient of each b. The data above the single solid horizontal line considers only the data-sets where all agent beliefs survived for the duration of the trial. The data shown below the single, solid horizontal line considers all data from Table 2

X	Y	$\rho_{x,y}^{RED}$	$\rho_{x,y}^{GREEN}$	$\rho_{x,y}^{BLUE}$
$\mathcal{B}_{b}$	pd_{avg}^{b}	0.999446	0.982713	0.996501
$\mathcal{B}_{b}$	μr_{vm}^{b}	0.070508	0.154952	0.428662
pd_{avg}^{b}	μr_{vm}^{b}	0.071228	0.232328	0.451288
$\mathcal{B}_{b}$	μr_{vm}^{b}	0.133879	-0.200710	0.417260
pd_{avg}^{b}	μr_{vm}^{b}	0.321438	-0.060922	0.817549

This chart more clearly illustrates that higher $\mathcal{B}_{b}$ values yield both higher μr_{vm}^{b} values and more variability in those values. For the sake of illustration, the RED, $GREEN$, and $BLUE$ belief labels may have been interchanged so that the following is always true: $\mathcal{B}_{RED} \leq \mathcal{B}_{GREEN} \leq \mathcal{B}_{BLUE}$. Since the labels are simply convenient ways of referencing the specific $\mathcal{B}_{b}$ values (which are all independent), this causes no change in the actual data analysis.

Figure 10. Agent Belief vs. $\mathcal{B}_{b}$: This chart illustrates ten trials with $\mathcal{B}_{RED} = 20\%$, $\mathcal{B}_{GREEN} = 30\%$, and $\mathcal{B}_{BLUE} = 50\%$. The y axis represents the actual average vivification rate for each represented trial

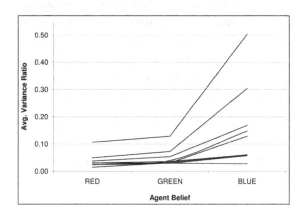

CONCLUSION

The goal of the research presented in this research was to establish that the manipulation of timing *variability* in temporally autonomous agent systems impacts the emergent population behavior. Message activation was incrementally explored via several unique simulation types. This research began by describing a system which loosely obeyed John Conway's *Game of Life* rules, but did so in a manner which required each agent to receive a simple "notification message" which prompted it to vivificate. The behavior of this mode of operation differed from that of our earlier "passive" *Threaded Selection* model in one fundamental way; the *Threaded Selection* model produced a "smooth" curve across all r_{vm} whereas the *Message Activation* model — though producing similar pd_{avg} and age_{avg} values — produced much less "smooth" curves (Figure 1). The reasonable conclusion which can be drawn from this is that, in the *Threaded Selection* model, the temporal variability of the single agent is the most influential variable. However, in the *Message Activation* model, the variability of entire neighborhood must be considered.

More fundamentally, this research examined a simple "agent society" where agents exchange beliefs in an attempt to actively alter the states of neighboring agents. Three distinct "beliefs" were defined (*RED* , *GREEN* , and *BLUE*) which simply represent the dominant state of any given agent at any given time. It was discovered that the temporal variability any given group of agents participating directly impacts the agent's ability to compete within its environment. Specifically, the higher degree of variability within a belief population, the lower survival rate of that belief. Conversely, agents participating in beliefs which had very low variability in vivification rates, would quickly dominate the environment. In other words, agents who attempt to influence their neighbors at fixed intervals are more likely to succeed than if the intervals are more sporadic.

Finally, this research examined the effects of automating the vivification variability to produce dynamically altered vivification variance ratios in an attempt to produce stable belief population ratios. In the experiments conducted, it was discovered that a population (of agents participating in a given belief) could potentially collapse in the early stages of a trial, but stabilization generally occurs very quickly and once stabilization does occur, it can be perpetuated by continuously fine tuning the vivification variables ratios. In only one trial — of 22 of this type represented in this paper — did a population ever collapse once apparent stability took hold.

Several interesting conclusions can be drawn from Table 3 alone. This table illustrates the statistical correlations between several independent and dependant variables in the trials. Foremost, it can be seen that the actual population ratio averages (throughout all trials) strongly correlate to the target population ratios, thus supporting the conclusion that "varying the variability" is a viable mechanism for maintaining stability and target belief ratios. However, the statistical correlation between the average population density (of a given belief) and average variance ratio is relatively weak, except in the beliefs with the largest target populations. In the cases where the "BLUE" belief target was 50% of the population, pd_{avg}^b correlated to μr_{vm}^b with $\rho \approx .818$, which indicates a strong correlation in the presence of an otherwise "highly chaotic" environment.

REFERENCES

Baray, C. (1998). Effects of population size upon emergent group behavior. *Complexity International, 06*. Available from http://journal-ci.csse. monash.edu.au/ci/vol06/baray/baray.html

Cantwell, J. (2005). A formal model of multi-agent belief-interaction. *Journal of Logic Language and Information, 14*(4), 397–422. doi:10.1007/s10849-005-4019-8

Conover, A. J., & Trajkovski, G. P. (2007, November 9–11). Effects of temporally asynchronous interaction on simple multi-agent behavior. In *Emergent agents and socialities: Social and organizational aspects of intelligence. technical report fs-07-04* (pp. 34–41). Menlo Park, CA: The American Association for Artificial Intelligence.

Conover, A. J. (2008a). *A simulation of temporally asynchronous agent interaction dynamics*. Unpublished doctoral dissertation, Towson University, 8000 York Road, Towson MD, 21252.

Conover, A. J. (2008b). A simulation of temporally variant agent interaction via passive examination. In S. G. Collins & G. P. Trajkovski (Eds.), *Agent-based societies: Social and cultural interactions*. Hershey, PA: IGI Global. (Publication Pending)

Deffuant, G., Neau, D., Amblard, F., & Weisbuch, G. (2001). Mixing beliefs among interacting agents. *Advances in Complex Systems, 3*, 87–98. doi:10.1142/S0219525900000078

Gardner, M. (1970, Oct). Mathematical games - the fantastic combinations of John Conway's new solitaire game, *Life. Scientific American*, 120–123. doi:10.1038/scientificamerican1070-120

Gaston, M. E., & desJardins, M. (2005). Agent-organized networks for dynamic team formation. In F. Dignum, V. Dignum, S. Koenig, S. Kraus, M. P. Singh, & M. Wooldridge (Eds.), *4rd international joint conference on autonomous agents and multiagent systems (AAMAS 2005), july 25-29, 2005, utrecht, the netherlands* (pp. 230–237). ACM. Available from http://doi.acm.org/10.1145/1082473.1082508

Lu, Q., Korniss, G., & Szymanski, B. K. (2006, October 12–15). Naming games in spatially-embedded random networks and emergent phenomena in societies of agents. In *Interaction and emergent phenomena in societies of agents* (pp. 148–155). Menlo Park, CA: The American Association for Artificial Intelligence.

Pasquier, P., & Chaib-draa, B. (2003). The cognitive coherence approach for agent communication pragmatics. In *Aamas* (pp. 544–551). ACM. Available from http://doi.acm.org/10.1145/860575.860662

Schilling, R. (2006, October 12–15). A project to develop a distributed, multi-agent communication architecture using message feedback. In *Interaction and emergent phenomena in societies of agents* (pp. 96–103). Menlo Park, CA: The American Association for Artificial Intelligence.

ENDNOTES

[1] Vivification is defined as the process by which an agent "wakes" to interact with its environment at either deterministic or nondeterministic intervals.

[2] The mechanism by which delay times are chosen is not discussed in this work, but it is important to note the during each agent's vivification cycle, a sleep time is randomly chosen within a given experimental range. The range remains fixed thought a given trial.

[3] Unless otherwise explicitly specified

Chapter 3
Statistical Properties of Social Group Evolution

Gergely Palla
Hungarian Academy of Sciences, Hungary

Tamás Vicsek
Hungarian Academy of Sciences, Hungary & Eötvös University, Hungary

ABSTRACT

The authors' focus is on the general statistical features of the time evolution of communities (also called as modules, clusters or cohesive groups) in large social networks. These structural sub-units can correspond to highly connected circles of friends, families, or professional cliques, which are subject to constant change due to the intense fluctuations in the activity and communication patterns of people. The communities can grow by recruiting new members, or contract by loosing members; two (or more) groups may merge into a single community, while a large enough social group can split into several smaller ones; new communities are born and old ones may disappear. According to our results, the time evolution of social groups containing only a few members and larger communities, e.g., institutions show significant differences.

INTRODUCTION

Until the recent past, *social network* research was based on questionnaire data, reaching typically a few dozen individuals (Granovetter, 1992; Wasserman, 1994; White, 1976). The main advantage of this approach is that it can provide very detailed information concerning the ties between people: what sort of acquaintance is it based on, how intense is the relation, whether it is mutual or not, what is the emotional background behind the connection, etc. However, a major drawback is that the size of the sample that can be generated this way is very limited, and as long as it is based solely on the opinion of the surveyed people, the strength of the ties remains subjective.

A major shift in paradigm begun to take place in this field around the millennium, when large datasets describing various social relations between people have become available for research (Barabási, 2003; Mendes & Dorogovtsev, 2003; Watts & Strogatz, 1998). Due to the rapid de-

DOI: 10.4018/978-1-60960-171-3.ch003

Copyright © 2011, IGI Global. Copying or distributing in print or electronic forms without written permission of IGI Global is prohibited.

velopment in informatics, the handling of *social networks* constructed from e-mail or phone-call records with more than a million nodes can be easily solved with present day computers. When compared to the questionnaire date, the information about the individual links is limited in these systems. However, the strength of the ties can be measured in more objective way, by e.g., aggregating the number of e-mails or phone-calls between the people. One of the first results obtained from the analysis of large scale social networks based on automated data collection was given by Onnela et al. (2007), providing empirical evidence for the famous Granovetter hypothesis (Granovetter, 1973) in a *mobile phone network*. Due to the richness of mobile phone data a series of other important studies followed along this line, dealing with problems spreading from human mobility patterns (González, Hidalgo & Barabási, 2008), through the laws of geographical dispersal of social connections (Lambiotte, Blondel, de Kerchove, Huens, Prieur, Smoreda & Van Dooren, 2008) to the spread of mobile phone viruses (Wang, González, Hidalgo & Barabási, 2009). Along with intense research of mobile phone networks, the field of complex network proliferated in other directions as well. The recently opened frontiers in this multidisciplinary area include the study of tagged networks (Cattuto, Loreto & Pietronero, 2007; Cattuto, Barrat, Baldassarri, Schehrd &Loreto, 2009; Palla, Farkas, Pollner, Derényi & Vicsek, 2008) and hyper-graphs (Zlatic, Ghoshal &Caldarelli, 2009; Ghoshal, Zlatic, Caldarelli & Newman, 2009), and the development of general network models, capable of producing random graphs with diverse properties (Leskovec, Chakrabarti, Kleinberg & Faloutsos, 2005; Mahadevan, Krioukov, Fall &Vahdat, 2006; Robins, Snijders, Wang, Handcock & Pattison, 2007; Palla, Lovász & Vicsek, 2010).

In this chapter our focus is on the *communities* (modules, clusters, or cohesive groups) of large *social networks*, associated with more densely linked parts. These structural sub-units can cor-

respond to families, friendship circles, or a tightly connected group of colleagues (Scott, 2000; Watts, Dodds, & Newman, 2002), and have no widely accepted unique definition (Everitt, 1993; Fortunato & Castellano, 2009; Girvan & Newman, 2002; Newman, 2004; Palla, Derényi, Farkas, & Vicsek, 2005; Radicchi, Castellano, Cecconi, Loreto, & Parisi, 2004; Shiffrin & Börner, 2004). Community finding turned out to be an important issue in other types of network systems as well (Knudsen, 2004), e.g., the location of multi-protein function al units in molecular biology (Ravasz, Somera, Mongru, Oltvai, & Barabási,, 2002; Spirin & Mirny, 2003) or finding sets of tightly coupled stocks in economy (Heimo, Saramäki, Onnela, & Kaski, 2007; Onnela, Chakraborti, Kaski, Kertész, & Kanto, 2003) can be crucial to the understanding of the structural and functional properties of the systems under investigation. Due to the importance of communities in complex network theory, the set of available community finding methods is vast (Fortunato & Castellano, 2009). Here we shall use the Clique Percolation Method*Clique Percolation Method* (Clique Percolation MethodCPM, Palla et al., 2005), which (due to its local nature) is especially suitable for studying *evolving communities*.

The frequent changes in the activity and communication patterns of individuals result in a constantly changing social network (Barabási et al., 2002; Ebel, Davidsen, & Bornholdt, 2002; Holme, Edling, & Liljeros, 2004; Liljeros, Edling, Amaral, Stanley, & Aberg, 2001), which can show non-trival effects e.g., in respect of the link density of the newly appearing nodes (Smith, Onnela & Johnson, 2007), the rewiring schemes of the already existing links (Lindquist, Ma, van den Driessche & Willeboordse, 2009), or the appearance of new links (Hu, Kaza & Chen, 2009, Liu & Deng, 2009). Naturally, such networks consist of *dynamically evolving communities*. Our knowledge of the mechanisms governing this underlying *community dynamics* is limited, but is essential for a deeper understanding of the development and self-optimization of the society as a whole (Hopcroft, Khan, Kulis, & Selman, 2004; Kossinets & Watts, 2006; Noh, Jeong, Ahn, & Jeong, 2005; Pollner, Palla, & Vicsek 2006). In this chapter we investigate in detail the time dependence of communities on a large scale and uncover the basic relationships of the statistical features of *community evolution* (Palla, Vicsek, & Barabási, 2007). We examine the community evolution in two systems of major interest, corresponding to the already introduced *mobile phone network* and a *co-authorship network* between collaborating scientists. Co-authorship networks provide another important field in complex network theory, where the studied graphs originate from scientists publishing research articles together. Due to the rapidly expanding online archives, data on the *time evolution* of such networks can be accessed rather easily. These datasets also provide an ideal ground for studying the evolution of scientific fields (Herrera, Roberts & Gulbache, 2010), the development of scientific paradigms (Cointet & Chavalarias 2008), or the processes of knowledge creation and information diffusion (Lambiotte & Panzarasa 2009; Ausloos & Lambiotte 2007).

Turning back to the investigation of *community evolution*, our study consists of the following main stages: creating series of networks from the given databases, locating static communities in the subsequent snapshots of the evolving networks, constructing evolving communities from the static snapshots, and finally, analyzing the statistic properties of the evolving groups, The observed communities show a number of elementary evolutionary steps in time, which range from community formation to breakup and merging. We find that large groups persist longer if they are capable of dynamically altering their membership, suggesting that an ability to change the composition results in better adaptability and a longer lifetime for social groups. Remarkably, the behavior of small groups displays the opposite tendency, the condition for stability being that their composition remains unchanged. We also show

that the knowledge of the time commitment of the members to a given community can be used for predicting the community's lifetime. These findings offer a new view on the fundamental differences between the dynamics of small groups and large institutions.

BACKGROUND

The Clique Percolation Method

As we already mentioned in the Introduction, communities correspond to dense parts of the networks, in which a member is more strongly connected to other members in the community than to the rest of the network. *Cliques* (maximal complete sub-graphs, in which every node is linked to every other node) correspond to the densest parts of a network; therefore, they serve as an ideal starting point to search for communities (Everett & Borgatti, 1998). However, limiting the community definition to cliques only would be too restrictive in most cases. *k-clique percolation* offers a similar, but more flexible alternative for network clustering (Derényi, Palla, & Vicsek, 2005; Palla et al., 2005; Ábel et al., 2005). The k-cliques correspond to complete sub-graphs of k nodes, and two k-cliques are said to be adjacent if they share k-1 nodes. In this approach a community is equivalent to a maximal set of k-cliques, in which we can reach any k-clique from any other k-clique through chains of k-clique adjacency. Such an object is analogous to a percolation cluster studied in the statistical physics literature; hence the method is called the Clique Percolation Method*Clique Percolation Method*. The communities defined this way can be best visualized with the help of a k-clique template (an object isomorphic to a complete graph of k nodes). Such a template can be placed onto any k-clique in the graph, and rolled to an adjacent k-clique by relocating one of its nodes and keeping its other k-1 nodes fixed. Thus, the k-clique communities of a graph are all

Figure 1.(a) Illustration of the k-clique template rolling at k=4. Initially the template is placed on A-B-C-D (left panel) and it is ``rolled'' onto the sub-graph A-C-D-E (middle panel). The position of the k-clique template is marked with thick black lines and black nodes, whereas the already visited edges are represented by thick gray lines and gray nodes. Observe that in each step only one of the nodes is moved and the two 4-cliques (before and after rolling) share k-1=3 nodes. At the final step (right panel) the template reaches the sub-graph C-D-E-F, and the set of nodes visited during the process (A-B-C-D-E-F) are considered as a k-clique community; (b) Two overlapping communities at k=4. The community of the gray nodes is sharing the black node with the community of the empty nodes

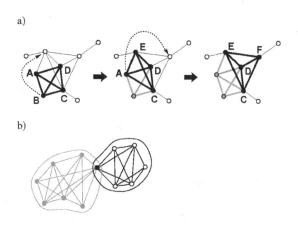

those sub-graphs that can be fully explored by rolling a *k*-clique template in them, but cannot be left by this template. An illustration of *k*-clique template rolling is shown in Figure 1a.

One of the main advantages of the Clique Percolation Method CPM is that it allows *overlaps between the communities*: a node can be part of several communities at the same time (see Figure 1b). This aspect can be very important in the analysis of social networks, since people can be members in multiple social groups in parallel, e.g., everybody belongs to both her/his family and her/his group of friends at the same time. An interesting example for the importance of overlaps in real systems is presented in a recent study of entrepreneurial groups by Vedres & Stark (2010). Another noteworthy property of the Clique Percolation Method CPM is that its definition is local: the community structure in the vicinity of a given node is not affected by the deletion/insertion of links far away. In contrast, in case of global methods, where the community structure is obtained

by optimizing the partition of the network with respect to a global parameter, the local modification of the network can cause a global change in the community structure.

In principle, the Clique Percolation Method CPM outlined above can be only applied to binary networks (i.e., to those with undirected and unweighted connections). However, an arbitrary network can always be transformed into a binary one by ignoring any directionality in the connections and keeping only those connections that are stronger than a threshold weight w^*. Changing the threshold is similar to changing the resolution (as in a microscope) with which the community structure is investigated: by increasing w^* the communities start to shrink and fall apart. A very similar effect can be observed by changing the value of k as well: increasing k makes the communities smaller and more disintegrated, but at the same time, also more cohesive. When we are interested in the community structure around a particular node, it is advisable to scan through a ranges of k and w^* values and monitor how the communities change. Meanwhile, when analyzing the modular structure of the entire network, the criterion used to fix these parameters is based on finding a modular structure as highly structured as possible. This can be achieved by tuning the parameters just below the critical point of the percolation transition. In this way we ensure that we find as many communities as possible, without the negative effect of having a giant community that would smear out the details of the modular structure by merging (and making invisible) many smaller communities.

Construction of the Studied Networks

The data sets we consider contain the monthly roster of articles in the Los Alamos *cond-mat archive* spanning 142 months, with over 30000 authors (Warner, 2003), and the complete record of phone-calls between the customers of a mobile phone company spanning 52 weeks (accumulated over two week long periods), and containing the communication patterns of over 4 million users (Onnela et al., 2007). Both type of collaboration events (a new article or a phone-call) document the presence of social interaction between the involved individuals (nodes), and can be represented as (time-dependent) links. In case of the mobile phone network*phone-call network* the connections where calls were initiated in only one direction were neglected, in consistency with the results of Hidalgo & Rodriguez-Sickert (2008) showing that reciprocal links in a *mobile phone network* tend to be stronger and more persistent. We assumed that in both systems the social connection between people had started some time before the collaboration/communication events and lasted for some time after these events as well. (E.g., the submission of an article to the archive is usually preceded by intense collaboration and reconciliation between the authors, which is in most cases prolonged after the submission

as well). Collaboration/communication events between the same people can be repeated from time to time again, and higher frequencies of collaboration/communication acts usually indicate closer relationship. Furthermore, weights can be assigned to the collaboration and communication events quite naturally: an article with n authors corresponds to a collaboration act of weight $1/(n-1)$ between every pair of its authors, whereas the costs of the phone-calls provide the weight in case of the mobile phone network*phone-call network*. Based on this, we define the link weight between two nodes a and b at time t as

$$w_{a,b}(t) = \sum_i w_i \exp\left(-\lambda\left(t - t_i\left(/w_i\right)\right),\right.$$

where the summation runs over all collaboration events in which a and b are involved (e.g., a phone-call between a and b), and w_i denotes the weight of the event i occurring at t_i. (The constant λ is a decay time characteristic for the particular social system we study). Thus, in this approach the time evolution of the network is manifested in the changing of the link weights. However, if the links weaker than a certain threshold w^* are neglected, the network becomes truly restructuring in the sense that links appear only in the vicinity of the events and disappear further away in time, as shown in Figure 2. for a randomly chosen connection in the mobile phone network*phone-call* network. The above method of weighting ties between people is very useful in capturing the continuous time dependence of the strength of connections when the information about them is available only at discrete time steps.

The *communities* in the studied system were extracted at each time step with the help of the Clique Percolation Method*CPM*. The actual values of the k and w^* parameters were $k=3$, $w^*=0.1$ in case of the co-authorship network, and $k=4$, $w^*=1.0$ in case of the mobile phone network*phone-call network*. In Figure 3a-b we show the local

Figure 2. The changing of the link-weight as a function of time for a connection in the mobile phone networkphone-call network. If a weight threshold of w*=1 is introduced, the link is present only inside the shaded intervals. Figure from the Supplementary Material of Palla et al. 2007

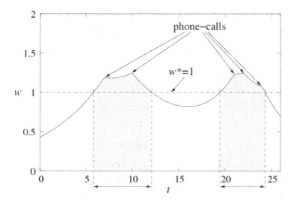

structure at a given time step in the two networks in the vicinity of a randomly chosen individual (marked by a rectangular frame). The communities (social groups represented by more densely interconnected parts within a network of social links) are coded with the different shades of gray, so that white nodes (and dashed edges) do not belong to any community, and those that simultaneously belong to two or more communities are shown in black. The two networks have rather different local structure: due to its bipartite nature,

the collaboration network is quite dense and the overlap between communities is very significant, whereas in the mobile phone networkphone-call network the communities are less interconnected and are often separated by one or more inter-community nodes/edges. Indeed, while the phone record captures the communication between two people, the publication record assigns to all individuals that contribute to a paper a fully connected clique. As a result, the phone data is dominated by single links, while the co-authorship data has many dense, highly connected neighborhoods. Furthermore, the links in the phone network correspond to instant communication events, capturing a relationship as it happens. In contrast, the co-authorship data records the results of a long term collaboration process. These fundamental differences suggest that any potential common feature of the community evolution in the two networks represent generic characteristics of community formation, rather than being rooted in the details of the network representation or data collection process.

Creating Evolving Communities

Since our focus is on *community evolution*, we need to find a method for "threading" the static snapshots of the communities (i.e., find a way to

Figure 3. (a) The local community structure at a given time step in the vicinity of a randomly selected node (marked by a rectangular frame) in case of the co-authorship network; (b) The same picture in the mobile phone networkphone-call network. Figure from Palla et al. 2007

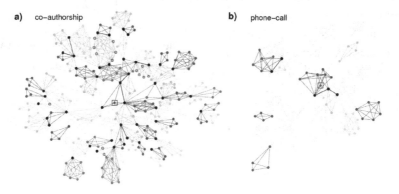

Figure 4. Possible events in the community evolution. When new members are introduced, the community grows, whereas leaving members cause decay in the size. Communities can merge and split, new groups may emerge and old ones can disappear. Figure from Palla et al. 2007

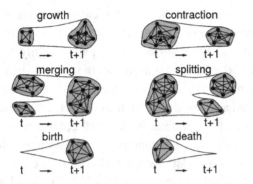

pinpoint the image or pre-image of a given community at the next or previous time step). The basic events that may occur in the life of a community are shown in Figure 4.: a community can grow by recruiting new members, or contract by loosing members; two (or more) groups may merge into a single community, while a large enough social group can split into several smaller ones; new communities are born and old ones may disappear. According to a recent study, the creation of new communities and community growth are the dominant processes in the co-authorship network (Lee, Kahng & Goh, 2008). Given that a huge number of groups are present at each time step, it is a significant algorithmic and computational challenge to match communities uncovered at different time steps. Naturally, the basic idea is to look for communities with similar membership. The importance of choosing a local community finding method becomes clear at this point. Suppose that the network suffers only localized minor changes between subsequent time steps: in this case we expect that the communities found at the unchanged parts of the network should remain the same. However, when using a global method, this is not guaranteed, since the drawback of these methods is that even a small local change in the network can reshuffle the entire community structure. Such an effect can result in strange fluctuations in the evolving communities even when the underlying sub-graph between the community members and the surrounding remains the same.

Turning to the technical details of the community matching, the basic idea of our algorithm is the following. For each consecutive time steps t and $t+1$ we construct a joint graph consisting of the union of links from the corresponding two networks, and extract the Clique Percolation MethodCPM community structure of this joint network (we thank I. Derényi for pointing out this possibility). Any community from either the t or the $t+1$ snap-shot is contained in exactly one community in the joint graph, since by adding links to a network, the Clique Percolation MethodCPM communities can only grow, merge or remain unchanged. Thus, the communities in the joint graph provide a natural connection between the communities at t and at $t+1$. If a community in the joint graph contains a single community from t and a single community from $t+1$, then they are matched. If the joint group contains more than one community from either time steps, the communities are matched in descending order of their relative node overlap, which is defined for a pair of communities A and B as

$$C(A,B) - \frac{|A \cap B|}{|A \cup B|},$$

where the nominator is given by the number of common nodes in A and B, and the denominator corresponds to the number of nodes in the union of the two communities. (For more details, see the Supplementary Information of Palla et al., 2007)

Statistics Related to Communities and Community Evolution

Coverage and Community Size Distribution

One of the most basic properties characterizing the partitioning of a network is the overall coverage of the community structure, i.e., the ratio of nodes contained in at least one community. When adjusting the k-clique size and the w^* weight threshold in the Clique Percolation Method CPM, one should also monitor the changes in the coverage: when k and w^* become too large, the coverage decreases, and the majority of the nodes are excluded from the communities.

Another important statistics describing the community system is the community size distribution, $p(s)$, defined as the number of communities of size s, divided by the total number of communities. For practical reasons, in some cases it is easier to use the cumulative community size distribution, $P(s)$, defined as the number of communities of size smaller than s, divided by the total number of communities. In other words,

$$P(s) = \sum_{s'=0}^{s-1} p(s').$$

Age, Lifetime and Auto-Correlation

The age, τ of a given community at time step t represents the number of time steps passed since its birth. The correlation between the age and other properties (e.g., the size) can provide interesting information about the typical behavior of communities at certain points in their life cycle. The lifetime τ^* is given by the number of steps between the birth and the disintegration of a community, and can be viewed as a simple measure of "fitness": communities having higher fitness have an extended life, while the ones with small fitness quickly disintegrate, or are swallowed by another community.

When interested in the study of the fluctuations in the membership of communities, the most natural tool is the auto-correlation function, defined as the relative overlap between two different states of the same community A:

$$C_A(t_1, t_2) \equiv \frac{\left| A(t_1) \cap A(t_2) \right|}{\left| A(t_1) \cup A(t_2) \right|}.$$

In this chapter we are interested in the behavior of the above function when the compared states are t steps apart, i.e., when $t_2 = t_1 + t$. More precisely, we shall study the average auto-correlation between two states of the same community t steps apart, which can be written as

$$C_A(t) \equiv \left\langle C_A(t_1, t_1 + t) \right\rangle_{t_1}.$$

A rapidly decaying auto-correlation function signals a dynamically changing community, in which the old members are replaced by newcomers at a fast rate, whereas for an absolutely static community $C(t)=1$.

Stationarity

As we shall see later, the above aspect, (namely whether a community is dynamically changing or static) can be crucial. To grasp this important property with a single parameter instead of a function, we introduce the *stationarity* (Palla et al., 2007) defined as the average the average correlation between subsequent states of a community:

$$\zeta \equiv \frac{\sum_{t=t_0}^{t_{max}-1} C(t, t+1)}{t_{max} - t_0 - 1},$$

where t_0 denotes the birth of the community, and t_{max} is the last step before the extinction of the community. A ς value close to unity signals a static community, whereas lower stationarity values correspond to more dynamic communities. In fact, the average ratio of members changed in one time step is given by 1- ς.

THE STATISTICAL PROPERTIES OF COMMUNITY EVOLUTION

Validation of the Communities

Before actually analyzing the community evolution, it is important to check whether the uncovered communities correspond to groups of individuals with a shared common activity pattern. For this purpose we compared the average weight of the links inside communities, w_c, to the average weight of the inter-community links, w_{ic}. For the co-authorship network w_c/w_{ic} is about 2.9, while for the mobile phone networkphone-call network the difference is even more significant, since w_c/w_{ic} is around 5.9, indicating that the intensity of collaboration/communication within a group is significantly higher than with contacts belonging to a different group.

While for coauthors the quality of the clustering can be directly tested by studying their publication records in more detail, in the mobile phone networkphone-call network personal information is not available. In this case the zip-code and the age of the users provide additional information for checking the homogeneity of the communities. In Figure 5a we show the size of the largest subset of people having the same zip code in the communities, averaged over the time steps, as the function of the community size s, divided by $<n_{rand}>$, representing the average over random sets of users. The significantly higher number of people with the same zip-code in the Clique Percolation MethodCPM communities as compared to random sets indicates that the communities usually correspond to individuals living relatively close to each other. It is of specific interest that $<n_{real}>/<n_{rand}>$ has a prominent peak at $s\approx35$, suggesting that communities of this size are geographically the most homogeneous ones. However, as Figure 5b shows, the situation is more complex: on average, the smaller communities are more homogeneous, but there is still a noticeable peak at $s\approx30$-35. In Figure 5a we also show the average size of the largest subset of members with an age falling into a three years wide time window, divided by the same quantity obtained for randomly selected groups of

Figure 5. (a) The black symbols correspond to the average size of the largest subset of members with the same zip-code, $<n_{real}>$, in the phone-call communities divided by the same quantity found in random sets, $<n_{rand}>$, as the function of the community size s. Similarly, the white symbols show the average size of the largest subset of community members with an age falling in a three year time window, divided by the same quantity in random sets; (b) The $<n_{real}>/s$ as a function of s, for both the zip-code (black symbols and the age (white symbols). Figure from Palla et al. 2007

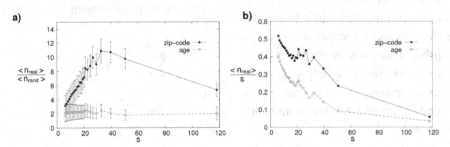

individuals. The fact that the ratio is larger than one indicates that communities have a tendency to contain people from the same generation, and the $<n_{rand}>/s$ plot indicates that the homogeneity of small groups is on average larger than that of the big groups. In summary, the phone-call communities uncovered by the Clique Percolation MethodCPM tend to contain individuals living in the same neighborhood, and with comparable age, a homogeneity that supports the validity of the uncovered community structure. (Further support is given in the Supplementary Material of Palla et al. 2007).

Basic Statistics

The overall coverage of the community structure was on average 59% in case of the co-authorship network, which is a reasonable coverage for the Clique Percolation MethodCPM. In contrast, we could only achieve a significantly smaller ratio for the mobile phone networkphone-call network. At such a large system size, in order to be able to match the communities at subsequent time steps in reasonable time we had to decrease the number of communities by choosing a higher k and w^* parameter ($k=4$ and $w^*=1.0$), and keeping only the communities having a size larger or equal to $s=6$. Therefore, in the end the ratio of nodes contained in at least one community was reduced to 11%. However, this still means more than 400000 customers in the communities on average, providing a representative sampling of the system. By lowering the k to $k=3$, the fraction of nodes included in the communities is raised to 43%. Furthermore, a significant number of additional nodes can be also classified into the discovered communities. For example, if a node not yet classified has link(s) only to a single community (and, if it has no links connecting to nodes in any other community) it can be safely added to that community. Carrying out this process iteratively, the fraction of nodes that can be classified into communities increases to 72% for the k=3 co-authorship network, and

to 72% (61%) for the $k=3$ ($k=4$) mobile phone network, which, in principle, allows us to classify over 2.4 million users into communities.

Now let us move onto the community size distribution of the mobile phone networkphone-call network, shown in Figure 6a for different time steps. They all resemble to a power-law with a high exponent. In case of $t=0$, the largest communities are somewhat smaller than in the later time steps. This is due to the fact that the events before the actual time step cannot contribute to the link-weights in case of $t=0$, whereas they can if $t>0$. In Figure 6b we can follow the time evolution of the community size distribution in the co-authorship network. In this case $t=0$ corresponds to the birth of the system itself as well (whereas in case of the phone-calls it does not), therefore the network and the communities in the network are small in the first few time steps. Later on, the system is enlarged, and the community size distribution is stabilized close to a power-law. In Figs.6c-d we show the number of communities as a function of the community size at different time steps in the examined systems. For the mobile phone networkphone-call network (Figure 6c), this distribution is more ore less constant in time. In contrast, (due to the growth of the underlying network) we can see an overall growth in the number of communities with time in the co-authorship network (Figure 6d). Since the number of communities drops down to only a few at large community sizes in both systems, we used size binning when calculating the statistics shown in the forthcoming Sections.

The Inter Relatedness of the Size, Stationarity and the Expected Life-Time

For evolving communities, we study first the relation between two basic quantities, the size s and age τ. According to Figure7a, s and τ are positively correlated: larger communities are on average older, which is quite natural, as commu-

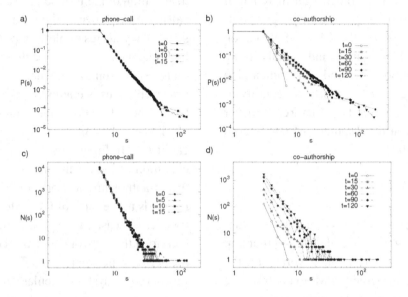

Figure 6. (a) The cumulative community size distribution in the mobile phone networkphone-call network at different time steps; (b) The time evolution of the cumulative community size distribution in the co-authorship network; (c) The number of communities of a given size at different time steps in the mobile phone networkphone-call network; (d) The time evolution of the number of communities with a given size in the co-authorship network. Figure from the Supplementary Material of Palla et al. 2007

nities are usually born small, and it takes time to recruit new members to reach a large size.

More interesting results can be obtained from the auto-correlation, $C(t)$, quantifying the relative overlap between two states of the same community t time steps apart. In Figure 7b we show the average time dependent auto-correlation function for communities born with different sizes. We find that in both networks, the auto-correlation function decays faster for the larger communities, indicating that the membership of the larger communities is changing at a higher rate (Palla et al., 2007). On the contrary, small communities change at a smaller rate, their composition being more or less static.

Figure 7. (a) The average age τ of communities with a given size (number of people) s, divided by the average age of all communities <τ>, as the function of s, indicating that larger communities are on average older; (b) The average auto-correlation function C(t) of communities with different sizes (the unit of time, is one month). The C(t) of larger communities decays faster. Figure from Palla et al. 2007

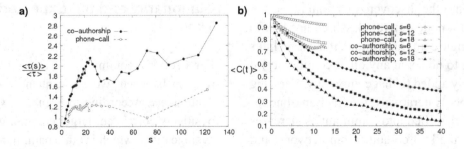

Figure 8. (a) The average life-span <τ> of the communities as the function of the stationarity ς and the community size s for the co-authorship network. The peak in <τ*> is close to ς=1 for small sizes, whereas it is shifted towards lower ς values for large sizes; (b) Similar results found in the mobile phone networkphone-call network. Figure from Palla et al. 2007*

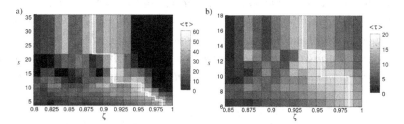

As we already described in the previous section, the above aspect of the communities can by quantified with the help of the stationarity. Now let us examine, how does the stationarity and the community size effect the lifetime, $τ^*$ of the communities. Figure 8a-b show the average life-span $<τ^*>$ (color coded) as a function of the stationarity ς and the community size s (both s and ς were binned). In both networks, for small community sizes the highest average life-span is at a stationarity value very close to one, indicating that for small communities it is optimal to have static, time independent membership. On the other hand, the peak in $<τ^*>$ is shifted towards low ς values for large communities, suggesting that for these the optimal regime is to be dynamic, i.e., a continually changing membership (Palla et al., 2007). In fact, large communities with a ς value equal to the optimal ς for small communities have a very short life, and similarly, small communities with a low ς (being optimal at large sizes) are disappearing quickly as well.

To illustrate the difference in the optimal behavior (a pattern of membership dynamics leading to extended lifetime) of small and large communities, in Figure 9 we show the time evolution of four communities from the co-authorship network. As Figure 9a indicates, a typical small and stationary community undergoes minor changes, but lives for a long time. This is well illustrated by the snapshots of the community structure, showing that the community's stability is conferred by a core of three individuals representing a collaborative group spanning over 52 months. While new co-authors are added occasionally to the group, they come and go. In contrast, a small community with high turnover of its members, (several members abandon the community at the second time step, followed by three new members joining in at time step three) has a lifetime of nine time steps only (Figure 9b). The opposite is seen for large communities: a large stationary community disintegrates after four time steps (Figure 9c). In contrast, a large non-stationary community whose members change dynamically, resulting in significant fluctuations in both size and the composition, has quite extended lifetime (Figure 9d). Indeed, while the community undergoes dramatic changes, gaining (Figure 9e) or loosing a high fraction of its membership, it can easily withstand these changes.

Adherence and Life-Time

The quite different stability rules followed by the small and large communities raise an important question: could an inspection of the community itself predict its future? To address this question, for each member in a community we measured the total weight of this member's connections to outside of the community, w_{out}, as well as to members belonging to the same community, w_{in}.

Figure 9. Time evolution of four communities in the co-authorship network. The height of the columns corresponds to the actual community size, and within one column the light gray color indicates the number of "old" nodes (that have been present in the community at least in the previous time step as well), while newcomers are shown with black. The members abandoning the community in the next time step are shown with mid gray colors, the shade depending on whether they are old or new. (This latter type of member joins the community for only one time step). From top to bottom, we show a small and stationary community (a), a small and non-stationary community; (b), a large and stationary community; (c) and, finally, a large and non-stationary community (d). A mainly growing stage (two time steps) in the evolution of the latter community is detailed in panel (e). Figure from Palla et al. 2007

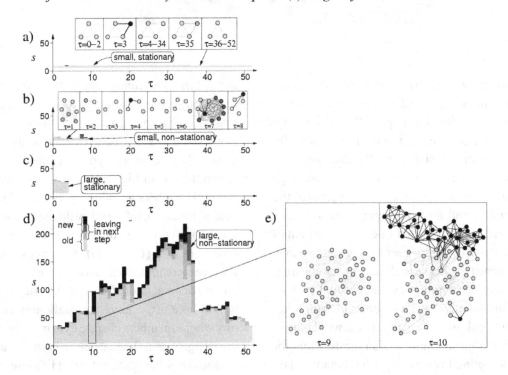

We then calculated the probability that the member will abandon the community as a function of the $w_{out}/(w_{out}+w_{in})$ ratio. As Figure 10a shows, for both networks this probability increases monotonically, suggesting that if the relative adherence of a user is to individuals outside a given community is higher, then it is more likely that he/she will leave the community (Palla et al., 2007). In parallel, the average time spent in the community by the nodes, $\langle\tau_n\rangle$, is a decreasing function of the above ratio (Figure 10a inset). Individuals that are the most likely to stay are those that commit most of their time to community members, an effect that is particularly prominent for the phone network.

As Figure 10a shows, those with the least commitment have a quickly growing likelihood of leaving the community.

Taking this idea from individuals to communities, we measured for each community the total weight of links (a measure of how much a member is committed) from the members to others, outside of the community, W_{out}, as well as the aggregated link weight inside the community, W_{in}. We find that the probability for a community to disintegrate in the next step increases as a function of $W_{out}/(W_{out} + W_{in})$, as shown in Figure 10b, and the lifetime of a community decreases with the $W_{out}/(W_{out} + W_{in})$ ratio (Figure 10b inset). This in-

Figure 10. (a) The probability p_l for a member to abandon its community in the next step as a function of the ratio of its aggregated link weights to other parts of the network, w_{out} and its total aggregated link weight $w_{out} + w_{in}$. The inset shows the average time spent in the community by the nodes, $<\tau_n>$, in function of $w_{out}/(w_{out} + w_{in})$; (b) The probability p_d for a community to disintegrate in the next step in function of the ratio of the aggregated weights of links from the community to other parts of the network W_{out} and the aggregated weights of all links starting from the community $W_{out} + W_{in}$. The inset shows the average life time $t<\tau^*>$ of communities as a function of $W_{out}/(W_{out} + W_{in})$. Figure from Palla et al. 2007

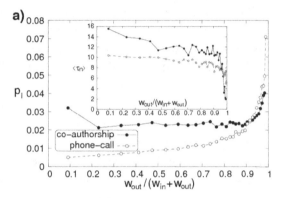
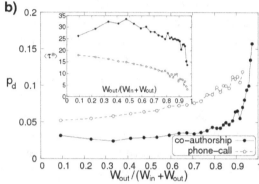

dicates that self-focused communities have a significantly longer lifetime than those that are open to the outside world (Palla et al., 2007). However, an interesting observation is that, while the lifetime of the phone-call communities for moderate levels is relatively insensitive to outside commitments, the lifetime of the collaboration communities possesses a maximum at intermediate levels of inter-collaborations (collaboration between colleagues who belong to different communities). These results suggest that a tracking of the individual's as well as the community's relative adherence to the other members of the community provides a clue for predicting the community's fate.

SUMMARY AND DISCUSSION

In summary, our results indicate a significant difference between smaller collaborative or friendship circles and institutions. At the heart of small cliques are a few strong relationships, and as long as these persist, the community around

them is stable. It appears to be almost impossible to maintain this strategy for large communities, however. Thus we find that the condition for stability for large communities is continuous changes in their membership, allowing for the possibility that after some time practically all members are exchanged. Such loose, rapidly changing communities are reminiscent of institutions that can continue to exist even after all members have been replaced by new members. For example, in a few years most members of a school or a company could change, yet the school and the company will be detectable as a distinct community at any time step during its existence. We also showed that the knowledge of the time commitment (or adherence) of the members to a given community can be used for predicting the community's lifetime. These findings offer a new view on the fundamental differences between the dynamics of small groups and large institutions.

To put our results into a wider concept, we note that the study of the time evolution of networks and restructuring modules seem to open a new frontier in multidisciplinary science, with a dynamically increasing number of publications in the very recent years. Here we pick only a few examples, having a closer relationship to the main results of our chapter. An important direction of research focuses on the origin of homophily in evolving social networks as presented by Kossinets & Watts (2009). Relating to this, the importance of distinguishing between homophily driven diffusion and influence-based contagion in dynamic networks was pointed out by Aral, Muchnik & Sundararajan (2009). An interesting alternative to the kinship or homophily models was given by Johnson, Xu, Zhao, Ducheneaut, Yee, Tita & Hui (2009), based on statistical analysis of the time evolution of online guilds and offline gangs.

The analysis of time evolving networks and restructuring communities provides challenges on the algorithmic and data handling level as well. Fenn et al. (2009) introduced a node-centric approach allowing to track the effects of the community evolution on the functional roles of individual nodes without having to track entire communities, whereas Mucha et al. (2010) developed a generalized framework of network quality functions allowing the study of community structure in a general setting encompassing networks evolving over time, having multiple types of links (this property is often referred to as multiplexity), and having multiple scales. A method for distinguishing between real trends and noisy fluctuations was presented by Rosvall & Bergstrom (2010), along with assigning significance to the partitioning of single networks.

The advances in these fields also trigger the development of new network models. The class of co-evolving network models is inherently well suited for describing time-dependent networks, providing a framework where the state of the nodes affect the rewiring of the links and vice versa. The recent achievements related to this approach include the description of an interesting fragmentation and recombination transition caused by competing time-scales (Vazquez, Gonzalez-Avella,

Eguiluz & San Miguel, 2007), and a study of the co-evolution of phases and connection strengths in a graph of oscillators (Aoki & Aoyagi, 2009). Studying game theory on networks is another related modeling framework, where the state of the system depends both on the topology of the connections between the players and the rules of cooperation between the players. This sort of approach can be used to model the development of altruistic behavior in human society (Eguiluz & Tessone, 2009). According to Kiss, Mihalik, Nanasi, Ory, Spiro, Soti, & Csermely (2009), cooperation can be also vital for the emergence of hierarchical complexity in evolving biological networks. Finally, we mention that ongoing group dynamics through coalescence and fragmentation plays an important part in the general model for human insurgency introduced by Bohorquez, Gourley, Dixon, Spagat & Johnson (2009).

REFERENCES

Ábel, D., Palla, G., Farkas, I., Derényi, I., Pollner, P., & Vicsek, T. (2005). *CFinder: Clusters and Communities in networks*. http:/www.cfinder.org/

Aoki, T., & Aoyagi, T. (2009). Co-evolution of Phases and Connection Strengths in a Network of Phase Oscillators. *Physical Review Letters, 102*, 034101. doi:10.1103/PhysRevLett.102.034101

Aral, S., Muchnik, L., & Sundararajan, A. (2009). Distinguishing influence-based contagion from homophily-driven diffusion in dynamic networks. *Proceedings of the National Academy of Sciences of the United States of America, 106*, 21544–21549. doi:10.1073/pnas.0908800106

Ausloos, M., & Lambiotte, R. (2007). Drastic events make evolving networks. *The European Physical Journal B, 57*, 89–94. doi:10.1140/epjb/e2007-00159-6

Barabási, A.-L. (2003). *Linked*. New York: Plume.

Barabási, A.-L., Jeong, H., Néda, Z., Ravasz, E., Schubert, A., &Vicsek, T. (2002). Evolution of the social network of scientific collaborations. *Physica A-Statistical Mechanics and its Applications 311*, 590-614.

Bohorquez, J. C., Gourley, S., Dixon, A. R., Spagat, M., & Johnson, N. F. (2009). Common ecology quantifies human insurgency. *Nature, 462*, 911–914. doi:10.1038/nature08631

Cattuto, C., Barrat, A., Baldassarri, A., Schehrd, G., & Loreto, V. (2009). Collective dynamics of social annotation. *Proceedings of the National Academy of Sciences of the United States of America, 106*, 10511–10515.

Cattuto, C., Loreto, V., & Pietronero, L. (2007). Semiotic dynamics and collaborative tagging. *Proceedings of the National Academy of Sciences of the United States of America, 104*, 1461–1464. doi:10.1073/pnas.0610487104

Cointet, J.-P., & Chavalarias, D. (2008). Multi-level science mapping with asymmetrical paradigmatic proximity. *Networks and Heterogeneous Media, 3*, 267–276.

Derényi, I., Palla, G., & Vicsek, T. (2005). Clique-Clique percolation in random networks. *Physical Review Letters, 94*, 160-202. doi:10.1103/PhysRevLett.94.160202

Ebel, H., Davidsen, J., & Bornholdt, S. (2002). Dynamics of social networks. *Complexity, 8*, 24–27. doi:10.1002/cplx.10066

Eguiluz, V. M., & Tessone, C. J. (2009). Critical behavior in an evolutionary ultimatum game with social structure. *Advances in Complex Systems, 12*, 221–232. doi:10.1142/S0219525909002179

Everett, M. G., & Borgatti, S. P. (1998). Analyzing Clique Overlap. *Connections, 21*, 49–61.

Everitt, B. S. (1993). *Cluster Analysis*. London: Edward Arnold.

Fenn, D. J., Porter, M. A., McDonald, M., Williams, S., Johnson, N. F., & Jones, N. S. (2009). Dynamic communities in multichannel data: An application to the foreign exchange market during the 2007-2008 credit crisis. *Chaos (Woodbury, N.Y.), 19*, 033119. doi:10.1063/1.3184538

Fortunato, S., & Castellano, C. (2009). Community structure in graphs. In E. A. Meyers (Ed.), Encyclopedia of Complexity and System Science. Berlin: Springer.Community

Ghoshal, G., Zlatic, V., Caldarelli, G., & Newman, M. E. J. (2009). Random hypergraphs and their applications. *Phys. Rew. E, 79*, 066118. doi:10.1103/PhysRevE.79.066118

Girvan, M., & Newman, M. E. J. (2002). CommunityCommunity structure in social and biological networks. *Proceedings of the National Academy of Sciences of the United States of America, 99*, 7821–7826. doi:10.1073/pnas.122653799

González, M. C., Hidalgo, C. A., & Barabási, A.-L. (2008). Understanding individual human mobility patterns. *Nature, 453*, 779–782. doi:10.1038/nature06958

Granovetter, M. S. (1973). The strength of weak ties. *American Journal of Sociology, 78*, 1360–1380. doi:10.1086/225469

Granovetter, M. S. (1992). *Decision Making: Alternatives to Rational Choice Models Economic Action and Social Structure: The Problem of Embeddedness*. Newbury Park, CA: SAGE.

Heimo, T., Saramäki, J., Onnela, J.-P., & Kaski K. (2007). Spectral and network methods in the analysis of correlation matrices of stock returns. *Physica A-Statistical Mechanics and its Applications 383*, 147-151.

Herrera, M., Roberts, D. C., & Gulbahce, N. (2010). Mapping the Evolution of Scientific Fields. *PLoS ONE, 5*, e10355. doi:10.1371/journal.pone.0010355

Hidalgo, C. A., & Rodriguez-Sickert, C. (2008). The dynamics of a mobile phone network. *Physica A, 387,* 3017–3024. doi:10.1016/j. physa.2008.01.073

Holme, P., Edling, Ch. R., & Liljeros, F. (2004). Structure and Time-Evolution of an Internet Dating Community.. *Social Networks, 26,* 155–174. doi:10.1016/j.socnet.2004.01.007

Hopcroft, J., Khan, O., Kulis, B., & Selman, B. (2004). Tracking evolving communities in large linked networks. *Proceedings of the National Academy of Sciences of the United States of America, 101,* 5249–5253. doi:10.1073/pnas.0307750100

Hu, D., Kaza, S., & Chen, H. (2009). Identifying Significant Facilitators of Dark Network Evolution. *Journal of the American Society for Information Science and Technology, 60,* 655–665. doi:10.1002/asi.21008

Johnson, N. F., Xu, C., Zhao, Z., Ducheneaut, N., Yee, N., Tita, G., & Hui, P. M. (2009). Human group formation in online guilds and offline gangs driven by a common team dynamic. *Physical Review E: Statistical, Nonlinear, and Soft Matter Physics, 79,* 066117. doi:10.1103/PhysRevE.79.066117

Kiss, H. J. M., Mihalik, A., Nanasi, T., Ory, B., Spiro, Z., Soti, C., & Csermely, P. (2009). Ageing as a price of cooperation and complexity. *BioEssays, 31,* 651–664. doi:10.1002/bies.200800224

Knudsen, S. (2004). *A Guide to Analysis of DNA Microarray Data.* Wiley-liss.

Kossinets, G., & Watts, D. J. (2006). Empirical analysis of an evolving social network. *Science, 311,* 88–90. doi:10.1126/science.1116869

Kossinets, G., & Watts, D. J. (2009). Origins of Homophily in an Evolving Social Network. *American Journal of Sociology, 115,* 405–450. doi:10.1086/599247

Lambiotte, R., Blondel, V. D., de Kerchove, C., Huens, E., Prieur, C., Smoreda, Z., & Van Dooren, P. (2008). Geographical dispersal of mobile communication networks. *Physica A, 387,* 5317–5325. doi:10.1016/j.physa.2008.05.014

Lambiotte, R., & Panzarasa, P. (2009). Communities, knowledge creation, and information diffusion. *Journal of Informatrics, 3,* 180–190. doi:10.1016/j.joi.2009.03.007

Lee, D., Kahng, B., & Goh, K.-I. (2008). Evolution of the coauthorship network. *Journal of the Korean Physical Society, 52,* S197–S202. doi:10.3938/jkps.52.197

Leskovec, J., Chakrabarti, D., Kleinberg, J., & Faloutsos, C. (2005). Realistic, mathematically tractable graph generation and evolution, using Kronecker multiplication. *Lecture Notes in Computer Science, 3721,* 133–145. doi:10.1007/11564126_17

Liljeros, F., Edling, Ch. R., Amaral, L. A. N., Stanley, H. E., & Aberg, Y. (2001). The Web of Human Sexual Contacts. *Nature, 411,* 907–908. doi:10.1038/35082140

Lindquist, J., Ma, J., van den Driessche, P., & Willeboordse, F. H. (2009). Network evolution by different rewiring schemes. *Physica D. Nonlinear Phenomena, 238,* 370–378. doi:10.1016/j. physd.2008.10.016

Liu, J., & Deng, G. (2009). Link prediction in a user-object network based on time-weighted resource allocation. *Physica A, 388,* 3643–3650. doi:10.1016/j.physa.2009.05.021

Mahadevan, P., Krioukov, D., Fall, K., & Vahdat, A. (2006). Systematic topology analysis and generation using degree correlations. *Computer Communication Review, 36,* 135–146. doi:10.1145/1151659.1159930

Mendes, J. F. F., & Dorogovtsev, S. N. (2003). *Evolution of Networks: From Biological Nets to the Internet and WWW*. Oxford, UK: Oxford University Press.

Mucha, P. J., Richardson, T., Macon, K., Porter, M.-A., & Onnela, J.-P. (2010). CommunityCommunity Structure in Time-Dependent, Multiscale, and Multiplex Networks. *Science, 328,* 876–878. doi:10.1126/science.1184819

Newman, M. E. J. (2004). Detecting community structure in networks. *The European Physical Journal B, 38,* 321–330. doi:10.1140/epjb/e2004-00124-y

Noh, J. D., Jeong, H. C., Ahn, Y. Y., & Jeong, H. (2005). Growing network model for community with group structure. *Physical Review E: Statistical, Nonlinear, and Soft Matter Physics, 71,* 036131. doi:10.1103/PhysRevE.71.036131

Onnela, J.-P., Chakraborti, A., Kaski, K., Kertész, J., & Kanto, A. (2003). Dynamics of market correlations: Taxonomy and portfolio analysis. *Physical Review E: Statistical, Nonlinear, and Soft Matter Physics, 68,* 056110. doi:10.1103/PhysRevE.68.056110

Onnela, J.-P., Saramäki, J., Hyvonen, J., Szabó, G., Lazer, D., & Kaski, K. (2007). Structure and tie strengths in mobile communication networks. *Proceedings of the National Academy of Sciences of the United States of America, 104,* 7332–7336. doi:10.1073/pnas.0610245104

Palla, G., Derényi, I., Farkas, I., & Vicsek, T. (2005). Uncovering the overlapping community structure of complex networks in nature and society. *Nature, 435,* 814–818. doi:10.1038/nature03607

Palla, G., Farkas, I. J., Pollner, P., Derényi, I., & Vicsek, T. (2008). Fundamental statistical features and self-similar properties of tagged networks. *New Journal of Physics, 10,* 123026. doi:10.1088/1367-2630/10/12/123026

Palla, G., Lovász, L., & Vicsek, T. (2010). Multifractal network generator. *Proceedings of the National Academy of Sciences of the United States of America, 107,* 7640–7645. doi:10.1073/pnas.0912983107

Palla, G., Vicsek, T., & Barabási, A.-L. (2007). Quantifying social group evolution. *Nature, 435,* 814–818. doi:10.1038/nature03607

Pollner, P., Palla, G., & Vicsek, T. (2006). Preferential attachment of communities: The same principle, but a higher level. *Europhysics Letters, 73,* 478–484. doi:10.1209/epl/i2005-10414-6

Radicchi, F., Castellano, C., Cecconi, C., Loreto, V., & Parisi, D. (2004). Defining and identifying communities in networks. *Proceedings of the National Academy of Sciences of the United States of America, 101,* 2658–2663. doi:10.1073/pnas.0400054101

Ravasz, E., Somera, A. L., Mongru, D. A., Oltvai, Z. N., & Barabási, A.-L. (2002). Hierarchical organization of modularity in metabolic networks. *Science, 297,* 1551–1555. doi:10.1126/science.1073374

Robins, G., Snijders, T., Wang, P., Handcock, M., & Pattison, P. (2007). Recent developments in exponential random graph (p*) models for social networks. *Social Networks, 29,* 192–215. doi:10.1016/j.socnet.2006.08.003

Rosvall, M., & Bergstrom, C. T. (2010). Mapping Change in Large Networks. *PLoS ONE, 5,* e8694. doi:10.1371/journal.pone.0008694

Scott, J. (2000). Social Network Analysis: A Handbook. London: Sage Publications.Social Network

Shiffrin, R. M., & Börner, K. (2004). Mapping knowledge domains. *Proceedings of the National Academy of Sciences of the United States of America, 101,* 5183–5185. doi:10.1073/pnas.0307852100

Smith, D. M. D., Onnela, J.-P., & Johnson, N. F. (2007). Accelerating networks. *New Journal of Physics, 9,* 181. doi:10.1088/1367-2630/9/6/181

Spirin, V., & Mirny, K. A. (2003). Protein complexes and functional modules in molecular networks. *Proceedings of the National Academy of Sciences of the United States of America, 100,* 12123–12128. doi:10.1073/pnas.2032324100

Vazquez, F., Gonzalez-Avella, J. C., Eguiluz, V. M., & San Miguel, M. (2007). Time-scale competition leading to fragmentation and recombination transitions in the coevolution of network and states. *Physical Review E: Statistical, Nonlinear, and Soft Matter Physics, 76,* 046120. doi:10.1103/PhysRevE.76.046120

Vedres, B., & Stark, D. (2010). Structural Folds: Generative Disruption in Overlapping Groups. *American Journal of Sociology, 115,* 1150–1190. doi:10.1086/649497

Wang, P., González, M. C., Hidalgo, C. A., & Barabási, A.-L. (2009). Understanding the Spreading Patterns of Mobile Phone Viruses. *Science, 324,* 1071–1076. doi:10.1126/science.1167053

Warner, S. (2003). E-prints and the Open Archives Initiative. *Library Hi Tech, 21,* 151–158. doi:10.1108/07378830310479794

Wasserman, S., & Faust, K. (1994). Social Network Analysis: Methods and Applications. Cambridge: Cambridge University Press. Social Network

Watts, D. J., Dodds, P. S., & Newman, M. E. J. (2002). Identity and search in social networks. *Science, 296,* 1302–1305. doi:10.1126/science.1070120

Watts, D. J., & Strogatz, S. H. (1998). Collective dynamics of 'small-world' networks. *Nature, 393,* 440–442. doi:10.1038/30918

White, H. C., Boorman, S. A., & Breiger, R. R. (1976). Social structure from multiple networks. I. Blockmodels of roles and positions. *American Journal of Sociology, 81,* 730–780. doi:10.1086/226141

Zlatic, V., Ghoshal, G., & Caldarelli, G. (2009). Hypergraph topological quantities for tagged social networks. *Phys. Rew. E, 80,* 036118. doi:10.1103/PhysRevE.80.036118

Chapter 4
Two Informational Complexity Measures in Social Networks and Agent Communities

António Jorge Filipe Fonseca
ISCTE, Portugal

ABSTRACT

Several informational complexity measures rely on the notion of stochastic process in order to extract hidden structural properties behind the apparent randomness of information sources. Following an equivalence approach between dynamic relation evolution within a social network and a generic stochastic process two dynamic measures of network complexity are proposed.

INTRODUCTION

Most of the statistical social network analysis methods rely on a fixed network structure. Earlier methods of dyadic statistical analysis manage to provide quantification on degrees of mutuality between actors and triadic analysis does a step forward allowing validation of theories of balance and transitivity about specific components of a network. Each of these constitutes a subset of a more general *k-sub graph analysis* based on *k-sub graph census* extracted from the network architecture. Some sort of frequency analysis is done over these censuses from which probabilistic distributions can be evaluated. More recent single

relational statistical analysis additionally allows the validation of statistic models through parametric estimation. Looking further for positional assumptions of groups of actors, stochastic block model analysis measure the statistical fitness of defined equivalent classes on the social network (Carrington, 2005) (Wasserman, 1994). All of these tools assume some sort a static network structure, a kind of snapshot of reality, over which statistical measuring is done and some degree of confidence is evaluated against real data. It is not of our knowledge any method of providing some sort of analysis on the dynamic structure of social networks in which the set of relations evolves over a certain amount of time. The method we propose has the purpose of allowing a probabilistic informational based evaluation of each actor's inner

DOI: 10.4018/978-1-60960-171-3.ch004

Copyright © 2011, IGI Global. Copying or distributing in print or electronic forms without written permission of IGI Global is prohibited.

Figure 1. A network that evolves over time. The arcs between the nodes represent all the interplay activity performed during the timeslot $nT, \left(1 \leq n \leq N\right)$

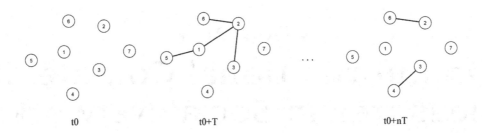

complex motivated behaviour on the process of relation change inside his network. The evaluation is supported on the measurement of the *Entropy Density* and after of the *Excess Entropy* over the stochastic relational changing. Measuring the evolution of this interplay complexity measure can provide some insights into each actor degree of inner structure pertaining to the specific kind of relation that the network is supposed to represent. *Entropy Density* and *Excess Entropy* are theoretical measures and for practical purposes only estimative can be obtained. The study of estimative computation for entropy is still subject to intense research in the Physics community. As the measurement only approaches the real relational entropy of each actor, it can be considered within the context of the set of members of the social network an absolute measure as the same estimate bias is applied to the community as an all.

NETWORK DYNAMICS AND INFORMATION

The complexity of the information that may be extracted from observations of a source, as a phenomenological observation of its behavior, without any prior knowledge of the source's internal structure, may reveal missed regularities and structural properties hidden behind the apparent randomness of the stochastic process that the source generates. This information can provide

useful clues in order to predict the source future behavior or its characteristic properties. In social network dynamics each actor generally performs some sort of action, communication acts; exchange of capital or economic goods or any other possible social interplay or attribute for which a well defined time limit and intensity can be pinpointed in time. This definition can generally be extended and even applied to objects as for example a correlation of goods purchased by each client of a supermarket. The agent that determines the dynamic nature of a network is primarily Time. Topologically a network that evolves as the one depicted in *figure 1* is completely defined as a set of graphs, each constituted by a set of nodes and link, eventually tagged with some intensity attribute, that have been established during a defined time slot *T* of the interval of observation. The sequence of the *n* time slot started at time t_0 pretend to report the dynamical relational evolution that the network is supposed to represent. There are some approaches to dynamic network that take into account possible resilience of links as an intensity attribute. In fact, the process of time partitioning can be tricky, dynamic features that appear relevant at some time slot durations can in fact be insignificant look at other time spans. There exist ways to circumvent this problem taking into account the kind of relation the network represents. For example normalizing the duration of the interplay through an inverse exponential

Figure 2. Growth of H(L) function of L. The picture also shows the metric entropy coefficient h_μ as the rate of increase with respect to l of the total Shannon entropy in the large L limit

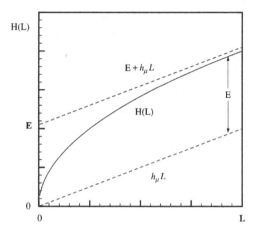

function of time slot duration can avoid some dependence on value of T.

Having a dynamic network and coding the combination of all the established links that each node performed during each time-slot, we obtain a relational stochastic process for that particular node. This process will symbolically represent the node relational evolution within the community. The extraction of informational quantities from this process is straightforward.

INFORMATIONAL MEASURES OF COMPLEXITY

Given a symbolic process $\overleftrightarrow{S} \equiv \cdots S_{-2}, S_{-1}, S_0, S_1, S_2 \cdots$ of random variables S_{T_i} that range over an alphabet A, taking sequence values $\cdots s_{-2}, s_{-1}, s_0, s_1, s_2 \cdots \in A$, the total Shannon entropy of *length-L* sequences of $\overleftrightarrow{S}$ is defined as (Cover, 2006):

$$H(L) = \sum_{s^L \in A^L} Pr(s^L) \log_2 Pr(s^L)$$

Where s^L are symbols belonging to these sequences of L length that represent combinations of symbols of A constituting the alphabet A^L. On a binary alphabet with $A^L = \{0,1\}$ and with $L=3$, $A^L = \{000, 001, 010, 011, 100, 101, 110, 111\}$. $H(L)$ is calculated over all the extension of the process $\overleftrightarrow{S}$ for any possible consecutive combination of L symbols. It happens that $H(L)$ is a non-decreasing function of L: $H(L) \geq H(L-1)$ and it is also a concave function:

$$H(L) - 2H(L-1) + H(L-2) \leq 0.$$

This fact can easily be understood if we notice that the size of A^L increases exponentially with L and so inversely does $Pr(s^L)$. Figure 2 depicts the growth of $H(L)$ function of increasing L length:

$$h_\mu \equiv \lim_{L \to \infty} \frac{H(L)}{L}$$

REDUNDANCY

The entropy rate h_μ quantifies the amount of *irreducible randomness* that remains after all the correlations and patterns embedded in longer and longer *length-L* sequence blocks are extracted from the entropy computation (Crutchfield, 2001). It is the rate at which the source transmits *pure randomness* and it is measured as *bits/symbol*. Since each symbol belongs to an alphabet of size $|A|$ the *Redundancy* within the source, R, is given by the difference between this maximum theoretical entropy rate, the *channel capacity* that is needed to transmit any optimally coded message from an arbitrary source using an alphabet A, $C = \log_2 |A|$, and h_μ:

$$R \equiv \log_2 |A| - h_\mu$$

The redundancy R is a measure of the information that an observer gains after expecting a maximally entropic uniform probability distribution from the source and actually learns the correct distribution $Pr\left(\overleftrightarrow{S}\right)$ of the sequence.

It is possible to define derivatives for $H(L)$. Having the first derivative we obtain the *apparent entropy rate* or *apparent metric entropy* at a given length L:

$$h_\mu(L) \equiv \Delta H(L)$$
$$= H(L) - H(L-1), L \geq 1$$

This derivative constitutes an *information gain*. The function $h_\mu(L)$ is an estimate of how random the source appears if only blocks of the process up to length L are considered. The difference between $h_\mu(L)$ and the true h_μ on the measure into the infinite L limit, give a related L-estimate, the *per-symbol L-redundancy*:

$$r(L) \equiv \Delta R(L) \equiv h_\mu(L) - h_\mu$$

$r(L)$ measures how the *apparent entropy rate* computed at a finite L exceeds the actual *entropy rate*. Any difference between the two indicates there is redundant information in the L-blocks in the amount of $r(L)$ bits. Interpreting $h_\mu(L)$ as an estimate of the source's unpredictability we can look further at the rate of change of $h_\mu(L)$, the rate at which the unpredictability is lost. This is given by the second order derivative:

$$\Delta^2 H(L) \equiv \Delta h_\mu(L) = h_\mu(L) - h_\mu(L-1)$$

PREDICTABILITY GAIN

The previous second order derivative provides a measure of the change, for each increment on the size of increasing larger L blocks, of the *metric entropy* estimate $h_\mu(L)$. This measure constitutes a *predictability gain* (Crutchfield, 2001). From the previous equation we can see that the quantity $-\Delta^2 H(L)$ measures the reduction in per-symbol uncertainty in going from $(L-1)$ to L block statistics. Computing how this derivative converges to the limit $L \rightarrow \infty$, which is to say that for every possible large combinations of symbols, we obtain the a *Total Predictability* G of the process.

G is defined as:

$$G \equiv \sum_{L=1}^{\infty} \Delta^2 H(L)$$

And as $h_\mu(L)$ is always positive it can be shown that $\Delta^2 H(L) \leq 0$ and also that:

$$G = -R$$

like R the unit of G is *bits/symbol*. For a periodic process $G = \log_2 |A|$, $h_\mu = 0$ so it assumes its maximum value for a completely predictable process. G however does not tell us how difficult it is to carry out any prediction, nor how many symbols must be observed before the process can be optimally predicted, but in fact give us a measure "disequilibrium" between the actual entropy rate of the process h_μ and the maximum possible entropy rate of a periodic process with the same alphabet A.

A finite L estimate of G is given by:

$$G(L) = H(1) + \sum_{l=2}^{L} [H(l) - 2H(l-1) + H(l-2)]$$

FINITARY AND INFINITARY PROCESSES

If, for all i and j, the probabilistic distribution of each symbol obeys the equality $Pr(S_i) = Pr(S_j)$, the probability distribution of the stochastic process:

$$Pr(\vec{S}) = Pr(\cdots, S_i, S_{i+1}, S_{i+2}, S_{i+3}, \cdots)$$

is given by: $Pr(\vec{S}) = \cdots Pr(S_i)Pr(S_{i+1})Pr(S_{i+2})\cdots$ and we say that the process is *independently and identically distributed*. If however the probability of the next symbol depends on the previous symbol, we then call the process *Markovian*:

$$Pr(\vec{S}) = \cdots Pr(S_{i+1} \mid S_i)Pr(S_{i+2} \mid S_{i+1})\cdots$$

In a general case, if the probability depends on previous R symbols of the sequence:

$$Pr(S_i \mid \cdots, S_{i-2}, S_{i-1}) = Pr(S_i \mid S_{i-R}, \cdots, S_{i-1})$$

Then we call this type of process an *order-R Markovian*. A *hidden Markov* process consists of an internal *order-R Markov* process that is observed by a function of its internal-state sequences. These are usually called *functions of a Markov chain* which we suppose is embedded inside the system. These kind of processes are considered *finitary* since any Markov Chain as a finite amount of memory.

Generally any stochastic process is said to be *finitary* if at the $L \to \infty$ limit:

$$H(L) \sim h_\mu L$$

$$\lim_{L \to \infty} \Delta H(L) = h_\mu,$$

$$\lim_{L \to \infty} \Delta^n H(L) = 0 \text{ for } n \geq 2$$

On a *finitary* process the *entropy rate* estimate $h_\mu(L)$ decays faster than $1/L$ to the actual entropy rate h_μ. Other way of defining a finitary process is to admit that the *Excess Entropy* E, the second measure we will examine, is finite on *finitary* processes and infinite otherwise.

EXCESS ENTROPY

In order to capture the structural properties of memory embedded into the system, we need to look at other entropy convergence integrals. Several authors (Packard,1982) (Grassberger,1986) (Li,1991) (Crutchfield,2001) defined a quantity named *Excess Entropy* E or *Complexity, Effective Measure of Complexity* or *Stored Information*, as measure of how $h_\mu(L)$ converges to h_μ. This quantity is expressed as:

$$E \equiv \sum_{L=1}^{\infty} \left[h_\mu(L) - h_\mu \right] = \sum_{L=1}^{\infty} r(L)$$

The unit of E is *bits*. Following the reasoning explained above this quantity gives us the difference between the per-symbol entropy conditioned on L measurements and the per-symbol entropy conditioned on an infinite number of measurements. As the source appears less random at length L by the amount $r(L)$ this constitutes a measure of information carrying capacity in the L-blocks that is not actually random but due instead to correlations. If one sums these individual per-symbol L-redundancy contributions we obtain the total amount of apparent memory in the source, which can be interpreted as an *intrinsic redundancy*. The entropy-rate convergence is controlled by this intrinsic redundancy as a property of the source. At each L we obtain additional information on the way about how $h_\mu(L)$ converges to h_μ, this information is not contained in $H(L)$ and $h_\mu(L)$ for smaller L. Thus each measure of $h_\mu(L)$ is an independent indicator of how $h_\mu(L)$ converges to h_μ. For *non-finitary* processes E does not converge at all. We will admit however, as we will deal with estimates for finite L relative within a definite context of similar estimates, that they provide an absolute characterization of *intrinsic redundancy* up to L-block estimates within the context. The structure of this quantified memory of the system cannot be analyzed within the framework of information theory, for this purpose complexity measures based on computation theory like *Kolmogorov Complexity* or *Logic Depth* must be used (Shannon, 1948)(Kolmogorov, 1965).

The excess entropy can also be seen as the mutual information between the left and right (past and future) semi-infinite halves of the process $\overset{\leftrightarrow}{S}$:

$$E = \lim_{L \to \infty} MI\left[S_0 S_1 \cdots S_{2L-L} ; S_{L+1} S_{L+2} \cdots S_{2L}\right]$$

Whenever this limit exist.

A finite L estimate of E is given by:

$$E = \sum_{l=1}^{L}\left[h_\mu(l) - h_\mu(L)\right]$$

$$= \sum_{l=1}^{L}\left[H(l) - H(l-1)\right] - L\left[H(L) - H(L-1)\right]$$

MEASURING COMMUNITY DYNAMICS

Having a social network or a community of actors which relations evolve over a specific time interval we now want to quantify each agent's degree of complex intentionality that determines dynamical structural change within the community network of interactions. Recalling the equivalence of relational change with a stochastic process examined in the above section, it is reasonable to establish a phenomenological equivalence between each agent's observed dynamical changing of relations process as a stochastic process eventually determined by each actor specific structure.

Assuming a community with N actors, we may divide the interval duration of our observation into K time slots of duration T. At each time slot k each agent or node n_i, $(1 \le i \le N)$ has a domain $A = 2^{N-1}$ of possibly different relation configurations c_i^k directly with other agents. The L-block entropy of this stochastic process C_i as A^L possibly different configurations c_i^l for each of the blocks which is given by:

$$H_i(L) = -\sum_{k=1}^{K-L} Pr(c_i^{kL}) \log_2 Pr(c_i^{kL})$$

where:

$$Pr\left(c_i^{kL}\right) = \frac{1}{A^L}\sum_{l=1}^{|A^L|} \delta_{c_i^{kL}, c_i^L} \, , \, c_i^{kL} \in A^L \, , \, c_i^L \in A^L$$

c_i^{kL} is the L-length configuration c_i^l that starts at time slot k.

Recalling the above definition of G, an estimate of the total predictability $G_i(L)$ for a time interval of K time slots, with a sufficiently large L (L can be as large as K, but we should note that the computational effort grows exponentially with the size L) is given by:

$$G_i(L) = Hi(1) + \sum_{l=2}^{L}\left[H_i(l) - 2H_i(l-1) + H_i(l-2)\right]$$

and an estimate of the excess entropy $E_i(L)$ for each agent of the community is given by:

$$Ei(L) = \sum_{l=1}^{L} \left[H_i(l) - H_i(l-1) \right] - L \left[H_i(L) - H_i(L-1) \right]$$

With respect to the definition of *total predictability* we can interpret $G_i(L)$ at the end of the network evolution observation, as the node or actor *n predictability*, which is an equivalent of measuring the periodicity of the actor's interplay within the community. An actor with a large amount of *predictability* should stick to regular patterns of relations both in time and in interplay with other actors. On the other hand the quantity $E_i(L)$ provides an estimate of the n_i node or actor magnitude of *complex subjective commitment* to its relational choices within the network. This means to have some kind of memory that dictates his relational patterns, in other word to be socially complex.

At this point we should note that these two measures, although egocentric and also estimates, should be considered absolute within the complete set of relations between nodes of the network. In fact, when both measures are using the same L estimate and are applied to the set of nodes as an all, they can be considered as an absolute measurement with respect to all the nodes of a particular observation. Then, when we are referring to the *complex subjective commitment* or *predictability* on some node on the context of one observation, we are considering two properties of the particular situated role of each node in respect to the particular kind of relation that the network is supposed to describe.

As we have stated above, there is an equivalence of E_i with the mutual information between the past and the future of the series of connections each node performs. Thus, we can see why E_i is adequately defined as a *commitment* towards a subjective preference for some dynamic pattern of relations within the network as opposed to no preference at all. The excess entropy E_i quantifies the magnitude of correlation between the past

observations of the set of relational patterns at each node with future observations and vice versa, thus reflecting the commitment of the node to enforce the observed set of patterns.

THE COMMUNITY OF AGENTS PARALLEL

Until now we have been considering normal human interactions, however these same two measures of complex social activity can also be applied to computer agent communities. Multi-agents systems normally implement some kind of protocol for message exchange that allows the agents to cooperate and coordinate (Weiss, 2000)(Shoham, 2009). The fine tuning of message exchanging and work distribution among agents can benefit from informational measuring of agent communication. The application of these two measures can provide useful tools to adjust agent communication in very sophisticated and complex agent environments.

AN EXAMPLE

In order to better illustrate the measures proposed on the previous section we will examine a hypothetical community of agents constituting an artificial social network with some given assumptions about the agent roles. A general human social network could be used instead. Let us consider the message exchange between agents during a defined period T. Admissibly we have a chronological log of all the messages which we partition at a fixed time intervals. Let us also assume that we want to restrict the focus of our study into a restrict subset of agents and that those agents have arbitrarily complex cognitive and communication capabilities:

1. One coordinator for a given task
2. A agent that performs part of the task
3. A directory facilitator

We want have some insight, having only logged timestamp; sender and receiver for each message, on the memory extent and role of each agent. Considering that we have *a posteriori* knowledge that these agents have the following roles:

1. The coordinator communicates only with the agents under his responsibility in order to perform his coordinated task. At fixed intervals he checks with a non coordinated agent the state of accomplishment of the task.
2. The coordinated agent periodically consults the coordinator in order to adjust his goal. Otherwise he just silently prosecutes his goal.
3. The directory facilitator randomly exchanges messages with every agent of the community at their request in order facilitate agent communication.

From this description we should expect to obtain at the end of our observation a great level of *predictability* for the working agent, a moderate level for the coordinator and vanishing levels for the directory facilitator. On the other hand the *subjective commitment* to patterns of communication should be greater for the coordinator as he should possess a greater amount of memory that should allows him to coordinate his well defined team of agents, a lesser one for the directory facilitator, as although communicating randomly within the community he should however reflect some patterns of communication behavior product of the system's global memory, and a lesser degree for the worker agent as he only communicates at regular interval with his single coordinator.

CONCLUSION

We strongly believe these two measures of egocentric social complexity have great potential on the evaluation of social networks. Actor or agent *social predictability* constitutes an important indicator in many evaluations. Also the *commitment to the community* is an important factor on distinguishing and characterizing its members. We should recall that the nature of the social relation that is evaluated for each particular network as direct influence on the interpretation of these measures. Social network science abstracts the nature of the relation from the actors involved. A dynamic relation, as we stated above, could mean communicating but also buying and selling or just having some kind of affinity between actors or agents. Thus the nature of the relation that is studied has direct impact on the nature of the measurements. Also a correct choice of sampling rate of the network timeline constitutes a critical matter that directly influences the results. For each dynamics, different time slot duration will have direct impact on the results obtained. This impact should be subject of further investigation, it is more or less obvious however that each dynamic process has his own time scale. This scale has thus direct influence on the correct choice of time partition. A concrete application of these measures to a real case scenario will follow.

REFERENCES

Carrington, P. J., Scott, J., & Wasserman, S. (2005). *Models and Methods in Social Network Analysis.* UK: Cambridge University Press.

Cover, T. M., & Thomas, J. A. (2006). *Elements of Information Theory.* US: John Wiley and Sons.

Crutchfield, J. P., & Feldman, D. P. (2001). Regularities unseen, randomness observed: Levels of entropy convergence. *Santa Fe Institute Working Papers* 01-02-012.

Grassberger, P. (1986). Toward a Quantitative Theory of Self-Generated Complexity [Springer Netherlands.]. *International Journal of Theoretical Physics, 25,* 907–938. doi:10.1007/BF00668821

Kolmogorov, A. N. (1965). Three approaches to the quantitative definition of information. *Problems of Information Transmission, 1*, 1–7.

Li, W. (1991). On the Relationship between Complexity and Entropy for Markov Chains and Regular Languages. *Complex Systems. Complex Systems Publications, 5*, 381–399.

Packard, N. H. (1982). Measurements of Chaos in the Presence of Noise. *Phd Thesis, University of California*

Shannon, C. (1948). A Mathematical Theory of Communicatio*n. Bell System Technical Journal, Bell Laboratories, 27*, 379-423, 623-656.

Shoham, Y., & Leyton-Brown, K. (2009). *Multiagent Systems – Algorithmic, Game-theoretic, and Logical Foundations*. US: Cambridge University Press

Wasserman, S., & Faust, K. (1994). *Social Network Analysis: Methods and Applications*. UK: Cambridge University Press.

Weiss, G. (2000). *Multiagent systems a modern approach to distributed artificial intelligence.* Cambridge MA USA: The MIT Press.

This work was previously published in International Journal of Agent Technologies and Systems (IJATS), edited by Goran Trajkovski, pp. 49-57, copyright 2009 by IGI Publishing (an imprint of IGI Global).

Chapter 5
Quantifying Disorder in Networks:
The von Neumann Entropy

Filippo Passerini
Humboldt-University, Germany

Simone Severini
University College London, UK

ABSTRACT

The authors introduce a novel entropic notion with the purpose of quantifying disorder/uncertainty in networks. This is based on the Laplacian and it is exactly the von Neumann entropy of certain quantum mechanical states. It is remarkable that the von Neumann entropy depends on spectral properties and it can be computed efficiently. The analytical results described here and the numerical computations lead us to conclude that the von Neumann entropy increases under edge addition, increases with the regularity properties of the network and with the number of its connected components. The notion opens the perspective of a wide interface between quantum information theory and the study of complex networks at the statistical level.

INTRODUCTION

The *von Neumann entropy* (or equivalently *quantum* entropy) was defined by von Neumann (1955) in his fundational work in quantum mechanics. Nowadays the von Neumann entropy is an important tool in quantum information theory (see Nielsen and Chuang (2001); Ohya and Petz (1993)). In the present work we first associate a graph to a quantum state, injectively. Then, we study the von Neumann entropy of the state itself.

Since the information contained in the state is nothing more but the information contained in the graph, with an easy abuse of language, we can say that we study the *von Neumann entropy of the graph*.

Our purpose is to get a feeling about the properties of a network that are readable through the Neumann entropy. During our discussion, we will guess that the properties highlighted by the entropy are related, even if not in a clear way, to the amount of symmetry in a graph. Entropy is axiomatically connected to the amount of disorder. Somehow, disorder and complexity may be seen

DOI: 10.4018/978-1-60960-171-3.ch005

Copyright © 2011, IGI Global. Copying or distributing in print or electronic forms without written permission of IGI Global is prohibited.

as different notions. Quantitative measures of complexity in networks have been described by Bonchev and Buck (2005), while in the theoretical computer science literature, there are many ideas for determining the complexity of a graph. It is in fact important that these ideas give rise to the study of so-called *parametrized complexity*. However, in our context, we are more directly interested in some efficiently computable quantity, which can say something about a network as a physical object, when we do not have an exact picture and with a possibly large number of vertices.

As a matter of fact, the notion opens the perspective of a wide interface between quantum information theory and the study of complex networks, at least at the statistical level.

From the technical point of view, we take a straightforward approach based on a faithful mapping between discrete Laplacians and quantum states, firstly introduced by Braunstein, Ghosh, and Severini (2006); see also Hildebrand, Mancini, and Severini (2008).

We interpret the set of eigenvalues of an appropriately normalized discrete Laplacian as a distribution and we compute its Shannon entropy. Let us recall that the Shannon entropy measures the amount of uncertainty of a random variable, or the amount of information obtained when its value is revealed. The topic is extensively covered by, *e.g.*, Cover and Tomas (1991).

It is not simple to give a combinatorial interpretation to the von Neumann entropy. Superficially, we give evidence that this can be seen as a measure of regularity, *i.e.*, regular graphs have in general higher entropy when the number of edges has been fixed. This is not the end of the story. Quantum entropy seems to depend on the number of connected components, long paths, and nontrivial symmetries (in terms of the automorphism group of the graph).

Fixed the number of edges, entropy is smaller for graphs with large cliques and short paths, *i.e.*, graphs in which the vertices form an highly

connected cluster. The remainder of the paper is organized as follows.

In the next section we introduce the required definitions and focus on first properties. By adding edges one by one to the empty graph (that is, the graph with zero edges), we attept to construct graphs with minimum and maximum entropy, respectively.

We then explore the influence of the graph structure on the entropy. We consider different classes of graphs: regular graphs, random graphs, and the star as an extremal case of scale-free graph (*i.e.*, graphs for which the degree distribution follows a power law). We have chosen these classes because these are well-studied and considered in many different contexts. The asymptotic behavior for large number of vertices shows that regular graphs tend to have maximum entropy.

We study numerically how the entropy increases when adding edges with different prescriptions. Once fixed the number of edges, the entropy is minimized by graphs with large cliques. In the concluding section, we will indicate a number of directions for future research.

The von Neumann Entropy

The state of a quantum mechanical system with a Hilbert space of finite dimension n is described by a *density matrix*. Each density matrix ρ is a positive semidefinite matrix with $\mathrm{Tr}(\rho) = 1$. Here we consider a matrix representation based on the combinatorial Laplacian to associate graphs to specific density matrices.

Let $G = (V, E)$ be a simple undirected graph with set of vertices $V(G) = \{1, 2, ..., n\}$ and set of edges

$$E(G) \subseteq V(G) \times V(G) - \{\{v, v\} : v \in V(G)\}$$

The *adjacency matrix* of G is denoted by $A(G)$ and defined by $[A(G)]_{u,v} = 1$ if $\{u, v\} \in E(G)$ and $[A(G)]_{u,v} = 0$, otherwise.

The *degree* of a vertex $v \in V(G)$, denoted by $d(v)$, is the number of edges adjacent to v. A graph G is d-*regular* if $d(v) = d$ for all $v \in V(G)$. Let d_G be the *degree-sum* of the graph, i.e. $d_G = \sum_{v \in V(G)} d(v)$. The *average degree* of G is defined by $\bar{d}_G := \tilde{n}^{-1} \sum_{v \in V(G)} d(v)$, where $\tilde{n}$ is the number of *non-isolated vertices*, that is vertices v such that $\{u, v\} \in E(G)$ for some $u \in V(G)$.

The *degree matrix* of G is an $n \times n$ matrix, denoted by $\Delta(G)$, having uv-th entry defined as follows: $\left[\Delta(G)\right]_{u,v} = d(v)$ if $u = v$ and $\left[\Delta(G)\right]_{u,v} = 0$, otherwise.

The *combinatorial Laplacian matrix* of a graph G (for short, *Laplacian*) is the matrix $L(G) = \Delta(G) - A(G)$. The matrix $L(G)$ is a major tool for enumerating spanning trees (via the Matrix-Tree Theorem) and has numerous applications (see Kirchhoff (1947), Biggs (1993); Grone, Merris, and Sunder (1990)). As a consequence of the Geršgorin disc theorem, $L(G)$ is positive semidefinite.

By these definitions, the Laplacian of a graph G scaled by the degree-sum of G is a density matrix: $\rho_G := L(G) / d_G = L(G) / \mathrm{Tr}\left(\Delta(G)\right)$. It is then clear that $\rho_G = L(G) / \tilde{n}\bar{d}_G$. The entropy of a density matrix ρ is defined as $S(\rho) = -\mathrm{Tr}(\rho \log_2 \rho)$.

Now, given the notion of Laplacian, we say that $S(\rho_G)$ is *the quantum entropy* (or, for short, *entropy*) of G. Let $\nu_1 \geq \nu_2 \geq \cdots \geq \nu_n = 0$ and $\lambda_1 \geq \lambda_2 \geq \cdots \geq \lambda_n = 0$ be the eigenvalues of $L(G)$ and ρ_G, respectively. These are related by a scaling factor, i.e. $\lambda_i = \nu_i / d_G = \nu_i / \tilde{n}\bar{d}_G$, for $i = 1, ..., n$. The entropy of ρ_G can be also written as $S(G) = -\sum_{i=1}^{n} \lambda_i \log_2 \lambda_i$, where $0 \log_2 0 = 0$, by convention. (See Grone, Merris, and Sunder

(1990), for a survey on Laplacian spectra.) Since its rows sum up to 0, then 0 is the smallest eigenvalue of ρ_G. The number of connected components of G is equal to the multiplicity of 0 as an eigenvalue.

The largest Laplacian eigenvalue is bounded by the number of non-isolated vertices, i.e., $\nu_1 \leq \tilde{n}$ (see Duval and Reiner (2002), Proposition 6.2); thus it follows immediately that $0 \leq \lambda_i \leq 1 / \bar{d}_G$, for $i = 1, ..., n$. It is important to remark that since $0 \leq \lambda_i \leq 1 / \bar{d}_G$, for $i = 1, ..., n$, $S(\rho_G)$ equals the Shannon entropy of the probability distribution $\{\lambda_i\}_{i=1}^{n}$.

If a general density matrix ρ has an eigenvalue 1 then the other must be 0 and $\rho = \rho^2$. In such a case, the density matrix is said to be *pure*; otherwise, *mixed*. For later convenience, we define the quantity $R(G) := n^{-1} \sum_{i=1}^{n} \frac{\nu_i}{d_G} \log_2 \frac{\nu_i}{d_G}$.

The *disjoint union* of graphs G and H is the graph $G' = G \cup H$, whose connected components are G and H. We denote by K_n the complete graph on n vertices. The simplest regular graph is the *perfect matching* $M_n := \bigcup_{j=1}^{n/2} K_2^{(j)}$. Let $\mathcal{G}_n$ be the set of all graphs on n vertices. The next fact was proved by Braunstein *et al.* (2006):

Theorem 1. *Let* G *be a graph on* $n \geq 2$ *vertices. Then* $min_{\mathcal{G}_n} S(G) = 0$ *if and only if* $G = K_2 \bigcup_j K_1^{(j)}$ *and* $max_{\mathcal{G}_n} S(G) = log_2(n - 1)$ *if and only if* $G = K_n$. *When* $n = 2$, *then* $min_{\mathcal{G}_2} S(G) = max_{\mathcal{G}_2} S(G) = 0$ *and* $G = K_2$.

For general density matrices, $S(\rho) = 0$, if ρ is a pure state; $S(\rho) = -\log_2 \frac{1}{n} = \log_2 n$ if $\rho = \frac{1}{n} I_n$, i.e., a completely random state. The analogue in $\mathcal{G}_n$ is K_n given that the spectrum or ρ_{K_n} is $\{\frac{1}{n-1}^{[n-1]}, 0^{[1]}\}$.

Figure 1. Plots of $S(G_i^{max})$ and $S(G_i^{min})$ (resp. solid and dashed line) as functions of the number of edges for $i = 1, 2, ..., n$

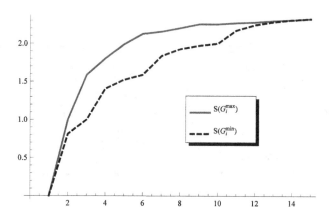

The next result bounds the variation of the entropy under edge addition. Let $G' = G + \{x,y\}$, where $V(G) = V(G')$ and $E(G') = E(G) \cup \{u,v\}$. An alternative proof could be given by invoking eigenvalues interlacing (Cvetkovic, Doob, and Sachs (1979)).

Theorem 2. *For graphs G and $G' = G + \{x,y\}$, we have $S(\rho_{G'}) \geq \dfrac{d_{G'} - 2}{d_{G'}} S(\rho_G)$.*

Starting from $K_2 \bigcup_j K_1^{(j)}$ (the graph with zero entropy) we can think of a discrete-time process in which we add edges so that the entropy is extremal (resp. maximum or minimum) at every step. Let us denote by G_i^{max} and G_i^{min}, $i \geq 1$, the graphs with maximum and minimum entropy at the i-th step, respectively.

Figure 1 contains $S(G_i^{max})$ and $S(G_i^{min})$ (resp. solid and dashed line) as functions of the number of edges $i = 1, 2, ..., 15$, for graphs in $\mathcal{G}_6$. The initial graph is $G_1^{max} = G_1^{min} = K_2 \bigcup_{j-1}^{6-l} K_1^{(j)}$; the final one is $G_{15}^{max} = G_{15}^{min} = K_6$. Each edge labeled by $j \leq i$ in the graph K_6 on the left (resp. right) hand side of Figure 2 is also an edge of G_i^{max} (resp. G_i^{min}).

This illustrates the steps for constructing every G_i^{max} and G_i^{min}. It turns out that the vertices of G_i^{max} tend to have "almost equal" or equal degree. In fact G_i^{max} is a $i/3$-regular graph, for $i = 3, 6, 9, 12$. On the other hand, $G_{l(l-1)/2}^{min} = K_l \bigcup_{j=1}^{6-l} K_1^{(j)}$, if $l = 3, 4, 5$. The meaning is without ambiguity: entropy is minimized by those graphs with *locally* added edges, *i.e.*, edges increasing the number of complete subgraphs (also called *cliques*).

Even if we consider graphs with only six vertices, it is already evident that long paths, nontrivial symmetries and connected components give rise to a larger increase of the entropy. This property is confirmed by further numerical analysis below.

Let $\mathcal{G}_{n,d}$ be the set of all d-regular graphs. For $G \in \mathcal{G}_{n,d}$, we have $\Delta(G) = dI_n$, and hence $\lambda_i = \dfrac{d - \mu_i}{\text{Tr}(\Delta(G))} = \dfrac{d - \mu_i}{dn}$, for $i = 1, 2, ..., n$, where μ_i denotes the i-th eigenvalue of $A(G)$.

Theorem 3. *Let G be a graph on n nonisolated vertices. If $lim_{n\to\infty} \dfrac{R(G)}{log_2 n} = 0$ then $lim_{n\to\infty} \dfrac{S(G)}{S(K_n)} = 1$. In particular, if $G \in \mathcal{G}_{n,d}$ then $lim_{n\to\infty} \dfrac{S(G)}{S(K_n)} = 1$.*

Figure 2. This figure shows two complete graphs K_6 with labeled edges. For the graph on the left hand side, the edge labeled by i is added at time i in order to construct G_i^{max}. The graph on the right hand side is the analogue drawing for G_i^{min}

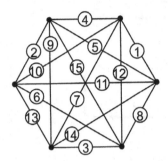 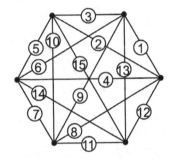

The *complete bipartite graph* $K_{p,q}$ has $V(K_{p,q}) = A \cup B$, where $|A| = p$ and $|B| = q$, and each vertex in A is adjacent to every vertex in B. The graph $K_{1,n-1}$ on n vertices is said to be a *star*.

Theorem 4. *Let $G \in \mathcal{G}_n$ with v such that $\{v, u\} \in E(G)$ for every u, and let*

$$lim_{n\to\infty} \bar{d}_G = d_\infty < \infty.$$

Then $lim_{n\to\infty} \frac{S(G)}{S(K_n)} \leq 1 - \frac{1}{d_\infty}$. In particular, the star $K_{1,n-1}$ saturates the bound, since $d_\infty = 2$, and

$$lim_{n\to\infty} \frac{S(K_{1,n-1})}{S(K_n)} = \frac{1}{2}.$$

Similarly to what we have done in the previous section, we observe how the entropy of a graph $G \in \mathcal{G}_n$ increases as a function of $|E(G)| = e$. Starting from $K_2 \bigcup_{j=1}^{n-2} K_1^{(j)}$, we consider four different ways of adding edges:

Random graphs with exactly e edges. These are constructed by chosing e pairs of vertices at random from the total number of pairs;

The graph $M_{2e} \bigcup_{j=1}^{n-2e} K_1^{(j)}$;

The graph $K_{1,(e+1)-1} \bigcup_{j=1}^{n-e-1} K_1^{(j)}$;

The graph $K_m \bigcup_{j=1}^{n-m} K_1^{(j)}$, where

$$m = \left\lceil \frac{1 + \sqrt{1 + 8e}}{2} \right\rceil.$$

Recall that adding isolated vertices to a graph does not change its entropy.

Figure 3 shows the case $n = 20$. It is evident that the entropy is larger for graphs with an high number of connected components. In this sense, M_n has relatively high entropy. The smallest entropy is obtained for complete graphs.

FUTURE RESEARCH DIRECTIONS

Normalized Laplacian. We have considered the combinatorial laplacian $L(G)$. There is a related matrix called *normalized Laplacian* and defined by $\mathcal{L}(G) = \Delta^{-1/2} L(G) \Delta^{-1/2}$ (by convention $[\Delta^{-1}]_{v,v} = 0$ if $d(v) = 0$). It results that $[\mathcal{L}(G)]_{u,v} = 1$ if $u = v$ and $d(v) \neq 0$, $[\mathcal{L}(G)]_{u,v} = -1 / \sqrt{d(u)d(v)}$ if $\{u, v\} \in E(G)$, and $[\mathcal{L}(G)]_{u,v} = 0$, otherwise (see Chung (1997) and Terras (1999)). If a graph has no isolated vertex then $\text{Tr}(\mathcal{L}(G)) = n$. Therefore, we can define the density matrix $\rho_G := \frac{\mathcal{L}(G)}{n}$. The entropy of $\hat{\rho}_G$ is then $S(\hat{\rho}_G) = -\text{Tr}$

Figure 3. Plots of the entropy of four different kind of graphs as a function of the number of edges $e = 1, 2, \ldots, 190$. The different plots represent different ways of adding edges to a graph with $n = 20$ vertices. The value of $S(R_{n,e})$ have been avaraged over 15 different random graphs, for each value of e

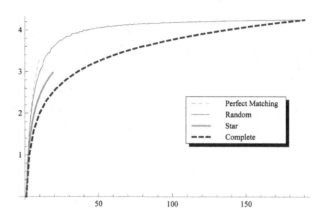

$(\dfrac{\mathcal{L}(G)}{n} \log_2 \dfrac{\mathcal{L}(G)}{n}) = -W + \log_2 n = -\dfrac{1}{n}$ T r $\left(\mathcal{L}(G) \log_2 \mathcal{L}(G)\right) + \log_2 n$. Since the eigenvalues of $\mathcal{L}(G)$ are in $[0,2]$, when limit $n \to \infty$, the quantity W remains finite. We may then conclude that when the number of vertices goes to infinity, the entropy $S(\hat{\rho}_G)$ tends to $S(\rho_{K_n})$. This fact provide s a motivation for dealing with $L(G)$ instead of $\mathcal{L}(G)$.

Algebraic connectivity. Let $a(G) = \nu_{n-1}$ be the *algebraic connectivity* of G (Fiedler (1973)). It is nonzero only if G is connected. The value of $a(G)$ quantifies the connectivity of G. Is there a relation between $a(G)$ and $S(\rho_G)$? Consider K_n and the n-cycle C_n, that is the connected 2-regular graph on n vertices. For these, $a(K_n) = n$ and $a(C_n) = 2(1 - \cos \dfrac{2\pi}{n})$. By Theorem 3, $\lim_{n \to \infty} S(C_n) = S(K_n)$. However the algebraic connectivity of the two graphs behave differently in this limit: $\lim_{n \to \infty} a(K_n) = \infty$ and $\lim_{n \to \infty} a(C_n) = 0$.

Eigenvalue gap. Let $b(G) = \mu_1 - \mu_2$ be the *eigenvalue gap* of G. This parameter determines the mixing time of a simple random walk on G (see Chung (1997)). If $G \in \mathcal{G}_{n,d}$ then $a(G) = b(G)$. Hence $\lim_{n \to \infty} b(K_n) = \infty$ and $\lim_{n \to \infty} b(C_n) = 0$. We can therefore state that $b(G)$ and $S(\rho_G)$ describe different properties of G at least on the basis of this basic observation.

A combinatorial definition. It is unclear whether $S(G)$ is related to combinatorially defined entropic quantities. For example, the Körner entropy defined by Körner (1973); see Simonyi (1995) for a survey. Also, the entropies defined by Riis (2007) and Bianconi (2008). Intuitively, any relation should be weak, because the quantum entropy depends on the eigenvalues. For this reason it describes some global statistical behaviour, with only partial control over combinatorial properties.

Beyond cospectrality. Graphs with the same eigenvalues have equal entropy. We have seen that also perfect matchings and complete graphs plus a specific number of isolated vertices have equal entropy, but are clearly noncospectral. Determine families of graphs with the same entropy remains an open problem.

Relative entropy. The quantum relative entropy is a measure of distinguishability between two states (see the review by Vedral (2001)). Given two graphs G and H, the *quantum relative entropy* may be defined as $S(G \parallel H) := -\text{Tr}(\rho_G \log_2 \rho_H) - S(\rho_G)$. What kind of relations between the two graphs are emphasized by the relative entropy? To what extent can this be used as a measure of distinguishability for graphs?

Mathematical open problems:

- Does the star $K_{1,n-1}$ have smallest entropy among all connected graphs on n vertices?
- Is the entropy strictly monotonically increasing under edge addition?

Further considerations. It is plausible that the von Neumann entropy of networks introduced in this chapter is the first known information theoretic parameter to distinguish between scale-free graphs and random graphs. In this way, we have given strength to the connection between quantum information theory and the theory of networks. Thanks to this relation, it is possible to use the concepts and the well developed mathematical framework of quantum information theory to study the statistical and topological properties of networks. On the other hand, the networks analysis could lead to new insights for information theory and thus this connection might be fruitful in both ways.

The von Neumann entropy is an efficiently computable parameter which may be used to control the algorithmic construction of networks where nodes/links are added sequentially under some constraints. For instance, minimizing or maximizing the entropy itself or imposing some relation between the entropy of the network under study and the entropy of a known graph. This might be useful for the study of the topological evolution of networks and a better understanding of adaptive networks, *i.e.*, networks where the topological evolution is related to dynamical processes defined on the nodes (Gross and Bla-

sius (2008)). In particular, it would be interesting to compute entropies during the evolution and compare it to the change of entropies of known physical systems.

This could help to understand why do networks evolve to certain kinds of specific topologies. For the case of adaptive networks, it might be interesting to study the interplay between the von Neumann entropy (seeing as a "topological entropy") and the entropy associated to the dynamical processes defined on the network itself. This might lead to a better understanding of some of the peculiar features of adaptive networks like the formation of complex regions or robust self-organization. The understanding of the interaction between the *dynamics of the network* and the *dynamics on the network* is of fundamental importance since many phenomena in nature are indeed described by adaptive networks (for example, in the analysis of traffic and road networks, epidemics, *etc.*).

Networks appear in many different areas of science. A somehow bold, but still interesting question that we may ask is the following one: do networks appearing in different contexts show different behavior in relation to their von Neumann entropy? That is, can we use the entropy as a parameter to characterize the restricted scientific context where the networks are defined? A similar research was performed looking at network motifs, *i.e.*, patterns of interconnections (as for example, specific subgraphs) that appear in a network with higher frequency with respect to the standad random graphs models (see Milo *et al.* (2002)). It results that networks describing the same class of phenomena (ecological food webs, genetic networks, the World Wide Web, *etc.*) share the same class of motifs. This kind of analysis is useful to shed light on the principles that are regulating the networks structure. The von Neumann entropy might contribute in this direction.

We have seen that the entropy, when the number of edges is fixed, is minimum for graphs with large cliques. From a mathematical point of view, it would be interesting to understand this behavior at a more formal level. This will provide a new spectral parameter for the analysis of cliques.

At a different, less operational level we might ask what is the physical meaning and what are the roles of the von Neumann entropy of networks. For instance, we might ask if this quantity can be really interpreted as a physical entropy and in that case we may wonder what is the microscopic degeneracy of states that is behind this macroscopic entropy. A trivial guess is that this degeneracy might be related to the number of co-entropic graphs. To keep in mind that a recurrent principle in physics is the maximization of the entropy. Thus, if the entropy introduced here is a genuine thermodynamical quantity, a relatively small entropy would be proper of open complex systems. Scale-free networks, showing a lower entropy respect to regular or random networks, would be associated to complex systems that are open, which is, not isolated from an environment (or, roughly speaking, subject to external changes). In some sense, the scale-free nature of a number of natural complex structure might be associated to the interaction with an external system.

PROOFS OF THE THEOREMS

Proof of Theorem 2

Chosen a labeling of $V(G)$, for $G \in \mathcal{G}_n$ we can write $A(G) = \sum_{\{u,v\}\in E(G)} A(u,v)$, where $A(u,v)$ is the adjacency matrix of a graph $G(u,v) := \{u,v\} \bigcup_{i=1}^{n-2} K_1$. We can then define an $n \times n$ diagonal matrix $\Delta(u,v)$ such that $[\Delta(u,v)]_{u,u} = [\Delta(u,v)]_{v,v} = 1$ and $[\Delta(u,v)]_{k,q} = 0$ if $u \neq v$. It follows that $\Delta(G) = \sum_{\{u,v\}\in E(G)} \Delta(u,v)$.

Then $\rho_G = \frac{1}{d_G} \sum_{\{u,v\}\in E(G)} (\Delta(u,v) - A(u,v))$. Let

$\{|1\rangle, |2\rangle, ..., |n\rangle\}$ be the standard basis of $\mathbb{C}^n$. By definition, $|i\rangle \equiv (0_1, 0_2 ..., 0_{i-1}, 1_i, 0_{i+1}, ..., 0_n)^T$. We associate the pure state

$$|\{u,v\}\rangle = \frac{1}{\sqrt{2}}(|u\rangle - |v\rangle)$$

to the edge $\{u,v\}$. Let $P(u,v)$ be the projector associated to

$$|\{u,v\}\rangle: P(u,v) = \frac{1}{2}(I_2 - \sigma_x).$$

Then

$$\rho_G = \frac{2}{d_G} \sum_{\{u,v\}\in E(G)} P(u,v)$$

and $\rho_{G'} = \frac{d_G}{d_{G'}} \rho_G + \frac{2}{d_{G'}} P(x,y)$.

It is well-known that the entropy S is concave (see Ohya and Petz (1993)):

$$S\left(\sum_{i=1}^{l} \alpha_i \rho_i\right) \geq \sum_{i=1}^{l} \alpha_i S(\rho_i),$$

where ρ_i are density matrices and $\alpha_i \in \mathbb{R}^+$. Hence $S(\rho_{G'}) \geq \frac{d_G}{d_{G'}} S(\rho_G) + \frac{2}{d_{G'}} S(\{x,y\})$. However, since $S(\{x,y\}) = 0$, the claim is true.

Proof of Theorem 3

When $G \in \mathcal{G}_n$, $\rho_G = \frac{L(G)}{n \, \bar{d}_G}$, where

$\bar{d}_G = \frac{1}{n} \sum_{v \in V(G)} d(v)$. Since $\lambda_i = \frac{\nu_i}{n d_G}$, we have

$$S(G) = -\frac{1}{n}\sum_{i=1}^{n} \frac{\nu_i}{d_G} \log_2 \frac{\nu_i}{d_G} + \frac{1}{n}\sum_{i=1}^{n} \frac{\nu_i}{d_G} \log_2 n.$$

Given that $\mathrm{Tr}\left(\rho_G\right) = \dfrac{\nu_i}{nd_G} = 1$, by taking

$R(G) := \dfrac{1}{n}\sum_{i=1}^{n}\dfrac{\nu_i}{d_G}\log_2\dfrac{\nu_i}{d_G}$, the quantum entropy

of G is given by $S(G) = -R(G) + \log_2 n$. Since $S(K_n) = \log_2(n-1)$, we have

$$S(G) = -R(G) + \frac{S(K_n)\log_2 n}{\log_2(n-1)}.$$

From this expression, we see immediately that if $\lim_{n\to\infty}\dfrac{R(G)}{\log_2 n} = 0$ then $\lim_{n\to\infty}\dfrac{S(G)}{S(K_n)} = 1$.

Now, let us consider $G \in \mathcal{G}_{n,d}$. Since $d(v) = d$ for every $v \in V(G)$, it follows that $\bar{d} = d$ and $\nu_i = d - \mu_i$. Given that for a d-regular graph $-d \le \mu_i \le d$, we have $0 \le \nu_i \le 2d$, for every $i = 1,...,n$. The quantity $R(G)$ is now given by

$$R(G) = \frac{1}{n}\sum_{i=1}^{n}x_i\log_2 x_i, \quad \text{where} \quad x_i = \frac{\nu_i}{d}, \quad \text{and}$$

$0 \le x_i \le 2$. The function $x_i\log_2 x_i$ assumes finite values in the range $[0,2]$. Thus $R(G)$ is also finite. In particular, since $R(G)$ is an average, it remains finite even if considering an arbitrary large number of vertices. This implies that the entropy for a d-regular graph tends to the entropy of K_n in the limit $n \to \infty$.

It may useful to remark two points:

- The density matrix of a perfect matching M_n is then $\rho_{M_n} = \dfrac{1}{n}\bigoplus_{n/2\,\text{times}}\begin{pmatrix}1 & -1\\ -1 & 1\end{pmatrix}$

  and $S(M_n) = -\dfrac{n}{2}\left(\dfrac{2}{n}\log_2\dfrac{2}{n}\right) = \log_2\dfrac{n}{2}$,

  because $\lambda_1^{\left[\frac{n}{2}\right]} = \dfrac{n}{2}$ and $\lambda_2^{\left[\frac{n}{2}\right]} = 0$. Thus, $S(M_n) = S(K_{n/2+1})$. For M_4 we have

$S(M_4) = S(K_3) = 1$. More generally, $S\left(M_{2^k}\right) = k - 1$.

- The entropy of $G \in \mathcal{G}_{n\to\infty}$ tends to the entropy of K_n if all the quantities $\dfrac{\nu_i}{d_G}$ remain finite, *i.e.*, $\lim_{n\to\infty}\dfrac{R(G)}{\log_2 n} = 0$.

Proof of Theorem 4

Let G be as in the statement. So, $d_1 = n - 1$. For a graph with at least one edge, Grone *et al.* (1992) (Corollary 2) proved that $\nu_1 \ge d_1 + 1$; for a generic graph on $\tilde{n} = n$ vertices, we know that $\nu_1 \le n$ (see Duval and Reiner (2002), Proposition 6.2). By these two results, $\nu_1 = n$. Thus, we have

$$R(G) = \frac{1}{n}\sum_{i=1}^{n}\frac{\nu_i}{d_G}\log_2\frac{\nu_i}{d_G} = \frac{1}{n}\log_2\frac{n}{d_G} + \frac{1}{n}\sum_{i=2}^{n}\frac{\nu_i}{d_G}\log_2\frac{\nu_i}{d_G}$$

and $\lim_{n\to\infty}\dfrac{R(G)}{S(K_n)} \ge \dfrac{1}{d_\infty}$.

Because $S(G) = -R(G) + \log_2 n$, we have $\lim_{n\to\infty}\dfrac{S(G)}{S(K_n)} \le 1 - \dfrac{1}{d_\infty}$. Now, the eigenvalues of $\rho_{K_{1,n-1}}$ are $\lambda_1^{[1]} = \dfrac{n}{2n-2}$, $\lambda_2^{[n-2]} = \dfrac{1}{2n-2}$ and $\lambda_3^{[1]} = 0$. Thus, the entropy is given by

$$S(K_{1,n-1}) = -\frac{n}{2n-2}\log_2\frac{n}{2n-2} + \frac{n-2}{2n-2}\log_2(2n-2)$$

and in the limit $n \to \infty$ we have the second part of the statement. Since $\bar{d} = \dfrac{2n-2}{n}$, it results $d_\infty = 2$ and the bound is saturated.

ACKNOWLEDGMENT

The authors would like to thank Yasser Omar, John Symons, Sven Banisch, Rui Lopes and Jorge

Louçã for their interest in this work and for helpful discussion. SS is a Newton International Fellow.

REFERENCES

Bianconi, G. (2008). The entropy of network ensembles. arXiv:0802.2888v2 [cond-mat.dis-nn]

Biggs, N. (1993). *Algebraic Graph Theory*. Cambridge, UK: Cambridge University Press.

Bonchev, D., & Buck, G. A. (2005). Quantitative Measures of Network Complexity. In Bonchev, D., & Rouvray, D. H. (Eds.), *Complexity in Chemistry* (pp. 191–235). Biology and Ecology. doi:10.1007/0-387-25871-X_5

Braunstein, S., Ghosh, S., & Severini, S. (2006). The laplacian of a graph as a density matrix: a basic combinatorial approach to separability of mixed states. *Annals of Combinatorics, 10*(3), 291–317. doi:10.1007/s00026-006-0289-3

Chung, F. R. K. (1997). *Spectral graph theory*. CBMS Regional Conference Series in Mathematics, 92. Published for the Conference Board of the Mathematical Sciences, Washington, DC. Providence, RI: American Mathematical Society.

Cover, T., & Thomas, C. (1991). *Elements of information theory*. New York: John Wiley. doi:10.1002/0471200611

Cvetkovic, D. M., Doob, M., & Sachs, H. (1979). *Spectra of graph theory and applications*. New York: VEB Deutscher Berlin, Academic Press.

Duval, A. M., & Reiner, V. (2002). Shifted simplicial complexes are Laplacian integral. *Transactions of the American Mathematical Society, 354*(11), 4313–4344. doi:10.1090/S0002-9947-02-03082-9

Fiedler, M. (1973). Algebraic connectivity of graphs. *Czechoslovak Mathematical Journal, 23*, 298–305.

Grone, R., Merris, R., & Sunder, V. (1990). The Laplacian spectrum of a graph. *SIAM Journal of Matrix Anaysis and Applications, 11*, 218–238. doi:10.1137/0611016

Gross, T., & Blasius, B. (2008). Adaptive Co-evolutionary Networks: A Review. *Journal of the Royal Society, Interface, 5*, 259–271. doi:10.1098/rsif.2007.1229

Hildebrand, R., Mancini, S., & Severini, S. (2008). Combinatorial laplacians and positivity under partial transpose. *Mathematical Structures in Computer Science, 18*, 205–219. doi:10.1017/S0960129508006634

Kirchhoff, F. (1847). Über die Auflösung der Gleichungen, auf welche man bei der Untersuchung der linearen Verteilung galvanischer Ströme gefuhrt wird. *Annalen der Physik und Chemie, 72*, 497–508. doi:10.1002/andp.18471481202

Körner, J. (1973). Coding of an information source having ambiguous alphabet and entropy of graphs. *In Proeedings of the 6th Prague Conference on Information Theory,* pp. 411-425.

Milo, R., Shen-Orr, S., Itzkovitz, S., & Kashtan, N., Chklovskii, & D., Alon, U. (2002). Network Motifs: Simple Building Blocks of Complex Networks. *Science, 298*, 824–827. doi:10.1126/science.298.5594.824

Nielsen, M. A., & Chuang, I. L. (2000). *Quantum computation and quantum information*. Cambridge, UK: Cambridge University Press.

Ohya, M., & Petz, D. (1993). *Quantum entropy and its use*. Berlin: Springer-Verlag.

Riis, S. (2007). Graph Entropy, Network Coding and Guessing games. arXiv:0711.4175v1 [math. CO]

Simonyi, G. (1995). Graph entropy. In L. L. W. Cook & P. Seymour (Eds.), *Combinatorial Optimization, vol 20 of DIMACS Series on Discrete Mathematics and Computer Science* (pp. 391-441).

Terras, A. (1999). *Fourier analysis on finite groups and applications. London Mathematical Society Student Texts, 43*. Cambridge, UK: Cambridge University Press. doi:10.1017/CBO9780511626265

Vedral, V. (2001). The role of relative entropy in quantum information theory. *Reviews of Modern Physics, 74*(1), 197–234. doi:10.1103/RevModPhys.74.197

von Neumann, J. (1955). *Mathematical Foundations of Quantum Mechanics*. Princeton, NJ: Princeton University Press.

Section 2
Emergencies

Chapter 6
Enhancing the Adaptation of BDI Agents Using Learning Techniques

Stéphane Airiau
University of Amsterdam, The Netherlands

Lin Padgham
RMIT University, Australia

Sebastian Sardina
RMIT University, Australia

Sandip Sen
University of Tulsa, USA

ABSTRACT

Belief, Desire, and Intentions (BDI) agents are well suited for complex applications with (soft) real-time reasoning and control requirements. BDI agents are adaptive in the sense that they can quickly reason and react to asynchronous events and act accordingly. However, BDI agents lack learning capabilities to modify their behavior when failures occur frequently. We discuss the use of past experience to improve the agent's behavior. More precisely, we use past experience to improve the context conditions of the plans contained in the plan library, initially set by a BDI programmer. First, we consider a deterministic and fully observable environment and we discuss how to modify the BDI agent to prevent re-occurrence of failures, which is not a trivial task. Then, we discuss how we can use decision trees to improve the agent's behavior in a non-deterministic environment.

DOI: 10.4018/978-1-60960-171-3.ch006

Copyright © 2011, IGI Global. Copying or distributing in print or electronic forms without written permission of IGI Global is prohibited.

INCORPORATING LEARNING IN BDI AGENTS

Introduction

It is widely believed that learning is a key aspect of intelligence, as it enables adaptation to complex and changing environments. Agents developed under the Belief-Desire-Intention (BDI) approach (Bratman, Israel, & Pollack, 1988) are capable of *simple* adaptations to their behaviors, implicitly encoded in their *plan library* (a collection of pre-defined *hierarchical plans* indexed by goals and representing the standard operations of the domain). This adaptation is due to the fact that *(i)* execution relies entirely on *context sensitive subgoal expansion*, and therefore, plan choices at each level of abstraction are made in response to the *current* situation; and *(ii)* if a plan happens to fail, often because the environment has changed unexpectedly, agents "backtrack" and choose a different plan-strategy.

However, BDI-style agents are generally unable to go beyond such level of adaptation, in that they are confined to what their pre-defined plan libraries encode. As a result, they cannot significantly alter their behaviors from the ones specified during their initial deployment. In particular, these agents are not able to *learn* new behaviors (i.e., new plans) nor to learn how to choose among plans—both plans and their contexts are hard-coded. In this work, we are concerned with the latter limitation. We therefore analyze BDI-based agent designs and identify opportunities and mechanisms for performing plan context learning in typical BDI-style agents. By doing so, agents can enjoy a higher degree of adaptability by allowing them to improve their plan selection *on the basis of analysis of experiences*.

Research in machine learning can be broadly categorized into *knowledge-rich* and *knowledge-lean* techniques. Whereas some researchers have proposed and investigated learning mechanisms that incorporate and utilize significant amounts of domain knowledge (DeJong & Mooney, 1986, Ellman, 1989, Kolodner, 1993), the large majority of popular learning techniques assume very little domain knowledge and are largely data, rather than model, driven (Aha, Kibler, & Albert, 1991, Booker, Goldberg, & Holland, 1989, Kaelbling, Littman, & Moore, 1996, Krause, 1998, Quinlan, 1986, Rumelhart, Hinton, & Williams, 1986). Research in multiagent learning (Alonso, d'Inverno, Kudenko, Luck, & J.Noble, 2001, Panait & Luke, 2005, Tuyls & Nowé, 2006) has also followed this trend. This is particularly unfortunate as practical multiagent systems are meant to leverage existing domain knowledge in order to facilitate scalability, flexibility, and robustness. For most such online, real-time multiagent systems, individual agents need to quickly and effectively respond to unforeseen events as well as to gradual changes in environmental conditions. In this context, the amount of experience and adaptation time available will be orders of magnitude less than what is assumed by offline knowledge-lean learning algorithms. As a result, techniques that take advantage of the available domain knowledge to aid and guide the learning and adaptation process are key to the development of successful agent learning approaches.

So, in the context of BDI agents, we foresee significant synergistic possibilities for combining *learning* and *reasoning* mechanisms. Whereas available domain knowledge of BDI agents can inform and direct embedded learning modules, the latter can incrementally adapt and update components of the reasoning module to "tune" the agents' behaviors. It may well be the case that while substantial knowledge is encoded at design-time, there are additional *nuances* which can be learnt over time that will eventually yield better overall performance. In this article, then, we discuss issues and propose preliminary techniques in order to refine coarse heuristics provided by the BDI programmer at design time for the purposes of doing plan selection, that is, we focus on mechanism for "improving" the *context conditions* of existing plans.

The rest of the article is organized as follows. In the next section, we provide an overview of the relevant aspects of typical BDI-style agents. We then discuss modifications to the BDI framework so as to include mechanisms for improving plan selection by refining the context conditions of plans. We do so by relying on a number of simplifying assumptions that make the scenario an "ideal" one. After that, we outline ways in which these assumptions may be lifted. We end the article by drawing conclusions and future lines of work.

BDI AGENT-ORIENTED PROGRAMMING

The BDI (Belief-Desire-Intention) model is a popular and well-studied architecture of agency for intelligent agents situated in complex and dynamic environments. The model has its roots in philosophy with Bratman's (Bratman, 1987) theory of practical reasoning and Dennett's theory of intentional systems (Dennett, 1987). BDI agent-oriented systems are extremely flexible and responsive to the environment, and as a result, well suited for complex applications with (soft) real-time reasoning and control requirements. There are a number of agent programming languages and development platforms in the BDI tradition, such as PRS (Georgeff & Ingrand, 1989), JAM (Huber, 1999), JACK (Busetta, Rönnquist, Hodgson, & Lucas, 1998), 3APL (Hindriks, Boer, Hoek, & Meyer, 1999), Jason (Bordini, Hübner, & Wooldridge, 2007).

In a BDI-style system, an agent consists, basically, of a belief base (akin to a database), a set of recorded pending events, a plan library, and an intention base. While the *belief base* encodes the agent's knowledge about the world, the *pending events* stand for the goals the agent wants to achieve/resolve. The *plan library* in turn contains plan rules of the form $e:\psi \leftarrow P$ encoding the standard

domain operation-strategy P (that is, a program) for handling an event-goal e when context condition ψ is believed to hold. Importantly, new *internal* events may be "posted" during the actual execution of program P. Lastly, the *intention base* accounts for the current, partially instantiated, plans that the agent has already committed to in order to handle or achieve some event-goal.

In some way or another, all the above agent programming languages and development environments capture the basic reactive goal-oriented behavior: a BDI system responds to events, the inputs to the system, by committing to handle one pending event-goal, selecting a plan rule from the library, and placing its plan-body program into the intention base. More concretely, these system generally follow Rao and Georgeff's abstract interpreter for rational agents (Rao & Georgeff, 1992) which, roughly speaking, is repeats the following steps (illustrated in Figure 1):

1. Select a *pending*—internal or external— *event* (if any).
2. *Update* beliefs, goals, and intentions—new information may cause the agent to update its beliefs and modify its goals and intentions.
3. Using the plan library, determine the set of *applicable plans* to respond to the selected

Figure 1. Architecture of a typical BDI agent system

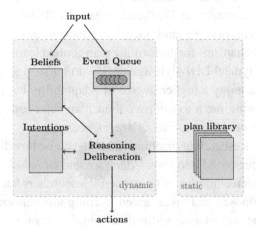

event, that is, identify those plans that are relevant to the event type and whose context condition are believed true.

4. *Choose one applicable plan* and push it into the intention structure, either as a completely new intention for an external event or by expanding the details of the intention that produced the internal event.

5. Select one intention and *execute* one or more steps on it. This execution may, in turn, generate new *internal* events.

For the purposes of this article, we shall mostly focus on the plan library, which contains the procedural domain knowledge of the domain by encoding the typical operations. Intuitively, a plan of the form $e:\psi\leftarrow P$ is meant to state that program P is a reasonable strategy to follow in order to address the event-goal e whenever ψ is believed to hold. Event e is referred as the trigger of the plan, ψ its context condition, and program P the plan's body. A plan body typically contains actions (*act*) to be performed in the environment, belief updates ($+b$ and $-b$ to add or delete a proposition, respectively) and tests (? φ) operations, and subgoals ($!e$) to post internal events which ought to be in turn resolved by selecting suitable plans for that event.

By grouping together plans which respond to the same event type, the plan library can be seen as a set of *goal-plan tree* templates, where goal (or event) nodes have children representing the alternative plans for achieving the goal, and in turn, plan nodes have children nodes representing the subgoals (or actions) of the plan. These structures, depicted in Figure 2, can be seen as "AND"/"OR" trees: for a plan to succeed all the subgoals and actions of the plan must be successful ("AND"); for a subgoal to succeed one of the plans to achieve it must succeed ("OR").

When a step in a plan happens to fail (e.g., an action cannot be executed, a test condition does not apply, or subgoal itself fails), this causes the whole plan to fail, and an alternative applicable plan for its parent goal is tried. If there are no alternative applicable plans, the parent goal itself fails, cascading the failure and search for alternative plans upwards one level in the goal-plan tree. It is exactly this context-sensitive search of alternative plans for a goal that enables BDI systems to robustly recover from failure situations, particularly, those where the environment has changed in an unexpected manner.

Interestingly, the structured information contained in the goal plan tree can also be used to provide guidance to the learning module. In particular, consider the context condition of plans, which are critical for guiding the execution of the agent program. A plan will not be used in the current state if its context condition is not satisfied. Incorrect or inadequate context conditions can lead to two types of problems. If the context condition of a plan is *over-constrained* and evaluates as false in some situations where the plan could succeed then this plan will simply never be tried in those situations, resulting in possible utility loss to the agent. On the other hand, if the context condition is *under-specified*, it may evaluate to true in some situations where the plan will be ineffective. Such "false triggers" will result in unnecessary failures, and although the agent may recover by choosing alternative plans, it may lose valuable time or waste resources unnecessarily, thereby losing utility. Hence, it would be preferable to learn from experience to avoid using plans that are unlikely to succeed at particular environmental states.

Figure 2. Goal-plan tree hierarchy

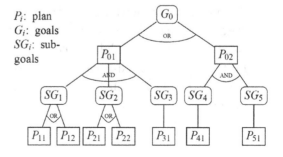

The rest of this article explores the issue of learning to improve the context conditions specified by the programmer.

REFINING THE CONTEXT CONDITIONS OF PLANS

We start by considering an idealized setting and explore ways in which plan selection could be refined based on experience. The "ideal" setting allows us to describe and understand the ideal situation, noting that non-trivial reasoning is already required if we are to eventually exclude all unnecessary failures.

The most straightforward way of refining plan selection is to gradually modify the context conditions of plans so as to make them more specific. We shall also briefly discuss a more subtle refinement that could be done by a smarter reasoner, regarding selection of plan *sequences* in specific situations.

Assumptions

In designing the idealized setting, we shall make a number of simplifying assumptions, namely:

a. The environment in which the agent is situated is assumed to be *deterministic* and *fully observable* by the agent. Thus action actions outcomes (including its success or failure) are always the same for each particular state and the agent always knows in which state she is in. This shall allow us to always make *correct* updates to context conditions.

b. The initial plans' context conditions provided at design-time are understood as *necessary conditions*, that is, as minimum constraints for the plan to succeed—our goal is not to repair "erroneous" context conditions, but to further refine them. This assumption amounts to the programmer encoding the knowledge she is *certain* about in the context condition of the agent, with the hope that the learning mechanism will complete the unknown "gaps."

c. Plan bodies are restricted to sequences of actions and subgoals, and intentions are executed in a linear manner, that is, without any interleaving. This removes the need to monitor for interactions between goals that could have an effect on success. Interleaving can be allowed, provided a suitable reasoning module can guarantee the linearization-equivalence of their executions with respect to the goals pursued.

d. Typical BDI failure recovery, under which different available options for a goal are tried when a plan ends up failing, is assumed *disabled*. Learning in the context of BDI failure recovery poses new challenges and issues that we have not considered at this point.

Besides these core restrictions, we should also make a number of technical assumptions:

- Beliefs and context conditions of plans are expressed in propositional logic. Let V denote the set of available propositions in the domain.

- The agent has a complete and correct axiomatization of the dynamics of the domain. This means that all changes to any variable $v \in V$ are explicit to the agent. This allows us to reason about changes caused by the agent, as opposed to those happening independently in the environment.

- A superset of all propositional variables that are (potentially) *relevant* for the success/failure of a plan P is known and defined at design-time. We shall refer to that set as R_p (of course, $R_p \subseteq V$). The idea is that although only some of the variables in R_p may be used to express the initial context condition of P, no variable outside such set may influence the success or failure of P. (A likely candidate for R_p can be identified as the set of variables that are accessed by some plan below the parent goal of P in the goal-plan tree.)

When s is a complete state of the world, we denote with $s[R_p]$, the tuple containing the values of propositions in R_p in state s.

Refining Context Conditions: The Ideal Case

We will now discuss the situations in which one can refine a context condition (to avoid failure due to poor plan choice) in a provably correct way.

Recall that the context condition of a plan indicates the situations in which the plan is expected to succeed, provided the right plan decisions are made for the sub-goals posted in the plan. Thus, for a BDI agent to be efficient, it is important that plans have accurate context conditions so that the right choices are made. There are two possible scenarios explaining a failure of a plan P in a state s:

a. There is no path in P's sub-tree that leads to a success of P. This means that the choice to use P under state s was not correct. The challenge here is to know whether everything in P's sub-tree has been attempted (without success).

b. The choice of a particular action or sub-goal within P's sub-tree was not correct. For example, suppose that within P's sub goal-plan tree, the agent faces a choice between two sub-plans, and only one is bound to succeed. When the agent decides to use the wrong sub-plan, P may also end up failing (this is exactly what BDI failure recovery would often help to address. However, in this work, we assume that BDI failure retry mechanism is "disabled."). In that case, the initial decision of using P was indeed cor-

rect, but a later (wrong) choice provoked the failure.

So, let us consider the example depicted by the plan-goal tree in Figure 2. Assume that (deterministic) plans P_{11}, $P_{12,}P_{21,}P_{22}$, and P_{31} each consists of a sequence of one or more atomic actions and suppose that plan P_{01} was chosen for execution at a state s. Suppose next that plan P_{11} is started in some state s to address subgoal SG_1, and that, after some steps, plan P_{11} happens to fail. Such failure will in turn cause the failure of goal SG_1 itself and of plan P_{01} as well (remember we assume no failure recovery so plan P_{12} would not be tried upon failure). The question then is: *when can we update the context condition of plan P_{01} to exclude state $s[R_{P01}]$?*

Observe that one cannot directly rule out (sub) state $s[R_{P01}]$ from P_{01}'s context condition as soon as P_{01} fails, since P_{01}'s failure could have been avoided had plan P_{12} been chosen instead for achieving SG_1. However, if we have previously recorded that option P_{12} has already failed in the past when started in a state s', such that $s'[R_{P12}]= s[R_{P12}]$, then we would be justified in updating the context condition of P_{01} to disallow (sub) state $s[R_{P01}]$. This is because *all* possible execution paths of P_{01} from state $s[R_{P01}]$ are bound to fail. Notice that this reasoning is valid only the assumptions that the domain is deterministic and fully-observable, and that R_p includes all the propositions that could influence, directly or indirectly, the success of plan P.

Let us now slightly modify the situation and assume the failure occurs in plan P_{31} instead, thus propagating upwards to P_{01}. In this case, it is correct to further constrain P_{01}'s context condition (to rule out substate $s[R_{P01}]$) *only if* all combinations of plan choices for previous subgoals SG_1 and SG_2 have been tried (in states compatible with $s[R_{P01}]$). Otherwise, plan P_{31} may have failed only due to an "incorrect" combination of plans for goals SG_1 and SG_2.

Nevertheless, there is some additional selection information that an agent could potentially use in such cases. For example, suppose that the failure of P_{31} occurred after having executed plans P_{11} and P_{21} to achieve SG_1 and SG_2, respectively. Then, one can conclude that, in the context of plan P_{01} and in states compatible with $s[R_{P01}]$, the combination of plans P_{11} and P_{21} is "bad" one, as it would eventually cause P_{31} to fail. In future cases, hence, the agent should avoid such combination of plan choices for achieving SG_1 and SG_2. Interestingly, however, this is *not* information that could be represented as part of the context condition of plans. The reason is that context conditions are *local* to their particular plans and do not take into account the various ways may be combined (in higher-level plans) to achieve different goals. Instead, one should see this knowledge as meta-level information that could be used by a (complex) plan selection function in order to choose (or exclude) particular paths through the goal-plan tree.

We close this section by pointing out an interesting application of *automated planning* in this context. In principle, the goal-plan tree has been initially designed so that if the context condition of a plan is met, there is indeed a path leading to a success of the plan. By refining the context condition of a plan (e.g., plan P_{31}), the agent could eventually rule out any successful execution for a plan higher up in the hierarchy (e.g., plan P_{01}). In such a case, it would be justified to also modify the higher level plan's context condition (e.g., the context of plan P_{01}). So, in general, once we have detected a failure and modified the corresponding failed plan's context condition (e.g., plan P_{31}'s context), we may want to propagate context modifications as far up the goal-plan tree as is justified. To that end, one could rely on automated planning, in particular, on *Hierarchical Task Network* (HTN) plan decomposition, as described in (Sardina, de Silva, & Padgham, 2006). The idea is to verify if, given the modifications done in lower-level plans, there is still a potential solution for a higher-level plan. If not, then we can update the higher-level plan's context condition, and so on. In our example, if after modifying the context condition of P_{31}, we attempt offline HTN planning on plan P_{01} from state s and fail to find a decomposition solution, then we can modify the context condition of P_{01} to exclude substate $s[R_{P01}]$: by offline reasoning we have already discovered that there is no valid decomposition for P_{01} in s.

REFINEMENT OF CONTEXT CONDITIONS IN NONDETERMINISTIC ENVIRONMENTS

The context in which we have discussed the refinement of plans' context conditions and the agent's plan selection function in the previous section can be seen as "ideal": *(i)* the environment is deterministic and fully observable; *(ii)* the (initial) context conditions are always necessary ones; and *(iii)* the success and failure of plans are always observable. Once we allow for *nondeterministic* actions, one can no longer update context conditions based on a single failure as proposed in the previous section. Nevertheless, the agent should, over time, be able to learn that certain states do tend to lead to failure, and to refine our plan selection accordingly.

Decision Trees (Mitchell, 1997) are a natural learning mechanism choice for this situation, since they can deal with "noise" (created by the non-determinism in our case) and they are able to support disjunctive hypotheses. What is more, a decision tree is readily convertible to *rules*, which are the usual representation of context conditions. We associate then a decision tree with *each plan* in the goal-plan tree. As we build up and record experiences, the decision tree will identify the conditions under which success and failure are likely, allowing us to modify context conditions in a similar way to our simple example in the previous section.

Typically, a decision tree is built *offline* from a set of data. In our case, though, we would like the agent to act as best she can, while accumulating experience so as to make improved decisions as more information is gathered. Algorithms for incremental induction of decision are available (Swere, Mulvaney, & Sillitoe, 2006, Utgoff, Berkman, & Clouse, 1997).

There are two important and inter-related questions to answer when using a decision tree to learn the context condition of a plan: *(a)* when is it justified to *record* data (in particular, failure data)? ; and *(b)* when and how the decision tree may be used for plan selection? The first issue involves deciding when a failure in a plan-node is meaningful for such node. The second one is related to plan applicability and actual plan selection, and how the current decision tree at hand can be used to determine whether a plan is applicable and which plan to choose among the applicable ones.

Recording Data in a Plan's Decision Tree

We have a decision tree linked to each plan, capturing the past experience of the agent in executing that plan. Upon execution of a plan, the agent must decide whether to incorporate the information about such execution into the corresponding plan's decision tree. This is particularly important if the plan happens to fail: Should the agent update the decision tree with failure information?

First of all, in a non-deterministic environment, there will inevitably be some "noise" in the data gathered and a plan P may fail where it generally works. One reason for plan P to fail is an (unexpected) change of some variable in R_p due to some environment factors outside the control of the agent. Such causes of failure should not lead us to conclude that plan P was a bad choice. Instead, one should monitor for and discard situations where the relevant variables for plan P have been affected outside of the agent's

control, so such failures would not be recorded (this assumes there is no correlation between P's execution and the unexpected changes in the environment). Alternatively, one could record them and assume that these data points will eventually be treated as noise. For simplicity, in our empirical investigation we did not consider any external effects so that the agent is the only one performing actions in the environment.

Based on the analysis done in the previous section, one could argue that it does not make sense to record the (failure) data for a plan P when P fails due to a poor choices made within P's sub-tree. Again, if plan P_{01} would have worked well had plan P_{12} been chosen instead of P_{11}, then the failure of P_{01} is in a sense spurious, corresponds to a false negative, and should not be recorded in P_{01}'s corresponding decision tree. Once accurate selections are regularly being made below P_{01}, we expect the system to indeed take into account failures and update P_{01}'s decision tree.

Considering this, our initial approach was to delay the collection of data for a plan P until all plans in P's sub-tree are considered accurate or stable enough. We call such approach *bottom up learning* (BUL). Note that this poses another non-trivial challenge, namely, deciding when a decision tree for a plan is accurate/stable enough, that is, close enough to its "real" ideal context condition. In our empirical evaluation, we use the naive approach of requiring a minimum number of data points (*minNumRecords*). Figure 3 determines, recursively, when **a** decision tree is considered stable or accurate enough at a given plan-node. Clearly, this is an extremely simplistic way of evaluating the "quality" of a decision tree at hand in a plan-node and, in future work, we shall be exploring more sophisticated accounts.

Inspired by the reasoning behind the "ideal" setting discussed in the previous section, the BUL bottom-up learning approach suffers from the drawback that it may in fact take a large number of execution instances before any data is collected for a plan P. This is particularly problem-

Figure 3.

```
Algorithm 1: StableDecisionTree(P)
    /* numRecords(P) is the number of instances recorded for plan P's decision
       tree                                                                   */
    if P is an action then
        // there is no sub-tree
        return (numRecords(P) > minNumRecords)
    else
        if (numRecords(P) > minNumRecords) then
            for each subgoal G_p of P do
                for each plan Q satisfying G_p do
                    if (not StableDecisionTree(Q)) then
                        return false;
            return true;
        else
            return false;
```

atic in the context of multi-agent systems, in which we may not expect to execute the same plans a large number of times in short periods of time. Because of that, we also experimented with what we call the *concurrent learning* approach (CL), in which the agent always collects data at all nodes, regardless of the decision trees' qualities down the hierarchy. Obviously, the proportion of false negative instances is expected to be higher than when using the BUL method, but more data will be collected at each node regardless of its level within the hierarchy. If the plan selection mechanism promotes some exploration to compensate for those false negative instances (see

below), it should still be possible to reach optimal behavior given enough instances.

The following Figure 4 shows the abstract procedure for deciding when to record an execution instance in a decision tree, depending on the strategy (BUL or CL) adopted.

Using Plans' Decision Trees for Plan Selection

The second issue to be addressed is the notion of plan applicability and plan selection in the context of the newly introduced decision trees. Typical BDI systems consider a plan applicable when its

Figure 4.

```
Algorithm 2: Record(Plan P, State s, boolean out)
    /* s:  world state when P was selected                              */
    /* out:  outcome of P's execution                                   */
    /* AddInstance(P,s,o):  add instance (s,o) to P's decision tree      */
    switch selectionMode do
        case CL
            numRecords(P) + +;
            AddInstance(P, s, out);
        case BUL
            if StableDecisionTree(P) then
                numRecords(P) + +;
                AddInstance(P, s, out);
```

context condition ψ is believed true; and a plan is selected for execution among the applicable set. In our context, it is expected that, besides the initial context formula provided at design time, the decision tree attached to a plan also influences the applicability and selection of a plan.

So, given that we have assumed that the context condition ψ of a plan (set at design-time by the BDI programmer) is a necessary condition, the agent first filters plans with respect to their initial contexts. If the context condition of a plan does not hold, the plan is *not* considered as a candidate for selection. Once a plan has passed its initial context condition, the agent may want to consider also its corresponding decision tree, in order to exploit the experience obtained so far.

Thus, key issues regarding the use of the decision trees are *(a)* when to begin using the trees; and *(b)* how to allow for plan exploration in order to "correct" possibly spurious entries. These issues, together with that as to whether it is better to delay the data collection for higher nodes until lower nodes are stabilized, are in fact the subject of our experimentation in the next section.

To address these issues we have considered the following three plan selection mechanisms that extend the standard BDI plan selection:

Simple Selection. In this plan selection approach, the agent uses the standard (random) plan selection among those plans considered applicable. However, in contrast with the standard BDI approach, a plan is considered applicable if its design-time context condition ψ holds and either its decision tree is not accurate/stable enough (under some account of stability; e.g., see Figure 3), or its decision tree is considered stable and provides a success rate higher than a given threshold (e.g., 50% success over past recorded instances).

Optimistic Selection. Under this account, the plan with the highest rate of success is selected. Such rate is obtained by computing the ratio between the number of positive and negative instances in the leaf nodes corresponding to the current state of the world in the relevant decision tree, provided such decision tree is considered stable enough. Otherwise, if the decision tree for a plan is not deemed stable yet, the highest rate is assigned to the plan. By doing that, we bias the plan selection to explore plans whose decision trees are not yet accurate enough so as to collect enough experience to bring them to a stable status.

Probabilistic Selection. Under this account, a plan is selected probabilistically according to the ratio of positive versus negative instances: the ratio between the number of positive and negative instances is computed as for the optimistic selection, and then, a plan is chosen with a probability *proportional* to the ratio of success (a minimal ratio is assigned to plans to avoid complete ruling out plans due to initial failures). In contrast with the two previous approaches, this method *always* takes into account the decision trees associated with plans, and as a result, there is no need to check for stability of decision trees. This is because all plans—even those that have unfortunately failed in their first executions—would have some chance to be eventually selected for execution, and thus, plan exploration is always guaranteed.

From a conceptual perspective, wee believe that the probabilistic plan selection mechanism provides the most suitable account for our extended BDI agents, since it does not require any notion of decision tree "stability" and it provides a parsimonious exploration-exploitation scheme. This was later corroborated our experiments (see below). by In some sense, one can view this plan selection approach as generalizing the standard *binary* BDI notion of plan applicability to a *graded* account of applicability.

A high-level representation of these selection accounts is shown in Figure 5.

Empirical Results

We conducted preliminary experiments to evaluate how agent performance is affected by the different issues discussed in previous sections. We concentrate on the following two issues:

Figure 5.

Algorithm 3: *Select*(State s, Goal g)

/* $pass\_context(PlanLibrary, g, s)$ selects the set of plans that satisfy goal g
and which context condition is satisfied in world state s. */
/* $rnd\_u(l)$: selects randomly item in the set l using a uniform probability
distribution */
/* $rnd\_w(l)$: selects randomly an item in the set l of pairs (e, w) where the
probability for selecting item e is proportional to w */
/* $Prob_{success}(P, s)$: proportion of positive instances in the leaf node of P's
decision tree for the state s */

$candidates \leftarrow pass\_context(PlanLibrary, g, s)$;
$applicable = \emptyset$;
switch *selectMode* **do**

   case *simple*
      for *all* $P \in candidates$ **do**
         if $StableDecisionTree(P)$ **then**
            if $(Prob_{Success}(P, s) > 0.5)$ **then**
               $applicable \leftarrow applicable \cup \{P\}$
         else
            $applicable \leftarrow applicable \cup \{P\}$:
      return $rnd\_u(applicable)$;

   case *optimistic*
      for *all* $P \in candidates$ **do**
         if $StableDecisionTree(P)$ **then**
            $applicable \leftarrow applicable \cup \{(P, Prob_{success}(P, s))\}$
         else
            $applicable \leftarrow applicable \cup \{(P, 1.0)\}$;
      $bestP \leftarrow \text{argmax}_{(P, w) \in applicable} w$;
      return $rnd\_u(bestP)$;

   case *probabilistic*
      for *all* $P \in candidates$ **do**
         if $StableDecisionTree(P)$ **then**
            $applicable \leftarrow applicable \cup \{(P, Prob_{success}(P, s))\}$
         else
            $applicable \leftarrow applicable \cup \{(P, 1.0)\}$;
      return $rnd\_w(applicable)$;

---

a. Selecting a plan when multiple plans are applicable. We tested the three different selection mechanisms presented in the previous section, namely, simple selection, optimistic selection, and probabilistic selection.

b. Collecting data instances to build the decision tree for each plan. We compared the BUL approach with the CL one for deciding when to consider an execution experiences meaningful for a plan node.

We set up a testbed program with 19 plans, 6 variables, and 4 levels in the goal-plan tree, which is depicted in Figure 6. In the experiments with deterministic environments, each plan leaf node had one action, which succeeded in a particular state and failed in all others. Thus, we expect the characterization of such state to be the context condition to be learnt for the corresponding plan. In non-deterministic experiments, actions also failed 10% of the time in the world states where they are expected to succeed (i.e., where their precondition holds).

Figure 6. Goal-plan tree used for the experiments

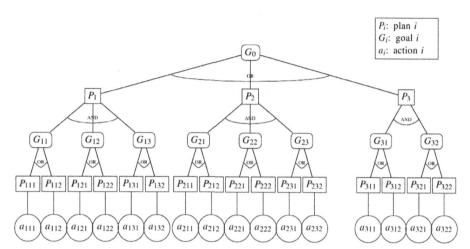

To make sure there is indeed space for learning, we ensured that from every possible world state, there is always some successful plan for the top-level goal. For all plans, the context condition initially specified by the programmer was empty (i.e., always true). At each iteration of the experiment, the state of the environment was randomly set and the top goal was posted. Recall that we have not taken into account the typical BDI failure recovery mechanism. A failure or success of the top level goal is recorded at the end of each iteration. As the agent collects data, decision trees are built at each plan node, using the J48 decision tree algorithm implemented in weka (Witten & Frank, 2005). Currently, we constantly keep rebuilding the decision trees; in future, we expect to use the incremental algorithm of (Swere et al., 2006).

Finally, we recall that, in the experiments reported in this article, we used the rather simplistic approach of waiting for some number of instances k for determining that a decision tree is considered reliable (see Figure 3).

Results

In the deterministic environment, one would expect to learn perfect behavior, and this was indeed corroborated by our experiments. Using BUL and $k=35$, we the agent achieved 100% success in selecting the right plan. Using CL with $k=35$, in contrast, the agent never achieved perfect behavior, as top level plans collected false negatives (i.e., a failure that was due to a wrong decision in the tree below, when a success was possible by making a correct decision). Nonetheless, CL managed to achieve perfect behavior when plan selection used a $k=50$: the additional data was sufficient to counteract the false negatives.

Figure 7 shows the performance level of the agent after learning, for different values of k. Differences are statistically significant for $k=10$ ($p=3.87e-05$), though this is no longer the case for $k\geq20$ ($p=0.23$, for $k=20$, $p=0.14$ for $k=35$). The figure also indicates the total number of instances required before performance converged, i.e., the decision tree did not change with further training instances. The number of total instances required varies greatly between the CL and BUL approaches. For example, with $k=50$, CL requires a little over 200 total instances to achieve perfect behavior, whereas BUL with $k=35$ requires a little over 800 instances. This is to be expected as, when using BUL, top-level plans in the goal-plan tree must wait for plans below to have collected enough data before collecting their own data.

Figure 7. Deterministic environment

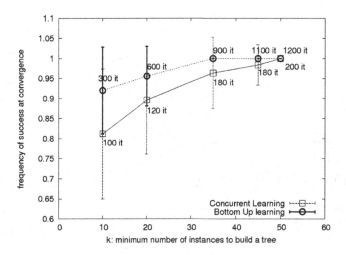

So, as expected, when using BUL, the agents can learn perfect behavior, but require sufficient number of instances ($k>35$) before using a tree and a (potentially) large total number of instances. Using CL, on the other hand, an agent can still learn to behave perfectly with higher values of k, but requires a much smaller number of total instances. It is unclear at this stage how the (lack of) complexity (size of the goal-plan tree, number of attributes, complexity of the real context conditions) of the scenario studied affects the relative values of the total instances required.

In the non-deterministic environment, we do not expect perfect behavior irrespective of how well agents have learnt the context conditions. Experimentally, with a 10% non-deterministic chance of failure, we can only achieve about 83% success (this can be shown to be correct analytically also). With $k=50$, CL produces an average success rate of 76% and BUL an average success rate of 79.5% (difference not statistically significant). The basic pattern in the non-deterministic case is the same as for the deterministic one. One can start using the decision trees with less data, without degrading performance, if using BUL. However, CL is able to achieve an optimal result faster overall by waiting longer before making any use of the learned information.

The above experiments were conducted using simple selection. Once we introduced probabilistic selection, we observed that CL was able to recover from its previous performance degradation. In the deterministic environment, using CL and $k=1$, probabilistic selection yielded 100% accuracy after a little over 200 instances. Plans that are successful early on are chosen more frequently. In the presence of false negative instances, a plan may be classified as not applicable, but it can still be selected due to the probabilistic selection mechanism. With more experience, the agent is likely to collect more positive instances, increasing then the likelihood of selecting the plan and therefore "correcting" the corresponding decision tree. For the non-deterministic environment, an average success rate of 83% was achieved after about 350 instances.

The experiments in Figure 8 compare the different selection mechanisms. These graphs are averaged over 10 runs. In the left graph, we set $k=20$. First, the graph shows that using CL is clearly better early on. The asymptotic behavior of all the mechanisms are identical (at least, no statistical difference). Interestingly, the probabilistic version seems to do somewhat better than the other two selection mechanisms. The right graph compares the use of a different update method when the

Figure 8. Comparison of the different approached in a non deterministic environment

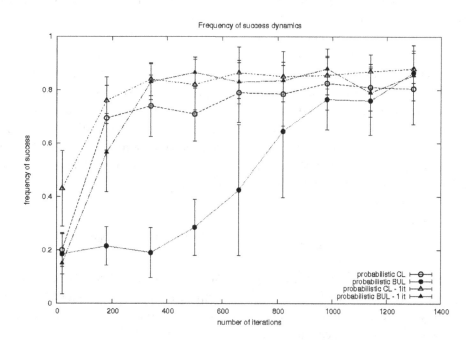

probabilistic selection is used. The curves noted "1 it" correspond to the case where $k=1$. One can see that CL in that case is better early on, and as good as BUL later on.

DISCUSSION AND CONCLUSION

In this article, we explored the use of learning to extend typical BDI agent systems. To implement a BDI agent system, the designer-programmer must provide each plan in the plan library with a context condition, stating when the plan may be used. Writing adequate context conditions for each plan may be a difficult, if not impossible, task. As context conditions play a central role in the overall performance of a BDI system, we propose to analyze past execution experiences to improve the context conditions of the plans. To that end, we assume that the BDI programmer sets initial necessary conditions for the success of each plan; and the task of the learning module is to *refine* such conditions to avoid or minimize re-occurrence of failures. We first studied an idealized setting,

where the environment is observable and totally deterministic, in order to get an understanding of the issues and challenges involved in the learning task. We showed that even within the simplified context, correctly refining the context conditions is not trivial. We then relaxed the assumption on determinism and discussed how to use decision trees to refine the context conditions. In particular, we discussed the issues of data collection in a decision tree and actual use of decision trees for the plan selection process.

Others have also used decision trees as a tool for learning plan context conditions. In (Phung, Winikoff, & Padgham, 2005), inductive learning was used to build a decision tree for deciding which plan to use. The instances observed between the update were used to estimate the accuracy of the tree, and when the tree was successful enough, it was used as the context condition. The problem faced by the learning agent is similar to ours when all initial context conditions are set to true. Their approach, however, is tailored to a particular example, and it is not clear how to generalize it. Hernandez et al. discussed learning from interpretation, which extends learning of decision trees (Guerra-Hernández, Fallah-Seghrouchni, & Soldano, 2004a, 2004b); as ours, their work is preliminary. The approach of (Jiménez, Fernández, & Borrajo, 2008) shares some of our goals, namely to tailor the behavior of an agent to its environment and its particular uncertainty. In the context of planning, the authors propose to use past experiences to learn the conditions of success of individual actions and encode the knowledge learnt in a relational decision tree. When a new problem arises, the planner takes advantage of the new knowledge. Our goal is to provide learning capabilities to a (generic) BDI agent, which generally do not engage in first principles planning. We are interested in learning the context condition of plans, rather than individual actions. When learning only the pre-conditions of actions, which are leaf nodes in a hierarchical structure, one is not faced with the issues and challenges we have discussed in this work.

The learning framework described in this article has several drawbacks and places for improvement. As noted before, the criterion used to test the accuracy-stability of decision trees is currently simplistic and more sensible criteria need to be tested. We expect more involved criteria would lead to an improvement on the robustness of learning. In addition, we are also interested in using algorithms that are designed to induce decision trees *incrementally* (Swere et al.., 2006, Utgoff et al.., 1997), rather than rebuilding the whole decision tree when a new instance is added to it. We shall also investigate the use of automated HTN planning to enhance the refinement of context conditions by checking for potential successful decompositions. This is because, although initially there may be a full decomposition for a plan P, this may not be the case anymore after some context conditions of sub-plans have been refined. One can then perform HTN offline planning to check if there is still a valid decomposition of P, and if not, then P's context conditions should also be updated (i.e., further restricted).

Finally, we point out that we have restricted our attention to the learning of plans' context condition. This type of learning has intrinsic limitations due to the locality property of such conditions. In particular, by modifying context conditions, the agent may be unable to learn interactions between plans or new means of achieving its goals. To that end, an account that modifies the meta-level plan selection function or the plan-goal hierarchy itself (e.g., by adding a new plan for a goal) would be necessary.

ACKNOWLEDGMENT

We would like to thanks María Inés Crespo for helping us with the editing of the document and the anonymous referees for their suggestions to improve the article.

REFERENCES

Aha, D. W., Kibler, D., & Albert, M. K. (1991). Instance-based learning algorithms. *Machine Learning*, 6(1), 37–66. doi:10.1007/BF00153759

Alonso, E., d'Inverno, M., Kudenko, D., Luck, M., & Noble, J. (2001). Learning in multi-agent systems. *The Knowledge Engineering Review*, 16(3), 277–284. doi:10.1017/S0269888901000170

Booker, L., Goldberg, D., & Holland, J. (1989). Classifier systems and genetic algorithms. *Artificial Intelligence*, 40, 235–282. doi:10.1016/0004-3702(89)90050-7

Bordini, R. H., Hübner, J. F., & Wooldridge, M. (2007). *Programming multi-agent systems in AgentSpeak using Jason. Wiley*. Series in Agent Technology. doi:10.1002/9780470061848

Bratman, M. E. (1987). *Intentions, plans, and practical reason*. Cambridge, MA: Harvard University Press.

Bratman, M. E., Israel, D. J., & Pollack, M. E. (1988). Plans and resource-bounded practical reasoning. *Computational Intelligence, 4*(4), 349–355. doi:10.1111/j.1467-8640.1988.tb00284.x

Busetta, P., Rönnquist, R., Hodgson, A., & Lucas, A. (1998). *JACK Intelligent Agents - Components for Intelligent Agents in Java* (Tech. Rep.): Agent Oriented Software Pty. Ltd, Melbourne, Australia. (Available from http://www.agent-software.com)

DeJong, G., & Mooney, R. (1986). Explanation-based learning: An alternative view. *Machine Learning, 1*, 145–176. doi:10.1007/BF00114116

Dennett, D. C. (1987). *The intentional stance.* MIT Press.

Ellman, T. (1989, November). Explanation-based learning: A survey of programs and perspectives. *ACM Computing Surveys, 21*(2), 163–221. doi:10.1145/66443.66445

Georgeff, M. P., & Ingrand, F. F. (1989). Decision making in an embedded reasoning system. In *Proceedings of the international joint conference on Artificial Intelligence* (pp. 972–978).

Guerra-Hernández, A., Fallah-Seghrouchni, A. E., & Soldano, H. (2004a). Distributed learning in intentional BDI multi-agent systems. In *Proceedings of the fifth Mexican international conference in Computer Science (ENC'04)* (pp. 225–232). Washington, DC, USA.

Guerra-Hernández, A., Fallah-Seghrouchni, A. E., & Soldano, H. (2004b). Learning in BDI multi-agent systems. In *Computational logic in multi-agent systems* (Vol. 3259, pp. 218–233). Springer Berlin / Heidelberg.

Hindriks, K. V., Boer, F. S. D., Hoek, W. V. D., & Meyer, J. J. C. (1999). Agent programming in 3APL. *Autonomous Agents and Multi-Agent Systems, 2*(4), 357–401. doi:10.1023/A:1010084620690

Huber, M. J. (1999, May). JAM: A BDI-theoretic mobile agent architecture. In *Proceedings of the third international conference on autonomous agents, (AGENTS'99)* (p. 236-243).

Jiménez, S., Fernández, F., & Borrajo, D. (2008). The PELA architecture: Integrating planning and learning to improve execution. In *Proceedings of the twenty-third AAAI conference on Artificial Intelligence* (AAAI'08) (pp. 1294–1299). Chicago, USA.

Kaelbling, L., Littman, M. L., & Moore, A. W. (1996). Reinforcement learning: A survey. *Journal of AI Research, 4*, 237–285.

Kolodner, J. (1993). *Case-based reasoning.* San Mateo, CA: Morgan Kaufmann.

Krause, P. J. (1998). Learning probabilistic networks. *The Knowledge Engineering Review, 13*(4), 321–351. doi:10.1017/S0269888998004019

Mitchell, T. M. (1997). *Machine learning.* McGraw Hill.

Panait, L., & Luke, S. (2005). Cooperative multi-agent learning: The state of the art. *Autonomous Agents and Multi-Agent Systems, 11*(3), 387–434. doi:10.1007/s10458-005-2631-2

Phung, T., Winikoff, M., & Padgham, L. (2005). Learning within the BDI framework: An empirical analysis. In *Proceedings of the 9th international conference on knowledge-based intelligent information and engineering systems (KES'05), LNAI volume 3683* (p. 282). Melbourne, Australia: SpringerVerlag.

Quinlan, R. J. (1986). Induction of decision trees. *Machine Learning, 1*, 81–106. doi:10.1007/BF00116251

Rao, A. S., & Georgeff, M. P. (1992). An abstract architecture for rational agents. In *Proceedings of the third international conference on principles of knowledge representation and reasoning* (KR'92) (p. 439-449). San Mateo, CA, USA.

Rumelhart, D., Hinton, G., & Williams, R. (1986). Learning internal representations by error propagation. In Rumelhart, D., & McClelland, J. (Eds.), *Parallel distributed processing (Vol. 1)*. Cambridge, MA: MIT Press.

Sardina, S., de Silva, L. P., & Padgham, L. (2006). Hierarchical planning in BDI agent programming languages: A formal approach. In *Proceedings of autonomous agents and multi-agent systems (AAMAS'06)* (pp. 1001–1008). Hakodate, Japan.

Swere, E., Mulvaney, D., & Sillitoe, I. (2006). A fast memory-efficient incremental decision tree algorithm in its application to mobile robot navigation. In *Proceedings of the 2006 IEEE/RSJ international conference on intelligent robots and systems* (pp. 645–650).

Tuyls, K., & Nowé, A. (2006). Evolutionary game theory and multi-agent reinforcement learning. *The Knowledge Engineering Review*, *20*(1), 63–90. doi:10.1017/S026988890500041X

Utgoff, P. E., Berkman, N. C., & Clouse, J. A. (1997). Decision tree induction based on efficient tree restructuring. *Machine Learning*, *29*(1), 5–44. doi:10.1023/A:1007413323501

Witten, I. H., & Frank, E. (2005). *Data mining: Practical machine learning tools and techniques* (2nd Edition ed.). Morgan Kaufmann, San Francisco.

This work was previously published in International Journal of Agent Technologies and Systems (IJATS), edited by Goran Trajkovski, pp. 1-18, copyright 2009 by IGI Publishing (an imprint of IGI Global).

Chapter 7
Reward Shaping and Mixed Resolution Function Approximation

Marek Grzes
University of Waterloo, Canada

Daniel Kudenko
University of York, UK

ABSTRACT

A crucial trade-off is involved in the design process when function approximation is used in reinforcement learning. Ideally the chosen representation should allow representing as closely as possible an approximation of the value function. However, the more expressive the representation the more training data is needed because the space of candidate hypotheses is larger. A less expressive representation has a smaller hypotheses space and a good candidate can be found faster. The core idea of this chapter is the use of a mixed resolution function approximation, that is, the use of a less expressive function approximation to provide useful guidance during learning, and the use of a more expressive function approximation to obtain a final result of high quality. A major question is how to combine the two representations. Two approaches are proposed and evaluated empirically: the use of two resolutions in one function approximation, and a more sophisticated algorithm with the application of reward shaping.

INTRODUCTION

In contrast to supervised learning, RL agents are not given instructive feedback on what the best decision in a particular situation is. This leads to the *temporal credit assignment problem*, that is, the problem of determining which part of the behaviour deserves the reward (Sutton, 1984). To address this issue, the iterative approach to RL

DOI: 10.4018/978-1-60960-171-3.ch007

applies backpropagation of the value function in the state space. Because this is a delayed, iterative technique, it usually leads to a slow convergence, especially when the state space is huge. In fact, the state space grows exponentially with each variable added to the encoding of the environment when the Markov property needs to be preserved (Sutton & Barto, 1998).

When the state space is huge, the tabular representation of the value function with a separate entry for each state or state-action pair becomes

Copyright © 2011, IGI Global. Copying or distributing in print or electronic forms without written permission of IGI Global is prohibited.

infeasible for two reasons. Firstly, memory requirements become prohibitive. Secondly, there is no knowledge transfer between similar states and a vast number of states need to be updated many times. The concept of value function approximation (FA) has been successfully used in reinforcement learning (Sutton, 1996) to deal with huge or infinite (e.g., due to continuous variables) state spaces. It is a supervised learning approach which aims at approximating the value function across the entire state space. It maps values of state variables to the value function of the corresponding state.

A crucial trade-off is involved in the design process when function approximation is used. Ideally the chosen representation should allow representing as closely as possible an approximation of the value function. However, the more expressive the representation the more training data is needed because the space of candidate hypotheses is larger (Mitchell, 1997). A less expressive representation has a smaller hypotheses space and a good candidate can be found faster. Even though such a solution may not be particularly effective in terms of the asymptotic performance, the fact that it converges faster makes it useful when applied to approximating the value function in RL. Specifically, a less expressive function approximation results in a broader generalisation and more distant states will be treated as similar and the value function in this representation can be propagated faster. The core idea of this chapter is the use of a mixed resolution function approximation, that is, the use of less expressive FA to provide useful guidance during learning and the use of more expressive FA to obtain a final result of high quality. A major question is how to combine the two representations. The most straightforward way is to use two resolutions in one function approximation. A more sophisticated algorithm can be obtained with the application of reward shaping. The shaping reward can be extracted from a less expressive (abstract) layer and used to guide more expressive (ground) learning.

To sum up: in this chapter we propose combining more and less expressive function approximation, and three potential configurations are proposed and evaluated:

- the combination of less and more expressive representations in one approximation of the value function,
- the use of less expressive function approximation to learn the potential function for reward shaping which is used to shape the reward of learning with desired resolution at the ground level,
- the synergy of the previous two, that is, learning the potential function from less expressive approximation and using it to guide learning which combines less and more expressive resolution in one FA at the ground level.

Our analysis of these ideas is based on tile coding (Lin & Kim, 1991) which is commonly used for FA in RL. The proposed extensions to RL are however of general applicability and can be used with different methods of function approximation, especially those which use basis functions with local support (Bishop, 1996).

The rest of this chapter is organised as follows. In the next section, function approximation with tile coding is introduced. Learning with mixed resolution tile coding and the algorithm which learns the potential function for reward shaping are discussed in two subsequent sections. Then, the experimental validation of the proposed extensions to RL is presented, and the last section summarises this chapter.

BACKGROUND

Tile coding is introduced in this section. In particular, the dependency of the resolution and the generalisation power of tile coding is highlighted and shown as a motivation for this work.

Function Approximation

The most straightforward approach to the representation of the value function is the state space enumeration with a separate value function entry associated with each state. There are several reasons why this approach may not be sufficient.

1. When the state space is huge, memory requirements may be prohibitive to store values for all enumerated states.
2. Neighbouring states usually have similar values of the value function. When learning with enumerated and represented individually states, only one particular state is updated during one Bellman backup. With this in mind it would be desirable if the update of the value function of one state could influence also values of neighbouring states.
3. Some global regularity in the feature space of the state representation may allow for broad generalisations in the representation of the value function (e.g., using multi-layer perceptron or more generally regression methods which use global basis functions Bishop, 1996).

Value function approximation methods take advantage of the fact that states with similar values of state features have in most cases a similar value of the value function, or that the global generalisation can be achieved. The idea is to represent the value function, *V(s)*, as a vector of parameters, $\theta \in R^d$, with d smaller than the number of states. In this way, the update of the value function according to one state is generalised across similar states (Sutton, 1996). The general form of this approach to the SARSA algorithm yields the following update rule:

$$\theta' = \theta + \alpha \delta_t(Q_\theta) \nabla_\cdot Q_\cdot(s, a) \qquad (1)$$

When linear function approximation is used, that is, when $Q_\theta = \theta^T \varphi$ where $\varphi : S \times A \to R^d$ defines basis functions then $\nabla_\theta Q_\theta(s, a) = \varphi(s, a)$. Linear function approximation is commonly used in practice, however little is known about its convergence properties. The only known theoretical results are due to Melo et al. (2008) who prove convergence under rather restrictive conditions (Szepesvari, 2009).

An interesting issue is how different regression methods address requirements listed at the beginning of this section. For example, the second issue can be addressed with function approximation based on local basis functions (e.g., radial basis functions Bishop, 1996) or linear averagers (Szepesvari, 2009; Gordon, 1995). Basis functions of this type are robust in preserving initialisation of the approximation and are also required by specific techniques which have tight requirements on used approximation. For example, proofs of convergence of fitted value iteration in (Gordon, 1995) require functions which are contraction mappings and linear averagers meet this requirement. The problem with these methods however is the fact that they do not address well the issue of the exponential state space explosion which is due to the Markov property. Approximation with global basis functions (which addresses the third issue from the list at the beginning of this section) is much more robust against the state space explosion due to global generalisation. The learning process is, however, more problematic in this case. The update of one state usually changes the value function of the whole state space (e.g., when linear regression or the multi-layer perceptron is used). This leads to problems with initialisation and exploration, because the current policy may be changing radically during learning. For this reason, methods like neural fitted Q iteration need to store <s,a,s'> triples and re-use them during training of the neural network (Riedmiller, 2005), i.e. a type of experience replay is applied (Lin, 1992).

Figure 1. Tile coding examples with a different resolution. Three tilings with tiles of three units in a) and six units in b)

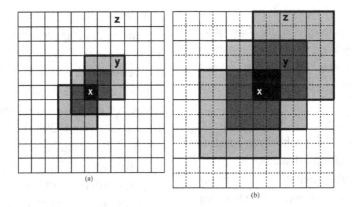

Value Function Approximation with Tile Coding

Value function approximation takes advantage of the fact that states with similar values of state features have in most cases a similar value of the value function. The idea is to represent the value function, V, as a vector of parameters, θ, with the size, N, of this vector smaller than the number of states. In this way the update of the value function according to one state is generalised across similar states (Sutton, 1996).

Function approximation should be fast and allow for online learning. Linear functions with updates based on gradient-descent methods meet this requirement. The linear approximation of the value function for action a can be expressed in the following form:

$$V^a(s) = \sum_{i=0}^{N-1} \theta^a_{\,i} \varphi_i(s), \qquad (2)$$

where $\varphi_i(s)$ is a basis function. The gradient-descent update rule for this approximation takes the form:

$$\theta' = \theta + \alpha \delta_t \varphi(s), \qquad (3)$$

where α is the learning rate and δ_t is the temporal difference:

$$\delta_t = r + \gamma V^{a'}(s') - V^a(s). \qquad (4)$$

The immediate reward is represented by r, γ is the discount factor, and s and s' are two consecutive states.

Tile coding (Sutton, 1996) is a particular method to define a basis function, $\varphi_i(s)$, for states or state-action pairs. This method partitions the input space into several displaced layers (tilings) of overlapping tiles. Each state can be allocated to exactly one tile in each tiling. Thus, $\varphi_i(s)$ takes value 1 for tiles it is allocated in and 0 otherwise. Figure 1 shows how it can be determined in a 2D space. Tiles allow for generalisation to neighbouring positions. For example, an update of the value function in position x has an impact on the value function in position y which may not be visited during the entire period of learning. One of the key motivations to propose the algorithms introduced in next two sections is the fact that coarser generalisation (see Figure 1b) allows for a more rapid propagation of the value function. This coarser generalisation means that the resulting representation is less expressive, but it can be used to guide learning of the value function with a more detailed representation.

Reward Shaping

When the agent is learning from simulation, the immediate reward, r, which is in the update rule of the SARSA algorithm given by equation:

$$Q(s,a) \leftarrow Q(s,a) + \alpha[r + \gamma Q(s',a') - Q(s,a)]. \tag{5}$$

represents the (only) feedback from the environment. The idea of reward shaping is to provide an additional reward which will improve the performance of the agent. This improvement can mean either faster learning or a better quality of the final solution, especially in the case of large domains. The shaping reward does not come from the environment. It represents extra information which is incorporated by the designer of the system and estimated on the basis of knowledge of the problem. The concept of reward shaping can be represented by the following formula for the SARSA algorithm:

$$Q(s,a) \leftarrow Q(s,a) + \alpha[r + F(s,a,s') + \gamma Q(s',a') - Q(s,a)], \tag{6}$$

where $F(s,a,s')$ is the general form of the shaping reward which in our analysis is a function $F : S \times S \rightarrow R$. A natural example of the potential function in navigation domains is the straight-line distance to the goal at the maximum speed. The shaping reward, $F(s,s')$, is then positive if, according to such a potential function, state s' is closer to the goal than state s.

Depending on the quality of the shaping reward, it can decrease the time the algorithm spends attempting suboptimal actions, thus it can improve exploration. This decrease is the main aim of applying reward shaping. Ng et al. (1999) defined formal requirements on the shaping re-

ward. In particular, the optimal behaviour of the (model-free) agent is left unchanged if and only if the shaping reward is defined as a difference of some potential function Φ of a source state s and a destination state s' (see Equation 7).

$$F(s,s') = \gamma \Phi(s') - \Phi(s) \tag{7}$$

This can be further clarified in the following way. When one has certain knowledge about the environment (knowledge which may help decrease the number of suboptimal actions the agent will attempt during learning), this knowledge can be used in different ways. In some cases the Q-table can be simply initialised based on this knowledge. The theoretical work of Ng et al. (1999) proved that if instead of initialising the Q-table, the same knowledge is used as a shaping reward, the final solution of the agent will not be changed. One of the most important implications of this fact is that it allows for a straightforward use of background knowledge in RL with function approximation. It is not an obvious task of how to use existing heuristics to initialise the Q-table which is represented, for example, as a multi-layer neural network (see Section 2.1 which introduces function approximation). The fact that reward shaping can be equivalent allows for a straightforward use of background knowledge in such cases. Heuristic knowledge can be easily given via reward shaping even when the function approximation with multi-layer neural networks is used. In the case of neural networks with global basis functions (Bishop, 1996) the use of reward shaping instead of Q-table initialisation (assuming that such an initialisation could be done easily) would have additional advantages. The consistent reward shaping would be given all the time during the learning process, whereas initialised values would change rapidly during temporal-difference learning.

The motivation for the need for potential-based shaping comes substantially from the work of Randløv (2001) who showed a domain in which a wrongly defined reward shaping changed the objective of learning. In the domain which involves learning to ride a bicycle towards a goal which is determined by the environment reward, the agent with the shaping reward was learning to ride in cycles without moving towards the goal, i.e. it was converging to a different policy than the one specified by the environment reward. In order to act optimally according to the environment reward, the agent has to navigate directly to the goal state while avoiding falling down. This example indicated deficiencies of reward shaping and lead to the theoretically grounded work of Ng et al. (1999) and Wiewiora (2003).

One problem associated with potential-based reward shaping is that often detailed knowledge of the potential function of states is not available or is very difficult to represent directly in the form of a shaped reward. When the shaping reward is computed as in Equation 7, the application of reward shaping reduces to the problem of how to learn the potential function, $\Phi(s)$, and in this chapter a method to address this issue is proposed. We suggest learning the potential function online as the value function of a coarse, abstract tile coding. At this time it is worth reconsidering that a particularly convenient potential function would be the one which is equal to the value function, that is, $\Phi(s) = V(s)$, which helps justify why roughly approximating the value function is a promising approach for reward shaping. The algorithm is introduced in the fourth section of this chapter.

Mixed Resolution Tile Coding

In this section we introduce a RL architecture that treats both the fine and coarse tilings as parts of the same function approximator. This straightforward idea can be easily found in Figure 1. Basically, two tilings with different resolution are used. The less expressive one with a coarse resolution is intended to allow for broader generalisation early and the more expressive with a fine resolution to yield refinement later on. Now, the value

function can be represented as two vectors of parameters θ^c and θ^f for coarse and fine tilings correspondingly. To these tilings correspond also two basis functions φ^c and φ^f. In this setting the value function is computed as:

$$V(s) = \sum_{i=0}^{N^c-1} \theta_i^c \varphi_i^c(s) + \sum_{i=0}^{N^f-1} \theta_i^f \varphi_i^f(s), \qquad (8)$$

where $N^c = \left|\theta^c\right|$ and $N^f = \left|\theta^f\right|$. For the value function computed in this way, the temporal difference can be evaluated in a standard way according to Equation 4 and vectors θ^c and φ^f updated according to the gradient descent rule in Equation 3.

This method allows for a natural coexistence of two resolutions in one function approximator. It can be seen as a method of obtaining and using high level knowledge to guide early learning.

The next section shows how to use this knowledge in a different way. Reward shaping is proposed as another way of using knowledge which is provided by the coarse resolution to speed up learning with a more detailed resolution

LEARNING THE POTENTIAL FUNCTION FOR REWARD SHAPING

We propose a RL architecture with two levels of tile coding. The first one learns an approximation of the Q-function at the ground RL level. The second, coarser one learns an abstract V-function which is used as the potential function to calculate the shaping reward (see Equation 7) for the ground level. The algorithm which is proposed here builds on two techniques existing in the field: 1) multigrid discretization used with MDPs (Chow & Tsitsiklis, 1991), and 2) automatic shaping which was recently proposed (Marthi, 2007).

Related Work

The multigrid discretization in the MDP setting (Chow & Tsitsiklis, 1991) was used to solve an MDP in a coarse-to-fine manner. While this technique is well suited to dynamic programming methods (a coarse problem at a high, abstract level can be solved and used at a more detailed, ground level), there was no easy way of merging layers with a different resolution when applied to RL algorithms. First such attempts were made by Anderson & Crawford-Hines (1994) and this problem was evident in their work. The need for knowledge of the topology of the state space is necessary in their solution to define how multiple levels are related, and this fact made the approach infeasible for RL tasks. It used a multigrid as a way of obtaining knowledge, but the mechanism to use this knowledge at a ground RL level was missing. We propose potential-based reward shaping as a solution to these problems. The ground RL algorithm does not have to be modified and knowledge can be given in a transparent way via an additional shaping reward. In this work, the idea of multigrid discretization is reflected in two different resolutions in tile coding.

In the automatic shaping approach (Marthi, 2007) an abstract MDP is formulated and solved. In the initial phase of learning, the model of an abstract MDP is built and after a defined number of episodes an abstract MDP is solved and its value function used as the value of the potential function for ground states. We propose an algorithm which applies tile coding with different resolutions to create ground and abstract levels. Instead of defining an abstract task as dynamic programming for solving an abstract MDP, we use RL to solve the abstract task online. RL with representation based on tile coding results in a natural translation between ground and abstract levels. Tile coding in itself can be easily applied in a multigrid fashion and because it has been mostly used with model-free RL and SARSA in particular (empirical results in the literature (Stone et al., 2005) show that SARSA is generally better than Q-learning when tile coding is used; the explanation is justified in the literature by the fact that SARSA is an on-policy method), it is sensible to apply RL for solving an abstract level problem. Tile coding is an important and popular function approximation method for model-free learning, and our approach meets requirements of model-free RL with tile coding. Our aim is to have more robust model-free learning with tile coding, while still enjoying all properties of model-free learning. Additionally, knowledge about the environment which is used to define tile coding at the ground level is sufficient to deploy our method in its basic form.

Work on tile coding which is related to this chapter was presented in (Zheng et al., 2006) where two function approximations with tile coding were also applied. In this case, Q- instead of the V-function is used at an abstract level. The high level, abstract Q-values are used to guide the exploration in the initial learning phase. This approach lacks the reference to the potential-based reward shaping as results in (Zheng et al., 2006) do not indicate a clear advantage of that method. Without the robust mechanism of potential-based reward shaping, the Q-function needed to be used at an abstract level. The usage of the V-function would require for example approximating transition probabilities. In our case, it is enough to learn only the V-function which can converge sufficiently faster to be useful for potential-based reward shaping.

The variable resolution discretization has been studied in the field (Munos & Moore, 2002). The idea is to split some cells (states) and bring a higher resolution to some areas of the state space in order to represent a better policy. Our approach can be seen as orthogonal to this technique because they could be combined together and bring their distinct merits to the overall solution. We learn the shaping reward which can be used to guide ground learning with a variable resolution discretization. The interesting question arises, whether a variable resolution could improve the process of learning a potential function when applied at an abstract level and focused on fast propagation of guidance. When applied at the ground level it is intended to play the opposite role, i.e. to provide a higher resolution where it is necessary (Munos & Moore, 2002).

The relationship of the number of tilings and the interval size was studied by Sherstov & Stone (2005). Their results show that a smaller number of tilings with wider intervals speeds up learning in initial episodes but hurts convergence at later stages. In contrast, narrower intervals (with preferably one tiling) slow down initial learning but lead to a higher quality of the final solution. Choosing in our algorithm a fine grained encoding with a small number of tilings at the ground level and coarse generalisation for reward learning can be seen as an easy way to have fast convergence at the beginning and good convergence at the end of learning.

Because in our algorithm learning takes place at two levels of abstraction, it is worth relating this approach to the general concept of hierarchical machine learning. Stone & Veloso (2000) proposed the universal idea of layered learning where the search space of hypotheses can be reduced by a bottom-up, hierarchical task decomposition into independent subtasks. Each local task is solved separately, and tasks are solved in a bottom-up order. The distinguishing feature of this paradigm is that the learning processes at different layers do not interact with each other and different machine learning algorithms can be used at different layers. In particular, RL was applied to learn in this architecture (Stone & Veloso, 2000), i.e. to learn at a particular layer. Because tasks are solved independently using results from learning at lower layers, the algorithm proposed in this chapter can be seen as a potential choice for selected subtasks.

When relating our algorithm to hierarchical reinforcement learning it is worth noting how the hierarchy interacts with reinforcement learning in such algorithms. Regardless of the type of abstrac-tion used to create hierarchy (e.g. state abstraction, hierarchical distance to the goal Kaelbling, 1993; Moore et al., 1999, feudal reinforcement learning Dayan & Hinton, 1993, temporal abstraction Parr & Russell, 1997; Sutton et al., 1999, or both state and temporal abstractions Dietterich, 2000) the hierarchy exists in the final representation of the solution, i.e. the policy is defined on this hierarchy, and learning may take place at all levels of the hierarchy simultaneously. The value function is a function of not only the ground states and actions but also some elements determined by the hierarchy (e.g., in Parr & Russell, 1997 HAMQ-learning maintains an extended Q-table $Q([s,m],a)$ indexed by a pair of states which includes state s and machine state m, and an action a at a choice point). In our algorithm the actual RL is not modified and the abstract level learning provides feedback which is given in a transparent way via reward shaping. There is also no need for knowledge about the hierarchical task decomposition, as in the basic case the knowledge which is used to design the state representation is sufficient to deploy this algorithm. In particular it can be applied to problems without a clear hierarchy.

A Novel Algorithm

Algorithm 1 summarises our approach, showing the key extensions to the standard version of SARSA(λ) with tile coding (Sutton & Barto, 1998). In our case learning at the ground level is the same as in standard SARSA(λ). The modification which is crucial for our discussion is the point where the SARSA(λ) algorithm is given shaping reward, $F(s,s')$, in Line 14 of Algorithm 1 where the temporal difference is computed. The way in which $F(s,s')$ is evaluated defines our extension.

The shaping reward, $F(s,s')$, is computed in Line 4 as the difference of the value function of current and previous states visited by the agent. Thus, $\Phi(s) = V(s)$ where V is the current estimate of the value function of the abstract RL task. This task is learned using temporal difference updates with tile coding (Lines 8 and 9) and symbols related to this learning process have subscript v in Algorithm 1. The mapping from state s to the set of tiles used at the abstract level is done in a straightforward way without any special knowledge. Basically, a lower resolution of tiles can be applied. However with optional, additional knowledge about the problem such a mapping can remove some state variables and appropriately focus abstract learning. It means that the less expressive representation can apply not only lower resolution but also remove some of the state variables.

RL at the abstract level is treated as a Semi-MDP (Semi-MDPs are extensions to MDPs in which the time between one decision and the next decision is taken into consideration as a real-valued or an integer-valued random variable (Hu & Yue, 2007)) since due to coarse tile coding an agent can be several time steps within the same position at the abstract level. The resolution of tile coding at the ground level should avoid such situations. For this reason time t is used when temporal difference in Line 8 is evaluated.

The generic function $reward_v(r)$ shows that abstract learning can receive an internally modified reward. According to our empirical evaluations $10^{-1}r$ gives good results on different domains where both the positive and negative reward is given. The division by factor 10 guarantees that the shaping reward extracted from an abstract V-function has smaller impact than the environment reward.

Use of Tilings

The algorithm has been shown as a generic approach to use two levels of tile coding. We combine this algorithm with the idea of mixed resolution function approximation which was introduced in

Algorithm 1. SARSA(λ)-RS: Gradient-descent SARSA(λ) with potential-based reward shaping from temporal difference learning of an abstract level value function.

```
 1:  repeat {for each step of episode}
 2:      V ← the abstract level v-function for state s
 3:      V '← the abstract level v-function for state s'; 0 if s' is a goal state
 4:      F(s,s') = γ_v V '- V
 5:      r_v = reward_v(r)
 6:      if r_v ≠ 0 or tiles for s ≠ tiles for s' at the abstract level then
 7:          t ← the number of time steps since the last update
 8:          δ_v = r_v + γ_v^t V '- V
 9:          Update approximation V(s) according to temporal difference δ_v
10:      end if
11:      Q ← the ground level state-action value for pair (s,a)
12:      Q'← the ground level state-action value for pair (s',a')
13:      if s' is not a goal state then
14:          δ = r + F(s,s') + γQ'- Q
15:      else
16:          δ = r - Q
17:      end if
18:      Update approximation of Q(s,a) according to temporal difference δ
19:  until s' is terminal
```

the third section of this chapter. This leads to two versions of Algorithm 1:

1. ground learning (Q-function) with only high resolution (fine tilings) and abstract learning (V-function) with low resolution (coarse tilings),
2. ground learning with both low and high resolution (according to the description in the third section of the chapter) and abstract learning with low resolution like in the first version.

Properties of the Algorithm

Even though the shaping reward is learned with a separate tile coding and separate vector of parameters, its performance is strictly correlated with relations between the Q- and V-function, in general, and the design of both levels of tiles. The following factors can thus have influence on the performance of Algorithm 1.

- $V(s)$ values learned at the abstract level are a function of only states whereas ground RL learns $Q(s,a)$ values in order to deal with unknown environment dynamics. This difference suggests that the positive influence of the potential function extracted from $V(s)$ should be higher with a larger number of actions $a \in A(s)$ because $V(s)$ learns only values of states whereas $Q(s,a)$ additionally distinguishes actions (there are more values to converge). Thus, $V(s)$ can converge faster than $Q(s,a)$ in the initial period of learning and can give positive guidance for learning $Q(s,a)$ at the ground level.
- There can exist structural dependencies between features in the state space. Such structural dependencies can be used to define a reduced representation at an abstract level. For example, a reduced number of

features can provide a high level guidance (e.g., goal homing). Detailed encoding at the ground level enables the algorithm to take into account other factors and world properties. Abstract learning with properly selected factors can result in a rapidly converging V-function which may improve slower converging ground learning.

- When the RL agent needs to learn on a problem with a wider range of values of state features with the same required granularity of function approximation (when the value function is very diverse and high granularity is necessary), the impact of learned reward shaping can be more significant. When tile coding at the abstract level applies a lower resolution, it reflects the situation given in Figure 1. Particularly in the initial period of learning, an abstract V-function can faster propagate information about highly rewarded areas than abstract Q-function.

Further sections test some of the aforementioned hypotheses on a range of RL tasks.

EXPERIMENTAL DESIGN

A number of experiments have been performed to evaluate extensions to RL proposed in two previous sections. The following configurations are tested. Their acronyms are defined here for the reference in the remainder of this chapter.

1. SARSA(λ): the standard version of the algorithm (Sutton & Barto, 1998).
2. Coarse: the standard version of SARSA(λ) with coarse tile coding.
3. Mixed: the standard version of SARSA(λ) with mixed resolution, that is, two tilings in one function approximator (according to Section 3).

4. RS: the algorithm introduced in Section 4 with coarse resolution at the abstract level and only fine resolution at the ground level.
5. Mixed-RS: like the previous version but with a mixed resolution for ground learning.

The following values of common RL parameters were used: $\lambda = 0.7$ (used at both levels), and $\lambda = 0$ (also at both levels) in the second series of experiments without eligibility traces, $\gamma = 0.99$, $\gamma_v = 0.99$, $\alpha = 0.1$ and $\alpha_v = 0.1$ (in both abstract and ground learning, the learning rate was being linearly decreased with each episode reaching 0.01 in the last episode). Values $\alpha = 0.1$ and $\lambda = 0.7$ were also used in the famous practical application of temporal difference learning: TD-gammon (Tesauro, 1992). In all experiments ε-greedy exploration strategy was used with ε decreasing linearly from 0.3 in the first episode to 0.01 in the last episode. Values of these parameters were chosen arbitrarily and the selection was guided by the most common settings from the relevant literature (Sutton & Barto, 1998; Tesauro, 1992). This value of ε is high enough to provide explorative behaviour, but small enough to ensure that the policy still drives exploration. All runs on all tasks were repeated 30 times and average results are presented in graphs. Following the evaluation process from recent RL competitions, the accumulated reward over all episodes was used as a measure to compare results in a readable way. It is worth noting that also the asymptotic performance can be explained using this type of graphs. Specifically, when two curves are parallel within a given number of episodes, it means that the asymptotic performance of two corresponding algorithms is the same. If one of these curves is steeper, it means that the asymptotic performance of the corresponding algorithm is better in the period under consideration. Error bars illustrating the standard error of the mean (SEM) are also presented. Statistical significance was checked with a paired sample Z test by setting the level of significance at $P < 0.05$.

The eligibility traces ($\lambda > 0$) are implemented in an efficient way (Sutton & Barto, 1998; Cichosz, 1995) at both levels. They are truncated when the eligibility becomes negligible. Specifically, the trace of N most recently visited states or state-action pairs is stored where $(\lambda\gamma)^N \geq 10^{-9}$. The value of eligibility is evaluated as: $e(\varphi_i(s,a)) = (\lambda\gamma)^t$ where t is the number of time steps since φ_i has been added to the trace. In this way, for all φ_i of the most recent pair (s,a), $t=0$ and it makes $e(\varphi_i(s,a)) = 1$ for all φ_i of this pair. It means that replacing eligibility traces are used (Singh & Sutton, 1996). For given values of parameters, $(\lambda\gamma)^N \geq 10^{-9}$, a maximum size of the trace is $N=56$.

EXPERIMENTAL DOMAINS

The following set of popular RL tasks were used as test domains in our experiments.

Mountain Car

The first experiments were performed on the mountain car task according to the description of Sutton & Barto (1998). This is one of the most famous RL benchmark problems. The car is situated in a steep-sided valley and its goal is to get out of this valley and ride to one of the hills (see Figure 2). Because the car's engine is not powerful enough, the car has to go certain distance up towards the opposite hill to get some momentum, and then accelerate towards the hill which corresponds to its goal.

The state space in this domain is described by the position p_t and velocity v_t of the car. There are three actions: backward, coast and forward. These actions correspond to car's acceleration a_t which has values -1, 0 and 1 correspondingly. The state is updated at each time step according to the following simplified physical model:

Figure 2. The mountain car task (Sutton & Barto, 1998)

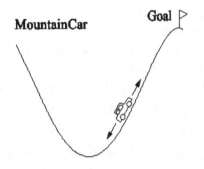

Figure 3. The car parking task (Cichosz, 1995). The domain state is described by $<xt, yt, \theta t>$

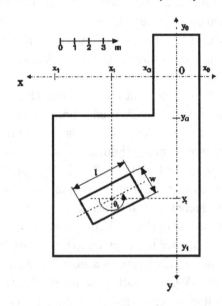

$$p_{t+1} = p_t + v_t, \qquad (9)$$

$$v_{t+1} = v_t + (0.001a_t) + (g\cos(3p_t)), \qquad (10)$$

where $g=0.0025$ is gravity. The range of state variables is bounded: $-1.2 \leq p_{t+1} \leq 0.5$ and $-0.07 \leq v_{t+1} \leq 0.07$. The goal state is reached when $p_{t+1} \geq 0.5$ for the main goal on the right hill and $p_{t+1} \leq -1.2$ for the negative goal on the left hill. In both cases, the episode ends and the new episode starts with the agent placed in a random position. An episode was also terminated, and the agent placed in a random position, after 10^3 steps without reaching any of the goal states. In our comparisons all tested algorithms were always evaluated on the same sequence of starting random positions for a fair comparison. It means that the random sequence of starting positions was selected before the experiment and all algorithms were tested on the same set of starting states. The agent received a reward of 1 upon reaching the goal state on the right hill and -1 on the left hill. This type of the reward functions was motivated by experiments of Munos & Moore (2002), as it makes the shape of the V-function more diverse (the car has to learn that it cannot go too much to the left). The goal of learning is to get to the right hill minimising the number of steps. Following Sutton & Barto (1998), 10 tilings

with 9×9 tiles were used for fine tilings and 6×6 for coarse tilings.

Car Parking

The car parking task comes from the existing RL literature (Cichosz, 1995, 1996). This is a simulated car parking problem (illustrated in Figure 3), where the goal of learning is to navigate the car to the garage so that the car is entirely inside of the garage. The car is represented as a rectangle in Figure 3 and cannot move outside of the driving area which is bounded by the solid line. This is an episodic task where the episode ends either when the car is successfully parked in the garage or when the car hits the wall of the bounded area. Each episode starts with the car placed in the same starting location (see below for exact coordinates). A reward of 100 was given upon entering the goal state. At all other time steps, the reward is 0.

The state space in this domain is described by three continuous variables: coordinates of the centre of the car, x_t and y_t, and the angle, θ_t, between the car's axis and the X axis of the coordinate system. There are three actions in the system: drive left, drive straight on, and drive right. These actions correspond to values of -5, 0, and 5 of the turn radius a_r which is used in equations below. These equations specify how state variables are updated after each time step τ.

1. if $r \neq 0$ then
   a. $\theta_{t+\tau} = \theta_t + \tau v / a_r$
   b. $x_{t+\tau} = x_t - a_r \sin(\theta_t) + a_r \sin(\theta_{t+\tau})$
   c. $y_{t+\tau} = y_t + a_r \cos(\theta_t) - a_r \cos(\theta_{t+\tau})$
2. if $r = 0$ then
   a. $\theta_{t+\tau} = \theta_t$
   b. $x_{t+\tau} = x_t + \tau v \cos(\theta_t)$
   c. $y_{t+\tau} = y_t + \tau v \sin(\theta_t)$

Velocity v was constant and set to 1 [m/s]. The time step $\tau = 0.5$[s] was used. The initial location of the car is: $x_t = 6.15$[m], $y_t = 10.47$[m], and $\theta_t = 3.7$[rad].

Two different configurations of the task were analysed in our experiments. The first one is with all geometrical parameters specified by Cichosz (1996). The dimensions are as follows: $w = 2$ [m], $l = 4$ [m], $x_0 = -1.5$ [m], $x_G = 1.5$ [m], $x_l = 8.5$ [m], $y_0 = -3$ [m], $y_G = 3$ [m], and $y_l = 13$ [m]. For this configuration, there were 6 tilings over one group of three state variables with $5 \times 5 \times 5$ tiles per tiling. The state space is defined in the same way as in (Cichosz, 1996). As this version of the problem is relatively small, the same tilings were used also for the V-value at the abstract level. In the second configuration, the size of the driving area was tripled with $x_l = 24.5$ and $y_l = 37$. Because of the larger size, the number of intervals was also tripled yielding $15 \times 15 \times 15$ tiles per tiling for fine tilings and $10 \times 10 \times 10$ for coarse tilings. The initial location of the car in this larger version of the domain was: $x_t = 22.15$ [m], $y_t = 24.47$ [m], and $\theta_t = 3.7$ [rad].

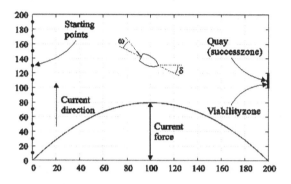

Figure 4. The boat task (Jouffe, 1998)

Boat

The problem is to learn how to navigate a boat from the left bank of the river to the quay on the right bank (see Figure 4). There is a strong non-linear current in the river. The boat starts in one of the ten possible starting positions on left bank and navigates to a narrow quay on the right bank (the sequence of random starting positions is the same within compared algorithms for a fair evaluation). The fact that there is strong non-linear current in the river requires precise use of continuous actions in this domain or at least a fine grained discretisation (Lazaric et al., 2007). Our implementation of this domain follows the description of Jouffe (1998) except for a narrower quay with its width set to $Z_s = 0.2$ and the random starting positions used recently by Lazaric et al. (2007) where this task was shown to be challenging for classical RL algorithms. This domain was used in our experiments to check the influence of the number of actions on the performance of our methods, because discretisation into a larger number of actions leads to better final results in this domain but also yields more time consuming learning.

The state of the environment is described by coordinates of the boat's bow, x and y in the range [0,200], and the angle δ between the boat's axis and the X axis of the coordinate system. The boat is controlled by setting the desired direction which is in the range $[-90°, 90°]$. The boat's bow coordinates are updated using the following equations:

$$x_{t+1} = \min(200, \max(0, x_t + s_{t+1} \cos(\delta_{t+1})))$$

$$y_{t+1} = \min(200, \max(0, y_t - s_{t-1} \sin(\delta_{t+1}) - E(x_{t+1})))$$

where E stands for the effect of the current and is expressed as: $E(x) = f_c(\frac{x}{50} - (\frac{x}{100})^2)$ where $f_c=1.25$ is the force of the current. The angle, δ_t, and speed, s_t, are updated according to:

$$\delta_{t+1} = \delta_t + I\Omega_{t+1}$$

$$\Omega_{t+1} = \Omega_t + ((\omega_{t+1} - \Omega_t)(s_{t+1} / s_{MAX)})$$

$$\Omega_{t+1} = \Omega_t + ((\omega_{t+1} - \Omega_t)(s_{t+1} / s_{MAX)})$$

$$s_{t+1} = s_t + (s_d - s_t)I$$

$$\omega_{t+1} = \min(\max(p(U_{t+1} - \delta_t), -45°), 45°)$$

where $I=0.1$ is the system inertia, ω the rudder angle, $s_{MAX}=2.5$ the maximum allowed speed of the boat, $s_d=1.75$ is the desired speed of the boat, and $p=0.9$ is the proportional coefficient required to compute the rudder angle according to a given value of the desired direction U_t.

The reward function is defined as follows. If the agent crosses left, top, or bottom boundary of the working area, the reward of -10 is given. If the quay is reached within its boundaries, that is, within the distance $Z_s/2$ from the centre of it (the success zone) where $Z_s=0.2$, the reward of 10 is always given. There is an additional viability zone defined around the quay. The width Z_v of this zone is 20. If the boat reaches the right bank within this zone (outside the success zone) the reward function is decreasing linearly from 10 to -10 relative to the distance from the success zone. Reaching the right bank outside of the viability zone yields the reward of -10.

RESULTS

Experimental results are discussed for each domain separately as they were designed to test different properties of the methods proposed in this chapter.

Mountain Car

The obtained results with eligibility traces (Figure 5) show that reward shaping with mixed function approximation (Mixed-RS) has the most rapid improvement. Mixed function approximation (Mixed) obtains the second best performance, though the cumulative reward is worse than in Mixed-RS with statistical significance after 2050 episodes. Mixed is better than SARSA(λ) with statistical significance after 230 episodes, than RS after 390 episodes, and better than Coarse after 940 episodes. When comparing other configurations, Coarse speeds up learning at the beginning, but asymptotically loses with a more detailed representation (refer to Section 5 to check how to read the asymptotic performance). The need of a more expressive representation becomes evident here. Learning with reward shaping (RS) offers good asymptotic properties, but its improvement is smaller than with mixed versions (Mixed and Mixed-RS). An interesting observation is that mixed representations, both with (Mixed-RS) and without (Mixed) reward shaping, improve learning right from early episodes and gain the best asymptotic performance. These results show, that RL can be boosted in a straightforward way just by combining two representations with different expressiveness in one function approximator (Mixed) and additional use of reward shaping (Mixed-RS) can lead to further improvement.

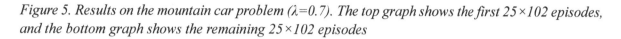

Figure 5. Results on the mountain car problem ($\lambda=0.7$). The top graph shows the first 25×102 episodes, and the bottom graph shows the remaining 25×102 episodes

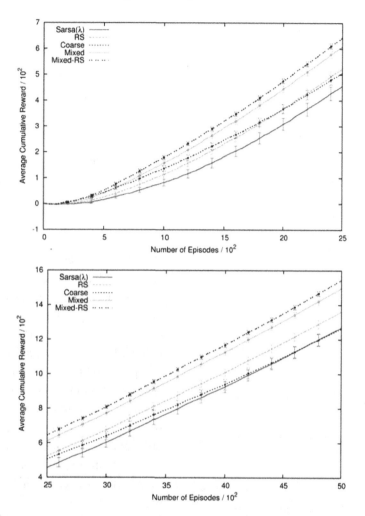

Another experiment on the mountain car task is reported in Figure 6 where $\lambda=0$ is used. In this case the advantage of Mixed and Mixed-RS is more evident. Mixed-RS is better than Mixed with statistical significance after 28 episodes. Mixed is better than Coarse after 2900 episodes and better than RS after 420 episodes. Also in this case, Coarse loses asymptotically with other methods. The overall observation from this experiment is that when learning without eligibility traces, our extensions lead to better absolute improvement.

Car Parking

In the car parking problem with the larger size of the working area, the type of knowledge which is learned from coarse tilings starts playing a more significant role. Figure 7 shows results for the original task. The task is relatively small here with a short distance to the goal (see the picture of this configuration in Figure 3) and our extensions do not bring improvement in this setting. But, the encouraging observation is that asymptotic convergence is not violated when our methods are used. There is no statistical significance between

Figure 6. Results on the mountain car problem (λ=0)

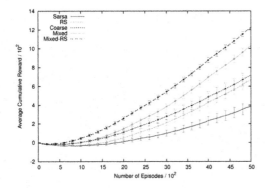

Figure 7. The car parking problem with original settings (λ=0.7)

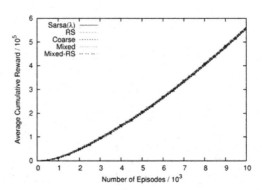

Figure 8. The car parking problem with the tripled size of the working area (λ=0.7)

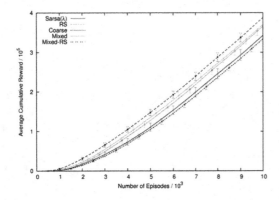

differences are less significant here, Mixed-RS gains the best performance. It can be noted here that the advantage of our extensions becomes more important on larger instances of problems. We can also try to find an explanation for the fact that reward shaping worked the best here, and RS in the initial period of learning in particular when compared to Mixed. We conjecture that the reason for this is that in order to reach the goal state the car needs to be in a very specific range of positions (it is easy to hit the wall) and learning with only mixed resolution was not able to lead to such an initial improvement because of the strict position to enter the goal. This seems to be a rational explanation when the experiment presented in Figure 10 is taken into consideration. In this case, when λ =0, methods which use reward shaping, that is, Mixed-RS and RS, work better than all other methods. There is however no statistical difference between Mixed-RS and RS. In Figure 9, the experiment on the original task and λ =0 is also presented. In contrast to results in Figure 7, eligibility traces are not used here and this time the basic version of SARSA(λ) gains better asymptotic performance (no statistical difference between SARSA(λ) and Mixed). This observation shows that on small problems the standard version of the algorithm may be sufficient.

any two methods in this experiment. In the second configuration, where the distance to the goal is bigger, goal-homing knowledge becomes more important. This is reflected in Figure 8. In this case two types of reward shaping yielded the best initial improvement with mixed resolution after them. However, Mixed obtains better final convergence than RS. Statistical tests are more informative here. There is no statistical significance between Mixed and RS, and also between Mixed-RS and Mixed. When comparing Mixed-RS and RS, the difference is statistically significant between episodes 600 and 4800. Mixed-RS is better than SARSA(λ) after 580 episodes and there is no statistical difference between Mixed and SARSA(λ). Even though the

Figure 9. The car parking problem with original settings (λ=0)

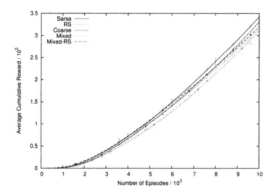

Figure 10. The car parking problem with the tripled size of the working area (λ=0)

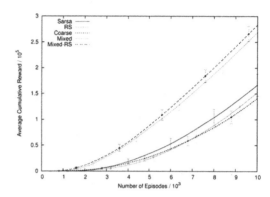

Figure 11. The boat problem with 5 actions (λ=0.7)

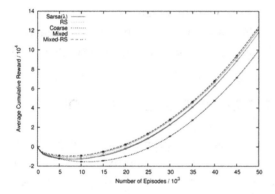

Boat

The agent controls the boat by the desired direction in the range [-90°,90°]. Experiments with discretization into 5, 20 and 40 values (actions) are reported. The same number of 5 tilings was used with 10×10×10 tiles for fine tilings and 8×8×8 tiles for coarse tilings.

Firstly results with eligibility traces are discussed. Figure 11 presents results with 5 actions. Differences, even though small, are statistically significant, particularly for Mixed and Mixed-RS when they are compared to other methods. Mixed-RS has better (with statistical significance) cumulative reward after 350 episodes than Mixed. And, Mixed is better than RS after 2000 episodes

and better than SARSA(λ) after 300 episodes. Learning in this version of the task progresses relatively well and, in effect, the coarse learning loses from early episodes. When 40 actions were used (Figure 13), the best performance was also due to reward shaping with mixed function approximation at the ground level (Mixed-RS) followed by learning with only mixed function approximation (Mixed). The difference between Mixed-RS and Mixed is statistically significant after 440 episodes and the absolute improvement is higher here than when 5 actions were used. Mixed is also better than RS after 6800 episodes. Additional experiments with 20 actions (see Figure 12) yielded results where reward shaping led to higher improvement than with 5 actions and lower than with 40 actions showing coherence with our hypothesis that our extensions are of particular interest when there are many actions $a \in A(s)$. The results of RS are between Mixed and pure SARSA(λ) in a similar way as in mountain car. RS with 40 actions converges faster in the initial phase of learning, at a pace similar to SARSA(λ) with only 5 actions, and obtains better results in the long run. The asymptotic performance of our algorithms is also very good. The problem of slow convergence of pure SARSA(λ) with 40 actions (i.e. the number of actions desired for this

Figure 12. The boat problem with 20 actions ($\lambda=0.7$)

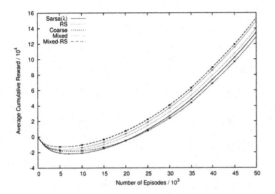

Figure 13. The boat problem with 40 actions ($\lambda=0.7$)

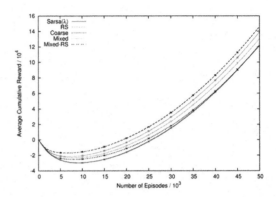

domain) which was pointed out by Lazaric et al. (2007) can thus be mitigated by our approaches.

The boat domain was also evaluated without eligibility traces, that is, with $\lambda=0$. Results of this experimentation are in Figures 14, 15 and 16 for 5, 20 and 40 actions respectively. In this case observations are different than in the previous study. Firstly, differences between algorithms are higher in terms of absolute difference in performance, the distances between curves are bigger with a similar size of intervals for the standard error of the mean. In all cases Mixed-RS performs better with statistical significance than other methods. Another important issue in this case is that the basic version of the SARSA(λ) algorithm performed very well in terms of asymptotic con-

vergence. When learning with eligibility traces, the improvement which our methods bring was smaller in terms of the absolute difference, but the asymptotic performance was also very good.

SUMMARY AND DISCUSSION

In this chapter, we propose using two hypotheses spaces, that is, function approximation with different levels of expressiveness in RL. Two approaches to obtain learning with mixed resolution are introduced and empirically evaluated when applied to tile coding. The results show that simultaneous learning at two levels and learning with mixed resolution FA can converge to a stable solution.

Figure 14. The boat problem with 5 actions ($\lambda=0$)

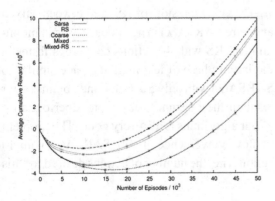

Figure 15. The boat problem with 20 actions ($\lambda=0$)

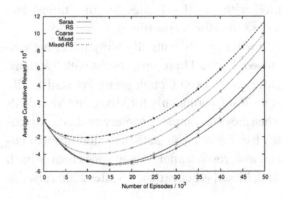

Figure 16. The boat problem with 40 actions (λ=0)

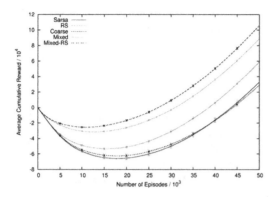

We conjecture that this is due to the fact that our experiments are based on the SARSA algorithm (on-policy temporal difference learning) which has been shown in the literature (Stone et al., 2005) to work better with function approximation than Q-learning.

Results on tasks selected according to different properties show that the application of our extensions to RL are especially beneficial when: 1) there are many actions in each state; 2) a high resolution of the policy is required (due to details in the environment) with a wide range of values of state variables, i.e. on the larger instance of the domain; 3) a high level guidance can be extracted from a subset of state variables.

Reward shaping with mixed FA at the ground level was the best in all runs on large instances. Actually, only in the car parking task with original size and λ=0 our approaches were not the best, and even then it was not statistically significant. Learning with only mixed FA was the second-best on two domains but reward shaping without mixed resolution was better on one domain, that is, when the path to the goal led via states with very constrained values of state variables (entering the parking space in the car parking task). Overall, the results show that reward shaping with mixed resolution FA at the ground level was the most successful.

The contribution of the algorithm is the improved convergence rate, especially in domains satisfying the properties outlined above.

The comparison between learning with λ>0 and λ=0 showed that our algorithms generally lead to better absolute improvement when λ=0, but good asymptotic properties were preserved in both cases in most experiments. Additionally, even with λ=0, our algorithms without eligibility traces faster gained a similar performance to SARSA(λ) with eligibility traces, that is, with λ>0. Eligibility traces, even when using a more efficient version (truncating is used in our experiments), yield certain computational overhead. With λ=0, only one backup is performed after each step and with λ=0.7 (and other relevant parameters according to our experimental design) the number of backups is N=56. The computational complexity is significant and was empirically observed during experimental evaluation. This observation indicates that with our methods applied without eligibility traces, a comparable convergence can be achieved at lower cost, because there is at most one backup of the V-function for each SARSA backup. Eligibility traces require significantly more updates. In contrast to eligibility traces, separate and external representation of knowledge is obtained in our method with reward shaping.

It is important to note that ideas proposed in this chapter do not require any explicit domain knowledge. In its basic form abstract learning can be defined using the same knowledge which is used to design tile coding at the ground level. The most straightforward approach is the use of wider intervals of high level tiles.

REFERENCES

Anderson, C., & Crawford-Hines, S. (1994). Multigrid Q-learning. *Technical Report CS-94-121*, Colorado State University.

Bishop, C. M. (1996). *Neural Networks for Pattern Recognition*. Oxford, UK: Oxford University Press.

Chow, C. S., & Tsitsiklis, J. N. (1991). An optimal one-way multigrid algorithm for discrete-time stochastic control. *IEEE Transactions on Automatic Control*, *36*(8), 898–914. doi:10.1109/9.133184

Cichosz, P. (1995). Truncating temporal differences: On the efficient implementation of TD(λ) for reinforcement learning. *Journal of Artificial Intelligence Research*, *2*, 287–318.

Cichosz, P. (1996). Truncated temporal differences with function approximation: Successful examples using CMAC. *In Proceedings of the 13th European Symposium on Cybernetics and Systems Research*.

Dayan, P., & Hinton, G. E. (1993). Feudal reinforcement learning. *In Proceedings of Advances in Neural Information Processing Systems*.

Dietterich, T. G. (2000). Hierarchical reinforcement learning with the MAXQ value function decomposition. *Journal of Artificial Intelligence Research*, *13*, 227–303.

Gordon, G. (1995). Stable function approximation in dynamic programming. *In Proceedings of International Conference on Machine Learning*.

Hu, Q., & Yue, W. (2007). *Markov Decision Processes with Their Applications. Advances in Mechanics and Mathematics*. New York: Springer.

Jouffe, L. (1998). Fuzzy inference system learning by reinforcement methods. *IEEE Transactions on Systems, Man and Cybernetics. Part C, Applications and Reviews*, *28*(3), 338–355. doi:10.1109/5326.704563

Kaelbling, L. P. (1993). Hierarchical learning in stochastic domains: Preliminary results. In *Proceedings of International Conference on Machine Learning*, (pp. 167-173).

Lazaric, A., Restelli, M., & Bonarini, A. (2007). Reinforcement learning in continuous action spaces through sequential Monte Carlo methods. *In Proceeding of Neural Information Processing Systems*.

Lin, C.-S., & Kim, H. (1991). CMAC-based adaptive critic self-learning control. *IEEE Transactions on Neural Networks*, *2*, 530–533. doi:10.1109/72.134290

Lin, L.-J. (1992). Self-improving reactive agents based on reinforcement learning, planning and teaching. *Machine Learning*, *8*, 293–321. doi:10.1007/BF00992699

Marthi, B. (2007). Automatic shaping and decomposition of reward functions. *In Proceedings of the 24th International Conference on Machine Learning*, (pp. 601-608).

Melo, F. S., Meyn, S. P., & Ribeiro, M. I. (2008). An analysis of reinforcement learning with function approximation. *In Proceedings of International Conference on Machine Learning*, (pp. 664-671).

Mitchell, T. M. (1997). *Machine Learning*. New York: McGraw-Hill.

Moore, A., Baird, L., & Kaelbling, L. P. (1999). Multi-value-functions: Efficient automatic action hierarchies for multiple goal MDPs. *In Proceedings of the International Joint Conference on Artificial Intelligence*, (pp. 1316-1323).

Munos, R., & Moore, A. (2002). Variable resolution discretization in optimal control. *Machine Learning*, *49*(2-3), 291–323. doi:10.1023/A:1017992615625

Ng, A. Y., Harada, D., & Russell, S. J. (1999). Policy invariance under reward transformations: Theory and application to reward shaping. *In Proceedings of the 16th International Conference on Machine Learning*, (pp. 278-287).

Parr, R., & Russell, S. (1997). Reinforcement learning with hierarchies of machines. In *Proceedings of Advances in Neural Information Processing Systems, 10.*

Randløv, J. (2001). *Solving Complex Problems with Reinforcement Learning.* PhD thesis, University of Copenhagen.

Riedmiller, M. (2005). Neural fitted Q iteration - first experiences with a data efficient neural reinforcement learning method. In *Proceedings of the European Conference on Machine Learning,* (pp. 317-328).

Sherstov, A. A., & Stone, P. (2005). Function approximation via tile coding: Automating parameter choice. *In Symposium on Abstraction, Reformulation, and Approximation,* (pp. 194-205).

Singh, S. P., & Sutton, R. S. (1996). Reinforcement learning with replacing eligibility traces. *Machine Learning, 22*(1-3), 123–158. doi:10.1007/BF00114726

Stone, P., Sutton, R. S., & Kuhlmann, G. (2005). Reinforcement learning for RoboCup-soccer keepaway. *Adaptive Behavior, 13*(3), 165–188. doi:10.1177/105971230501300301

Stone, P., & Veloso, M. (2000). Layered learning. *In Proceedings of the 11th European Conference on Machine Learning.*

Sutton, R. S. (1984). Temporal credit assignment in reinforcement learning. PhD thesis, Department of Computer Science, University of Massachusetts, Amherst.

Sutton, R. S. (1996). Generalization in reinforcement learning: Successful examples using sparse coarse coding. *Advances in Neural Information Processing Systems, 8,* 1038–1044.

Sutton, R. S., & Barto, A. G. (1998). *Reinforcement Learning: An Introduction.* Cambridge, MA: MIT Press.

Sutton, R. S., Precup, D., & Singh, S. P. (1999). Between MDPs and Semi-MDPs: A framework for temporal abstraction in reinforcement learning. *Artificial Intelligence, 112*(1-2), 181–211. doi:10.1016/S0004-3702(99)00052-1

Szepesvari, C. (2009). *Reinforcement learning algorithms for MDPs.* Technical Report TR09-13, Department of Computing Science, University of Alberta.

Tesauro, G. (1992). Practical issues in temporal difference learning. *Machine Learning, 8,* 257–277. doi:10.1007/BF00992697

Wiewiora, E. (2003). Potential-based shaping and Q-value initialisation are equivalent. *Journal of Artificial Intelligence Research, 19,* 205–208.

Zheng, Y., Luo, S., & Lv, Z. (2006). Control double inverted pendulum by reinforcement learning with double CMAC network. *In The 18th International Conference on Pattern Recognition,* (pp. 639-642). IEEE Computer Society.

Chapter 8

Inductive Logic Programming and Embodied Agents:
Possibilities and Limitations

Andrea Kulakov
University of Sts Cyril and Methodius, Macedonia

Joona Laukkanen
The American University of Paris, France

Blerim Mustafa
University of Sts Cyril and Methodius, Macedonia

Georgi Stojanov
The American University of Paris, France

ABSTRACT

Open-ended learning is regarded as the ultimate milestone, especially in intelligent robotics. Preferably it should be unsupervised and it is by its nature inductive. In this article we want to give an overview of attempts to use Inductive Logic Programming (ILP) as a machine learning technique in the context of embodied autonomous agents. Relatively few such attempts exist altogether and the main goal in reviewing several of them was to find a thorough understanding of the difficulties that the application of ILP has in general and especially in this area. The second goal was to review any possible directions for overcoming these obstacles standing on the way of more widespread use of ILP in this context of embodied autonomous agents. Whilst the most serious problems, the mismatch between ILP and the large datasets encountered with embodied autonomous agents seem difficult to overcome we also found interesting research actively pursuing to alleviate these problems.

INTRODUCTION

Open ended learning, particularly in intelligent (sometimes also called cognitive) robotics, is

regarded as the ultimate milestone in the development of the discipline. Ideally, an autonomous robot enabled with its sensors and actuators, after spending some time in an unknown environment, would come up with some knowledge about that environment. That knowledge would then be used

DOI: 10.4018/978-1-60960-171-3.ch008

Copyright © 2011, IGI Global. Copying or distributing in print or electronic forms without written permission of IGI Global is prohibited.

to gain more knowledge (in a sort of a bootstrapping process) and/or enhance performance in specific tasks. Preferably the open-ended learning should be unsupervised and by its nature it is inductive. Based on the sensory motor traces the robot should come up with learned constructs that would help it interpret the incoming sensory flux in a more abstract manner. In other words, the learned constructs would help the robot develop higher level perception which would group and integrate the low level sensory input into coherent perceived scenes and possibly temporal narratives.

Open-ended learning is also referred to as *task-independent* or *task non-specific*. Different mechanisms are then needed in order to guide the behavior of the robot and quite often researchers talk about *internal motivation systems*. In this context *artificial curiosity* is understood to be the mechanism that would drive these robots to do *something* rather than *nothing* (for an overview of different implementations of artificial curiosity as well as more general *internal value systems* please see (Stojanov and Kulakov, 2006). Sometimes artificial curiosity is explicitly referred to as *goal-generation mechanism*.

Given the properties of Inductive Logic Programming (capability to learn new concepts given positive and negative instance of the concept and some amount of background knowledge) its choice for artificial agent capable of open-ended learning may seem natural. Another advantage of ILP is that its output is easily understandable and easily modifiable by the human user. Background knowledge would be provided by the innate knowledge of the agent, and the agent itself would sample its environment for positive and negative examples.

This article is organized in the following way: In section one, we give a brief introduction of ILP, we mention some theoretical limitations which we deem relevant to understand the range of applicability of ILP in robotics, and finally we enumerate the areas where it has been applied with considerable success.

The second section is devoted to the review of six papers reporting on research efforts to apply ILP in the context of robotics. We analyze individually what the goals of these projects were and evaluate what the lessons are that can be learned from these efforts; what are the encouraging results, and on the other hand, what are the difficulties that were encountered with ILP.

In section three we summarize how some of the problems that have emerged while applying ILP in robotics have been addressed.

Finally, in the last section we take a look at several approaches that we judge promising when pursuing an increase in ILP performance to cope with the requirements of intelligent robotics.

ILP: A Brief Introduction

Inductive Logic Programming (ILP) is the intersection of inductive learning and logic programming (LP) (Lavrac & Dzeroski, 1994), a field of interest and great promises in the early 90's. From inductive learning, ILP inherits the goal of inducing hypothesis from observations and by using LP's representational mechanism it overcomes the representational limitations of propositional logic and the difficulties in using substantial background knowledge.

On the other hand, ILP extends the computational logic by investigating induction as opposed to the traditional usage of deduction as the basic mode of inference (e.g. *exploitation* of a PROLOG program). While computational logic describes deductive inference from logic formulae provided by the user, ILP describes the inference of logic programs (which can be thought of as describing *concepts*) from samples (positive and negative instances of the concepts being learnt) and some background knowledge.

The main distinction between ILP and the related areas of inductive inference such as **grammar induction** (Biermann & Feldman, 1972), **finite state automata induction** (Moore, 1956), **Turing Machine induction** (Biermann

Figure 1.

$$B = \begin{Bmatrix} parent(ann, mary) \\ parent(ann, tom) \\ parent(tom, eve) \\ parent(tom, ian) \\ female(ann) \\ female(mary) \\ female(eve) \end{Bmatrix}, E^+ = \begin{Bmatrix} daughter(mary, ann) \\ daughter(eve, tom) \end{Bmatrix}, E^- = \begin{Bmatrix} daughter(tom, ann) \\ daughter(eve, ann) \end{Bmatrix}$$

$$H = \{daughter(X, Y) \leftarrow female(X), parent(Y, X)\}$$

& Krishnaswamy, 1976) and **LISP induction** (Summers, 1975) is the emphasis on universal representation, which should have provided it a much wider application. The output of ILP is easily understandable and easily modifiable by the user by simply deleting or adding complete clauses or literals, without worrying about the ordering. The semantics of logic programs are also closely related to their syntax, and logic programs allow the same representation for examples, background knowledge and hypotheses.

ILP infers new knowledge by inducing hypotheses given some background knowledge and a set of positive and negative samples $(B + E^+ + E^- \Rightarrow H)$. The hypotheses need to be both complete with respect to the positive and consistent with respect to the negative samples. We'll have a look at the sample given in Lavrac & Dzeroski (1994): (See Figure 1).

In this example ILP is given some background knowledge on parenthood and gender and evidence on the target predicate that needs to be learned, *daughter/2*. From this background knowledge and the examples ILP is then able to learn a definition of the notion of *daughter*. For a detailed description of the theory and usage of ILP we refer the reader to (Lavrac & Dzeroski, 1994), (Bratko & Muggleton, 1995) and (Muggleton & De Raedt, 1994). There are many popular implementations of ILP, and we'll reference only some of them: MIS (Shapiro, 1983), MARVIN (Sammut & Banerji, 1986), MARKUS (Grobelnik,1992), LINUS (Lavrac et al., 1991) and FOIL (Quinlan, 1990).

Main Application Areas of ILP

ILP is not the only player in the realm of inductive inference today, but opposed to other computational techniques, such as statistical regression or neural networks, ILP outputs are logic rules, easily understood by humans. Its main applications are also in fields where this feature is critical, that is in domains in which the concepts to be learned can not be easily described in an attribute-value fashion. These domains can roughly be grouped in two groups: **scientific discovery and knowledge acquisition** as a field with an ever gaining popularity, and the **developing of programming assistants**.

In the field of scientific discovery and knowledge acquisition, success of ILP can be credited to the fact that it is one of the few techniques coming from the world of AI that produces knowledge that is:

- publishable in a reference journal in the application area
- understandable and meaningful to the scientists in the application area
- produced with a general purpose tool, not a modification specifically adjusted to the application area

Below is a representative list of representative applications of ILP in scientific discovery and knowledge acquisition:

- It is shown in (King et al., 1992) that ILP can be used in **drug design**, because of its capability to construct rules which predict the activity of untried drugs. Rules are constructed from examples of drugs with known medical activity. The accuracy of the rules is found higher than the traditional statistical methods. Moreover, the understandable rules provide more insight, thus, reducing the number of compounds for testing;
- (Bergadano et al., 1988) gives an example of ILP usage in the field of **protein secondary shape prediction** where the usage of background knowledge combined with ILP's ability to describe structural relations boosted the accuracy of predictions by over 20%;
- In (Feng, 1992) ILP is used as a tool for **satellite diagnosis**. Using the model of the satellite's power system, a correct set of rules for diagnosing power failures could be developed in a simple temporal formalism in which each predicate had an associated timestamp;
- In (Lavrac et al., 1993) ILP was successfully used in **rheumatology** as incorporating background relational knowledge provided by an expert improved the quality of the rules that were induced;
- **Finite Element Mesh** design is accomplished using ILP in (Dolsak & Muggleton, 1992) and (Dolsak et al., 1998). These methods and models are widely used by engineers and scientists to analyze stress in physical structures.

ILP is also frequently used in the area of programming assistants. Programming assistants are tools that assist a programmer in the design and development of software. Within this field, ILP is found useful in a variety of tasks such as:

- **Logic Program Synthesis** (Deville & Lau, 1993), a technique of deriving efficient programs from an inefficient implementation or from a specification and in the extreme case, even from examples only;
- **Inducing properties of databases** and **knowledge base updating** (De Raedt & Lavrac, 1993), which are a straightforward use of ILP for normalization or gaining further insights from the database/knowledgebase. This application is continuously gaining popularity within the field of **data mining**;
- Program testing and debugging which is another well known ILP application since the grounding work of Shapiro on the MIS (Shapiro, 1983);

Limitations of ILP

The main theoretical problem with ILP is the problem of **learnability.** The process of forming and refining hypothesis is *not always convergent*, that is, not all hypotheses are learnable. Two major approaches are in use as a guide towards forming convergent hypotheses:

- **Identification in the limit** (Gold, 1967): derived from computability theory, and dealing with finite time convergence of a learning procedure on an infinite example stream;
- **Probably-Approximately-Correct (PAC)** (Valiant, 1984) learning: derived from cryptography and computational complexity theory and dealing with probabilistic identification from finite (polynomial) sets of examples;

Another major problem in ILP, closely related to learnability, is determining whether a **provabil-**

ity relation is decidable or not. Two provability relations are being used in ILP; implication and subsumption. For instance, it is proven in (Marcinkowski & Pacholski, 1992) that a Horn clause program consisting of a set of ground facts, one ground query, and one Horn clause with three literals is **not decidable in the general case**. The authors of (Schmidt-Schauss, 1988) also prove that a Horn clause program consisting of one ground fact, one ground query, and two Horn clauses with two literals is **not decidable in the general case**. For more detailed and formal analysis of the identified classes of decidable and non-decidable programs, the reader is referred to (Jappy et al., 1996).

Further, ILP also has a range of other well-studied theoretical limitations:

1. **ILP can only be applied in strictly closed domains**. This is a significant limitation and determines the dominant usage of ILP for closed-domain applications (see previous section on application domains); any attempt to apply ILP beyond these domains would require considerable extensions of the basic paradigm;

2. **ILP is sensitive to data imperfections**. (Lavrac & Dzeroski, 1994) states that noise, insufficiently covered samples, inexactness and missing values as major imperfections. Some ideas are even given on overcoming them but ILP remains within the closed domain applications.

3. **Size of the search space** is usually too large (different biases (syntactic, semantic) are proposed for restricting the size) (Muggleton & De Raedt, 1994).

The mentioned limitations clearly place ILP within the realm of domain-specific closed-world learning of relations, largely determining its main usage to remain in the fields mentioned earlier.

By now, then, we can already predict what the difficulties are that would be encountered by any

attempts to apply plain ILP in the domain of real world robotics. In the case of autonomous open-ended learning, for example, it would be hard, or even impossible to use this original version of ILP, since it means giving up on the added biases and user interaction, which significantly affects the performance of ILP. We will elaborate on this point in the section that follows.

ILP IN ROBOTICS

Because of the aforementioned limitations of ILP, we would argue that it is not a big surprise that ILP has not been used extensively in robotics, because, in its original version, it was found to be impractical and unsuitable for robotics learning.

In this part of the article, we will review several papers related to five research projects directly dealing with ILP and physical agents. We believe that the selected projects are fairly representative with respect to the advantages, limitations, as well as the open issues in the application of ILP in robotics.

The papers (Klingspor et al., 1996) and (Rieger, 1995) present the authors' experiences of an attempt to use ILP techniques for predicate invention induced by sensory-motor data of a robot. The aim of this project was to build more convenient Human-Robot Interface where the commands sent to the robot were to be grounded in the robot's sensory-motor apparatus. On one hand, the user would specify the robot's task in a way that would be more natural for human users, while on the other hand, human users would more easily understand the robot's actions. They have used a scenario for moving the robot through an exit (Figure 2).

The first issue, that they were faced with, was how to learn higher level concepts from the raw sensory-motor traces. Abstraction from the sensory-motor data was deemed necessary, because learning high-level concept predicates directly from sensor data and robot movements was found

Figure 2. The room with the robot traces (Adapted from (Rieger, 1995))

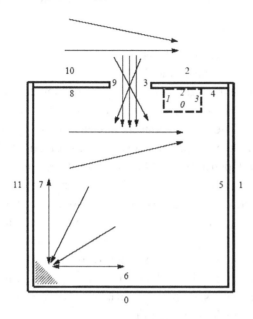

Figure 3. An abstraction hierarchy (adapted from (Rieger, 1995))

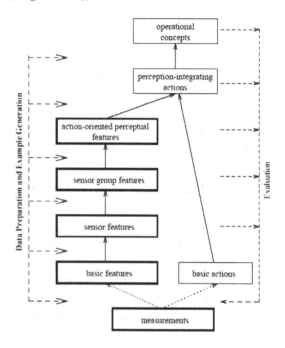

infeasible. The following observation from (Klingspor et al., 1996) is quite illustrative regarding the need to introduce multiple abstraction levels: "It became clear, that misclassifications at lower levels of abstraction do not result in the misclassification of concepts at higher levels of abstraction. If, for instance, the measurements of one sensor are not right, the sensor group may nevertheless deliver the correct pattern. This is due to (learned) rules that demand three sensors of a group to derive the same pattern before this pattern is said to hold for the sensor group. In this way, the hierarchy of learned concepts contributes to the robustness of learning results.". Figure 3 shows the abstraction hierarchy that was proposed.

The authors clearly state that real-world domains, such as robotics, are characterized by an enormous amount of data. In order to apply learning successfully, it is crucial to provide the learning algorithms only with relevant background knowledge, which is far from a trivial task. It would be possible to apply some sort of preprocessing to the raw sensory-motor readings that would reduce the dimensionality of the input data. This would prevent the algorithm from being **overloaded with irrelevant information**, which slows down the learning process and may even cause the algorithm to find results of **poor quality**.

Several stages of this proposed abstraction hierarchy require explicit human intervention:

- Perceptual features are classified by hand, through the time-consuming generation process of examples and background knowledge.
- Given a set of positive and negative examples, the human user has to decide which examples are to be included in a training/test set.
- The authors provide a method, *case selection*, which allows the user to specify, which defining predicates with which features should be included in the back-

ground knowledge for a given set of target predicates.

Apparently, in this case we cannot talk of unsupervised learning. Indeed, published critiques of this approach state that it needs "some type of prior background knowledge, either a predefined domain theory in the form of initial operators, or external instruction and knowledge on how to perform the transformation." (Garcia-Martinez et al., 2000) and that "Having an AI designer providing the robots with an adequate representation has a major drawback: it is fixed, ad-hoc representation. Any change of setting (e.g. museum instead of an AI lab) may require a new perceptual description" (Bredeche et al., 2003).

The authors themselves were aware that "the coupling between the knowledge-base and the robot is manual, i.e., the data exchange is realized by an engineer who loads the basic actions derived by the knowledge-based system into the robot system and loads the sensor data of the robot into the knowledge-based system." (Klingspor et al., 1996). There is no report so far that they have avoided this human-in-the-loop intervention.

The most important findings that can be extracted from their attempt are that:

- Learning high-level concepts directly from sensor data and robot movements is not likely to produce good results;
- The application of ILP to sensor and action data goes beyond standard (see previous section) ILP applications;
- Real-world domains, such as robotics, are characterized by an enormous amount of data. In order to apply learning successfully, it is essential to apply heavy preprocessing of the sensory-motor data; providing the learning algorithms with a fair amount of relevant background knowledge also seems to be a must;

- For successful learning, human intervention is required (their method *case selection)*;

In order to address some of these issues they have expanded the ILP rules to Probabilistic Automata and to Hidden Markov Models. For example, if we look at a learned concept as a FSA, sometimes several concepts are identified with the final state of the automaton. In this case, the authors developed a Hidden Markov Model to account for these ambiguities by splitting the final state into several unambiguous ones by introducing nondeterministic transitions to the newly generated states, and by associating probabilities with the non-deterministic transitions. During the learning phase the training data is used to derive relative frequencies, which are then taken as estimates for the transition probabilities.

This was not the only attempt to expand the ILP rules to Hidden Markov Models. In (Bostrom, 1998), it is explained how ILP works on sequences and how we can equate the invented predicates to a deterministic Finite-State-Automaton. As we believe that these sort of extensions of ILP are useful for its application in robotics, we will give a detailed example from (Bostrom, 1998). Given the following general theory:

(c1) p([ ]).
(c2) p([a | L]):- p(L).
(c3) p([b | L]):- p(L).

together with the positive examples $E^+ =$ {p([a,a,a,b,b]), p([a,a,b,b,b,b])} and the negative examples $E^- =$ {p([a]), p([a,b,a])}, the corresponding positive sequences are {c2c2c2c3c3c1, c2c2c3c3c3c3c1} and the negative sequences are {c2c1, c2c3c2c1}.

The general theory and the automation are used to construct the following hypothesis:

p([a | A]):- p(A).
p([b | A]):- p_1(A).

Figure 4. Finite state automaton (adapted from (Bostrom, 1998))

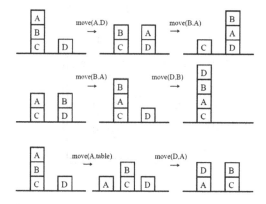

Figure 5. Narratives in the Blocks'world (adapted from (Lorenzo, 2002))

p_1([ ]).
p_1([b | A]):- p_1(A).

In the second part of (Bostrom, 1998) this system is modified in order to learn Hidden-Markov-Models, as an extension to the Finite-State-Automata, where the state transitions are explicitly modeled by their probabilities.

Other attempts to use ILP in the robotics domain also date from the mid 1990's and they will be further explained below.

In (Lorenzo, 2002), non-monotonic narrative formalisms were used to represent actions and their consequences.

Looking at Figure 5 each narrative consists of a representation of the initial position of blocks given by the predicate *holds/2*, the actions executed and the effects produced by the actions, represented with the predicates *happens/2* and *caused/3* respectively. As an example, consider the first narrative of Figure 5 as represented in Figure 6.

These kinds of narratives were used in addition to ILP and certain success was achieved. Despite the success, the authors have noticed the problem with concurrent actions and their ramifications; the actions can support, but can also even cancel, each other's effects meaning that the effect predicates need to consider all subsets of cancel-ing actions for each effect. This, as the authors explain, "makes the descriptions of actions cumbersome and difficult for complex domains, and consequently harder to learn".

We might add that in multi-agent systems, where the agents concurrently act in the environment, such representations of action's causes and effects combined with ILP seem impractical. Finally in the conclusions of (Lorenzo, 2002) it is stated that: "Further work needs to be done to show the adaptation to more and increasingly more complex scenarios, and with different noise levels, e.g., to improve its adequacy for dealing with real robot's environments."

In a similar paper by the same group (Lorenzo & Otero, 2000), their intentions are described to continue towards: "[...] more real domains, with a larger number of fluents (objects) and actions and with different noise and uncertainty levels. The most challenging domain is Cognitive Robotics that is concerned with high-level cognitive functions of robots that reason, act and perceive

Figure 6.

holds($clear(a), 0$)	happens($move(a, d), 1$)	happens($move(b, a), 2$)
holds($clear(d), 0$)	caused($on(a, b), f, 1$)	caused($on(b, c), f, 2$)
holds($on(a, b), 0$)	caused($on(a, d), t, 1$)	caused($on(b, a), t, 2$)
holds($on(b, c), 0$)	caused($clear(b), t, 1$)	caused($clear(c), t, 2$)
holds($on(c, table), 0$)	caused($clear(d), f, 1$)	caused($clear(a), f, 2$)
. . .		

Figure 7. A maze field (Adapted from (Inuzuka et al., 2000))

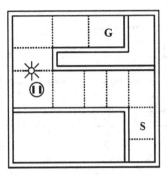

POSSIBILITIES TO OVERCOME THE DIFFICULTIES

In this section we will try to summarize the main difficulties that have been encountered in the attempts to apply ILP in robotics, how some researchers try to deal with them and will give some guidance on how these difficulties could possibly be overcome given the latest developments in the relevant areas of machine learning.

Summarizing the Difficulties

In some sense the difficulties that have been reported by authors that have tried to apply the original ILP paradigm could have been predicted by looking at the theoretical limitations of ILP. Robots which are supposed to function in a real world, in a non structured environment (e.g. as opposed to robot scientist: (King, 2005))

1. Operate in an open domain par excellence; real world environments are inherently uncertain;
2. Their sensors, and actuators usually provide high dimensional data that are inherently noisy;
3. Face the problem of scalability of ILP to handle large amount of data;

Moreover, most of the real world phenomena and linguistic concepts are inherently fuzzy, ambiguous, and probabilistic. This becomes crucial if the goal of a robotic project is to come up with a robot that would go in the wild and gain insights about its environment.

Overcoming Difficulties by Oversimplifying the Environment

Faced with the difficulties, researchers have sometimes been tempted to make the real world robotic system fit into the ILP framework. This is perhaps not surprising as the complexity in robotics

in changing, incompletely known, unpredictable environments. In this case, an almost complete description of robot's actions and its environment is required, which is a time consuming task (as shown in (Klingspor et al., 1996).

Still, the most direct and least encouraging critique on the use of ILP in robotics comes from Japanese authors (Inuzuka et al., 2000). They consider the problem of controlling a Khepera robot that would go from an initial position to a goal position in a maze, which was constructed as shown in Figure 7, while learning the robot's control by induction of relational concepts using iteratively collected examples.

The authors clearly stated: "ILP has been intensively studied because it can be applied to complex and structural domains, where the first-order language is necessarily to express objects. Instead of the merit, we can find that the ILP is not very good at the domains of robot learning. Even for simple tasks, such as following a visible target, which we describe in this article, it is not easy to acquire appropriate rules by ILP method." (Inuzuka et al., 2000)

Hence, the overall impression is that the only somewhat successful results thus far are in simulations in the rather limited blocks-world domain, not different from the one used by Shakey-the-robot in the early days of robotics research in the early '70s.

Figure 8. Problem environments in AI (Adapted from Russel & Norvig, 2002)

Task Environment	Observable	Deterministic	Episodic	Static	Discrete	Agents
Crossword puzzle	Fully	Deterministic	Sequential	Static	Discrete	Single
Chess with a clock	Fully	Strategic	Sequential	Semi	Discrete	Multi
Poker	Partially	Stochastic	Sequential	Static	Discrete	Multi
Backgammon	Fully	Stochastic	Sequential	Static	Discrete	Multi
Taxi driving	Partially	Stochastic	Sequential	Dynamic	Continuous	Multi
Medical diagnosis	Partially	Stochastic	Sequential	Dynamic	Continuous	Single
Image-analysis	Fully	Deterministic	Episodic	Semi	Continuous	Single
Part-picking robot	Partially	Stochastic	Episodic	Dynamic	Continuous	Single
Refinery controller	Partially	Stochastic	Sequential	Dynamic	Continuous	Single
Interactive English tutor	Partially	Stochastic	Sequential	Dynamic	Discrete	Multi

is often overwhelming. To emphasize this point, it is very illustrative to look at the only chapter on robotics in the most influential and widely used textbook about AI today "AI: The Modern Approach" (Russel & Norvig, 2002), devoted to this issue of complexity.

The authors first give a classification of environments where some artificial agent is supposed to operate: (Figure 8)

As the authors put it:

*As one might expect, the hardest case is partially observable, stochastic, sequential, dynamic, continuous, and multi-agent. It also turns out that most real situations are so complex that whether they are really deterministic is a moot point. For practical purposes, they must be treated as stochastic. **Taxi driving** is hard in all these senses.*

While the robotic learning should be capable of functioning in the most complex environment – the real world, what is done even today in some robotics research, is to simplify the problem environment and make it like the environment of the crossword puzzle problem. That is, to make it: **fully observable** (by using global coordinates, overhead cameras, etc), **deterministic** (by shrinking the objects to avoid their accidental rotation and by other carefully tailored objects and actions), **static** (by having only static objects), **discrete** (by forwarding and turning the robot in steps)

and **single-agent.** Only then some programs for Data Mining using ILP are able to learn notions in terms that are practical, from gathered sensory motor data. Even when the environment is reduced in such a way that it can be expressed by a regular-expression, the ILP programs have time constraint problems, if the number of the defining predicates is larger than 7, but most importantly, these ILP programs have theoretical problems even if the number of literals is larger than 2 (Kietz & Dzeroski, 1994).

By no means should these types of solutions (which simplify the environment) be considered satisfactory.

Dealing with Uncertainty

Much of the complexity in robotic systems arises from uncertainty. In the book (Russel & Norvig, 2002) (page 923), in the chapter for Robotics, the authors describe uncertainty as a key characteristic of robotics problems and devote elaborated discussion to it:

In robotics, uncertainty arises from partial observability of the environment and from the stochastic (or unmodeled) effects of the robot's actions. Errors can also arise from the use of approximation algorithms such as particle filtering, which does not provide the robot with an exact belief state even if the stochastic nature of the environment is modeled perfectly.

[...] Planning paths through configuration space is already a challenging problem; it would be worse if we had to work with a full probability distribution over states. Ignoring uncertainty in this way works when the uncertainty is small.

Unfortunately, ignoring the uncertainty does not always work. In some problems the robot's uncertainty is simply too large. For example, how can we use a deterministic path planner to control a mobile robot that has no clue where it is? In general, if the robot's true state is not the one identified by the maximum likelihood rule, the resulting control will be suboptimal. Depending on the magnitude of the error this can lead to all sorts of unwanted effects, such as collisions with obstacles.

The field of robotics has adopted a range of techniques for accommodating uncertainty.

This approach has already come within reach of the solution of the taxi-driving environment (the most difficult in AI problems) in a recent DARPA Urban Challenge (Voelcke, 2007, November) where autonomous vehicles where racing in an almost usual urban environment.

Indeed, the trend today seems to be to combine pure logic with probabilistic reasoning which has become the target of a wealth of research lately (to name a fraction of the research, consider for example the recently published papers about Markov Logic Networks (Richardson & Domingos, 2006), about Probabilistic Logic Learning (De Raedt & Kersting, 2004) and about unifying Logical and Statistical AI (Domingos et al., 2006), then the recently organized conference (progic07: The Third Workshop on Combining Probability and Logic, special focus: Probabilistic Logics and Probabilistic Networks - 2007) or the book

"Probabilistic Logic Networks" (Goertzel et al., 2008 in press).

One of the authors of (Cohen & Page, 1995) have given later in (Page, 2000) several directions for future ILP research. Of these directions the first two are most relevant for robotics:

- incorporating explicit probabilities into ILP
- stochastic search

Lately, C. D. Page has been working in the field of Bioinformatics, where work has resulted in successful combination of ILP and Bayesian Networks to form a new approach called Statistical Relational Learning (Getoor & Taskar, 2007, November):

Inductive Logic Programming (ILP) is the study of automated inductive learning where the knowledge representation used is first-order definite clause logic (as embodied in the language Prolog). The richness of the representation makes ILP particularly well-suited to domains such as organic chemistry and molecular biology, natural language processing, and telecommunications, where examples are easily described as sets of objects (e.g., atoms in a molecule) together with relations that hold among those objects (e.g., bonds or distance relations). Because of the close correspondence between logic and databases, ILP is a leading approach to directly mining databases with multiple relational tables. Statistical Relational Learning (SRL) combines explicit representation of uncertainty, as in Bayesian networks and related graphical model approaches, with the ability to analyze relational data.

Certainly, SRL offers a way to model uncertainty but, again, its applicability in robotics should be further explored as modeling uncertainty comes with the price tag of increased time complexity.

Dealing with High Dimensionality and Noise

Noise reduction techniques vary from general purpose to specific purpose techniques depending on the application. General purpose noise reduction techniques are techniques developed for removing standard modeled noise (Gaussian noise, white noise etc.) using linear convolution filters (FIR cut-off, averaging filter, Gaussian filter etc.). Specific purpose noise reduction techniques are techniques developed based on specific knowledge about the non-standard type of noise that one is trying to remove. These techniques are generally non linear; for instance, the median filter is a technique developed for removing granular noise.

Similarly, dimensionality reduction techniques can also be divided into general purpose and application-specific techniques. Principal Component Analysis (PCA) is an example of a general purpose dimensionality reduction technique. PCA transforms the multidimensional input signal so that

- the components of the input vectors are orthogonal and de-correlated,
- the resulting orthogonal components are sorted so that the ones with greater variations come first, and
- the components with no variations are completely eliminated.

Application-specific techniques are various techniques for feature extraction, i.e. extraction of meaningful features from the signal in a useful format (variable, vector, XML etc.). Examples of meaningful feature-vectors from the camera sensory stream, for example, could be the color-histogram, the edge-histogram etc.

These techniques look promising to be applied in the early stage of the preprocessing of the input which is supposed to go to the ILP learning algorithm.

Addressing the Scalability Issue

One way to scale performance is to employ inductive learning in incremental fashion. This allows using a partial instance memory so that part of the examples can be dismissed and subsequent learning need not consider all examples all over again.

The AQ-PM method for training example selection (Maloof & Michalski, 2000), for example, uses the learned concepts to find those examples (both positive and negative) that are critical for a concept's definition, those situated at the concept's boundaries. Only these examples are stored whilst others are discarded. Since fewer examples need to be considered when learning concepts this lowers both memory consumption and learning time. In (Biba, Basile, et al., 2006; Biba, Ferilli, et al., 2006) a system is presented that uses a fast external storage for storing the terms. The database solution provides faster access to the terms than using a full memory approach and further, the database is used to store links between concepts and the clauses in the concepts as well as links between clauses and the examples that the clauses cover. Storing these links is useful when refining hypothesis as it suffices to check only the examples that are possibly affected; examples previously covered by a clause, during the specialization of the clause or the negative examples for the concept in question when the clause is generalized. This reduces again the number of checks that need to be performed and hence it shortens the learning time.

Even if not quite of order of magnitude, the improvements in learning time that could be realized, especially with the latter mentioned system, seem rather encouraging. Whilst arguably still rather an optimization than anything else (considering the size of the problem), in some specific and still very limited situations improvements of this magnitude could just prove decisive.

CONCLUSION

In this article we gave an overview of attempts to use ILP in robotics. Not many such attempts exist and already studying the theoretical limitations of ILP provided an initial understanding why this is the case. Whilst ILP has its strengths and there are areas where ILP is successfully used, it has serious problems when used in robots operating in unstructured, real-world environments. Virtually all the research projects that we reviewed had, although with very different goals, faced almost the same problems related to open-endedness of the real-world environments, inherent noise in the sensory-motor apparata, and finally the size of the hypothesis space.

It is clear that the choice for the use of ILP in robotics was led by the idea of easier human-robot interaction and understanding. In the last decade, ILP seemed as promising machine learning technique for robotics, but this choice has proven as inadequate for operation in a real-world robotics.

Although it is likely that the problems will remain difficult to solve, our review into the research aiming to overcome these problems shows that there are also a number of methods that could help at least to alleviate the problems. These findings lead us to think that a combination of methods such as

- introduction of a probabilistic component in the LP setup;
- introducing layers of abstractions where lower layers perform heavy preprocessing of the raw sensory-motor flux and the learning algorithms are applied to the higher level concepts;
- tackling scalability using incremental-ILP supported by external vast and fast DB storage;

We believe that the combination of the above methods possibly with the introduction of innovative heuristics may significantly improve the performance of ILP in robotics, although it wouldn't be counted as ILP anymore.

The results from the research on reasoning by analogy seem like a rather good point to start looking for candidates for new heuristics. The idea of reasoning by analogy is to use old knowledge in order to explain new observations. We are not however aware of any research projects where ILP would have been used in conjunction with reasoning by analogy.

Finally, motivation and inner value systems should be in the core of any open ended learning system. Inner value system can be a powerful bias in the search of the hypothesis space. Although it is far from trivial to incorporate motivation and inner value systems in a, say, purely symbolic ILP system, we believe that it is a path worth pursuing.

ACKNOWLEDGMENT

The work described in this article has been partially funded by the European Commission's Sixth Framework Programme under contract no. 029427 as part of the Specific Targeted Research Project XPERO ("Robotic Learning by Experimentation").

REFERENCES

Bergadano, F., Giordana, A., & Saitta, L. (1988). Concept acquisition in noisy environments. *IEEE Transactions on Pattern Analysis and Machine Intelligence, 10*, 555–578. doi:10.1109/34.3917

Biba, M., Basile, T. M. A., Ferilli, S., & Esposito, F. (2006). Improving Scalability in ILP Incremental Systems. Proceedings of CILC 2006 - Italian Conference on Computational Logic, Bari, Italy, June 26-27.

Biba, M., Ferilli, S., Esposito, F., Di Mauro, N., & Basile, T.M.A. (2006). A Fast Partial Memory Approach to Incremental Learning through an Advanced Data Storage Framework.

Biermann, A. W., & Feldman, J. A. (1972). On the synthesis of finite-state machines from samples of their behavior. *IEEE Transactions on Computers*, *C*(21), 592–597. doi:10.1109/TC.1972.5009015

Biermann, A. W., & Krishnaswamy, R. (1976). Constructing programs from example computations. *IEEE Transactions on Software Engineering*, *2*(3). doi:10.1109/TSE.1976.233812

Bostrom, H. (1998). Predicate Invention and Learning from Positive Examples Only. In Proceedings of the Tenth European Conference on Machine Learning. (pp 226-237). Springer Verlag.

Bratko, I., & Muggleton, S. (1995). Applications of Inductive Logic Programming. *Communications of the ACM*, *38*(11), 65–70. doi:10.1145/219717.219771

Bredeche, N., Chevaleyre, Y., Zucker, J.-D., Drogoul, A., & Sabah, G. (2003). *A meta-learning approach to ground symbols from visual percepts. Robotics and Autonomous Systems journal, special issue on Anchoring Symbols to Sensor Data in Single and Multiple Robot Systems*. Elsevier.

Cohen, W.W. & Page, C.D. (1995). Learnability in Inductive Logic Programming: Methods and Results. New Generation Computing 13(1-2)

De Raedt, L., & Kersting, K. (2004). Probabilistic Logic Learning. *SIGKDD Explorations*, *2*(2), 1–18.

De Raedt, L., & Lavrac, N. (1993). The many faces of inductive logic programming. In Proceedings of the 7th International Symposium on Methodologies for Intelligent Systems: Lecture Notes on Artificial Intelligence, Springer-Verlag.

Deville, Y., & Lau, K. (1993). Logic Program Synthesis. Journal of Logic Programming, Special Issue.

Dolsak, B., Bratko, I., & Jezernik, A. (1998). Knowledge base for finite-element mesh design learned by inductive logic programming. *AIEDAM*, *12*(2), 95–106.

Dolsak, B., & Muggleton, S. (1992). The application of inductive logic programming to finite element mesh design. In Muggleton, S. (Ed.), Inductive Logic Programming, 453-472, Academic Press, London.

Domingos, P., Kok, S., Poon, H., Richardson, M., & Singla, P. (2006). Unifying Logical and Statistical AI. In Proceedings of the Twenty-First National Conference on Artificial Intelligence 2-7, Boston, MA.

Feng, C. (1992). Inducing temporal fault diagnostic rules from a qualitative model. In Muggleton, S. (Ed.), *Inductive Logic Programming*. London: Academic Press.

Garcia-Martinez, R. (2000). An Integrated Approach of Learning, Planning, and Execution. *Journal of Intelligent & Robotic Systems*, *29*, 47–78. doi:10.1023/A:1008134010576

Getoor L. & Taskar B. (2007, November). Introduction to Statistical Relational Learning, MIT Press.

Goertzel, B., Ikle, M., Goertzel, I. L. F., & Heljakka, A. (2008, in press). Probabilistic Logic Networks: A Comprehensive Framework for Uncertain Inference, Springer.

Gold, E. M. (1967). Language identification in the limit. *Information and Control*, *10*, 447–474. doi:10.1016/S0019-9958(67)91165-5

Grobelnik, M. (1992). MARKUS: An optimized Model inference System. Workshop on Logical Approaches to Machine Learning, Tenth European Conference on AI, Vienna, Austria.

Inuzuka, N., Onda, T., & Itoh, H. (2000). Learning Robot Control by Relational Concept Induction with Iteratively Collected Examples. In Wyatt, J., & Demiris, J. (Eds.), *EWLR 1999, LNAI 1812* (pp. 71–83). Springer-Verlag Berlin Heidelberg.

Jappy, P., Nock, R., & Gascuel, O. (1996). Negative Robust Learnability results for Horn Clause Programs. International Conference on Machine Learning, Barri, 258-265.

Kietz, J.-U., & Dzeroski, S. (1994). Inductive Logic Programming and Learnability, SIGART Bulletin, Vol. 5, No. 1.

King, R. (2005). The Robot Scientist Project. In the Proceedings of the 8th International Conference on Discovery Science, Lecture Notes in Artificial Intelligence Vol. 3735.

King, R., Muggleton, S., Lewis, R., & Sternberg, M. (1992). Drug design by machine learning: The use of inductive logic programming to model the structure activity relationships of thrimethorpin analogus binding to dihydrofolate reductase. *Proceedings of the National Academy of Sciences of the United States of America, 89*(23), 11322–11326. doi:10.1073/pnas.89.23.11322

Klingspor, V., Morik, K., & Rieger, A. (1996). Learning Concepts from Sensor Data of a Mobile Robot. *Machine Learning, 23*(2/3), 305–332. doi:10.1023/A:1018245209731

Lavrac, N., & Dzeroski, S. (1994). *Inductive Logic Programming: Techniques and Applications.* New York: Ellis Horwood.

Lavrac, N., Dzeroski, S., & Grobelnik, M. (1991). *Learning nonrecursive definitions of relations with LINUS* (pp. 265–281). Berlin: Fifth European Working Session on Learning.

Lavrac, N., Dzeroski, S., Pirnat, V., & Krizman, V. (1993). The use of background knowledge in learning medical diagnostic rules. *Applied Artificial Intelligence, 7*, 273–293. doi:10.1080/08839519308949989

Lorenzo, D. (2002). Learning non-monotonic causal theories from narratives of actions, In Proceedings of The 9th International Workshop on Non-Monotonic Reasoning NMR'2002, Toulouse, France.

Lorenzo, D., & Otero, R. P. (2000). Learning to reason about actions. In Horn, W. (Ed.). Proceedings of the Fourteenth European Conference on Artificial Intelligence, IOS Press, Amsterdam.

Maloof, M., & Michalski, R. (2000). Selecting examples for partial memory learning. *Machine Learning, 41*, 27–52. doi:10.1023/A:1007661119649

Marcinkowski, J., & Pacholski, L. (1992). Undecidability of the Hornclanse implication problem. In Proc. 33rd Annual IEEE Symposium on Foundations of Computer Science, pages 354-362.

Moore, E. F. (1956). Gedanken-experiments on sequential machines. In Shannon, C.E. & McCarthy, J., (Ed.), Automata Studies, 129-153, Princeton University Press, Princeton, NJ.

Muggleton, S., & De Raedt, L. (1994). ILP: Theory and Methods. Journal of Logic Programming, 19 and 20, 629-679.

Page, D. (2000). ILP: Just Do It. In Proceedings of Computational Logic 2000, Lloyd, Dahl, Kerber, Lau, Palamidissi, Pereira, Sagiv, Stuckey (Eds), Berlin: Springer, LNAI 1861, pp. 25-40.

Quinlan, J. (1990). Learning logical definitions from relations. *Machine Learning, 5*(3), 239–266. doi:10.1007/BF00117105

Richardson, M., & Domingos, P. (2006). Markov Logic Networks. *Machine Learning, 62*, 107–136. doi:10.1007/s10994-006-5833-1

Rieger, A. (1995). Data preparation for inductive learning in robotics. In Working Notes of the IJCAI Workshop on Data Engineering for Inductive Learning.

Russel, S., & Norvig, P. (2002). *AI: The Modern Approach*. Pearson Education, Inc.

Sammut, C., & Banerji, R. (1986). Learning concepts by asking questions. Machine Learning: An Artificial Intelligence Aproach, II, 167-191, Morgan-Kaufmann, San Mateo, CA.

Schmidt-Schauss, M. (1988). Implication of clauses is undecidable. *Theoretical Computer Science, 59,* 287–296. doi:10.1016/0304-3975(88)90146-6

Shapiro, E. Y. (1983). *Algorithmic program debugging.* MIT Press.

Stojanov, G., & Kulakov, A. (2006). On Curiosity in Intelligent Robotic Systems. AAAI Fall Symposia, Arlington, VA, USA, October 12-15.

Summers, P. D. (1975). Program construction from examples. PhD thesis, Yale University, New Haven, CT.

Valiant, L. G. (1984). A theory of the learnable. *Communications of the ACM, 27,* 1134–1142. doi:10.1145/1968.1972

Voelcke, J. (2007, November). Autonomous Vehicles Complete DARPA Urban Challenge. IEEE Spectrum.

This work was previously published in International Journal of Agent Technologies and Systems (IJATS), edited by Goran Trajkovski, pp. 34-49, copyright 2009 by IGI Publishing (an imprint of IGI Global).

Chapter 9
Cognitive Robotics and Multiagency in a Fuzzy Modeling Framework

Goran Trajkovski
Algoco eLearning Consulting, USA

Georgi Stojanov
The American University in Paris, France

Samuel Collins
Towson University, USA

Vladimir Eidelman
Columbia University, USA

Chris Harman
Swarthmore College, USA

Giovanni Vincenti
Gruppo Vincenti, S.r.l., Italy

ABSTRACT

Fuzzy algebraic structures are a useful and flexible tool for modeling cognitive agents and their societies. In this article we propose a fuzzy algebraic framework where the valuating sets are other than the unit interval (lattices, partially ordered sets or relational structures). This provides for a flexible organization of the information gathered by the agent (via interactions with the environment and/or other agents) and enables its selected use when different drives are active. Agents (Petitagé, ANNA, POPSICLE and Izbushka), which are instantiations of our model, are also given in order to illustrate the use of this framework, as well as its possible extensions.

DOI: 10.4018/978-1-60960-171-3.ch009

Copyright © 2011, IGI Global. Copying or distributing in print or electronic forms without written permission of IGI Global is prohibited.

INTRODUCTION

Powerful tools, capable of capturing relevant parts of the world, as well as flexible enough to enable customized views of behaviors, are necessary when observing and calibrating cognitive agents in single and multiagent environments. This need becomes even more apparent when observing the interaction between the agent and the environment, the agents themselves, and while studying the emergence of new phenomena in such setups. Due to the extension of ranks, fuzzy structures enable for a more flexible and anthropomorphic toolset for frameworks within which we study the agents, environment, interaction, and other related phenomena.

When fuzzifying crisp algebraic and relational structures, we usually change the rank of the characteristic function of either the carrier of the structure, or of the operations/relations of the systems (observed as sets themselves) from the two-element set $\{0, 1\}$ to the unit interval $[0, 1]$. For our modeling purposes, we introduce further generalizations. The unit interval is a special case of a lattice, every lattice a partially ordered set (poset), and each poset a relational structure. For our cognitive model, we utilize algebraic structures valued by lattices (L-fuzzy structures), posets (P-fuzzy structures), and relational structures (R-fuzzy structures).

Within these efforts, in this article we observe fuzzy algebraic structures as a base for our interactivist model of agency. Based on their experiences from the stay in an initially unknown environment, our agents build associations of expectancies of the general form $percept_1$-$action_0$-$percept_2$ (meaning that if it perceives $percept_1$ and applies $action_0$ it expects to see $percept_2$) and attribute to them drive-related emotional contexts. The exploration of the environment is governed by a Piagetian inborn scheme, a sequence of actions that an agent aims to execute in its search for a place where it can satisfy its active drive(s).

We will be presenting the below consideration using language as if applied to an autonomous mobile agent in a 2D environment, executing actions like forward, left, etc. This simplification does not hurt the exposition on the approach when applied to other types of environments (3D, cyberspace etc.), and actions (different from actual physical movements from one spot in the environment to another).

The article is organized as follows. Section 2 gives the cognitive agency and fuzzy algebraic preliminaries needed for the presentation of the cognitive agent in Section 3. Section 4 gives examples of cognitive agents within the fuzzy algebraic framework: Petitagé, our first complete cognitive agent, and its implementation in PYRO; ANNA, a cognitive agent with a neural network approach to learning; POPSICLE, as an environment for harvesting information from human subjects for the purpose of calibrating the simulation models; Izbushka, an agent-environment that couples with users, defining its goals via the interaction with the human partner. The last section overviews the article and gives directions for further research.

PRELIMINARIES

Below we present our view on agency and multiagency, as well as the fuzzy algebraic structure preliminaries necessary to introduce our new fuzzy algebraic definition of the cognitive agent.

Cognitive Agency

Crucial to the agent's performance is the intrinsic representation of its environment that it builds when it interacts with the environment (or other agents). Due to perceptual resolution, problems such as perceptual and/or cognitive aliasing arise (Trajkovski 2007). For example, two locally distinct places of the environment might be perceived the same way by the agent. All that the agent can rely on at that point is the context of the place it is in, as (unlike approaches in traditional Artificial Intelligence) it is not being spoon-fed the whole environment. The term context here refers to experiences that the agent has had immediately preceding its arrival at its present position. The agent enters the environment as a blank slate, and proceeds to build a functional representation of it. The agent's behavior depends on the inborn scheme of action that it tries to execute, and it notes the percepts that result from the execution of a subpart of its scheme, as inspired by the infant development studies of Jean Piaget (1973).

In our analyses, we distinguish between two distinct classes of perspectives in observing a given environment: ontology (ALF - Agent Learning Framework), as the view of the designer (meta-observer), and gnoseology, the view of the individual agent, as formalized below (Trajkovski & Vincenti 2005). Due to sensory restrictions in realistic environments, the two views do not coincide. We refer to the phenomenon when two locally distinct places are perceived the same by an agent as perceptual aliasing. Let $V = \{v_1, v_2,..., v_n\}$ be vertices denoting locally distinct places in the environment that can be reached by the agent, and $A = \{s_1, s_2,..., s_m\}$ the action repertoire of an agent, i. e. the set of actions it is able to perform. Then the structure $G = (V, A, r)$ (where $r \subseteq (V \times V) \times A$, $((u, v), s) \in r$ if and only if the agent is taken from $u \in V$ to $v \in V$ by the action $s \in A$) shows where the agents ends up after the execution of each one of its actions.

Also, let $L = \{l_1, l_2,..., l_k\}$ be a set of labels (perceptual resolution of an agent) and $f:V \to L$ a surjective mapping (perceptual aliasing), that denotes what an agent sees when located at vertex V. Then the quintuple

$$G'' = (V, A, L, r, f)$$

will denote the ontology (ALF). The relation r induces the structure $r''' \subseteq (L \times L) \times A$ (such that $((f(v_1), f(v_2)), s) \in r'''$ if and only if $((v_1, v_2), s) \in r)$. The triplet

Figure 1. The main components of our cognitive agent

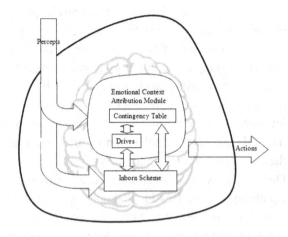

$$G''' = (L, r''', A)$$

now represents the gnoseology of a given agent.

As we said, the agent (Figure 1) enters the environment as a blank slate. Based on the topology of the environment (and especially the positions of the obstacles) the agent will execute (or not) actions from its inborn scheme. The successful actions executed from the scheme and the percepts associated with the actions in the subscheme build the intrinsic representation of the environment of the agent. Bumping into an obstacle (a wall) increases pain. The drive to avoid pain is omnipresent during an agent's sojourn in any environment.

The governing procedure (Figure 2) of the learning process is the building of the intrinsic representation of the environment that serves as a working memory for the individual agent. Its content is based on the experiences an agent has had while being in the given environment. The agent's actions are determined by the action sequence in the inborn scheme. The agent tries to execute the next action in the scheme; if the trial is successful, it records the perceptual context of the place where the action relocated it. By the time the agent has tried to execute all the actions in its scheme, it has executed a subscheme (a

Figure 2. The learning procedure in our cognitive agent (Stojanov, Trajkovski & Božinovski 1997)

```
Generate_Intrinsic_Representation (G: Interaction_Graph, ξ: Schema; GIR: Assotiative_Memory, D: SetOfDrives)
BEGIN_PROCEDURE
        Initialize (R_A = ∅) ;
        Initialize_Position (G; Position) ;
        Try (Position, ξ; (B_1, S_1) ) ;
        Add ([ (λ, λ), (B_1, S_1) ]; R_A) ;
        WHILE (Active_Drive_Not_Satisfied) DO
        BEGIN_WHILE
                Try (Position, ξ; (B_2, S_2) ) ;
                Add ([ (B_1, S_1), (B_2, S_2) ]; R_A) ;
                (B_1, S_1) : = (B_2, S_2) ;
        END_WHILE
        Propagate_Context ((B_1, S_1), drive; GIR).
END_PROCEDURE


Try (Position: Location_In_Interaction_Graph, ξ: Schema; (B, S) : Percepts_Actions_Pair)
BEGIN_PROCEDURE
        S: = λ;
        TryIn (Position, ξ; (Add (S, Currfent_Percept), B) ) ;
        REPEAT
                TryIn (Position, B; (Add (S, Current_Percept), B)
        UNTIL NOT enabled (B)
END_PROCEDURE


Propagate_Context (d: drive; GIR: Assotiative_Memory)
BEGIN_PROCEDURE
        N: = 0;
        WHILE (B_1, S_1) ∈ Projection_2 (GIR) DO
        BEGIN_WHILE
                Projection_3 (GIR) : = exp (-N) ;
                INC (N)
        END_WHILE
END_PROCEDURE
```

sequence of actions that are a subset of those in the scheme, and follow the relative order of precedence of execution as the order in the scheme), and "remembered" the percepts seen during the execution of the subscheme. At this time it checks to see if it had experienced the same subscheme-perceptual context pairs before, creating an expectation for the experience to follow. If the expected experience does not occur as it has in the past, the agent registers a surprise while attempting to execute the inborn scheme again.

Once the agent finds a place in the environment that satisfies its active drive (say hunger), it propagates a positive emotional context back to all of the experiences recorded since the last activation of the drive. The emotional context, a value discussed in context of a drive only, is a measure of usefulness of a given experience on the way to satisfying a drive. For more details and experiments relative to the emotional context of experiences in an agent, see (Trajkovski 2003, 2007).

Multiagency Considerations

As we move from the single agent to the multiagent environments, we need to model the inter-agent interaction on a higher level than the interaction between the agent and the physical environment. If the agents do not register each other except as part of the physical environment, the discussion collapses to one about a discrete union of individual agents in single agent dynamic environments.

With the promise of mirror neurons (Rizzolatti et al. 1996) as being the human hardware for imitation, the phenomenon of imitation is receiving a lot of attention lately as a model of early learning. We adopt it as a model for exchanging experiences between the agents in our multiagent society. Our cognitive agents are equipped with a special sensor especially for sensing other akin agents in the same environment. Sensing another agent takes the agent into imitation mode, during which information about the environment relative to the active drive (s) is being exchanged (Trajkovski

2002), as well as concepts, or even proto-linguistic constructs (Bisbey & Trajkovski 2005).

Fuzzy Algebraic Structures

Inspired by our previous work in the domain of L-fuzzy lattices (Tepavčević & Trajkovski 2001), here we give an approach to fuzzification of algebraic structures that we use in the next section as grounds for our fuzzy model of cognitive agents. The discussion will mainly be focused on the fuzzification of the structures by replacing the valuating structure, the unit interval, with a complete lattice (L-fuzzy structures), whereas the P- and R- generalizations will be mentioned only at the beginning of the section to illustrate the general approach that can be followed for all structures discussed in the context of L-fuzzification. Therefore, unless specifically denoted, the term fuzzy structure in this article relates to L-fuzzy structures.

When we fuzzify a set, we change the rank of the characteristic function of the set and explore the augmentation of features in the generalized set, attributed mostly by what the valuating lattice brings into the picture.

Let $(L, \wedge, \vee)$ be a complete lattice with bottom 0 and top 1, and let X be a nonempty set. Then the mapping $\mu: X^2 \to L$ is an L-fuzzy relation on the set X. Let $p \in L$. Then the p-level cut of μ is the mapping $\mu_p: X^2 \to \{0, 1\}$, such that $\mu_p(x, y) = 1$ if and only if $\mu(x, y) \geq p$. An L-fuzzy relation is reflexive if for all $x \in X$, $\mu(x, x) = 1$; it is weakly reflexive if for all pairs x, $y \in X$, $\mu(x, x) \geq \mu(x, y)$; antisymmetric if for all pairs x, $y \in X$, $x \neq y$: $\mu(x, y)$ $\wedge \mu(y, x) = 0$; transitive if for all x, y, $z \in X$: $\mu(x, y) \wedge \mu(y, z) \leq \mu(x, z)$.

For the P- and R- fuzzy structures, the valuating structure is a poset, and a relationship structure with the UP (unique projection) property respectively. If $R = (S, \rho)$ is a relational system with a carrier S and relation ρ, and the relation ρ_1 is defined via

$$\rho_1(x) = \{y \in S \mid (y, x) \in \rho\}, x \in S$$

and if for all elements

$$x, y \in S, x \neq y \Rightarrow \rho_1(x) \neq \rho_1(y)$$

then the system is said to have the UP property (Šešelja & Tepavčević 1995).

The straightforward approach to fuzzifying an algebraic structure would be to fuzzify the characteristic function of the carrier. But, as we can observe the operational (and/or relational) set of the structure as sets, we can fuzzify their characteristic functions. We will illustrate some of the choices that we have examined in the case of L-fuzzy lattices, and eventually we will see that with minimal interventions, the three approaches derive structures that can be easily re-represented into any of the other two: by fuzzification of the characteristic function of the carrier (L^M fuzzy lattices), by fuzzification of the ordering (L^O fuzzy lattices), and by fuzzification of both the carrier membership and the ordering simultaneously (Šostak fuzzy lattices). Also, by choosing different generalizations of the definitions of L-fuzzy lattices, we get two different classes of L-fuzzy lattices, the second a super class of the first. In the first definition we insist for the level cuts to be sub-lattices of the carrier structure, whereas for the second we only require the cuts to be lattices per sé. We will be denoting the valuating lattice as $L = (L, \leq)$, and its corresponding algebraic version will be denoted by the triplet $(L, \wedge, \vee)$. The conversion, i.e. re-representation of a lattice from the relational representation into the algebraic and vice versa are well known (Birkhoff 1984).

If $(M, \wedge_M, \vee_M)$ is a crisp lattice, then the mapping $\mu: M \to L$ is an L^M fuzzy lattice of type 1 if all of its p-cuts ($p \in L$) are sublattices of M (Figure 3). If all the cuts are lattices per sé, and not necessarily sublattices of M, then we are talking about L^M fuzzy lattices of type 2 (example in Figure 4). Šostak lattices are defined when the fuzzification of both the characteristic function

Figure 3. All cuts of the fuzzy lattice

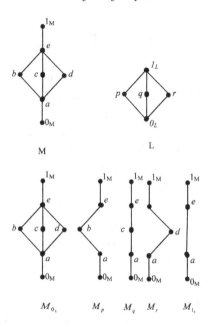

Figure 4. Not all cuts of the fuzzy lattice

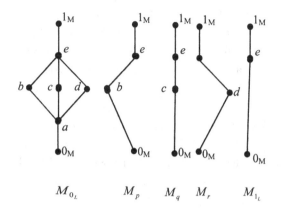

of the lattice carrier, and of the ordering relation happen simultaneously.

Are sublattices of $M = \{0_M, a, b, c, d, e, 1_M\}$, when valued by $L = \{0_L, p, q, r, 1_L\}$ via μ. Thus μ is an L-fuzzy lattice of type 1.

Are sublattices of $M = \{0_M, a, b, c, d, e, 1_M\}$, when valued by $L = \{0_L, p, q, r, 1_L\}$ (with orderings as in Figure 3) via μ, but they are still all lattices per sé. Therefore μ is an L-fuzzy lattice of type 2.

The L^M fuzzy lattices of type 1 bear some nice properties that give us alternative ways of defining attributes of the agent. For example, $\mu: M \to L$ is an L^M fuzzy lattice of type 1 if and only if for all x, y∈M both of the following inequalities hold simultaneously (Tepavčević & Trajkovski 2001): $\mu(x \wedge_M y) \geq \mu(x) \wedge_L \mu(y)$, and $\mu(x \vee_M y) \geq \mu(x) \wedge_L \mu(y)$, or if and only if $\mu(x \wedge_M y) \vee_L \mu(x \vee_M y) \geq \mu(x) \wedge_L \mu(y)$. Analogous theorems can be proven for L^M fuzzy lattices of type 2.

Now, let's observe L-fuzzy lattices obtained by fuzzification of the ordering relation in a crisp lattice (L^O fuzzy lattices). We assume here that the valuating lattice $(L, \leq)$ is complete, with bottom

0_L and top 1_L. Moreover, the notation L' would stand for the linear sum $L' = 0 \oplus L$, where 0 is a special one-element lattice, and 0 is not an element of L. Let $\rho: M^2 \to L'$ be an L-fuzzy relation, and for p∈L', the following set is defined

$$= \{x \in M \mid \rho_p(x, x) = 1\}.$$

If M is nonempty, then the pair (M, ρ), where $\rho: M^2 \to L'$ is an L-fuzzy relation, is an L^O fuzzy lattice of type 1 if and only if the structure (M, ρ_0) is a lattice and all of its p-cuts (p∈L) are its sublattices. Respectively, we shall be talking about type 2 lattices if the p-cuts are lattices per sé, not necessarily sublattices of M. We need to mention here that a p-level relation ρ_p is a sublattice of, when it is observed as a candidate for a lattice over the following set

$$= \{x \in M \mid \rho_p(x, x) = 1\}.$$

Alternatively, $\rho: M^2 \to L'$ is an L^O type 1 lattice if and only if the following conditions hold (Trajkovski 1997):

1. ρ is a weak fuzzy ordering relation;
2. For all x, y∈M, there exists an element S∈M, such that for all $p \in \{0_L\} \cup \{p \in L \mid x, y \in \}$

$\rho(x, S) \geq p$ and $\rho(y, S) \geq p$, and for all $s \in M$, $\rho(x, s) \geq p \wedge \rho(y, s) \geq p \Rightarrow \rho(S, s) \geq p$;

3. For all $x, y \in M$, there is an element $I \in M$, so that for $p \in \{0_L\} \cup \{p \in L \mid x, y \in \}$ $\rho(I, x) \geq p$, and $\rho(I, y) \geq p$, and for all $i \in M$, $\rho(i, x) \geq p \wedge \rho(i, y) \geq p \Rightarrow \rho(i, I) \geq p$.

We have also given algorithms for conversion from the L^O to L^M fuzzy lattices of type 1 and vice versa as follows (Trajkovski 1998). Let $\mu: M \to L$ be an L^M fuzzy lattice of type 1, where $(M, \wedge, \vee)$ is a lattice and let $L' = 0 \oplus L$. Then, the mapping $\rho: M^2 \to L'$ defined by

$$\rho(x, y) = m(x) \wedge_L m(y) \text{ for } x \leq y$$

and $\rho(x, y) = 0$, otherwise is an L^O fuzzy lattice of type 1. Moreover, M_p and (ρ_p), for $p \in L$ are the same (crisp) sublattices of M. Conversely, if $\rho: M^2 \to L'$ is an L^O fuzzy lattice of type 1, where $L' = 0 \oplus L$ is a complete lattice with a unique atom 0_L, top element 1_L and the bottom element 0. Then, the mapping $\mu: M \to L$ defined with $\mu(x) = \rho(x, x), x \in M$, is an L^M fuzzy lattice of type 1, with a reference lattice. Moreover, the cuts μ_p and $(, \rho_p)$ are the same sublattices of M for fixed $p \in L$. The same algorithm can also be applied for rerepresentation of fuzzy lattices of type 2.

Then the mapping $\mu: M \to L$ is a Šostak-M lattice (L^M fuzzy lattice of type 3) if all of its p-cuts ($p \in L$) are posets whose ordering relation is a subset of the ordering of the lattice M. Similarly, if $\mu: M \to L$ and $\rho: M^2 \to L$, are mappings such that for all $x, y \in M$: $\rho(x, y) \leq m(x) \wedge_L m(y)$, the pair (μ, ρ) is a Šostak-O (L^O fuzzy lattice of type 3) fuzzy lattice. The two structures of type 3 are equivalent, and are congruent to Šostak's definitions of fuzzy categories (Šostak 1997).

THE COGNITIVE AGENT

The Fuzzy Definition of an Agent

The main motivation for considering alternatively-valued fuzzy algebraic structures as a framework for modeling cognitive agents comes from well known psychological studies on human drives and motivation. It is believed (after Maslow (1954)) that human drives are hierarchical in nature. As drives are a central part of our definition of an agent, and as the agent needs different parts of the operative memory to function when different drives are active, the definition of the cognitive agent is easy to state. We use the previous definitions of ontology and agent gnoseology, and choose for $D = (D, \leq)$ (the nonempty set D has cardinality R) to be the lattice (poset, relational structure) of drives of the agent, ordered by a binary relation of hierarchy $\leq \subseteq D \times D$. Drives, as previously stated, are central to our cognitive agent (Figure 1).

The vector-valued mapping $f: V \to \{0,1\}^R$, visible by the designer, and defined via

$$f(v_j) = (e_1, e_2, \ldots, e_R), v_j \in V, j = 1, 2, \ldots, n,$$

defines the scheme of supply in the environment. The component e_i ($i = 1, 2, \ldots, R$) of has $f(v_j)$ a zero value if the i-th drive of the agent cannot be satisfied at v_j, or 1 otherwise (Further, instead of constants, the e_i's can be functions of supply for the different vertices, and would denote the amount of drive satisfiers, such as food, or water, at a given point in time). The vector-valued mapping $d: T \to \{0,1\}^R$ (T-discrete time set), is the drive activation pattern for the agent. The i-th component of d at a given time tells us whether the i-th drive is active.

So, now the structure $G_{GIO} = (V, A, L, D, d, r, f, \phi)$ represents the ALF/ontology, the context within which us as designers, design our experiments for observations.

Let $\Sigma \subseteq A^*$ and let $\xi = b_1 b_2 \ldots b_k$ be the inborn scheme of the agent. A subscheme of ξ is any sequence of actions..., $i_j = 1,2,\ldots k$, $i_1 < i_2 < \ldots < i_p$. We will denote by B_ξ the set of all possible subschemes of ξ. The longest possible subscheme that can be executed from a given vertex v^* is said to the filter of ξ in v^*.

We will now define the relation τ, of key importance in the theory, as a fuzzy binary relation valued by the structure of drives:

$$t: (B_x \times L^*)^2 D \to \times [0,1]$$

where L^* is the set of all possible sequences of perceptions (labels), defined as follows:

$$t((B_i, S_i), (B_j, S_j)) = (d_w, e_w),$$

If there is such a node $v^* \in V$, such that after executing the filter B_i while experiencing a perceptual string S_j, the agent gets to execute a filter B_j and registers S_j. e_w is the emotional context of the expectancy $(B_i, S_i), (B_j, S_j)$ for the drive d_w and is a measure of how useful the expectancy has been in satisfying the drive d_w. So, now, the quadruplet $AA = (L, A, D, \tau)$, where L is the set of percepts, A the agent's action repertoire, D the set of drives, and τ the agent's intrinsic representation of the environment is the formal definition of a cognitive agent. This is congruent with our definition of an agent (Trajkovski 2007), as any manmade or artificial artifact exhibiting autonomy, proactivity and intentionality.

Given a set of agents C, specifying when and where they entered the environment, (G_{GIO}, C) defines the multiagent environment. If all agents in C are the same in the sense of drives, schemes and learning algorithms, we speak of a homogenous society; otherwise the society is heterogeneous. Further considerations of the issues in the societies can be found in (Trajkovski 2007). Central to the societies of agents is inter-agent communication, as a method for exchanging information. In the next section we discuss some of the modalities that we have experimented with.

EXAMPLES OF AGENTS BASED ON THE FRAMEWORK

Petitagé, Our First Complete Cognitive Architecture

Petitagé (pronounced: /pee-ah-zhe/) was our first complete "cognitive architecture" (Stojanov, Božinovski & Trajkovski 1997). It was inspired by a simple add-on mechanism to an existing behavior control mechanism in an autonomous agent (Stojanov et al., 1995). This idea is fairly simple, i.e. the architecture of some autonomous system is controlled by the "Control Mechanism"; it computes whatever should be done given the particular sensory input. The augmented architecture has an Expectancy Module (EM) which maintains a table of triplets where one row has the form of (Sensory_readings_at_t, Action_taken_at_t, Expected_sensory_readings_at_t+1), where t denotes time.

Initially, the expectancy module table is empty, and it is filled (it learns) as the agent interacts with an environment. After a while, it can predict the consequences of some action taken in a particular context, and it controls the agent, speeding up its performance, since the EM basically is a look-up table. However, when an expectancy is not met (e. g. cases where there are some changes in the environment) an expectancy break signal is sent to the control mechanism and it computes the new output value for the actuators.

This architecture was inspired by Edward Tolman's expectancy construct (1948). Tolman, a neobehaviorist has stressed the role of anticipation, and the need for some internal (mentalistic) structures to be introduced in the basic behaviorist stimulus-reaction (S-R) paradigm, in order to account for the results of some of his rats-in mazes experiments (Tolman & Hoznik 1930, Tolman

1932). Thus, the basic representational unit is the expectancy unit S_1-R-S_2 (stimulus-reaction-stimulus), and it incorporates both sensory and motor information. Therefore, if the agent is assumed to be able to build a network of such expectancy units, then various experimental results have natural explanations.

The next challenge was how to account for situations where different places the agents visits collapse into the same sensory image S (e. g. if the agent is facing a corner of a square room, which corner is it?).

Perceptual aliasing is a common problem in agency, and has been neglected or avoided by traditional Artificial Intelligence since its inception. For example, it was shown that the majority of reinforcement learning (RL) algorithms are properly treated within the dynamic programming framework (Barto et al. 1995). RL methods which use dynamic programming as a mathematical framework require that the environment be represented to the agent via some set of distinct labels (i. e. different "S"s for every place). This puts constraints on the domains where such methods could be used. In our opinion, the major problem is not learning the path to the goal if you have a model of the environment given as an implicit or explicit graph, but to autonomously come up with such a representation.

Jean Piaget's genetic epistemology and the wealth of experimental data and theoretical musings looked to us as a natural departing point. In a nutshell, his theory of cognitive development in humans is a process of a) spontaneous execution of inborn sensory-motor schemes b) building partial ordering in this space of modified, and newly formed schemes, as a result of the processes of assimilation and accommodation; c) interiorization of these operations by the acting agent. Naturally, the notion of scheme is central in our cognitive agent architecture.

Agents built on the basis of the architecture described in the previous section successfully solved navigational problems where classical

reinforcement learning (RL) architectures were helpless because of perceptual aliasing. However, this was not the main intention with this architecture. The idea was to leave the task of building an intrinsic representation of the environment to the agent itself, which we consider to be far more important. Further refinement of this basic model meant looking for regularities in the stream of enabled schemes. As a higher level of abstraction, we have added a mechanism for detection of cycles in the stream of enabled schemes. A cycle is detected when the same sequence of enabled scheme accompanied with the same perceptual strings is encountered for more than n times where n is a heuristically determined constant. Having completed an enabled scheme while in a cycle, the agent can decide not to follow the actions dictated by the next enabled scheme, but to perform a random action instead, and possibly end up in a different cycle. The action is then memorized as connecting those two cycles.

Details of the Implementation of Petitage in PYRO

PYRO (PYthon RObotics) provides for easy control of either a physical or simulated robot through abstracted access to all of the robots controls (Blank et al. 2005). Examples of abstracted robot controls utilized in this implementation are: movement, rotation, camera vision, robot grippers, and sonar range sensors. The abstraction of these devices allows for immediate immersion into the project's implementation, rather than typical pre-project middling with complicated robot controls.

In this implementation, the robot's action repertoire is simple - it includes four compass directions: north, south, east and west, navigation towards a goal in sight and a dynamic obstacle avoidance function. The robot's inborn scheme is crucial to robot movement within the environment: the robot follows a direction until a collision is imminent, then turns in the direction away from the minimum sensor reading. The robot is equipped with sonar

Figure 5. Robot's operating environment with food and eight frontal sensors shown

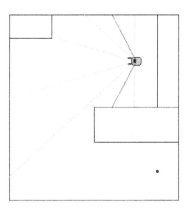

Figure 6. Example of situations when perceptual aliasing occurs. Although the robot the agent is at three locally distinct places, due to sensory limitations, it perceives them as identical

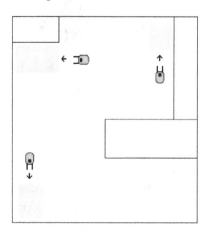

sensors and several devices which facilitate goal satisfaction and environmental navigation.

Depending on specification, eight or sixteen sensors project radially outward from the robot, and these sensors detect the respective distance from the robot to an object in the environment. These sensors serve as the robot's 'eyes' and allow for environmental categorization of similar sensor readings. The robot is also equipped with a camera used exclusively for detecting nearby food. The camera utilizes a blobify function to draw a box around red objects and reports back the pixel dimensions of the box. This allows for smooth navigation to food once in close proximity (assuming food is in front of robot's path). The robot is equipped with a gripper capable of storing and deploying a red puck (food).

The robot's environment is infinitely changeable, but testing was performed in a relatively simple single agent setting (Figure 5). As discussed above, a common problem for any robot performing goal-directed environmental navigation is perceptual aliasing. In Figure 6, we show the test environment with areas of possible perceptual aliasing highlighted.

Within our framework, environmental navigation and goal finding require that a robot have a sensor matching system capable of recognizing a remembered state. Artificial neural networks

(ANNs) have been shown to be successful categorizers (Luger 2002). For this reason, it seemed intuitive that a neural network would be well suited to recognizing various environmental states. The fuzzy ARTMAP neural network is one of the logical choices for categorizing and recognizing previously visited states because of its proficiency self-organizing analog multidimensional maps (Carpenter et al. 1992). Via Figure 7 we can diagnose regions of perceptual aliasing in the environment.

Our model describes a method of remembered interaction with the environment that relies on a contingency table for lookup of previously visited states, where each row of a contingency table represents a state. Each of the previously visited states has associated with it a number in the unit interval [0, 1] referred to as emotional context that has inherent information about reliability and favorability. The emotional context essentially links two environmental states and the robot's movement between the two. The emotional context must exceed a defined reliability threshold in order for the robot to take action based on the information contained in a given row.

Figure 7. (a) The defined environmental regions; (b) juxtaposed with the environment as classified by the agent; note the areas of perceptual aliasing in Figure 6 present a challenge for the agent

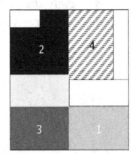 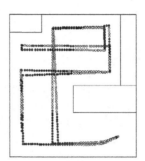

The robot operates with two tables at all times. The first stores the robot's moves in chronological order to allow for easy context propagation. Context propagation occurs when the robot's goal is met (in this case food is found and gripped). Emotional context propagation involves looking through the entire path the robot took to the goal. The last move taken from a given environmental region is recorded and is deemed favorable, meaning, its emotional context is increased. The environmental regions are ensured to be accurate within the context propagation function by checking that the region is identified consecutively at least five times in the chronological table. The rows with favorable context are then inserted into the contingency table. Insertion into the contingency table entails looking through the table for an identical row (one with the same region and compass direction identified) ; if there is an identical row, the context of that move is increased accordingly; otherwise, the row is inserted normally.

The second (contingency) table is prioritized based on emotional context and only stores rows that have a favorable context. The second contingency table is searched through before every execution of the inborn scheme in hopes of identifying a direction to follow that would lead the robot to food. In order for a row of the second contingency table to be acted upon, the emotional context associated with the given row must surpass an experimentally optimized reliability threshold.

This means that the robot must find food several times and establish sufficiently reliable routes and, as a counterpoint, moves with unproven reliability are suppressed, a biologically inspired solution to effective goal satisfaction (Figure 8).

Multiple Homogenous Agents

In the multiagent system, the interaction of the agents within the environment is correspondent to the human action of direction giving. The exchange is complicated by the fact that one robot has no access to the internal state of the other. This means that the direction giving is not consensual. The direction-receiving robot acts as a pickpocket, taking the information contained in the other robot's contingency table, and appropriately assimilating the information into its own contingency table. Once a fellow robot has been identified in the robot's line of sight, the contingency table is usurped (Figure 9). This contingency table sharing models a type of shared cognition that accelerates the robot's learning rate, in terms of contingency table robustness, and, consequently enables the robot to execute more favorable actions in search of food.

ANNA

ANNA (Artificial Neural Network Agent) is an extension of the fuzzy cognitive agents in our

Figure 8. (a) Average numbers of steps to perceiving the place where the hunger drive can be satisfied versus the number of activation of the hunger drive (Trajkovski 2007). The data depicted here is from 50 consecutive activations of the hunger drive (x-axis). On y-axis, the average steps to food (range 0-8) are shown, measured in number of contingency table associations (cognitive maps hops), and not actual actions. After the first five activations of the drive, the number of average steps stabilizes. (b) Average number of steps to food in environments with two different ratios of perceptual aliasing (percepts/labels), for the 10-50th activation of the hunger drive. The squares represent numbers of associations used to find food in the case of lower aliasing ratio. (0-8 is the range of the y-axis).

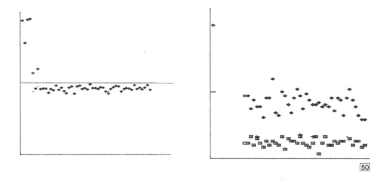

framework towards a congruent continuous model of cognition. The advantage in parallel distributed systems, such as those implemented in ANNA, lies in effective adjustment and assimilation to dynamic environments. The continual model replaces the contingency table as the control structure for an agent navigating an environment; memory and learning take place through the specific neural network architecture and algorithms. The agent builds

Figure 9. A multiagent setup in PYRO. The darker robot has identified the other and is obtaining its contingency table

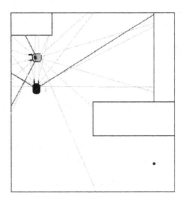

an intrinsic representation of the environment by a process of node connection strength adjustments within the neural network. The emotional context attribute of each entry in the contingency table is taken care of by the combination of connection strengths and values of the nodes in the neural network. This may superficially seem to be a haphazard reassignment of the emotional context, however, on closer inspection there are several strong analogous functional consequences.

Emotional context provides a measure of the usefulness of an action taken in fulfillment of a specific drive, and thus actions that are not performed frequently are probably fruitless, and are thus removed from the table. In a neural network, actions not frequently taken are also "forgotten" due to weight adjustments that continuously take place in accordance with current actions. After an activation of a drive, the agent navigates the environment until achieving fulfillment of the drive, and then the neural network is subsequently trained. In this way, connection strength adjustments correspond to gain in satisfaction due to completion of a drive, and just as random weights are useless, so are actions without an emotional context. Conversely, actions with a positive emotional context have a raised probability of being executed. Likewise, fulfilling actions provide reinforcement learning for the network and raise the probability of future execution.

Neural Network Architecture

Two different neural network architectures were examined experimentally to evaluate the interactivist claim that an internal representation emerges through agent-environment interaction and navigation. In both cases the action repertoire has been abstracted to simple four-directional compass headings. The first is designed to examine goal-directed behavior. A Multilayered Perceptron (MLP) feedforward network is used with the backpropagation method for weight adjustment (Widrow & Lehr 1990). A three input sequence is presented; consisting of the past action-percept pair, as well as the current percept (Figure 10).

The output is the next action that should be executed from the agents subscheme. The externally imposed goal is to follow red-colored tiles while navigating the environment to satisfy the hunger drive. The success of the agent's internal representation of the environment is judged on several parameters related to attainment of the desired goal. The network is trained in a supervised fashion using an offline training method consisting of a predefined training set with several input and expected output pairs taken from the environment. The training takes place in an incremental fashion, with each training epoch consisting of a randomly selected training pair being introduced to the network and the error back propagated. This process is repeated with the agent navigating the environment between trainings until the error between the neural network output and expected output for the training patterns is acceptably reduced.

The second architecture examines the predictive power of the network in determining future

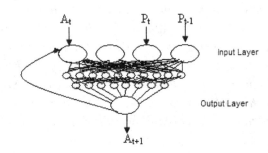

Figure 10. ANNA's ARTMAP-IC architecture

executable action sequences from the agent's inborn scheme. Here we use a neural network based on the Adaptive Resonance Theory (ART). An ARTMAP-IC network (Carpenter & Markuzon 1998) is used to provide the functionality of stable, dynamic and supervised training. In addition, the network is specially suited to handle inconsistent cases where input vectors may be identical but correspond to different outcomes. These cases are directly related to the perceptual aliasing problem, and the ARTMAP-IC has a methodology to handle them with successful probabilistic predictions. In dynamical systems parlance, the network is a self-organizing map, making a correspondence between the input vector and output action sequence, with system activity in creating accurate expectancies being the arbiter of the success of the self-organization. The input is exactly the same as described above, however, a four-action subscheme is attempted in place of the one-action sequence above. The network is trained in an online fashion until network convergence occurs when the network maximizes the percentage of patterns recognized.

ANNA in Action

The simple color-coded environments that were used in the simulation experiments are shown in Figure 11.

Statistical analyses of parameter dynamics are shown in Figures 12, 13, 14, 15, 16, and 17. The success in the goal-directed MLP network was

Figure 11. Training environments E₁ (a), E₂ (b), and E₃ (c) with the dot representing agent starting locations in the respective environment

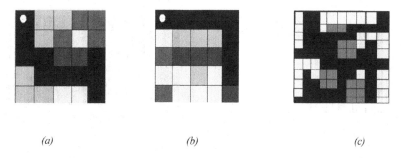

(a)   (b)   (c)

Figure 12. Amount of pain (running into obstacles) observed during 600 epochs of incremental training with 1000 time steps in between training in E₁ (a) and E₂ (b)

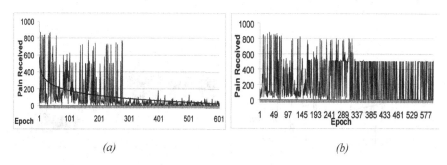

(a)   (b)

Figure 13. Percentage of trajectory during each iteration carried out over red tiles in E₁ (a) and E₂ (b)

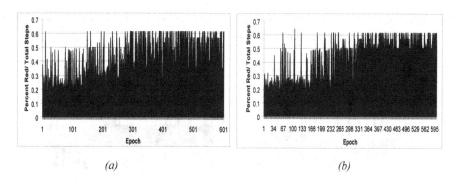

(a)   (b)

measured via observed pain, the percentage of red-colored tiles taken of the total steps taken, and if drive fulfillment was achieved.

There is evidence, provided by the experiments conducted in E₁ focusing on goal-directed behavior, that convergence, observable through incremental improvements in performance, is always achieved. This is not surprising because the training set was designed specifically focusing on this environment. The performance of the MLP network in E₂ and E₃ is systematically less positive, with convergence being achieved in only a number of cases. This is also expected due to lack of robustness in the MLP network architecture when presented with new cases.

Figure 14. Binary representation of either drive fulfillment (1-finding food) or unsuccessful finish after allotted amount of time has elapsed (0) in E_1 (a) and E_2 (b)

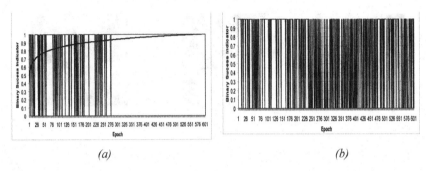

(a)   (b)

Figure 15. Observed surprise -- occurring when the actual executable subscheme is greater than expected -- measured out of every ten time steps while the agent navigates the environment E_1 (a) and E_3 (b)

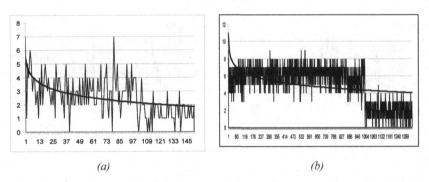

(a)   (b)

Figure 16. Pain measurements -- occurring when the expectancy is violated with an actual action sequence that is less than expected -- measured out of every ten time steps, in E_1 (a) and E_3 (b)

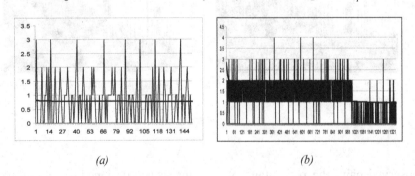

(a)   (b)

The ARTMAP-IC network output correct expectancies of allowable action subscheme's approximately 79% of the time after appropriate exposure in the environment of 1000 (E_1) -10000 (E_3) time steps. This suggests that the agent was able to form a functional internal representation of the hidden structure in the environment. More importantly, the network exhibits fast learning and robustness toward new input-output patterns (learning without forgetting of past experience).

We are currently considering two possibilities for interagent communication in a society of AN-

Figure 17. Correct predictions of executable action sequence over time in the environment E_1 (a) and E_3 (b)

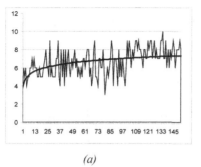

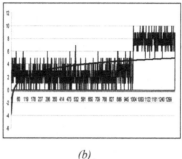

(a)   *(b)*

NAs. In Connection Strength Trading (CST) the more experienced agent, $ANNA_1$, normalizes its connection strengths in an analog [0, 1] range and multiplies the trainee's, $ANNA_2$'s, corresponding connection strengths by its own values. To clarify, if a specific set of node connections (e.g. n_{11}-n_{18}) in $ANNA_1$'s neural network have become strong due to their successful decision making ability leading to drive fulfilling actions, $ANNA_2$ will have its own corresponding n_{11}-n_{18} node connections multiplied by a proportionately high number to ensure that those nodes will be more prominent in its decision making process in the future. CST replaces the contingency table pickpocketing in the previous multiagent model with a weight proportion adjustment. This is a promising route because although weights are created randomly in each test case, and thus result in differing final connection strengths; the connection strengths after training suggests that certain patterns and proportions emerge that can be exploited. In Training Set Passing (TSP) the more experienced agent presents the trainee with a training set which it has created through its own interaction with the environment, thus effectively passing on its experience. The training set is collected from sensory percept-action pairs in the immediately surrounding area of the environment, since this is where the agents met and the trainee's acquired knowledge will most likely be directly applicable.

POPSICLE, A Tool for Calibrating Models with Data from Human Subjects

Humans are the only linguistically competent agents. As humans are able to filter out other stimuli, they can emulate agents as defined in our framework. The set of stimuli and the action repertoire are defined by telling participants what inputs they should pay attention to and what possible motor actions they are allowed to do. Examples would consist of statements like: "On the screen you will be seeing patterns like this (demonstration of the patterns). " To define the action repertoire, the subject might be told: "You are allowed to press or not to press these buttons (experimenter shows the buttons to the subject)." Schemes are defined similarly. One example would be this contingency scheme: "Follow the tiles colored yellow". Here is an example of external goal creation: to define the "react as fast as you can" goal the participant is told: "find the food." With the assumption that the human agent is paradigmatic for the cognitive agent, we extracted data on human subjects to inform our model of simulated cognitive agents.

The experimenter can now observe various aspects of the agent's pathway through that particular environment. Of course, of particular interest are the structures that emerge during the agent-environment interaction. These are the networks of concepts and behaviors, and because

Figure 18. Designer's view on one of the environments used in POPSICLE (Trajkovski et al. 2006)

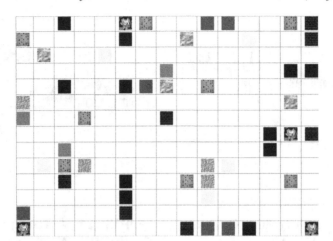

they are not directly observable the experimenter has to reconstruct them out of the agent's observable parameters.

A Java program (the tester) guides the POPSICLE (Patterns in Orientation: Pattern-Aided Simulation Interactive Context Learning Experiment) experiment. The tester presents a series of environments; each is a simple maze made of colored tiles with obstacles. Using separate keys, the agents move up, down, left and right in the given designer visible environment. However, what the agent (subject) sees is different from the designer's view, as shown in Figures 18 and 19.

Subjects are exposed to the environment on two different contextual levels. Context 0 presents the subject with a single colored tile. There are no clues given to whether it is possible to move North, South, East or West. The subject must use trial and error to navigate. In Context 1 the subject is given the tile that she is on and the adjoining tiles. All the tiles show their respective colors. This includes the colors for obstacles, which are black, and the goal, which is gray. The borders are represented by black squares, although they are not identified as borders specifically.

The participants in the experiment work in pairs, one of whom is referred to as a primary

Figure 19. A subject's view in Context 1. The center tile is the tile of current position. The upper tile is the current position square and is a black obstacle

user, and the other as her partner. Each portion of the POPSICLE experiment is 3 minutes long, after which both participants are asked to discuss their observations and to record their conceptualizations in a questionnaire. Detailed analysis of a POPSICLE experiment can be found in (Trajkovski & Conover 2007). The POPSICLE environment can be modified to accommodate any kinds of experimental scenarios, and it is for that purpose that we have developed the CVS repository of methods.

Izbushka (named after the Slavic folk character Baba Yaga's semi-sentient hut) represents work in Cognitive Multiagency based on the framework presented in this article, and takes it in the domain of heterogeneous online societies, designed to elicit insight into emergent, virtual networks and organizations. Izbushka is actually an online environment-agent that structurally couples with human agents in the course of its creation. At first, Izbushka is just a blank screen; human agents clicking onto squares or striking keys illuminate different patterns, shapes, colors or elicit different sounds. Absent from the environment is any sense that human agents are "correct" or "incorrect" in their inputs. At the same time human agents are interacting with Izbushka, Izbushka is interacting with them, changing the hierarchies of its drives through the framework of interactivist-expectative agency. Izbushka's programmed drives (in no particular order) include: 1) proliferation (filling the screen) ; 2) completing all of the notes in a chromatic scale; 3) changing from one color into another; 4) building a pattern or 5) interrupting a pattern. Human agents will anticipate some "drive" from Izbushka (that they will articulate as the "point" or "goal" of Izbushka), but what they do not know is that the execution of these drives depends upon their inputs. That is to say, to Izbushka, the inputs of human agents are the environment it must navigate; its hierarchy of drives are an intrinsic representation of the environment it perceives. This, in turn, changes the kinds of outputs from Izbushka and, therefore,

the environment perceived by the human agents. Multiple human agents (or non-human agents) will be able to log on to Izbushka simultaneously and, together, co-create a dynamic environment displaying emergent complexity, i.e., one whose final shape cannot be reduced to the actions of individual agents (Sawyer 2001). Ultimately, our goal is to run Izbushka with human-agents drawn from around the world whose simultaneous actions on Izbushka anticipate the shape of other emergent behaviors online. Implementation details on Izbushka can be found at (Trajkovski et al. 2006).

While interacting with Izbushka, participants generate data in several ways, among them realtime logs of the dynamic environment, a log/cache of keystrokes and the concomitant drives activated by Izbushka. Secondly, we interview human participants about their impressions, asking them to narrate the process by which they literally "make sense" out of Izbushka. This is, following the insights of Francisco Varela, a record of perception-as-enaction, something actively constructed by participants rather than given a priori (Varela 1999).

Izbushka extends our considerations based on the framework in both theoretical and practical directions. With Izbushka there is no pre-given environment. Instead, the "environment" can only be enacted through the interactions of agents, an autopoietic creation, where agents are creating themselves (Varela et al. 1991, Maturana & Varela 1980).

In fact, agents are the environments for other agents. In Bruno Latour's actor-network theory, our technologies impose back upon us, structuring our interactions even as we ascribe our human behaviors onto them (Latour 1979). With Izbushka, we have expanded actor-network theory to accommodate the opposite case, when non-human agents arrogate behavior onto us, and we, in turn, impose back upon them.

With Izbushka, human and non-human agents are both imbricated in the co-creation around a dynamic environment ontologically inseparable from those agents. This is what might be called a properly multi-agent system, where, as Woolridge (2002) has said, there is no such thing as a "single-agent" system; we would be mistaken in defining any one agent as ontologically prior to that system.

CONCLUSION AND DIRECTIONS FOR FURTHER RESEARCH

We have given a formal framework based on fuzzy algebraic structures for modeling cognitive agents in single and multiagent settings. The model relies on an extension of the Zadehian definition of fuzzy sets that are valued with the unit interval [0, 1] to structures that are valued with lattices, posets, or relational structures. We give overviews of cases where we have used this framework with uniagent environments (Petitagé), a neural network control structure (ANNA), a human-machine interfacing agent (POPSICLE), and a coupling environment-agent in a heterogeneous setting (Izbushka). The case studies and selected results illustrate the power of this fuzzy–based framework.

Extendable ideas from this research have overarching implications for the burgeoning subfields interrelated with Artificial Intelligence and disciplines that have recently emerged from it. Cybersociology finds fuel in the form of information about specific methodologies used and theories implemented in the study of cognitive robotics, contributing to an overall maturation of the field. Specifically, our fuzzy algebraic paradigm emerges as an effective, biologically inspired framework to work under. Cyberanthropology is similarly galvanized by a wealth of data describing the emergent behavior of uniagent, multiagent and human-computer systems. Cognitive science is also benefited from the anthropomorphic explanatory power of our modeled behavioral systems. The reciprocity between cognitive science and cognitive robotics is balanced by providing insights into human action patterns and decision-making

heuristics from a detached and empirically verifiable viewpoint.

By expanding upon the transition from the discrete to a continuous model and its promise, as well as more realistic environments with heterogeneous agents, we hope to more closely model human agency. The expectation is that the emergent behavior will be more adaptive to environmental inconsistencies, capable of exhibiting creative solutions when presented with novel problems. Such a robust system would be consistent with human support systems and would advance the capabilities of the artificial agents to a point of irrefutable demonstrated intelligence through group cognition.

REFERENCES

Barto, A. G., Bradtke, S. J., & Singh, P. S. (1995). Learning to act using real-time dynamic programming. *Artificial Intelligence*, *72*(1), 81–138. doi:10.1016/0004-3702(94)00011-O

Birkhoff, G. (1984). *Lattice Theory*. Providence: Amer. Math. Soc.

Bisbey, P., & Trajkovski, G. (2005), Rethinking Concept Formation for Cognitive Agents. REU Technical Report. Available online at http://pages. towson. edu/gtrajkov/REU/2005/Paul/Paul. pdf (accessed 3 December 2005).

Blank, D., Kumar, D., Meeden, L., & Yanco, H. (2005), The Pyro toolkit for AI and robotics. Available online at Pyro Robotics web site: http://www. pyrorobotics. org/?page = PyroPublications (accessed 25 July 2005).

Carpenter, G. A., Grossberg, S., Markuzon, N., Reynolds, J. H., & Rosen, J. H. (1992). Fuzzy ARTMAP: A Neural Network Architecture for Incremental Supervised Learning of Analog Multidimensional Maps. *IEEE Transactions on Neural Networks*, *3*(5), 698–713. doi:10.1109/72.159059

Carpenter, G. A., & Markuzon, N. (1998). ART-MAP-IC and medical diagnosis: Instance counting and inconsistent cases. *Neural Networks, 11*, 323–336. doi:10.1016/S0893-6080(97)00067-1

Carpenter, G. A., & Markuzon, N. (1998). ART-MAP-IC and medical diagnosis: Instance counting and inconsistent cases. *Neural Networks, 11*, 323–336. doi:10.1016/S0893-6080(97)00067-1

Latour, B., & Woolgar, S. (1979). *Laboratory Life*. Beverly Hills: Sage.

Luger, G. F. (2002). *Artificial Intelligence: Structure and Strategies for Complex Problem Solving*. New York: Addison-Wesley.

Maslow, A. (1954). *Motivation and Personality*. New York: Harper and Bros.

Maturana, H. R. & Varela, F. J. (1980), Autopoiesis and Cognition: The Realization of the Living. Boston Studies in the Philosophy of Science, 42.

Piaget, J. (1973). *The Child's Conception of the World*. London: Paladin.

Rizzolatti, G., Fadiga, L., Gallese, V., & Fogassi, L. (1996). Premotor cortex and the recognition of motor actions. *Brain Research. Cognitive Brain Research, 3*(2), 131–141. doi:10.1016/0926-6410(95)00038-0

Sawyer, K. (2001). Emergence in Sociology. *American Journal of Sociology, 107*(3), 551–586. doi:10.1086/338780

Šešelja, B., & Tepavčević, A. (1995). Partially Ordered and Relational Valued Fuzzy Relations I. *Fuzzy Sets and Systems, 72*, 205–213. doi:10.1016/0165-0114(94)00352-8

Šostak, A. (1997). Fuzzy categories versus categories of fuzzily structured sets: Elements of the theory of fuzzy categories. Mathematik-Arbeitspapiere. *Categorical Methods in Algebra and Topology, 48*, 407–439.

Stojanov, G., Božinovski, S., & Trajkovski, G. (1997). Interactionist-Expectative View on Agency and Learning. *IMACS Journal of Mathematics and Computers in Simulation, 44*, 295–310. doi:10.1016/S0378-4754(97)00057-8

Stojanov, G., Stefanovski, S., & Božinovski, S. (1995), Expectancy Based Emergent Environment Models for Autonomous Agents. Proc 5th International Symposium on Automatic Control and Computer Science, Iasi, Romania.

Stojanov, G., Trajkovski, G., & Božinovski, S. (1997). *The Status of Representation in Behavior Based Robotic Systems: The Problem and a Solution, Proc* (pp. 773–777). Orlando, FL: Systems, Man and Cybernetics.

Tepavčević, A., & Trajkovski, G. (2001). L-fuzzy Lattices: An Introduction. *Fuzzy Sets and Systems, 123*, 209–216. doi:10.1016/S0165-0114(00)00065-8

Tolman, E. C. (1932). *Purposive Behavior in Animals and Men*. New York: Appleton-Century–Crofts.

Tolman, E. C. (1948). Cognitive Maps in Rats and Men. *Psychological Review, 55*, 189–208. doi:10.1037/h0061626

Tolman, E. C., & Honzik, C. H. (1930). 'Insight' in Rats. *University of California Publications in Psychology, 4*, 215–232.

Trajkovski, G. (1997), Fuzzy Relations and Fuzzy Lattices. MSc Thesis. SS Cyril and Methodius University, Skopje, Macedonia.

Trajkovski, G. (1998), An approach towards defining L-fuzzy lattices. Proc. NAFIPS'98, Pensacola Beach, FL, 221-225.

Trajkovski, G. (2002). MASIVE: A Case Study in Multiagent Systems. In Engineering, I. D., & Leaning, A. (Eds.), *Yin, H., Allison, N., Freeman, R., Keane, J., Hubbard, S* (pp. 249–254). Springer Verlag.

Trajkovski, G. (2003), Environment Rrepresentation in Multiagent Systems, PhD Thesis, SS Cyril and Methodius University, Skopje, Macedonia.

Trajkovski, G. (2007). *An Imitation-Based Approach to Modeling Homogenous Agents Societies*. Hershey: Idea Group.

Trajkovski, G., & Collins, S. (2007). (in press). Autochthony through Self-Organization:Interactivism and Emergence in a Virtual Environment. *New Ideas in Psychology*.

Trajkovski, G., Collins, S., Braman, J., & Goldberg, M. (2006), Coupling human and nonhuman agents, Proc 2006 AAAI Fall Symposium Interaction and Emergence in Societies of agents. AAAI Press, in press.

Trajkovski, G., & Conover, A. (2007). On a Software Platform for MASIVE Simulations. In Trajkovski, G. (Ed.), *An Imitation-based approach to modeling homogenous agents societies* (pp. 136–166). Hershey: Idea Group.

Trajkovski, G., & Stojanov, G. (1998). Algebraic Formalization of Environment Representation. In Tatai, G., & Gulyas, L. (Eds.), *Agents Everywhere* (pp. 59–65). Budapest: Springer.

Trajkovski, G., & Vincenti, G. (2005), A Fuzzy Framework for Modelling Multiagent Societies, Proc NAFIPS 2005, Ann Arbor, MI.

Varela, F., Thompson, E., & Rosch, E. (1991). *The Embodied Mind*. Cambridge: MIT Press.

Varela, F. J. (1999). The specious present: a neurophenomenology of time consciousness. In Petitot, J., Varela, F. J., Pachoud, B., & Roy, J.-M. (Eds.), *Naturalizing Phenomenology: Issues in Contemporary Phenomenology and Cognitive Science* (pp. 266–314). Stanford: Stanford University Press.

Widrow, B., & Lehr, M. A. (1990). 30 years of adaptive neural networks: perceptron, Madaline, and backpropagation. *Proceedings of the IEEE*, *78*(9), 1415–1442. doi:10.1109/5.58323

Wooldridge, M. (2002). *An Introduction to Multiagent Systems*. Chichester: John Willey & Sons.

This work was previously published in International Journal of Agent Technologies and Systems (IJATS), edited by Goran Trajkovski, pp. 50-73, copyright 2009 by IGI Publishing (an imprint of IGI Global).

Chapter 10

Interactions in Context–Zero:
Towards Conceptual Adaptation through the Izbushka Agent

James Braman
Towson University, USA

ABSTRACT

Designing computer interfaces and other technologies that interact with users in adaptive ways that attempt to emulate natural styles of learning is generally difficult. As technology has become common in our daily interactions, adaptive interfaces are key in helping users in many situations. In this chapter the preliminary investigation with the intelligent agent Izbuhska is discussed, along with how it can be used to collect various data from users in an attempt to understand how they perceive the program and "learn" while interacting. Izbushka as a tool will help to generate new ways of understanding and conceptualizing interaction by presenting users with a "zero-context" environment. Izbushka presents users with a unique interface in an attempt to study user interactions that lack traditional metaphors or ontological grounding typical in many computer interfaces. The Izbushka agent is our first step towards filtering our preconceived metaphorical ideas in order to generate new understanding of human-computer interaction.

INTRODUCTION

The evolution of technology and its integration into the many facets of modern society has created new forms of communication and interaction. Aspects of the "Information Age" have been infused into our daily routines in a way that has fundamentally altered our modes of thinking about

such technology and interaction itself, requiring changes in the way we structure and use information. It is important to understand how we have been impacted by technology and how these new mediums are understood and conceptualized as our perceptions have changed. Technology often creates a sense of immersion during its use as we project conceptualized versions of ourselves into these spaces (Dede, 2009). Many virtual and artificial spaces create environments that bypass the

DOI: 10.4018/978-1-60960-171-3.ch010

Copyright © 2011, IGI Global. Copying or distributing in print or electronic forms without written permission of IGI Global is prohibited.

normal physical boundaries associated with real life and real time face to face interaction. As part of the synergistic changes brought on by technology, our models, methods and abilities to interact with computers and within these environments should also change. The design and implementation of the human element in human-computer interaction should be thought of as a variable itself and as an artifact of our culture that dynamically adjusts with changes in our technologies (Trajkovski, 2007).

Society and many of its functions have become increasingly dependent on these technological artifacts. The internet alone has been growing at exponential rates with new links and data being updated and added constantly. We are surrounded by information; data is thrust at us in many forms often causing us to become overloaded or confused. Users can typically become frustrated and anxious especially when using many standard technologies we often take for granted such as word processors, email and while surfing the Net (Ceaparu, 2004). Given all of this data, even with the best programs, users want information presented in a way that is understandable and well structured. While working with vast amounts of information they will want to be able to filter, select and restructure it, with least possible effort (Shneiderman, 2005). Many of the interfaces for applications and interactive environments are counter intuitive thus adding to user frustration and sharpening the learning curve for understanding the application and the information that it is trying to provide. How can we then create an interface that a user can fully utilize and interact with, in a way that will closely relate to his or her natural learning style, so that it can be used in the most efficient and successful way? This question takes us to the main of the purpose of our investigation with the Izbushka interface agent as we try to discover new ways to help solve interface and learning problems between technology and human users. With the Izbushka agent prototype and some preliminary experiments, we begin to

investigate how users understand and perceive "information" presented by the agent.

BACKGROUND

Through the use and investigation of intelligent agents we can study human-computer interactions in ways that are new and unconventional. Agents can be used to study various emergent behaviors that occur when users interact with technology. These behaviors and interaction patterns are what shape and drive many interfaces. Only by changing our perception and developing new ideas can we truly understand the best methods in which humans and machines learn and interact together. It is not in our best interest to create interfaces or rely only on our current methodologies and metaphorical constructs for current computer environments and software; we need to truly have an understanding of human perception in these contexts in order to develop the best ways of interaction. Through the interaction with computers and other technology, the process has generally "been structured through metaphors drawn from physical spaces… and through certain assumptions about the user derived from pre-existing, physical relationships" (Trajkovski, 2007). Some preconceived metaphors commonly shared between users of internet and other technology that are grounded in the real physical world include: online shopping, shopping carts, virtual classrooms, chat rooms, desktops, multi-user dungeons, e-books, email etc. Many computer related metaphors are drawn from real objects or real physical spaces or interactions. Our investigations seek to find new and different ways to interact in these environments in ways that are not grounded in such preconceived metaphors.

To investigate these concepts an environment-agent named Izbushka was developed that will be used to collect data and study emergent interactions between human and non-human agents. The results from these interactions can be used to understand ways in which people and machines "learn", interact, form multi-agent societies and form metaphors which are used to make sense of, and characterize computer agency and computer interaction" (Trajkovski, 2007). Izbushka has been created to help us understand interaction "as a simultaneous cognitive, social and cultural event" while studying "emergent forms of learning, communicating and behaving" in this environment (Trajkovski, 2007). Izbushka and its human user learn together and structurally couple to form a multi-agent system, as Izbushka adapts to the input yielded by the human user. In this chapter the Izbushka agent will be discussed in detail along with the results of some preliminary studies with human subjects interacting with the agent. Izbushka as a tool will help to generate new ways of understanding and conceptualizing interaction by presenting users with a "zero-context" environment. What we mean by a zero-context is an environment is "that is in many ways inexplicable and unfamiliar – i.e., without evident goals, familiar "spaces" or language" (Trajkovski, 2007).

The Izbushka Agent

The Izbushka environment-agent is an interactive, reactive, hybrid (artificial + human coupled) intelligent agent composed of both an emergent and a "top-down" hierarchy of drives (Trajkovski, 2007). Izbushka serves as our context-zero tool while coupling with its user during interaction with the program. Izbushka was designed with the key purpose of helping to "[understand] heterogeneous multi-agent systems, and observing emergent phenomena in such agent societies" (Trajkovski, Collins, Braman, Goldberg, 2006). Through the use and implementation of the Izbushka agent we hope to: 1. Understand how people learn in this multi-agent environment (Izbushka as a user-coupled interface / MAS) 2. Understand some of the design issues involved in constructing such an agent. 3. Better understand how humans conceptualize these dynamic environments. (How does a variation in perception/context level affect the

user?) These seemingly separate questions are all part of the same question, which is how human and non-human agents interact and learn, and importantly how do they learn together. How can we design an environment agent that can couple with the user and serve as a bridge or "medium" between the environment and the user? In this chapter the aim is not to answer all of these large complex questions, but begin to look at how the user and an agent can learn together and conceptualize the presented environment.

The agent serves as an extension to the user while interacting with both the current simulated world and the human user. "It is a common perception that in human-computer interactions, humans perceive the agents as extensions of their physical lives into virtual spaces" (Trajkovski et al, 2006). Placing a human in a totally new and unknown environment in which they cannot bring any preconceived metaphorical notions or concepts of the outside physical world to the simulated space allows us a unique opportunity to study the learning process in a multi-agent environment. Once the user eventually learns how to traverse the simulated world, we then can both investigate how the human and how the agent perceive the current world state and interaction. Does the user develop new metaphors and ways of perception related to the physical world or do they perceive it in a way that is similar to the current mainstream perceptions? Through the use of Izbushka we hope to observe and "find new, generative metaphors for understanding multi-agent systems in the course of our analysis, i.e., that properly emergent phenomena, neither reducible to individual elements nor higher-order collectivities, presents the possibility of the novel and unexpected" (Trajkovski, 2007).

To understand the Izbushka agent lets first look at the environment representation and how both Izbushka and the human user interact within. Izbushka creates a simple grid based world composed of an $N \times N$, 2-dimensional space, where the value of N can be defined at the start of the simulation. Traversable areas within the environment

Figure 1. Sample of Izbushka's hidden environmental state

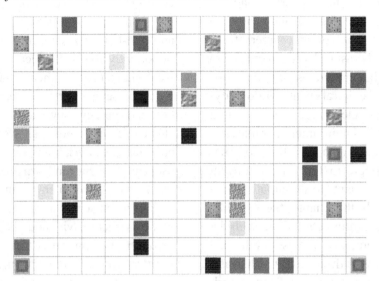

in which the users can occupy (the user can only occupy one square at one instance) are presented as a blank white square. All other colors or patterned squares are obstacles of the environment, where the user can not move. If a user happens to "bump" into an obstacle or container edge of the environment a sound is played alerting the user to that obstacle. At the start of the simulation, once the value of N is known, Izbushka creates a random environmental state configuration. If the experimenter wishes to use a static map at start-up, Izbushka has the capability to load in pre-configured map. Figure 1 shows a sample of a random environment at a particular instance that was created by Izbushka. Figure 2 then shows all possible types of obstacles in the simulation.

The user interacts within the environment by only using the standard arrow keys on the keyboard. Users are also limited to movements only in the four cardinal directions North, South, East and West. The user cannot move outside the boundaries of the environment nor can they move into or through an obstacle. Taking concepts from Smith and Mosier (1986) Data entry guidelines, this minimal input action limitation is beneficial as it "reduces the memory load on the users" and "fewer input actions mean greater operator productivity and usually fewer chances for error" (Shneiderman, 2005). This movement limitation in the user interface is beneficial as it creates function. We wish to create a unique environment and interface to be as unconventional as possible. The visual display to the human user is unique as Izbushka automatically "blacks out" all locations in the environment that are not in the current context field of perception. The environment as

Figure 2. Possible obstacle types

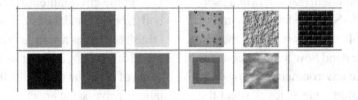

Figure 3. View in Context 0 in a 3 x 3 grid

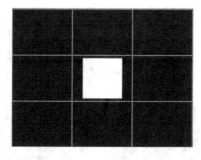

shown in Figure 1 is never viewable to the user, but only to Izbushka. Another main feature of the Izbushka environment is that as the user "moves" through the environment by the use of the arrow keys, the user does not actually see the move. The display gives the impression that the underlying environment is shifting and not the user. This is another way in which we try to filter out any possible preconceived metaphorical notions of space or traversal as well as to see what new ways a user can interact in this fashion.

In an attempt to filter out any preconceived metaphors of physical, social and cultural notions that a user may bring to the interaction process, we created Izbushka as our "zero context" environment and tool. Our use of the term "Context" refers to the general perception of an agent (in this case the human user) in its current environment. It should be noted that a true context level can not ever truly be at a "zero" level since "there's always contexts, schema, syntax and so on" in perception involved with the program and its use. (Trajkovski et al, 2006). To compensate for this fact we can utilize an environment that is non-standard in nature and other wise "uncanny" (Trajkovski, 2007). In our zero context methodology we only allow the perception of the human agent's current locale in the environment. By default, Izbushka always starts the user in zero-context mode. All other aspects of the environment including any other empty and traversable spaces or obstacles of all types are "blanked" out and not visible to the user. The Izbushka agent however has the

perceptual ability of the entire environment. Figure 3 shows an example of context-0 in a 3 x 3 grid simulation. Note that the center square is the subject's current location in the space, while all other areas of perception are un-perceivable.

So how then does one perceive anything in context-0? How does one perceive an environment where one can not use his or her senses such as taste, smell, touch? Vision is limited to only viewing your current location and nothing more. The only sense left in to utilize is that of sound. Sound can be utilized in programs to aide a user in such things as navigation. Izbushka in the same sense in the zero-context setting, uses sound alone to helps the user discover and learn the "correct" path to follow. Izbushka allows the user to traverse the space based on sound in context 0. Each type of movement is associated with a sound type as well as if an obstacle is hit. The user must develop their cognitive map of the environment without seeing it with their eyes per say, but by visualizing in with sound. In investigating human-agent interaction we proposed to develop Izbushka in a way that allowed interaction "without ontologically grounding these interactions based on physical environments or physical interactions" (Trajkovski, 2007). Using a nonstandard and otherwise unpredictable interface for our experiment, users will have a greater propensity for confusion. This confusion and uncanny design in interface can lead to knew ways of interaction and learning allowing for alternative ways at looking at human computer interaction. Izbushka does utilize other context levels but limits this to what we call context-1 and context-2 perception. The use of the different context levels is based on how well Izbushka "believes" the human agent has learned the environment and makes a decision as to what context level to use next. A context level of zero is used initially then is gradually advanced to one and then to two. The following figures show examples of human perception in a sample environment at the various context levels. Again traversable/empty spaces are denoted by a

Figure 4. View in Context 1 for a 3 x 3 grid

Figure 5. View in Context 2 for a 5 x 5 grid

blank white space where all obstacles are a space of any other color or pattern. Context one and Context two are shown in Figure 4 and in Figure 5 respectively.

Perception in context 1 is limited to the current locale (Center square) and the contents of the four surrounding squares in each of the 4 cardinal directions.

Perception in context 2 is in essence, "context 1 of context 1". Visibility of the four cardinal squares (context 1) is added to the squares of the previous context 1 configuration giving us context 2 perception. As the user's current Cartesian (x,y) position moves, so does all of the corresponding field of perception. If the user moves close to a container edge of the simulated space, the field will not show anything, and temporarily become smaller.

Looking at Figure 6, we can abstractly see how the agent works. Input is sent to the program and interpreted as numeric representations of the user's actions. Also the current level of the user's perception is also sent as data to the agent. The sending, interpretation and processing of the human data is referred to in the figure as "Pre-processing". Internally in the program this is where the data is interpreted and sent to various modules contained within the agent. Data from this phase is also sent to a database recording module where input and actions are time stamped and recorded along with the context levels. Data from these phases are then passed to deeper functions and objects

within the agent that interpret the data. This data is combined with the perceptual data sensed by the agent from the environment. This phase is labeled "Interface coupling & decision rules", this is where Izbushka decides on what to change in the environment thus changing the interface and contributing to the human interface coupling process. Izbushka in this phase also attempts to realize if the human user should change context levels if the agent feels that the user has learned. The drives and decisions rules of Izbushka are hierarchal in nature and based upon subsumption architecture. Once Izbushka has decided on what to display to the user, these changes are sent to Izbushka's recording object. The "Action and Learning" Phase takes the decision data from the previous step and updates its internal variables that contain its memory and knowledge of the interaction process. Next the changes are made to the environment directly, as Izbushka is the only agent in the system with the ability to make any changes. The action made to the environment can be perceived by the human user immediately. The new environmental state that is perceived by the user starts the process over again.

Izbushka contains several behavior modules that take sensory input from both the environment and the human user. The basis for Izbushka's action was derived from the idea of behavioral models from the subsumption architecture approach (Nillson, 1998). Using this type of architecture we can decompose the overall aspects of

Figure 6. Izbushka Agent Model

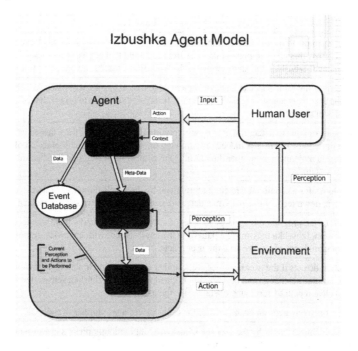

Izbushka's complex behavior into several simple layers of abstraction. Each function receives an input, and based on that information if certain criteria are met, makes a decision to change the environment. Once he agent has perceptively recognized that an event has occurred, the behavioral modules take some corresponding action (Bigus, Bigus, 2001). Variables in the various modules store data that monitor human actions over periods of time. It has been noted that "surprisingly complex behaviors can emerge from the interaction of relatively simple reactive machines with a complex environment" (Nillson, 1998).

Table 1 shows the Izbushka behavioral conditions that drive Izbushka to change the environment. Some are driven by user action and some proactively by the agent. Other actions are made in an attempt to help the user "learn" during the interaction process.

By placing human and non-human agents into interactions with Izbushka with "no immediately apparent goals beyond the self-organization of the human/non-human multi-agent system itself

with the ultimate goal of studying the representations produced by the interacting agents" we can properly understand and study any possible emergent phenomena (Trajkovski 2006). The "goals" of the human agent will emerge in the course of the interaction between the human user and the Izbushka agent. "The "goal" of the human agent will be to discern the goal of the simulation" (Trajkovski et al, 2006). For the Izbushka experiment human participants were asked to interact with Izbushka as long as they wanted, but for at least ten minutes (as shown). These test sessions were conducted in a classroom setting with each person having their own instance of Izbushka running on their machine. Once the sessions were complete, each participant completed a survey.

For the experiment, a total of twenty-one volunteers were asked to participate. Each participant was told only that a study was being conducted on human-agent interaction and how people and computers learned together. Users were not told anything about Izbushka, the Izbushka environment, the presentation of the environment (as far

Table 1. Izbushka Behavioral Conditions

Behavior Module	Function
1	If the user attempts to move outside of the simulation space and strikes an edge, *N* times, Izbushka will build a wall of objects across that edge, to prevent the user from touching that edge again. Eventually as the user moves through the environment Izbushka will start removing the wall. Barrier walls are removed faster at lower context levels.
2	If a user strikes the same space at an environment edge then Izbushka will place one obstacle at that location to prevent the user from attempting the move again. If the user still tries to go off that edge of the environment, then function 1 will also activate.
3	This module attempts to detect if a user is only moving in one direction for a period of moves without moving in any other directions. If a user is indeed only moving one way, Izbushka will place an obstacle in front of the user's path to force a movement in another direction. If the context level is high, Izbushka may place a group of obstacles in the user's path.
4	Izbushka looks for a certain movement pattern given by the user's directional moves. The default pattern is "up, up, down, down, down left". If this pattern is detected, certain random obstacles are added to the environment.
5	At the start of the program the agent picks a set of coordinates and marks them as special. If the user happens to go to that location, Izbushka may make a pattern in the environment with obstacles, remove obstacles or add obstacles in a few random locations to see how the user reacts.
6	This function detects if the user becomes stuck, either because of their actions in the environment or because Izbushka has made a change and accidentally trapped the user. If Izbushka senses that the user is trapped, then the agent will clear a path by removing obstacles for the user.
7	Izbushka proactively adds an obstacle after the users moves a set number of times
8	After so many moves input by the user the Izbushka agent randomly picks a location on the map. If the currently picked location is an obstacle, the agent will remove it.

as the display characteristics or the concept of context levels). Each participant was told only that they would interact with the Izbushka program and then afterward, asked to complete a survey. Users were also told only to use the four arrow keys (up, down, left, right) and that the other keys would not function and would have no effect. The obstacles in the Izbushka environment are placed at random at the beginning of the programs execution; neither the human user nor the Izbushka agent know or control the initial environmental configuration. Figure 7 shows a typical "before and after" picture of the underlying environmental configuration. The left most portion of the figure represents the initial configuration and the right most portion represents the environment over a period of time where the human and non human agent have interacted.

When participants were first presented the program for the experiment, users started in context level 0. At this context level the environment can only be sensed through sound; even at this

Figure 7. Environment state before and after interaction

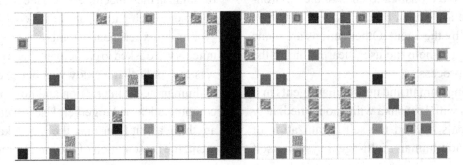

Figure 8. Typical Learning Curve of Users (Average)

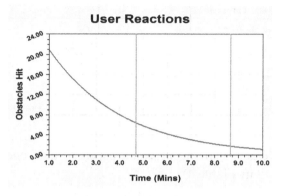

Figure 9. Izbushka Agent Reaction over time (Average)

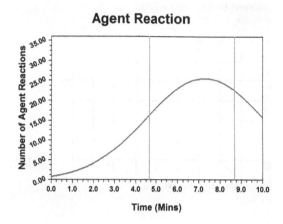

limited "view", participants could gain knowledge of the interaction process and related movement and objects by certain associated sounds or sound patterns. Successful moves were associated with more pleasant sounds, while non-successful sounds were less pleasant (i.e. attempting to go off the edge of the environment produces a loud and annoying explosion). As the user interacted with the program over time, the context level of the simulation was increased by the Izbushka agent. Over time and over increased context levels, users typically learned more about the environment, what actions were associated with the different sounds and what obstacles to avoid. This learning process occurred for all users even if they did not realize that the Izbushka environment was based of the notion of a maze like environment. The general learning curve for typical users can be seen in Figure 8 below. The X-axis shows events over time, while the Y-axis represents an average number of obstacles hit. The vertical lines that divide the graph show the change from a lower context to a higher context. These bars are placed at the average time it takes to change context levels. The graph shows a decrease in the number of obstacles hit over time as the context levels increase. A user starts at context 0 and then increased to context 1 and then following to context 2.

During the interaction with the user, the Izbushka agent made various changes to the environment based on its behavior modules and the input it sensed from the user and environment. The following figure shows the various changes that the Izbushka agent made over time. The figure shows the average number of changes made to the environment at each minute of interaction. It is important to note that some behavior modules may un-do other modules in the hierarchy of drives. For example if the number of modifications at one instance is twenty, it does not necessarily mean that Izbushka placed twenty new obstacles in the environment. The agent may have deleted, added or moved that many obstacles in combination during that time frame. It is approximate.

Figure 9 shows the average number of reactions performed by Izbushka. It can be observed that Izbushka increased its reaction during context 0 and into context 1, where after about 7.5 minutes into the interaction, it started to decline. The amount of Izbushka's reactions declined during context 2 until the end of the simulation.

Table 2. Participant Computer Usage

Average Computer Usage per week	Frequency	Percentage (*n=21*)
Less than one hour	0	0%
Two to five hours	2	9.5%
Six to ten hours	3	14.3%
Ten hours and more	16	76.2%

Table 3. Participant Internet Usage

Average Internet Usage per week	Frequency	Percentage (*n=21*)
Less than one hour	0	0%
Two to five hours	3	14.3%
Six to ten hours	2	9.5%
Ten hours and more	16	76.2%

Participant Demographic Information and Survey Data

This section presents the demographic information as well as results collected from the post experiment questionnaire. A total of 21 participants were utilized in the experiment. Of the participants, 14 were male (66.6%) and 7 were female (33.3%). The average age overall for the participants was 28.9 years, and by gender the average age of male participants was 24.9 years and female participants had an average age of 32.9 years.

Each person was asked the average time spent on the computer each week and the average time they spend on the internet each week as shown in Table 2 and in Table 3 respectively.

Participants were asked to list the general activities they performed on the computer on

Table 4. Participant Computer Activity

Computer Activity	Frequency
Email	15
Internet (general)	9
Programming	9
Word Processing / Excel	8
Administrative Tools	2
Chat / Instant Messaging	2
Using Databases	2
Music	1
Financial Program	1

average. Participants could list more than one activity (Table 4).

Those in the experiment were also asked to rate their overall "computer experience" on a scale on 1 to 10 (1 representing no experience and 10 representing an expert user). Overall participants rated themselves at an average of 8.6 on the scale. Females in the study had an average self rating of 7.6 while males had an average self rating of 9.1. In part 1 question 5 of the survey, participants were asked if they had ever participated in any online classes or were ever involved in any distance learning via the internet. Overall 52.4% of participants responded "Yes" while the remaining 47.6% responded "No". Many of these questions were asked in order to gain insight on how users interacted with the computer generally.

Part two of the survey was concerned in discovering how the users felt about the interaction with Izbushka and how they understood the purpose of the interaction and how they interpreted the program. Part two consisted of eight questions where they could express their feeling on several important related topics. Question 1 was a four part question consisting of four separate Likert scales ranging from 1 to 10 asking for their overall general reaction to the program. On the scale ranging from Terrible to Wonderful (1-10) the average user rating was 6. On the scale ranging from Frustrating to Satisfying (1-10) the average user rating was a 5. On the scale rating the Izbushka program from Dull to Stimulating (1-10) the average rating was a 6. On the scale from 1 to 10 rating the program from Difficult to Easy the average rating was a

Table 5. Surprises in program interaction

Was there anything surprising or unusual about the program?
Appearance of Patterns and Pictures
Limited view
Environment shifted
Did not understand the goal
The sounds that represented movements and pictures
Limited control

Table 6. Evaluating purpose

What do you believe is the purpose of the program?
A Game
Color pattern formation
To create sound patterns
To study human learning or their ability to navigate
To navigate with limited scope of visibility
Maze with a limited view
To see how many movements can be made in a period of time
Cognitive testing

7. The remaining seven questions from part two of the questionnaire consisted of asking the user several open ended questions in order to see how each participant felt about their interaction with the program. Question two asked the participants if they felt anything was surprising or unusual about the program. A generalization of the answers can be seen below in Table 5.

Next, participants were asked what they believed was the purpose of the program. Participants were not told what they were trying to achieve. As part of the research we wanted to see what the user perceived as the goal or purpose of the simulation. Table 6 shows the general responses given by the participants in answering this question.

The next question asked users specifically if they were able to reach the "goal" of the simulation. If they were able to reach the goal, they were asked to describe how they were able to do so. Table 7 shows the results to the first part of the question; Table 8 shows typical answers that describe how they were able to reach their individual goal.

Participants were then asked if they found any portion of their interaction either satisfying or frustrating. 61.9% responded that they felt frustrated while the remaining 38.1% said they felt more satisfied then frustrated by the experience. Question 6 asked users to express how they felt about the color patterns / scheme that were presented by the program and if it had any meaning to them in particular. We wanted to know if certain colors or color formation were important in the users understanding of the process. Some users may view certain colors or patterns differently then perhaps other users. Table 9 lists responses from this question on the reaction to color patterns.

Participants were also asked to explain and express how they felt about the environment that was presented. The results from this question can be seen below in Table 10.

The last question of part two, asked if they felt they were able to learn what was happening in the simulation. 52.4% of the participants said

Table 7. Goal achievement during simulation

Able to Reach goal	Frequency	Percentage
No	11	52.4%
Yes	6	28.6%
Unsure	4	19.0%

Table 8. Ways goal was achieved

Describe how you were able to do so?
Avoided exploding sounds
Removed obstacles from the side
Avoided Obstacles
Made certain patterns appear
Made certain sounds

Table 9. Reaction to color patterns

Express your feelings on the color patterns expressed in the program. What did they mean to you?
Colorful / Vibrant
Blues were calming
Represent solid objects
Fire and water tile needed to be avoided. Represented danger
Walls / obstacles
Black represents a boundary or nothingness
White squares traversable.

Table 10. Reaction to environment

Explain how you felt about the environment presented by the program
Unusual / confusing / strange
Easy to interact with
Helpful with navigation
Simple / simplistic
Was a Maze
Did not like the limited view
Was easier as more was shown

Table 11. Usefulness of audio in navigation

Helpfulness of audio	Frequency	Percentage
Not at all	0	0%
Somewhat helpful	8	38.1%
Helpful	8	38.1%
Very helpful	5	23.8%

"Yes" they were able to learn what was happening while 47.6% said that "No" they did not learn what was happening in the simulation. Part 3 was focused on evaluating user navigation in the environment. Question 1 asked user's to rate how helpful audio output assisted them in navigating the environment. Likewise, question 2 asked how the visual output helped in their navigation (as far as the various levels of context presented). Question 3 was focused on how the graphics in the environment affect their ability to navigate. The responses for these questions are shown in Table 11, Table 12 and in Table 13 respectively.

Table 12. Usefulness of visual output in navigation

Helpfulness of Visual	Frequency	Percentage
Not at all	2	9.5%
Somewhat helpful	6	28.6%
Helpful	7	33.3%
Very helpful	6	28.6%

Twelve participants reported "yes" that they felt lost or confused and the remaining 9 participants said "No". The final question asked users, again using a scale 1 to 10, to rate the likely hood they would have used this program if they happened to have come across it on their own. With 1 being A "Not likely" rating and 10, representing "Very likely", on average users reported a 4 on how likely they were to use the program. This survey yielded interesting results and feelings expressed by the participants.

DISCUSSION OF RESULTS

It can be argued that the users were able to learn how to navigate the environment with the Izbushka agent (based on their individual interpretation of the goal) observing that the number of obstacles encountered decreased over time. The first section

Table 13. Helpfulness of Graphics during interaction

Helpfulness of Graphics in the program	Frequency	Percentage
Had no affect	3	14.3%
Made it more confusing	5	23.8%
Helpful	9	42.9%
Very helpful	4	19.0%

of figure 8 represents the number of obstacles hit in context 0; context 1 is presented by the second section of the graph and context 2 data is shown in the last section of the graph. As the user was able to see a larger portion of the environment (as in an increased context level) they would learn to avoid the obstacles. If one looks at each section individually however, interestingly enough the same phenomena can be observed in each context level. Even when a user remains in context-0, users typically learn to avoid obstacles through the use of sound patterns as presented in the graph. Human learning can also been seen in context 1 and context 2; the average number of obstacles hit decreases in each context level separately as does it decrease overall through the entire simulation.

In evaluating the graph in figure 9, the number of reactions made by Izbushka can be observed as a function of reactions over time. The number of reactions the agent made was measured by adding the number of reactions of each behavior module for each minute (averaged). The number of reactions starts to increase over the time period where the human user interaction is in context 0. This increase in reactions continues where the user remains in context 1, until about minute 7.5, where at that point the number of reactions starts to decline. This decrease in the amount of agent reaction continues through the remainder of the simulation while the user remains in context 2.

An interesting phenomenon can be observed when one considers both graphs from both the human and non human agent simultaneously. The Izbushka agent responds to the human agent's increase of "erroneous" moves during context 0. One can see a gradual increase in Izbushka's reactions during the context 0 time interval. By the time the human users perceive the environment in context 1 mode, they begin to make more moves in the environment thus increasing the human and non human agent coupling process resulting in an increase in the Izbushka agent reaction and a decrease in human "mistakes" or obstacles hit. This increase in the amount of moves can also be

explained by the "novelty of the new stimulus" and that it increases one's need for exploration (Macedo & Caroso, 2004). Curiosity is often associated with an increase of exploration and a common "psychological construct that has been closely related with this type of behavior (Macedo & Caroso, 2004). Exploration can often be seen as a motivation for learning. During context 1, the human agent makes more moves, but less erroneous moves, thus causing the reactions of the intelligent agent to decline near the start of context 2; the agent to eventually make less reactive moves during this later time interval. When the human agent has learned more about the environment there is less interaction by the agent. To clearly restate the interpretation of the graphs, as the human agent interacts with the environment they hit many obstacles as they are learning in the environment, increasing the reaction of the intelligent agent. As the number of obstacles hit decline, the amount of changes to the environment made by the Izbushka agent decreases.

FUTURE WORK

Besides general improvement of the agent, the next step with the Izbuhska agent is to extend the program from a 2D maze like environment to a 3D space. Using the virtual world of Second Life®, a more realistic version of the environment can be created where the user would have to navigate the space via their avatar (Braman *et al*, 2007). Various context levels can be simulated by limiting camera controls through the use of an attachable HUD (Head-up Display) or in combination of darkening areas of the surrounding environment. Using a 3D version of Izbushka we can explore new ways of interaction and how users learn in different types of spaces. Figure 10 illustrates the beginning of a 3D recreation. Figure 11 illustrates an avatar inside the environment in context-0 and Figure 12 illustrates an avatar in context-1.

Figure 10. *Beginning Build of the Izbushka Environment in Second Life*

Figure 11. *Avatar in Context-0*

CONCLUSION

The increase use of computer technology and its incorporation into our daily lives has and will continue to change our conceptualization of technology and that of human computer interaction of all forms. The various computer environments, in which users interact with and learn, provide rich mediums for exploration and potential applicability for future growth for the field of computer science. The Izbushka agent while coupled with the human user interacting within the simulation yielded some interesting results on how users interacted and perceived the program. Through this interaction we were able to see how an agent could

Figure 12. *Avatar in Context-1*

be coupled with the user as part of the interface. The Izbushka agent itself as coupled with the human user chose what to display based on its own hierarchy of drives and through the input given by the human user during the learning process. Our goal through the interaction of these agents in our experiment by placing both human and non human agents together was to study the results of interaction and emergent behavioral phenomena.

Human agents while using computer technology often conceptualizes the interaction as metaphors based on there own interpretation and understanding of real interaction in the "real world". Izbushka as a 0-context tool used during computer interaction was used to filter out these preconceived metaphorical ideas in order to generate new understanding of human computer interaction. Human understanding and the ways in which we learn are one of the main shaping forces in designing usable and functional systems based on our perception. As our technology changes and encompass the various types of agents, systems will become more heterogeneous in nature. Experiments like Izbushka are just one step in understanding and gathering information about new ways to build interfaces that are closely related to individual use and personal style. Our aim is to continue this research with Izbushka as we improve and modify its functionally and user-coupling abilities to collect deeper and more meaningful data.

REFERENCES

Bigus, J. (2001). *Constructing Intelligent Agents Using Java*. Second Edition. New York: Wiley Computer Publishing.

Braman, J., Jinman, A., Trajkovski, G. (2007). Towards a Virtual Classroom: Investigating Education in Synthetic Worlds. *The AAAI Fall Symposium. Emergent Agents and Social and Organizational Aspects of Intelligence*. Arlington, VA.

Ceaparu, I., Lazar, J., Bessiere, K., Robinson, J. & Shneiderman, B. (2004). Determining Causes and Severity of End-User Frustration *International Journal of Human-Computer Interaction*, 17, 3, (2004), 333-356.

Dede, C. (2009, January). Immersive Interfaces for Engagement and Learning. *Science*, *323*(5910), 66–69. doi:10.1126/science.1167311

Macedo, L., Cardoso, A. (2004). *Exploration in Unknown Environments with Motivational Agents*. AAMAS 04'. July 19-23. New York.

Nilsson, N. (1998). *Artificial Intelligence: A New Synthesis*. San Fransico, CA: Morgan Kaufman Publishers, Inc.

Shneiderman, B., Plaisant, C. (2005). Designing the user interface. *Strategies for effective human-computer Interaction 4th edition*. University of Maryland, College Park. Addison Wesley. 2005.

Smith, S., Mosier, J. (1986). Guidelines for Designing User Interface Software, Report ESD-TR-86-278, Electronic Systems Division, MITRE Corporation, Bedford, MA. Available from National Technical Information Service, Springfield, VA.

Trajkovski, G. Collins, S. Braman, J., & Goldberg, M. (2006). *Coupling Human and Non-Human Agents*. The AAAI Fall Symposium: Interaction and Emergent Phenomena in Societies of Agents. Arlington, VA.f

Trajkovski, G. (2007). *An Imitation-Based Approach to Modeling Homogenous Agent Societies*. Hershey, PA: Idea Group Publishing.

Chapter 11
Norm Emergence with Biased Agents

Partha Mukherjee
University of Tulsa, USA

Sandip Sen
University of Tulsa, USA

Stéphane Airiau
University of Amsterdam, The Netherlands

ABSTRACT

Effective norms can significantly enhance performance of individual agents and agent societies. We consider individual agents that repeatedly interact over instances of a given scenario. Each interaction is framed as a stage game where multiple action combinations yield the same optimal payoff. An agent learns to play the game over repeated interactions with multiple, unknown, agents. The key research question is to find out whether a consistent norm emerges when all agents are learning at the same time. In real-life, agents may have pre-formed biases or preferences which may hinder or even preclude norm emergence. We study the success and speed of norm emergence when different subsets of the population have different initial biases. In particular we characterize the relative speed of norm emergence under varying biases and the success of majority/minority groups in enforcing their biases on the rest of the population given different bias strengths.

INTRODUCTION

Recent literature in multiagent systems show a significant increase in interest and research on normative systems which are defined as (Boella, Torre, & Verhagen, 2008):

A normative multiagent system is a multiagent system organized by means of mechanisms to represent, communicate, distribute, detect, create, modify, and enforce norms, and mechanisms to deliberate about norms and detect norm violation and fulfillment.

Norms or conventions routinely guide the choice of behaviors in human societies and plays

DOI: 10.4018/978-1-60960-171-3.ch011

Copyright © 2011, IGI Global. Copying or distributing in print or electronic forms without written permission of IGI Global is prohibited.

a pivotal role in determining social order (Hume, 1978). Conformity to norms reduces social frictions, relieves cognitive load on humans, and facilitates coordination. This is because individuals conform to norms assuming others are going to do the same (Lewis, 1969). Typically norms facilitate social interactions by enabling interacting agents choose actions without social enforcement, that result in coordinated behavior, e.g., driving on appropriate sides of the road. Norms may be adhered to in human societies because they facilitate the functioning of individuals, or because of the threat of social disapproval (Posner, 2000) or acceptance by individuals of desired conduct (Elster, 1989).

Computational agents, too, often have to coordinate their actions and adoption and adherence to norms can improve the efficiency of agent societies. A large class of interactions between self-interested agents (players) can be formulated as stage games with simultaneous moves made by the players (Genesereth, Ginsberg, & Rosenschein, 1986). Such stage games often have multiple equilibria (Myerson, 1991), which makes coordination uncertain. While *focal points* (Schelling, 1960) can be used to disambiguate such choices, they may not be available in all situations. Norms can also be thought of as focal points evolved through learning (P. H. Young, 1996) that reduce disagreement and promote coherent behavior in societies with minimal oversight or centralized control (Coleman, 1987). Norms can therefore have economic value to agents and help improve their efficiency. Norms in human societies, however, can also prevent flexibility and do not necessarily efficiency. In addition, different societies may evolve different norms to solve the same coordination problem, norms may shift over time, and can have varying degrees of stability (H. P. Young, 2008). Hence, the systematic study and development of robust mechanisms that facilitate emergence of stable, efficient norms via learning in agent societies promises to be a productive research area that can improve coordination in and thereby functioning of agent societies.

Establishment of social norms may come about by top-down influences like official edicts and role models, bottom-up processes driven by local customs, and lateral diffusion of established norms between related interaction types (H. P. Young, 2008). Most research on norms in multiagent systems focus on the *legalistic view* where norms are used to shape the behavior of open systems without using sanctions to enforce desirable behavior. In this approach norms are typically logically specified using a normative language (García-Camino, Rodríguez-Aguilar, & Sierra, 2005) from which rules of behavior can be automatically derived (Silva, 2008). Our approach to norm emergence from personal interactions is based on the *interactionist view* which adopts a bottom-up view of individual adoption of norms because of alignment of goals and utilities between agents in a population (Castelfranchi, 1998, 2003). In addition to the appeal of distributed, rather than centralized approach, the process of norm emergence can also facilitate efficiency and promote fairness (Binmore, 1994, 2005).

While researchers have studied the emergence of norms in agent populations, they typically assume access to significant amount of global knowledge (Epstein, 2001, Kandori & Rob, 1995, P. H. Young, 1993, 1996). For example, all of these models assume that individual agents can observe sizable fraction of interactions between other agents in the environment. While these results do provide key insights into the emergence of norms in societies where the assumption of observability holds, it is unclear if and how norms will emerge if all interactions were private, i.e., not observable to any other agent not involved in the interaction.

To study the important phenomenon of emergence of social norms via private interactions, we use the following interaction framework. We consider a population of agents, where, in each interaction, each agent is paired with another agent randomly selected from the population. Each agent then is learning concurrently over repeated interactions with randomly selected members from the population. We refer to this kind of learning *social learning* to distinguish from learning in iterated games against the same opponent (Fudenberg & Levine, 1998). Our experiments involve symmetrical games with multiple pure-strategy equilibria with the same payoff.

In previous work on learning in games, the opponent is fixed. In our *social learning framework* (Mukherjee, Sen, & Airiau, 2007, Sen & Airiau, 2007), the opponent is unknown and different at each iteration. In past work (Mukherjee et al., 2007, Sen & Airiau, 2007), we have considered a society of agents where opponents use the same learning algorithm, but we assume that agents did not have an initial bias to play a particular policy. We have also studied the effect the presence of non-learning agents playing a fixed strategy, and we observed that few agents were able to bias the emergence of one norm. In both cases, we observe that a norm always emerges when the learning agents' policy is initially set with a uniform probability distribution. In this article, our goal is to provide experimental results that throw light on the dynamics of the emergence of norms by studying the effect of an initial bias in the policy of the learners. For example, do we observe the convergence of a norm in a 2-action game when the policy of 50% of the agent is initially set to play action 1 and the policy of the other agent is initially set to play action 2? We investigated a number of related issues: the effect of population size playing with an initial bias, agents playing with varying initial biases, multiple populations with opposite policies, multiple populations with bias differentials etc.

RELATED WORK

The need for effective norms to control agent behaviors is well-recognized in multiagent societies (Boella & Torre, 2003, Vázquez-Salceda, Aldewereld, & Dignum, 2005). In particular, norms are key to the efficient functioning of electronic institutions (García-Camino, Rodríguez-Aguilar, Sierra, & Vasconcelos, 2006). Most of the work in multiagent systems on norms, however, has centered on logic or rule-based specification and enforcement of norms (Dignum, Kinny, & Sonenberg, 2002, Vázquez-Salceda et al., 2005). Similar to these researches, the work on normative, game-theoretic approach to norm derivation and enforcement also assumes centralized authority and knowledge, as well as system level goals (Boella & Lesmo, 2002, Boella & Torre, 2003). While norms can be established by centralized diktat, a number of real-life norms evolve in a bottom-up manner, via "the gradual accretion of precedent" (P. H. Young, 1996). We find very little work in multiagent systems on the distributed emergence of social norms. We believe that this is an important niche research area and that effective techniques for distributed norm emergence based on local interactions and utilities can bolster the performance of open multiagent systems. We focus on the importance for electronic agents solving a social dilemma efficiently by quickly adopting a norm. Centralized social laws and norms are not sufficient, in general, to resolve all agent conflicts and ensure smooth coordination. The gradual emergence of norms from individual learning can facilitate coordination in such situations and make individuals and societies more efficient.

In our formulation, norms evolve as agents learn from their interactions with other agents in the society using multiagent reinforcement learning algorithms (Panait & Luke, 2005, Tuyls & Nowé, 2006). Most multiagent reinforcement learning literature involves two agents iteratively playing a stage game and the goal is to learn policies to reach preferred equilibrium (Powers & Shoham, 2005). Another line of research considers a large population of agents learning to play a cooperative game where the reward of each individual agent depends on the joint action of all the agents in the population (Tumer & Wolpert, 2000). The goal of the learning agent is to maximize an objective function for the entire population, the world utility.

Figure 1.

Algorithm 1: Interaction protocol.

---
for *a fixed number of epoch* **do**
$\quad$ **repeat**
$\quad\quad$ remove randomly agents p_{row} and p_{col} from the population ask each agent to
$\quad\quad$ select an action;
$\quad\quad$ send the joint action to p_{row} and p_{col} for policy update;
$\quad$ **until** *all agents have been selected during the epoch* ;

The social learning framework we use to study norm emergence in a population is somewhat different from both of these lines of research. We are considering a potentially large population of learning agents. At each time step, however, each agent interacts with a single agent, chosen at random, from the population. The payoff received by an agent for a time step depends only on this interaction as is the case when two agents are learning to play a game. In the two-agent case, a learner can adapt and respond to the opponent's policy. In our framework, however, the opponent changes at each interaction. It is not clear *a priori* if the learners will converge to useful policies in this situation.

SOCIAL LEARNING FRAMEWORK

The specific social learning situation for norm evolution that we consider is that of learning "rules of the road". In particular, we will consider the problem of which side of the road to drive in and who yields if two drivers arrive at an interaction at the same time from neighboring roads. (It might seem to the modern reader that "rules of the road" are always fixed by authority, but historical records show that "Society often converges on a convention first by an informal process of accretion; later it is codified into law." (P. H. Young, 1996) We will represent each interaction between two drivers as a *n*-person, *m*-action stage game. These stage games typically have multiple pure strategy equilibria. In each time period each agent is paired with a randomly selected agent from

the population to interact. An agent is randomly assigned to be the row or column player in any interaction. We assume that the stage game payoff matrix is known to both players, but agents cannot distinguish between other players in the population. Hence, each agent can only develop a single pair of policies, one as a row player and the other as a column player, to play against any other player from the agent population. The learning algorithm used by an agent is fixed, i.e. an intrinsic property of an agent.

When two cars arrive at an intersection, a driver will sometimes have another car on its left and sometimes on its right. These two experiences can be mapped to two different roles an agent can assume in this social dilemma scenario and corresponds to an agent playing as the row and column player respectively. Consequently, an agent has a private bimatrix: a matrix when it is the row player, one matrix when it is the column player. Each agent has a learning algorithm to play as a row player and as a column player and learns independently to play as a row and a column player. An agent does not know the identity of its opponent, nor its opponent's payoff, but it can observe the action taken by the opponent (perfect but incomplete information). The protocol of interaction is presented in Figure 1.

We have considered a homogeneous society of agents where the WoLF-PHC (Bowling & Veloso, 2002) learning algorithm is chosen for learning norms. WoLF-PHC (Win or Learn Fast - policy hill climbing) can learn mixed strategies. Though WoLF is guaranteed to converge to a Nash equilibrium of the repeated game in a 2-person,

2-actions game against a given opponent, it is not clear whether it is guaranteed to converge in social learning.

EXPERIMENTAL STUDY

We are now presenting experimental results exploring the influences of the following issues on the norm emergence.

Same initial bias: we study the case where a subset of the population has the same bias to choose one norm over the other, the remaining agents in the population do not have an initial bias. We study the influence of two parameters: the size of the biased population and the strength of the initial bias.

Agents starting with opposite bias: we study the case where 50% of the agents in the society have a strong initial bias for one norm and the remaining 50% have an initial bias for the other norm. We vary the proportion of agents initially set with one norm to investigate how fast a majority norm will emerge in the social environment.

Population sizes with varying bias differentials: we have investigated the emergence of norms when a bias differential is introduced among the learners. If a certain size of population has an initial bias of x% to choose an action then the remaining learners have that of y% to choose the other action as we have considered 2-person 2-action game. So a bias differential exists in the society of learners. We like to study the outcome in terms of percentage of runs averaged for emergence of majority norm by varying the bias differentials and the number of learners playing with opposite biases.

We are now presenting the scenario used for our study before presenting the results.

Table 1. Stage game corresponding to interaction at a traffic intersection (G- go, Y_L- yield left, Y_R – yield right)

	G	Y_R
G	-1, -1	3, 2
Y_L	2, 3	1, 1

SOCIAL DILEMMA SCENARIO

One typical example of the use of norms or convention is to resolve social dilemmas. A straightforward example of this is when two drivers arrive at an intersection simultaneously from neighboring streets. While each player has the incentive of not yielding, myopic decisions by both can lead to undesirable accidents. Both drivers yielding, however, also creates inefficiency. Ideally, we would like norms like "yield to the driver on right", which serves all drivers in the long run. Hence, the dilemma is resolved if each member of the population learns to "yield" as a row (column) player and "go" as a column (row) player. The player that yields gets a lesser payoff since it is losing some time compared to the other player. The players know whether they are playing as a row or a column player: the row player sees a car on its right, and the column player sees a car on its left. The action choices for the row player are to go (G) or yield to the car on the right (Y_R), and they are go (G) or yield to the car on the left (Y_L) for the column player.

We model this coordination game using the payoffs presented in Table 1. Note that for a social norm to evolve, all agents in the population has to learn any one of the following policy pairs: (a) (row:G, col: Y_L), i.e., yield to the car on the left, or (b) (row: Y_R, col:G), i.e., yield to the car on the right. We say a norm has emerged in the population when all learners make the corresponding choice except for infrequent random exploration.

Figure 2. Iterations required for a norm to emerge in a society where the 20% of population is only biased in one action

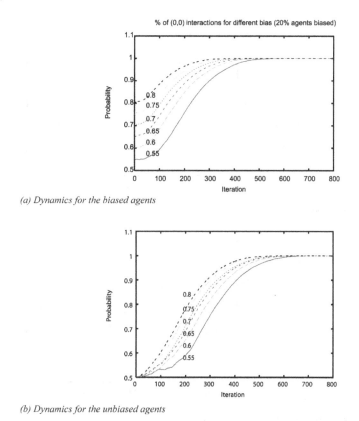

(a) Dynamics for the biased agents

(b) Dynamics for the unbiased agents

Influence of Agents Biased in One Option with Varying Bias Values

Our previous work shows that a norm always emerges when the agents have no initial bias. It takes some time for the agents to decide which norm is going to be used, and it is not clear what causes the decision. Is it the influence of few learners that converge faster? Or is it due to a large portion of the agents having a small bias for one norm? In this experiment, we test the latest hypothesis: if a subset of the population has an initial bias, the norm should emerge faster. We study the speed of emergence of a norm when we vary the proportion of the agent with the same initial bias, and the strength of the bias.

In this experiment we vary the number of agents playing with different biases for choos-

ing the norm to yield to the car on the left (i.e. go when the agent plays as a row player and Y_L when the agent is playing as a column player), while the remaining agents are initially unbiased. The norm that emerges is always the norm that had an initial bias. Figure 2(a) and Figure 3(a) represent the dynamics of the agents with an initial bias, and Figure 2(b) and Figure 3(b) represent the dynamics of the agents with no initial bias. In Figures 2(a) and 2(b), 20% of the population has an initial bias. We observe that the norm emerges faster among the agents that started with an initial bias compared than among the agents that started with no bias. In addition, the stronger the bias, the faster the speed of emergence of the norm. For example, the emergence of the norm is faster when the initial bias of the agent is 0.8 ($\approx$ 500 iterations) than when the value of the bias is

Figure 3. Iterations required to emerge a norm in a society where the 80% of population is only biased in one action

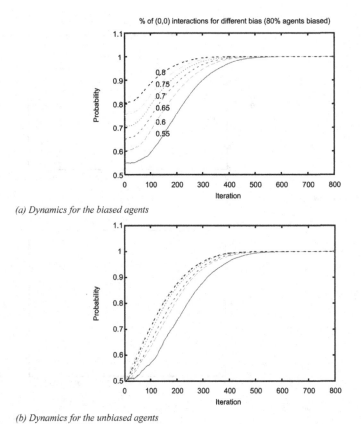

(a) Dynamics for the biased agents

(b) Dynamics for the unbiased agents

0.55 (≈ 675 iterations). In Figures 3(a) and 3(b), the proportion of agent that has an initial bias is 80%. Among the agents that were initially biased, the speed of emergence of the norm is comparable when the proportion of agent with initial bias is 20% or 80%. However, among the agent that started unbiased, the speed of emergence is faster when 80% of the population has an initial bias.

Influence of Agents Starting with Opposite Policies

So far we have considered a society where a certain percentage of learners are biased in choosing one particular norm and the remaining population is unbiased. We have observed that the norm that

Figure 4. Society with 225 agents using WoLF, averaged over 1,000 runs. The population converges 490 times to (G, Y_L) and 510 times to (Y_R, G)

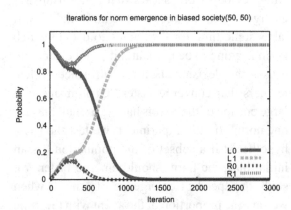

Figure 5. Society with 225 agents using WoLF, averaged over 1,000 runs. The population converges 100% of the times to (G, Y_L)

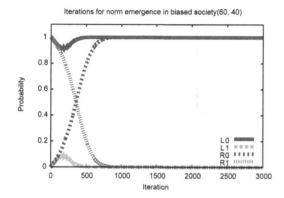

Iterations for norm emergence in biased society(60, 40)

always emerges is the norm which had an initial bias. Now we consider 50% of the population will start with the policy to yield to the car on the right, and the other 50% starts with the policy to yield to the car on the left. For example in a population of 225 agents using WoLF, over 1000 runs we observed that the norm "yield to the left" emerged 490 times and the norm "yield to the right" emerged 510 times. We present the learning dynamics for a run in Figure 4. In (Sen & Airiau, 2007), non-learning agents playing a fixed pure strategy are also present in the population. Our scenario is different from the scenario there are equal number of fixed agents playing pure strategy 'yield to the left' or pure strategy 'yield to the right'. In (Sen & Airiau, 2007), the presence of only 4 agents playing one norm influences the entire population to almost always converge that norm.

We have run the experiment by increasing the number of agents with an initial bias for the norm to 'yield to the left' to 60%, the remaining 40% of the population initially using the norm to 'yield to the right'. It is observed from Figure 5 that the norm that emerges is always the norm that was initially chosen by the majority of agents. Comparing Figures 4 and 5, we observe that the speed of emergence of the norm is significantly faster

when the split of the population is 60%/40% than when it is 50%-50% ($\approx$ 750 iterations instead of $\approx$ 1250

Influence of Population Sizes with Varying Bias Differentials

In the previous set of experiments, we have studied some special cases. First we considered the case where all agents that have an initial bias have the same bias for the same norm, and we studied the influence of the strength of the bias. Then, we studied the case where agents have a maximum initial bias (initially, the agent chooses one norm with probability 1), though different agents may prefer different norms, and we studied the influence of the proportion of agents that initially prefer one norm over the other on the speed of emergence of a norm. In this section, we propose a more general study of the influence of the bias. We assume that

- All agents start with an initial bias;
- All agents that have a bias for the same norm have the same value for the initial bias.

If the proportion of agents that initially prefer norm a is more than 50%, we say that a is the majority norm, and the other norm is the minority one. Hence our study has three parameters:

x: is the proportion of the population corresponding to the majority, hence $0.5 \leq x \leq 1$;

y: the bias of the preferred norm for the set of agents that are in the majority;

z: the bias of the preferred norm for the set of agents that are in the minority;

We refer to $(y-z)$ as the **bias differential** and $2x-1$ as the **population differential** (note that as $0.5 \leq x \leq 1$, $0 \leq 2x-1 \leq 1$).

We now investigate, in a systematic way, the influence of the bias and population differentials

Figure 6. 2-D and 3-D plot for norm convergence when bias differentials exist in the society

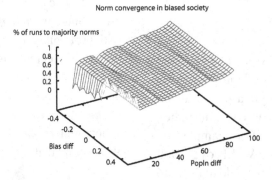

(a) Nature of the percentage of runs that varies with different biased differentials

(b) The surface, generated by the influence of bias and population differential on % of runs averaged for convergence of majority norms

on the nature of the norm that emerges. We present the results in Figures 6(b) and 6(a).

In Figure 6(b),

- The x-axis is the population bias.
- The y-axis is the bias difference. For a bias difference of 0.45, the majority has an initial bias of 1 and the minority one of 0.55; thereafter, the minorities bias is incremented by 0.5 and the majority bias is decremented by 0.5 (produces a bias difference of 0.1 in one step) until the bias difference is -.45. The 0 bias corresponds to the case where the majority and minority have an initial bias of 0.775 (see Table 2).
- The z-axis represents the percentage of times that the norm of the majority emerges

In Figure 6(a), we represent the percentage of time the norm of the majority emerges as a function of the population bias for some fixed values of the bias difference (i.e., we slice Figure 6(b) for a fixed value of the bias difference).

Let us consider the scenario where the population differential is 90% and the bias differential is -0.45. That case corresponds to the case where the majority is formed by 95% of the population and has a bias of .55, and the minority is formed by 5% of the population with a bias of 1 (see Table 2). For this scenario, we observe that the norm of the majority always emerges.

When the bias differential is positive, the majority has a higher bias compared to the minority (see Table 2). In that case, the norm that emerges is the norm of the majority, irrespective of the population difference. This is to be ex-

Table 2. Bias differential table

Majority bias	Minority bias	Bias differential
1	0.55	.45
0.95	0.6	0.35
0.90	0.65	0.25
0.85	0.70	0.15
0.80	0.75	0.05
0.775	0.775	0
0.75	0.8	-0.05
0.70	0.85	-0.15
0.65	0.9	-0.25
0.60	0.95	-0.35
0.55	1	-0.45

pected as the agents in the majority have also the stronger bias.

When the bias differential is negative, it means that the bias of the minority is stronger than the bias of the majority. In other words, the minority contains fewer agents, but their bias is much stronger and may influence undecided agents. In such cases the norm preferred by the minority may ultimately be adopted by everyone. When the bias of the minority is very strong and the one of the majority is weak, the norm of the majority emerges only if the size of the majority is extremely large. For example, when the bias difference is -0.45, the minority has a bias of 1, the majority a bias of .55, if the population differential is lower than 70 (i.e., if the size of the majority smaller than 85%), the norm of the minority will always emerge!

With this bias differential, the size of the majority has to be 95% before its preferred norm always emerges. In general, for negative bias differential, there are three regions:

1. A minimum population differential below which the minority norm always emerges;
2. A range of population differential in which increasing the population differential increasing the likelihood of the majority norm emerging,

3. And a maximum population differential above which the majority norm always emerges.

Also as the bias difference between the minority and the majority norm followers increase, it takes more population differential for the majority to bring about a certain likelihood of its preferred norm emerging (the curves shift to the right in Figure 6).

CONCLUSION

We investigated a bottom-up process for the evolution of social norm that depends exclusively on individual experiences rather than observations or hearsay. Our social learning framework requires each agent to learn from repeated interaction with anonymous members of the society. In past work, we have assumed that the learners did not have an initial bias for one norm over another one, and under that hypothesis, we always observed the emergence of a norm.

In this work, we investigate the influence of the bias of the initial policy of a learner on the norm that emerges. We empirically showed that if all agents have a bias for the same norm, the norm emerges faster than when agents do not have initial bias. Then we showed that when all agents have a strong bias, a norm always emerge and is the one of the majority. The larger the margin between the majority and the minority, the faster the convergence. Finally, we provided a more general study of the influence of the initial bias where all agents have an initial bias, and agents that initially prefer the same norm have the same bias. For example, our study shows that when the majority has a weak bias and the minority a strong one, the size of the majority must be over a threshold for the norm preferred by the majority to emerge.

In future works, we would like to complete the general study presented under *Influence of population sizes with varying bias differentials* as we have only presented results about a particular relationship between the initial bias of the majority and minority. When the agents initially start with no bias, after some iterations, they start to have a small bias. We would like to use the study to see whether we can determine when the norm is actually chosen by the agents: after a few iterations, the bias induced by the random interactions between the agents may be enough for one norm to emerge for sure.

REFERENCES

Binmore, K. (1994). *Game theory and the social contract, vol. i. playing fair*. Cambridge, MA: MIT Press.

Binmore, K. (2005). *Natural justice*. Oxford: Oxford University Press. doi:10.1093/acprof:oso/9780195178111.001.0001

Boella, G., & Lesmo, L. (2002). A game theoretic approach to norms. *Cognitive Science Quarterly*, *2*(3–4), 492–512.

Boella, G., & van der Torre, L. (2003). Norm governed multiagent systems: The delegation of control to autonomous agents. In *Iat '03: Proceedings of the ieee/wic international conference on intelligent agent technology* (p. 329-335). Washington, DC, USA: IEEE Computer Society.

Boella, G., van der Torre, L., & Verhagen, H. (2008). Introduction to the special issue on normative multiagent systems. *Autonomous Agents and Multi-Agent Systems*, *17*(1), 1–10. doi:10.1007/s10458-008-9047-8

Bowling, M. H., & Veloso, M. M. (2002). Multiagent learning using a variable learning rate. *Artificial Intelligence*, *136*(2), 215–250. doi:10.1016/S0004-3702(02)00121-2

Castelfranchi, C. (1998). Modeling social action for ai agents. *Artificial Intelligence*, *103*(1–2), 157–182. doi:10.1016/S0004-3702(98)00056-3

Castelfranchi, C. (2003). Formalising the informal? dynamic social order, bottom-up social control, and spontaneous normative relations. *Journal of Applied Logic*, *1*(1–2), 47–92. doi:10.1016/S1570-8683(03)00004-1

Coleman, J. S. (1987). Norms as social capital. In Radnitzky, G., & Bernholz, P. (Eds.), *Economic imperialism: The economic approach applied outside the field of economics*. New York, NY: Paragon House.

da Silva, V. T. (2008). From the specification to the implementation of norms: an automatic approach to generate rules from norms to govern the behavior of agents. *Autonomous Agents and Multi-Agent Systems*, *17*(1), 113–155. doi:10.1007/s10458-008-9039-8

Dignum, F., Kinny, D., & Sonenberg, L. (2002). From desires, obligations and norms to goals. *Cognitive Science Quarterly*, *2*(3–4), 407–430.

Elster, J. (1989). Social norms and economic theory. *The Journal of Economic Perspectives*, *3*(4), 99–117.

Epstein, J. M. (2001). Learning to be thoughtless: Social norms and individual computation. *Computational Economics*, *18*(1), 9–24. doi:10.1023/A:1013810410243

Fudenberg, D., & Levine, D. K. (1998). *The theory of learning in games*. Cambridge, MA: The MIT Press.

García-Camino, A., Rodríguez-Aguilar, J., & Sierra, C. (2005). Implementing norms in electronic institutions. In *Proceedings of the fourth international conference on autonomous agents* (p. 667-673). New York, NY: ACM Press.

García-Camino, A., Rodríguez-Aguilar, J. A., Sierra, C., & Vasconcelos, W. (2006). A rule-based approach to norm-oriented programming of electronic institutions. *ACM SIGecom Exchanges*, *5*(5), 33–41. doi:10.1145/1124566.1124571

Genesereth, M., Ginsberg, M., & Rosenschein, J. (1986). Cooperation without communications. In *Proceedings of the national conference on artificial intelligence* (p. 51-57). Philadelphia, Pennsylvania: The MIT Press.

Hume. (1978). *A treatise of human nature*. Oxford, England: Oxford University Press.

Kandori, M., & Rob, R. (1995, April). Evolution of equilibria in the long run: A general theory and applications. *Journal of Economic Theory*, *65*(2), 383–414. doi:10.1006/jeth.1995.1014

Lewis, D. K. (1969). *Convention: A philosophical study*. Cambridge, MA: Harvard University Press.

Mukherjee, P., Sen, S., & Airiau, S. (2007, May). Norm emergence in spatially constrained interactions. In *Proceedings of aamas 2007 workshop on adaptive and learning agents (alag-07)* (pp. 79–83).

Myerson, R. B. (1991). *Game theory: Analysis of conflict*. Cambridge, MA: Harvard University Press.

Panait, L., & Luke, S. (2005). Cooperative multi-agent learning: The state of the art. *Autonomous Agents and Multi-Agent Systems*, *11*(3), 387–434. doi:10.1007/s10458-005-2631-2

Posner, E. (2000). *Law and social norms*. Cambridge, MA: Harvard University Press.

Powers, R., & Shoham, Y. (2005). New criteria and a new algorithm for learning in multi-agent systems. In *Proceedings of nips*.

Schelling, T. C. (1960). *The strategy of conflict*. Havard University Press.

Sen, S., & Airiau, S. (2007, January). Emergence of norms through social learning. In *Proceedings of the twentieth international joint conference on artificial intelligence (ijcai'07)* (pp. 1507–1512). Menlo Park, Ca: AAAI Press.

Tumer, K., & Wolpert, D. H. (2000). Collective intelligence and Braess' paradox. In *Proceedings of the seventeenth national conference on artificial intelligence* (p. 104-109). Menlo Park, CA: AAAI Press.

Tuyls, K., & Nowé, A. (2006, March). Evolutionary game theory and multi-agent reinforcement learning. *The Knowledge Engineering Review*, *20*(1), 63–90. doi:10.1017/S026988890500041X

This work was previously published in International Journal of Agent Technologies and Systems (IJATS), edited by Goran Trajkovski, pp. 71-84, copyright 2009 by IGI Publishing (an imprint of IGI Global).

Chapter 12
Governance Mechanisms in Web 2.0:
The Case of Wikipedia

Christopher Goldspink
Incept Labs, Australia

ABSTRACT

This chapter documents the findings of research into the governance mechanisms within the distributed okok known as Wikipedia. It focuses in particular on the role of normative mechanisms in achieving social self-regulation. A brief history of the Wikipedia is provided. This concentrates on the debate about governance and also considers characteristics of the wiki technology which can be expected to influence governance processes. The empirical findings are then presented. These focus on how Wikipedians use linguistic cues to influence one another on a sample of discussion pages drawn from both controversial and featured articles. Through this analysis a tentative account is provided of the agent-level cognitive mechanisms which appear necessary to explain the apparent behavioural coordination. The findings were to be used as a foundation for the simulation of 'normative' behaviour. The account identifies some of the challenges that need to be addressed in such an attempt including a mismatch between the case findings and assumptions used in past attempts to simulate normative behaviour.

INTRODUCTION

This chapter presents the findings of primary research into governance mechanisms operating within anonymous computer mediated production environments, now commonly referred to as Web 2.0. In this case the platform examined is Wikipedia. The chapter is presented in two parts. The first deals with theory relevant to both understanding and modelling the effect of rules and norms on social self-regulation in computer mediated environments such as Wikipedia. Alternative theories of governance relevant to Web 2.0 are discussed. The concept of norms is identified as central to understanding Web 2.0 governance. The concept of norms is, however, problematic from a social theoretical standpoint as it points to conflicting origins of order. This is considered

DOI: 10.4018/978-1-60960-171-3.ch012

Copyright © 2011, IGI Global. Copying or distributing in print or electronic forms without written permission of IGI Global is prohibited.

briefly in the context of the micro-macro/structure-agency debate. An emergentist account of norms is argued as necessary to describe the relationship in a way which can be made operational.

The second part of the chapter provides a fine grained analysis of how speech acts are used by Wikipedian's to influence one another. The relationship between these (micro) speech acts and emergent (macro) patterns of social regulation are described. Through this analysis a tentative account is provided of the individual, social and technological artefacts which appear necessary to explain the behavioural coordination observed within Wikipedia discussion pages. This analysis was designed to support identification of the minimum mechanisms which would need to be included in a multi-agent simulation which would support the further study of social self regulation in Web 2.0.

Wikipedia was chosen, as when people encounter it for the first time and learn how it works, they commonly express surprise. The expectation is that an open collaborative process of such magnitude should descend into chaos. Yet Wikipedia has thrived, growing rapidly since its inception and spinning off many non-English language equivalents. Furthermore, Wikipedia has been shown to produce credible encyclopaedic articles (Giles, 2005) without the top down controls typically employed for this type of production. While the number of rules and etiquettes have also grown rapidly from the original 'no rules' standpoint (Sanger, 2005), Wikipedia appears so far to have avoided the formation of an editorial elite or oligarchy (Konieczny, 2009). Wikipedia therefore offers fertile ground for understanding the mechanisms of governance at play in this form of Web 2.0 environment.

Wikipedia's sheer size, the extent to which every transaction is logged, and its length of time under development offers a valuable and rare source of social science data (Medelyan, Milne, Legg, & Witten, 2009). For those of us interested in understanding and modelling the

dialectic between individual behaviours and social structures and order, Wikipedia is attractive, as the way in which people can influence one another is constrained when compared to non-computer mediated environments. In Wikipedia actions at the level of the individual are restricted to communicative (speech) acts and edits.

This research focuses on how speech acts are employed by editors to influence the behaviour of others. Particular attention is given to how editors use the illocutionary force of utterances (Searle, 1969) and deontic commands to influence one another to comply to rules, etiquettes and social norms and the role these play in the actual order observed.

Conclusions are drawn about how the order observed in Wikipedia may be explained as well as the apparent influence of social artefacts, goals and the wiki technology on the achievement of that order.

PART ONE: THEORY RELEVANT TO UNDERSTANDING SOCIAL REGULATION IN COMPUTER MEDIATED ENVIRONMENTS

Governance Theory

According to the relevant Wikipedia article, the word 'governance' derives from the Latin that suggests the notion of "steering". The concept of governance is used in a number of disciplines and a wide range of contexts and the range and type of steering mechanisms differ depending on whether the focus is with States or institutions. While both have been applied to understanding Web 2.0, it is most common (and arguably most appropriate) to use institutional concepts of governance. Institutional steering mechanisms may be: formal (designed rules and laws) or informal (emergent as with social norms); extrinsic (involving contracts and/or material incentives) or intrinsic (involving values and principles); and the mechanisms by which governance operates may be top down (imposed by authority) or bottom up (invented by the participants as a basis for regulating each other).

Theories vary with respect to the mechanisms advanced and the emphasis placed on different mechanisms. Theory is also advanced for different purposes: to explain or to prescribe. In broad terms the debate is often dichotomised with economics derived theories (Agency and Transaction Cost) on one side and sociological theories (stewardship) on the other (see J. H. Davis, D. Schoorman, & L. Donaldson, 1997; Donaldson & Davis, 1991). Depending on the position of the advocate these may be presented as antithetical or as viable alternatives for different contexts.

Agency theory derives from neo-classical economics and shares the foundational assumption of agent utility maximization (Jensen & Meckling, 1976). Advocates argue that many productive transactions involve *principals* who delegate tasks to *agents* to perform on their behalf (Donaldson & Davis, 1991). This gives rise to what is known as the 'principal's dilemma'. Simply stated this dilemma asks *'how can the principal ensure that the agent will act in its interest rather than on the basis of self-interest?'* Note that this dilemma arises from the assumed self-interested nature of agents – it is a dilemma intrinsic to the assumptions upon which the theory is based even though this is argued to have empirical support. Two general solutions are offered: the use of formal contracts and sanctions and the use of material incentives.

Critics argue that not all human decisions are made on the basis of self-interest. Sociological and psychological models of governance posit various alternatives: some remain committed to assumptions of rational action and goal seeking, while others address issues of power or various forms of intrinsic motivation, including a desire to conform to social norms. These latter positions generally form the basis of theories of *stewardship* (J. H. Davis, D. F. Schoorman, & L. Donaldson, 1997).

While these two broad sets of ideas form the backdrop to most debates about governance, in traditional institutions increased recourse has also been made to Transaction Cost Economics (TCE) (Coase, 1993, 1995; Williamson, 1996). TCE is concerned with the relative merit of alternative governance arrangements for differing production environments. Oliver Williamson (1985), a key contributor, states *'The choice of governance mode should be aligned with the characteristics of the transaction...'*. Principals are presented with a continuum of possible ways of trying to achieve effective regulation from open markets to hierarchy. Both of these are seen as imposing costs (agency costs for hierarchy and transaction costs for markets). The aim is to combine them to achieve an optimum balance between these costs. This 'balancing' implies a top down rational decision making role for institutional managers.

More recently two additional categories of governance have been added to the TCE family – 'networks' and 'bazaars'. Both have arisen to explain the emergence of production and exchange arrangements which do not seem to fit on the market-hierarchy continuum. Both Network Governance (Candace Jones, William S Hesterly, & Stephen P Borgatti, 1997) and Bazaar Governance (Demil & Lecocq, 2003) are argued to be particularly relevant to understanding the flexible structures associated with Open Source production and Web 2.0. Demil & Lecocq (2003: 8) cite Jones et al (1997: 916) and argue that network governance:

...involves a select, persistent, and structured set of autonomous forms [agents] engaged in creating products or services based on implicit and open ended contracts to adapt to environmental contingencies and to coordinate and safeguard exchanges. These contracts are socially – not legally – binding.

The final sentence highlights the key difference between network and more conventional TCE mechanisms. To achieve cooperation the network form of governance relies on social control, such as *'occupational socialization, collective sanctions, and reputations'* rather than on formal authority.

Bazaar governance is also argued to rely heavily on the mechanism of reputation (Demil & Lecocq, 2003: 13). Reputation is assumed to provide the incentive to become involved and to comply with group expectations and norms. Unlike network systems, however, agents are free to enter or leave the exchange process – there are no obligations to become or to remain engaged. Raymond (1999) states that *'contrary to network governance, free-riders or opportunistic agents cannot be formally excluded from the open-source community'*.

To summarise:

- Free markets are characterised by: a lack of obligation to engage in a transaction; low interdependence between parties involved with the exchange; and transactions regulated only by price. Within a pure market the individual identities of the transacting parties are not important.

- In Hierarchies, there are formal contracted obligations on all parties, these are maintained by fiat but may also be supported by wider formal institutions e.g. Courts. Obligations are associated with formal position making the official (role) identity of the parties the key determinant of the relationship.

- Within network structures, exchanges are regulated using relational contracts – there is a formal obligation to remain engaged even though specific actions and operational responsibilities may not be included in a contract. There is also some reliance on social norms– the socialised position of actors becomes important. Exchange commitments may be relatively short lived and persist only so long as they offer mutual benefit.

- With bazaar governance there is no obligation on any party to perform particular duties or even to remain engaged: there are low entry and exit costs. There are few formal mechanisms for policing or sanction but sufficient regulation is achieved by means of shared task, reciprocity norms and/or informal group sanctioning with participants influenced by their desire to build reputation.

Understanding the Role of Norms

As can be seen, 'norms' are argued to play a role in a number of theories of governance, with their being particularly significant in Stewardship, Network and the Bazaar theories. Sociologists have long argued that norms are fundamental mechanisms for social regulation. What though is a 'norm'? How do norms emerge and how are they influenced and by what?

Gibbs (1981) argues that *'Sociologists use few technical terms more than norms and the notion of norms looms large in their attempt to answer a perennial question: How is social order possible?'*. Not surprisingly then the concept has been incorporated into a wide range of alternative and often competing bodies of theory.

Therborn argues (2002: 868) that people follow norms for different reasons. The extremes run from habit or routine to rational knowledge of consequences for self or the world. Between these lie:

- Identification with the norm or values – linking sense of self (identity) to the norm source (person, organization or doctrine) often leading to in-group-out-group.
- Deep internalization – self-respect – done independently to what others are doing.

Bicchieri (2006: 59) provides a rare hint at the cognitive process involved stating:

To 'activate' a norm means that the subjects involved recognise that the norm applies: They infer from some situational cues what the appropriate behaviour is, what they should expect others to do and what they are expected to do themselves, and act upon those cues.

This suggests a complex process of self-classification (how am 'I' situated with respect to this group and what is the nature of the situation in which 'I' find myself, does a norm pertain to 'me' in this situation and under what conditions and to what extent am I obliged to comply?).

Norms then may involve mechanisms as simple as mimicry or copying, through to the exercise of conscious and deliberate action based on an assessment of a situation as salient to the exercise of a particular way of acting.

In attempting to explain how norms operate the literature can be divided into two fundamentally distinct groups. In the social philosophical tradition (Lewis, 1969) norms are seen as a particular class of emergent social behaviour which spontaneously arise in a population. From this perspective, a 'norm' is a pattern identified by an observer ex-post. The defining characteristic of the pattern is the apparently prescriptive/proscriptive character: people behave 'as if' they were following a rule. This is a bottom up account – from micro to macro.

By contrast, the view offered by the philosophy of law sees norms as a *source* of social order. This standpoint assumes the prior existence of (powerful) social institutions and posits them as the source of rules, which, when followed, lead to social patterns. This is a top down account – from macro to micro.

These positions appear antithetical although following the work of Berger and Luckman (1972) each may be seen as a part of a dialectic whereby emergent social patterns become reintegrated and formalised in institutions. This dialectical account of the relationship between the individual and the collective has formed the focus of many social theories over the years, including the well known theories of Bourdieu, Habermas and Giddens. These have all foundered on the failure to specify the mechanisms by which the individual shapes the social and the social constrains the individual.

Emergence

The concept of emergence has long been invoked to explain the nature of the relationship between micro and macro in many scientific disciplines (Ablowitz, 1939; Clayton, 2006; Davies, 2006; Emmeche, Koppe, & Stjernfelt, 1997; Goldstein, 1999; Holland, 1998). It has recently become central to accounts of the behaviour of complex systems and is behind the growing interest in the role of computer simulation for the study of such systems (Kennedy & Eberhart, 2001; Richardson, 2002).

As we discuss more extensively in 'Agent Cognitive Capabilities and Orders of Social Emergence' (C. Goldspink & Robert Kay, 2008), the concept has been advanced within three distinct streams: *philosophy*, particularly of science and mind; *systems theory*, in particular complex systems; and *social science* where it has largely been referred to under the heading of the micro-macro link and/or the problem of structure and agency. While the concept remains somewhat controversial (Goldstein, 1999), what has been largely agreed is that social structure and individual agency come together in *activity* or in *body-hood* – the specific psycho-motor state at the instant of enaction. Both Vygotsky and Giddens, for example, focus on action as the point of intersection between human agency and social structures and it is implicit in Bourdieu's *habitus* also.

We have argued elsewhere (Goldspink, 2008; Goldspink & Kay, 2007; Chris Goldspink & Robert Kay, 2008), as has Sawyer (2003; 2005) that accounts of emergence drawn from the natural sciences are insufficient to deal with social emergence. Specifically we have argued that such approaches fail to conceive of or deal with what Ellis (2006) and Gilbert (2002) have referred to as 'orders of emergence'. It is to be expected that different orders of emergence may be supported by different levels of agent capability. This is arguably a fundamental issue for those of us interested in simulating social behaviour.

The EU funded project (Sixth Framework Programme - Information Society and Technologies- Citizens and Governance in the Knowledge Based Society) titled "Emergence In the Loop: simulating the two way dynamics of norm innovation" (EMIL) was intended to advance our understanding of the mechanisms of social emergence. To provide some empirical grounding, the research into Wikipedia described in the next part was designed and conducted by the author while with the Centre of Research in Social Simulation (CRESS), an EMIL partner. CRESS is located within the Department of Sociology at the University of Surrey. The conclusions of this chapter are, however, those of the author.

PART TWO: AN EMPIRICAL STUDY OF INFLUENCE MECHANISMS IN WIKIPEDIA

The Nature of Wikipedia as a Domain of Coordinated Social Behaviour

Wikipedia belongs to the Open Source movement as it has adopted the Open Source License. It was originally designed to operate under the umbrella of a conventional hierarchical form of governance and its unanticipated success as a radical governance experiment makes it a particularly interesting case study. It was anticipated that findings in relation to the Wikipedia may have some wider relevance to understanding the open source phenomena but also serve to cast light on mechanisms which underpin human institutions– particularly those that are more normative in nature. In order to be able to judge the degree of generalisation that may be possible it is first important to identify the distinctive features of the Wikipedia.

Wikipedia grew out of an earlier Web encyclopaedia project called Nupedia founded by Jimmy Wales with Larry Sanger appointed as its first editor-in-chief. From its inception Nupedia was linked to a free information concept and thus the wider open source movement. Nupedia used traditional hierarchical methods from compiling content with contributors expected to be experts. The resulting complex and time consuming process and an associated lack of openness have been argued to explain the failure of the Nupedia. Sanger (2006a; 2007a), however, questions this view, arguing that the expert model was sound but needed to be simplified.

Sanger was introduced to the WikiWiki software platform in 2001 and saw in it a way to address the limitations hampering Nupedia. The inherent openness of the Wikiwiki environment was, however, seen as a problem so Wikipedia began as an experimental side project. Sanger notes that a majority of the Nupedia Advisory Board did not support the Wikipedia, being of the view '...*that a wiki* could *not resemble an encyclopaedia at all, that it would be too informal and unstructured*' (Sanger, 2007a). However the intrinsic openness of Wikipedia attracted increasing numbers of contributors and quickly developed a life of its own. Almeida et al (2007) note that growth in articles, editors and users have all shown an exponential trajectory. From Sanger's earlier comments it is clear that he had been surprised at the rate of development and of the quality achieved by the relatively un-coordinated action of many editors. Sanger remains committed to the value of expert top down editing having gone on to found Citizendium (Sanger, 2006b, 2007b).

The Debate over Governance in Wikipedia

The use and enforcement of principles and rules has been an ongoing issue within the Wikipedia community with a division emerging between the founders and within the wider community about whether rules were necessary and if they were, how extensive they should be and how they should be policed. The power to police rules or impose sanctions has always been limited by the openness of the technology platform. Initially Sanger and Wales, were the only administrators with the power to exclude participants from the site. In 2004 this authority was passed to an Arbitration Committee which could delegate administrator status more widely. The Arbitration Committee is a mechanism of last resort in the dispute resolution process, only dealing with the most serious disputes. Recommendations for appointment to this committee are made by open elections with appointment the prerogative of Wales.

In the early stages Sanger argues the need was for participants more than rules and so the only rule was 'there is no rule'. The reason for this, he explains, was that they needed to gain experience of how wikis worked before over prescribing the mechanisms. However, *'As the project grew and the requirements of its success became increasingly obvious, I became ambivalent about this particular "rule" and then rejected it altogether'* (Sanger, 2007a). However, in the minds of some members of the community, it had become 'the essence' of Wikipedia.'

In the beginning, complete openness was seen as valuable to encourage all comers and to avoid them feeling intimidated. Radical collaboration – allowing everybody to edit everyone's (unsigned) articles – also avoided ownership and attendant defensiveness. Importantly it also removed bottle necks associated with 'expert' editing. That said the handpicking of a few core people is regarded by Sanger as having had an important and positive impact on the early development of Wikipedia. Sanger argues for example *'I think it was essential that we began the project with a core group of intelligent good writers who understood what an encyclopaedia should look like, and who were basically decent human beings'* (2005). In addition to 'seeding' the culture with a positive disposition, this statement highlights the potential

importance of establishing a style consistent with the Encyclopaedia genre – a stylistic model which might shape the subsequent contributions of others.

Sanger argues that in the early stages 'force of personality' and 'shaming' were the only means used to control contributors and that no formal exclusion occurred for six months, despite there being difficult characters from the beginning. The aim was to live with this 'good natured anarchy' until the community itself could identify and posit a suitable rule-set. Within Wikipedia rules evolved and as new ones were needed they were added to the 'What Wikipedia is not' page'. Wales then added the 'Neutral Point of View' (NPOV) page which emphasised the need for contributions to be free of bias. The combination of clear purpose and the principle of neutrality provided a reference point against which all contributions could be easily judged. Sanger regards the many rules, principles and guidelines which have evolved since as secondary and not essential for success.

How do newcomers learn these (ever increasing) rules and do they actually influence behaviour? Bryant et al (2005) suggest that there is evidence of 'legitimate peripheral practice', a process whereby newcomers learn the relevant rules, norms and skills by serving a kind of apprenticeship. These authors argue that this is evident in new editors of Wikipedia initially undertaking minor editing tasks before moving to more significant contributions, and possibly, eventually, taking administrative roles. These authors tend to project a rather idealistic view of involvement, however, overlooking a key attribute of the wiki environment –newcomers have the same rights as long standing participants and experts and this mechanism for socialising newcomers can be effectively bypassed.

In some Open Source environments (such as Open Source Software) it is possible to gain reputation which may be usable in the wider world. The commitment to the community is often explained (for an excellent overview see Rossi, April, 2004) by arguing that a desire for reputation increases compliance. However, in the Wikipedia environment there is no list of contributors to which an editor can point as evidence of their contribution (although they can self-identify their contributions on their user page). Contributions are, in essence, non attributable. In the case of Wikipedia identification with product, community and values appears a more likely reason for remaining involved than does reputation.

In a study specifically designed to study the conflict and coordination costs of Wikipedia, Kittur, Suh, Pendleton, & Chi (2007: 453) note that there has a been a significant increase in regulatory costs over time. '*...direct work on articles is decreasing, while indirect work such as discussions, procedure, user coordination, and maintenance activity (such as reverts and anti-vandalism) is increasing*'. The proportion of indirect edits (i.e. those on discussion or support pages) has increased from 2% to 12%. Kittur et al cite an interview respondent as stating '*the degree of success that one meets in dealing with conflicts (especially conflicts with experienced editors) often depends on the efficiency with which one can quote policy and precedent.*' (Kittur et al., 2007: 454). This suggests that force of argument supported by the existence of the formal rules and etiquette are important to the governance process. This is however based on ex post attributions.

Wiki Technology: The Artefact

Wiki technology has a *very flat learning curve:* contributing is extremely simple. There are few technical impediments confronting novice users. Wiki platforms are *intrinsically open* supporting decentralised action unless modified to control or restrict access. *Division of labour emerges* as editors choose which pages interest them and which they want to focus on contributing to or maintaining.

Wikipedia has added a number of facilities which support the ready detection and correction of vandalism. *Watch lists* support users in taking

responsibility for the oversight and monitoring of particular topics. Changes made to a page are logged using a *history list* which supports comparison between versions as well as identifying the time and date of any change and the ID of who made that change. The *reversion* facility supports the rapid reinstatement of the page content. Lih (2004: 4) attributes significance to this feature noting that '*This crucial asymmetry tips the balance in favour of productive and cooperative members of the wiki community, allowing quality content to emerge*'. and Stvilia et all (2004: 13) note that '*By allowing the disputing sides to obliterate each others contributions easily, a wiki makes the sides interdependent in achieving their goals and perhaps surprisingly may encourage more consensus building rather than confrontation*'.

Stvilia, Twidale, Gasser, & Smith (2005) among others identify *discussion pages* as an important '*...coordination artefact which helps to negotiate and align members perspectives on the content and quality of the article.*' Discussion pages provide an opportunity for managing minor disputes about content or editing behaviour and for movement towards the agreement.

Ciffiolilli (2007) has argued that a significant consequence of these technical features is the way in which they alter transaction costs (Coase, 1993; Williamson & Winter, 1993). Transaction costs result from information overheads associated with complex coordination. However, the technology does not cancel other costs of coordination and control. These are commonly referred to as agency costs and the highly open nature of the wiki may increase them. In hierarchies, this cost is evident in the cost of command and control (management overhead) whereas in the Open Source environment they are borne by the participating community (and not necessarily equitably). The cost burden will be less where there is a high level of self-regulation and lower where a lack of goal alignment or low social commitment leads contributors to disregard others and act individualistically or opportunistically. The efficacy of cultural control will be influenced by factors such as the homogeneity of the user group and that group's propensity for self-organisation (endogenous norm formation), rates of turnover of the group, and the effect of external perturbation of the group or of the task on which they are working. This may also be subject to feedback effects: reduced norm compliance may lead to higher turnover and reduced commitment, further reducing norm compliance for example.

In conclusion then, Wikipedia is a volunteer open source project characterised by low ties between contributors, no formal obligations and very few means for the exercise of formal sanction. There is a low level of reciprocity with contributors under no obligation to maintain engagement. The wiki technology is open, inviting many to the task and imposing low costs to participation while reducing transaction costs. There is however high reliance on pro-social behaviour dominating if agency costs (borne by individuals) is not to lead to high turnover and possible governance failure. The anonymity of Wikipedia precludes any significant reputation effects outside of the small group of co-editors who maintain extended involvement with an article and to a very limited degree the wider Wikipedia community.

Wikipedians have produced a set of permissions, obligations, rules and norms which have been documented in guidelines and etiquettes as well as embedded in technical artefacts such as style bots. The need for and effect of these is however controversial. From a governance perspective there are relatively few means within Wikipedia by which formal control can be exercised using these rules and the community relies instead on the use of informal or 'soft' control. These mechanisms need to be effective in the face of perturbation from 'vandals' (task saboteurs), 'trolls' (social saboteurs), as well as turnover of contributors in the context of a task which can require the accommodation of emotionally charged and value based issues.

Analysis of Governance Micro-mechanisms

In Wikipedia there are two classes of activity: editing; and conversation about editing. This paper is not concerned with the editing activity (although this is to be considered in future research) but with the self-organising and self-regulating phenomena which make it possible. Insight into this can be gained by examining the Discussion pages which accompany many of the articles rather than the articles themselves. The activity on the Discussion pages comprises a series of 'utterances' or speech acts between contributors about editing activity and the quality of product. On the face of it then, these pages should provide a fertile source of data to support analysis of how governance operates in the Wikipedia, in particular informal or 'soft' governance.

Within these pages we expected to see attempts by editors to influence the behaviour of one another through the only means available to them – communicative acts. We anticipated that these may exhibit some regularity which would allow us to examine both the range and type of events that led to the explicit invocation of rules and norms and which revealed emergent influence patterns which were themselves normative. We wanted also to examine what conventions prevailed and how these compared and interacted with the goal of the community and its policies. A convention is defined here as a behavioural regularity widely observed by members of the community. Policies include explicit codes of conduct as well as guidelines (etiquettes) and principles.

Methodology

For the study we randomly selected a sample of Discussion pages associated with both Controversial and Featured articles. At the time of the study (May/June 2007) there were 583 articles identified by the Wikipedia community as controversial.

The featured articles are more numerous. At the time of the study there were approximately 1900 of them. The analysis reported here is based on a sample of nineteen Controversial and eleven Featured articles. The most recent three pages of discussion were selected for analysis from each Discussion page associated with the article included in the sample.

These were subjected to detailed coding using the Open Source qualitative analysis software WeftQDA. Both qualitative and quantitative analysis was performed. The latter was undertaken by re-processing the coded utterances such that each utterance constituted a case and each applied code a variable associated with that case. This data set was then analysed using SPSS.

A number of coding schemes for natural speech were considered before choosing to use the Verbal Response Mode (VRM) taxonomy (Stiles, 1992). VRM has been developed over many years and used in a wide range of communication contexts. Stiles defines it as *'a conceptually based, general purpose system for coding speech acts. The taxonomic categories are mutually exclusive and they are exhaustive in the sense that every conceivable utterance can be classified.'* (Stiles, 1992: 15). The classification schema is attractive where there is a need (as here) to capture many of the subtleties of natural language use that derive from and rely on the intrinsic flexibility and ambiguity of natural language yet map them to a more formal system needed for computer simulation.

Additional codes were applied to identify: valence, subject of communication, explicit invocation or norms or rules and the associated deontic and trigger, whether the receiver/s accepted the illocutionary force of the utterance and the ID and registration status of the person making the utterance.

There were 3654 utterances coded in these thirty three documents.

Findings

Style of Communication

There was a statistically significant correlation between the article group (Controversial vs Featured) and broad style of communication. This was however very small at -0.078 (p=.01 2-tailed). This difference was most apparent when examined at the level of specific styles. Both groups had approximately similar proportions of neutrally phrased utterances (approximately 64%). Nearly one quarter (22.5%) of all utterances in Featured articles were positive compared to only eleven percent in controversial sites. By comparison nearly one quarter (23.9%) of all utterances in controversial sites were negative compared to fourteen percent for featured. The positive styles of 'affirming', 'encouraging' and 'acknowledging' were significantly overrepresented in the featured articles but underrepresented in the controversial articles. The reverse was the case for the negative styles of 'aggressive', 'contemptuous' and 'dismissive'.

There was a statistically significant correlation between the broad style of communication and the editor status. The correlation was again very low at -.054 (p=.01 two tailed).

Overall, the most common positive utterance was affirming (4.7%) closely followed by encouraging (4.7%) and acknowledging (4.3%). The most common negative utterance was dismissive (8.2%) followed by defensive (6.4%) and contemptuous (3.5%).

All the Wikipedia discussions sampled reflected a strongly neutral-objective *style* (although from the qualitative observations it was apparent that the content was sometimes far from objective or balanced). The statistically significant difference between Controversial and Featured sites was in the relative balance of positive and negative utterance and was not so great as to explain the different status awarded the associated articles.

Validation

Within speech act theory (Habermas, 1976; Searle, 1969), validation refers to whether an utterance made by one speaker is accepted, rejected, ignored or let go unquestioned by the intended recipient/s.

In the Wikipedia sample half of all utterances were accepted without question. A further eighteen percent were explicitly accepted by at least one editor; eleven percent were explicitly rejected and a substantial twenty two percent were ignored. Twenty five percent of positive style utterances were accepted by at least one editor compared to eighteen percent of neutral and only nine percent of negative. By comparison only two percent of positive utterances were rejected compared to nine percent of neutral and twenty six percent of negative. Positive utterances were more likely to be accepted without question (61%) compared to negative (21.7%) and neutral (54.4%). Negative comments were more likely to be ignored (44.1%) compared to neutral (18.2%) and positive (11.4%).

From this we can conclude that positive utterances are more likely to be validated than negative, but that overall, a significant number of utterances are ignored or rejected.

Normative and Rule Invocation

Overall 5.2% of all utterances involved norm or rule invocation. This meant that Wikipedia rules were invoked 122 times and general social norms a further 77 times in 3654 utterances. This overall number was contributed to disproportionately by three (outlier) articles in the sample. Rules were most commonly invoked in response to neutral style communication (63.9%) followed by twenty seven percent in response to a negative style. Only nine percent of positive style utterances were responded to with a rule invocation. By comparison, norms were most commonly invoked in response to negative style utterances (53.2%) followed by neutral (44.2%) and then positive (2.6%). The difference in likelihood of invocation by style was statistically significant (p=.001).

A Wikipedia rule invocation was most likely to be triggered by the *form* of an article (44.9%) an *edit action* (22%); an *article fact* or a *person's behaviour* (both 16%). A norm was most likely to be triggered by a *person's behaviour* (35.6%), an *edit action* (23.3%), *article form* (21.9%), or *article fact* (19.2%). This pattern did not differ to a significant degree between the Featured and Controversial sites.

Nearly three quarters (73.6%) of rule invocations had the implicit deontic of 'it is obligatory' Norms also were most likely to carry this deontic (61.3%). The second most likely deontic was 'it is permissible that' (9.7%).

While there was no statistically significant difference in the degree to which either norms or rules were invoked between the Featured and Controversial articles, there was a qualitative difference in the role norm and rule invocation played. In Controversial discussions, social norms and rules were most likely to be invoked against the behaviour of an editor who was of a different view (group?) while in Featured sites, norms and rules were somewhat more often used by the editor as a reflection on their own contribution – i.e. involved a level of self-check. This might take the form of a statement such as 'I know this is not NPOV but.....'.

Registered vs. Non-registered Users

There was no statistically significant difference in the likelihood for either registered or non-registered users to invoke norms or rules. There was a statistically significant difference between registered and non-registered editors (p=.000) when it came to validation. Registered editors were more likely than non-registered to be explicitly accepted (18.7% of utterances compared to 13.9%), less likely to be rejected (9.9% compared to 13.7%), considerably less likely to be ignored (18.3% compared to 34.7%) or unquestioned (53.1% compared to 37.6%). Qualitatively, however, it was much more common that un-registered users would make suggestions before undertaking edits, particularly in the Features articles, so their behaviour was less likely to attract action or comment.

Non-registered editors were more likely to make negative style utterances (24.3% compared to 18.5%) and less likely to make positive utterances (9.5% compared to 17.4%). This difference was significant (p=.000).

Influence through Illocutionary Force

The theory of speech acts distinguishes between the meaning of an utterance and its pragmatic intent. With the VRM coding frame used in this research each utterance is coded twice, once to capture the semantic form and again to capture the use of language to exert (illocutionary) force (Searle, 1969). A typical utterance may have a *form* which differs from the *intent*. The utterance 'could you close the door?', for example, has the form of a *question* but the intent of *advisement:* the speaker intends the listener to close the door. In VRM, the relationship of form to intent is expressed, using the statement "in service of" (Stiles, 1992). In this example the question 'could you close the door' is 'in service of' the advisement 'close the door'. In standard presentation this is recorded as (QA).

Edification in service of Edification (EE) is the most frequent form of utterance in the Wikipedia sample – 37% of all utterances were of this mode. The Edification mode is defined as deriving from the speaker's frame of reference, making no presumption about the listener and using a neutral (objective) frame of reference shared by both speaker and listener. This mode is informative, unassuming and acquiescent. As a strategy for influencing others it reflects attempts to convince by neutral objective argument.

The second most common mode is that of Disclosure in service of Disclosure (DD). Disclosure is defined as being from the speaker's experience, making no presumption, but being framed using the speaker's frame of reference. This is summarised as informative, unassuming but directive.

Unlike EE mode, DD mode represents an attempt by the speaker to impose or have the listener accept the speaker's frame. Twelve percent of all utterances adopted this form.

The third most common mode is Disclosure in service of Edification (DE). The DE mode represents an utterance which is from the speaker's frame of reference but as if it is neutral or from a shared frame. Eight percent of all utterances used this mode. This is a somewhat neutral mode where the speaker offers clearly labelled personal knowledge as information.

The fourth most common mode is Advisement in service of Advisement (AA). AA mode represents speech from the speaker's experience, which makes presumptions about the listener and adopts the speaker's frame of reference. It can be summarised as informative, presumptuous and directive. It commonly takes the form of 'you should....' Approximately 7% of utterances were in this mode. A further 12% of utterances have the directive pragmatic intent of advisement masked by using a less presumptuous form – that of Edification or Disclosure.

Significantly, utterances associated with politeness (such as acknowledgements 5%) and with discourse which aims at mutual understanding, such as confirmation (1.5%) and reflection (1%), were very rare in the Wikipedia sample.

Discussion of Findings

What is significant about the utterance strategies is that they typically involve an exchange of assertions delivered with a neutral – i.e. non-emotive style. There are very few explicit praises, or put downs, and few niceties like explicit acknowledgements of one another. Seldom do contributors refer to one another by name – the exchanges are rather impersonal. This does not tally with what one would expect if the Wikipedia etiquette (http://en.wikipedia.org/wiki/Wikipedia:Etiquette) had been institutionalised. The Featured articles conform a little more closely with what one would expect than do the Controversial, but if we assume that the etiquette captures the community's ideal, the emerged patterns do not conform to that 'ideal' to the extent that might be expected in either case. Similarly we see low levels of questioning or of reflection (i.e. feeding back the words of the speaker to check understanding or to come to better understand the other's intentions). This is arguably inconsistent with the task needs – to reach consensus on controversial topics. The frequency with which utterances were ignored also suggested low engagement by participants in the discussion. All of this would seem to need some explanation.

The absence of any expression of acknowledgement of emotions and/or similarity of attitude (homophilly) among many contributors suggests that Wikipedia lacks many of the qualities of verbal exchange that would identify it as strong community. It is more consistent with being a place to share coordination of a task. This could suggest that the goal is the primary orienting point. However, the lack of quality of discourse needed to achieve consensus is more indicative of a brief encounter between different and established milieux which struggle to find common understanding rather than of a community committed to a common goal (Becker & Mark, 1997). This might suggest that the shared goal may be subordinate to more personal goals by a considerable proportion of contributors. Or it may be that the technology and environment will support no more than this.

The Wikipedia environment supports saboteurs who can use the opportunity afforded by the open and anonymous platform to use identity deception i.e. to mimic the language and style of an 'expert' or to present as a genuine editor while trying to pursue a personal or political agenda hostile to the aims or interests of the Wikipedia. We found no direct evidence of this behaviour in the pages we sampled even though the discussions about controversial articles provide particularly fertile ground for such sabotage. Nevertheless the threat of it could have an overall influence on the type of communication conventions which arise. Editors may, for example, display reserve and suspicion, withholding trust and taking conventional signals of authority and identity (Donath, 1998) as unreliable. The first principle in the Wikipedia etiquette is 'assume good faith'. To do so would, however, leave the process more vulnerable to 'troll' activity.

Utterance strategies between registered and unregistered editors did not vary greatly, although unregistered editors were more likely to use disclosure intent and more likely to ask questions (possibly associated with the increased likelihood that they are relatively new to Wikipedia). They are also more likely to be negative – reflecting their potentially lower commitment to the article or the community.

Qualitatively there was considerable evidence of mind reading (theory of mind) – i.e. editors appeared to form judgements about the intent of others on relatively little information. There was, however, little evidence of the use of utterance strategies to better understand or check these theories of mind. Some editors, particularly in the Controversial discussions appeared quick to judge and then follow response patterns consistent with those judgements (e.g. ignoring or accepting utterances of others). There were also few instances of renegotiated patterns of communication style. Positions and styles stayed relatively constant over the period of the interaction. Only occasionally would an editor modify his/her style significantly if challenged. Of the rule invocations 26% were accepted, a similar proportion were rejected or ignored and the remainder went unquestioned (but generally had no affect on behaviour). This is consistent with norms being triggered by a limited range of cues which allow individuals to locate themselves and select identities appropriate to a context and which then remain essentially stable. The invocation of rules and norms appears to have little to no immediate effect on behaviour although it is not clear if it has an effect in subsequent behaviour as this cannot be ascertained from the available data.

CONCLUSION AND FUTURE WORK

In this study we set out to identify mechanisms which underpin the emergence of systemic self-organisation in a volunteer on-line global institution. The aim was to specify the mechanisms involved in order to support the design of a simulation architecture suitable for the wider study of normative mechanisms. The findings have challenged some of our assumptions and expectations, in particular:

- The more detailed and specific behavioural etiquette seems to have little influence on the overall character and style of interaction.
- The overall quality of interaction of editors falls short of the range and quality of communicative style characteristic of a community and that would be consistent with what one would expect, given the nature of the task.
- Most regulation is achieved without the need for frequent explicit invocation of rules or norms. Rather, behaviour seems to accord to a convention which editors quickly recognise and conform to. Alternatively the behaviour may reflect norms acquired elsewhere and carried over into their online behaviour. This then minimally accommodates what needs to be done to satisfy the task in a context of potentially heterogeneous personal goals.
- There was a lack of evidence of active negotiation of expectations and standards and convergence of behaviour towards a norm. Within the discussion pages there appeared to be little obvious norm innovation, evolution, adaptation or extension. This suggests that on first encounter with Wikipedia, editors read a set of cues as to what constitutes appropriate or acceptable behaviour and then accommodate it. Alternatively the order observed may be largely attributable to the prior socialisation of participants with local norms and rules playing a very minor part in supporting task regulation.
- While there is a difference between controversial and featured sites this is minimal and the quality of the interaction cannot explain the difference in status. Similarly there appeared to be little in the subject matter of the two groups of articles which would explain the difference – both contained subject matter which was contestable and subject to significantly diverse opinion.

Wikipedia is not a market as there is no tradable product or price, either in a conventional sense or in the form of tradable reputation. Nor is Wikipedia a command hierarchy: the openness of the wiki platform and the low cost of joining and leaving preclude formal control as a primary means for governance. Neither is Wikipedia well described by the network theory of governance as there is no obligation to maintain involvement. While it might be expected that the Bazaar Governance would apply, the absence of a reputation mechanism suggests that it may be better considered through the more general lens of stewardship theory. Even here, there is no role for moral leadership but rather a diffused willingness to comply with certain minimum standards on the part of a sufficient majority.

There is no clear basis to argue that the apparent order is a direct result of the use of deontic commands associated with social norms and environment specific rules. Despite the fact that the community has been a prolific rule generator, they appear to play a minor role. Contributors demonstrate a style which is broadly inconsistent with these rules and not a good fit with the task.

Overall though there is order and it appears to be emergent. The mechanisms which underpin this emergence have not been revealed by the analysis undertaken to date although some hypotheses can be tentatively suggested. The neutral-objective style may be a consequence of the anonymity and open nature of the environment – leading to a suspension of trust. It may propagate as new comers copy the pattern through a process of behavioural cueing. It is possible also that the order is due to pro-social behaviour internalized and brought to the task. The volunteer nature of Wikipedia, and the level of commitment required, is likely to mean that long term editors reflect a pro-social disposition (Penner, Dovidio, Piliavin, & Schroeder, 2005). In this context a little norm/rule invocation may go a long way if not by influencing immediate behaviour then by encouraging future compliance and/or by giving incentive for non-compliers to leave. The relatively small difference in overall style apparent in relation to the diverse range of articles may have little to do with the specific communicative behaviours adopted in communication about that article but rather due to the chance association of individuals at a given point of time and how this subtle process of encouragement and dissuasion plays out over time. Such a view is quite different from that modelled in past attempts to simulate social norms.

REFERENCES

Ablowitz, R. (1939). The Theory of Emergence. *Philosophy of Science*, 6(1), 16. doi:10.1086/286529

Almeida, R. B., Mozafari, B., & Cho, J. (2007). *On the Evolution of Wikipedia*. Paper presented at the International Conference on Weblogs and Social Media

Becker, B., & Mark, G. (1997). *Constructing Social Systems through Computer Mediated Communication*. German National Research Center for Information Technology.

Berger, P. L., & Luckman, T. (1972). *The Social Construction of Reality*. New York: Penguin.

Bicchieri, C. (2006). *The Grammar of Society*. Cambridge, UK: Cambridge University Press.

Bryant, S. L., Forte, A., & Bruckman, A. (2005). *Becoming Wikipedian: Transformation of Participation in a Collaborative Online Encyclopedia*. Paper presented at the GROUP 05.

jCiffolilli, A. (2007). Phantom Authority, self-selective recruitement and retention of members in virtual communities: The case of Wikipedia [Electronic Version]. *FirstMonday*, 8. Retrieved 20 April 2007 from http://firstmonday.org/issues/issue8_12/ciffolilli/index.html.

Clayton, P. (2006). Conceptual Foundations of Emergence Theory. In Clayton, P., & Davies, P. (Eds.), *The re-Emergence of Emergence: The Emergentist Hypothesis from Science to Religion*. Oxford, UK: Oxford University Press.

Coase, R. H. (1993). The Nature of The Firm. In Williamson, O. E., & Winter, S. G. (Eds.), *The Nature of the Firm: Origins, Evolution and Development*. New York: Oxford University Press.

Coase, R. H. (1995). *Essays on Economics and Economists*. Chicago: University of Chicago Press.

Davies, P. (2006). The Physics of Downward Causation. In Clayton, P., & Davies, P. (Eds.), *The Re-Emergence of Emergence: The Emergentist Hypothesis from Science to Religion*. Oxford, UK: Oxford University Press.

Davis, J. H., Schoorman, D., & Donaldson, L. (1997). Towards a Stewardship Theory of Management. *Academy of Management Review*, 22(1), 20–47. doi:10.2307/259223

Davis, J. H., Schoorman, D. F., & Donaldson, L. (1997). Towards a Stewardship Theory of Management. *Academy of Management Review*, 22(1), 20–47. doi:10.2307/259223

Demil, B., & Lecocq, X. (2003). *Neither market or hierarchy or network: The emerging bazaar governance*. Université Lille/Institut d'Administration des Entreprises.

Donaldson, L., & Davis, J. H. (1991). Stewardship Theory or Agency Theory: CEO Governance and Shareholder Returns. *Australian Journal of Management, 16*(1), 49–65. doi:10.1177/031289629101600103

Donath, J. S. (1998). Identity and deception in the virtual community. In Kollock, P., & Smith, M. (Eds.), *Communities in Cyberspace*. London: Routledge.

Ellis, G. F. R. (2006). On the Nature of Emergent Reality. In Clayton, P., & Davies, P. (Eds.), *The Re-Emergence of Emergence: The Emergentist Hypothesis from Science to Religion*. Oxford, UK: Oxford University Press.

Emmeche, C., Koppe, S., & Stjernfelt, F. (1997). Explaining Emergence: Towards an Ontology of Levels. *Journal for General Philosophy of Science*, (28): 83–119. doi:10.1023/A:1008216127933

Gibbs, J. P. (1981). *Norms, Deviance and social control: Conceptual matters*. New York: Elsevier.

Gilbert, N. (2002). *Varieties of Emergence*. Paper presented at the Social Agents: Ecology, Exchange, and Evolution Conference Chicago.

Giles, J. (2005). Internet Encyclopaedias go head to head [Electronic Version]. *Nature*. Retrieved 20 April 2007 from http://www.nature.com/news/2005/051212/full/438900a.html.

Goldspink, C. (2008). *Towards a socio-ecological View of emergence: the reflexive turn* Paper presented at the Embracing Complexity: Advancing ecological understanding in organization EGOS Summer Workshop.

Goldspink, C., & Kay, R. (2007). *Social Emergence: Distinguishing Reflexive and Non-reflexive modes*. Paper presented at the AAAI Fall Symposium: Emergent Agents and Socialities: Social and Organizational Aspects of Intelligence.

Goldspink, C., & Kay, R. (2008). *Agent Cognitive Capabilities and Orders of Emergence: critical thresholds relevant to the simulation of social behaviours'*. Paper presented at the AISB Convention, Communication, Interaction and Social Intelligence.

Goldspink, C., & Kay, R. (2008). Agent Cognitive Capability and Orders of Emergence. In Trajkovski, G., & Collins, S. (Eds.), *Agent-Based Societies: Social and Cultural Interactions*.

Goldstein, J. (1999). Emergence as a Construct: History and Issues. *Emergence, 1*(1), 49–72. doi:10.1207/s15327000em0101_4

Habermas, J. (1976). Some Distinctions in Universal Pragmatics: A working paper. *Theory and Society, 3*(2), 12.

Holland, J. H. (1998). *Emergence: from chaos to order*. Reading, MA: Addison Wesley.

Jensen, M. C., & Meckling, W. H. (1976). Theory of the firm: Managerial behavior, agency costs, and ownership structure. *Journal of Financial Economics, 3*, 305–360. doi:10.1016/0304-405X(76)90026-X

Jones, C., Hesterly, W. S., & Borgatti, S. P. (1997). A General Theory of Network Governance: Exchange Conditions and Social Mechanisms. *Academy of Management Review, 22*(4), 911–945. doi:10.2307/259249

Jones, C., Hesterly, W. S., & Borgatti, S. P. (1997). A General Theory of Network Governance: Exchange Conditions and Social Mechanisms. *Academy of Management Review, 22*(4), 911–945. doi:10.2307/259249

Kennedy, J., & Eberhart, R. C. (2001). *Swarm Intelligence* (1 ed.). London: Academic Press.

Kittur, A., Suh, B., Pendleton, B. A., & Chi, E. H. (2007). *He Says, She says: Conflict and coordination in Wikipedia*. Paper presented at the Computer/Human Interaction 2007, San Jose USA.

Konieczny, P. (2009). Governance, Organization, and Democracy on the Internet: The Iron Law and the Evolution of Wikipedia. *Sociological Forum*, *24*(1), 162–192. doi:10.1111/j.1573-7861.2008.01090.x

Medelyan, O., Milne, D., Legg, C., & Witten, I. H. (2009). Mining meaning from Wikipedia. *International Journal of Human-Computer Studies*, *67*, 716–754. doi:10.1016/j.ijhcs.2009.05.004

Penner, L. A., Dovidio, J. F., Piliavin, J. A., & Schroeder, D. A. (2005). Prosocial behavior: Multilevel perspectives. *Annual Review of Psychology*, *56*, 365–392. doi:10.1146/annurev. psych.56.091103.070141

Richardson, K. A. (2002). *On the Limits of Bottom Up Computer Simulation: Towards a Non-linear Modeling Culture*. Paper presented at the 36th Hawaii International Conference on Systems Science, Hawaii.

Rossi, M. A. (April, 2004). *Decoding the "Free/Open Source (F/OSS) Puzzle" - a Survey of Theretical and Empirical Contributions*. Unpublished Working paper. University of Sienna.

Sanger, L. (2005). The Early History of Nupedia and Wikipedia: A Memoir [Electronic Version]. *Slashdot*. Retrieved 12 April 2007 from file:///C:/ data/surrey/Case%20Studies/wikipedia/early%20 history%20of%20nupedia%20and%20wikipedia. htm.

Sanger, L. (2006a). The Nupedia myth [Electronic Version]. *ZDNet.com* from http://talkback.zdnet. com/5208-10535-0.html?forumID=1&threadID= 22228&messageID=422549&start=-39.

Sanger, L. (2006b). *Why Make room for experts in web 2 [Electronic Version]*. Retrieved 12 April 2007 from http://www.citizendium.org/roomfor-experts.html.

Sanger, L. (2007a). The Early History of Nupedia and Wikipedia: A Memoir [Electronic Version]. *Slashdot*. Retrieved 12 April 2007 from file:///C:/ data/surrey/Case%20Studies/wikipedia/early%20 history%20of%20nupedia%20and%20wikipedia. htm.

Sanger, L. (2007b). *Why the Citizendium Will (probably) succeed* [Electronic Version]. Retrieved 13 April 2007 from http://www.citizendium.org/ whyczwillsucceed.html.

Sawyer, K. R. (2003). Artificial Societies: Multiagent Systems and the Micro-macro Link in Sociological Theory. *Sociological Methods & Research*, *31*, 38. doi:10.1177/0049124102239079

Sawyer, K. R. (2005). *Social Emergence: Societies as Complex Systems*. Cambridge, UK: Cambridge University Press. doi:10.1017/ CBO9780511734892

Searle, J. R. (1969). *Speech Act: An Essay in the Philosophy of Language*. Cambridge, UK: Cambridge University Press.

Stiles, W. B. (1992). *Describing Talk: A Taxonomy of Verbal Response Modes*. Thousand Oaks, CA: Sage.

Stvilia, B., Twidale, M. B., Gasser, L., & Smith, L. C. (2005). *Information Quality Discussions in Wikipedia*. Illinois: Graduate School of Library and Information Science.

Therborn, G. (2002). Back to Norms! On the Scope and Dynamics of Norms and Normative Action. *Current Sociology*, *50*(6), 17. doi:10.1177/0011392102050006006

Williamson, O. E. (1996). *The Mechanisms of Governance*. New York: Oxford University Press.

Williamson, O. E., & Winter, S. G. (1993). *The Nature of The Firm: Origins, Evolution and Development*. New York: Oxford University Press.

Section 3
Applications

Chapter 13

A Multi–Agent Machine Learning Framework for Intelligent Energy Demand Management

Ying Guo
CSIRO ICT Centre, Australia

Rongxin Li
CSIRO ICT Centre, Australia

ABSTRACT

In order to cope with the unpredictability of the energy market and provide rapid response when supply is strained by demand, an emerging technology, called energy demand management, enables appliances to manage and defer their electricity consumption when price soars. Initial experiments with our multi-agent, power load management simulator, showed a marked reduction in energy consumption when price-based constraints were imposed on the system. However, these results also revealed an unforeseen, negative effect: that reducing consumption for a bounded time interval decreases system stability. The reason is that price-driven control synchronizes the energy consumption of individual agents. Hence price, alone, is an insufficient measure to define global goals in a power load management system. In this chapter the authors explore the effectiveness of a multi-objective, system-level goal which combines both price and system stability. The authors apply the commonly known reinforcement learning framework, enabling the energy distribution system to be both cost saving and stable. They test the robustness of their algorithm by applying it to two separate systems, one with indirect feedback and one with direct feedback from local load agents. Results show that their method is not only adaptive to multiple systems, but is also able to find the optimal balance between both system stability and energy cost.

DOI: 10.4018/978-1-60960-171-3.ch013

Copyright © 2011, IGI Global. Copying or distributing in print or electronic forms without written permission of IGI Global is prohibited.

INTRODUCTION

As technology advances, consumers become increasingly more power hungry. This causes many countries, including Australia, to suffer from an increasing gap between electricity supply and demand (Hou, 2007; US, 2002). The traditional way of tackling such a problem is to increase supply by investing heavily in infrastructure and building more generators. Alternatively, power load management can reduce levels of power consumption on the demand side, and hence reduce the level of energy required to run appliances, saving money and reducing the risk of inadequate supply (Sutton, et. al. 1998; Wilson, et. al. 2003).

Electricity distribution is a complex system, consisting of loads, generators, and transmission and distribution networks (Guo, et. al. 2005). To control this physical system, generators and retailers bid into a market that balances supply and demand while ensuring safe network operation. Demand and price fluctuate quickly and loads that are responsive in real time can have high value to retailers and networks. This scenario is ideal for the adoption of multi-agent technology (Dimeas, et. al. 2004; McArthur, et. al. 2005). A network of autonomous agents can be overlaid on the physical distribution network, controlling customer loads and, where available, local generators (Borenstein et. al. 2002; Hagg, et. al. 1995; Li, et. al. 2008; Platt, 2009; Ygge, 1998).

Australia's Commonwealth Scientific and Industrial Research Organisation (CSIRO) is developing an energy management and control system that consists of an agent network to be installed at multiple levels of the electricity distribution network (James, et. al. 2006; Li, et. al. 2007; Li, et. al. 2007; Zeman, et. al. 2008). This system has a three-level architecture consisting of the following types of agents: 1) the top-level *broker agent*; 2) the middle-level *group agent* and 2) the bottom-level *appliance agent*.

Appliance agents are responsible for the low-level management of consumption for each end-use device. At the bottom level, appliances can be intelligently switched on or off based on customer preferences (Guo, et. al. 2005). A cluster of such agents is then managed by a group agent on the middle level (Li, et. al. 2007; Ogston, et. al. 2007). The group agents also receive an energy quota from an upper-level broker agent representing the needs of electricity market participants and network operators. This energy quota is a limit on the total energy consumption for a group of appliances.

In this paper, we focus on the intelligent management of the broker agent -- that is, how to choose the optimal strategy to provide the real-time quota to the group agent. As the top level in the system, the broker agent needs to incorporate information from the market (such as the current local price of energy) as well as input from group agents (Guo, 2007). The broker agent is required to manage the risk of exposure to volatile wholesale pool prices and reduce strain on the network.

Energy price can change dramatically when the demand is very high such as a hot summer afternoon. Because market energy prices and weather conditions are dynamic, we chose to use one of the machine learning algorithms, the reinforcement learning (RL) framework, as an online learning approach. The two usual approaches to reinforcement learning are model-free and model-based. Model-free algorithms perform well for simple problems. Because the energy market is a dynamic system which exhibits unpredictable properties such as the price of energy, we cannot easily generate a model beforehand. Hence we use the model free RL algorithm – Q-learning. To cope with the dynamic nature of the energy market, we enable the reward matrix to update towards the optimum (which is different from conventional RL) while the agent learns the environment. We present this approach and its application for setting the system-level goal. The experimental results show that by using this method, the broker agent is not only adaptive to multiple systems, but is also able to find an optimal balance between both system stability and energy cost.

The remainder of this paper is organised as follows. Section 2 outlines our approach and Section 3 describes the RL learning process. In Section 4, we present experimental results in a simulated environment. Finally, conclusions based on these experiments are given in Section 5.

PROBLEM DESCRIPTION

Australian Energy Network Model

In Australia, the National Electricity Market Management Company Limited (NEMMCO) was established in 1996 to administer and manage the National Electricity Market (NEM), to develop the market and continually improve its efficiency. Figure 1 shows the typical Australian energy and financial flow under management of NEMMCO. Within such flow structure, wholesale trading in electricity is conducted under a spot market where supply and demand are instantaneously matched in real-time through a centrally-coordinated dispatch process. Generators offer to supply the market with specific amounts of electricity at particular prices. From all offers submitted, NEMMCO determines which generators are to produce electricity by meeting prevailing demand in the most cost-efficient way. NEMMCO then dispatches these generators into production. A dispatch price is determined every five minutes, and six dispatch prices are averaged every half-hour to determine the spot price for each trading interval for each of the regions of the NEM. NEMMCO also sets a maximum spot price of $10,000 per Megawatt hour. This is the maximum price at which generators can bid into the market. During most times of the year, the spot price is low (less than $20 per Megawatt hour), but every now and then, it can also be very high (near or at the maximum price), when there is a peak demand. This occurs when energy supply is under extreme pressure,

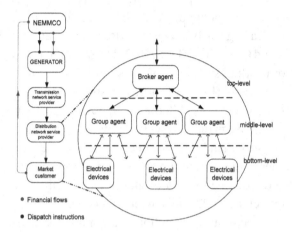

Figure 1. An energy network model. Left: Typical Australian energy and financial flow. Right: Enlarged three-level multi-agent structure for our system

such as when there is extreme high temperature on a hot summer day.

Electricity is not economically storable, and being a volatile commodity, production is subject to rigid, short-term capacity constraints. Since demand is highly variable, this means there will be times when there is plenty of capacity and the only incremental costs of producing electricity are fuel, operating and maintenance costs. At other times, the capacity constraint will be binding, causing the incremental cost to increase greatly and market prices to rise (Borenstein, et. al. 2002; US, 2002; Wilson, et. al. 2002).

Multi-Agent Architecture Placement

For NEMMCO, the highest priority is power system reliability. To improve reliability of the power system and avoid the maximum spot price, one approach is to intelligently reduce the peak demand. To do so, we design an energy management architecture as shown in Figure 1. This structure is comprised of two layers (bottom-level & middle level) of energy distribution agents, and one layer of consumption manager agents (top-level). This tri-level architecture can be easily outlined in a

Figure 2. Exchange of information between Broker and Group Agent

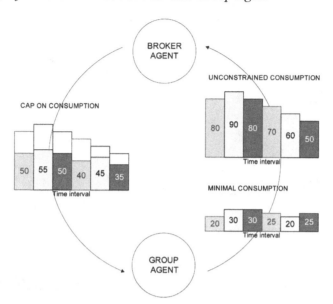

bottom-up fashion. On the consumption level, the energy usage of electrical devices or appliances may be controlled, to a varying degree, by the device-manager agents that switch on and off the power supply to the device. A cluster of such agents, grouped together according to physical or market driven factors, are managed by a group agent on the lower distribution level (Guo, et. al. 2008; Li, et. al. 2007; Ogston, et. al. 2007). The group agent, in turn, receives a group quota from an upper-level distribution agent, referred to as the broker agent. The broker agent, which can view the spot price as well as the group demand requirements, defines the quota in order to achieve system-level goals, described in Section 2.4.

The Role of Broker Agent

The goal of the broker agent is to retrieve up-to-date information on the market and demand requirements, make dynamic, informed decisions on local energy consumption limits and propagate this information down to the group agent. The information passed to a group agent is referred

to as a *cap*, and is the upper limit of energy consumption allocated to a particular group.

The sequence of events for deciding a cap in the broker agent is as follows. Firstly, the broker agent communicates with external parties to obtain knowledge of current and historical data, such as the latest market price, regional demand, local weather, etc. Secondly, the broker agent communicates with the group agent to gain knowledge of local energy demand requirements. These local energy demand requirements are expressed as two sets of information: 1) the minimal achievable consumption of the group and 2) the unconstrained (default) consumption of the group. Here minimal is defined as the total minimal consumption over an entire future market cycle interval (e.g., five minute interval). The unconstrained (default) consumption of the group refers to the total consumption of the group when agents operate under normal conditions without external influence (see Figure 2). Lastly, the broker agent calculates the cap on the next market cycle interval for the group agent using all information available to it. The cap calculated by the broker lies inclusively between

Figure 3. Imposing a strict cap on consumption creates future oscillations in demand

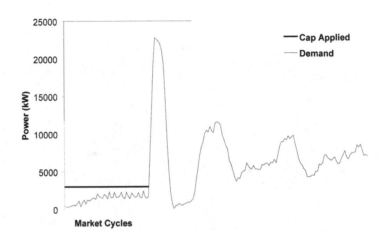

the values of the constrained and unconstrained plans sent from the group agent.

One would assume that an optimal cap function would be the minimal achievable consumption for the group; that is, restricting the agent energy consumption levels to the lowest possible value that the system can cope with. In fact, when imposing a minimal cap, electricity which is not consumed in one period will usually need to be consumed at a later time. The longer a minimal cap is imposed, the more devices are pushed to a stressful limit, so that when the cap is released, all appliance agents, having been energy-starved, choose to switch on at that point, causing demand to increase rapidly. This result is demonstrated in Figure 3, which shows the total power demand of a system of one hundred simulated refrigerators: when a strict cap is imposed in the first half hour, a peak level in consumption occurs when the cap is released. Such peak demand can cause negative effects such as shortage in energy provision or a peak price. System stability is then threatened. Hence the broker agent needs to define a cap which not only reduces energy costs, but also avoids instability within the system.

Cap Function Definition

We assume the capped value of collective energy consumption is imposed over a period T. The cap can be expressed as a constant that directly defines the limit or as a time varying, piece-wise function. The *cap function, $L(t_j)$*, where $t_0 \le t_j < t_0 + T$, is represented in the following form:

$$L(t_j) = l_j \left(\kappa_{un}(t_j) - \kappa_{min}(t_j) \right) + \kappa_{min}(t_j) \qquad (1)$$

where the *cap ratio, $l_j \in [0,1]$*, is a time invariant, $t_j = t_0 + j\delta, j \in Z$, $J = \{j \in Z : 0 \le j\delta < T\}$, $\kappa_{un}(t)$ is the unconstrained consumption of the group, and $\kappa_{min}(t)$ is the minimal consumption of the group. Here δ is the market cycle interval. We also assume that $\kappa_{un}(t)$ and $\kappa_{min}(t)$ are time invariant during each interval.

This function defines a sequence of percentages over T, where cap ratio $l_j = 0$ means the cap is equivalent to the minimal consumption $\kappa_{min}(t_j)$, $l_j = 1$ means the cap is equivalent to the unconstrained consumption $\kappa_{un}(t_j)$. When $0 < l_j < 1$, the cap is chosen to be a value between $\kappa_{min}(t_j)$ and $\kappa_{un}(t_j)$, calculated by $L(t_j)$.

THE LEARNING METHOD FOR OPTIMAL CAP SELECTION

Reinforcement Learning

The main goal now is to find an algorithm that the broker agent can use to set an near-optimal cap for the group agent. The judgment of the "optimal" cap can be measured based upon two important elements:

- **Cost**: the global cost of utilizing energy;
- **System stability**: the energy demand distribution along the time dimension.

In this optimization problem, there is insufficient information to apply a supervised learning methodology. In typical supervised learning algorithms, sample input-output pairs are required to be learnt from. The broker agents in our problem have no a-priori knowledge of "correct" cap settings. The dynamic nature of the energy market is yet another reason why the application of a supervised learning methodology is unsuitable. The market changes its behavior due to many direct and indirect factors such as local temperature, weather condition, market spot price and predicted demand.

It is therefore necessary to use a learning methodology which allows the agent to learn its behavior online based on feedback from the environment. We choose one of the most popular reinforcement learning (RL) approaches, Q-learning, to allow the broker agent to learn from experience. Behavioral learning is adaptive with time, allowing RL to cope with control of a dynamic system, such as energy demand. Adopting behavioral learning provides the added advantage that there is little need for the broker agent to know about the system. The broker agent can learn how to set the cap through trial-and-error interactions with the environment.

For Q-learning, a matrix R is used to model the environment reward system (Watkins, et. al. 1992).

Then, another matrix, named Q, is put into the brain of the agent that will represent the memory of what the agent has learned through experience. In our problem, because of the non-stationary and dynamic nature of the energy system, the environment may be different for the same agent action. To cope with this problem, we enable the R matrix to be updated in parallel with learning the Q matrix. The pseudo code of this method is presented in Table 1.

State Space Definition

To initialize the learning algorithm, we first need to define the state space, the action space and the action reward / penalty function. In our problem, the energy demand, the electricity price, and the cap are real values. To simplify the algorithm, we first transform these values into discrete quantities.

Three energy demand (d) states are {low, medium, high} using two thresholds D_L and D_H:

$$d = \begin{cases} low & as\ d < D_L \\ medium & as\ D_L \leq d < D_H \\ high & as\ D_H \leq d \end{cases}.$$

Two electricity price (P) states are {normal, abnormal}:

$$P = \begin{cases} normal & when\ P < \$100\ /\ MWh \\ abnormal & when\ P \geq \$100\ /\ MWh \end{cases}$$

- Cap ratio (l) states are {50%, 70%, 80%, 90%, 100%}. The cap function $L(t)$ can then be calculated according to equation (1) as the action.

We define the combination of the energy demand d, the electricity price P, and the cap ratio l as the state $s=(d, P, l)$. Hence the size of the state space s is: 3x2x5=30 in this case. The above

Table 1. The Learning Approach

Initialize environment reward matrix R: elements equal to $-\infty$

Initialize the discount-rate parameter γ ($0 \leq \gamma \leq 1$)

Initialize the Q matrix as a zero matrix

Set episode counter to one

WHILE episode counter is less than or equal to total number of episode

• Decide the initial state – random select l_1, read in $\kappa_{un}(t_0)$, $\kappa_{min}(t_0)$, $P(t_0)$

　• DO while not read end of current episode

o Select l_i among all possible actions for current state

o Using l_i to calculate $d(t)$ and go to the next state

　　o Get next state based on all possible actions

　　o Calculate immediate reward w using eq. (3)

　　o Update R matrix: $R(s, l) \leftarrow (R(s, l) + w)/2$

　　o Update Q matrix:

$$Q(s_t, l_t) \leftarrow R(s_t, l_t) + \gamma \max_l Q(s_{t+1}, l)$$

　• ENDDO

ENDWHILE

---

threshold and discrete settings are predefined according to properties of the Australian market. We will show in the experimental section that such simple discretization and small state space still provides good results for the broker agent. Note that we can always enlarge the state space by defining finer discrete thresholds.

Learning Process for Cap Selection

The broker agent is first initialized with an allocation of group agents under its control. $\kappa_{un}(t_0)$ is the initial unconstrained consumption plan (request) sent from the group agent, along with the minimal consumption plan $\kappa_{min}(t_0)$ for the group. On initialization, the broker agent also receives environmental state information such as $P(t_0)$, the market electricity price at $t = t_0$.

Firstly, the group agent sends the plan information to the broker agent. The broker then calculates an initial cap $L(t_1)$ using equation (1), with a randomly chosen l_1. This cap is propagated down to group agents which then adjust the consumption profiles of their loads. The real energy consumed

$d(t_1)$ is reported to the broker agent when the current market cycle is complete. The broker agent's state at time t_1 is decided as $s(t_1) = \left(d(t_1), P(t_1), L(t_1)\right)$. Here, the real energy consumed $d(t)$ is mainly decided by previous cap and previous plans $\kappa_{un}(t-1)$, $\kappa_{min}(t-1)$. Hence it is defined as:

$$d(t) = \kappa_{un}(t) + \beta * (1 - l_{t-1}) * \left(\kappa_{un}(t-1) - \kappa_{min}(t-1)\right) \tag{2}$$

where β is an effect-factor which describes the side effect of the cap from the previous time step (ref. to Figure 3).

At the *Nth* time step, a reward is provided as:

$$w = -(\alpha \sum_{j=1}^{N} P_j \times d_j + \sigma^2), \tag{3}$$

The reward function has a two-fold purpose, as described in Section 3.1, which is reflected in the function as two separate terms. The first term gives a reward based on the cost of energy in the previous N time units. The second term gives a reward based upon the variation σ^2 of the cap $L(t)$. The parameter α is a weight which reflects the importance between these two measurements.

The pseudo code of the algorithm is as in Table 1. During each training session (each episode), the broker agent explores the environment (represented by Matrix R) and retrieves the reward w until the end of the learning process. The purpose of training is to enhance the "brain" of the broker agent, represented by the Q matrix. More training will result in a finer-tuned Q matrix that can be used by the agent to make optimal decisions.

The feedback mechanism within the system creates a flow-on effect of decisions. That is, a different cap which is chosen within one market cycle will result in different energy requirements for following cycles. This flow-on effect is represented in the algorithm as the discount-rate parameter γ, which has a range of 0 to 1 ($0 \leq \gamma \leq 1$). If γ is closer to zero, the agent will tend to consider only immediate reward. If γ is closer to one, the agent will consider future reward with greater weight, willing to delay the reward. The size of the R matrix is decided by the number of states. That is, a 30x30 matrix. It is initialized to be a matrix with values of negative infinity because there is no knowledge about the environment, hence no reward. The R matrix is then updated as a function of the immediate reward at each time step. We can perform learning of the R matrix whilst also learning the Q matrix simultaneously. The R matrix dynamically adjusts to suit the non-stationary environment, including complex effects such as the market, group agent demand and weather.

EXPERIMENTS

In this section, we will show how the above learning approach is applied to the broker agent that can choose an optimal strategy to provide the real-time quota to the group agent. We will consider two different scenarios separately.

Scenario One: Without Direct Feedback from Group Agent

Because the electricity market price and demand cannot be strongly affected when total electricity devices under demand management is a small proportion of the whole market. We started our first experiments with such scenario that the cap setting does not directly cause group agents to change their consumption. Hence the indirect effect is calculated by equation (2). For this scenario, the NEMMCO datasets were used.

Data Preparation

The price and demand values chosen fell in the January 2006 period, shown in Figure 4. There were several price peaks during this month for the NSW state of Australia, where the highest value was \$529.95 on 23rd January 2006. In fact, the highest demand (12674.6 MWh) also occurred on the same day.

To generate the learning samples, we firstly cut the datasets into pieces (episodes) where each piece has 5 data points as $E_m = \{(d_1, P_1)(d_2, P_2)(d_3, P_3)(d_4, P_4)(d_5, P_5)\}$.

Experiments

With each episode E_m, we learn the R matrix and Q matrix using the following update rule. Firstly, we read in (d_1, P_1), and randomly select a cap ratio l_1. The immediate reward can be calculated according to equations (2) and (3). Another random selected cap is defined as l_2. With the calculated d_2 (using eq. (2)), the next state is then fixed. Hence the corresponding value in the R matrix is updated using the immediate reward, and so is the $Q(s,l)$. In our experiments, we set parameters $\gamma = 0.8$, and $\beta = 0.2$. Using data for the entire

Figure 4. NEMMCO Demand and price data of January 2006 for the NSW region of Australia

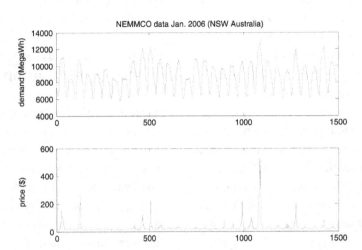

month, the first half of the episodes were used for learning the R and Q matrices and the latter half were used for testing.

Experimental results are shown in Figure 5, Figure 6 and Figure 7. Because the reward matrix R is learnt online, the reward function (3) is crucial to the learning results. With the different choice of α in the reward function (3), different cap optimization results were achieved. When the optimization was focused on the cost of demand, the capped demand was kept low (below 10,000 Megawatts for the majority of the time in Figure 5). Smaller demand creates instability in the cap ratio (see top figure in Figure 5). On the other hand, if we put too much emphasis on cap stability, energy demand and cost were ignored, leading to the results in Figure 6.

The best results, illustrated in Figure 7, negotiated the balance between demand cost and system stability. Clearly, the low cap matches the high price very well. When low market prices occurred, the cap was released to 90% of demand requested, avoiding future demand oscillation (as shown in Figure 3).

Scenario Two: With Direct Feedback from the Group Agent

For this scenario, the recently developed CSIRO multi-agent platform (Prokopenko, et. al. 2007) was used. In this platform, cap setting in one market cycle or time step directly affects the group agents' demand consumption for the next time step. Hence, equation (2) is no longer required.

Within this architecture, when a group agent receives a consumption limit, and subsequently determines that it is below the normal collective requirement (unconstrained demand), it will then modify the devices' plans to delay their electricity usage whilst also minimizing the impact on the appliances (level of interference) or their operations (e.g. average temperature in a refrigerator). Placing a constraint on the level of consumption for one market cycle will increase the level of required consumption for that agent in the following market cycle. Details of the system architecture are described in the paper by Li, et. al. (2007).

Data Preparation

Datasets of demand were generated by the CSIRO demand management simulator. In these experiments we simulate 100 appliances (refrigerators)

Figure 5. Cap setting where optimization is focused on minimizing demand and cost. Top: Cap chosen by broker agent; Bottom: Unconstrained consumption vs. capped energy consumed

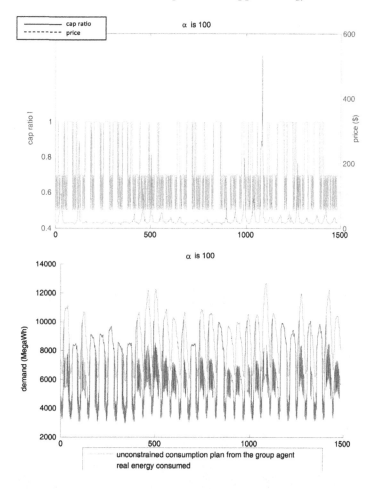

Figure 6. Cap setting where the optimization focus is on system stability

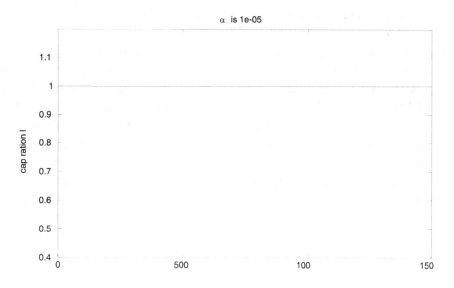

Figure 7. Cap setting where optimization is based on balancing cost and system stability. Top: Cap chosen by the broker agent; Bottom: Unconstrained consumption vs. capped energy consumed

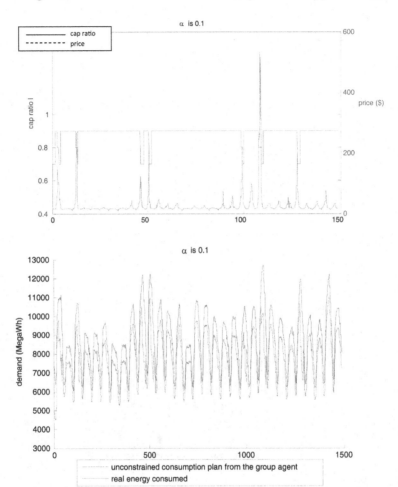

Experiments

with randomly selected cycle times between 30 and 50 mins. The temperature bounds of all appliances are between 1 and 10 degrees Celsius. All appliances are rated at 1000kW, consuming an average of 1000kW per hour. Price data used was retrieved from NEMMCO archives for January 2005 for the NSW region of Australia. Experiments were simulated over a period of one month, with 5 minute time intervals for each market cycle. The unconstrained demand and price profiles are shown in Figure 8.

For this scenario, the *R* and *Q* matrices were learnt over the first half of the month, before the resultant *Q* matrix was tested for the remainder of the month. When optimization focused on the cost of demand, the capped demand was kept low, producing similar results to Scenario One. When the cap was chosen as a compromise between system stability and cost, results were again similar to Scenario One, illustrated in Figure 9. The real energy consumed is lower than the unconstrained

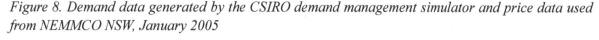

Figure 8. Demand data generated by the CSIRO demand management simulator and price data used from NEMMCO NSW, January 2005

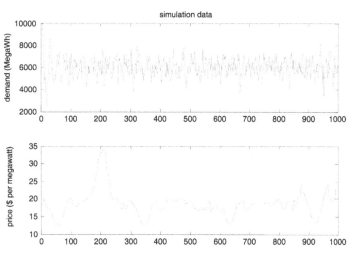

consumption plan from the group agent, while the system stability is achieved as well. These experiments demonstrate the ability for the algorithm to be applied to a real-time environment where direct feedback is implemented. Because comparable results were achieved for this scenario, the assumption (equation (2)) can be used when the cap optimization approach is used for other market systems where the closed loop in Figure 2 does not exist.

CONCLUSION

The electricity market is a dynamic system, where demand and price can fluctuate dramatically. Demand management is a recent attempt to control fluctuations in energy requirements at the appliance level, hence reducing the cost of energy provision. Using agent technology, devices can monitor and control their consumption, essentially delaying their energy usage when the demand for electricity is high. This architecture provides benefits to multiple stakeholders, including monetary relief to consumers, as well as relief to the energy network infrastructure.

Initial experiments on reducing energy consumption for short periods were conducted in order to quantify cost savings for high price periods. These experiments revealed an unpredictable effect of system instability when system constraints were released (Figure 3). In order to achieve lower cost without compromising system stability, we propose a learning method to set system-level goals. Using this learning approach, we are able to define a dual-purpose reward function to train the system on increasing system stability as well as reducing energy cost.

Experiments using our method were conducted within a simulated feedback system as well as a closed-loop system. For our non-closed system (Section 4.1, Scenario One), we simulate feedback within the system using a function which allows us to parameterize the flow-on effect of reducing demand. For our closed-loop system (Section 4.2, Scenario Two), we include models of individual appliance agents, which are directly affected when constraints are placed on the system. For both scenarios, the experimental results show that the energy consumption cost is reduced with a stable system while the broker agent implements the control strategies learnt by our algorithm.

Figure 9. Cap setting where the optimization focus is on load demand and cost. Top: Cap chosen by the broker agent; Bottom: Unconstrained consumption vs. capped energy consumed

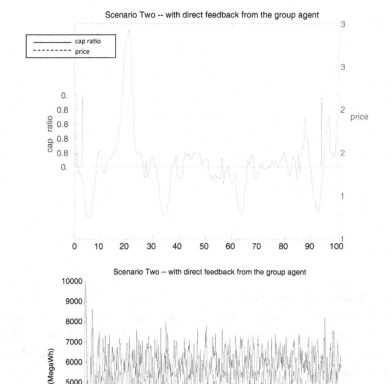

Conducting experiments in multiple environments illustrates the adaptability of our learning method for energy demand management. Results show a compromise can be met between system stability and cost. The method we introduce uses only a small state space for both the decision and reward matrix but still produces effective outcomes. For future work, we wish to explore alternative methods for setting system-level goals. A reduction in parameter space and/or in training time whilst also providing system stability and cost reduction would be ideal.

ACKNOWLEDGMENT

Our thanks to Astrid Zeman, Geoff James, Geoff Poulton, and Mikhail Prokopenko for valuable discussion.

REFERENCES

Borenstein, S., Jaske, M., & Rosenfeld, A. (2002). *Dynamic pricing, advanced metering, and demand response in electricity markets. Center for the Study of Energy Markets. Paper CSEMWP-105.* University of California.

Dimeas, L., & Hatziargyriou, N. D. (2004). Operation of a multi agent system for microgrid control. *IEEE Transactions on Power Systems*, *20*(2), 1447–1455.

Guo, Y. (2007). *Cap optimisation for broker agent*. *Technical Report*. CSIRO.

Guo, Y., Li, J., & James, G. (2005). Evolutionary optimization of distributed energy resources. Advances *in Artificial Intelligence, 18th Australian Joint Conference on Artificial Intelligence*. (3809 of Springer LNCS, pp.1086-1091).

Guo, Y., Li, R., Poulton, G., & Zeman, A. (2008). A simulator for self-adaptive energy demand management. *Second IEEE International Conference on Self-Adaptive and Self-Organizing Systems (SASO)*, Italy.

Hägg, S., & Ygge, F. (1995). *Agent-oriented programming in power distribution automation – an architecture, and language, and their applicability*. Licentiate thesis, Lund University.

Hou, I. (2007). International Energy Outlook 2007. *Energy Information Administration*, http://www.eia.doe.gov/

James, G., Cohen, D., Dodier, R., Platt, G., & Palmer, D. (2006). A deployed multi-agent framework for distributed energy applications. *Proceedings of the Fifth international Joint Conference on Autonomous Agents and Multi-agent Systems*. AAMAS '06. New York: ACM Press, 676-678.

Kaelbling, L. P., Littman, M., & Moore, A. (1996). Reinforcement learning: A survey. *Journal of Artificial Intelligence Research, 4*, 237–285.

Li, J., Poulton, G., & James, G. (2007). Agent-based distributed energy management. *The 20th Australian Joint Conference on Artificial Intelligence*. Gold Coast, Queensland, Australia, 2-6 December.

Li, J., Poulton, G., James, G., Zeman, A., Wang, P., Chadwick, M., & Piraveenan, M. (2007). Performance of multi-agent coordination of distributed energy resources. *WSEAS Transactions on System and Control, 2*(1), 52–58.

Li, R., Li, J., Poulton, G., & James, G. (2008). Agent Based Optimisation Systems for Electrical Load Management. Proc. First *International Workshop on Optimisation in Multi-Agent Systems (OPTMAS), in conjunction with Seventh Conference on Autonomous Agents and Multi-Agent Systems*, 60-68, Estoril, Portugal, May.

Li, R., & Poulton, G. (2007). *Optimal management of multiple resource consuming devices during periods of supply restriction*. Technical Report, CSIRO, May.

McArthur, S. D. J., & Davidson, E. M. (2005). Concepts and approaches in multi-agent systems for power applications. *Proceedings of the 13th International Conference on Intelligent Systems Application to Power Systems*. Nov.

Ogston, E., Zeman, A., Prokopenko, M., & James, G. (2007). Clustering distributed energy resources for large-scale demand management, *First International Conference on Self-Adaptive and Self-Organizing Systems (SASO)*.

Platt, G. (2009). *Smart agents: an intelligent way to manage and control energy*. http://www.csiro.au/science/SmartAgents.html

Prokopenko, M., Zeman, A., Guo, Y., & Li, R. (2007). *Hierarchy-based aggregation studies*. Technical Report, CSIRO, September.

Sutton, R. S., & Barto, A. G. (1998). *Introduction to reinforcement learning*. Cambridge, MA: MIT Press.

Watkins, C., & Dayan, P. (1992). Q-learning. *Machine Learning, 8*(33), 279–292. doi:10.1007/BF00992698

Wilson, B., & Deck, C. A. (2002). The effectiveness of low price matching in mitigating the competitive pressure of low friction electronic markets. *Electronic Commerce Research, 2*(4).

Wilson, B., Rassenti, S. J., & Smith, V. L. (2003). Controlling market power and price spikes in electricity networks, demand-side bidding. *Proceedings of the National Academy of Sciences of the United States of America, 100*(5).

Ygge, F. (1998). *Market-oriented programming and its application to power load management*, Ph.D. Thesis. Lund University.

Zeman, A., Prokopenko, M., Guo, Y., & Li, R. (2008). Adaptive Control of Distributed Energy Management: A Comparative Study. *Second IEEE International Conference on Self-Adaptive and Self-Organizing Systems (SASO)*, Italy.

Chapter 14

A Step–By–Step Implementation of a Multi–Agent Currency Trading System

Rui Pedro Barbosa
University of Minho, Portugal

Orlando Belo
University of Minho, Portugal

ABSTRACT

With this chapter the authors intend to demonstrate the potential practical use of intelligent agents as autonomous financial traders. The authors propose an architecture to be utilized in the creation of this type of agents, consisting of an ensemble of classification and regression models, a case-based reasoning system and an expert system. This architecture was used to implement six intelligent agents, each being responsible for trading one of the following currency pairs with a 6-hour timeframe: CHF/JPY, EUR/CHF, EUR/JPY, EUR/USD, USD/CHF and USD/JPY. These agents simulated trades during an out-of-sample period going from February of 2007 till July of 2010, having all achieved an acceptable performance. However, their strategies resulted in relatively high drawdowns, and much of their profit disappeared once the trading costs were factored into the trading simulation. In order to overcome these problems, they integrated the agents in a multi-agent system, in which agents communicate their decisions to each other before sending the market orders, and work together to eliminate redundant trades. This system averaged out the returns of the agents, thus eliminating much of the risk associated with their individual trading strategies, and also originated considerable savings in trading expenses. Their results seem to vindicate the usefulness of the proposed trading agent architecture, and also demonstrate that there is indeed a place for intelligent agents in financial markets.

INTRODUCTION

The foreign exchange market, or Forex market, is the place where currency prices are set. The

DOI: 10.4018/978-1-60960-171-3.ch014

participants in this market can be divided in three main groups: banks, brokers and clients (Shamah, 2003). Central and commercial banks provide the bulk of liquidity, while brokers act as intermediaries for clients, which can range from multinationals to individual speculators. Trading

Copyright © 2011, IGI Global. Copying or distributing in print or electronic forms without written permission of IGI Global is prohibited.

in the Forex market is accomplished with the buying and selling of currency pairs. The price of a currency pair states the price of the base currency in terms of another currency. For example, USD/JPY is the price of the United States Dollar expressed in Japanese Yen. A price of 107.57 for the USD/JPY pair means we need 107.57 JPY to buy 1 USD. To profit from price movements in this pair, we should buy USD/JPY lots (go long) if we expect the USD to become more valuable compared to the JPY, or sell USD/JPY lots (go short) if we expect the JPY to become more valuable compared to the USD. Buying the currency pair actually means buying the base currency and selling the other currency, while selling the currency pair means selling the base currency and buying the other one. Closing an open trade is achieved by performing the opposite operation, i.e., buying the currency that was sold and selling the one that was bought. When a trade is closed, the resulting profit or loss can be expressed in pips. A pip is the smallest possible change in the price of a currency pair. For the USD/JPY pair, a pip corresponds to a price movement of 0.01.

The Forex market is quite different from any other financial market. The most remarkable differences are the nonexistence of a central marketplace and the fact that it is available 24 hours a day. Currency prices continuously rise and fall throughout the week, in reply to the constant flow of news and reports being released, and periods of high volatility are frequent. For this reason, trading currencies is always associated with a great deal of risk. The objective of our research is to implement agents that can manage this risk, and that can trade profitably in this market. We will start by devising the mechanism that the agents use to predict currency price movements. Different implementations will be tested, from using a simple standalone classification or regression model to using an ensemble of models. The practical use of these data mining models in financial time series prediction has already been extensively studied. Yao and Tan (2000) obtained empirical evidence of the usefulness of artificial neural networks in the development of profitable Forex trading strategies. Franses and Griensven (1998) reported similar results, and demonstrated that artificial neural networks can often perform better than linear models. The same conclusion was achieved by Kamruzzaman and Sarker (2003), which showed that artificial neural networks can outperform traditional time series prediction models, such as the autoregressive integrated moving average. But artificial neural networks are not the only models that have been shown to make reasonably accurate Forex predictions. Gençay (1999) compared the performance of nearest neighbour regression models with artificial neural networks using different sets of currency price data, and concluded that the nearest neighbour models performed better. Tay and Cao (2001) used different types of financial data to compare the predictive capability of both artificial neural networks and support vector machines, and concluded that the support vector machines made better predictors.

Some studies have also shown the advantages of more complex prediction strategies. Abraham (2002) used the price data of several currencies to compare the accuracy of artificial neural networks with the accuracy of hybrid predictors, and concluded that the hybrid solutions performed better. Pavlidis, Tasoulis, Plagianakos, Siriopoulos and Vrahatis (2005) obtained better results with a hybrid approach when compared with several nearest neighbour models. Yu, Lai and Wang (2005), with a hybrid solution consisting of artificial neural networks and an expert system, were able to create a trading strategy that was profitable under simulation. Singh and Fieldsend (2001) tested their hybrid system using the Santa Fe competition datasets (Weigend & Gershenfeld, 1993) and obtained interesting results for most datasets, but not the one containing the currency price data. Cao (2003) applied support vector machines experts to those same datasets, and reported acceptable results. Many other articles have been published on this subject, with most demonstrating the potential of some classification and regression models to be used in the implementation of profitable Forex trading strategies.

So far, accuracy has been the preferred way to measure the performance of financial prediction models. Of the previously mentioned studies, only the ones by Yao and Tan (2000), Yu et al. (2005) and Pavlidis et al. (2005) used the profit or the rate of return to measure the models' performance. The others use primarily the accuracy predicting price direction (for classification) or the predicted prices' mean squared error (for regression). However, from a trader's point a view, accuracy is not the best way to evaluate a trading strategy. Higher accuracy does not necessarily translate into higher profit, because the profit of several accurately predicted trades can be wiped out by a single losing trade. A low mean squared error is also not a guarantee that a model can produce profitable predictions (Swingler, 1994). For this reason, and in contrast with previously published articles, we will be focusing on two other performance gauges to determine the usefulness of a model: the accumulated profit obtained from simulating trades with its predictions (using out-of-sample data), and the maximum drawdown during the course of that simulation. The maximum drawdown, loosely defined as the maximum accumulated loss experienced after a series of trades, is an important measure of how risky a trading strategy was in the past. This statistic is very important when analyzing Forex trading strategies, because currency investments are usually leveraged, i.e., done with borrowed funds. A big drawdown greatly decreases the monetary resources available for trading, which can either prevent the trader from opening new traders or even trigger a margin call. Our research will also differ from much of what other researchers have published in that we will not be implementing tools that can be used by human traders to facilitate their trading activity. Instead, we intend to implement autonomous agents that can actually replace human traders. In fact, we intended to go one step further, and

create systems that can replace traditional hedge funds. We believe this type of activity is a perfect fit for the use of agent technology. As Jennings and Wooldridge (1998) point out, one situation in which it makes sense to use agent technology is when an intelligent agent is an appropriate metaphor for a given functionality. Consider the inner workings of a hedge fund, i.e., an investment company that can buy or short sell a wide range of financial instruments. The typical hedge fund employs several traders, each being responsible for negotiating a specific set of financial instruments, with the objective of obtaining the best return possible. The traders likely cooperate with each other, in order to optimize the return of the hedge fund as a whole. Clearly, a multi-agent system is a natural metaphor for this type of organization, with the intelligent trading agents playing the part of the human traders. We should point out that, with this metaphor, we are not implying that being a successful financial trader is in any way correlated with being intelligent. In fact, we intended to demonstrate in this chapter that profitable trading can be the result of chance alone. Disregarding profitability, the software trading agents in our hedge fund scenario can be considered intelligent in the sense that they can act rationally, i.e., they can exhibit autonomous goal-oriented behaviour.

Depending on how they are programmed, intelligent trading agents can have several advantages over their human counterparts. The most obvious is their ability to work 24 hours a day, uninterrupted. This is especially important if they are participating in the Forex market, which is open 24 hours a day. The agents are also not susceptible to having their judgment clouded by fear or greed, unless these emotions somehow arise from their implementation. Finally, using powerful hardware and a fast network connection, they will be able to make decisions and open/close trades much faster than any human ever could. If a trading strategy is based solely on number crunching, it is obvious that an intelligent agent will always be able to beat its human counterpart. Considering these advantages, there is clearly some practical interest in the development of intelligent trading agents. We will begin our research with the design of a generic agent architecture that can be used in the implementation of this type of agents. This architecture will be composed of three modules, namely:

1. the prediction module, responsible for forecasting the direction of the price of a financial instrument;
2. the empirical knowledge module, responsible for deciding how much to invest in each trade;
3. the domain knowledge module, responsible for incorporating expert knowledge into the trading decisions, among which the timing for closing open trades.

The contribution of each module to the trading performance will be demonstrated with the step-by-step implementation of an intelligent agent, which will be responsible for trading the USD/JPY currency pair with a timeframe of 6 hours. Once the usefulness of the proposed agent architecture has been demonstrated, we will use it to create five other currency trading agents, which will be integrated in a multi-agent system that can act as a real life autonomous hedge fund.

A HYBRID ARCHITECTURE FOR INTELLIGENT TRADING AGENTS

In order to trade a financial instrument without supervision, an intelligent agent will need to be able to make several decisions. This implies being capable of answering questions such as:

*   When should a financial instrument be bought or short sold?
*   How much should be invested in each trade?

*   When should an open trade be closed?

The way a trading agent answers these questions will depend on what it is trying to achieve. Since our objective is to create agents that mimic the activity of typical hedge fund traders, their goal should be to try to obtain the maximum profit possible while simultaneously minimizing the risk. We can measure how well an agent achieves this objective by using two metrics: the return on investment and the maximum drawdown. The return on investment is the ratio between the profit the agent was able to obtain and the capital that was initially available. The maximum drawdown, on the other hand, measures the historical maximum peak to valley decline in the agent's equity, i.e., the maximum accumulated loss experienced while trading. Rather than using the raw values of the return and the maximum drawdown to measure the agents' performance, we will be utilizing two related metrics. The first is the ratio between the total return and the maximum drawdown. We named it the RMD ratio:

$$RMD\,ratio = \frac{Return\,Since\,Inception}{Maximum\,Drawdown\,Since\,Inception}$$

The RMD is a pain-to-gain ratio similar to the Calmar (Young, 1991) and the MAR ratios, which are frequently used by investors to compare the results of different investment funds. It allows us to measure the risk adjusted performance of a trading strategy in the past. The higher a strategy's RMD ratio, the bigger its return is in comparison to the maximum drawdown. Strategies with higher RMD ratios are theoretically better suited for using leverage because, assuming they maintain the same level of performance going forward, augmenting the leverage will increase the return much more than it will increase the drawdown. The other metric that we will use in conjunction with the RMD ratio is the return per trade, which can be calculated by dividing the total return on investment by the total number of trades. A high return per trade is extremely important because there are costs associated with real life trading. These costs include, among other things, commissions, spreads and slippage. If the return obtained in each trade is not high enough to at least make up for its cost, the trader will lose money. It is not uncommon for strategies that seem very profitable on paper to fail miserably once trading costs are taken into consideration.

Now that we have defined the metrics with which the trading agents will be evaluated, we can define their goals accordingly: they should follow a trading strategy that will maximize the RMD ratio and also maximize the return per trade. In the sections that follow we will present an agent architecture that is meant for the development of intelligent agents that can trade with these objectives in mind.

Predicting the Direction of the Price Using Data Mining

Just like the human entities they attempt to mimic, trading agents need to be able to decide when to buy or short sell a financial instrument. As previously described, many studies have shown that data mining models can be used in this task. We will be following a similar strategy, with the incorporation of a model-based prediction mechanism in the agents' architecture. This mechanism can be implemented using a multitude of strategies (Barbosa & Belo, 2009). The simplest approach is

training a data mining model to predict the direction of the price of the financial instrument that will be traded. The model's predictions can then be utilized to decide if the instrument should be bought or sold short. In order to demonstrate this methodology, we trained seven different models using historical data for the USD/JPY currency pair. Details on the training attributes and parameters will be provided later. For now, we will be focusing only on the models' performance. The USD/JPY raw data was segmented into instances, each corresponding to a period of 6 hours. Five of the models were trained for classifying the data, in order to be able to predict the direction of the price of the currency pair in subsequent 6-hour periods. These predictions corresponded to one of two classes: "the price of the USD/JPY pair will increase in the next 6 hours" or "the price of the USD/JPY pair will decrease in the next 6 hours". The other two data mining models were trained for regression using the same data. Instead of predicting the direction of the price, their job was to predict the exact USD/JPY percentage price change in subsequent 6-hour periods. These forecasts were then converted into one of the classes: if the model predicted a negative price change, its class prediction was "the price will decrease in the next 6 hours", otherwise it was "the price will increase in the next 6 hours". Each of the seven data mining models was utilized to implement a simple trading bot, according to the architecture shown in figure 1.

Figure 1. Architecture for implementing trading bots with a simple prediction mechanism

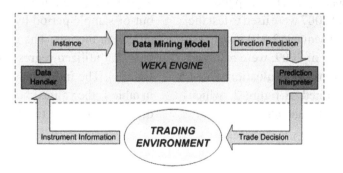

Figure 2. Historical USD/JPY prices since 1975. There are two things worth noting in this chart. First, it is clear that the prices in the training data are considerably less volatile than in other periods in the past. Second, the price changes in the out-of-sample data seem quite different from those in the training data, which means the data mining models should have a hard time making accurate predictions

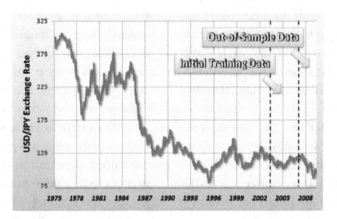

Notice we are using the term "trading bot" instead of "intelligent trading agent", because the entities implemented with the architecture shown in figure 1 cannot be considered intelligent. While they can act autonomously, they are just simple hardcoded programs that lack the ability to adapt to changes in market conditions. Their behaviour is also not guided by the objectives that we defined for our intelligent agents: to maximize the return while attempting to minimize the risk.

Each of the seven bots was configured to open trades according to the predictions of its model. The Weka data mining software and API (Witten & Frank, 2005) was utilized to train each model, using a specific set of attributes. The training instances were extracted from historical data corresponding to the period between May of 2003 and December of 2006, for a total of around 4,000 instances. The 50 instances that makeup the first 2.5 weeks of January of 2007 were used to test the models. Finally, the subsequent 2,510 instances, up to the middle of May of 2009, were reserved for out-of-sample performance evaluation. These three periods are delimited in figure 2, which shows the USD/JPY exchange rate since 1975.

Once the implementation of the seven bots was completed, each made predictions for the 2,510 out-of-sample instances, and trades were simulated accordingly. As previously mentioned, each instance corresponded to a 6-hour period, thus our trading simulation implies that the bots would open a new trade every 6 hours, starting Sunday at 18:00 GMT till Saturday at 00:00 GMT. For each instance, if a bot's model predicted a price increase, a long trade was simulated; if it predicted a price decrease, a short trade was simulated. If the forecast turned out to be accurate, the absolute value of the USD/JPY percentage price change in the corresponding period was added to the bot's return, otherwise it was subtracted. Notice that this methodology for calculating the profit implies that the bots were using a fixed trade size throughout the simulation. Figure 3 shows the cumulative return obtained in the out-of-sample period by the bots that used classification models. The cumulative return of the bots that utilized regression models is shown in figure 4. The individual results are summarized in table 1; the values shown are gross returns that do not account for trading costs.

Figure 3. Cumulative return of the bots that used standalone classification models to trade the USD/ JPY currency pair (excluding the trading costs)

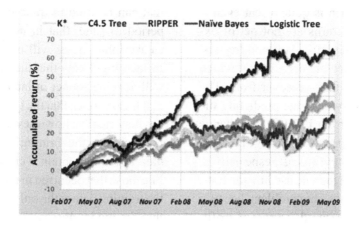

Figure 4. Cumulative return of the bots that used standalone regression models to trade the USD/JPY currency pair (excluding the trading costs)

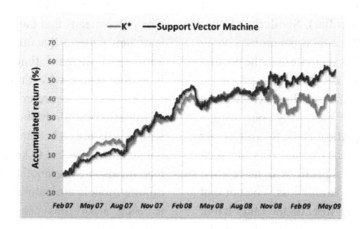

Table 1. Simulation results of the bots that used standalone models to trade the USD/JPY currency pair (excluding the trading costs)

Model	Return (%)	Max DD (%)	RMD Ratio	Return/Trade (%)	Accuracy (%)	Trades
K* (classification)	11.6	14.8	0.79	0.0046	52.4	2,510
C4.5 Decision Tree	35.1	13.6	2.58	0.0140	53.2	2,510
RIPPER Rule Learner	45.0	11.0	4.08	0.0179	52.9	2,510
Naïve Bayes	29.7	17.1	1.74	0.0118	52.1	2,510
Logistic Model Tree	63.7	10.0	6.37	0.0254	54.3	2,510
K* (regression)	42.8	18.7	2.29	0.0170	52.9	2,510
Support Vector Machine	56.0	12.6	4.43	0.0223	53.4	2,510

We were surprised to see that all the bots were able to achieve a positive return at the end of the simulation period, which is quite a feat even if we consider that the returns are not net of expenses. Still, these are not particularly good results. Several bots experienced big drawdowns, which took them several months to recover from. The bots were also not very accurate predicting the short term direction of the USD/JPY exchange rate. This was not unexpected. Exchange rates are very "noisy" and hard to forecast, especially at shorter timeframes like the one used by the bots. But this is not necessarily a big problem, because successful trading is measured in terms of profitability, not accuracy. Higher accuracy does not always translate into higher profit, as we can see in the bots' results: the least accurate bot (which used a naïve Bayes classifier) was almost three times more profitable than the least profitable bot (which used a K* classifier). Similarly, the bot that used the RIPPER model was simultaneously more profitable and less accurate than the bot that used the C4.5 decision tree. The worst performing bot in the group was the one that predicted the direction of the USD/JPY exchange rate using a K* classifier. Its insignificant 0.0046% return per trade means that, once the trading costs are taken into account, the bot's profit will more than likely turn into a considerable loss. The bot that used the logistic model tree, on the other hand, achieved impressive results. It was not only the most profitable and most accurate of all, but also the one with the lowest maximum drawdown. Its RMD ratio for the simulation period was 6.37. This means that, if we repeated the simulation using leverage, the increase in the final return would be 6.37 times bigger than the increase in the maximum drawdown. On the flip side, the bot's return per trade was just 0.0254%, which should barely make up for the trading costs.

Overall, the bots' results indicate that a prediction mechanism based on a single data mining model is not good enough to be used in the implementation of an autonomous trading agent.

Picking the best model is only easy in hindsight. And even if we are lucky enough to pick a model that can be used to trade profitably for a given period of time, that in no way guarantees that catastrophic losses will not occur in the future. In fact, it is likely that the model's performance will degrade sooner or later. If we look at figure 2, it is easy to see that the USD/JPY exchange rate has historically shown several patterns which are not visible in the training data. In particular, this data does not contain a crash in the pair's price like those that occurred in the '70s and '80s. Since the training data is the only source of information that the model possesses, it will only be able to recognize the patterns that it learned from it. If history were to repeat itself, and another crash occurred in the USD/JPY price, the model would more than likely not be able to recognize these patterns. The "train once, use forever" methodology also means that the bot will not be able to learn new patterns that might occur in the future, no matter how many times they happen, which is another reason why it might eventually fail.

One way to overcome this problem would be to periodically retrain the data mining model with new data, as it becomes available. While this would enable the bot to keep learning over time, it could also lead to another problem. Many data mining models are naturally unstable, i.e., their learning algorithms can originate completely different models from relatively similar training sets. Such is the case with C4.5 decision trees (Quinlan, 1993), for example. Were we to retrain one of these trees with more data, the resulting decision tree could be completely different from the original, potentially degrading the performance of the prediction mechanism. The bot would then keep opening trades based on the predictions of an inaccurate model, which could eventually lead to its ruin. This is the main problem with using a single model for making the predictions: if the market dynamics change and the model's performance worsens, the bot has no means to adapt to these changes, and will continue to trade until it goes bankrupt. An implicit requirement for an autonomous trading agent is that it must be able to at least try to survive extreme changes in market conditions, also known as black swan events (Taleb, 2007). For this reason, we needed to keep looking for a more "intelligent" prediction mechanism, one that would make the agents more resilient to this type of events.

A research-proven alternative to making predictions based on a single data mining model is to use an ensemble of models. Several empirical studies, such as those by Sollich and Krogh (1996) or Opitz and Maclin (1999), have demonstrated that a committee of classifiers can frequently outperform the predictive ability of a single classifier. Bagging, boosting and stacking are among the most well-established ensemble techniques. Bagging (Breiman, 1996) is the simplest of the three. It consists of an ensemble of models of the same type that are trained using different training sets, with the models' predictions being aggregated by majority voting. This technique is especially useful if the models use an unstable training algorithm. Boosting (Schapire, 1990) uses a different strategy. It iteratively creates new models that are more accurate predicting the instances that were misclassified by previously trained models. This is accomplished by reweighting the data after each model is trained: instances that were misclassified gain weight, while accurately classified instances lose weight. Thus, the next model to be trained will focus primarily on the most problematic instances. The resulting ensemble performs classification using weighted voting, with the weight of each vote being proportional to the accuracy of each model. This method is most commonly used with weak learners, i.e., simple and relatively inaccurate models like decision stumps. Boosting can frequently turn these weak learners into strong learners. Stacking (Wolpert, 1992) differs from both bagging and boosting in that it combines models of different types. The votes of the models in the ensemble are aggregated by a meta-learner, i.e., a data mining model that learns how

best to combine the predictions of these models. Besides bagging, boosting and stacking, many other ensemble techniques have been proposed in data mining literature. We developed our own technique using a step-by-step methodology, starting with a simple ensemble consisting of the seven models that were previously tested. This ensemble was integrated in an architecture component named "prediction module", which is responsible for feeding the instance data to the models, and for aggregating their predictions. A simple USD/JPY trading agent was built around this module, in compliance with the architecture shown in figure 5. As depicted in this figure, the agent obtains updates regarding the financial instrument's price from the trading environment, and uses the predictions of the ensemble to open new trades.

Our first implementation of the prediction module aggregated the models' prediction by simple majority voting. In other words, the same weight was given to the class prediction of each of the seven models in the ensemble, therefore the ensemble prediction for each instance was simply the class with the most votes. Using this strategy, the USD/JPY trading agent simulated a trade for each of the 2,510 out-of-sample instances. The agent's cumulative return throughout the simulation period is shown in figure 6, in comparison with the results of the best and the worst trading bots that were previously tested.

The agent achieved a RMD ratio of 2.23, with a 0.0131% return per trade. Compared with the simpler trading bots, its performance was average. This is more or less what we expected. The ensemble does not perform as well as its best model, nor as bad as its worst, because it is averaging the models' performances. This is actually a good thing: in the long run, the ensemble-based prediction mechanism should be more robust than a mechanism based in a single model, because even if some of its models become out-of-sync with the market, their poor accuracy should be mitigated by the predictions of the other models.

Figure 5. Architecture for implementing trading agents that use the prediction module to make trading decisions

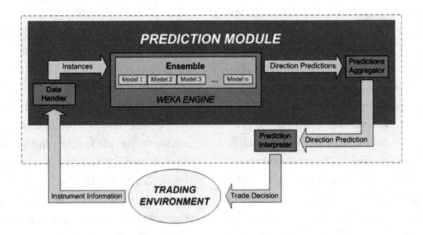

The simpler trading bots do not possess this type of redundancy, because their decisions are based on the predictions of a single data mining model.

The ensemble used in the aforementioned trading simulation was composed of data mining models of entirely different types, ranging from decision trees to lazy classifiers and regression models. Being this different, it is fair to assume that some of them might be more accurate when the instrument's price is trending upward, while others might perform better when the price is trend-

ing down. It is possible that building a prediction mechanism that can capitalize on each model's accuracy under different market conditions might improve the profitability of the agent. In order to test this assumption, we modified the implementation of the prediction module: it still used an ensemble with the exact same models, but each model's vote now had its own specific weight, with these weights being updated over time. To make the weights proportional to the models' accuracy, the following equations were used:

Figure 6. Cumulative return of the USD/JPY trading agent that used an ensemble of models with equal weights to make predictions (excluding the trading costs). The results obtained with the best and the worst trading bots are also shown, for comparison purposes

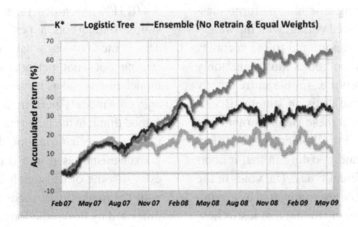

Figure 7. Cumulative return of the USD/JPY trading agent that used an ensemble of models with dynamic accuracy-based weights to make predictions (excluding the trading costs). Results obtained with an ensemble with equal weights are also shown

$$Long\ AF = \frac{Accuracy\ predicting\ long\ trades}{100} - 0.5 \quad (1)$$

$$Short\ AF = \frac{Accuracy\ predicting\ short\ trades}{100} - 0.5 \quad (2)$$

Before each prediction, and considering only the last n trades, the prediction module used equations 1 and 2 to calculate each model's long accuracy factor and short accuracy factor. We set n to 50 because we wanted the weights to be based in the models' performance under the most recent market conditions. Once all the models made their predictions, the weights of their votes were chosen according to their long or short accuracy factors: if a model predicted a price increase, the weight of its vote was its long accuracy factor; if it predicted a price decrease, the weight of its vote was its short accuracy factor. If a model's vote had a negative weight, it was set to zero; in practical terms, this signified that the model's prediction was ignored. The aggregation of the models' predictions was accomplished by adding the weights of the votes of the models that predicted a price increase, and then subtracting the weights

of the votes of the models that predicted a price decrease. If the resulting value was greater than zero, then the final ensemble prediction was that the price would increase in the following period; if it was lower than zero, the ensemble prediction was that the price would decrease; finally, if it was exactly zero, the prediction mechanism would not make a prediction, and the agent would not trade. This last condition meant that, if all models were showing poor accuracy in the recent past, the agent would be "smart" enough to stop trading until their accuracy improved. The simulation results for the USD/JPY trading agent, using this new implementation of the prediction module, are shown in figure 7; these results are compared with the performance of the simpler agent that used an ensemble with equal weights.

The new agent obtained a RMD ratio of 2.31, slightly better than the ratio of the agent that used the ensemble with equal weights. The 0.0122% return per trade, on the other hand, was not as good. While the simulation consisted of 2,510 out-of-sample instances, the agent only performed 2,327 trades. This means that, during the simulation, the agent temporarily stopped trading because all its data mining models were showing poor accuracy. In other words, all the models' votes

Figure 8. Cumulative return of the USD/JPY trading agent that used an ensemble of models with dynamic profit-based weights to make predictions (excluding the trading costs)

had negative weights, thus the prediction module stopped making predictions. Overall, we cannot say that, for this agent and timeframe, using dynamic accuracy-based weights in the prediction module was a significant improvement over using equal weights.

As already mentioned, from a trader's point of view, profit is much more important than accuracy. Therefore, it might make more sense to base the models' vote weights on their past profitability, instead of their accuracy. To accomplish this, we made another change to the prediction module. It acted exactly the same way as in the previous implementation, but the models' vote weights were now based on their profitability, as given by the following equations:

$$Long\ PF = \frac{\sum returns\ of\ profitable\ long\ trades}{\sum |\ returns\ of\ unprofitable\ long\ trades\ |} - 1 \tag{3}$$

$$Short\ PF = \frac{\sum returns\ of\ profitable\ short\ trades}{\sum |\ returns\ of\ unprofitable\ short\ trades\ |} - 1 \tag{4}$$

Just like with the previous module implementation, these equations were used before each prediction to calculate each model's long and

short profit factor in the last 50 trades. If a model predicted a price increase, the weight of its vote was its long profit factor, and if it predicted a price decrease, the weight of its vote was its short profit factor. The simulation results using this new version of the USD/JPY trading agent are shown in figure 8. For comparison purposes, the results obtained with the other module implementations are also shown.

The chart in figure 8 shows that, for this specific financial instrument and timeframe, using profit-based vote weights was a better strategy than using accuracy-based weights. The new agent achieved a RMD ratio of 3.50 and a return per trade of 0.0227%, both metrics showing an improvement over previous implementations of the prediction module. It only made 2,339 trades, which means that trading was halted temporarily during the simulation, because all the agent's models were making unprofitable predictions in the recent past.

We have seen how an agent's performance varies when its prediction mechanism is changed from a single standalone model to an ensemble of models with equal or dynamic vote weights. These models remained static throughout the course of the simulations, unable to learn new patterns while the trades were being performed.

Figure 9. The split between the training and the test data at a specific point in the simulation. The training set grows as time goes by, while the test set remains the same size and contains the most recent data

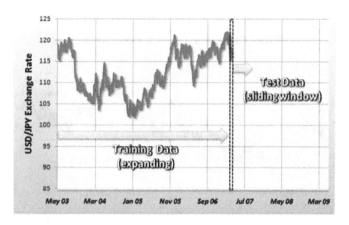

As previously referred, it is fair to assume that the data that was used to train the models does not contain all the information they need to keep making accurate predictions indefinitely. After each prediction, once a trade is simulated, there is always a new instance available; it is possible that periodically retraining the models with these new instances might improve their accuracy over time. However, since some of the models can be unstable, it is necessary to make sure that the retrained models perform at least as well as they did before retraining. We implemented a new version of the prediction module to test this strategy. Before each prediction, this module split all the available instances in two datasets: the test set, with the most recent 50 instances, and the training set, with all the rest. Using these two sets of data, the following sequence of steps was applied to each model in the ensemble before each prediction:

1. The model was retrained using the training set.
2. The retrained model was utilized to make class predictions for all the test instances, and trades were simulated accordingly; using the results of this simulation, the overall accuracy factor of the retrained model was calculated with the following equation:

$$Overall \ AF = \frac{Accuracy}{100} - 0.5 \qquad (5)$$

3. If the overall accuracy factor of the retrained model was higher than or equal to the overall accuracy factor of the model before retraining, then the retrained model replaced it in the ensemble. Otherwise, the retrained model was discarded.

This algorithm ensured that the agent kept learning over time, because its models were periodically retrained with a growing training set. Figure 9 illustrates this concept of a growing training set, coupled with a test set that moves like a sliding window. By using the accuracy in the last 50 trades to decide if a model should be replaced by a retrained version of itself, the prediction module was able to ensure that, at any given point in time, the ensemble contained models that were performing as good as possible under the most recent market conditions.

An agent was implemented using this new version of the prediction module. Its performance throughout the simulation period is shown in figure 10. We used equal vote weights in this simulation, i.e., the ensemble prediction was decided by simple majority voting.

Figure 10. Cumulative return of the USD/JPY trading agent that used an ensemble with periodical retraining and replacement of models based on accuracy (excluding the trading costs). Also shown are the results obtained with the simpler prediction module, which did not retrain the models

Much to our surprise, the results obtained with the new agent were considerably worse than those obtained with the simpler agent that did not retrain the models. It achieved a RMD ratio of 1.48, and a return per trade of just 0.0112%. Not a very impressive performance by any standards.

Once again, we attempted to improve the agent's performance by making the prediction module focus on the profit. Instead of using the overall accuracy factor to decide when a retrained model should become a part of the ensemble, we made it use the overall profit factor, for which we defined the following equation:

$$Overall\ PF = \frac{\sum returns\ of\ profitable\ trades}{\sum |\ returns\ of\ unprofitable\ trades|} - 1$$

(6

This new implementation of the prediction module ensured that a retrained model only replaced the original model in the ensemble if it was determined that it would have been at least as profitable as the original in the most recent 50 trades. The agent's cumulative return in the simulation period, using this new strategy, is shown in figure 11.

The agent obtained a RMD ratio of 1.61 and a return per trade of 0.0142%. This was slightly better than the performance of the accuracy-based solution. Nevertheless, this improvement was still not big enough to justify the computational overhead that results from periodically retraining the models.

Up to this point, we have tested two different strategies for improving the performance of a trading agent. First, we tried to create an agent with the ability to adapt itself to different markets conditions, by assigning dynamic vote weights to the data mining models in its prediction module. Next, we tried to create an agent that could keep learning over time, by retraining the models in its ensemble before each prediction. Obviously, the next step should be to create an agent with both capabilities. To accomplish this, a new prediction module was implemented. It used dynamic weights based on the long and short accuracy factors (equations 1 and 2), and retrained and replaced models based on the overall accuracy factor (equation 5). The agent's return, using this prediction module, is shown in figure 12.

This new strategy showed promising results: the agent achieved a RMD ratio of 4.70 and a return per trade of 0.0183%. We expected to

Figure 11. Cumulative return of the USD/JPY trading agent that used an ensemble with periodical retraining and replacement of models based on profit (excluding the trading costs). Results obtained with the other two strategies (no retraining and retraining with replacement based on accuracy) are also shown

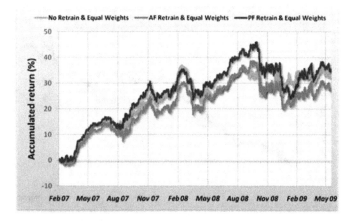

obtain even better results by focusing on the profit instead of the accuracy. To accomplish this, we created another prediction module. It used dynamic vote weights based on the models' long and short profit factors (equations 3 and 4), and retrained and replaced models according to their overall profit factor (equation 6). With this new prediction module, the agent achieved the results shown in figure 13.

The performance of the new agent was significantly better than that of any of the previously tested solutions. Its RMD ratio was 5.35 and its return per trade was 0.0260%. Table 2 contains the simulation results for all the prediction module implementations that were tested. Clearly, this last strategy was the one that showed the biggest potential. Considering its empirical results, this prediction mechanism seems good enough to be used as a building block in the development of a completely autonomous trading agent. For this reason, we selected this particular implementation of the prediction module to be

Figure 12. Cumulative return of the USD/JPY trading agent that used an ensemble with retraining and dynamic vote weights based on accuracy (excluding the trading costs). The results of the simpler agent (with no model retraining and equal vote weights) are also shown

Figure 13. Cumulative return of the USD/JPY trading agent that used an ensemble with retraining and dynamic vote weights based on profit (excluding the trading costs). The results obtained with some other versions of the prediction module are also shown

used in the creation of "smart" trading agents. Besides being profit-oriented, it should allow the agents to keep learning over time and to adapt to changes in market dynamics, hence taking them one step closer to being completely autonomous.

A recap of the algorithm used by the selected module is shown in figure 14. We should note that, according to this algorithm, the decision to replace a model in the ensemble with a new version of itself trained with more data is based on the profitability shown with the test data. This means that the models' selection is based on how well they perform with the test instances. This is not a good data mining strategy. Just because a

model was able to make profitable predictions for a small set of test data, that does not mean it will be able to do so for new, unseen data. To put it another way, a model that cannot generalize well from the training data might be able to make profitable predictions for several test instances due to chance alone. This is indeed a problem, and could result in some subpar models ending up as part of the ensemble. However, this flaw is mitigated by the way the prediction module works: first of all, if the model is indeed a bad predictor, the prediction module will decrease the weight of its vote in the ensemble's forecast; it might even set it to zero, meaning that the model's pre-

Table 2. Simulation results of the USD/JPY trading agent using different prediction module implementations (excluding the trading costs)

Model	Return (%)	Max DD (%)	RMD Ratio	Ret/Trade (%)	Accuracy (%)	Trades
Equal weights	32.9	14.8	2.23	0.0131	53.4	2,510
Dynamic weights (AF)	28.4	12.3	2.31	0.0122	52.6	2,327
Dynamic weights (PF)	53.1	15.2	3.50	0.0227	53.0	2,339
Retrain (AF)	28.0	18.9	1.48	0.0112	53.1	2,510
Retrain (PF)	35.5	22.1	1.61	0.0142	53.6	2,510
Retrain & Dynamic weights (AF)	43.1	9.2	4.70	0.0183	52.5	2,362
Retrain & Dynamic weights (PF)	61.8	11.5	5.35	0.0260	52.2	2,375

Figure 14. Pseudo-code for the algorithm used by the prediction module to forecast the direction of the price of a financial instrument for a given target period

```
Split the available instances in two datasets: the test set with the most recent n instances, and
the training set with all the rest.

For each model in the ensemble:
    For each instance in the test set, make the model predict its class and use the prediction to
    simulate a trade.
    Use the simulation results to calculate the model's overall profit factor (equation 6), long
    profit factor (equation 3) and short profit factor (equation 4).
    Retrain the model with the training set.
    For each instance in the test set, make the retrained model predict its class and use the
    prediction to simulate a trade.
    Use the simulation results to calculate the retrained model's overall profit factor (equation
    6), long profit factor (equation 3) and short profit factor (equation 4).
    If the overall profit factor of the retrained model is greater than or equal to the overall
    profit factor of the model before retraining:
        Replace the model in the ensemble with the retrained model.
    Else:
        Discard the retrained model.
    Use the model in the ensemble to make a prediction for the target period.
    If it predicts a price increase:
        Set the weight of its vote to its long profit factor.
    If it predicts a price decrease:
        Set the weight of its vote to its short profit factor.
    If the weight is a negative number:
        Set it to zero.
Add the weights of the votes of all the models that predict a price increase, and subtract from
this value the weights of the votes of all the models that predict a price decrease.
If the resulting value is greater than zero:
    Predict a price increase in the target period.
Else if it is lower than zero:
    Predict a price decrease in the target period.
Else:
    Do not make a prediction for the target period.
Once the target period ends, create a new instance and add it to the available data.
```

dictions will be completely ignored. Also, the module will continuously try to replace an unprofitable model with a more profitable retrained version of itself. This flaw in the module's algorithm actually demonstrates its greatest strength: it is capable of ignoring the predictions of inaccurate models and of replacing bad predictors in the ensemble, and is able to temporarily stop making forecasts if all its models suddenly become bad predictors. However, this ability to spot the bad models is not instantaneous. Only after several inaccurate forecasts will the module be able to determine that a given data mining model is out-of-sync with the market. Still, even if there is some lag, bad models do end up being ignored

or replaced sooner or later, and this characteristic is key to the agent's autonomy.

Choosing the Trade Size Using Empirical Knowledge

The prediction module enables the trading agents to automatically decide when to buy or short sell a financial instrument. However, in order to lower the trading risk, the agents also need to be able to make decisions regarding how much to invest in each trade. They should be prepared to use smaller trade sizes when the perceived risk is bigger, and to avoid trading when the expected return is negative. The agents that were implemented according to the architecture in figure 5 completely lacked this skill. They used the same size for the all trades, which is a rather simplistic money management strategy. We attempted to make the agents smarter by creating a new module, with which we intended to improve their trading decisions. The aim of this module was to assist the agents in deciding how much to invest in each trade, i.e., enabling them to select an appropriate trade size according to specific conditions. For each potential trade, this module enabled the agent to decide between three possible sizes: if a trade was expected to be profitable, a standard, user-defined trade size was used; if there were doubts regarding the trade's potential profit, half the standard trade size was used; finally, if a trade was expected to be unprofitable, the trade size was set to zero, which in practical terms meant that the agent would not make that trade. This mechanism was designated "empirical knowledge module", because it uses information from previous trades to decide the size of future trades. The module's implementation was accomplished with a case-based reasoning system. In this system, each case corresponds to a previously executed trade, and contains the following information:

- the price direction forecasted by the prediction module;
- the price direction forecasted by each model in the prediction module's ensemble;
- the return obtained with the trade.

This mechanism attempts to capitalize on the higher profitability associated with certain combinations of model predictions, which is something that is empirically evident. For example, looking at the trades performed by the agents in previous simulations, it is clear that those carried out when all the models make the same prediction, i.e., all predict a price increase or all predict a price decrease, are in general more profitable than those performed when the predictions are mixed. The empirical knowledge module was integrated in a new agent architecture, shown in figure 15.

The architecture depicted in figure 15 inserts a new step in the agents' decision process. Before a trade is opened, the prediction module forwards the details of its forecast to the empirical knowledge module. The case-based reasoning system then proceeds to retrieve from its database all the cases with the same ensemble prediction and the same combination of models' forecasts. The

Figure 15. Architecture for implementing trading agents using the prediction module, which forecasts the direction of the price, in conjunction with the empirical knowledge module, which decides the trade size

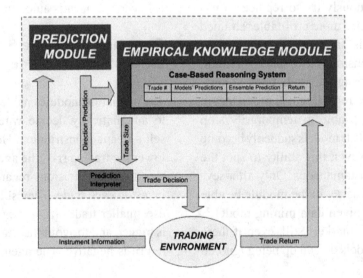

overall profit factor of the retrieved cases is then calculated with equation 6, and the resulting value is used to decide on how much to invest in the trade that is about to be opened: if the profit factor is less than or equal to a predefined threshold, the agent does not trade; if it is greater than or equal to another predetermined threshold, the agent uses the standard trade size; if it is between the two thresholds, the agent uses half the standard size. A more detailed description of this algorithm is shown in figure 16.

We used the architecture from figure 15 to implement a new agent to trade the USD/JPY currency pair. Its return during the simulation period is presented in figure 17. Its performance is shown in comparison with that of the simpler agent that was previously tested, which was based on the architecture in figure 5.

Figure 16. Pseudo-code of the algorithm utilized by the empirical knowledge module to select the trade size to use in a given target period

```
Get the ensemble's and the models' price direction forecasts for the target period from the
prediction module.

Retrieve from the database all the cases with the same combination of predictions.

While the number of retrieved cases is lower than a user-defined minimum:
    Remove the last model's prediction from the search and retrieve the cases again.

Calculate the overall profit factor of the retrieved cases (equation 6).

If the profit factor is greater than or equal to a user-defined threshold:
    Make the trade size equal to the standard size.

Else if it is lower than another user-defined threshold:
    Make the trade size equal to zero.

Else:
    Make the trade size equal to half the standard size.

Once the trade is closed, inserted a new case in the database.
```

Figure 17. Cumulative return of the USD/JPY trading agent that is based on the combination between the prediction module and the empirical knowledge module (excluding the trading costs). The return obtained with the simpler USD/JPY trading agent, which only used the prediction module, is also shown for comparison purposes

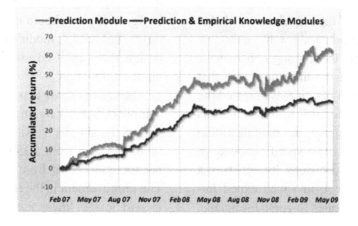

The chart in figure 17 shows that adding the empirical knowledge module to the implementation of the USD/JPY trading agent actually hurt its final return. At first sight, this does not look like an improvement. But the smaller return is something that was to be expected. The goal of the empirical knowledge module was to lower the risk, by making the agent skip trades and put less money on the line under certain circumstances. Since the agent took fewer chances, we were not surprised to see that its return was lower than it would have been if it used a fixed trade size. One should expect lower risk to come at the expense of lower potential profits. However, compared to the simpler agent, the RMD ratio of the new agent increased from 5.35 to 5.66. This confirms that the empirical knowledge module did work as expected: it improved the agent's performance, by making its trading strategy less risky. Equally important was the substantial decrease in the number of trades, from 2,375 to 1,688. This decrease means that, during the simulation, the agent skipped several trades due to its empirical knowledge module predicting they were going to be unprofitable. On the flip side, the return per trade of the new agent dropped from 0.0260% to 0.0210%, which means that the significant decrease in the number of trades was not big enough to make up for the smaller return.

Integrating Domain Knowledge into the Trading Decisions

Both the prediction and the empirical knowledge modules were designed to allow the agents to learn from their empirical trading experiences. However, there is always some knowledge that cannot be learned from practice. We created the "domain knowledge module" to overcome this problem. As its name implies, this module's main responsibility is to use domain-specific knowledge to improve the trading decisions. It consists of a rule-based expert system, in which expert human traders can insert rules to guide the agents'

actions. These rules can be related to many different aspects of trading. For example, they can define low liquidity periods in which the agents should not trade. Or they can be used to make the agents close trades when a certain profit or loss is reached. This type of rules can have a very significant impact on an agent's performance. For example, a take-profit rule, i.e., one that makes the agent close a trade when it reaches a specific profit, can turn trades that would otherwise be unprofitable into profitable trades. Whenever a take-profit rule is used, a trade will be profitable as long as, during the prediction's target period, the price moves in the forecasted direction at least up to the predefined take-profit target. If the price later reverses course, the agent will not be impacted because it will have already closed the trade to lock in the profit. Thus, even if an agent opens a trade based on an inaccurate prediction, it will still make a profit in those circumstances.

In order to test the domain knowledge module's contribution to the performance of our trading agent, we designed a new agent architecture, shown in figure 18. The domain knowledge module was implemented using the JBoss Drools rule engine.

According to this new design, the domain knowledge module is responsible for making the trading decisions, based on both the price direction prediction and the expert-defined rules. Following our previous methodology, this architecture was utilized to implement a new USD/JPY trading agent. Its performance under simulation is shown in figure 19. We should note that, since the empirical knowledge module was not a part of the design, the agent used a fixed trade size throughout the simulation.

Our results show that the return of the more complex USD/JPY trading agent was smaller than that of the simpler version. However, its RMD ratio increased from 5.35 to 5.78, and its return per trade increased from 0.0260% to 0.0438%. The improvement in the return per trade was due in part to the lower number of trades, which

Figure 18. Architecture for implementing trading agents using the combination between the prediction module, which forecasts the direction of the price, and the domain knowledge module, which makes the actual trading decisions

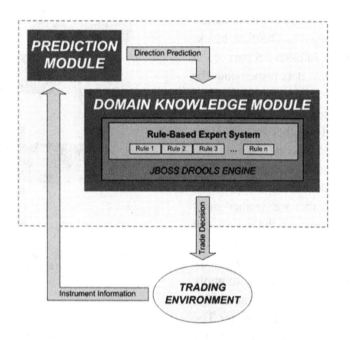

dropped from 2,375 to 1,205. This relatively low number of trades signifies that the rules in the agent's domain knowledge module prevented it from simulating trades for more than half of the 2,510 out-of-sample instances. Clearly, adding

the domain knowledge module to the agent's architecture resulted in a considerable improvement to its trading strategy. The rules that made this improvement possible will be discussed later.

Figure 19. Cumulative return of the USD/JPY trading agent that is based on the combination between the prediction module and the domain knowledge module, compared to the agent that used only the prediction module (excluding the trading costs)

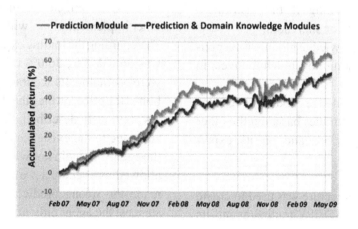

The Trading Agent Architecture

In previous sections, we described three building blocks that can be utilized in the implementation of autonomous trading agents. The first block, the prediction module, is an essential part of the agent architecture, because it is responsible for making the price direction forecasts that allow the agents to decide when to buy or short sell a financial instrument. The other two building blocks, the empirical knowledge module and the domain knowledge module, were combined with the prediction module and tested separately. According to the metrics that we deemed most important, the RMD ratio and the return per trade, both modules were able to improve the performance of the USD/JPY trading agent. We would expect an agent with the ability to apply both empirical knowledge and expert knowledge to its trading decisions to perform even better. The three building blocks were therefore integrated in what constitutes our final proposal for a trading agent architecture. This architecture, shown in figure 20, is meant to be used as the basis for the rapid implementation of intelligent agents that can trade different types of financial instruments.

Our intelligent trading agent architecture defines the modules' responsibilities as follows:

- the prediction module is responsible for forecasting the direction of the instrument's price; its forecasts are utilized as suggestions regarding if the instrument should be bought or short sold;
- the empirical knowledge module is responsible for suggesting how much to invest in each trade;
- the domain knowledge module is responsible for opening trades based on the other modules' suggestions and on its expert rules.

The proposed architecture was used to create a truly "intelligent" USD/JPY trading agent. Its

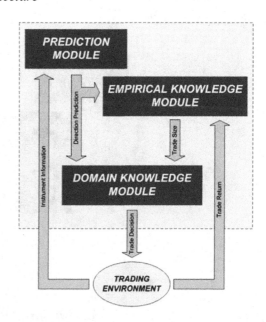

Figure 20. The intelligent trading agent architecture

cumulative return throughout the simulation period is shown in figure 21, in comparison with the return obtained with simpler agent implementations. The simulation results obtained with all the different module combinations that were tested are summarized in table 3.

Figure 21 shows that, compared to simpler implementations, our final intelligent USD/JPY trading agent did not achieve as much profit. Nevertheless, when designing the agent architecture, we put the emphasis on capital preservation rather than profit maximization. In this aspect, the final intelligent agent outperforms all the other implementations, with a RMD ratio of 8.57. Disregarding the trading expenses, its success rate was 56.0%, i.e., 56.0% of the simulated trades were profitable. Its accuracy predicting the direction of the price, on the other hand, was just 53.8%. As previously described, this disparity was possible due to the existence of a take-profit rule in the agent's domain knowledge module. This rule allowed it to secure a profit in trades for which it made the wrong predictions. Out of 2,510 instances, the agent only made 1,146 trades. Since

Figure 21. Cumulative return obtained using different module combinations to trade the USD/JPY currency pair (excluding the trading costs). The intelligent agent uses all three modules to make its trading decisions

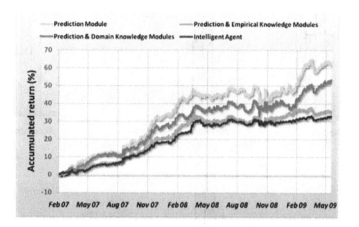

its accuracy and success increased as we added more modules to its architecture, we can conclude that the modules did indeed allow the agent to avoid several unprofitable trades.

While the USD/JPY trading agent achieved a relatively good performance, there is not much we can conclude from its results, as they might have been just a fluke. Its success could be due to a simple stroke of good luck, which would eventually disappear if it continued to trade after the simulation period. Even if there is no way to know for sure if that was really the case, we can at least calculate the probability of it being so. In order to do this, we created a "dumb" USD/JPY trading bot that made random decisions regarding when to buy or short sell a financial instrument. This

bot was based on the architecture shown in figure 1, only we replaced the data mining model with a "coin-flipping" mechanism that made random predictions regarding the direction of the USD/JPY exchange rate. We used the bot to perform 100 trading simulations, each run consisting of the 2,510 out-of-sample instances that were utilized to evaluate the USD/JPY intelligent trading agent. The histograms in figure 22 synthesize the bot's performance in these 100 runs.

We expected the bot's lack of skill to be reflected in its overall performance. That was clearly the case: the average return for the 100 runs was close to 0%, and the average accuracy was around 50%. Without considering the trading cost, which would have a significant negative

Table 3. Simulation results of the USD/JPY trading agent using different module combinations (excluding the trading costs)

Module combination	Ret (%)	Max DD (%)	RMD Ratio	Ret/Trade (%)	Accuracy (%)	Success (%)	Trades
Prediction Module	61.8	11.5	5.35	0.0260	52.2	52.2	2,375
Prediction & Empirical Knowledge Modules	35.4	6.3	5.66	0.0210	53.4	53.4	1,688
Prediction & Domain Knowledge Modules	52.8	9.1	5.78	0.0438	52.4	54.7	1,205
Intelligent Agent	32.7	3.8	8.57	0.0285	53.8	56.0	1,146

Figure 22. Histograms with the results of the 100 trading simulations performed by the USD/JPY trading bot that made random buy and short sell decisions (excluding the trading costs)

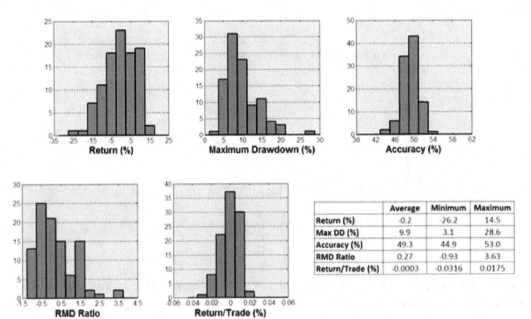

	Average	Minimum	Maximum
Return (%)	-0.2	-26.2	14.5
Max DD (%)	9.9	3.1	28.6
Accuracy (%)	49.3	44.9	53.0
RMD Ratio	0.27	-0.93	3.63
Return/Trade (%)	-0.0003	-0.0316	0.0175

impact on the return, this is the type of performance that one should expect from a trading strategy that relies on chance alone. The bot's best simulation run ended with a return of 14.5% and a RMD ratio of 3.63, which compares poorly with the intelligent agent's 32.7% return and 8.57 RMD ratio. Clearly, it seems improbable that our agent could have obtained this kind of performance just because it was lucky. Nevertheless, even if none of the bot's simulation runs ended with a RMD ratio over 3.6, it is certainly possible it could happen if we kept repeating the simulations. Bayesian statistics can be utilized to calculate the credible intervals surrounding the probability of that happening. We start with the assumption that there is no prior information regarding the probability of a bot achieving a RMD ratio greater than 3.6, i.e., if we keep repeating the simulation, the proportion of runs that finish with a RMD ratio over 3.6 can be anywhere between 0 and 1. The prior distribution for this proportion is, therefore, uniform. Next, we combine this prior distri-

bution with a binomial distribution summarizing the results of our 100 runs' sample, which yields a beta distribution. We can use this posterior distribution to calculate credible intervals for the proportion of runs in the population that might finish with a RMD ratio over 3.6. According to this methodology, we can say with 95% confidence that the probability that a sequence of random predictions throughout the simulation period could result in a RMD ratio over 3.6 is between 0.00025 and 0.03587. This demonstrates that, while possible, it is not very probable that a "dumb" trading bot could achieve a performance as good as the one obtained by our intelligent agent. More importantly, we can extrapolate from these credible intervals that it is very unlikely that the USD/JPY trading agent could owe its success to a series of lucky trades. Nevertheless, even if the agent proved to be a skilful trader in the simulation period, we cannot be sure it will continue to do so going forward. In the financial trading business, past performance is never a guarantee of future results.

For this reason, we needed to come up with a strategy that could accommodate for the possibility that a trading agent could become unprofitable in the future. This strategy will be described in the next section.

A DIVERSIFIED FOREX INVESTMENT STRATEGY

Following the implementation of the USD/JPY trading agent, we created five other agents using the proposed agent architecture, one for each of the following currency pairs: EUR/USD, EUR/JPY, EUR/CHF, USD/CHF and CHF/JPY. Similarly to the USD/JPY agent, the new agents were trained to open a trade every 6 hours: the first at midnight, followed by trades at 6 AM, 12 PM and 18 PM GMT. The agents closed each trade at the end of the corresponding trading period, before making a new prediction and opening a new trade; depending on the rules in the domain knowledge module, it is also possible that an agent could close a trade before the end of the period. We picked the 6-hour timeframe for two reasons: first, the historical price data we were able to gather online only went as far back as 2003, hence a relatively short timeframe was needed, so that enough instances could be extracted from the raw data to train the models; second, by using this timeframe, the agents would be opening trades at times that do not usually coincide with the release of any major reports, such as interest rate decisions or the nonfarm payrolls employment change. Currency prices can become extremely volatile around the time these reports are published, which frequently leads to bigger bid-ask spreads and slippage that make it more difficult to trade profitably.

We configured the prediction modules of the all the Forex trading agents using the following settings:

- The models in each agent's ensemble were selected using an automatic program that trained numerous models with random attributes and parameters, and selected the 7 most profitable according to a small set of test data. This number of models seemed like a good compromise between speed and redundancy: the ensembles were small enough that their predictions could be made at the speed required for real life trading, and they were sufficiently diversified to allow the agents to adapt to changes in market dynamics. The training instances utilized by the selection algorithm were compiled from historical price data obtained from Oanda Corporation, starting in the middle of 2003 up to December of 2006, for a total of around 4,000 instances per pair. In order to select the best models, the selection algorithm tested them with a small dataset, which consisted of only 50 instances, corresponding to the first 2.5 weeks of January of 2007. The final composition of the 6 ensembles is shown in tables 4 through 9. Among the attributes used in the training instances are the hour of the day, the day of the week, lagged percentage price changes (LAG) and the current class or price change; the selection algorithm also utilized attributes that professional traders regularly use in technical analysis, such as moving averages (MA), the relative strength index (RSI), the Williams %R (WIL) and the rate of change (ROC); notice that, while the classification models try to predict the next class ("the price will increase in the next 6 hours" or "the price will decrease the next 6 hours"), the regression models try to predict the percentage price change in the next period, after which the prediction is converted into one of the classes (if the forecasted price change is negative, the class prediction is "the price will decrease in the next 6 hours", otherwise the class

Table 4. Composition of the ensemble of the EUR/USD agent

Model	Attributes	Prediction
Naive Bayes	hour (nom), day of week (nom), % price change	Class
Support Vector Machine	hour (nom), day of week (num), MA(2), RSI(11), ROC(12)	% Change
CART Decision Tree	hour (nom), day of week (nom), LAG(2), RSI(2), ROC(2), ROC(5)	Class
Support Vector Machine	hour (nom), day of week (nom), MA(6), MA(4), MA(3), % price change	% Change
Least Median Squared Linear Regression	hour (nom), day of week (nom), LAG(5), LAG(4), LAG(3), LAG(2), LAG(1), % price change	% Change
Instance-Based K*	hour (nom), day of week (nom), price direction	% Change
Gaussian Radial Basis Function Network	% price change, hour (num), day of week (nom), MA(12), ROC(4)	Class

prediction is "the price will increase in the next 6 hours").

- The test data sliding window, depicted in figure 9, was set to 50 instances. This means that, before each forecast, the prediction modules use the last 50 instances to test the models and recalculate their profit factors; as previously described, these values are used to define the vote weights, and to decide if a model should be replaced with a newer version that was trained with more data. Our decision to utilize a sliding

window with only 50 instances was based on the following reasons:

- Most financial price series exhibit heteroskedasticity (Franses, 1998); this implies that the volatility is clustered, with long periods of low volatility usually being followed by short periods of high volatility. Since the weights of the models' votes are based on their profitability according to the test instances, the test set needs to be kept relatively small, so that these weights can change quickly

Table 5. Composition of the ensemble of the EUR/JPY agent

Model	Attributes	Prediction
Nearest-Neighbour Classifier	price direction, hour (nom), day of week (num), MA(8), MA(12), RSI(15)	Class
Support Vector Machine	price direction, hour (num), day of week (nom), LAG(7), WILR(25), ROC(7)	% Change
CART Decision Tree	hour (num), day of week (num), MA(8)	Class
PART Decision List	price direction, hour (nom), day of week (num), RSI(21), ROC(7)	Class
Instance-Based K*	price direction, hour (nom), day of week (num), WILR(11), ROC(7)	% Change
Instance-Based K*	price direction, hour (nom), day of week (num), MA(8), RSI(12), RSI(20)	Class
Support Vector Machine	hour (num), day of week (nom), MA(7)	% Change

Table 6. Composition of the ensemble of the EUR/CHF agent

Model	Attributes	Prediction
RIPPER Rule Learner	% price change, hour (num), day of week (nom), WILR(24), RSI(27), RSI(39), RSIS(8)	Class
Multinomial Logistic Regression Model	price direction, hour (num), day of week (nom), RSI(18), RSI(28)	Class
CART Decision Tree	price direction, close price, hour (num), day of week (num), LAG(5), RSIS(7), ROC(20), ROC(21)	Class
Support Vector Machine	% price change, RSI(9), RSI(25)	% Change
Instance-Based K*	price direction, MA(11), LAG(1), WILR(8), ROC(1)	% Change
Gaussian Radial Basis Function Network	price direction, hour (num), WILR(17), RSI(23), ROC(3)	% Change
C4.5 Decision Tree	price direction, hour (num), day of week (nom), LAG(1), WILR(11), RSI(14)	Class

whenever the market enters a period of higher volatility. In other words, the shorter the test set, the faster the agents can adapt to changes in the market dynamics.

○ The sliding window methodology specifies that the new instance that becomes available at the end of each trading period should be turned into a test instance, while the oldest instance in the test set should be turned into a training instance. This implies that, the shorter the test set, the faster the newer instances will be used for training the models. Hence, the shorter the test set, the faster the agents will be able to learn new patterns.

These two reasons demonstrate why it is important to use a relatively small sliding window of test data. However, if it is too small, the weights could become erratic. The smaller the test set, the more susceptible they will be to the outliers in the data, which could make them less reliable. Using a sliding window with 50 instances seemed like a good compromise. This size meant that, for

Table 7. Composition of the ensemble of the USD/JPY agent

Model	Attributes	Prediction
Instance-Based K*	hour (nom), day of week (nom), MA(6), price direction	Class
C4.5 Decision Tree	hour (nom), day of week (nom), MA(6), price direction	Class
RIPPER Rule Learner	hour (nom), day of week (nom), price direction	Class
Naive Bayes	hour (nom), day of week (nom), % price change	Class
Logistic Decision Tree	hour (nom), MA(6), price direction	Class
Instance-Based K*	hour (nom), day of week (nom), MA(6), price direction	% Change
Support Vector Machine	hour (num), day of week (num), MA(10), MA(2), % price change	% Change

Table 8. Composition of the ensemble of the USD/CHF agent

Model	Attributes	Prediction
Gaussian Radial Basis Function Network	hour (num), LAG(6), WILRS(6), WILRS(34)	Class
K-Nearest Neighbours Classifier	hour (num), LAG(1), LAG(6), WILR(24)	% Change
Pace Regression	hour (num), day of week (num), MA(4), LAG(4)	% Change
Support Vector Machine	hour (nom), LAG(4), WILR(7), WILR(23)	Class
Nearest-Neighbour Classifier	close price, hour (nom), day of week (nom), LAG(6), WILR(31), RSIS(22), ROC(35)	Class
CART Decision Tree	price direction, hour (num), WILR(14)	Class
Support Vector Machine	hour (nom), day of week (num), MA(11), RSI(2), RSI(29)	% Change

each prediction, the weights of the models' votes would be based on their profitability in the preceding 2.5 weeks of trading. The agents' empirical knowledge modules, responsible for suggesting the amount to invest in each trade, were configured with the following settings:

- After retrieving the cases from the database and calculating their profit factor, the size of the prospective trade was set to zero if that profit factor was less than or equal to zero. Thus, if previous similar trades were

mostly unprofitable, the new trade was not opened.

- If the profit factor was between zero and 1.5, the trade size was set to half the user-defined standard amount.
- If the profit factor was greater than or equal to 1.5, the trade size was made equal to the standard amount. Hence, the agents only traded the maximum quantity allowed when similar trades in the past showed considerable profit.

Table 9. Composition of the ensemble of the CHF/JPY agent

Model	Attributes	Prediction
Gaussian Radial Basis Function Network	price direction, hour (nom), day of week (num), MA(32), LAG(6), WILRS(7), RSI(32), ROC(32)	Class
CART Decision Tree	price direction, hour (num), MA(37), WILR(34), WILRS(13), WILRS(37), ROC(4), ROC(22)	Class
Naive Bayes	% price change, close price, LAG(5), LAG(8), WILRS(39), RSIS(16)	Class
Best-First Decision Tree	price direction, close price, hour (num), day of week (nom), MA(20), MA(34), WILRS(11), RSI(32)	Class
Alternating Decision Tree	% price change, day of week (nom), WILR(6), WILRS(13), RSI(7), ROC(3)	Class
RIPPER Rule Learner	close price, hour (nom), day of week (num), LAG(8), WILR(4), WILRS(17), RSI(40)	Class
Support Vector Machine	hour (num), day of week (nom), WILR(30)	% Change

• At least 3 cases were required in order to calculate the profit factor. If the case-based reasoning system was not able to find enough similar trades in the database, it would retrieve the cases again using less restrictive conditions; this was accomplished by removing the last model's prediction from the information to match, and then repeating the search.

The final step in the implementation of the Forex trading agents was to configure their domain knowledge modules. This was accomplished with the following set of rules:

• Do not trade if it is Christmas Day, New Year's Day or Good Friday; this rule was necessary to prevent the agents from trading in low liquidity days, in order to avoid the increase in volatility that might occur due to there being a smaller number of traders in the market.

• Skip the first and the last trades of the week, i.e., the trades on Sunday at 18 PM and on Friday at 18 PM GMT; these trades were prevented because the Forex market is usually less liquid during those periods, and consequently the prices are more prone to erratic behaviour.

• Only open a new trade if there is not already a trade open with the same settings, i.e., the same direction and size; to put it another way, if at the end of the trading period there is a trade open that already provides the agent the exposure it wants for the following period, then it can just keep that trade open, instead of closing it and opening a new one; this rule is important because it eliminates the costs associated with redundant trades.

• Close a trade if it reaches a profit equal to 2/3 of the average price range (in percentage) in the previous 5 periods; these take-profit targets are calculated using the following equation, with n set to 5:

$$tp(n) = 100 \times \frac{\sum_{i=1}^{n} \left(\frac{max_i - min_i}{open_i} \right)}{n} \times \frac{2}{3} \qquad (7)$$

where min_i, max_i and $open_i$ are the minimum, maximum and opening prices in the previous i^{th} period. The reason for using this equation is that it allows the agents to set take-profit targets according to the most recent price volatility: the profit goal will increase when the prices are more volatile, and decrease when the prices are more stable. To ensure that the profit target is never too small to make up for the trading costs, the actual value the agents use in their take-profit orders is given by the maximum between 0.15% and the value calculated with equation 7.

Once the implementation of the Forex trading agents was concluded, we used them to simulate trades for the period between February of 2007 and August of 2010, which corresponds to 3,844 out-of-sample instances. Their cumulative return throughout this period is shown in figures 23 and 24, and the simulation results are summarized in table 10.

The results shown in table 10 offer empirical evidence against the efficient market hypothesis (Fama, 1970). All the agents were able to obtain a positive return at the end of the simulation period, and their average accuracy predicting the direction of the exchange rates was well over 50%; both achievements would be unlikely if the Forex market was completely efficient.

Overall, the agents' performance can be considered impressive. Their RMD ratios clearly demonstrate their ability to trade profitably without taking too much risk. However, there is always the possibility that these successful trading performances were just a fluke, or the result of specific market conditions during the simulation period. Hence, there is no way to tell if the agents

Figure 23. Cumulative return of the CHF/JPY, EUR/CHF and EUR/JPY trading agents (excluding the trading costs)

Figure 24. Cumulative return of the EUR/USD, USD/CHF and USD/JPY trading agents (excluding the trading costs)

would be able to keep trading profitably going forward. For this reason, it would be unwise to utilize just one agent to trade real funds. That would be the equivalent of "putting all the eggs in one basket", which is definitely not the safest or the smartest way of investing. Fortunately, there is a time-proven strategy for overcoming this problem; it is known as investment diversification, and consists in investing in various uncorrelated financial instruments simultaneously, in order to decrease the risk of owning each of them individually. The reasoning behind this strategy is simple: losses incurred while trading some of the instruments can be compensated by gains obtained while trading others, which should yield a smoother overall return. By making the six Forex agents share the monetary resources (Barbosa & Belo, 2010), we can easily implement this type of strategy. In order to do so, we just need to evenly

distribute the trading capital between them, and ensure that all their losses and gains are credited in the same brokerage account. Compared to the agents' individual results, the cumulative return of the diversified strategy should be considerably less volatile, which should make it safer in the long run.

Figure 25 shows a representation of this diversified investment strategy. The agents are spread across multiple hosts, so that they can make predictions and open trades faster. They use the same brokerage account, share the monetary resources, and open trades at the same time, all without communicating with each other. The simulation results obtained with this diversified strategy, using the six Forex agents, are shown in figure 26.

The diversified strategy achieved a return of 37.9%, with a maximum drawdown of just 2.1%.

Table 10. Simulation results of the Forex trading agents (excluding the trading costs)

Agent	Return (%)	Max DD (%)	RMD Ratio	Ret/Trade (%)	Accuracy (%)	Success (%)	Trades
CHF/JPY	48.2	7.2	6.69	0.0269	53.7	55.9	1,792
EUR/CHF	23.9	4.4	5.44	0.0133	53.3	55.5	1,803
EUR/JPY	42.1	9.6	4.37	0.0244	52.7	55.6	1,724
EUR/USD	24.4	8.9	2.75	0.0133	53.2	56.8	1,842
USD/CHF	53.6	4.5	11.87	0.0299	54.0	57.1	1,795
USD/JPY	35.3	5.5	6.38	0.0198	52.7	55.1	1,783

Figure 25. An agent-based diversified Forex investment strategy. For clarity's sake, only 4 agents are represented. The agents use the same trading account to interact with the market, and share the monetary resources in that account. In what regards to their investment decisions, they are completely independent of each other

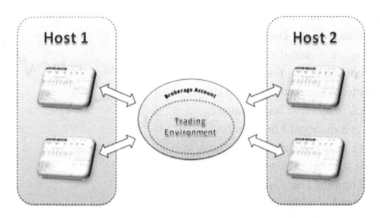

Its RDM ratio was 18.11, with a return per trade of 0.0035%. Looking at the chart in figure 26, the performance obtained with this strategy is close to perfect. The return curve has a pronounced positive slope, which is proof of the strategy's profitability, but more importantly this curve is very smooth, which indicates that trading was virtually risk free during the simulation period. This improvement in the drawdowns is exactly what we were hoping to attain. By averaging the performances of the six agents, the diversified strategy is not as profitable as the best agent, nor as unprofitable as the worst; its real advantage lies in that fact that, by allowing the losses of some of the agents to be offset by the gains of others, it can achieve a much smaller maximum drawdown, without sacrificing too much profit. This makes it well suited for the use of leverage, which should originate even better returns. Our trading simulation has confirmed that, as expected, investment diversification is an invaluable risk management strategy.

The results obtained with the trading agents and the diversified investment strategy seem to vindicate the usefulness of the trading agent architecture that we proposed. However, as one would expect, things cannot be that simple. Successful

financial trading is far from an easy feat, and it would be naïve to expect all agents to be able to trade profitably in real life. From a practical point of view, the simulation results we got were simply too good to be true. The detail that makes all the difference is the fact that, so far, none of the trading simulations has accounted for the trading costs, the "nemesis" of short term investment strategies. Therefore, even if we can conclude from our tests that the agents were indeed able to find several patterns in the price data, that does not necessarily mean that they would be able to use that information to trade profitably in real life.

Figure 26. Cumulative return of the diversified Forex investment strategy (excluding the trading costs)

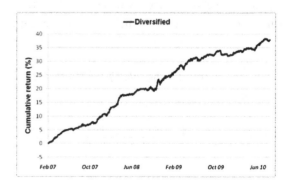

Considering the agents' small return per trade, it is obvious that any trading expenses should have a significant impact on their profitability. In order to perform a more realistic evaluation of the trading performance of the proposed diversified investment strategy, we defined a fixed cost per trade and recalculated the agents' cumulative return. We tried to base this cost on actual real life trading expenses: we defined a fixed commission of 3 pips per trade, which is more or less what we should expect to pay at a discount Forex market maker. The cumulative return obtained with the diversified investment strategy, when the agents are subjected to this trading cost, is shown in figure 27 and summarized in table 11.

Much to our disappointment, most of the profit of the diversified investment strategy disappears once the trading costs are taken into account. With a return of just 8.4%, and a comparatively high maximum drawdown of 5.6%, this strategy has now lost all its appeal for real life trading. The drop from 56.0% to 53.0% in the percentage of successful trades means that many of the agents' profitable trades turned into losses once the costs of the trades were considered. The problem here is easy to identify: too much capital is being wasted with commissions, because the agents are performing too many trades. Also, it seems like the 6-hour timeframe used by the agents might be too short, because the price variation of the currency pairs in these time periods is frequently too small to make up for the trading costs. Hence, in order to implement a safe and profitable trading system that could actually be deployed in real life, we had two choices: increase the agents' trading timeframe, or decrease the number of trades they

Figure 27. Cumulative return of the diversified Forex investment strategy (including the trading costs)

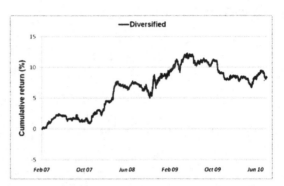

make (without affecting their return). The first option should decrease the impact of the trading costs, because the potential return in each trade would be greater compared to cost of the trade. Since we did not have enough training data (increasing the timeframe meant that we would have fewer instances to train the agents), we decided to focus on the second option, which led to an interesting challenge: trying to make the agents produce the exact same return, while doing fewer trades. In the next section we present our solution to this problem.

THE MULTI-AGENT FOREX TRADING SYSTEM

When we first started designing the trading agent architecture, we established that the agents would be evaluated according to their RMD ratio (a pain-to-gain measure of how much risk they incur to make a profit) and their return per trade (a measure

Table 11. Simulation results of the diversified Forex investment strategy (excluding and including the trading costs)

Strategy	Return (%)	Max DD (%)	RMD Ratio	Ret/Trade (%)	Accuracy (%)	Success (%)	Trades
Diversified (gross)	37.9	2.1	18.11	0.0035	53.3	56.0	10,739
Diversified (net)	8.4	5.6	1.52	0.0008	53.3	53.0	10,739

of their sensitivity to the trading costs). In the previous section, we successfully demonstrated that investment diversification can be used to improve the agents' overall RMD ratio. However, net results showed that we still needed to increase their return per trade, in order to create agents that can actually be deployed in the market to trade real funds. Obviously, this can be accomplished by either increasing the total return, without increasing the number of trades, or by decreasing the number of trades required for obtaining that same return. As previously mentioned, increasing the investment timeframe could prove beneficial, as it should allow the agents to make more profit per trade. The alternative to this change, which would force us to retrain all the agents with different instances, would be to come up with a way for the agents to make the same return using less trades. By capitalizing on the specificities of the Forex market, we were able to devise a strategy for that. Whenever an agent buys a currency pair, it is in fact buying the base currency and selling the other currency. When it shorts the currency pair, it is selling the base currency and buying the other one. For example, if the EUR/USD trading agent buys $100,000 of the currency pair, and the EUR/USD price is 1.3990, its market exposure will be long €71,500 and short $100,000. If, at the same time, the USD/JPY agent buys $100,000 of its pair, and the USD/JPY price is 89.90, its exposure will be long $100,000 and short ¥8,995,000. If we combine the market exposure of the two agents, the end result is long €71,500 and short ¥8,995,000. This exact same exposure could be obtained by simply buying $100,000 of the EUR/JPY pair. Therefore, in this particular situation, two trades could be replaced with just one. The unleveraged capital required for obtaining the desired exposure would also be cut in half, from $200,000 to $100,000. Now let us imagine that the EUR/JPY agent predicted a price decrease, and short sold its currency pair with a trade size of $100,000. Considering the decisions of the three agents, we are now faced with the following sce-

nario: the EUR/USD agent is expecting the price of the euro to increase in comparison to the U.S. dollar, the USD/JPY agent is expecting the price of the U.S. dollar to increase in comparison to the Japanese yen, and the EUR/JPY agent is expecting the price of the euro to decrease in comparison to the Japanese yen. Clearly, there is a contradiction in these forecasts. If the prices of the three pairs actually moved in the predicted directions, it would create an obvious triangular arbitrage opportunity. The Forex market is efficient enough not to allow these type of temporary profit opportunities to happen often, if ever. If we add up the exposure of the three agents, we will be able to see that, even though there are three trades open, there is no actual exposure to the market. The three trades cancel each other out, i.e., no matter how much the prices move, the sum of the return of the three trades will always be zero. Therefore, in these circumstances, a perfect replacement for the three trades would be to not open any trades at all; that way, the agents would not pay any commissions, and would not tie up any capital. This example shows that, as is, the currency trading agents utilized in our diversified investment strategy are making a lot of redundant trades.

As previously described, each agent makes an investment decision concerning its currency pair at the beginning of each trading period. There are 5 different possibilities for this decision: buy using the standard, user-defined size; buy using half the standard size; do not trade; short using half the standard size; and finally, short using the standard trade size. This means that, for every period, there are 15,625 ways of combining the decisions of the six agents (that is the total number of permutations with repetition, or 5 to the power of 6). Most of these decision combinations can be transformed into a smaller set of trades that yield the same market exposure. We devised an algorithm to accomplish that, and will describe it with an example. Let us consider that the standard trade size was set to $100,000, and that the decisions of the six agents for a given 6-hour period were:

- Short $50,000 of EUR/USD,
- buy $100,000 of EUR/JPY,
- short $100,000 of EUR/CHF,
- buy $50,000 of USD/JPY,
- short $100,000 of USD/CHF,
- short $100,000 of CHF/JPY.

If considered separately, these decisions would result in 6 new trades being opened, and would require $500,000 of unleveraged capital. In order to minimize the number of trades, we start by calculating the market exposure that each decision would produce:

- -$50,000 in EUR and +$50,000 in USD;
- +$100,000 in EUR and -$100,000 in JPY;
- -$100,000 in EUR and +$100,000 in CHF;
- +$50,000 in USD and -$50,000 in JPY;
- -$100,000 in USD and +$100,000 in CHF;
- -$100,000 in CHF and +$100,000 in JPY;

Next, we add up all the exposures, so as to calculate the total desired exposure per currency:

- -$50,000 in EUR;
- $0 in USD;
- -$50,000 in JPY;
- $100,000 in CHF.

Now that we have determined the actual market exposure corresponding to the decisions of the 6 agents, we need to compute the smallest set of trades that can yield that exposure. In order to do so, we start by picking the currency with the biggest positive exposure and the currency with the biggest negative exposure. In this example, they are the $100,000 in CHF and the -$50,000 in EUR. The smallest of these, in absolute value, is the size of the first trade. In this case the smallest is $50,000, which means the first trade must give us an exposure of $50,000 in CHF and -$50,000 in EUR, with the remaining $50,000 in CHF being saved for the next iteration of the algorithm. The trade that can produce this exposure is either

buying $50,000 of CHF/EUR or short selling $50,000 of EUR/CHF. While none of the agents trades the CHF/EUR, there is one that trades the EUR/CHF; hence, it will be responsible for short selling $50,000 of EUR/CHF. We now repeat the same step, using the currency exposure that was left after the previous iteration:

- $0 in EUR;
- $0 in USD;
- -$50,000 in JPY;
- $50,000 in CHF;

The remaining exposure can be obtained by either buying $50,000 of CHF/JPY, or short selling $50,000 of JPY/CHF. Thus, the CHF/JPY agent will be responsible for buying $50,000 of CHF/JPY. All the exposure has now been accounted for, which means that no other trades are needed. Thus, our algorithm was able to transform the initial set of 6 prospective trades into just 2, which will yield the exact same exposure. The required unleveraged capital also decreased, from $500,000 to $100,000. Clearly, enabling the agents to communicate their decisions to one another before opening trades, and using this algorithm to optimize the number of trades opened, will result in considerable savings. Hence, this is the perfect setting for implementing a multi-agent system. We defined a simple negotiation protocol for this system:

- whenever an agent is started, it must inform all other agents that it will become a part of the system; likewise, it must warn the other agents before leaving the system;
- after an agent makes an investment decision for a given trading period, instead of opening the corresponding trade, it communicates this decision to all other agents;
- once an agent receives all the trading decisions for a given period, it uses the previously described algorithm to compute the smallest set of trades that can yield the desired overall exposure; if its currency pair

Figure 28. The status message format. The action tag is used to specify if the agent that is stipulated in the pair tag is entering or exiting the system

```
<status>
        <pair>EUR/USD</pair>
        <action>IN</action>
</status>
```

Figure 29. The decision message format. The pair tag stipulates the currency pair traded by the agent; the price tag contains the most up-to-date price for that pair; the size tag is a code for the agent's decision: 2 for buying the standard trade size, 1 for buying half the standard trade size, 0 for not trading, -1 for shorting half the standard trade size, and -2 for shorting the standard trade size

```
<decision>
        <pair>EUR/USD</pair>
        <price>1.3990</price>
        <size>2</size>
</decision>
```

appears in the computed set, it opens the corresponding trade, otherwise it just waits until the next period.

This protocol is easily understood. At any given point in time, all the agents know which other agents are in the system. When the time comes to open a trade, they make their predictions, and cooperate with each other by communicating their intentions (i.e., the trades they plan to open). Once they receive all the decisions, each agent will compute the smallest set of trades that can achieve the corresponding overall market exposure. Since they all use the same algorithm with the same inputs, they will all compute the same set. Once this is done, each agent just needs to check if the computed set contains a trade involving its pair. If that is the case, it opens that trade; otherwise, it just waits for the next trading period, when a new combination of decisions will be generated.

Communication in this multi-agent system is accomplished with a simple ad-hoc XML-based language. This language consists of just two types of messages. The *status* message is utilized by agents to communicate their entry or exit from the system, while the *decision* message is utilized to communicate their trading decisions. The formats of these messages are shown in figure 28 and figure 29, respectively.

Figure 30 shows a representation of the proposed multi-agent Forex trading system. Compared to the simpler diversified investment strategy, depicted in figure 25, this system adds the inter-agent communication functionality that

allows the agents to minimize the number of trades opened in each trading period. In our implementation of the system, the inter-agent communication (with the aforementioned XML messages) is handled by the Apache ActiveMQ message broker. Communication with the Forex market is achieved using the proprietary API of a currency broker, which allows the agents to send orders to the market, receive currency price updates, and obtain information regarding the status of their trades. This system is highly scalable: agents can be moved freely between hosts, and new hosts can be added to support a growing number of agents.

The return obtained with the multi-agent system in the simulation period, using the six Forex agents and considering the trading costs, is shown in figure 31 and table 12; for comparison purposes, we also show the return obtained with the simpler diversified investment strategy (in which the agents were not aware of each other).

The improvement in the trading results is very clear in figure 31. The reason why the multi-agent system performs much better than the diversified strategy is the fact that, besides being able to decrease the number of trades, it is also able to decrease the capital requirements. What this means, from a practical point of view, is that the agents can use a bigger trade size when they are part of the multi-agent system. We will explain this phenomenon with an example. Consider we

Figure 30. The multi-agent Forex trading system. For clarity's sake, only 4 agents are represented. The thinner arrows represent the inter-agent communication, while the wider arrows represent the agents' interactions with the market

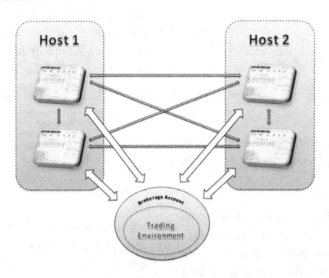

Figure 31. Cumulative return of the multi-agent diversified investment strategy (including the trading costs). The return of the simpler diversified strategy is shown in comparison

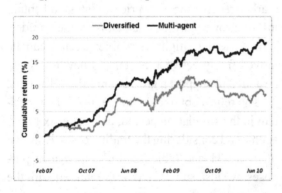

had $100,000 available for investing, and did not want to use any leverage initially. If we were to use a single agent to trade, we would set its standard trade size to $100,000. If, on the other hand, we wanted to use the diversified investment strategy with six agents, we would need to divide that amount between them; hence, their standard trade size would be set to $16,667. While we might expect to do the same when the six agents

are integrated in a multi-agent system, that would actually be a waste of resources. Going through all the 15,625 possible decision combinations, and the corresponding minimal sets of trades computed by the agents, we can verify that the maximum number of trades in any of those sets is 3. Also, the maximum volume, i.e., the maximum amount of capital invested simultaneously, is only 4 times the standard trade size (versus 6 times for the simpler diversified strategy). Therefore, in order to maximize the utilization of the monetary resources, the standard trade size for the agents in the multi-agent system should be made equal to the initial capital divided by 4, or $25,000. That is 50% higher than the amount used by the agents in the simpler strategy. The bigger trade size signifies that, using the same money and subject to the same leverage restrictions, the agents in the multi-agent system can open trades with a much bigger market exposure. These results in bigger profits, which explains the much better return of the multi-agent system compared to the simpler diversified strategy. Obviously, the lower number of trades also contributed to this improvement.

Table 12. Comparison between the simulation results of the multi-agent system and the simpler diversified strategy (including the trading costs)

Strategy	Diversified without inter-agent communication	Diversified multi-agent
Return (%)	8.4	18.9
Maximum Drawdown (%)	5.6	2.2
RMD Ratio	1.52	8.46
Return/Trade (%)	0.0008	0.0029
Total Trades	10,739	6,543
Simultaneous trades (maximum possible)	6	3
Simultaneous volume (maximum possible)	6 × standard trade size	4 × standard trade size
Standard trade size (unleveraged investment)	initial capital / 6	initial capital / 4

When integrated in the multi-agent system, the agents opened 39% less trades than when trading isolated. Thus, they spent a lot less money in commissions, which allowed the system to reach the end of the simulation period with a positive unleveraged return of 18.9%. This is an acceptable profit after 3.5 years of trading, but far from exceptional. Nevertheless, we should not be discouraged by this unimpressive return. By making the agents use leverage, the system's profit in real life could be substantially higher. The multi-agent system seems to be well suited for trading with borrowed funds, because its small maximum drawdown and high RMD ratio indicate its strategy is relatively risk free. For example, if we allowed for a maximum initial leverage of 5:1 (i.e., the agents' standard trade size would be set to 5 times the initial capital divided by 4), the system's return would be 5 times bigger, or 94.7%. However, using leverage also increases the risk of the trading strategy; the bigger risk can be seen in the system's new maximum drawdown, which would also be 5 times bigger, or 11.2%. Nevertheless, even with the greater risk, this would be an excellent performance by any standards.

CONCLUSION

We began our research with the objective of demonstrating the potential use of intelligent agents as a replacement for human traders. Implicitly, we were assuming that speculative financial trading is not just a game of chance, but rather an activity in which success is determined by skill instead of luck. This is an arguable premise, at least among those who believe in rational and efficient markets. However, as we see it, the numerous bubbles and crashes in asset prices that have occurred in the last decade have already proven, beyond doubt, that financial markets are anything but rational. This implies that, from time to time, it is entirely possible that an asset's market price will be at odds with its intrinsic value. We set out to create autonomous agents that would attempt to capitalize on those temporary profit opportunities. We proposed an architecture intended for the development of this type of entities, and used it to implement six Forex trading agents. These agents were tested with several years' worth of out-of-sample data, and their overall performance, measured in terms of return and maximum drawdown, was acceptable. However, we found that their accuracy was, in general, very disappointing. This was not totally unexpected. Even if financial markets are not completely efficient, the changes in financial instruments' prices will still be extremely hard to predict, because there are simply too many uncontrollable variables affecting them (especially at the shorter timeframes that our agents were using). Fortunately, the low accuracy turned out not to be a very significant problem. The main objective of the proposed agent architecture is to optimize the profit, rather than the accuracy, because profit is the ultimate goal in financial trading. Seeing that most agents were profitable in the simulation period, even without being very accurate, meant that they were able to predict the most important trades, i.e., those in which the price movements were bigger. Still, even if high accuracy is not a requirement for successful trading, it is likely that improving the agents' precision would also increase their profitability. We believe one might be able to achieve this improvement by using better attributes to train the agents. In our experiments, we only utilized training attributes that could be applied to different types of financial instruments; it is possible that, by using more specific attributes according to the investment vehicle being traded (like interest rate differentials, GDP growth or jobless rates for Forex pairs), we might be capable of creating much better predictors.

While our agents' results before commissions were very promising, they became much less impressive once we accounted for the trading costs. These expenses are bound to have a negative effect on the performance of all types of financial investors, because they lower the probability that the trades will be profitable. That is the reason why "bad" trading strategies (i.e., those that present no advantage over coin-flipping) will always have a negative expected return. In regard to the described agents, the adverse impact of the trading costs was exacerbated by the short timeframe they were using to open and close trades: since they did not allow enough time for the instruments' prices to change significantly in each trading period, their potential profit per trade was too low compared to the

trading expenses, and thus the risk/reward ratio of their trades was too high. Clearly, the best solution to this problem would be to increase the agents' trading timeframe, which would in turn increase the range of the instruments' prices (thus allowing for bigger potential profits, while the trading fees would remain the same). Longer timeframes might also improve the accuracy of the agents, because the price data would not be as noisy. Nonetheless, we opted for keeping the shorter timeframe, and attempted to improve the agents' performance by integrating them in a multi-agent system, for which we defined a negotiation protocol. The main objective of this system was to do away with redundant trades, in order to eliminate unnecessary expenses, and also to lower the trading risk through investment diversification. This last objective was particularly important, because the big variance in the agents' simulation results, as well as the well-known limitations of backtesting results versus real life performance, meant that we could not blindly trust any of them to trade real funds independently, as nothing guaranteed that they would be profitable in the future. Just as we hoped for, the simulation results obtained with the multi-agent systems were a big improvement over the individual performances of the trading agents that composed them, both risk-wise and profit-wise. This validated our expectations that proper investment diversification is an essential requirement, if we are to develop an investment system with the potential to be consistently profitable in the long run.

All things considered, we can conclude that the proposed trading agent architecture did indeed allow for the creation of trading agents whose actions resemble those of successful human traders. With varying competency, they showed the ability to adapt to sudden changes in market conditions, which is the single most important skill when working in such uncertain environments. Furthermore, by aggregating these agents, we were able to implement a multi-agent system that can emulate the inner workings of a small autonomous hedge fund, with the potential to yield a reasonable return with relatively low risk. Obviously, the number of agents used in this system was still too small. Increasing the number of agents, as well as adding agents that could trade other financial instruments (like stocks or futures) would greatly improve the investment diversification, which should in turn lead to a much safer multi-agent trading system.

In our opinion, the fact that we were able to implement a relatively successful multi-agent system using six intelligent trading agents is, in itself, an interesting contribution to the field of applied artificial intelligence, in general, and to the field of agency in particular. However, the potential we see in the proposed agent architecture is way more important than those particular results. Throughout our research, we had to use a "one size fits all" methodology to implement the agents, in order to remove any doubts that their performance in the simulation period could be biased due to excessive tweaking. We believe that much better returns could be obtained if the agents were individually fine-tuned, according to the financial instruments they were meant to trade. This would mean, for example, manually selecting the data mining models in their prediction modules, using better attributes to train these models, and selecting the most appropriate timeframe for each agent, according to the price volatility of the instrument that it was going to trade. Defining specific expert rules in their domain knowledge module should also prove beneficial, as should the individual optimization of their empirical knowledge modules. For example, instead of making the agents use the same standard trade size, the best performing could be allowed to trade bigger amounts. Allowing them to compound the gains and to trade with borrowed funds would also greatly improve their performance, as our leveraged results showed. One more thing to consider is that, just like in real life, some trading agents might eventually need to be "fired", and replaced with better agents. While we did not do this in our experiments, to avoid survivorship bias, it is

definitely something to consider in a live trading system. This all goes to show that there is still a lot of room for improvement in the multi-agent system that was presented as a prospective autonomous hedge fund. And this points to what we consider to be the highlight of our work: we have demonstrated the enormous potential that there is for the utilization of this type of systems in financial trading. In particular, our research opens the door to the creation of intelligent hedge funds based on multi-agent systems consisting of hundreds of individually fine-tuned trading agents, each using a specific timeframe and instrument combination, so as to maximize the investment diversification.

Overall, we believe the objective with which we started this research has been fulfilled. We have clearly demonstrated that there is a place for intelligent agents in financial markets, and have described a possible way to implement them. This conclusion is likely to be of interest to the investment community at large.

REFERENCES

Abraham, A. (2002). *Analysis of hybrid soft and hard computing techniques for Forex monitoring systems*. Proceedings of the 2002 IEEE International Conference on Fuzzy Systems, pp. 1616-1622.

Apache Active, M. Q. (n.d.). Retrieved from http://activemq.apache.org/

Barbosa, R., & Belo, O. (2009). A Step-By-Step Implementation of a Hybrid USD/JPY Trading Agent. *International Journal of Agent Technologies and Systems*, *1*(2), 19–35.

Barbosa, R., & Belo, O. (2010). *Multi-Agent Forex Trading System* (pp. 91–118). Agent and Multi-Agent Technology for Internet and Enterprise Systems.

Breiman, L. (1996). Bagging Predictors. *Machine Learning*, *24*(2), 123–140. doi:10.1007/BF00058655

Cao, L. (2003). Support vector machines experts for time series forecasting. *Neurocomputing*, *51*, 321–339. doi:10.1016/S0925-2312(02)00577-5

Fama, E. (1970). Efficient Capital Markets: A Review of Theory and Empirical Work. *The Journal of Finance*, *25*(2), 383–417. doi:10.2307/2325486

Franses, P. (1998). *Time series models for business and economic forecasting*. Cambridge, UK: Cambridge University Press.

Franses, P., & Griensven, K. (1998). Forecasting exchange rates using neural networks for technical trading rules. *Studies in Nonlinear Dynamics and Econometrics*, *2*(4), 109–114.

Gençay, R. (1999). Linear, non-linear and essential foreign exchange rate prediction with simple technical trading rules. *Journal of International Economics*, *47*, 91–107. doi:10.1016/S0022-1996(98)00017-8

JBoss Drools. (n.d.). Retrieved from http://jboss.org/drools

Jennings, N., & Wooldridge, M. (1998). *Applications of Intelligent Agents. Agent Technology: Foundations* (pp. 3–28). Applications, and Markets.

Kamruzzaman, J., & Sarker, R. (2003). Comparing ANN based models with ARIMA for prediction of Forex rates. *ASOR Bulletin*, *22*(2), 2–11.

Oanda Corporation. (n.d.). Retrieved from http://www.oanda.com/

Opitz, D., & Maclin, R. (1999). Popular ensemble methods: an empirical study. *Journal of Artificial Intelligence Research*, *11*, 169–198.

Pavlidis, N., Tasoulis, D., Plagianakos, V., Siriopoulos, C., & Vrahatis, M. (2005). Computational intelligence methods for financial forecasting. *Lecture Series on Computer and Computational Sciences*, *1*, 1–4.

Quinlan, J. (1993). *C4.5: Programs for Machine Learning*. San Fransico, CA: Morgan Kaufmann.

Schapire, R. (1990). The Strength of Weak Learnability. *Machine Learning*, *5*(2), 197–227. doi:10.1007/BF00116037

Shamah, S. (2003). *A Foreign Exchange Primer*. West Sussex, UK: Wiley Finance.

Singh, S., & Fieldsend, J. (2001). Pattern matching and neural networks based hybrid forecasting system. *Advances in Pattern Recognition - ICAPR 2001*, pp. 72-82.

Sollich, P., & Krogh, A. (1996). Learning with Ensembles: How over-fitting can be useful. *Advances in Neural Information Processing Systems*, *8*, 190–196.

Swingler, K. (1994). Financial prediction: some pointers, pitfalls and common errors. *Neural Computing & Applications*, *4*(4), 192–197. doi:10.1007/BF01413817

Taleb, N. (2007). *The Black Swan: The Impact of the Highly Improbable*. New York: Random House.

Tay, F., & Cao, L. (2001). Application of support vector machines in financial time series forecasting. *Omega*, *29*(4), 309–317. doi:10.1016/S0305-0483(01)00026-3

Weigend, A., & Gershenfeld, N. (1993). *Time series prediction: forecasting the future and understanding the past*. Boulder, CO: Westview Press.

Weka, A. P. I. (n.d.). Retrieved from http://www.cs.waikato.ac.nz/ml/weka/.

Witten, I., & Frank, E. (2005). *Data Mining: Practical machine learning tools and techniques* (2nd ed.). San Francisco, CA: Morgan Kaufmann.

Wolpert, D. (1992). Stacked generalization. *Neural Networks, 5*(2), 241–259. doi:10.1016/S0893-6080(05)80023-1

Yao, J., & Tan, C. (2000). A case study on using neural networks to perform technical forecasting of Forex. *Neurocomputing, 34*(1), 79–98. doi:10.1016/S0925-2312(00)00300-3

Young, T. (1991). Calmar Ratio: A Smoother Tool. *Futures, 20*, 40.

Yu, L., Lai, K., & Wang, S. (2005). Designing a hybrid AI system as a Forex trading decision support tool. *Proceedings of the 17th IEEE International Conference on Tools with Artificial Intelligence*, pp. 89-93.

Chapter 15
Modeling a Multi–Agents System as a Network:
A Metaphoric Exploration of the Unexpected

Tanya Araújo
Technical University of Lisbon (TULisbon), Portugal

Francisco Louçã
Technical University of Lisbon (TULisbon), Portugal

ABSTRACT

The article presents an empirically oriented investigation on the dynamics of a specific case of a multi-agents system, the stock market. It demonstrates that S&P500 market space can be described using the geometrical and topological characteristics of its dynamics. The authors proposed to measure the coefficient R, an index providing information on the evolution of a manifold describing the dynamics of the market. It indicates the moments of perturbations, proving that the dynamics is driven by shocks and by a structural change. This dynamics has a characteristic dimension, which also allows for a description of its evolution. The consequent description of the market as a network of stocks is useful for the identification of patterns that emerge from multi-agent interaction, and defines our research, as it is derived from a system of measure and it is part of the logic of a defined mathematics.

INTRODUCTION

In the very first page of his highly regarded novel, One Hundred Years of Solitude, Gabriel Garcia Marquez writes that, when arriving at Macondo and discovering so many unknown objects, Aurelio Buendia had to point out these things because no words were defined for them. This metaphor of the process of metaphorisation is an apt description of

the scientific process itself, as science points out to what it ignores: denotation generates connotation. Even when science is defined as a self-contained logic, as mathematics, it dares into the territories of the unknown and of the unexpected; the more rigorous, the more daring it ought to be.

Yuri Manin (Manin, 1991), in the paper "Mathematics as Metaphor", commented precisely on this metaphoric quality of mathematics:

DOI: 10.4018/978-1-60960-171-3.ch015

Copyright © 2011, IGI Global. Copying or distributing in print or electronic forms without written permission of IGI Global is prohibited.

Considering mathematics as a metaphor, I want to stress that the interpretation of the mathematical knowledge is a highly creative act. In a way, mathematics is a novel about Nature and Humankind. One cannot tell precisely what mathematics teaches us, in much the same way as one cannot tell what exactly we are taught by "War and Peace".

The epic "War and Peace" tells us much about Humankind, as the rigor of mathematics proposes to do. In each case, an exploration into the nature of evolution and change is at stake. The metaphors consequently produced, either as imaginary descriptions or as precise formal models, suggest new interpretations that therefore produce new meanings. Mathematics is semantics.

In particular, complexity - a metaphor of natural and social relations to be precisely analyzed by mathematical methods – defines an approach which is more insightful to understand dynamics than traditional determinism and positivism. In this article, we argue that this metaphor is powerful enough to suggest new methods to interpret the emergence of new patterns in the dynamics of the a multi-agents system.

Here, a stochastic geometry is applied to describe the structural change in the stock market for the last years. The description of the market as a network of stocks suggests evidence for a transition of regimes, measures its dynamics and provides a graphic description of the ongoing process.

Structure Generation in Complex Systems

The research on Complex Systems uses plenty of metaphorical developments where the interpretation of the mathematical knowledge (the creative process) gives place to at least two different (and apparently conflicting) perceptions of the system. The description of Complex Systems generally follows one of two strategies, describing the multi-agents system as:

A. **Simple systems with complex behavior:** They are simple systems because they are characterized by few degrees of freedom. Nevertheless the display unpredictable behavior: deterministic and yet apparently random. A rich literature has been based on this hypothesis. The mathematical tools are those used in non-linear dynamics, namely: ergodic invariants, measure theory, algebra and set theory.

B. **Complex systems with simple collective dynamics:** They are complex systems because they are characterized by having many degrees of freedom. Nevertheless their collective dynamics display patterns that can be observed at different levels. These patterns usually obey to Scale Laws, giving place to the emergence of simple structures that contrast to the huge amount of complexity that defines the individual components of the system. The mathematical tools are those above mentioned plus Graph Theory. When this is the strategy to approach a Complex System one, graph theory is used to characterize the emerging structures from a network modeling perspective.

Figure 1 provides a schematic description of the leading strategies to approach complexity. The arrows and the shaded circles indicate the route to be followed and the topics to be covered in this article.

For the interpretation of the apparently random financial market behavior, it is usual to compute some Ergodic Invariants (Lyapunov exponents, entropy measures) as an alternative to traditional modeling of stochastic processes. In the example here considered, we approach the stock market complexity from the Collective Dynamics perspective. To this end, a stochastic geometry technique is used to describe structural change. Due to their unpredictable behavior eluding so many established models, stock markets have been widely discussed as an example of complex

Figure 1. A schematic description of the leading strategies to approach complexity

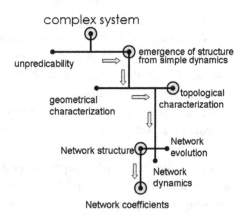

systems. As a result of such efforts, in recent years new methods were suggested in order to describe the dynamics of changes in the behavior of complex markets. Because the huge amount of available data, some interesting methods are based on empirically oriented and computationally highly demanding approaches.

This article applies a stochastic geometry technique designed to highlight the definition of a simple object that emerges from the collective behavior of a complex system. In the current case, the market is described according to the evolution of the 424 stocks consistently measured in the S&P500 index for 1998-2008.

The stochastic geometry proceeds to the metaphorical representation of a stock market as a cloud of points in the space. The use of a properly defined distance (computed from the correlation coefficients between stock returns) gives a meaning to geometric and topological notions in the study of the market.

Given that set of distances between points, our geometrical metaphor discusses three semantic questions:

1. Has the cloud a characteristic dimension?

This is, in other words, the embedding question: what is the smallest manifold that contains the set which has obviously many degrees of freedom? Our strategy is based upon the intuition that, if the proportion of systematic information present in correlations between stocks is small, then the corresponding manifold is a low-dimensional entity, which can be described.

2. Has the cloud any typical shape?

Again, the intuition is that, if the cloud is described as a low dimensional object, its dynamics can be observed as the evolution of its form as it is shaped by the occurrence of bubbles and crises. In portfolio optimization models, when the systematic and unsystematic contributions to the portfolio risk are distinguished, the former is associated to the correlation between stocks (collective structure) and the later to the individual variances of each stock. Consequently, the leading directions obtained from surrogate data may be taken as reference values that represent the characteristic size with which it contributes to the shape of a market whose components were uncorrelated. They correspond to the characteristic size of the individual (isolated) components of the market. On the other hand, the leading directions obtained from actual data represent the characteristic size of each structure emerging from the dynamics of the market, that is, associated to each leading direction of the market space.

3. Finally, does the evolution of the cloud follow any specific pattern?

Groups of stocks, having their position on the cloud determined by the distance metric, are observed to evolve in a synchronous fashion, particularly under the impact of periods of market turbulence.

As in other fields of science (Stanley, 2000), synchronization in the market plays an important role in the identification of abnormal periods. When the stock market is investigated, synchronization is at the root of the modification of the shape of the geometric object describing the market dynamics. Here a geometrical and topological approach is proposed in order to address these three questions.

This article is organized in the following way: the next section presents a stochastic geometry technique which is particularly convenient to approach the complexity of financial markets from a structure generation perspective. We start by describing the financial market through the application of that geometrical technique which set the basis for the presentation of a topological characterization of this complex system. The third section is dedicated to the topological description of the corresponding market space, being initiated with a presentation of some relevant network coefficients, it includes the presentation of the network of stocks that result from the behavior financial agents. The article ends with the appropriate conclusions and the outline of future research work.

THE GEOMETRICAL CHARACTERIZATION

From the set of stocks and their historical data of returns over the time interval, and using an appropriate metric (as in Mantegna, 1999; Mantegna & Stanley, 2000), we compute the matrix of distances between the stocks. Considering the prices (p) for each stock, and their daily returns

$$r(k) = \log(p_t(k)) - \log(p_{t-1}(k)) \tag{1}$$

a normalized vector

$$\vec{\rho}(k) = \frac{\vec{r}(k) - \langle \vec{r}(k) \rangle}{\sqrt{n\left(\langle \vec{r^2}(k) \rangle - \langle \vec{r}(k) \rangle^2\right)}} \tag{2}$$

is defined, where n is the number of components (number of time labels) in the vector $\vec{\rho}(k)$. With this vector one defines the distance between the stocks k and l by the Euclidian distance of the normalized vectors.

$$d_{ij} = \sqrt{2(1 - C_{ij})} = \left\| \vec{\rho}(k) - \vec{\rho}(l) \right\| \tag{3}$$

with C_{ij} being the correlation coefficient of the returns $r(i)$, $r(j)$.

After the distances (d_{ij}) are calculated for the set of N stocks, they are embedded in $\Re^D$, where $D \leq N - 1$, with coordinates $\left\{ \vec{x}(k) \right\}$. The center of mass $\vec{R}$ is computed and coordinates reduced to the center of mass.

$$\vec{R} = \frac{\sum_k \vec{x}(k)}{k} \tag{4}$$

$$\vec{y}(k) = \vec{x}(k) - \vec{R} \tag{5}$$

and the inertial tensor

$$T_{ij} = \sum_k y_i(k) y_j(k) \tag{6}$$

is diagonalized to obtain the set of normalized eigenvectors $\{ \lambda_i, \vec{e}_i \}$. The eigenvectors $\vec{e}_i$ define the characteristic directions of the set of stocks. The characteristic directions correspond to the eigenvalues (λ_i) that are clearly different from those obtained from surrogate data. They define a reduced subspace of dimension d, which carries the systematic information related to the market correlation structure.

This corresponds to the identification of empirically constructed variables that drive the market and, in this framework, the number of surviving eigenvalues is the effective characteristic dimension of this economic space.

It was empirically found that markets of different sizes, ranging from 70 to 424 stocks, across different time windows (from one year to 35 years) and also from different market indexes (S&P500 and Dow Jones), have only six effective dimensions (Araújo & Louçã, 2007; Vilela Mendes, 2003).

In the next section we will apply such a dimensional reduction in the construction of new network coefficients that revealed particularly suitable to the identification of both normal and turbulent periods.

THE TOPOLOGICAL CHARACTERIZATION

The fact that d_{ij} is a properly defined distance gives a meaning to geometric notions and geometric tools in the study of the market. Moving towards a topological description of the market space, we start by visiting some relevant network coefficients to be applied in the topological characterization of market spaces.

Networks of agents play an important modeling role in fields as diverse as computer science, biology, ecology, economy and sociology. An important notion in these networks is the *distance* between two agents. Depending on the circumstances, distance may be measured by the strength of interaction between the agents, by their spatial distance or by some other criterium expressing the existence of a link between the agents.

Network Coefficients

Based on the notion of distance, global parameters have been constructed to characterize the connectivity structure of the networks. Two of them are the *clustering coefficient* and the *characteristic path length*. The characteristic path length is the average length of the shortest path connecting each pair of agents. The clustering coefficient measures the average probability that two agents, having a common neighbor, are themselves connected. These coefficients are sufficient to differentiate randomly connected networks from ordered networks and from *small world* networks. In ordered networks, the agents being connected as in a crystal lattice, clustering is high and the characteristic path length is large too. In randomly connected networks, clustering and path length are low, whereas in *small world* networks (Watts, 1998) clustering may be high while the path length is kept at a low level.

The coefficient of clustering and the characteristic path length capture structural differences, which in turn have implications on the robustness and adaptability of the networks. Besides those two well know coefficients, new characteristic coefficients have been introduced to characterize richer connectivity structures. To characterize additional information on the structure of the networks we have earlier introduced (see reference (Araújo & Vilela Mendes, 2000) new quantities to measure these properties, namely:

• Adaptability

When the networks being studied acquire a structure while learning a function, a relevant indicator of the network structure is, the extent to which, the acquired structure adapt itself to the representation of another function (Araújo & Vilela Mendes, 2000)

• Robustness

In the context above described, it is important to quantify the extent to which do the acquired structures succeed in keeping the same functionality when some of their connections are suppressed (Araújo & Vilela Mendes, 2000)

- Cooperation, antagonism

These coefficients are targeted at capturing the relative strengths of the connections above and below a chosen threshold value (zero for directed graphs).

- Continuous Clustering and Residuality coefficients, which are described below.

Continuous Clustering

Clustering Coefficient and the Characteristic Path Length usually apply to graph structures that are connected and sparse. When the networks we work with are fully-connected structures, a first step is targeted at obtaining a sparse representation of the network. Using the distance matrix d_{ij} to construct the minimal spanning tree connecting the N securities, as in Mantegna (Mantegna, 1999) we might then apply the graph theoretical notion of clustering to the spanning tree. However this construction neglects part of the information contained in the distance matrix. Instead we introduce a notion of "continuous clustering" as follows:

$$C = \frac{\sum\limits_{i \neq j \neq k}^{N} V_{ij} V_{ik} V_{jk}}{\sum\limits_{j \neq k}^{N} V_{ij} V_{ik}} \qquad V_{ij} = e^{-d_{ij}/\bar{d}} \qquad (6)$$

Where V_{ij} represents the *neighbour degree* of stocks i and j.

Measuring continuous clustering allows for capturing variations occurring in the structure of the market spaces. To improve such characterization, the residuality coefficient was also defined.

Residuality Coefficient

Residuality relates the relative strengths of the connections above and below the threshold value L.

$$R_t = \frac{\sum\limits_{d_t(i,j) \leq L} d_t(i,j)}{\sum\limits_{d_t(i,j) > L} d_t(i,j)} \qquad (7)$$

being L is the highest threshold distance value that insures connectivity of the whole network in the hierarchical clustering process.

These measures permit the identification of variations of the structure of the geometric object describing the dynamics of the market.

RESULTS

In this section, we show how, starting from a stochastic geometry approach, the evolution of financial markets creates a structure, which may be described by geometrical and topological coefficients. How the structures are affected by the occurrence of abnormal events is also studied. A central issue in structure creation is how, departing from the individual characteristics of such a complex system, network properties contribute to the understanding of macro (aggregate) economic behaviors.

Describing the resulting structure as a network of agents allows for the characterization of the collective dynamics of such a complex system. The application of some of the network coefficients earlier presented helps to emphasize the interplay between agent modeling approaches and the experimental perspective.

Geometrical Characterization of the S&P500 Stock Market

The application of the stochastic geometry technique earlier described to the set of 424 stocks present in the S&P500 stock market generated the geometrical manifold presented in Figure 2.

The shape of the cloud is close to a spherical one whenever the cloud represents a situation of business-as-usual, when the market is closed to

Figure 2. Market space described along the three dominant directions for a turbulent period

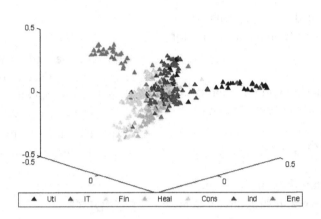

a stochastic universe. On the contrary, the shape of the geometric object representing the market is severely disturbed (acquiring prominences) whenever a crisis occurs. This is due to the synchronization and clustering processes, mostly following sectoral lines, as we proved before (Vilela Mendes, 2003; Araujo & Louçã, 2007; Araújo & Louçã, 2008).

To characterize the additional information on the structure of the market spaces, we computed the coefficient R, which quantifies the distribution of the intensity of the correlations among stocks present in the S&P500 market space along the 10 years.

Figure 3 show the evolution of the coefficient of Residuality for the last 10 years, exhibiting clear evidence of a change of regime for the last years, and furthermore, measuring the impact of the largest recent perturbations in the stock market, the crisis of 2000-2001 and 2007-2008. In particular, the subprime crises, as shown by the seismography, shows evidence for this change of regime, as the frequent episodes of perturbation become the rule in the highly synchronized market.

Topological Characterization of the Resulting Networks of Stocks

The previous results (Figure 2) suggest that, as the markets suffer a crash, there is a distortion in the dominant directions representing its leading variables. But our data prove as well that such distortion follows a sectoral pattern. Consequently,

Figure 3. The evolution of the coefficient R captures the emergence of highly correlated groups of stocks and detect how peculiar it is the crisis from the Winter 2008

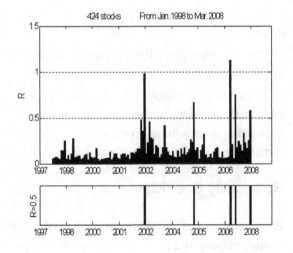

we discuss in this section the form of collective dynamics emerging under threat, using a graph representation of the network of stocks.

From the matrix of distances between stocks (equation 1) computed in the reduced six dimensional space over a time window of 22 days, we apply the hierarchical clustering process to construct the minimal spanning tree (MST) that connects the N securities. Then the Boolean graph B_D^6 is defined by setting $b(i,j)=1$ if $d^6(i,j) \leq \dfrac{L_{D^6}}{2}$ and $b(i,j)=0$ otherwise, where L_D^6 is the smallest threshold distance value that assures connectivity of the whole network in the hierarchical clustering process.

Of course, this network behaves very differently when business-as-usual dominates and whenever a crash occurs, as revealed by Figures 4 and 5. These figures show in their first sub-plots the whole network of companies, while the other seven sub-plots show the sectoral networks of Energy, Industry & Materials, Consumer, Health Care, Finance, Information Technology and Utilities stocks. The sectoral networks built from

August 2000 data (Fig. 4) are sparse and sparseness predominates even in the cases of Financial and Energy sectors. Conversely, the majority of the networks for March 2008 exhibit a very high degree of connectivity, which is particularly intense in the Industry, Utilities, Financial and Energy sectors.

It is also obvious that the nature of the shock and the evolution of the market produce different sectoral dynamics. As Figure 5 highlights, for the ongoing recession, the dominant impacts were in the Financial and Utilities sectors, whereas for the case of the 2001 crisis the impacts were more intense on Technologies, Industry and Energy.

This figure shows the structure of each crisis, as measured according to the density of relations among sectors; the subprime crisis is concentrated in the financial and utilities sectors, in contradistinction to other episodes of turbulence, such as the crash after 9.11, concentrated in the energy and industry sectors, as Fig.5 shows. The profile of each of the crisis can consequently be described and measured following the indications of this topology.

Figure 4. The August 2000 period of 'business as usual' displays few synchronous companies, in almost every sector contrasting to strong synchronization among stocks in the last month of the period under scrutiny

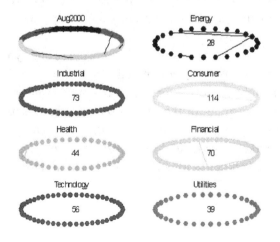

Figure 5. Strong synchronization among stocks in the last months of the current recession

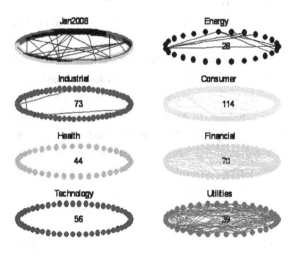

Results, as indicated in Figure 5, show that the amount of highly correlated (short-distant) fluctuations in the network of stocks whenever a crash occurs is very large. These networks display a large amount of distances whose values are below the endogenous threshold. This is due to the emergence of a relevant set of highly correlated fluctuations of the stock returns during market shocks forcing several *weak* correlated fluctuations to leave this category. Although the values of the overall network distances decrease with crashes, the emergence of highly correlated groups of stocks occupying the prominences in the market distorted shape leads to an increase of the value of the endogenous threshold L_D^6. As a consequence, the number of distances below L_D^6 tend to be much higher than the number of those that remain above the endogenous threshold, leading to a significant increase of the values of R.

During the Subprime Crisis, R reaches 1.4, while the same coefficient computed for normal periods rests below 0.5 (computing R from surrogate data yields typical values around 0.025). The evolution of R confirms our previous results, identifying the major crashes in the period and detecting how peculiar it is the current crisis. The Subprime Crisis constitutes one of the highest peaks in the evolution of R for the period under consideration.

Synchronization in the market is related to the occurrence of bubbles and crashes and it is at the root of the disproportionate impact of public events relative to their intrinsic information content. This applies to unanticipated public events but also to pre-scheduled news announcements. In this sense, connectivity patterns as those dictated by sectoral dynamics and the relative distributions of 'weak' and 'strong' connections provide useful insight on synchronization and market shocks.

Furthermore, using the $L_D^6/2$ threshold to filter the distances, we describe a network of companies whose stocks are required to be close enough in order to be connected. The notion of 'state' is then defined according to the connectedness of different companies, with those sharing the same state displaying synchronous behavior.

From the boolean graph B_D^6 we define s(i)=1 if $\exists$ j | b(i,j)=1 and s(i)=0 otherwise. In so doing, we are able to identify, along different periods of observation, those companies that are connected (being closer than the threshold distance) to at least one other companies in the whole network of companies.

The space of the synchronous companies in our population is described in Figures 6 to 8. Stocks are disposed on seven rings, whose color is determined accordingly to each specific sector (Energy, Industry & Materials, Consumer, Health Care, Finance, Information Technology and Utilities). Over the rings, the position of each stock is determined by its order number. However, those evidencing a non-synchronous (s(i)=0) evolution are missing, otherwise (s(i)=1) they are indicated with colors accordingly to the corresponding sector. Figure 6 to 8 exhibit monthly observations.

The plots in Fig.6 show that in March 1998, a period of 'business as usual' there are few synchronous companies, in almost every sectors, except in the Energy one. Conversely, in September 2001, almost every sector displays a highly synchronous set of stocks. The last plot in Figure 7 orders the synchronous movements evidencing the sectoral dynamics as showed in March 2008, where synchronization prevails in Industry, Utilities, Financial and Energy sectors. On the contrary, in August 2000, a period of 'business as usual' there are few synchronous companies, in almost every sectors.

The three plots in Fig.8 show the strong synchronization pattern among stocks in the last 3 months of the Winter 2008 crisis. As they clearly demonstrate for the case of the subprime crisis, synchronization is related to the occurrence of market shocks and, furthermore, the dynamics of the stocks of firms tend to follow sectoral patterns.

Figure 6. The calm period of March 1998 contrasting to September 2001, when almost every sector displays a highly synchronous set of stocks

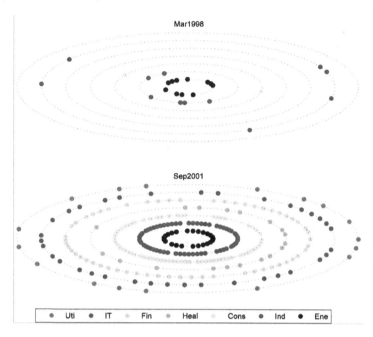

Figure 7. The August 2000 period of 'business as usual' displays few synchronous companies, in almost every sector contrasting to strong synchronization among stocks in the last month of the Winter 2008 crisis

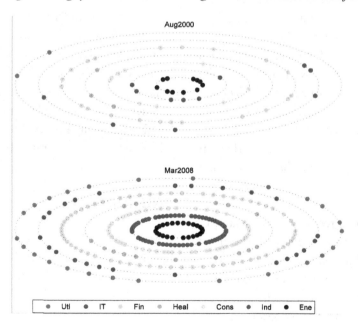

Figure 8. Strong synchronization among stocks in the last months of the Winter 2008 crisis

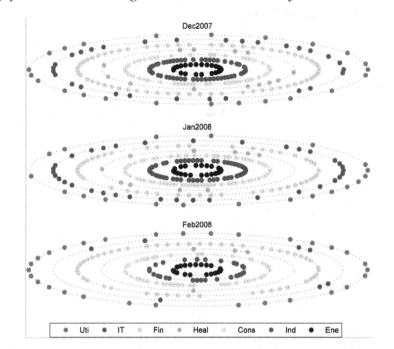

CONCLUSION AND FUTURE WORK

The construction of the S&P500 market space allowed for a description of the evolution of the market for the period under consideration, identifying the shock waves of crashes and measuring their impacts. Pursuing our strategy of investigation on the topological aspects of the stocks behavior, we computed the coefficient *R*, which captures the relative distribution of the distance values below and above the threshold distance. This index provided information on the evolution of the cloud describing the dynamics of the markets. It indicates the moments of perturbations, proving that the dynamics is driven by shocks and by a structural change.

Reconsidering our three questions, an answer is provided by this empirical approach. The cloud has a characteristic dimension, which allows for a description projecting its typical shape and identifying the patterns of its evolution. The index R is useful for this identification of shape and patterns and defines our research, as it is derived from a

system of measure and it is part of the logic of a defined mathematics. The conception of the Collective Dynamic of this object, the metaphor implicit in our method, is part of the effort to point out those things we still ignore, as the late Colonel Aurelio Buendia would say.

Our future research work is planned to focus on the trade-off between redundancy and efficiency in a network of agents. In the context of many complex systems, the underlying network structures are redundant rather than optimally efficient, as already emphasized long ago by von Neumann (von Newman, 1956).

REFERENCES

Araújo, T., & Louçã, F. (2007). The Geometry of Crashes - A Measure of the Dynamics of Stock Market Crises. *Quantitative Finance*, 7(1), 63–74. doi:10.1080/14697680601019530

Araújo, T., & Louçã, F. (2008). The Seismography of Crashes in Financial Markets. *Physics Letters. [Part A], 372,* 429–434. doi:10.1016/j.physleta.2007.07.079

Araújo, T., & Vilela Mendes, R. (2000), Function and form in networks of interacting agents. *Complex Systems, 12.*

Manin, Y. I. (1991). Mathematics as Metaphor. *Proceedings of the International Congress of Mathematicians* (pp. 1665-1671), Kyoto, Japan.

Mantegna, R. N. (1999). Hierarchical Structure in Financial Markets. *The European Physical Journal B, 11,* 63–74. doi:10.1007/s100510050929

Mantegna, R. N., & Stanley, H. E. (2000). *An Introduction to Econophysics: Correlations and Complexity in Finance.* Cambridge: Cambridge University Press.

Stanley, E. H. (2000). Exotic Statistical Physics: Applications to Biology, Medicine, and Economics. *Physica A, 285,* 1–17. doi:10.1016/S0378-4371(00)00341-1

Vilela Mendes, R., Araújo, T., & Louçã, F. (2003). Reconstructing an Economic Space from a Market Metric. *Physica A, 323,* 635–650. doi:10.1016/S0378-4371(03)00014-1

von Neumann, J. (1956). Probabilistic logics and the synthesis of reliable organisms from unreliable components. In S.E. McCarthy (Eds.), *Automata Studies.* Princeton: University Press.

Watts, D., & Strogatz, S. (1998). Collective dynamics of small-world networks. *Nature,* 393.

This work was previously published in International Journal of Agent Technologies and Systems (IJATS), edited by Goran Trajkovski, pp. 17-29, copyright 2009 by IGI Publishing (an imprint of IGI Global).

Chapter 16
Accounting Implications in Virtual Worlds

Jorge A. Romero
Towson University, USA

ABSTRACT

With the rapid growth and development of virtual world applications such as Second Life, created by Linden Lab, where virtual goods and services are exchanged for currency, there are real world implications with regard to taxes and financial regulations. This chapter discusses some of the accounting implications in virtual worlds related to virtual goods, intangible assets, tax issues, real estate issues, copyright issues, and presents a model of utility maximization in virtual environments, specifically, Second Life, based on the income generated by users. The virtual world of Second Life differs from games where users have to follow certain paths or game options. Events and transactions inside Second Life do not pause when a user exits the virtual environment (Chodorow, 2010). Second Life is designed to give users control over all activities in order to foster user creation and self-expression. It is this unique characteristic that is creating a whole new realm for business that is currently unregulated. For example, some activities that may be considered illegal in real life may not be illegal in the virtual world, and this adds a layer of complexity (Kennedy, 2009). Clearly Second Life is not a game; it is a virtual environment that has real world implications (Schlimgen 2010). These virtual worlds are becoming an increasingly important part of life for many users that spend a lot of time and money not only developing their virtual world identities but also doing business in those virtual environments (Kennedy, 2009). The market for virtual items was estimated to exceed U.S. $2.1 billion in 2007 (Lehdonvirta, 2009), and the virtual income that some users generate represents their real-world income (Bonifield and Tomas, 2008). In fact, many users are making a substantial living out of their virtual income, even generating an equivalent of more than $100,000 in real world dollars (Hemp, 2006). On average, Second Life members spend $1.5 million per day on virtual transactions, including virtual real estate transactions (Alter, 2008). While it is difficult to get an accurate estimate of the number of Second Life users due to the dynamic environment, and one in which one user may be represented by more than one avatar, Second Life is estimated to have more than 6.6 million active users from around the world (Moran, 2007), up from a handful of users in 2003 when Second Life started to gain popularity (Wiki Second Life, 2010).

DOI: 10.4018/978-1-60960-171-3.ch016

Copyright © 2011, IGI Global. Copying or distributing in print or electronic forms without written permission of IGI Global is prohibited.

VIRTUAL GOODS

Virtual worlds, such as Second Life, have a unique economic characteristic in which members use real money to buy virtual goods (Bonifield and Tomas, 2008). Virtual goods include characters, items, currencies and tokens that are available for sale in virtual environments. Virtual items are interconnected, which means that the item does not exist in isolation and it does not disappear when the creator logs off the virtual environment (Lehdonvirta, 2009).

In general, brand assets, knowledge assets, and managerial assets are called intangible assets, and they are not included in the balance sheet because it is difficult for accountants to value them under the Generally Accepted Accounting Principles (GAAP) reliability criterion. Intangible assets are listed in the balance sheet only when they are acquired in the market and therefore this is a real valuation (Penman, 2003). Intangible assets in real life do not exist physically (e.g. brands). In a similar manner, the goods in virtual worlds do not exist physically in real life, but may be considered as intangible assets in the real world. Moreover, goods in virtual worlds can be delivered electronically, buyers and sellers do not have physical contact with goods, and there is no physical presence of the virtual goods. A user may be represented by several avatars; therefore an additional layer of complexity is anonymity due to the fact that the buyer is an avatar and not the user directly. All of these factors mean that for accountants asset valuation in this context is not an easy task.

VIRTUAL MONEY

Second Life has similarities with EBay (www.ebay.com), where users trade goods in exchange for money. In order to acquire goods inside Second Life, users can convert their U.S. dollars, Euros, or other currencies into Linden dollars, and vice

versa. Linden dollars work in a similar fashion to any other foreign currency (Chung, 2008; Freeman, 2008).

Firms and entrepreneurs are seeing virtual worlds as an opportunity and a new channel to do business and advertise. For instance, fashion designer Giorgio Armani has a store in Second Life that resembles its main store located in Milan (Bonifield and Tomas, 2008). In addition to many smaller firms, large firms such as Dell, General Motors, Toyota, Nissan, Mercedes-Benz, Coca-Cola, and Nike have also stores inside Second Life. Some of them sell their products; others use their shops for branding, or to obtain customer feedback (Bonifield and Tomas, 2008). Virtual Worlds may be the equivalent of adding another dimension to business transactions.

In a real economy, money is defined as having the following two characteristics: money as a medium of exchange, and money as a temporary store of value (Hirshleifer, 1988). So, do Linden dollars really have the characteristics of real world currency? Can Linden Dollars be considered real money? In the case of Second Life, Linden dollars are only used inside the virtual world Second Life which we can say is the equivalent of a geographical boundary, but this does not affect the fact that we can classify Linden Dollars as a currency because they still have the two basic properties of money mentioned above: it is a medium of exchange inside the virtual world, and can be used as a temporary store of value and users can do any transaction like in the real world. Also, real currencies are usually used within a geographical boundary (Yamaguchi, 2004). In the case of the Linden dollar, there is an exchange rate and therefore it is valuable in the real world and people may accept it as a means of payment. Lindex is the official Second Life currency exchange.

Linden Labs has changed their policy related to virtual banks after the collapse of Ginko Financial in August 2007, and as of January 2008, if someone wants to have an ATM inside Second Life or offer interest on an investment in Second

Life, then they need to show proof of a government registration in order to avoid cases of fraud that have happened in the past (Second Life News Center, 2008).

Although virtual currencies seem to have the same properties as real currencies, there is one main difference: in a real economy there is a central bank that monitors closely the supply of money (Lehdonvirta, 2005). In virtual worlds this does not exist. Also, according to Second Life (2010), the exchange rate between Linden Dollars and U.S. Dollars has remained stable in the last years, but if these virtual economies continue to grow and develop at such rapid rates, are we going to start seeing inflation that affect price levels in virtual economies?

TAX

The real money transactions in virtual worlds are causing the Internal Revenue Service (IRS) and other regulatory institutions to pay attention to these virtual worlds (Bonifield and Tomas, 2008). Due to the dynamic nature of the Internet and virtual world applications, both of which evolve at such a rapid rate with increasingly complex transactions, tax laws may not be keeping up, thus creating uncertainties about the interpretation and application of real world tax laws in this virtual world context. There is much debate about federal income tax related to virtual transactions and whether tax should be applicable for every transaction or when the money is exchange for real money. The U.S. Congress (Congress of the United States. 2006), and the Internal Revenue Service-IRS (National Taxpayer Advocate, I.R.S. 2008) acknowledge the complexity of the issue and are looking at it, but state and use tax have not being discussed much thus far.

In addition to tax applicability at the federal level, we can also see this issue at the state level. The Streamlined Sales and Use Tax Agreement (SSUTA) also acknowledges the complexity of the

issue of online sales and discusses the requirements and effects on sales tax laws in-state sales and use tax. SSUTA discusses the taxability of products that are sold and delivered only electronically, and the sale of digital code. Digital code may include transactions in virtual worlds. SSUTA tries to provide transparency and to require states to follow certain provisions (Duncan and Andre, 2009).

Based on the interpretation of the U.S. Constitution, the U.S. Supreme Court has imposed limits on the ability of states to apply sales and use taxes (Schlimgen 2010). If sales and use tax is imposed in Second Life, the development of virtual worlds may be delayed and blocked in some ways by the additional regulations that may be imposed to virtual transactions, but on the other hand taxing virtual transactions may help states increase their tax collection target (Schlimgen, 2010).

One view is that income generated in Second Life should be recognized in the real world only when users convert their Linden dollars into real world currency (Chung, 2008). However, this model may have some tax advantages for users, allowing users to cash out their Linden dollars in different accounting periods from the actual transactions, thus providing opportunities to manipulate tax reporting.

Another view proposes that each transaction in Second Life should be taxed regardless if the user exchanges none, some or all of the money to real currency, therefore Linden dollars should be treated as a cash equivalent (Lederman, 2007). In this view, these transactions should be seen as equivalent to those that occur on EBay and therefore taxed accordingly. However, this raises the question of what tax rate to apply and under what jurisdiction would it be applied.

Independently of these contrasting views, implementing taxation in virtual worlds is complicated because income should be taxed only once for the same user (taxpayer). For instance, if the user invested $100 (after tax money) to buy some land inside Second Life and after some time he sold the land for the equivalent of $150 and cashed this money out of Second Life, then tax should be calculated based on the difference between $150 and $100 which is a gain of $50. Tax should not be applied to the whole $150 that has been cashed out; otherwise double tax will be applied to the first $100. In addition, taxing land in Second Life is more complex because now Second Life does not allow users to own virtual land, therefore virtual land may not be considered as property. Moreover, in real life, when property is subject to wear and tear, the property can be depreciated over a period of time in accordance to its useful life, but this may not be the case in Second Life (Chodorow, 2010). So, the question is: what kind of mechanisms will have to be in place in order to enforce tax in virtual worlds?

MODEL

Selling virtual goods in order to generate a utility in real money is a common picture in Second Life. The idea is to understand the utility generation process in virtual worlds in relation to real world income. Users can purchase virtual items (including virtual land) using real money. This virtual money plays an important role in real economies because there is an exchange rate. In economics, an agent in real life tries to maximize his utility function based on the consumption of goods, and the maximization of utilities is based on level of happiness of the agent (Hirshleifer, 1988).

In the case of a virtual environment, we can expect a similar behavior, with the difference that one user can be represented by more than one avatar "i" in the virtual world, where i=0, 1,.., j-1, j. Castronova (2003) developed a model to calculate the utility function of a user that operates in several virtual worlds. Following the model proposed by Castronova (2003), the utility function of a user in one virtual world (e.g. Second Life) can be expressed in the following way:

$$U = \Sigma_i \, u_i(t_i, f_i)$$

Where: U: the total utility of the user u_i: the utility of avatar i f_i: It is the unique characteristics of avatar "i" because each avatar may be playing a different role inside the virtual world. Therefore, each avatar in the virtual world has his own utility function. The incentive for a user to spend money in the virtual world will depend in the utility function of each of his avatars. t_i: the time that a specific user can spend in the virtual world as avatar "i"

Because the time that a user can spend in the virtual world is limited to T_0, therefore the time that this user has for each avatar is also constrained by T_0 as follows:

$$\Sigma t_i \leq T_0$$

If a user is represented by only one avatar, his utility function should be similar to the utility function of a user in real life, but the difference is that in a virtual world if a user spends more time trying to maximize the utility of a specific avatar, the available time for the remaining avatars will be reduced, and therefore their opportunities to maximize the utility functions of the other avatars will be limited (Yamaguchi, 2004).

If there are two avatars: The total utility of a user is equals to the utility of avatar "a" plus utility of avatar "b" as follows $U=Ua+Ub$, subject to the following constraint $t_a+t_b \leq T0$ (see Figure 1).

We can generalize the utility maximization model of user in virtual worlds in the following way:

$$\text{Max } U = \text{Max } (\Sigma_i \, u_i(t_i, f_i))$$

Subject to $\Sigma t_i \leq T_0$

OTHER CONSIDERATIONS

Real Estate Property

In the past, Linden Lab used to push the ownership of virtual land in Second Life, and real money was

Figure 1.

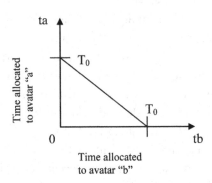

Time allocated
to avatar "b"

used to purchase virtual land. But more recently, Second Life has revised its end user agreement due to a dispute involving virtual real estate properties.

In 2006, Pennsylvania resident Marc Bragg sued Linden Lab, arguing that the company unlawfully confiscated U.S. $8,000 in virtual assets claiming that he acquired his property exploiting a loophole in their system. Linden Lab claimed that he violated Second Life's terms of agreement (Claburn, 2006). Linden Lab tried to compel to the arbitration of a court in San Francisco, but the court denied the motion. Both parties ended up settling out of court (Cavaretta, 2010).

After this incident, Linden Lab revised the service terms of Second Life, and virtual property can no longer be owned by Second Life users (Cavaretta, 2010). Instead, when users acquire virtual land, they only receive a limited license and users are forced to agree to these terms in order to continue using the service (Second Life-Terms of Service, 2010).

In reaction to this change in end user license agreement, there is a new class action lawsuit against Linden Lab for altering users' ownership rights on virtual property. As Cavaretta (2010) states, this action by Linden Lab could be equivalent to the confiscation of property, which introduces a whole new set of legal implications Cavaretta (2010).

With these changes, the legal status of online assets comes under question (Claburn, 2006).

Specifically, because users cannot obtain a deed for virtual property and they cannot depreciate the value of the property, then, who owns property in Second Life or other virtual world applications?

Intellectual Property

Intellectual property includes copyrights, trademarks, and patents. With regard to intellectual property, there are several issues involving copyrights, trademarks, and privacy rights, especially when users using their inspiration create characters and trade them inside and outside the virtual world. There are several lawsuits involving intellectual property in the virtual world (Bonifield and Tomas, 2008). Terms of service may be voided if courts find them unjust (Claburn, 2006).

Copyright laws safeguard owners against illegal use or duplication of intellectual work, but the scope and details of protection may be different from country to country, and this is of important interest in virtual worlds where users are from all over the world. Owners of original work need to register their work with the corresponding copyright office in order to be protected (Bonifield and Tomas, 2008). For instance, in the United States, the U.S. Copyright Act found in Title 17 of the U.S. Code provides the details governing copyright law in the U.S. The World Intellectual Property Organization (WIPO) is an agency of the United Nations that tries to promote copyright protection internationally (WIPO, 2010).

A trademark is a distinctive name, symbol, word, or phrase used by individuals, firms, or other entities in order to uniquely identify their goods (Bonifield and Tomas, 2008). In a similar way to copyright laws, trademark laws may be different from country to country. Therefore, trademark protection is also very important in virtual worlds. WIPO also tries to promote trademark protection internationally (WIPO, 2010).

DISCUSSION

As the Internet has been playing an increasingly important role in real economies, the trend of e-commerce sales continues to go up and states may continue losing more tax revenue (Le, 2007). The availability of the Internet altered the way of doing business, because it allows buyers and sellers to have access to information in a fast and inexpensive way. Something similar may be happening with the availability of virtual worlds. Therefore, government regulation is more likely to develop in the areas of taxation and intellectual property.

Virtual worlds can open opportunities to browse and test real world items in the virtual world without the need to go in person to a store. Virtual worlds have obvious effects on real economies because new job opportunities are created. For instance, 18-year-old Mike Everest has accumulated $35,000 only buying and selling virtual animal skins and virtual weapons in Entropia Universe (www.entropiauniverse.com); 17-year-old Kristina Koch, in her first week, accumulated $50 designing and selling virtual fairy wings and wizard's robes for avatars in Second Life (Alter, 2008).

Second Life still has some limitations for business transactions such as the following: credit cards are not accepted inside Second Life and only Linden dollars are accepted inside Second Life. Firms cannot link their supply chain management system with their virtual store and they do not have control of Second Life servers. Also, Second Life has high requirements related to software and hardware, therefore the number of customer that can be attracted to use Second Life may be limited because not all of them may have access to computers that meet the minimum hardware and software requirements.

Further research is needed because virtual worlds are rapidly evolving and new questions and issues involving taxes and currency transactions arise continuously. A better understanding of the tax implications of virtual world transactions will help companies, and users to develop business strategies and tax planning.

REFERENCES

Alter, A. (2008). My Weekend Journal; My Virtual Summer Job. *Wall Street Journal (Eastern Edition)*. New York: May 16. p. W.1.

Bonifield, C., & Tomas, A. (2008). Intellectual Property Issues for Marketers in the Virtual World. *Brand Management*, *16*(8), 571–581. doi:10.1057/bm.2008.41

Castronova, E. (2003). Theory of the Avatar. *CESifo Working Paper 863*. California State University at Fullerton.

Cavaretta, M. (2010). Linden Lab's 'Second Life' in a Catch-22 over Virtual Property, *Information Week*, July.

Chodorow, A. (2010). Tracing Basis through Virtual Spaces. *Cornell Law Review*, *95*(2).

Chung, S. (2008). Real Taxation of Virtual Commerce. *Virginia Tax Review*, 28(3).

Claburn, T. (2006). Virtual Worlds Collide with Real Laws. *Information Week*, December.

Congress of the United States. (2006). *Virtual Economies Need Clarification, Not More Taxes.* Congress of the United States, Joint Economic Committee, Press Release #109-98.

Duncan, H., & Andre, M. (2009). What's News in Tax: Sales and Use Taxation of Digital Products. *KPMG's What's News in Tax*.

Freeman, P. (2008). Trade foreign currencies online. *Money*, *105*, 84–85.

Hemp, P. (2006). Avatar-Based Marketing. *Harvard Business Review*, *84*(6), 48–57.

Hirshleifer, J. (1988). *Price Theory and Applications* (4th ed.). New York: Prentice-Hall, Inc.

Kennedy, R. (2009). Law in Virtual Worlds. *Journal of Internet Law*, April.

Kobrin, S. (2001). Territoriality and the Governance of CyberSpace. *Journal of International Business Studies*, *32*(4), 687–704. doi:10.1057/palgrave.jibs.8490990

Le, C. (2007). The honeymoon's over: states crack down on the virtual world's tax-free love affair with e-commerce. *Houston Business & Tax Law Journal*, *7*(2), 395–423.

Lederman, L. (2007). *Stranger than Fiction: Taxing Virtual Worlds*. New York University Law Review, Vol. 82; Indiana Legal Studies Research Paper No. 76. Retrieved December 23, 2008 from http://ssrn.com/abstract=969984

Lehdonvirta, V. (2005). Virtual Economics: Applying Economics to the Study of Game Worlds. *Proceedings of the 2005 Conference on Future Play*, Lansing, MI.

Moran, G. (2007). *CyberSocializing. Financial Planning*. Retrieved December 23, 2008 from http://www.financial-planning.com/asset/article/528451/cybersocializing.html

National Taxpayer Advocate. (2008). *I.R.S* (pp. 213–233). Annual Report to Congress.

Papagiannidis, S., Bourlarkis, M., & Li, F. (2008). Making Real Money in Virtual Worlds: MMORPGs and Emerging Business Opportunities, Challenges and Ethical Implications in Metaverses. *Technological Forecasting and Social Change*, *75*, 610–622. doi:10.1016/j.techfore.2007.04.007

Penman, S. (2003). *Financial Statement Analysis and Security Valuation* (2nd ed.). New York: McGraw-Hill/Irwin.

Schlimgen, R. (2010). Virtual World, Real Taxes: A Sales and Use Tax Adventure Through Second Life Starring Dwight Schrute. *Journal of Law. Science & Technology*, *11*(2), 877–899.

Second Life News Center. (2008). *UPDATE 3 - Linden bans Second Life banks*. Retrieved August 8, 2010 from http://secondlife.reuters.com/stories/2008/01/08/breaking-linden-bans-second-life-banks/index.html

Second Life-Terms of Service. (2010). *Second Life, Terms of Service*. Retrieved July 29, 2010 from http://secondlife.com/corporate/tos.php?lang=fr-FR.

Wiki Second Life. (2010). *Second Life*. Retrieved August 8, 2010 from http://wiki.secondlife.com/wiki/History_of_Second_Life

World Intellectual Property Organization. (n.d.). Retrieved from http://www.wipo.int/portal/index.html.en. Accessed July 28, 2010.

Yamaguchi, H. (2004). An Analysis of Virtual Currencies in Online Games. *Social Science Research Network*. Retrieved July 29, 2010 from http://papers.ssrn.com/sol3/papers.cfm?abstract_id=544422

Chapter 17
Multi–Agent–Based Simulation of University Email Communities

David M.S. Rodrigues
ISCTE – Lisbon University Institute, Portugal

ABSTRACT

In this chapter, a study on informal communication network formation in a university environment is presented. The teacher communication network is analyzed through community detection techniques. It is evident that informal communication is an important process that traverses the vertical hierarchical structure of departments and courses in a university environment. A multi-agent model of the case study is presented here, showing the implications of using real data as training sets for multi-agent-based simulations. The influence of the "social neighborhood," as a mechanism to create assortative networks of contacts without full knowledge of the network, is discussed. It is shown that the radius of this social neighborhood has an effect on the outcome of the network structure and that in a university's case this distance is relatively small.

INTRODUCTION

Networks are pervasive in our lives. They are everywhere, from the Internet, to biology, to social relations or economics (M. Newman, Barabasi, & Watts, 2006). The notion of a connected world is one that we assume is prevalent as a foundation. The connectedness of daily things prevails, even when one segments it into sub-networks.

Everything seems related, in some sense, to everything else.

In communication, the notion of networks is always present. Formal and informal relations arise from the interplay of actors during communication processes. Traditionally, networks have been categorized into four types, or classes: lattice networks, that are very regular and rigid, where a certain pattern is repeated *ad infinitum*; random networks, in which every connection is established according to some probability p_c; small-world networks that are somewhat in

DOI: 10.4018/978-1-60960-171-3.ch017

Copyright © 2011, IGI Global. Copying or distributing in print or electronic forms without written permission of IGI Global is prohibited.

between random networks and lattice networks, and have high transitivity and short average path lengths; and finally scale-free networks that have the same type of structure at different levels, with a characteristic hub and spoke structure, where every connection is made according to the degree of existing connections. In this scenario, informal communication networks seem to be formed according to other types of rules, as they can't truly be mapped into one of those four types of networks. These non-trivial networks, arise from the "social" aspect of these kinds of networks and several authors have discussed the problems of those four types of networks in failing to explain social networks. The problems that informal social communication networks present make them well-suited to be tested under new models of network formation and actor interplay. Multi-agent-based simulation is a popular field where these ideas can be tested and where ideas can be benchmarked.

In the next sections, we discuss the mechanisms presently available for community detection, mainly those developed with networks in mind, and we discuss some application of these algorithms to informal email communication systems through a case study. Also, we present a multi-agent model developed for exploring the influence of using real data in simulation and to test the idea of a "social neighborhood" in the formation of informal assortative communication networks.

COMMUNITY DETECTION ALGORITHMS

Community detection can be very useful for performing an exploratory analysis of data, and its usage transverses several domains, from statistics to computer science, biology or psychology. In every science, it is necessary to deal with empirical data, and one of the first classifications that one tries is to group the data according to some property that might manifest itself similarly inside

the groups. Several algorithms and techniques have been devised to accomplish this partitioning (Fortunato, 2010), but in practice all are faced with situations where a good partitioning isn't accomplished, and new methods have to be devised. Some methods are robust, and can be used effectively to classify groups with sets of data that are very heterogeneous. On the other hand, some are very specific to certain problems and need initial conditions that are particular to make its results appropriate (Shortreed, 2006).

The span of techniques and algorithms that tackle the problem of classification and identification of communities in graph representations of data has seen a great amount of interest and developments in the past few years. The field isn't confined only to traditional methods like graph partitioning, hierarchical clustering, partitional clustering and spectral clustering. There is a new set of divisive methods based on modularity, dynamical algorithms, spectral algorithms, and based on statistical inference that populated this field with several possible approaches on how to obtain information about structure (mainly social, but not limited to) that can be organized in the form of a graph (Fortunato, 2010).

Looking into more detail at some clustering techniques for networks, these can be divided into two main classes, according to the approach they take to the partitioning problem: global or local. In global strategies, the network is taken as a whole and usually a general property is used to divide the network, separating all of its members into clusters. One example of these techniques is hierarchical clustering algorithms like Girvan-Newman (Girvan & Newman, 2001) that use edge betweenness as the property of interest. In local algorithms, the strategy uses some local patterns when considering which points belong to each cluster. Clique percolation (Palla, Derényi, Farkas, & Vicsek, 2005) uses the notion of cliques to identify groups or modules.

Hierarchical Clustering is a type of partitioning strategy that produces a dendrogram from the breaking down of a complete graph. Two sub-classes of this type of partitioning are available, according to the way the dendrogram is built. One is a bottom-up approach, where one starts by considering each node as being a member of its own community, and then the process runs iteratively, merging communities according to some maximal value of a quality function. These are called hierarchical agglomerative methods. In other subclasses, there are the divisive methods of hierarchical clustering, where one considers that all nodes belong to one single initial community and then the process to construct the dendrogram is by breaking the communities iteratively into sub-communities up to the point where all nodes are attributed to communities with one node. The path of divisions is also based on the "optimal" value of some property, usually one that measures the strength of the connections between communities. This sub-class is known as a hierarchical divisive.

Two examples of these methods are the Girvan-Newman (Girvan & Newman, 2001) algorithm (GNA) and the Clauset-Newman-Moore algorithm (CNM) (Clauset, Newman, & Moore, 2004). The former is a hierarchical divisive algorithm, while the latter is agglomerative. GNA uses the edge betweenness to determine which edges can be safely removed from the network and iteratively removes them, splitting the network into sub-networks to construct the final dendrogram. The point in the dendrogram where the "optimal" cut is achieved is then given by a property called modularity (M. E. J Newman & Girvan, 2003). This property is based on a previous work where "assortative mixing" was defined (M. E. J Newman, 2002) to take into account the fact that some networks presented a tendency for vertices to be connected to other vertices that are like them in some way. In CNM, the modularity itself is used as the measure to determine which sub-communities to join, and from all different joining possibilities, it chooses the one that presents the maximal value of modularity. The "optimal" point to cut

the dendrogram is then where the value of the modularity is maximal.

The Girvan-Newman algorithm can be succinctly described as follows:

1. Calculate the edge betweenness for all edges in the graph.
2. Remove the edge with highest value of edge betweenness.
3. Recalculate edge betweenness for all edges affected by the previous removal.
4. Repeat from step 2 until there are no edges left in the graph.

The Clauset-Newman-Moore algorithm is described as follows:

1. Calculate the increase in modularity for every possible join in the network.
2. Select the join that maximizes the increase in modularity and merge both communities.
3. Repeat until there's only one community.

Both of these algorithms use the notion of modularity to determine the optimal point to cut the dendrogram. As said, it is an improvement on the notion of assortative mixing. "The modularity is, up to a multiplicative constant, the number of edges falling within groups minus the expected number in an equivalent network with edges placed at random" (M. E. J. Newman, 2006).

Although modularity has proven itself to be useful as a quality function to measure network optimal partitions, it presents a resolution problem discussed by Fortunato and Barthelemy (Fortunato & Barthelemy, 2006). They provided evidence that modularity-based methods might not be able to identify the existence of communities with a size smaller than a certain threshold. The value of the threshold for the size of the cluster depends on the total size of the network and the degree of connections between communities. The authors calculated a limit given as

$$l_s < 2l_R^{\min} = \sqrt{2L} \qquad (1)$$

where l_s is the number of internal connections of each community S, l_r^{min} is the extreme resolution limit and L is the total number of connections in the network. The authors proposed that when such conditions arise in algorithms that use the modularity property, the communities should be checked in further detail to see if it is possible to identify sub-communities inside them. One way is the re-use of the same algorithms applied to these communities.

The use of algorithms based on modularity can be enhanced by coupling them with spectral clustering techniques, where an initial modularity matrix is calculated and, from it, the first eigenvector is extracted to define the division of nodes into communities.

Spectral clustering takes advantage of the Laplacian matrix of the graph. Several techniques have been developed and according to the definition used in construction of the Laplacian matrix, they have different particularities. In essence, spectral clustering uses the Laplacian matrix L and a weight matrix W. The main idea is that one starts by constructing a similarity matrix based on a similarity measure between nodes. Then, a Laplacian matrix is constructed, and one proceeds to calculate the first k eigenvectors of L. A new matrix U is constructed with the k eigenvectors as columns. Each line of this matrix is then considered a point in $\mathbf{R}^k$ and this set of points is then partitioned using a simple *k-means* algorithm (von Luxburg, 2007). From this basic idea, several spectral partitioning methods have been devised, using non-normalized and normalized Laplacian matrices, and fuzzy spectral clustering, the nearest neighbor clustering, etc. (Jain, Murty, & Flynn, 1999).

All of the previous methods and strategies use a global approach to the community detection problem. They classify nodes from an outside global perspective. This accounts for some of the misses

Figure 1. Example of a clique chain with k=3

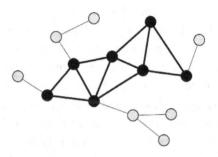

and pitfalls of almost every method. Alternatively, other methods use a local approach. One of these methods is based on the notion of complete subgraph. Inspired by the percolation theory, from the mechanical statistics (Stauffer & Aharony, 1994), the clique percolation method (Palla, et al., 2005) looks for chains of cliques of clique size k and define communities by the entire network that can be reached through a particular k-clique chain. Also, the method allows for overlapping communities, with some members belonging to different communities. This is one aspect that global methods don't usually take into account.

In clique percolation, one says that two cliques of size k are connected if they share k-1 common vertices. In the case of Figure 1, we can see in black the community of size $k=3$. Each triangle ($k=3$) shares with its immediate neighbors two vertices ($k-1$).

Despite all the techniques available at the moment not all of them are applicable in all situations. This is in part due to the lack of a unified definition of what a community is and in part to the almost chaotic evolution that this field had in the past years without precise guidelines (Fortunato, 2010). This means that graph clustering by it alone isn't capable of answering all the questions about the social system studied and other ideas, like using information theory / mutual information to detect structure in the network might be helpful (Rodrigues & Louçã, 2009) and agent based

COMMUNITY DETECTION IN EMAIL NETWORKS

One of the greatest interests in the email classification problem is due to the necessity of filtering emails to avoid the spread of spam. Several methods for the detection and elimination of those kind of messages have been proposed: tests based on semantic analysis, Bayesian tests, black lists and white lists provide good results, but create another problem: false positives (Garriss, et al., 2006). Besides these traditional methods, one approach that has been recently employed, takes advantage of the knowledge that one might have of the social structure of the social network that the user is in. The technique proposed by Kim (Kim, 2007) uses a spectral decomposition of the Laplacian matrix, built from the headers of the messages received in the user's inbox. From this decomposition of the network of contacts into sub-networks, the authors are able to classify each of the sub-networks according to their clustering coefficient. The authors state that sub-networks where the clustering coefficient is high can be classified as spam-free. In their tests, they achieved 100% accuracy in the classification of emails from the test case.

Besides the natural interest in detecting and classifying spam email, the analysis can be directed to legitimate emails in order to find other properties of the networks that emerge from the exchange of messages.

In a study made in the Hewlet-Packard Labs, Tyler et al. (Tyler, Wilkinson, & Huberman, 2003) conducted an analysis of the email logs to detect the informal structure of the relations and interests networks that were formed. With this study, they tried to understand the dynamics of information inside the company laboratory. They showed that these informal networks coexist along with the formal organizational structure and do serve the organization at different levels, like in conflictive objective resolution or in the definition of internal projects. They also found that informal communication networks work as a mean of learning and knowledge transmission inside the company. Due to the value that these communities present for organizations, they developed an automated method to identify these sub-networks. They used a set of email logs that had one million exchanged messages over a two-month period. They defined the minimum number of messages between two people for a connection to exist. This minimum number of messages passed between any two vertices defines the threshold that one can vary to construct the graph. They found that the graphs constructed in this manner were power-law for high thresholds. The algorithm used to divide the graph into modules was based on the Freeman's betweenness (Freeman, 1977) applied to edges and the algorithm is similar to Girvan-Newman algorithm (Girvan & Newman, 2001).

In another study at the university of Kiel, Germany, Ebel et al. (Ebel, Mielsch, & Bornholdt, 2002) studied the email network of the university from the logs of email servers for a 112-day span. Each node of the network corresponds to a student and the connections indicated the passing of messages between them. They found that the resulting network had an average degree of 2,88. Also, they verified that the degree distribution fell under a power-law with an exponential behavior in the tail of the distribution (for degree>100). The power law had an exponent of 1,81. When measuring the clustering of the network, the authors found that the network had a neighborhood effect due to the emails exchanged outside the network, lowering the clustering values but was still 1 or 2 orders of magnitude greater than the expected value for random networks with an equal degree of distribution.

UNIVERSITY EMAIL NETWORK

The development of simulations *in silico* based on agents has become popular in recent years as computational costs have plunged. One aspect that has been of great interest in recent articles is the modeling of real data, with the inclusion of the interaction of agents with the outside world (Janssen & Ostrom, 2006). Also, to tackle the problems of these kinds of techniques, new programming languages have been developed, so agents can explore the ambient outside the simulation (Dastani, 2008).

In this research, the idea of neighborhood influence on the formation of informal communication networks was tested. A model was created that includes real data in the simulation to allow the system to train itself in creating a dynamic solution for the problem. Using different training data sets, the influence of the amount of training in the outcome of the simulation results was assessed.

One of the greatest problems when creating a multi-agent simulation with real data is to find the balance between total freedom of the system and a strict rule-based simulation. If the model isn't constricted enough, one might obtain results that are very difficult to interpret. On the other hand, if the rules/history are strict, the simulation will simply reproduce what was fed via the training set and will be applicable only to that particular data, without being general enough for application in other areas. The main objective is to explore this middle ground, where new features might arise and the simulation can still capture the structure of the real data.

Solutions

The study of a university's informal communication network based on email messages was done through the case study of ISCTE–Lisbon University Institute. This allowed for the inference of the structure of the underlying network from the real data. The ISCTE email network presented some

Table 1. Adoption ratio of ISCTE email service

Sub-network	Members	Total	Ratio
Teachers	395	1153	34,3%
Students	279	11698	2,4%
Employees	197	197	46,2%

interesting aspects that made it a good candidate for a case study:

- Access to raw data from the logs of email servers. Under a privacy directive, all data was stripped of indentifying information.
- Volume of the data. The dimensions of the data allowed us to cross-reference it with other systems, namely the educational management system Fenix.[1]
- Several sub-networks available to study: teachers, students and employees.
- Communities known *à priori,* like the departments or courses to which teachers and students are associated.

The analysis of the networks revealed that students have low adoption rates of the service provided by the university, instead preferring external services. Employees had a higher ratio of adoption followed by teachers, as in Table 1.

With these results, only the teachers' network was analyzed in detail. Two global hierarchical clustering algorithms were used: the Girvan-Newman and the Clauset-Newman-Moore. Both use the modularity as a quality function for the partitioning. Investigation of the overlapping communities was done via the clique percolation algorithm and a k-core analysis was also conducted to find hierarchical clusters inside the teachers' network. The results are summarized in Table 2.

The number of departments/sections in ISCTE log files is 14, but from the analysis, only Girvan-Newman found the same number of components. Clauset-Newman-Moore gave a smaller number

Table 2. Analysis of the teachers' network for different clustering methods

Method	Ambit	Components	Groups	n. classified nodes
Girvan-Newman	Global	14	14	395
Clauset-Newman-Moore	Global	7	7	395
k-core	Local			
k=1		1	-	395
k=2		1	-	355
k=3		1	-	326
k=4		1	-	291
k=5		1	-	262
k=6		1	-	245
k=7		1	-	216
k=8		1	-	174
k=9		1	-	78
Clique Percolation	Local			
k=3		2	9	300
k=4		2	10	195
k=5		3	8	105
k=6		2	2	35
k=7		2	2	19

of communities, at 7. Both of the algorithms had a maximal value of modularity (Q) nearly 0,6 (0,588 for the former and 0,585 for the latter) and presented communities that didn't match exactly those defined by the departments of ISCTE, indicating a transversal communication process. When analyzing this phenomenon via the clique percolation method, it was found that for $k=3,4,5$ the number of groups found is in the range of the hierarchical clustering algorithms. This indicated that those communities overlapped and informal communication processes were transversal to the vertical organizational structure of ISCTE.

CIUCEU MODEL

From the observed results of the community detection analysis, a multi-agent based simulation (MABS) was developed. The Comunicação Informal entre Utilizadores de Correio Electrónico Universitário (CIUCEU) model was developed using MASON (Luke, et al., 2009). There are three different types of agents: the social entity, the teacher and two agents that control, train and monitor the simulation. The simulation has three types of agents: one representing the social entity teacher and two agents that take care of monitoring and training. These two agents allow the system to be trained and generate events and collect data or export data into formats for post-simulation processing.

During the data-collecting period of 62 days, we collected 7,376 message exchanges between teachers. The network formed by theses messages had an average degree of 10. The average degree is the final global value, and it doesn't take into account the process of acquiring new contacts. Looking at Figure 2, we can see that a power law governs the average degree growth, and we

Figure 2. Log plot of the average degree with the number of events. Grows with a power law with an exponent of 0,65. The red line is the average degree after each event and the black line is the fitting line, putting into evidence the power law growth of the average degree during the 62-day period

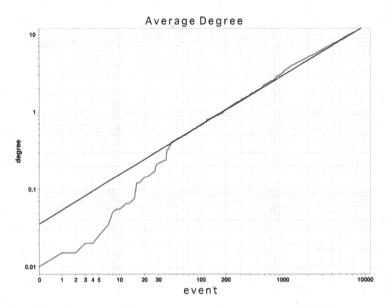

found that this had the exponent value of 0,593. In reality, the network of real connections doesn't grow indefinitely, and some sort of mechanism of removal of acquaintances has to take place. This process can occur faster than the removal of friendships that tend to last longer. As the span of the data was only of 62 days, this process of removal of acquaintances was not considered important and therefore was not included.

The degree distribution of the network reveals a non-trivial decay in the distribution of the degree probability as shown in Figure 3. This fact differs from the other findings for email systems, where a power law is observed. One can say from the data that there seems to co-exist 2 regimes: one for degrees lower than 13 and another regime for degrees above 13, where a power law of an exponent of 3.357 is observed. The main reason is probably that we are dealing with a sub-set of the email usage of teachers, as we are only considering messages exchanged within the email service provided by ISCTE. From the logs, we found that there were a considerable number of messages

being sent to and from external service providers. This indicated a low adoption of the ISCTE email service, which affected the results.

With this knowledge, the CIUCEU model was designed to run in two stages. First, a training regime of the agents was run, where the agents reproduced a sub-set of the collected data, and second a free regime where the agents could send and receive messages according to the model. This way, it was possible to include real data into the simulation.

Initially, the agents didn't have any contacts in their address book, and during the training phase, they reproduce the events that occurred in the training set. After each message was sent, the teachers updated their contact lists and re-calculated the probabilities of future contacts based on the number of previously exchanged messages. When the simulation entered the free regime, each step represented an event and the agent that had the opportunity to send a message did so to someone in their social neighborhood. The notion of social neighborhood is the group of

Figure 3. Degree distribution of the teachers network

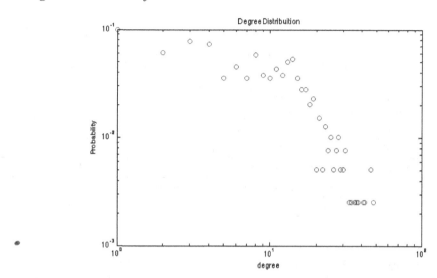

teachers who can be reached from the previously established message exchanges and are within a certain geographic distance of the teachers in question. The premise about this is that even not having previously exchanged messages with someone, one might have a high probability of knowing and contacting someone who is a contact of one of their contacts. The social neighborhood was explored up to geographic distances of 5 from the *ego* teacher. This idea alone is not sufficient to account for the network's growth. If, for example, an event opportunity arises for a teacher that didn't have any previous contacts and therefore had an empty contact list, he or she couldn't initiate a message as the probability of contacting any other teachers would be zero and his or her social neighborhood would consist of only himself/herself. This implies that besides the mechanism described before, a residual probability of sending messages must exist.

The CIUCEU model is described in detail in the following sections, according to the overview, design concepts and detailed (ODD) principles (Polhill, Parker, Brown, & Grimm, 2008).

Purpose

The purpose of this model is to provide evidence of the influence of "social neighborhoods" in the creation of informal communication-based networks of in the email system. The model serves as a means to study the influence of using real data in the outcome of community structures in the simulation, given that its understanding might be of interest for sampling problems or predictive cases.

State Variables and Scales

Agents: The system consists of agents who represent teachers integrated in the email system of a university or faculty. Each teacher is assigned to a department. This assignment can be random or through an input file in cases where training data exits.

Time: The time in the model is not continuous, but discrete. Each moment of time (a time step) corresponds to an event of sending one email message to one or more recipients. To determine the total simulation run time, the training set and the training percentage are used to determine the total runtime of the simulation. This means messages

Table 3. Model parameters, description of used values

Parameter	Description	Default Value
Vizinhanca	Distance used for the local transitivity	2
ProfDepart	Training file with the mapping between an numeric ID and the real departments in ISCTE	<text file>
Ficheiro	Training file with the sequence of events, one each line in the form sender recipient1 recipient2… recipientN	<text file>
Treino	Puts the model in training regime if activated	Active
PercMutation	Residual probability of establishing a random connection.	4.0×10^{-4}
PercTreino	Fraction of real data that was used in the training file	[0,1]
NumDepartamentos	The number of departments for simulations without training sets.	15
NumProfessores	The number of teachers for simulations without training sets.	395

exchanged during the 62 days were transformed into a sequence of events and the total number of events was then used as the total time steps of the simulation.

Event generator: This system controls the training process of the agents, who are responsible for putting the simulation into the training or free regime. At each time step, the event generator makes the right teacher reproduce the data in the training set during the training regime. In the free regime, the event generator selects one teacher as the sender and this teacher produces an event. At each time step, only one event occurs, and this is why the decision process was removed from the teacher-agent and was fed into the event generator.

Process Vision and Event Scheduling

The model assumes that the maintenance of social networks has a cost that in the long term implies a limit on the number of friends that one can have. This limitation comes from the idea that relations will deteriorate if not reinforced over time with new contacts. This is obviously not true for all relations. But as stated, for this particular case study where the time span was short (62 days), this rate of diminishing of relation strength is negligible. The model also uses the idea that connections are made preferentially between people who are homophiles. This characteristic is evidenced through an assortative mixing sub-model for the establishment of new connections.

The model in Figure 4 goes through a variable initialization phase, checking if the simulation has been put into the training mode. If it has, the data from the department teachers can be loaded and the simulation will create the agents accordingly. Then the simulation control is passed to the scheduler. If the simulation is in a free regime, the agents will be created according to the *NumDepartamentos* and *NumProfessores* variables. Afterwards, the scheduler takes control of the simulation and run it until the calculated runtime or until a user stop.

The scheduler defines the time step of the simulation as three sub-steps or levels as shown in Figure 5. The scheduling is discrete, being time and an abstract unit accounted for by the passage of events sent. At each simulation step, only one message is processed and sent from one sender to one or multiple recipients. If the case the simulation is in the training regime, the events are processed according to the training file by reading the next event in the file and sending orders to the respective teachers to complete the required task. The simulation is in free regime, then one teacher is selected randomly and ordered to send a message according to the model rules.

Figure 4. State diagram of the model run

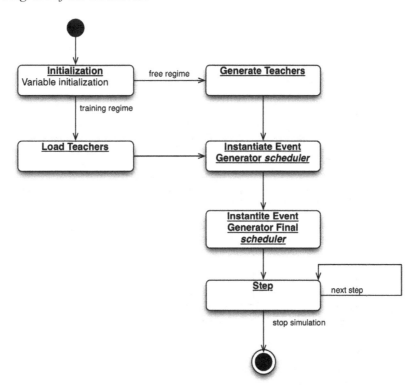

After the first sub-step, if the simulation is in free regime, then it is implemented as the residual probability of establishing a connection. At the end of the step, the third sub-step takes care of statistical calculations and model probabilities updated for all agents. Then the steps are incremented and the process repeated.

Design Concepts

Event: Taking the data structure into consideration, one event is the process of sending one email message. This means that any event has one (and only one) sender and one or several receivers.

Training: The CIUCEU model allows for the inclusion of real data to train its agents. This makes the probability of establishing connections to be derived directly from the historic values of real data instead of using aggregate results to define a distribution would then be imposed. A correlation defined by aggregate data would also not be local but global. The use of training data allows for local variations, even if globally the system tends to the present, the same global aggregate correlation as the fraction of the training data used tends to 1.

Emergence: The notion of emergence in CIU-CEU is found in the appearance of networks with structure. This means that within communities, the edge density is higher than the density of edges connecting communities and is higher than a random network density. The emergence of structure as a global property isn't defined beforehand. Only local rules are defined that control the establishment of connections between different teachers, the assortative mixing and the local transitivity. The global phenomenon of structure formation is then considered as the emergent phenomenon of the model.

Neighborhood: The model implements an algorithm that generates networks with assortive

Figure 5. State diagram of the 3-phase step implemented by the scheduler of the model

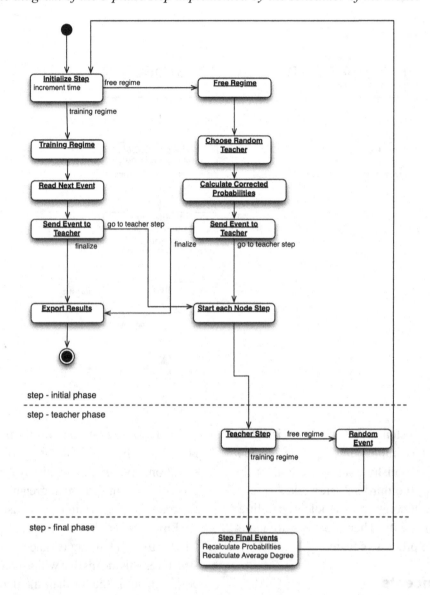

mixing and high transitivity, without using the traditional preferential attachment model of scale-free networks. This is because the latter model implies a global connection of the network and is, in fact, not possible in social networks. In CIU-CEU, agents only have a local understanding of their neighborhood. This mean that any assortative mixing sub-model or decision-making model that the agent does has to be confined to some notion of knowledge distance or, in this case, "social

neighborhood." When we have a distance of 1, then all of these local networks are *ego* networks, in which the central node has only contacts with its immediate *alters*. When the distance is 2, the *ego* knows its immediate *alters* and also their *alters*. This "social neighborhood" is then the set of teachers who are at a geodesic distance less or equal to a certain value.

Reciprocity: Although the sending of email messages is a directed act, the model assumes the reciprocity in terms of social relations. One connection from A to B has the same weight as that from B to A. This is due to the idea that social relations arise from the interaction and not necessarily from the direction. The model can be easily adapted to produce directed networks where reciprocity fails.

Knowledge: The agents have a local vision of the system through the probability distribution of establishing new contacts. This vision isn't global as it wouldn't be in social systems. The usage of a probability distribution for the establishment of contacts' accounts to this as a probability of 0, then in practice means the impossibility of establishing a contact. This probability is built from previous contacts and because of the notion of "social neighborhood," is expanded to include the connections of *alters* to other teachers to whom the *ego* doesn't yet have contact.

Initialization

The model is initialized in a 2D space where agents are placed randomly. They are insulated from the training data in the same number and attributes as the departments of ISCTE. This is done to allow the correspondence of events that will be used later for training the agency during the simulation run. The placement of the agents in a 2D space is arbitrary because there isn't a mapping between the physical and the topological spaces, but it presents the benefit of allowing the coupling of visualization algorithms to the simulation. After the initialization process, the simulation control is passed to the scheduler.

Entry and Training Data

The model is initiated with data from a file that has a mapping between each teacher's ID and his or her attributes, including department. The second set of data corresponds to a fraction of the exchanged messages between teachers, collected

Table 4. Example of the training data (edge file) for CIUCEU

```
0 1 2
3 4
7 8
7 9
10 11
12 13 14 15
16 17
...
```

during the 62 days of analysis. In Table 4. we can observe the first 7 lines of the training file.

Sub-Models

Random number generator: The generation of random numbers occurs when the simulation is in a free regime. It is used in the attribution of events to agents, allowing them to send messages to other agents. The uniform pseudo-random "*Mersenne twister*" generator was used (Matsumoto & Nishimura, 1998).

Assortative mixing: The idea that agents connect with other similar agents is achieved through the value of their degree. For a set of agents $X=<x_1,..., x_n>$ with a degree distribution of $<k_1, ..., k_n>$ and an historical probability distribution $<p_1,...,p_n>$, the corrected probability pc for the connection between agents i and j is given by:

$$pc_{i,j} = \frac{\dfrac{p_j}{1 + |k_i - k_j|}}{\sum_j \dfrac{p_j}{1 + |k_i - k_j|}} \qquad (2)$$

Using this expression, the corrected probability will take into account the degree of difference between the two agents, making a certain connection more probable if the degrees of the edges are similar and less probable otherwise.

Transitivity: High transitivity is achieved through the application of the assortative mixing sub-model only for a subset of agents in a social neighborhood of the sender. The probability of establishing a connection in this social neighborhood is defined as dependent on the geodesic distance. For agent i, j, and l and a geodesic distance d, where j and l are connected ($d_{j,l}=1$) and the distance between i and l is d ($d_{i,l}=d$), one can define a probability:

$$p^*_{i,l} = \frac{1}{d^a} \, p_{j,l} \tag{3}$$

The value of p^* represents an adjustment of the probability of connection over a certain distance. The parameter a will be a measure of how distance influences this probability. As it is necessary to calculate this probability over all possible geodesic paths, it is necessary to normalize the probabilities of connections to guarantees, so that $\sum p^*_{i,l} = 1$. This will give the normalized probability of $p_{i,l}$:

$$p_{i,l} = \frac{\sum_{GeoPath} p^*_{i,l}}{\sum_k \sum_{GeoPath} p^*_{i,l}} \tag{4}$$

Random Events: As previously discussed, the coupling of the sub-models for transitivity and assortative mixing isn't enough to guarantee that one obtains a giant component. This occurs because both sub-models allow only connections between nodes that are themselves already connected (degree >0). This implies that the model wouldn't be able to create new connections to isolated nodes. Therefore, it is necessary to introduce a small residual probability that for each event generated, a connection is possible to/from someone with a degree of zero.

Results

The model was initially tuned for the value of the residual probability with 50% of training data,

neighborhood of 1 and parameter of $a=4$, using as a control value the average degree, that had to be less than 10% of the real data. We found a value of 4.0×10^{-4} for the residual probability of events to be adequate.

The model was tested for fractions of the training data set between 10% and 90% and for values of the neighborhood between 1 and 5 to evaluate the impact of the neighborhood and the fraction of training used.

The real data showed that the average degree grows according to a power law of 0,593. For every run, we calculated the average degree, the density of the network, the average path length and the clustering coefficient. For all of these, the Clauset-Newman-Moore (Clauset, et al., 2004) algorithm was run to obtain an indication of the value of the maximal modularity of the network and to observe the results in the network structure.

The observed results of Figure 6 show that the final average degree of the simulation is very different from the observed real data for the case of low training fraction coupled with a neighborhood (v) greater than 1. Also, the increase in neighborhood seems to tend to a limiting impact, considering that this influence is controlled by the parameter a in the definition of the influence of *alters* of *alters*.

The density of the final network is naturally correlated with the final average degree of the network as the number of nodes kept the same.

The training fraction seems not to have a strong influence on the final average path length of the network for a neighborhood of 1 as the final results are almost constant. On the other hand, the usage of a value greater than 1 for the neighborhood has a strong impact in the average degree, presenting lower-than-expected simulation results. There is also a limiting factor for which for high values of v the results tend to a limiting plateau.

Measuring the clustering coefficient showed that the model with neighborhood 1 presents low values for low training fractions. This was expected as it corresponds to a situation where

Figure 6. Average degree vs. Training Fraction and Neighborhood (v)

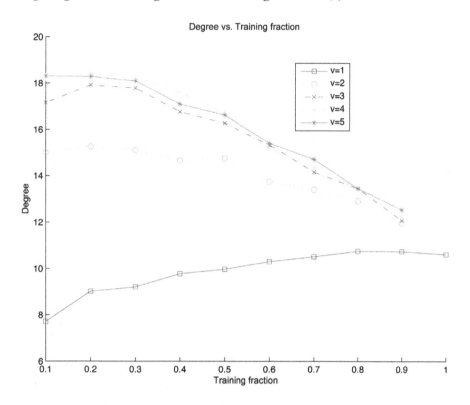

Figure 7. Density vs. Training Fraction and Neighborhood (v)

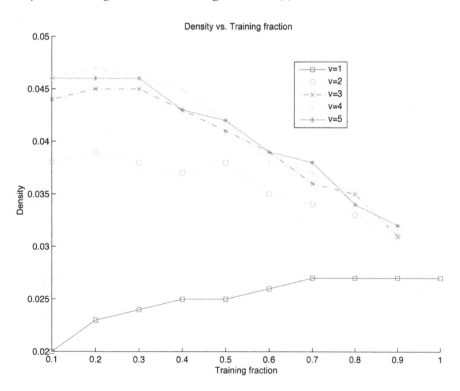

Figure 8. Average Path Length vs. Training Fraction and Neighborhood (v)

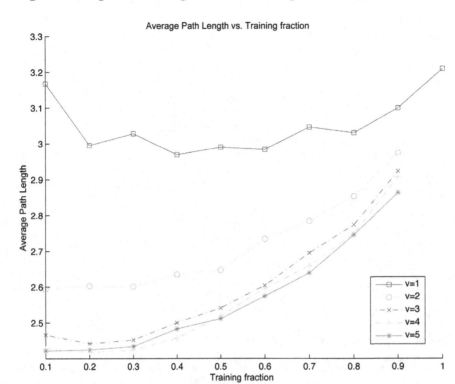

Figure 9. Clustering Coefficient vs. Training Fraction and Neighborhood (v)

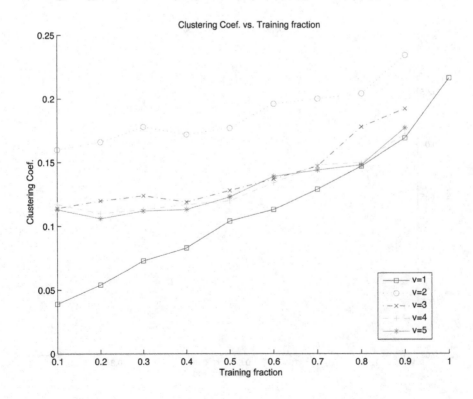

Figure 10. Modularity vs. Training Fraction and Neighborhood (v)

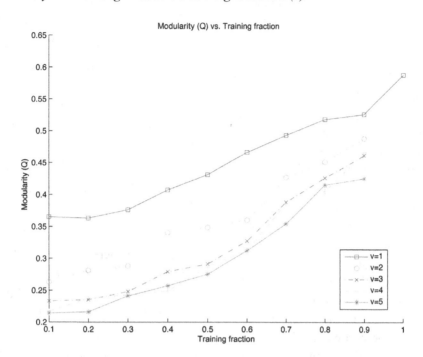

connections are only possible with previously connected agents. When the value of the social neighborhood increases (v=2), the results show that even with small training fractions, the model presents values of clustering similar to those of the real data. Curiously, an increase in the value of the social neighborhood has a negative effect on the coefficient clustering. This seems to indicate that first order neighbors and their *alters* are the most important agents for the establishment of informal social networks.

Looking at the model behavior in terms of structure of the communities formed, it is observed that the increase in the neighborhood has a negative effect on the value of modularity. If one thinks of communities as modules with a higher edge density than the density of inter-community edges, the increase in the social neighborhood will allow border nodes to have a higher probability of connecting to agents in other communities and therefore increase the inter-community edge density. In terms of the training fraction influence, it is observed that even for 10% of training, the

simulation still presents a structure of (Q>0.3) for v=1.

CONCLUSIONS AND PERSPECTIVES

The analyses of the informal communication networks in ISCTE showed that vertical hierarchies are very loose and that communication traverses departments. This is clearly shown with the clique percolation. The communication network seems to be centralized in terms of previous contacts, with a small social neighborhood affecting its dynamics. The extent of the influence of this social neighborhood to other networks of one's life is still not explored and might be useful to include in multi-network studies. The use of training data in simulations shows that even with a small fraction of training data it is possible to capture the latent structure of the original network.

The study of networks is receiving a great deal of attention from the research communities.

The coupling of networks with social simulations and real data inputs is becoming very important to understand, and could help create policies for the social reality that we live in. The present trend is to try and study the dynamics of these social networks. More important than understanding networks' structures in a synchronic perspective, recent trends are searching for ways to take into account the diachronic study of networks.

Another perspective for this work is to include attributes of the nodes in the network representation. These types of tagged networks can include semantic data from the real data and therefore might give insight into details otherwise not present in the previous approach.

Also, it might be useful to apply the techniques exposed previously to multi-level networks. This will allow the integration of the different social networks in which one participates in a global vision of its dynamics. Studying the way a work network affects friends' networks or hobby networks or even connects these networks to a geographical space is of great interest and might help explain the notion of one's territory (Symons, Louçã, Morais, & Rodrigues, 2007).

REFERENCES

Clauset, A., Newman, M. E. J., & Moore, C. (2004, August). *Finding community structure in very large networks. cond-mat/0408187*, from http://arxiv.org/abs/cond-mat/0408187 http://dx.doi.org/10.1103/PhysRevE.70.066111

Dastani, M. (2008). 2APL: a practical agent programming language. *Autonomous Agents and Multi-Agent Systems, 16*, 214–248. doi:10.1007/s10458-008-9036-y

Ebel, H., Mielsch, L.-I., & Bornholdt, S. (2002). Scale-free topology of e-mail networks. *Physical Review E: Statistical, Nonlinear, and Soft Matter Physics, 66*, 035103. doi:10.1103/PhysRevE.66.035103

Fortunato, S. (2010). Community detection in graphs. *Physics Reports-Review Section of Physics Letters, 486*(3-5), 75–174.

Fortunato, S., & Barthelemy, M. (2006, July). *Resolution limit in community detection. physics/0607100*, from http://arxiv.org/abs/physics/0607100 http://dx.doi.org/10.1073/pnas.0605965104

Freeman, L. C. (1977). A Set of Measures of Centrality Based on Betweenness. *Sociometry, 40*(1), 35–41. doi:10.2307/3033543

Garriss, S., Kaminsky, M., Freedman, M. J., Karp, B., Mazières, D., & Yu, H. (2006, May). *Abstract RE: Reliable Email.* Paper presented at the Proceedings of the 3rd Symposium on Networked Systems Design and Implementation, San Jose, CA.

Girvan, M., & Newman, M. E. J. (2001, December). Community structure in social and biological networks. *cond-mat/0112110*, from http://arxiv.org/abs/cond-mat/0112110

Jain, A. K., Murty, M. N., & Flynn, P. J. (1999). Data clustering: a review. *ACM Computing Surveys, 31*(3), 264–323. doi:10.1145/331499.331504

Janssen, M. A., & Ostrom, E. (2006). *Empirically Based, Agent-base models. Ecology and Society 11(2).* Resilience Alliance.

Kim, U. (2007). Analysis of Personal Email Networks using Spectral Decomposition. *International Journal of Computer Science and Network Security, 7*(4), 185–188.

Luke, S., Balan, G. C., Sullivan, K., Panait, L., Cioffi-Revilla, C., Paus, S., et al. (2009). MASON Multiagent Simulation Toolkit.

Matsumoto, M., & Nishimura, T. (1998). Mersenne twister: a 623-dimensionally equidistributed uniform pseudo-random number generator. *ACM Transactions on Modeling and Computer Simulation, 8*(1), 3–30. doi:10.1145/272991.272995

Newman, M., Barabasi, A.-L., & Watts, D. J. (2006). *The Structure and Dynamics of Networks:* (1 ed.). Princeton University Press.

Newman, M. E. J. (2002, September). *Mixing patterns in networks*. cond-mat/0209450, from http://arxiv.org/abs/cond-mat/0209450

Newman, M. E. J. (2006). Modularity and community structure in networks. *Proceedings of the National Academy of Sciences of the United States of America*, *103*(23), 8577–8582. doi:10.1073/pnas.0601602103

Newman, M. E. J., & Girvan, M. (2003, August). Finding and evaluating community structure in networks. *cond-mat/0308217*, from http://arxiv.org/abs/cond-mat/0308217

Palla, G., Derényi, I., Farkas, I., & Vicsek, T. (2005). Uncovering the overlapping community structure of complex networks in nature and society. *Nature*, *435*, 814–818. doi:10.1038/nature03607

Polhill, J. G., Parker, D., Brown, D., & Grimm, V. (2008). Using the ODD Protocol for Describing Three Agent-Based Social Simulation Models of Land-Use Change. *Journal of Artificial Societies and Social Simulation*, *11*(2), 3.

Rodrigues, D. M. S. (2009). *Detecção de Comunidades no Sistema de Correio electrónico Unviesritário*. Lisboa: ISCTE - Instituto Superior de Ciências do Trabalho e da Empresa.

Rodrigues, D. M. S., & Louçã, J. (2009). *Mutual information to assess structural properties in dynamic networks*. Paper presented at the European Conference on Complex Systems, Warwick.

Shortreed, S. (2006). *Learning in Spectral Clustering*.

Stauffer, D., & Aharony, A. (1994). *Introduction To Percolation Theory* (1 ed.): CRC.

Symons, J., Louçã, J., Morais, A., & Rodrigues, D. (2007, November 9--11, 2007). *Detecting emergence in the interplay of networks in AAAI Technical Report FS-07-04*, Arlington, Virginia.

Tyler, J. R., Wilkinson, D. M., & Huberman, B. A. (2003). Email as spectroscopy: automated discovery of community structure within organizations (pp. 81-96), Kluwer, B.V.

von Luxburg, U. (2007). A Tutorial on Spectral Clustering. *Statistics and Computing*, *17*(4), 395–416. doi:10.1007/s11222-007-9033-z

ENDNOTE

[1] The Fenix system is an integrated management system developed by IST for university and educational environments and is deployed at ISCTE. Fenix aims to provide a set of components for the on-line campus activities. For more details, please visit https://fenix-ashes.ist.utl.pt/fenixWiki/.

Chapter 18

Impact on Learner Experience:
A Qualitative Case Study Exploring Online MBA Problem-Based Learning Courses

J. Heather Welzant
Laureate Education, Inc., USA

ABSTRACT

This qualitative case study investigated how the integration of a Problem-Based Learning (PBL) curriculum in an online MBA program impacted the learner experience. The learner experience included three stances as created by Savin-Baden (2000). The stances were personal, pedagogical and interactional. The overarching theme was to examine the experiences of eight learners all in different BPL courses and at different stages in an online MBA program (the beginning, the middle and at the end of the program). The primary research question was: How does problem-based learning (PBL) in online MBA courses impact the learner experience? Purposeful sampling, specifically multiple variation sampling was chosen. The data was collected in accordance with Yin's (2003) five key components derived from documentation, archival records and interviews. The variety of data collection methods served to triangulate sources corroborating findings and offsetting the pitfalls of any one given method. Data analysis consisted of the constant comparison method using NVivo7 as the primary data management tool. Key findings correlated with the Savin-Baden (2000) study revealing how the stances were interdependent upon one another.

INTRODUCTION

Learner experience (Savin-Baden, 2000) was defined as a way to research learners in a unique context and understand how the learners view themselves in that context. The learner experience also investigates students' experiences in relation to the MBA PBL courses as a new paradigm in research that illuminates people and lives as three-dimensional not just as human subjects without history or a future. This qualitative case study included three stances created by Savin-Baden (2000); personal, pedagogical and interactional.

DOI: 10.4018/978-1-60960-171-3.ch018

Copyright © 2011, IGI Global. Copying or distributing in print or electronic forms without written permission of IGI Global is prohibited.

A stance is the sense of one's attitude, belief or disposition towards a particular context, person or experience (Savin-Baden, 2000, p.56). Personal stance was defined in the Savin-Baden (2000) study as "the way in which staff and students see themselves in relation to the learning context and give their own distinctive meaning to their experience of that context" (p.55). Pedagogical stance was defined in the Savin-Baden (2000) study as "the ways in which people see themselves as learners in particular educational environments" (p.55). Finally, interactional stance was also defined in the Savin-Baden (2000) study as "the ways in which learners work and learn in groups and construct meaning in relation to one another" (p.56).

The overarching theme was to examine the experiences of eight learners all in different BPL courses and at different stages in an online MBA program (the beginning, the middle and at the end of the program). The Primary research question was: How does problem-based learning (PBL) in online MBA courses impact the learner experience? The four secondary questions were:

1. How do learners view themselves in relation to the learning context? (Personal Stance)
2. How do learners give unique meaning to their experience within the learning context? (Personal Stance)
3. How do learners perceive themselves in the online MBA PBL course? (Pedagogical Stance)
4. How do learners work and learn in groups and construct meaning in relation to one another? (Interactional Stance)

PROBLEM DESCRIPTION

Problem-Based Learning (PBL) as related to online graduate business and management courses was valuable to study as most research to date has been primarily collected from the medical profession. Evidence does exist that that there is

a growing interest for more research into the benefits of PBL across other curricula. The Academy Assembly of Collegiate Schools of Business' new standards for accreditation looks more specifically at learning outcomes as the basis of continuous improvement in management education (Coombs & Elden, 2004).

Based on the new standards for accreditation, Coombs and Elden (2004) expect more research as necessary to support PBLs expansion. The authors continued by offering advice on critical areas in need of further studies. Among the many needs uncovered, PBL experts discussed the need for more research into the learner experience. Much of the literature in this area offers recommendations on the implementation of PBL, but minimal information regarding the intricacies and challenges of the approach exists (Savin-Baden, 2000). The current research available focuses on important concerns about how PBL is viewed, utilized and implemented (Savin-Baden, 2000).

An expectation exists that PBL will make a difference in learning however; not discussed is the reality of the anticipated difference in the learners' lives. For instance, "there is little research to date that has explored the impact upon staff and student's lives" (Savin-Baden, 2000, p.5). Haggis (2002) asserted that "the processes involved in teaching and learning remain in a 'black box' which is still largely unexplored" (p.207). Looking more in-depth at the personal experiences of learning has value and thus far has untapped potential in research. Learning theories and styles are not the only predictors of success in learning. The four learning styles (converger, diverger, assimilator and accommodator) developed by Kolb and Fry (1975) do not address the interaction or perception of the learner to learning nor does the model delve into the complexities of learning.

Often during the process the learners experience is what makes learning possible and significant. The different models of learning styles developed by experts are useful for assisting learners with comprehending different approaches to learning. The models do not get to the heart of the students lived experience. In the field of qualitative research, the criterion is to allow theories to unfold from circumstances (Creswell, 1998). Past studies on PBL emerged with frameworks imposed on data in ways that did not allow for the materialization of human action and experience. Research is missing a valuable piece of information regarding how PBL increases student recognition about established opinions and values in the context of the world of work within the educational framework (Savin-Baden, 2000). It is not widely known to what extent the integration of PBL in MBA programs impacts the learner experience.

The rationale for the study was based on a lack of intelligent discussions regarding the intricacies embedded in the learner experience. More studies on the individuality of the learner experience, rather than on adults as a general category would have broader implications in the area of student performance. For example, there is the potential to glean insights into the complexities involved with student learning experiences, to conduct new ways of "thinking about factors and influences which may be crucial in determining successes and failures in formal learning situations" (Haggis, 2002, p.211). The researcher established a need for more research, especially exploring through qualitative tactics PBLs impact on the learner experience. The majority of studies outlined in the literature review found were action learning/ research and quantitative studies. Difficult to locate were specific studies on learner experience.

REVIEW OF LITERATURE

The review of the PBL literature uncovered five main themes in the data available. The themes were problem-based learning in general, PBL in relationship to management education, the benefits and challenges of PBL, adult learning

theories, and the learner experience specifically related to PBL.

The first theme was in reference to problem-based learning in general. PBL is a constructivists approach to adult education that emphasizes the transfer of knowledge through solving real work scenarios (Coombs & Elden, 2004). Students are taught through a series of challenges, presented through ill-structured scenarios, developed in co-ordination with a facilitator, which closely mirror real life working issues.

The second theme outlined during the literature review was PBL in Management Education. Chaharbaghi and Cox (2001) identified how PBL has grown in significance in professional education. Even though the prime area of attention has been in the medical field, PBL has the potential for all professions.

The third theme uncovered during the literature review involved the benefits and challenges of PBL. The possibilities abound with PBL applications in higher education. The most obvious reason PBL is gaining ground in other professions is due to the significant benefits derived from its application.

The fourth theme uncovered during the literature review was regarding adult learning theory. With the invention of the internet, adult learning theory has been put to the test in online classrooms. However, the teachings of adult learning theory experts like Knowles, Brookfield, Cross and Merriam remain solid theories educators adhere to (Knowles, 1990). Adult learning theory experts approach this new medium for learning from a constructivist philosophy. This approach is less content focused and more learner-centered.

The fifth theme uncovered during the literature review was regarding learner experience. Savin-Baden's (2000) empirical study explored faculty and student's experiences of PBL across multiple disciplines and educational environments and derived a unique context to define learner experience.

METHODOLOGY

The methodology chosen for this case study was similar to Yin's (2003) approach to designing case studies. The researcher connected data to be collected with the proposed research question(s) and followed Yin's (2003) five key components: (a) the study's research question(s); (b) it's propositions, if any; (c) the unit(s) of analysis; (d) the logic were used for the case study; (e) the criteria for interpreting the findings. The identified population was eight online graduate business students each in different PBL courses and at different stages of the MBA program. Purposeful sampling, specifically multiple variation sampling was chosen. The data collected in accordance with Yin's (2003) five key components were documentation, reflection journals and interviews as the sources of evidence. These three sources of evidence served to triangulate sources corroborating findings and offsetting the pitfalls of any one given method (Swanson & Holton, 1997).

Data was received electronically and saved on a hard drive, jump drive and hard copies were printed out and filed. As advocated by Gall, Gall and Borg (2003), the researcher conducted informal analyses during data collection since data was emerging during the process. This proved advantageous because the researcher learned during informal analysis that students shared team assignments. The researcher subsequently deemed this to be an issue. All future data collection did not include any team work due to ethical and privacy reasons. Finally, since experts such as Creswell (1998), Merriam (1998), Yin (2003) and Stake (1995) recommend pilot tests for interview questions, the researcher implemented this practice which proved to also be beneficial.

Over the course of a two week period, six students assisted with pilot testing the interview questions. The experience revealed some issues with the initial interview questions, established the time requirements needed to conduct the interview and uncovered some technical and procedural issues with the methodology.

DATA ANALYSIS

Once pilot tests were conducted and all data was collected, data analysis became a reality. Data analysis consisted of an analysis using the constant comparison (Glaser and Strauss, 1999) method using NVivo7 as the primary data management tool. All data collected through student class documents, reflection journals and interviews was input into NVivo for data management and analysis purposes. Fourteen themes emerged from the NVivo data analysis.

Specifically, the emergent themes developed into three broader categories: personal stance; pedagogical stance; interactional stance. The three stances were known and planned for in advance based on the Savin-Baden (2000) study. Within the personal stance category, the following themes were identified: adjustment, challenging, confidence, faculty interaction and feedback and overwhelming. Within the pedagogical stance category comprehension, different perspectives and skill levels, real world application, researching and time constraints themes emerged. Finally, within the interactional stance category, the themes uncovered were faculty interaction, favorable, team work and unfavorable.

RESULTS

After a careful review and analysis of the data presented, the researcher reached two main conclusions. The conclusions include a comparison to the Savin-Baden (2002) study which led to a discussion of the relevance to human performance improvement models and an optimal learning experience. The conclusions drawn answer the primary research question and the four secondary research questions.

Comparison to the Savin-Baden (2002) Study

"The framework of dimensions of the learner experience comprises three stances: personal stance, pedagogical stance and interactional stance" (Savin-Baden, 2000, p58). The framework in the researcher's study was intentionally designed to mirror the Savin-Baden (2000) study. In the Savin-Baden study (2000) each stance is comprised of a number of domains. Domains as defined by Savin-Baden (2000) are "the overlapping spheres within each stance"(p.56). The case study's fourteen themes are the equivalent to Savin-Baden's domains. Collectively, these three stances and fourteen themes answer the primary research question: How does problem-based learning (PBL) in online MBA courses impact the learner experience?

The Savin-Baden (2000) study resulted in the personal stance connecting with five domains. The domains were fragmentation, discovering myself, defining my future self, placing myself in relation to my 'life world,' and re-placing myself: knowing the world differently. This case study also uncovered five themes (domains). However, the themes that emerged different from Savin-Baden's (2000) were adjustment, challenging, confidence, faculty interaction and feedback and overwhelming. The five different themes that emerged in this case study answer the first two secondary research questions in regards to the Personal Stance: (a) How do learners view themselves in relation to the learning context; and (b) How do learners give unique meaning to their experience within the learning context?

The adjustment, challenging and overwhelming themes each had different elements that corresponded with Savin-Baden's (2000) fragmentation. Fragmentation occurs when learners in a PBL format are challenged by the current sense of self and by the way they see the world and act in it. The challenge is a result of PBL encouraging students to create a body of knowledge and

make independent decisions about what counts as knowledge. An example is *Student A's* comments that "class was originally frustrating when a person is analytical and wants a solution rather than thinking about what is missing" (personal communication, April 3, 2007). Another example is when *Student C* commented,

How the course offers unfamiliar concepts that the learner is not used to practicing as most of the concepts are out of the scope of responsibility at work. The combination of unfamiliarity and lack of experience in HRM has me fumbling over myself at times (personal communication, April 10, 2007).

Both these comments were noted in the adjustment theme. Finally, similarities of fragmentation also exist in the challenging theme when *Student D* said,

The terms early on in the course were still quite foreign for me. I had to work much harder to understand and how to translate the information into every day work. It appears that my peers are beginning to respond differently as well so maybe I am not alone in the learning. (personal communications, April 10, 2007)

The confidence theme from the case study correlates well with Savin-Baden's (2000) re-placing myself: knowing the world differently. The awareness of 'knowing the world differently' captures the idea of how learners will frame the learning experiences for themselves, are able to formulate alternate perspective and value their own understanding of what is being learned. Aspects of 'knowing the world differently' were noticeable from the confidence theme when *Student A* said,

After completing further research on what a gap analysis is and how one should be done, I was more confident in my completed assignment. There were several readings that interested me this week

and understanding the theories and models behind the ideas was helpful. (personal communication, April 3, 2007)

Also related, *Student C* revealed that PBL "builds confidence in ones abilities and in each problem resolved gives more confidence to speak out and be creative and push forward on new problems that may arise" (personal communication, April 10, 2007).

The Savin-Baden (2000) study resulted in the pedagogical stance connecting with four domains. The domains were reproductive pedagogy, strategic pedagogy, pedagogical autonomy and reflective pedagogy. The case study uncovered five themes (domains). Yet, the themes were different from Savin-Baden's (2000) and were recorded as comprehension, different perspectives and skill levels, real world application, researching and time constraints. The five different themes that emerged in this case study answer the third secondary research question in regards to the Pedagogical Stance: How do learners perceive themselves in the online MBA PBL course?

Some elements of reproductive pedagogy (Savin-Baden, 2000) have similarities with comprehension and time constrains. Likewise, aspects of strategic pedagogy correlate well with some of the comprehension and researching themes. Pedagogical autonomy has some common elements with comprehension and real world themes. Finally, the reflective pedagogy relates to some aspects of the different perspectives and skill level theme. A specific example of the related reproductive domain with comprehension is when *Student E* said,

Sometimes when I read the material I don't really get it right away, but I have found that if I go and research the topics in the university library and read more about it, I understand a lot faster. I continually learn more about my style of learning in every class. (personal communication, April 5, 2007)

Further, several other examples of reflective pedagogy relating to the different perspectives and skill level theme are as follows:

1. *Student B* said "Open to the new subject matter but also the feedback I am getting from classmates or the instructor on the understanding." (personal communication, April 4, 2007)

2. *Student D* said "Take my learning that much further and give it everything I have; sharing with classmates b/c of the diversity; so much you can take that can enhance your learning as well." (personal communication, April 10, 2007)

3. *Student F* said "Interaction and working together on team; correlated well together. Been other classmates I have had that you push each other to keep going when you feel ready to quit. Need someone pushing and backing you." (personal communication, March 31)

The same comparisons can be drawn in Savin-Baden's (2000) interactional stance which consists of the ethic of individualism, validated knowing through 'real talk', connecting experiences through interaction and transactional dialogue. The case study formulated four themes (domains) through data collection. The themes were faculty interaction, favorable, team work and unfavorable. The four different themes that emerged in this case study answer the fourth and final secondary research question in regards to the Interactional Stance: How do learners work and learn in groups and construct meaning in relation to one another?

The Savin-Baden (2000) study did not focus on faculty involvement or on team work. This case study's interviews and reflection journals revealed a major emphasis on faculty and team work from the participants of the case study. The themes that did emerge in the interactional stance do have similarities with Savin-Baden (2000) domains. For instance, the connecting experiences through interaction mirrors some data collected from the favorable theme. The following represent some similar examples:

1. *Student G* said "I not only obtained valuable information from my instructor but from my classmates as well. I am eager to soak up and retain as much valuable information for the remainder of this course." (personal communication, March 19)
2. *Student F* said "I always love finding out about other work places and how management runs certain departments in that office for that particular business. I like how our teacher spreads out the assignments every other day. It makes it a lot easier to get the assignments done in my opinion." (personal communication, Saturday March 31, 2007)
3. *Student E* said, "I interacted very well with others this week. Everyone seemed to be in the same boat as me, ready for the class to be over, but still trying to grasp all the concepts. There was a lot of discussion on the concepts and how they relate to each person's work environment." (personal communication, April 5, 2007)

One key conclusion that can be drawn from a review of the fourteen themes in the three categories (or stances) is how the themes (domains) can overlap and how the stances are interdependent upon one another depending on the individual learner. Savin-Baden (2000) commented on the same findings, "The interrelationship between the stances can be seen through the manner in which student's pedagogical stances impacted upon their perceptions of themselves as a group members, which in turn was often centered in their personal stance" (p.66). For example, *Student H's* pedagogical stance was grounded in obtaining the best possible grade in the course. The need for high achievement and earning A's or a 4.0 might be rooted in *Student H's* personal stance. *Student H* has always earned A's throughout life

and anything less is unacceptable. The cross over of the pedagogical and personal stance for *Student H* impacted the learner's interactional stance.

A review of the themes for interactional stance and the comments made by *Student H* during the interview and in the reflection journals support previous findings by Savin-Baden (2000). Some comments made by *Student H* support the cross over of stances and the importance of earning an A for this learner. In the interactional category under the team work theme *Studen H* revealed all of the following:

1. The week started out with high-hopes for our learning team. Every one spoke to the importance of getting things on time. Unfortunately, the experience wasn't quite as high as expected.
2. I'm tired of being the one in charge and editor-in-chief. I miss my team from 503 where we really were a team, not a collection of essays that got submitted in one paper.
3. Very few of the teams I've been on are collaboration. Some are actually toxic where you need to struggle for every piece of information. It leaves you shouting at your computer as if the other team members could hear, "Don't you understand that what you do affects my grade?" (personal communications, April 11, 2007)

While it was never the intent to generalize the findings of this case study, the significance of the striking similarities between this qualitative case study and the Savin-Baden (2000) study can serve as the foundation for constructing grounded theory on the learner experience.

Relevance to Human Performance Improvement and an Optimal Learning Experience

The data collected, analyzed and research questions all warrant a discussion about the relevance to human performance improvement (HPI) and the optimal learning experience. One critical conclusion from the data analysis was the overwhelming aspect of the first week of class and the adjustment period needed by all students in the study. Some examples of learner comments from the adjustment theme during data analysis are as follows:

1. *Student B* shared from the Week 1 reflection journal, "There was a lot of information to grasp so some of my posts were not very thought provoking for other classmates as I was struggling to gain an understanding myself first." (personal communication, April 4, 2007)
2. *Student C* shared from the Week 1 reflection journal, "Adjustment at first and a challenge." (personal communication, April 10, 2007)
3. *Student E* shared from the Week 1 reflection journal, "shared from the Week 1 reflection journal." (personal communication, April 5, 2007)
4. *Student F* shared from the Week 1 reflection journal, "The first week of class is always scary and exciting both because you do not know what is going to happen or what is going to be expected of you." (personal communication, March 31, 2007)

Another aspect of data collection and analysis that divulged some serious challenges for the students was online team work. One can review the Interactional Stance with the four themes to gather how the majority of the discussion was on the challenges of the team experience. Here is an example of one comment to support the analysis from *Student F* "We also had a person in our Learning Team that did not check in after the 22nd and we had no idea if she was going to submit any information on the Learning Team paper that was due Monday" (personal communication, March 31, 2007).

The combination of the adjustment, feelings of being overwhelmed, and challenges of team work all might be alleviated with a human performance improvement intervention. Since many online universities today are for-profit, student retention, a positive learning experience and the bottom line health of the organization are of the utmost importance. The HPI model of the business analysis, performance analysis, cause analysis, intervention selection, intervention implementation and the evaluation of results could be implemented to determine the optimal intervention to address the student challenges (Piskurich, 2002). The end result would be higher student retention, an optimal learning experience and a boost in the university's bottom line. Some possible interventions might involve a student training session, student tutorials or a student mentoring program.

GENERAL INSIGHTS

Qualitative analysis would not be complete without discussing some of the aspects of data analysis that were not necessarily a part of the emerging themes but were worth mentioning. According to Stake (1995) analysis is a process that gives meaning to first impressions as well as to final reporting. Analysis is the processing of taking something a part. The process revealed some patterns or themes but looking deeper into aspects of the analysis that do not correlate to themes can also be of value. The aspect of the data analysis which was interesting to note was the learner's perceptions of a pure online MBA PBL Program with the 9-step model in the learner's program. Students perceived that they learned more about using the model and less about the content of the course. Yet, overall students perceived that PBL has high value, is rewarding and has meaningful real world applications.

All the learners attend the same online university and all the courses (10 in total) use a PBL approach, most with the same 9-step model as the tool to solve a business problem related to the content of the course. Throughout the course of the interviews the background questions shed some light on students' perceptions of learning in this format. Overall, the impressions were mixed. Some spoke generally and in favor of the program while others were concerned that content was not being captured in full as noted by *Student H*, "Too much emphasis on the steps and not enough put on content" (personal communication, April 11, 2007). *Student H* is a 4.0 student and an experienced manager.

Previous research into PBL in management education cautions universities from engaging in a pure PBL curriculum. According to Smith (2005), while the benefits of PBL are attractive, entire business schools courses and curriculum should not be converted to PBL. Smith (2005) emphasized two main attributes of management that limit PBLs execution in business education. Common sense indicates that business is not just about problem solving and making decisions. Instead, a manager is operation and maintenance focused. Day to day a manger runs the organization and students not only need to understand what is involved with decision making and running the organization but also with situational awareness and an understanding of organizational culture and other basic knowledge. In addition, when managers address problems to be solved, "their efforts are less dominated by gathering information from secondary sources then is the case with physicians" (Smith, 2005, p.372). Instead, managers rely on experience and collecting information informally from staff.

Smith (2005) discussed multiple benefits of PBL as improving knowledge and retention, increases understanding of material, improves focus and practice-relevant knowledge, improves knowledge integration, promotes thoughtfulness, develops teamwork, leadership and social skills, develops life-long learning and motivates student learning. Combs and Elden (2004) advocated for

PBL because one advantage is creating a problem solving context in a classroom setting that is realistic and relevant to an actual real world problem to be solved. The application of real world problems guides students to continuance of life-long learning (Milne & McConnell, 2001). "PBL meets the ideal of a lifelong learner with an inquiring mind, helicopter vision, information literacy, a sense of personal agency, and a repertoire of learning skills" (p.68).

While the purpose of the case study was not to prove any of the benefits of PBL, through an examination of the students' course work, the weekly reflection journals and in the telephone interviews all of the above themes evolved. A review of all three stances and fourteen is overwhelmingly positive about PBL with some challenges identified. The intent of the study is not to generalize these findings across all online MBA programs but the outcomes do contribute to the field of higher management education and so support the benefits identified in previous research.

SIGNIFICANCE OF THE STUDY

The fact that the results of data collection and analysis of the case study complement the Savin-Baden (2000) study support the notion that while learners do have different learning styles and may be a certain kind of thinker, the way students construct the learning experience is as unique as people are diverse. In the past educators assume PBL is only for mature thinkers and learners when in fact the examination of the learner experience demonstrates this is simply not true.

The end result is the potential for PBL has yet to be realized in all forms of education not just with online MBA programs. The implications of this study and the Saven-Baden (2000) study might reach beyond online MBA programs and the results might cross over not only to into other academic disciplines in higher education but could also have implications for K-12 education as well. Savin-Baden (2000) upheld that,

It is only by engaging with issues such as the organizational culture into which problem-based learning is placed, and the kind of model being offered, that it will be possible to bring to the fore the underlying agenda for adopting problem-based learning, which in turn can help students to understand the reasons for its implementation. (p.146)

The conclusions drawn about integrating HPI with learners in an online MBA PBL program support the significance of the study's impact on learner experience. A student intervention to boost student performance assists with the much needed data on the details related to actual learning and teaching situations (Haggis, 2002). The student interventions combined with the thick descriptions produced with data analysis might open the minds of higher education decision makers whose previously would not consider a PBL course format. Again, the influence could translate to other academia as well.

The general insights support PBL's emersion in other settings as well. From all eight participants the overwhelming perception is favorable about PBL and the application of what is being learned to real world settings. Haggis (2002) asserted that "the processes involved in teaching and learning remain in a 'black box' which is still largely unexplored" (p.207). By conducting this study, the researcher looked more in-depth at the personal experiences of learning and demonstrated the value of this information and to date this kind of research still has untapped potential in research. Learning theories and styles are not the only predictors of success in learning. The four learning styles (converger, diverger, assimilator and accommodator) developed by Kolb and Fry (1975) do not address the interaction or perception of the learner to learning nor does the model delve into the complexities in learning.

CONCLUSION AND RECCOMENDATIONS

In general, the significance and implications of this study defined a need for an expansion of PBL in all aspects of education. With this information comes a need for more investigation into the "lived curriculum" (Savin-Baden, 2000, p.146). Translated, the "lived curriculum" gets to the epicenter of what actually occurs in a PBL setting for staff, faculty and most importantly for students. Even with all the existing studies, the impact of a PBL curriculum remains largely a mystery. Studies that explore critical concerns of learning frameworks, learner characteristics (not just learning styles), and learning 'in relation' (p.146) are essential for proper curriculum development, for student retention, and to ensure an optimal learning experience.

Impact of PBL Classes on Student Motivation

Several of the articles examined in the literature review touched on student motivation. For instance, Milne and McConnell (2001) discuss PBLs effectiveness on self-directed learning and on increasing levels of motivation. However, no specific research was tied to those findings just a general discussed was included with the extensive review of the developments in PBL. Similarly, the Chung and Chow (2003) article on *Promoting Student Learning Through a Student-Centered Problem-Based Learning Subject Curriculum* was a qualitative study largely focused on student perceptions of learning and learning experiences and only touched on motivation. Even so, the findings are not generalizable to a larger audience since the study was on such a small group of participants. Very little quantitative research was uncovered on the impact of PBL classes on student motivation. A study utilizing the Motivated Strategies for Learning Questionnaire (MSLQ) to a large sample size might contribute to generalizing the findings to the larger audience of motivation and PBL.

Using HPI Models to Improve Student Performance in PBL Classes

The field of Human Performance and Improvement is growing while at the same time enrollment at online for-profit universities is also on the rise. A study using the HPI Model designed to improve student performance in PBL classes is unique and cutting edge. Learning online can be overwhelming as evidence from the results of data collection for this case study. The combination of the adjustment, feelings of being overwhelmed, and challenges of team work all might be alleviated with human performance improvement interventions. Since many online universities today are for-profit, student retention, a positive learning experience and the bottom line health of the organization are of the utmost importance. The HPI model of the business analysis, performance analysis, cause analysis, intervention selection, intervention implementation and the evaluation of results could be implemented to determine the optimal intervention to address the student challenges (Piskurich, 2002). The end result would be higher student retention, an optimal learning experience and a boost in the university's bottom line.

Exploring Issues with Assessment and PBL

During the literature search, the researcher also considered the challenges of assessment within a PBL curriculum. Brownell and Jameson (2004) specifically address the issues with assessment in PBL in the research on *Problem-Based Learning in Graduate Management Education: An Integrated Model and Interdisciplinary Application* but it is more of an afterthought and appears at the end of the article. The issue is most educators are experienced with assessing cognitive skills through exams. "PBLs extended focus on the effective behavior domains, however, requires a shift in the way student learning is assessed" (p.572). Also unique is how PBL is more of an iterative process

and continuous change unfolds throughout solving a complex problem. More research is needed to help those already invested in PBL and to entice others to adapt a PBL curriculum.

Long-Term Implications

A comprehensive Literature Review for this case study, the potential to research the long term implications of PBL surfaced. Most studies are contained in the short-term and longitudinal studies were hard to identify. Only one study, the Kanet and Barut (2003) study, of PBLs effectiveness at Clemson University was located. The study was longitudinal and took place from 1995 until 1999. The study is already dated and the field of education as related to PBL could greatly benefit from any longer-term effectiveness studies. Upon finding favorable results, perhaps PBL would be more widely accepted and utilized in the broad spectrum of education?

RECENT DEVELOPMENTS IN PBL RESEARCH

Since this case study was conducted mid-2007, this section will explore recent developments in PBL research related to multiple disciplines in higher education. A scan of recent developments between 2007 and the present revealed two primary areas of focus in the literature. The areas of focus were the impact of advancement in technology and the impact of the process and flow of PBL within online classrooms in higher education.

Technological advancements since 2007 have enabled instructional designers and faculty to minimize the gap between real-world and classroom requirements by implementing PBL in the curriculum (Reynolds & Hancock, 2010). In order to solve authentic scenarios, PBL is considered more than the structure of the curriculum. According to Reynolds and Hancock (2010), PBL is "the cognitive and inquiry process students must engage to solve real-world problems" (p. 177). *WebCaseStudy.com* (Zimitat, 2007) is one example of a technique used to simulate authentic learning using PBL. The focus of the Zimitat's 2007 study was to "report on the process of capturing community of practice knowledge for case studies to support student learning" (p. 321).

Savin-Baden et al.(2010) examined PBL in immersive virtual worlds (IVW) and the impact on the learning environment which has implications on the PBL process. The study resulted in the formation of a template that instructors can "adapt to the integration of new learning strategies (embedded in new learning theories such as PBL and in new literacy practices) and new learning spaces" (p. 129). Technology used for delivery of PBL curriculum is indeed an important part of the process. Clearly, more research needs to be conducted on proper integration of the use of advanced technology within a PBL curriculum.

One major conclusion of the original case study on the impact of the learner experience indicated was how more research was needed investigating the "lived curriculum" (Savin-Baden, 2000, p.146). The "lived curriculum" is what actually occurs in a PBL setting for staff, faculty and most importantly for students. Since the 2007 research on learner experience, studies have evolved that explore critical concerns of the learning frameworks, process, and flow of PBL. As previously indicated, this research is essential for proper curriculum development, for student retention and to ensure an optimal learning experience within an online PBL curriculum.

Vardi and Ciccarelli (2008) studied the use of PBL in tertiary-level allied health online course in Australia. The researchers dealt head on with the range of issues that cause dysfunction and distract students from optimal learning in order to examine the "lived experience" of these students. The man issues identified were heavy workload, inadequate preparation, and group participation problems. The research was grounded in seven critical strategies to address the challenges (2008).

The end result demonstrated how positive results could be achieved when the process is understood and strategies are put into place to reduce the challenges students experience in a PBL curriculum.

Barrett's 2010 study titled "The problem-based learning process as finding and being in flow" complimented Vardi and Ciccarelli research. Barrett (2010) ascertained that

experiencing and understanding the PBL process as a process of finding and being in flow, students would be in a better position to transfer their use of this process to a wide range of situations, in higher education, and in different workplaces (p. 173).

Finally, while more research has emerged on technological advances assisting with the process and delivery of PBL as has research on the framework, process and flow, the field of PBL could benefit greatly from studies focused on technology as part of the process of the "lived experience." By pulling all these pieces together, the acceptance and effective use of PBL in online curriculum in higher education would have an even greater impact on authentic student learning in a globally expansive workplace.

REFERENCES

Barrett, T. (2010). The problem-based learning process of finding and being in flow. *Innovations in Education and Teaching International, 47*(2), 165–174. doi:10.1080/14703291003718901

Brownell, J., & Jameson, D. (2004). Problem-based learning in graduate management education: an integrative model and interdisciplinary application. *Journal of Management Education, 28*, 558–577. doi:10.1177/1052562904266073

Chaharbaghi, K., & Cox, R. (2001). Problem-based learning: potential and implementation issues. *British Journal of Management, 6*, 249–256. doi:10.1111/j.1467-8551.1995.tb00098.x

Chung, J., & Chow, S. (2003). Promoting student learning through a student-centered problem-based learning subject curriculum. *Innovations in Education and Teaching International, 41,* 157–168. doi:10.1080/1470329042000208684

Coombs, G., & Elden, M. (2004). Introduction to the special issue: problem-based learning as social inquiry - PBL and management education. *Journal of Management Education, 28,* 523–535. doi:10.1177/1052562904267540

Creswell, J. W. (1998). *Qualitative Inquiry and Research Design; Choosing Among Five Traditions.* Thousand Oaks, CA: Sage Publications.

Gall, M. D., Gall, J. P., & Borg, W. R. (2003). *Educational research an introduction.* Boston: Pearson Education.

Glaser, B. & Strauss, A. (1999). *The discovery of grounded theory: Strategies for qualitative research.* New York: Aldine De Gruyer.

Haggis, T. (2002). Exploring the 'black box' of process: a comparison of theoretical notions of the 'adult learner' with accounts of postgraduate learning experience. *Studies in Higher Education, 27,* 207–220. doi:10.1080/03075070220119986

Kanet, J., & Barut, M. (2003). Problem-based learning for production and operations management. *Decision Sciences Journal of Innovative Education, 1,* 99–118. doi:10.1111/1540-5915.00007

Knowles, M. (1990). *The adult learner: A neglected species.* Houston, TX: Gulf Publishing.

Kolb, D. A., & Fry, R. (1975). *Toward an applied theory of experiential learning. Theories of Group Process.* London: John Wiley.

Merriam, S. B. (1998). *Qualitative research and case study applications in education.* San Francisco: Jossey-Bass.

Milne, M., & McConnell, P. (2001). Problem-based learning: a pedagogy for using case materials in accounting education. *Accounting Education, 10,* 61–82.

Piskurich, G. (2002). *HPI essentials.* Alexandria, VA: American Society of Training and Development.

Reynolds, J. M., & Hancock, D. R. (2010). Problem-based learning in a higher education environmental biotechnology course. *Innovations in Education and Teaching International, 47*(2), 175–186. doi:10.1080/14703291003718919

Savin-Baden, M. (2000). *Problem-based learning in higher education: untold stories.* Philadelphia: SRHE and Open University Press.

Savin-Baden, M. (2010). Situating pedagogies, positions and practices in immersive worlds. *Educational Research, 52*(2), 123–133. doi:10.1080/00131881.2010.482732

Smith, G. (2005). Problem-based learning: can it improve managerial thinking. *Journal of Management Education, 29,* 357–378. doi:10.1177/1052562904269642

Stake, R. (1995). *The art of case study research.* Thousand Oaks, CA: Sage Publications.

Swanson, R., & Holton, E. (1997). *Human resource development research handbook –linking research and practice.* San Francisco: Berrett-Koehler Publishers.

Vardi, I., & Ciccarelli, M. (2008). Overcoming problems in problem-based learning: a trial of strategies in an undergraduate unit. *Innovations in Education and Teaching International, 45*(4), 345–354. doi:10.1080/14703290802377190

Yin, R. K. (2003). *Case Study Research Design and Methods.* Thousand Oaks, CA: Sage Publications.

Zimitat, C. (2007). Capturing community of practice knowledge for student learning. *Innovations in Education and Teaching International, 44*(3), 321–330. doi:10.1080/14703290701486753

Chapter 19
Towards Learning 'Self' and Emotional Knowledge in Social and Cultural Human–Agent Interactions

Wan Ching Ho
University of Hertfordshire, UK

Kerstin Dautenhahn
University of Hertfordshire, UK

Meiyii Lim
Heriot-Watt University, UK

Sibylle Enz
Otto-Friedrich-Universitaet Bamberg, Germany

Carsten Zoll
Otto-Friedrich-Universitaet Bamberg, Germany

Scott Watson
University of Hertfordshire, UK

ABSTRACT

This article presents research towards the development of a virtual learning environment (VLE) inhabited by intelligent virtual agents (IVAs) and modelling a scenario of inter-cultural interactions. The ultimate aim of this VLE is to allow users to reflect upon and learn about intercultural communication and collaboration. Rather than predefining the interactions among the virtual agents and scripting the possible interactions afforded by this environment, we pursue a bottom-up approach whereby inter-cultural communication emerges from interactions with and among autonomous agents and the user(s). The intelligent virtual agents that are inhabiting this environment are expected to be able to broaden their

DOI: 10.4018/978-1-60960-171-3.ch019

Copyright © 2011, IGI Global. Copying or distributing in print or electronic forms without written permission of IGI Global is prohibited.

knowledge about the world and other agents, which may be of different cultural backgrounds, through interactions. This work is part of a collaborative effort within a European research project called eCIRCUS. Specifically, this article focuses on our continuing research concerned with emotional knowledge learning in autobiographic social agents.

INTRODUCTION

In addition to the popular utilisation of social agent simulations in areas such as education and academic research, nowadays immersive online virtual worlds allow social agents to be further enhanced through highly frequent interactions with human users. For example, Second Life (Linden Research, 2005), as a well-known and quickly evolving virtual society, has attracted millions of users to experience a new kind of social interaction in a virtual space. Powerful PCs, fast broadband connections and advanced 3D graphics offer users this alternative online reality. Interestingly, users' social activity in such a virtual society involves high levels of cultural and emotional learning, as many real cases demonstrate that are reported by Ananthaswamny (2007). How well can we expect intelligent virtual agents (IVAs) to be able to cope with interactions similar to those that human users experience in a comparable social context?

To answer this question, one of the primary goals from our research project eCIRCUS (2006) "Education through Characters with emotional-Intelligence and Role-playing Capabilities that Understand Social interaction" is to promote intercultural empathy. Cross-cultural conflicts have been the source of violent acts in many countries worldwide, including conflicts involving people who come to live in a different country. This background forms a strong motivation for our goal to develop a virtual learning environment (VLE) that supports intercultural learning and fosters intercultural empathy skills for its users. Through developing an educational role-play game named ORIENT with character-based emergent narrative (Aylett et al, 2005), we aim to establish a fun way to educate boys and girls at the age of thirteen

to fourteen years in the UK and Germany. The learning outcomes will be designed specifically for children native to the host countries and will be used by the entire school class.

Not surprisingly, in virtual worlds like Second Life or other popular online games, the large international user population and the freedom given to individuals to openly "live" in the environment introduce a certain level of difficulty in intercultural communication. Naturally most users can handle problems emerging from cultural differences – without much effort they can understand both verbal and non-verbal expressions from other characters, which may be either non-player characters (NPCs) or avatars controlled by other users who may be from different backgrounds[1]. To achieve the same level of social and cultural understanding, IVAs are expected to have an *interdependent* (rather than *independent*) "self" – being more attentive to themselves and sensitive to others[2] (Markus & Kitayama, 1991). Consequently, they need to have the ability to be aware of cultural differences and to learn from others. Therefore, we argue that IVAs will benefit from a type of memory which records events that are meaningful to the agent personally and also allows them to extend their knowledge about others' cultural expressions.

Like human beings, these agents should also respond to a stimulus situation with mediation by cognitive processing at several different stages. As reported by social psychologists (Wyer & Srull, 1989; Kim & Ko, 2007), effects of two factors play an important role in most phases of social and cultural information processing: (a) the affect or emotion that one experiences at the time information is processed and a judgment or decision is made, and (b) the agent's "self"[3]. If we assume that one's own emotional reaction to a stimulus is essentially an aspect of oneself, and emotions can be both cause and effect in relation to one's perceptions, then these two factors are clearly related.

In the psychological literature, two different definitions of emotion are commonly used. According to one tradition emotion is viewed as a set of internal cognitive processes of self-maintenance and self-regulation, e.g. Young defined emotion as an "acute disturbance of the individual as a whole" (Young, 1936, p. 263). Another tradition views emotion as an adaptive and organising response because it can motivate forces and direct activity (Salovey & Mayer, 1990). Both definitions seem to naturally assume that these cognitive processes or responses are universal (e.g. Plutchik, 1994), however, the emotional experience is very much culture-based (Solomon, 1984). The reason is that "emotional meaning is a social rather than an individual achievement – an emergent product of social life" (Lutz, 1988; p. 5). Furthermore, like our thoughts and the language that we use to express them, meaning and regulation of emotion are also shaped by "the interest of cultural cohesion", as pointed out by Bruner[4] (1990, p. 58).

To create the dynamic representation of different meanings of agents' emotions, it is beneficial to use schemas for agents' long-term memory that record significant events (events that are meaningful from the agent's point of view). Since the 1920s, psychologists like Bartlett (1932) have been illustrating that humans appear to deal with complex structural knowledge by using memory schemata – not by storing everything in a 'semantic bin' which works like a warehouse. In computational terms, the memory schema provides us with empty slots to be filled in by recalling meaningful episodic information from our long-term memory. This whole remembering process involves memory reconstructions of one's past experiences and thus produces coherent narratives[5] based on meaningful events which tend to be unforgettable in one's life. Psychologists

in recent decades identified this type of episodic long-term memory with personally significant events for individuals as *autobiographic memory* (Conway, 1990).

In light of our interests in agents' cultural and emotional learning using computational autobiographic memory, this article reports our ongoing research into the emergence of agents' knowledge about the "self" and emotion in social simulations. We aim to develop a minimal cognitive agent architecture with essential components for IVAs to perform cultural understanding, to extend emotional knowledge and thus eventually to be able to empathise with other agents or human users. In the rest of the article, we first review psychological literature illustrating cognitive representation of emotion concepts in human long-term memory. Next we discuss research in IVAs using emotional models. Then we introduce autobiographic memory for IVAs and our previous research using autobiographic agents with emotional expressions for narrative storytelling. Following that, we briefly introduce ORIENT (Overcoming Refugee Integration using Empathic Novel Technology) – a software application that is being developed that aims at helping teenagers in emotional and social learning. The next section illustrates several important modules in our agent architecture to support the implementation of agents' personality and emotion, and the integration of autobiographic memory for extendable emotional knowledge for individual agents. Finally, future work is discussed in the concluding section.

BACKGROUND

In this section we introduce some essential ideas that support our study in cultural and emotional learning for IVAs. These ideas are very much interdisciplinary, and they cover mainly the areas including 1) *the presentation of emotion concepts in human long-term memory,* 2) *empathy,*

Figure 1. Cognitive representation of the emotion concept "sad"

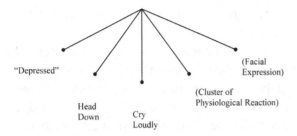

3) *memory and emotion*, and 4) *computational autobiographic agents*. We will illustrate the interrelations that exist between them.

Representation of Emotion Concepts

Culture not only impacts the language that we use, non-verbal behaviour that we display, our gender roles, etc, but also influences our emotional expressions. Here we specifically focus on agents' emotions because much psychological research has shown that emotion plays a critical role in our memory-encoding, decision-making, interaction with others, and overall, intelligence (Salovey & Mayer, 1990). To create socially "friendly" IVAs, emotion is certainly a critical component to be integrated into the agent architecture. From this perspective, representing concepts of emotions is fundamentally important in agents' memory.

In psychology, the way that humans encode concepts of different emotions has been commonly identified as a type of semantic representation. Emotion concepts, together with other concepts of semantic knowledge, are stored permanently in our long-term memory. Wyer & Srull (1989) suggested that, like concepts of personality, each emotion can be also conceptualised as a central node attaching different configurations as features. They further explained that these features may include verbal labels, representation of overt behaviours, etc. As an example, Figure 1 illustrates

their idea about the cognitive representation of the emotion concept of "sad".

Understandably, features attached to the central node are derived from social learning. They are, however, not only used for expressing the internal emotional state of oneself; more interestingly, in social interactions they are often used directly to interpret others' emotions. Consider the following scenario: A mother who observes her young son slamming the house door or performing another behaviour that she personally labels as "angry" may ask him "Why are you angry?". Therefore, emotion concepts stored in the long-term memory are crucial to daily life because the retrieval of these concepts can often help process observable information in interaction with others and in the process of making a decision of how to react or respond to the situation.

Believable Agents and Modelling Emotion

Research on believable agents in Artificial Intelligence (AI), inspired by work on believable characters in the Arts, has been pioneered by the Oz project under the guidance of Joe Bates. A believable character is "... one that provides the illusion of life, thus permitting the audience suspension." (Bates 1994, p. 122). Work on believable agents in AI has grown significantly, a detailed overview in believable emotional agents can be found in (Loyall, 1997).

Integrating an emotion model into the design of an agent architecture is important for believable interactive virtual agents in applications such as computer games or training software. Marsella and Gratch (2003) utilised appraisal processes from the OCC model (Ortony et al, 1988) for believable characters that perform in various applications. They state that appraisal variables enable agents to characterize the significance of events from the individual's perspective as the interpretation of each event is altered by an agent's own beliefs, desires and intentions, and past events. To continue this research direction with computational autobiographic memory, our previous work developed a mechanism that creates *significant experience* for believable virtual characters through OCC appraisal processes (Ho et al. 2007a).

Empathy

In addition to inferring others' internal states, emotion concepts are fundamentally important for the *empathic process*. Empathy refers to "any process where the attended perception of the object's state generates a state in the subject that is more applicable to the object's state or situation than to the subject's own prior state or situation" (Preston & de Waal, 2002, p. 4). Contemporary empathy research agrees on two main aspects of the empathic process, one is cognitive, and the other is affective in nature (Davis, 1996; 2006). Both aspects are clearly relevant to our research. Cognitive empathy focuses on the "intellectual or imaginative apprehension of another's condition or state of mind without actually experiencing that person's feelings" (Hogan, 1967, p. 308), resulting in an understanding of the target's inner state. Affective empathy is described as "a vicarious affective response to another's feeling" (Hoffman, 1977). Therefore, learning emotional expressions from another culture seems to rely on the understanding of internal states of the members of the culture and creating affective evaluative reactions towards them.

Furthermore, there can be two types of development for emotional reactions during the empathic process (Davis, 2006): 1) Through a repeated simultaneous experience of an emotional expression in a target person and an emotion in the observer, 2) through associative processes, which work similarly, but rely more on memory representations of past experiences of the observer; these associations may emerge from visual perception of expressions or situational cues.

Autobiographic Memory and Emotion

Being aware of how high level empathic processes help in increasing the cultural understanding of others, we now study further a rather basic but essential concept of attributing emotion to a specific kind of episodic memory – *autobiographic memory*. In psychology, autobiographic memory has been introduced as memory that contains significant and meaningful personal experiences for a human being (Nelson, 1993). It serves important functions in providing the basis for social interaction, maintenance of a dynamic self-concept as well as the representation of the meaning of concepts (Conway, 1990). Moreover, when memories were plotted in terms of age-at-encoding highly similar life-span memory retrieval curves were observed: the periods of childhood amnesia[6] and the reminiscence bump[7] were the same across cultures – suggesting that there are culturally invariant features of autobiographical memory that yield structurally similar memories across cultures (Conway et al, 2005).

In the literature on human memory, it has been widely acknowledged that events associated with emotional experiences partly constitute highly available memory. Psychologists and cognitive scientists also propose that when experiencing an event with emotional content, a human's cognitive system is more fully engaged in processing that event, in comparison to the processing of events which are not clearly associated with any strong emotional experience. This view can be further elaborated with respect to the frequency of rehearsal (Conway, 1990) – in that highly emotionally intense events are more readily available for retrieval.

Personally significant events which are directly involved in the self memory structure, like first time experiences, can have stronger impacts on humans' lives by creating a pre-existing knowledge structure for other similar events (Conway, 1990). These life events, together with events with emotions, indicate that central knowledge structures relating to the self have been employed in representing autobiographic memory. Nevertheless, studies e.g. from Markus & Kitayama (1991) suggest that emotional processes may differ from the nature of the self-system. They further pointed out that both 1) the predominant eliciting conditions, and 2) the intensity and frequency of emotions expressed and experienced by individuals, vary dramatically according to one's construal of the self.

Computational Autobiographic Agents

Conceptually, an autobiographic agent is an embodied agent which dynamically reconstructs its individual history (autobiography) during its life-time (Dautenhahn, 1996). This individual history helps autobiographic agents to develop individualised social relationships and to communicate with others, which are characteristics of social intelligence. It has been suggested that autobiographic memory for agents may also lead to more appealing and human-like engaging interactions, making the agents more pleasant and acceptable to humans.

Different types of computational memory architectures for Artificial Life autobiographic agents have been developed and experimentally evaluated in our previous research work, e.g. in (Ho et al, 2006). These architectures include memory modules which are commonly acknowledged in psychology: short-term, long-term, and positively and negatively categorised memories. In a series of simulation experiments we showed that agents embedded with these computational autobiographic memories outperform Purely Reactive agents that do not remember past experiences in surviving in both static and dynamic environments.

In the paradigm of developing synthetic agent architectures, we previously proposed that 1)

knowledge representations in the computational autobiographic memory can be based on general episodes that agents have experienced and 2) goal structure, emotion, and attention processes support and are influenced by the autobiographic knowledge (Ho & Watson, 2006). Autobiographic knowledge may also support long-term development and learning in synthetic agents as they gain new experience from acting in each new situation.

Our previous research also includes the investigation of how the engagement of users can be increased in an interaction through the inclusion of believable agents with their own emotions and autobiographic memory (Ho et al, 2007a; 2007b). Specifically, in Ho et al. (2007a), we incorporated the psychological view that emotions can arise in response to both internal and external events. More importantly, both types of events have "*a positively or negatively valenced meaning*" (Salovey & Mayer 1990, p. 186) for an individual agent.

More recently our study in Ho et al. (2008) shows that, embedded with communicative autobiographic memory, agents' behaviours can be understood as intentional, narratively structured, and temporally grounded. Furthermore, the communication of experience can be seen to rely on emergent mixed narrative reconstructions combining the experiences of several agents.

Earlier in this article we discussed the semantic representation of emotion concepts and how these concepts can be learnt. Now we define *learning* in this article as more than just acquiring knowledge. Agents use the emotional knowledge to improve their performance – in the sense of achieving believability and performing cultural interactions with other agents and human users. We therefore focus on low level symbolic learning for agents aiming to increase their cultural and emotional knowledge through gaining experiences from interactions with other agents/users and using autobiographic memory.

CULTURAL AND EMOTIONAL LEARNING FOR SOCIAL AGENTS

This section presents the challenge of creating IVAs that are able to extend their emotional knowledge based on cultural interactions with other agents or users. We start with identifying several limitations of existing research in the area. We then introduce the software application ORIENT developed within the eCIRCUS project, the agent architecture and examples of story scenarios in which agents' intercultural learning ability is required for human-agent interactions. Next, we present our agent architecture design and specify the *minimum requirements* for agents embedded with computational autobiographic memory in ORIENT to be able to learn emotional knowledge through social and empathic interactions.

Issues and Challenges

As discussed in the background section, humans represent concepts of emotion in long-term semantic memory. Importantly, these concepts are *not* innate but each individual forms them either from one's own cultural inheritance (i.e. knowledge acquired via folk tales, books or other media etc.) or from past meaningful personal experiences. For this reason, we may not be able to infer others' emotions from purely observable information during the interaction. Instead, backed up by the reviewed psychological literature, we argue that both cultural background knowledge as well as autobiographical experiences of a person or an agent play an important role in recognising and learning others' emotional expressions.

One possible approach is to create a synthetic culture for a group of agents, so that each agent can have the same set of semantic knowledge for emotional expressions that represent their culture – this is our first step in the current implementation of ORIENT, which will be introduced in the next subsection. Unfortunately, when these agents are

interacting with users in different circumstances, this set of *static* semantic knowledge is too limited.

Since developing a personality model which is valid across cultures is also essential to our research, we suggest re-interpreting cultural dimensions in terms of personality traits. According to Triandis & Suh (2002), the basic personality traits in the Big Five model (Costa & McCrae, 1992) are the most suitable to incorporate cultural dimensions. They argue that 1) the Big Five model is applicable to a wide variety of cultures, 2) traits are supposedly biologically based and they show the same pattern of developmental change in adulthood, and, most importantly, 3) acculturation effects can be found in the predicted direction. To give an example of point 3: if people live as part of a culture different from their own, then their behaviour and attitudes are likely to change by acclimatising to the lived in culture.

Overall, the Big Five model represents five replicable, broad dimensions of personality: Extraversion, Agreeableness, Conscientiousness, Neuroticism and Openness to experience. These five dimensions are, however, descriptive concepts that focus on illustrating how human behaviour can be traced back to psychological variables and their interplay. Therefore, they still need to be explicated in low-level structures and processes for our implementation.

With the consideration of the developmental stages that a person may pass through, the transition includes social and psychological changes. Hence, one shall undergo a time of important changes, which can be a cause of conflict, and a positive development of personality or a clearer sense of psychological identity (Piaget, 1952). Computationally capturing these changes from all agent interactions requires a careful design specification of episodic memory that allows agents to remember those significant events. Therefore, in addition to the underlying personality model that the agent might be using, computational autobiographic memory is necessary here to establish the learning of emotional knowledge and to emphasise the cultural differences of a particular individual.

Furthermore, although we discussed above that empathy is a crucial psychological process to understand others' internal states, modelling the empathic or similar processes, such as Theory of Mind (Premack & Woodruff, 1978; Baron-Cohen, 1991; Leslie, 1994), for agents is a highly challenging task. In the research field of believable IVAs, researchers have attempted to create empathic agents by, for example, using a data-driven affective architecture with human teaching examples (McQuiggan & Lester, 2006), or analysing human users' physiological responses through skin conductance and electromyography to guide the animated interface agents in performing empathic behaviour (Prendinger et al, 2006). However, in both examples the agent's emotional knowledge is predefined by the designer and is not extendable.

Integrating emotion into agents' behaviour modulation mechanisms has recently been widely studied, e.g. as part of a large European project called HUMAINE (HUMAINE, 2004). However, not many studies of agents' emotional learning based on culture can be found. One can imagine the difficulties: learning new emotion concepts means to match the particular expression the user shows with his/her internal emotional states – however, typically virtual agents can neither perceive the user's facial expression nor detect their physiological changes easily in real-time.

We argue that the first important step towards creating IVAs with abilities of learning emotional knowledge about other cultures, and ultimately empathising with others, is to enable the agents' long-term learning from *meaningful* events. For example, through remembering its significant experiences in the past agent_A learned that event_X always has a negative impact on its internal states and thus it generates a dislike emotion. Agent_A, after sometime, creates a concept *"event_X is harmful and leading to a dislike emotion"* and an associated *avoidance* action.

With this conceptual knowledge derived from its own experiences, initially agent_A assumes that all other agents whom it meets have the same concept. Therefore when agent_A sees agent_B expressing a dislike emotion, it automatically infers that event_X (or similar events that have a same effect) has happened to agent_B. Afterward, intuitively agent_A expresses its concern to agent_B and expects agent_B's "feedback". The feedback can be either a confirmation of the concept or an unexpected result, both of them will lead to an update of agent_A's existing concept for event_X and thus increase agent_A's cultural emotional knowledge. Note that the complete description of empathic processes is shown in the next subsection *Specifications for computational autobiographic memory*.

In addition to embedding computational autobiographic memory in the agent architecture, it is also essential to consider the "minimum requirements" as specifications for agents interacting with users or other agents. We aim to achieve that, eventually, both the agent's long-term "self" and emotional knowledge can emerge from such social and cultural interactions.

The Character-Based Approach

In this section we elaborate the character-based approach, with the features that computational autobiographic memory can provide, as a potential solution to address the issues we raised above. In order to allow our agents to adapt themselves to distinct cultures and to be able to establish empathic relations with others, the computational autobiographic memory model focuses on agents' knowledge representations and how information retrieved from autobiographic memory can support agents' goal processing with the PSI theory's "needs" as a foundation (see below for a detailed explanation of the PSI theory). In this model, meaningful episodic knowledge derived from an agent's past experience forms events, episodes, themes and life periods[8] in a bottom-up fashion.

Each of them has an abstraction generated for representing general meanings to the agent itself during different periods of its lifetime in a temporal sequence. The technical design for this model can be found in (Ho et al, 2007b).

The main advantage of our autobiographic memory model is that it attributes changes of internal states (e.g. emotions) in action-situation patterns to show the significance (to an agent itself) of past episodic experience. Thus this approach improves agents' learning and adaptation. Moreover, various levels of abstraction can feature the production of narrative storytelling for describing agents' past experiences as well as forming changeable personalities. Using autobiographic memory knowledge to bias planning current goals is particularly suitable in creating dramatic acting for synthetic agents.

Since the full description of the story scenario in ORIENT (eCIRCUS, 2006) goes beyond the scope of this article, we provide 1) the design of a fundamental personality model with its integration into the main architecture, 2) an example of the story scenario, and more importantly, 3) the detailed specifications of requirements for computational autobiographic memory based on the design for the ORIENT scenario and user-agent interaction.

Personality Model and Agent Architecture Implementation

In ORIENT we aim to use the descriptive trait concepts from Big Five for modelling personality. However, in order to allow agents to generate realistic and expressive behaviours in real-time from the personality model, it is not possible to simply use those five static parameters as initiated. It means that we will need to create a set of low-level internal states for agents (as main characters interacting with users in the game) to capture the dynamic changes of these states and to map the Big Five personality traits into them. As pointed

out by Schaub (1999), this approach will involve three levels of modelling work:

1. Descriptive level (Big Five) that provides information regarding each main character's general tendency in five (trait) dimensions.
2. Behavioural level (e.g. being friendly, aggressive) indicates characters' expression based on their personality during the game-play.
3. Low-level implementations of the system that generate behaviour through internal states (e.g. needs, intentions and goals)

The first step is to define the value of each character's personality trait using the Big Five dimensions[9]. Story writers for the ORIENT scenario and psychologists collaborate and revise these trait values based on the original design of each character in the story. Then these (1st level) trait values will be "translated" into low-level internal states (3rd level) for generating characters' motivations, intentions and goals. Finally, we expect that agents' behaviour (2nd level) will emerge from the dynamics of internal states, computational autobiographic memory and planning processes happening in the agent architecture.

To create the low-level system, the first step is to integrate the motivation module from PSI theory proposed by psychologist Dietrich Dörner (Dörner, 2003; Dörner & Hille, 1995). The original PSI theory is based on the idea that humans are motivated emotional-cognitive beings; therefore it integrates cognitive processes, emotions and motivation. The motivation module in our agent architecture includes existential "needs" (*Existence Preservation*, *Species Preservation* and *Affiliation*), and intellectual "needs" (*Competence* and *Certainty*). By mapping the corresponding Big Five trait values predefined by the story writers and psychologists to the set-point (threshold) of each need, an individual character's dynamic personality is created. For example, if character A was defined as a person who is secretive, wise

Table 1.

Big Five trait	PSI needs
Neuroticism	Many needs are highly activated at the same time
Extraversion	High need for affiliation
Agreeableness	Needs are generally not very activated or need long to exceed threshold
Conscientiousness	High need for competence and certainty
Openness	Low need for certainty, high need for competence

and rarely speaking to new people, then part of his Big Five traits are: High Conscientiousness, low Extraversion and low Agreeableness. Therefore the relevant set-points for PSI needs translated from traits are: High Competence, High Certainty and Low Affiliation. Table 1 shows a brief guideline for the translation from Big Five traits to PSI needs. Note that the mapping from traits to needs is not one-to-one in most cases.

All needs of each agent must be maintained in order to "survive" in the game environment. Therefore individual agents will try to reduce the deviation of each of their own need from the set-point as much as possible at all times. Intentions of an agent are built according to the strength (as determined by the deviation) of a need, the success probability to satisfy the need from the semantic knowledge, past significant experiences in autobiographic memory, and urgency (the timeframe to satisfy a need). Whenever a need deviates from the set point, it activates the corresponding intentions. In the case when several intentions are active in a given time, the strongest one will be selected and executed. To help depict the main ideas of the motivation-based architecture as well as the interactions between the computational autobiographic memory and other components, the overall design of the agent architecture is shown in Figure 2.

After the integration of needs for intention generation, we also utilise three types of behaviour modulators from PSI theory:

- **Activation:** Similar to the psychological concept of "arousal", activation represents the preparedness for perception and reac-

Figure 2. ORIENT agent architecture that links components such as needs, goals, emotion and autobiographic memory

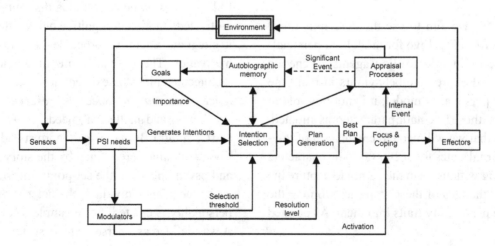

tion on the agent – speed of information processing. It increases with the general pressure from the motivation system and the strength of the currently active intention. For example, if the environment poses threats to the agent and its activation level is high, we will expect a short reaction time from the agent – it needs relatively quick cognitive adaptations for the satisfaction of current needs. As a result, only superficial perception and planning may be observed. Thus the agent will be highly cautious and try to adapt its responses to the environmental conditions.

- **Selection threshold:** To prevent the currently active intention to be easily replaced by another equally strong intention, a selection threshold increases the strength of the current intention and prevents oscillation of behaviour by giving priority to the currently active intention. Therefore, low selection threshold means that the agent is easily distracted from its current intention, and vice versa.

- **Resolution level:** Resolution level determines the carefulness and attentiveness of an agent's behaviour – the accuracy of cognitive processes, e.g. perception, planning, action regulation. It changes inversely to the activation value. Generally when the resolution level of the agent is high, it performs more extensive memory retrieval and generates either more alternative plans or a very detailed plan for achieving a selected intention.

Altogether these three modulators in the agent architecture establish the dynamic model of emotion as modulation of "cognition" (here we refer to "cognition" as an agent's perception, action-selection, memory access and planning). This unique aspect was derived from PSI theory, in which emotions are not explicitly defined but emerge from modulation of information process-

ing and adaptation to the environment, see Hille (2007) for details. In this case, an agent's complex behaviours become apparent due to the value of these modulators modified by needs.

Taking other agents and events from the environment into account, not only will they be internally represented symbolically in the agents' semantic memory (world knowledge), but the proposed agent architecture will also include their individual influence on the low-level needs. The strength of the influence is dependent upon an agent's personality specification, and is also affected by its own culture, and its existing experiences. Details of events which have brought significant impact to any of the agent's internal needs, together with other agents involved (if there were any), will be stored in the autobiographic memory for guiding the agent's future emotional and behavioural responses to the same type of events or agents. The relevant process is named *appraisal*, in line with other approaches to modelling emotions in IVA architectures, e.g. (Marsella & Gratch, 2003). Similar to our previous work (Ho, 2007a), for the interpretation of different types of emotional impact, e.g. in order to generate an agent's personal narrative, we utilise the OCC taxonomy (Ortony et al, 1988) as appraisal variables in the architecture.

Therefore, we also project the low-level needs to these appraisal variables. For example, *Like/Dislike* refers to how an event impacts the character's need for *affiliation*; *Desirability (of an event to oneself)* is determined by whether it satisfies or threatens to some extend the character's overall needs; *Desirability (for others)* – depending on how an event affects the other character's needs – is indeed important for an agent's cultural and emotional knowledge learning, and defined by a self-as-first-person evaluation process (see the next subsection *Empathising with others* for details). Furthermore, *Praiseworthiness*[10] is influenced by the agent's need for *certainty* and need for *competence*, also taking into account the social and cultural background of individuals.

At the beginning of an interaction with a user or other agents, each agent's internal needs will be initialised with random values together with a set of predefined "personality thresholds". Based on the level of deviation that each of its current needs has, it generates intention(s) and activates goal(s) that are relevant to the perceived circumstances. The goal with the highest priority to be executed can be determined by the fact that it can satisfy the current most deviated need. Moreover, the agent's competence level plus the past experiences in its autobiographic memory will provide information for the calculation of the success probability for a particular goal. Therefore, both goal importance and goal success probability will be used to manage intention and thus action selections.

We believe that, at a certain level, the composition of an agent's internal needs, goals and autobiographic memory in the architecture can attribute "meanings" to its emotional expressions. During the processes of appraisal, the agent evaluates both 1) internally, the effect of the coping action that it has carried out on its needs and 2) externally, the environmental changes based on that action. This mechanism allows agents with autobiographic memory to link their emotional expressions (for either internal or external events) to the changes of their internal needs. More importantly, their autobiographic memory records these "event-needs" relations as part of their life experiences, and thus they are able to infer the meaning of other agents' emotional expressions.

An Example from ORIENT Story Scenario

ORIENT is focused on friendship and integration strategies and is aimed at 13-14 year olds. It involves small groups of users interacting with a 3D virtual environment populated by intelligent agents from different fantasy cultures, using innovative communication and control devices and a mission that requires the teenage users to work together with the ORIENT cultures to save the planet. The users' task is to interact with each of the cultures through a number of engagement scenarios with the ultimate aim of saving the planet.

One of the scenarios will be a formal meal where agent_C has invited agent_D, which is from another culture on the planet, to join. The impact to agent_C's internal needs starts when it observes agent_D perform (what is to agent_C) a completely novel ritual when eating – the perceived situation reduces the level of both *certainty* and *competence* because agent_D's actions conflict with its own knowledge and expectation. This will then lead to an increase for these needs, and therefore, agent_C will adapt its future behaviour to take into consideration what they have just experienced. Since agent_C finds no relevant actions in the past to cope with the current situation, through the processes of *Intention Selection* and *Plan Generation* it chooses an emotional coping strategy with the display of *surprised* emotion to agent_D. The coping behaviour and changes to internal needs, together with the context as well as the reaction from agent_D are encoded in agent_C's autobiographic memory as a significant experience.

Since agent_D is from another culture, it may have a different reaction when perceiving agent_C's ritual. This is due to the inclusion of the Big Five which provides a foundational personality for each agent to show their own differences form others. The difference of reaction further leads to self-reflection and the creation of empathy – being aware of how others behave (see next subsection for details).

Generally when encountering an unexpected situation, how much agents adjust their behaviour will depend on their personality and past experiences individually. In the same way each significant event, that brings changes to their needs and triggers the elicitation of their emotion, allows them to learn from experience. Therefore, the learning of cultural emotional knowledge can emerge from intercultural agent-agent and user-agent interactions.

Specifications for Computational Autobiographic Memory

Given that the agent architecture supports both motivation-based personalities and appraisal models, the next key step is to produce the requirements that guide the integration of computational autobiographic memory. On the one hand these requirements are important to the conceptual specification of the overall architecture for ORIENT agents. On the other hand they are necessary in providing a method to validate the implementation of computational autobiographic memory.

Agents with "a life": Autobiographic Memory stores and re-constructs significant experiences that an agent derives from a *long-term interaction* with its environment and surroundings (objects, other agents, human users). By using the rich amount of information in autobiographic memory, the agent can largely extend its *temporal horizon* (Nehaniv & Dautenhahn, 1998; Nehaniv, 1999) which serves as an important foundation for an agent's planning process. The extended temporal horizon means that an agent's autobiographic memory and the remembering process provide 'extrasensory' meaningful information for the agent to modulate or guide its immediate or future behaviour – planning for future actions and story-telling about past or imagined events.

For example, it can relate the current situation to some particular moments in its memory, and then an action can be chosen based on the outcome desired by the agent. Therefore, ORIENT agents with autobiographic memory can be seen as "having a life" – a relatively long period of time – through developing such a kind of *interaction history*.

Repeated user-agent interactions: To facilitate the development of autobiographic memory, we aim to have users *interact repeatedly with the same* agent for a considerable amount of time in ORIENT. On the one hand, with an initial semantic world knowledge which is consistent with the agent's cultural background, the users' input can often violate an agent's expectations and thus create significant events in its autobiographic memory. On the other hand, while learning a specific culture in ORIENT, it is important for users to create a long-term relationship with an agent from that culture. This relationship has two important aspects: 1) the behaviour performed by the agent precisely reflects its culture – avoiding knowledge inconsistency which may be created by other agents or users that the agents is interacting with; 2) users can easily relate a currently perceived experience from a particular situation to past interactions with a specific agent. The latter aspect indicates that individualised interactions, as opposed to anonymous ones, can be more effective in learning other cultures for users in ORIENT.

Most importantly, a long-term relationship implies that users are familiar with the agent – understanding its personality through typical reactions to external events. This allows users not only to infer the agent's cultural background easily, but also to naturally engage empathically with the agent in various special occasions.

Forming relationships with agents: Other game characters in ORIENT which can provide pieces of information as cues for users to solve problems can be modelled as reactive agents (no autobiographic memory architecture) with the sole purpose of guiding users in ORIENT. In contrast, in long-term relationships developed through repeated interactions between the agent with autobiographic memory and users, both sides can gradually recognise each other's role e.g. as friend, ally, or enemy, etc. From this perspective, user-agent interactions in ORIENT emerge socially – the relationship drives the agent to behave differently when users are present, and also to behave differently in interactions with alternative users. This aspect also facilitates the link between an agents' emotion and attitude. Furthermore, agents' narratives can also be personalised for users – reconstructing events from autobiographic memory based on the history of the users' interaction.

Supporting Emotional Coping: In Ho et al (2007a) we showed that FearNot! agents (child-like characters inhabiting a virtual environment designed to teach school children how to better cope with bullying) possessing a simplified version of autobiographic memory can express their emotion by remembering past significant events (Ho et al, 2007; Dias et al, 2007). In FearNot! a user can interact with a victim character by offering potential coping strategies, after watching episodes of bullying take place in a virtual school environment. Our aim in the ORIENT agent architecture is to utilize the process of expressing emotion as one of the coping strategies when the agent is experiencing an unexpected situation.

Based on the information available to the agent from its autobiographic memory, a new set of goals will need to be formed in order to cope with the current unexpected situation and to reduce this discrepancy between expected and actual events. If no relevant information can be found to re-formulate the goals, the agent will be forced to fall back on emotion-based coping strategies. In our previous work (Dias et al, 2007), the agent architecture FAtiMA was implemented with a series of appraisal mechanisms and emotion-based coping strategies rooted in the OCC model (Ortony et al, 1998).

In addition to influencing the normal goal formulation process, agents with emotion can also generate coping strategies in the case that their autobiographic memory is lacking. Finally, these new coping strategies are themselves encoded into the autobiographic memory and can be used in the future to create and continuously update the working "self" to support the goal accomplishment.

Empathising with others: In ORIENT, we aim to create a concrete agent model with autobiographic memory and a feasible approach to enable agents to, at a certain level, "understand[11]" and thus empathise with others. The idea is to allow agents, by reconstructing past experiences, to reach the perceived physical-psychological states (e.g. emotions) of the target agents as closely as possible – perception of the target agent's feelings is a projection of the self. From the long-term autobiographic memory base, agents can remember past experiences which associate with specific physical-psychological states individually, as described in Ho et al (2007b). When a target agent's physical-psychological states are perceived by the empathiser (an agent that possesses autobiographic memory) then the empathiser will attempt to "imagine" a series of events in order to understand the target agent's situation. This first step models cognitive empathy. Afterward, through rehearsing the relevant experiences (internally re-perceiving these events from memory), the empathizing agent reaches similar physical-psychological states. This second step models affective empathy. At the end of this process the empathiser will express its physical-psychological states to the target agent; the target agent then may receive this empathy and feel experientially "understood", as suggested by Dautenhahn (1997, p. 20) "the concept of 'experiential understanding' can be described by dynamic mechanisms of resonance and synchronization". She further proposed that the metaphor of viewing artefacts as dynamic systems, studying interactions between an artefact and its environment, and correlating them with dynamics inside the agent could be a useful approach to experiential grounding of 'social understanding' in agents. The computational modelling of empathy discussed in this article is inspired by this view.

Based on the empathy cycle (Dautenhahn, 1997, Barrett-Lennard, 1993) the following necessary requirements and steps for modelling empathy in agents with autobiographic memory are suggested:

1. The "willingness" of the empathising agent after perceiving the target agent's physical-psychological states: a precondition for empathy to occur is to listen personally with truly interested attention and non-judging receptivity (Barrett-Lennard, 1997).

2. The available experience of the empathising agent: this enables the agent to "imagine" and thus "understand" the target agent's situation – remembering experiences, based on its own experiences or told by other agents, to allow an agent to reach the similar physical-psychological states that the target agent is currently in.

3. Rehearsal of the most appropriate experience: after all relevant experiences are retrieved from the autobiographic memory base and reconstructed with general event representations (Ho et al, 2007b), the empathiser selects the most similar experiences to rehearse internally[12]. The selected experience can bring the closest physical-psychological states (perceived from the target agent) to a) itself – if the experience is from its own or to b) other agents – if the experience was derived from story-telling or observation. Note that the reconstruction and selection of the most appropriate event is based on the empathiser's own perspective, therefore cultural differences may create 'difficulties' for this agent to have a good understanding of the target agent's situation. This exploration of such 'difficulties' is very relevant for ORIENT in order to support intercultural empathy.

4. Verbal or other behavioural expression toward the target agent: based on the selected experience that was rehearsed internally, the empathiser performs a certain behaviour to show its understanding of the situation to the target agent.

5. Finally, the target agent will receive empathy and thus feel "understood". Cultural differences may again create problems for the target agent to understand the expressed empathising action from the empathizer.

With this set of minimum requirements given to both agent architecture design and human-agent interaction specification, the *autobiography* of each agent can be richly developed and thus the agent can react to situations in a more believable (human-like) way. Based on the psychologically inspired approach, we can assume that 1) the agent's conceptualisation of emotional knowledge becomes more solid because meaning is now assigned to the individual agent's memory contents, e.g. as emotional impact; and 2) the inference of another's emotions based on unique subsets of internal physiological reactions can be established through the empathic processes.

As a result of having a dynamic personality model, appraisal processes and specifications of computational autobiographic memory for the implementation of the ORIENT agent architecture, we expect that agents in ORIENT can achieve social learning of the "self" and emotion knowledge from other cultures in their autobiographic memory. Eventually the selective memory encoding processes for emotion concepts from an agent will include: observing the target agents' behaviour, empathising, receiving feedback and exchanging experiences through communication with the agent.

CONCLUSION

In this article we discussed how agents can extend their emotional knowledge in social and cultural interactions with other agents or users. The computationally feasible and psychologically supported approach we proposed here for the implementation of IVAs integrates computational autobiographic memory with a cross-cultural personality model and the specification of requirements that facilitate the interactions. Essentially, computational autobiographic memory consists of temporal and episodic information encoded with sensory and emotional contents. As discussed in the previous section, it is critical to enable agents to have this kind of "autobiography" to derive the meaning of emotions and thus to learn new emotion concepts from another culture.

The main direction for this work is to complete the technical implementation of both the personality model and the computational autobiographic memory and the integration of them into the main agent architecture for game characters in ORIENT. As described in the previous section, the main agent architecture will be developed based on the PSI theory, and the emotion and appraisal models from the OCC taxonomy. Autobiographic memory will then play an important role in generating emotions and perception within the character's "mind", e.g. the character may perform individual emotional reactions while encountering other characters or users. In order to achieve this, appraisal variables must be dynamic and determined from the agent's experiences through the information stored in autobiographic memory. We also aim to carry out an evaluation in order to study whether the proposed memory model can increase the believability and interactivity of agents in the game played by different users.

Another future direction is to explore the social interaction between users and agents through gestures. Since using gestures can be a way to express one's emotion, and meanings of a gesture may vary in different cultures, this part of the research can extend the current approach of cultural and emotional knowledge learning for both users and agents. It is supposed that at any time the user can perform any gesture in front of game characters, but some gestures might have very different connotations depending on the context of the social and cultural interaction. Currently our project is examining the possibility of using the Nintendo Wii Remote[13] for recognising users' gestures as new input interface for ORIENT.

Finally, we are also interested to investigate *group* simulations in cultural learning and interactions. As reported by studies in psychology, the peer-group is increasingly important to adolescents and 90% of them identify themselves with a peer group (Palmonari et al, 1992). Also, according to the group socialization theory (Harris, 1996), teenagers' identities are shaped more by their peers than their parents because of peer pressure present in their environment. Therefore, modelling power relationships and the structure among members within a group is interesting – the expression of an agent's emotion can be influenced by both cultural background and the position of the member in the group.

ACKNOWLEDGMENT

This work was partially supported by European Community (EC) and is currently funded by the eCIRCUS project IST-4-027656-STP. The authors are solely responsible for the content of this publication. It does not represent the opinion of the EC, and the EC is not responsible for any use that might be made of data appearing therein.

REFERENCES

Ananthaswamny, A. (2007). Technology virtual worlds: a life less ordinary offers far more than just escapism. *New Scientist, 195*(2618), 26–27. doi:10.1016/S0262-4079(07)62147-2

Aylett, R., Louchart, S., Dias, J., Paiva, A., Vala, M., Woods, S., & Hall, L. (2006). Unscripted Narrative for Affectively Driven Characters [IEEE Computer Society.]. *IEEE Computer Graphics and Applications, 26*(3), 42–52. doi:10.1109/MCG.2006.71

Baron-Cohen, S. (1991). Precursors to a theory of mind: Understanding attention in others. In Whiten, A. (Ed.), *Natural theories of mind: Evolution, development and simulation of everyday mindreading* (pp. 233–251). Oxford: Basil Blackwell.

Barrett-Lennard, G. T. (1993). The phases and focus of empathy. *The British Journal of Medical Psychology, 66*, 3–14.

Barrett-Lennard, G. T. (1997). The recovery of empathy – toward others and self. In Bohard, A. C., & Greenberg, L. S. (Eds.), *Empathy reconsidered – new directions in psychotherapy* (pp. 103–121). Washington, DC: American Psychological Association. doi:10.1037/10226-004

Bartlett, F. C. (1932). *Remembering: A Study in Experimental and Social Psychology*. Cambridge, Great Britain: Cambridge University Press.

Bates, J. (1994). The role of emotion in believable agents. *Communications of the ACM, 37*(7), 122–125. doi:10.1145/176789.176803

Bruner, J. (1990). *Acts of Meaning*. Cambridge, MA/London: Harvard University Press.

Conway, M. A. (1990). *Autobiographical Memory: An Introduction*. Buckingham: Open Univ. Press.

Conway, M. A., Wang, Q., Hanyu, K., & Haque, S. (2005). A cross-cultural investigation of autobiographical memory: On the universality and cultural variation of the reminiscence bump. *Journal of Cross-Cultural Psychology, 36*(6), 739–749. doi:10.1177/0022022105280512

Costa, P. T., & McCrae, R. R. (1992). *Revised NEO Personality Inventory (NEO PI-R) and NEO Five Factor Inventory. Professional Manual*. Odessa, Florida: Psychological Assessment Resources.

Dautenhahn, K. (1996). Embodiment in animals and artifacts. In *AAAI FS Embodied Cognition and Action*, pp 27-32. AAAI Press. Technical report FS-96-02.

Dautenhahn, K. (1997). I could be you: The phenomenological dimension of social understanding. *Cybernetics and Systems, 28*, 417–453. doi:10.1080/019697297126074

Davis, M. H. (1996). *Empathy: A social phsychological approach*. Westview Press: A Division of Harper Collins Publishers.

Davis, M. H. (2006). Empathy. In Stets, J. E., & Turner, J. H. (Eds.), *Handbook of the Sociology of Emotions* (pp. 443–466). New York: Springer. doi:10.1007/978-0-387-30715-2_20

Dias, J., Ho, W.C., Vogt, T., Beeckman N., Paiva, A., & Andre, E. (2007). I Know What I Did Last Summer: Autobiographic Memory in Synthetic Characters. *Proceedings of Affective Computing and Intelligent Interaction 2007*, ACM Press.

Dörner, D. (2003). The mathematics of emotions. In F. Detje, D. Dörner & H. Schaub (Eds.), *Proceedings of the Fifth International Conference on Cognitive Modeling*, (pp. 75-79), Bamberg, Germany, Apr, 10-12 2003.

Dörner, D., & Hille, K. (1995). Artificial souls: Motivated emotional robots. *In Proceedings of the International Conference on Systems, Man and Cybernetics*, (pp. 3828-3832).

eCIRCUS (2006). http://www.e-circus.org/. Last accessed: 30-Nov-2007.

Harris, J. R. (1995). Where is the child's environment? A group socilization theory of development. *Psychological Review, 102*, 458–489. doi:10.1037/0033-295X.102.3.458

Hille, K. (2007). *A theory on emotion.* http://web.unibamberg.de/ppp/insttheopsy/dokumente/Hille_A_theory_of_emotion.pdf, 2007. Last accessed: 18-Dec-2007.

Ho, W. C., Dautenhahn, K., & Nehaniv, C. L. (2006). A study of episodic memory based learning and narrative structure for autobiographic agents. In *Proceedings of Adaptation in Artificial and Biological Systems, AISB 2006 conference, 3*, 26-29.

Ho, W. C., Dautenhahn, K., & Nehaniv, C. L. (2008). Computational Memory Architectures for Autobiographic Agents Interacting in a Complex Virtual Environment: A Working Model. *Connection Science, 20*(1), 21–65. doi:10.1080/09540090801889469

Ho, W. C., Dias, J., Figueiredo, R., & Paiva, A. (2007a). *Agents that remember can tell stories: integrating autobiographic memory into emotional agents. Proceedings of Autonomous Agents and Multiagent Systems (AAMAS)*. ACM Press.

Ho, W. C., & Watson, S. (2006). Autobiographic knowledge for believable virtual characters. *Intelligent Virtual Agents 2006 (IVA 2006)*, Springer LNAI, (pp. 383-394).

Ho, W. C., Watson, S., & Dautenhahn, K. (2007b). AMIA: A Knowledge Representation Model for Computational Autobiographic Agents. *Proceedings of IEEE International Conference on Development and Learning (ICDL) 2007*.

Hoffman, M. L. (1977). Sex differences in empathy and related behaviors. *Psychological Bulletin, 84*, 712–722. doi:10.1037/0033-2909.84.4.712

Hogan, R. (1969). Development of an empathy scale. *Journal of Consulting and Clinical Psychology, 33*, 306–316. doi:10.1037/h0027580

HUMAINE. (2004). http://emotion-research.net/. Last accessed, 25-Nov-07.

Kim, H. S., & Ko, D. (2007). Culture and self-expression. In Sedikides, C., & Spencer, S. (Eds.), *Frontiers of social psychology: The self*. New York: Psychology Press.

Leslie, A. M. (1994). Pretending and believing: Issues in the theory of ToMM. *Cognition, 50*, 211–238. doi:10.1016/0010-0277(94)90029-9

Leung, K., & Bond, M. H. (1984). The impact of cultural collectivism on reward allocation. *Journal of Personality and Social Psychology, 47*, 793–804. doi:10.1037/0022-3514.47.4.793

Linden Research. (2005). http://www.secondlife.com/. Last accessed, 9-Nov-07.

Loyall, A. B. (1997). *Believable Agents*. PhD thesis, Carnegie Mellon University, Pittsburgh, Pennsylvania. CMU-CS-97-123.

Lutz, C. (1988). *Unnatural emotions*. Chicago: University of Chicago Press.

Markus, H. R., & Kitayama, S. (1991). Culture and the self: Implications for cognition, emotion, and motivation. *Psychological Review, 98*(2), 224–253. doi:10.1037/0033-295X.98.2.224

Marsella, S., & Gratch, J. (200)3, Modelling coping behaviour in virtual humans: Dont worry, be happy, *Autonomous Agents and Multiagent Systems (AAMAS)*, ACM Press, (pp. 313–320).

McQuiggan, S. W., & Lester, J. C. (2006). Learning empathy: a data-driven framework for modeling empathetic companion agents. *Proceedings of the fifth international joint conference on autonomous agents and multiagent systems (AAMAS 06)*, Hakodate, Japan, (pp. 961-968).

Nehaniv, C. L. (1999). Narrative for artifacts: Transcending context and self. *Narrative Intelligence*, ser. AAAI Fall Symposium 1999. AAAI Press, pp. 101–104, Technical Report FS-99-01.

Nehaniv, C. L., & Dautenhahn, K. (1998). Semigroup expansions for autobiographic agents. In *Proceedings of the First Symposium on Algebra, Languages and Computation*. Osaka University, 77–84.

Nelson, K. (1993). The psychological and social origins of autobiographical memory. *Psychological Science, 4*, 7–14. doi:10.1111/j.1467-9280.1993.tb00548.x

Ortony, A., Clore, G., & Collins, A. (1988). *The Cognitive Structure of Emotions*. Cambridge University Press.

Palmonari, A., Pombeni, L., & Kirchler, E. (1992). Evolution of the self concept in adolescence and social categorization processes. *European Review of Social Psychology, 3*, 287–308. doi:10.1080/14792779243000096

Pike, K. L. (1954). Emic and etic standpoints for the description of behavior. In K.L. Pike (Ed.), *Language in relation to a unified theory of the structure of human behavior. Part I,* 8-28. Glendale California: Summer Institute of Linguistics.

Plutchik, R. (1994). *The psychology and biology of emotion.* New York: HarperCollins.

Premack, D. G., & Woodruff, G. (1978). Does the chimpanzee have a theory of mind? *The Behavioral and Brain Sciences, 1,* 515–526. doi:10.1017/S0140525X00076512

Prendinger, H., Becker, C., & Ishizuka, M. (2006). A study in users' physiological response to an empathic interface agent. *International Journal of Humanoid Robotics, 3*(3), 371–391. doi:10.1142/S0219843606000801

Preston, S. D., & de Waal, F. B. M. (2002). Empathy: Its ultimate and proximate bases. *The Behavioral and Brain Sciences, 25,* 1–72.

Rubin, D. C., Rahhal, T. A., & Poon, L. W. (1998). Things learned in early adulthood are remembered best. *Memory & Cognition, 26*(1), 3–19.

Salovey, P., & Mayer, J. D. (1990). Emotional Intelligence. *Imagination, Cognition and Personality, 9,* 185–211.

Schaub, H. (1999). Die Person als Synergieeffekt. Persönlichkeit als Ergebnis der Interaktion basaler Informationsverarbeitungsprozesse. Presentation at *the 8. Herbstakademie „Selbstorganisation in Psychologie und Sozialwissenschaften"* 27.-29.9.1999 in Jena, Germany.

Solomon, R. C. (1984). Getting angry: The Jamesian theory of emotion in anthropology. In Shweder, R. A., & LeVine, R. A. (Eds.), *Culture theory: Essays on mind, self, and emotion* (pp. 238–254). Cambridge: Cambridge University Press.

Tomasello, M. (1999). *The Cultural Origins of Human Cognition.* Harvard University Press.

Triandis, H. C., & Suh, E. M. (2002). Cultural influences on personality. *Annual Review of Psychology, 53,* 133–160. doi:10.1146/annurev.psych.53.100901.135200

Wetzler, S. E., & Sweeney, J. A. (1986). Childhood amnesia: An empirical demonstration. In Rubin, D. C. (Ed.), *Autobiographical memory* (pp. 202–221). Cambridge, UK: Cambridge University Press.

Wyer, R. Jr, & Srull, T. (1989). *Memory and Cognition in its Social Context.* Hillsdale, New Jersey: Lawrence Erlhaum.

Young, P. T. (1936). *Motivation of behavior.* New York: John Wiley & Sons.

ENDNOTES

[1] Developmental psychologist Tomasello argues that many unique characteristics of humans are elaborations of one trait that arises in human infants at about nine months of age: the ability to understand other people as intentional agents (Tomasello, 1999).

[2] Markus and Kitayama (1991) argue that the independent and interdependent views of the self in psychology can have a systematic influence on different aspects of cognition, emotion and motivation. They suggest that, in many cultures of the world, the Western notion of the self is seen as an *independent* entity "containing significant disposition attributes and as detached from context". Next they point out, however, that in many other constructs the self is viewed as *interdependent* with the surrounding context, and it is the "other" or "the "self-in-relation-to-other" that is focal in individual experience.

[3] Note, we do not claim that the artificial agents possess a concept of "self" comparable to that of e.g. human beings. We are using this concept in a computational sense

with reference to an autobiographic memory architecture.

4   Bruner (1990) quotes the results of Barlett's serial reproduction experiments in *Remembering* (1932), namely that the most distinctive characteristics of human memory schemata are 1) being under control of an affective cultural "attitude", and 2) any "conflicting tendencies" likely to disrupt individual poise or to menace social life are likely to destabilize memory organization.

5   In this article we define narrative as "a story being told by, perceived by, or remembered (reconstructed) by an agent", thus a narrative requires a story and an agent interpreting this story. The agent's motivations, goals and other internal states, as well as the context of when and where the story is being told, perceived or remembered, will influence how the story is being (re-)created. 'Narrative story-telling' refers to the specific process of how a story is being told by an agent.

6   Childhood amnesia suggests that children from birth to approximately 5 years of age do not seem to form extensive personal episodic memories. For details, see (Wetzler & Sweeney, 1986).

7   The reminiscence bump is the effect in the temporal distribution of autobiographical memory which suggests that people tend to recall more personal events from adolescence and early adulthood (10-25 years) than personal events from other lifetime periods (Rubin et al, 1986).

8   Life-period' or 'life-time' of an agent refers to the computational duration of its memory, in the sense of how long the agent interacts with and remembers experiences in its environment.

9   Note that we are not using the Big Five model to operationalise cultural differences in agents. We use it to create roles for a virtual role-play approach which is only an aid or auxiliary means to implement personality differences in agents through need states. Personality dimensions such as the Big Five can be compared across cultures – empirical data shows that their meaning is comparable across different cultures in each dimension (Pike, 1954; Leung & Bond, 1984).

10   Praiseworthiness is the action that an agent performed a praise- or blame-worthy behaviour, from the observer's point of view. Therefore it relates to an agent's abilities to 1) predict the consequences of actions (*need for certainty*) and 2) master problems and tasks, e.g. satisfy one's needs.

11   Note that "understanding" as used in this article in a computational sense refers to the agent's ability to relate experiences to its internal states and past experiences, it does not relate to the phenomenological nature of understanding in biological systems.

12   Rather than assigning the physical-psychological states associated with a past experience directly to an agent, rehearsing this experience is necessary to allow the agent to have another comprehension of this event based on the existing semantic knowledge and activated goals. Furthermore, when an agent rehearses a past experience internally, both the importance and endurance of this experience in the agent's memory are increased.

13   Please refer to the official Nintendo Wii controllers website: http://wii.nintendo.com/controller.jsp.

This work was previously published in International Journal of Agent Technologies and Systems (IJATS), edited by Goran Trajkovski, pp. 51-78, copyright 2009 by IGI Publishing (an imprint of IGI Global).

Compilation of References

Ábel, D., Palla, G., Farkas, I., Derényi, I., Pollner, P., & Vicsek, T. (2005). *CFinder: Clusters and Communities in networks*. http:/www.cfinder.org/

Ablowitz, R. (1939). The Theory of Emergence. *Philosophy of Science, 6*(1), 16. doi:10.1086/286529

Abraham, A. (2002). *Analysis of hybrid soft and hard computing techniques for Forex monitoring systems*. Proceedings of the 2002 IEEE International Conference on Fuzzy Systems, pp. 1616-1622.

Aha, D. W., Kibler, D., & Albert, M. K. (1991). Instance-based learning algorithms. *Machine Learning, 6*(1), 37–66. doi:10.1007/BF00153759

Almeida, R. B., Mozafari, B., & Cho, J. (2007). *On the Evolution of Wikipedia*. Paper presented at the International Conference on Weblogs and Social Media

Alonso, E., d'Inverno, M., Kudenko, D., Luck, M., & Noble, J. (2001). Learning in multi-agent systems. *The Knowledge Engineering Review, 16*(3), 277–284. doi:10.1017/S0269888901000170

Alter, A. (2008). My Weekend Journal; My Virtual Summer Job. *Wall Street Journal (Eastern Edition)*. New York: May 16. p. W.1.

Ananthaswamny, A. (2007). Technology virtual worlds: a life less ordinary offers far more than just escapism. *New Scientist, 195*(2618), 26–27. doi:10.1016/S0262-4079(07)62147-2

Anderson, C., & Crawford-Hines, S. (1994). Multigrid Q-learning. *Technical Report CS-94-121*, Colorado State University.

Antonia, D. Remembering when. (2002). *Scientific American, 66*, September.

Aoki, T., & Aoyagi, T. (2009). Co-evolution of Phases and Connection Strengths in a Network of Phase Oscillators. *Physical Review Letters, 102*, 034101. doi:10.1103/PhysRevLett.102.034101

Apache Active, M. Q. (n.d.). Retrieved from http://activemq.apache.org/

Aral, S., Muchnik, L., & Sundararajan, A. (2009). Distinguishing influence-based contagion from homophily-driven diffusion in dynamic networks. *Proceedings of the National Academy of Sciences of the United States of America, 106*, 21544–21549. doi:10.1073/pnas.0908800106

Araújo, T., & Louçã, F. (2007). The Geometry of Crashes - A Measure of the Dynamics of Stock Market Crises. *Quantitative Finance, 7*(1), 63–74. doi:10.1080/14697680601019530

Araújo, T., & Louçã, F. (2008). The Seismography of Crashes in Financial Markets. *Physics Letters. [Part A], 372*, 429–434. doi:10.1016/j.physleta.2007.07.079

Araújo, T., & Vilela Mendes, R. (2000), Function and form in networks of interacting agents. *Complex Systems, 12*.

Copyright © 2011, IGI Global. Copying or distributing in print or electronic forms without written permission of IGI Global is prohibited.

Ausloos, M., & Lambiotte, R. (2007). Drastic events make evolving networks. *The European Physical Journal B, 57,* 89–94. doi:10.1140/epjb/e2007-00159-6

Aylett, R., Louchart, S., Dias, J., Paiva, A., Vala, M., Woods, S., & Hall, L. (2006). Unscripted Narrative for Affectively Driven Characters [IEEE Computer Society.]. *IEEE Computer Graphics and Applications, 26*(3), 42–52. doi:10.1109/MCG.2006.71

Bainbridge, W. (2007). The scientific research potential of virtual worlds. *Science, 317,* 473. doi:10.1126/science.1146930

Banchoff, T. (1966). *Beyond the third dimension.* New York: Scientific American Library.

Barabási, A.-L. (2003). *Linked.* New York: Plume.

Barabási, A.-L., Jeong, H., Néda, Z., Ravasz, E., Schubert, A., & Vicsek, T. (2002). Evolution of the social network of scientific collaborations. *Physica A-Statistical Mechanics and its Applications 311,* 590-614.

Baray, C. (1998). Effects of population size upon emergent group behavior. *Complexity International, 06.* Available from http://journal-ci.csse.monash.edu.au/ci/vol06/baray/baray.html

Barbosa, R., & Belo, O. (2009). A Step-By-Step Implementation of a Hybrid USD/JPY Trading Agent. *International Journal of Agent Technologies and Systems, 1*(2), 19–35.

Barbosa, R., & Belo, O. (2010). *Multi-Agent Forex Trading System* (pp. 91–118). Agent and Multi-Agent Technology for Internet and Enterprise Systems.

Baron-Cohen, S. (1991). Precursors to a theory of mind: Understanding attention in others. In Whiten, A. (Ed.), *Natural theories of mind: Evolution, development and simulation of everyday mindreading* (pp. 233–251). Oxford: Basil Blackwell.

Barrett, T. (2010). The problem-based learning process of finding and being in flow. *Innovations in Education and Teaching International, 47*(2), 165–174. doi:10.1080/14703291003718901

Barrett-Lennard, G. T. (1993). The phases and focus of empathy. *The British Journal of Medical Psychology, 66,* 3–14.

Barrett-Lennard, G. T. (1997). The recovery of empathy – toward others and self. In Bohard, A. C., & Greenberg, L. S. (Eds.), *Empathy reconsidered – new directions in psychotherapy* (pp. 103–121). Washington, DC: American Psychological Association. doi:10.1037/10226-004

Bartlett, F. C. (1932). *Remembering: A Study in Experimental and Social Psychology.* Cambridge, Great Britain: Cambridge University Press.

Barto, A. G., Bradtke, S. J., & Singh, P. S. (1995). Learning to act using real-time dynamic programming. *Artificial Intelligence, 72*(1), 81–138. doi:10.1016/0004-3702(94)00011-O

Bates, J. (1994). The role of emotion in believable agents. *Communications of the ACM, 37*(7), 122–125. doi:10.1145/176789.176803

Baum, P., Yang, D.-S., & Zewail, A. (2007). 4D visualization of transitional structures in phase transitions by electron diffraction. *Science, 318,* 788–792. doi:10.1126/science.1147724

Becker, B., & Mark, G. (1997). *Constructing Social Systems through Computer Mediated Communication.* German National Research Center for Information Technology.

Bergadano, F., Giordana, A., & Saitta, L. (1988). Concept acquisition in noisy environments. *IEEE Transactions on Pattern Analysis and Machine Intelligence, 10,* 555–578. doi:10.1109/34.3917

Berger, P. L., & Luckman, T. (1972). *The Social Construction of Reality.* New York: Penguin.

Bianconi, G. (2008). The entropy of network ensembles. arXiv:0802.2888v2 [cond-mat.dis-nn]

Biba, M., Basile, T. M. A., Ferilli, S., & Esposito, F. (2006). Improving Scalability in ILP Incremental Systems. Proceedings of CILC 2006 - Italian Conference on Computational Logic, Bari, Italy, June 26-27.

Biba, M., Ferilli, S., Esposito, F., Di Mauro, N., & Basile, T.M.A. (2006). A Fast Partial Memory Approach to Incremental Learning through an Advanced Data Storage Framework.

Bicchieri, C. (2006). *The Grammar of Society*. Cambridge, UK: Cambridge University Press.

Bickhard, M., & Campbell, D. (n.d). Emergence: www. lehigh.edu/~mhb0/emergence.html. Retrieved February 18, 1999.

Biermann, A. W., & Feldman, J. A. (1972). On the synthesis of finite-state machines from samples of their behavior. *IEEE Transactions on Computers*, *C*(21), 592–597. doi:10.1109/TC.1972.5009015

Biermann, A. W., & Krishnaswamy, R. (1976). Constructing programs from example computations. *IEEE Transactions on Software Engineering*, *2*(3). doi:10.1109/TSE.1976.233812

Biggs, N. (1993). *Algebraic Graph Theory*. Cambridge, UK: Cambridge University Press.

Bigus, J. Bigus, J. (2001) *Constructing Intelligent Agents Using Java*. Second Edition. New York: Wiley Computer Publishing.

Binmore, K. (2005). *Natural justice*. Oxford: Oxford University Press. doi:10.1093/acprof:o so/9780195178111.001.0001

Binmore, K. (1994). *Game theory and the social contract, vol. i. playing fair*. Cambridge, MA: MIT Press.

Birkhoff, G. (1984). *Lattice Theory*. Providence: Amer. Math. Soc.

Bisbey, P., & Trajkovski, G. (2005), Rethinking Concept Formation for Cognitive Agents. REU Technical Report. Available online at http://pages. towson. edu/gtrajkov/REU/2005/Paul/Paul. pdf (accessed 3 December 2005).

Bishop, C. M. (1996). *Neural Networks for Pattern Recognition*. Oxford, UK: Oxford University Press.

Blank, D., Kumar, D., Meeden, L., & Yanco, H. (2005), The Pyro toolkit for AI and robotics. Available online at Pyro Robotics web site: http://www. pyrorobotics. org/?page = PyroPublications (accessed 25 July 2005).

Boella, G., & Lesmo, L. (2002). A game theoretic approach to norms. *Cognitive Science Quarterly*, *2*(3–4), 492–512.

Boella, G., van der Torre, L., & Verhagen, H. (2008). Introduction to the special issue on normative multiagent systems. *Autonomous Agents and Multi-Agent Systems*, *17*(1), 1–10. doi:10.1007/s10458-008-9047-8

Boella, G., & van der Torre, L. (2003). Norm governed multiagent systems: The delegation of control to autonomous agents. In *Iat '03: Proceedings of the ieee/wic international conference on intelligent agent technology* (p. 329-335). Washington, DC, USA: IEEE Computer Society.

Bohm, D. (1980). *Wholeness and the implicate order*. New York: Routledge & Kegan Paul.

Bohorquez, J. C., Gourley, S., Dixon, A. R., Spagat, M., & Johnson, N. F. (2009). Common ecology quantifies human insurgency. *Nature*, *462*, 911–914. doi:10.1038/nature08631

Bonchev, D., & Buck, G. A. (2005). Quantitative Measures of Network Complexity. In Bonchev, D., & Rouvray, D. H. (Eds.), *Complexity in Chemistry* (pp. 191–235). Biology and Ecology. doi:10.1007/0-387-25871-X_5

Bonifield, C., & Tomas, A. (2008). Intellectual Property Issues for Marketers in the Virtual World. *Brand Management*, *16*(8), 571–581. doi:10.1057/bm.2008.41

Booker, L., Goldberg, D., & Holland, J. (1989). Classifier systems and genetic algorithms. *Artificial Intelligence*, *40*, 235–282. doi:10.1016/0004-3702(89)90050-7

Bordini, R. H., Hübner, J. F., & Wooldridge, M. (2007). *Programming multi-agent systems in Agent-Speak using Jason. Wiley*. Series in Agent Technology. doi:10.1002/9780470061848

Borenstein, S., Jaske, M., & Rosenfeld, A. (2002). *Dynamic pricing, advanced metering, and demand response in electricity markets. Center for the Study of Energy Markets. Paper CSEMWP-105*. University of California.

Bostrom, H. (1998). Predicate Invention and Learning from Positive Examples Only. In Proceedings of the Tenth European Conference on Machine Learning. (pp 226-237). Springer Verlag.

Bowling, M. H., & Veloso, M. M. (2002). Multiagent learning using a variable learning rate. *Artificial Intelligence*, *136*(2), 215–250. doi:10.1016/S0004-3702(02)00121-2

Braman, J. Jinman, A. Trajkovski, G. (2007) Towards a Virtual Classroom: Investigating Education in Synthetic Worlds. *The AAAI Fall Symposium. Emergent Agents and Social and Organizational Aspects of Intelligence*. Arlington, VA.

Branas-Garza, P., Espinosa-Fernandez, L., & Serrano-del-Rosal, R. (2007). Effects of gender and age on retrospective time judgements. *Time & Society*, *16*, 1. doi:10.1177/0961463X07074104

Bratko, I., & Muggleton, S. (1995). Applications of Inductive Logic Programming. *Communications of the ACM*, *38*(11), 65–70. doi:10.1145/219717.219771

Bratman, M. E. (1987). *Intentions, plans, and practical reason*. Cambridge, MA: Harvard University Press.

Bratman, M. E., Israel, D. J., & Pollack, M. E. (1988). Plans and resource-bounded practical reasoning. *Computational Intelligence*, *4*(4), 349–355. doi:10.1111/j.1467-8640.1988.tb00284.x

Braunstein, S., Ghosh, S., & Severini, S. (2006). The laplacian of a graph as a density matrix: a basic combinatorial approach to separability of mixed states. *Annals of Combinatorics*, *10*(3), 291–317. doi:10.1007/s00026-006-0289-3

Bredeche, N., Chevaleyre, Y., Zucker, J.-D., Drogoul, A., & Sabah, G. (2003). *A meta-learning approach to ground symbols from visual percepts. Robotics and Autonomous Systems journal, special issue on Anchoring Symbols to Sensor Data in Single and Multiple Robot Systems*. Elsevier.

Breiman, L. (1996). Bagging Predictors. *Machine Learning*, *24*(2), 123–140. doi:10.1007/BF00058655

Brownell, J., & Jameson, D. (2004). Problem-based learning in graduate management education: an integrative model and interdisciplinary application. *Journal of Management Education*, *28*, 558–577. doi:10.1177/1052562904266073

Bruner, J. (1990). *Acts of Meaning*. Cambridge, MA/London: Harvard University Press.

Bryant, S. L., Forte, A., & Bruckman, A. (2005). *Becoming Wikipedian: Transformation of Participation in a Collaborative Online Encyclopedia*. Paper presented at the GROUP 05.

Busetta, P., Rönnquist, R., Hodgson, A., & Lucas, A. (1998). *JACK Intelligent Agents - Components for Intelligent Agents in Java* (Tech. Rep.): Agent Oriented Software Pty. Ltd, Melbourne, Australia. (Available from http://www.agent-software.com)

Callender, C., & Edney, R. (2001). *Introducing time*. Santa Cruz, CA: Aerial Press.

Cantwell, J. (2005). A formal model of multi-agent belief-interaction. *Journal of Logic Language and Information*, *14*(4), 397–422. doi:10.1007/s10849-005-4019-8doi:10.1007/s10849-005-4019-8

Cao, L. (2003). Support vector machines experts for time series forecasting. *Neurocomputing*, *51*, 321–339. doi:10.1016/S0925-2312(02)00577-5

Carpenter, G. A., Grossberg, S., Markuzon, N., Reynolds, J. H., & Rosen, J. H. (1992). Fuzzy ARTMAP: A Neural Network Architecture for Incremental Supervised Learning of Analog Multidimensional Maps. *IEEE Transactions on Neural Networks*, *3*(5), 698–713. doi:10.1109/72.159059

Carpenter, G. A., & Markuzon, N. (1998). ARTMAP-IC and medical diagnosis: Instance counting and inconsistent cases. *Neural Networks*, *11*, 323–336. doi:10.1016/S0893-6080(97)00067-1

Carrasco, C., & Mayordomo, M. (2005). Beyond employment: Working time, living time. *Time & Society*, *14*, 231–259. doi:10.1177/0961463X05055195

Carrington, P. J., Scott, J., & Wasserman, S. (2005). *Models and Methods in Social Network Analysis.* UK: Cambridge University Press.

Castelfranchi, C. (1998). Modeling social action for ai agents. *Artificial Intelligence, 103*(1–2), 157–182. doi:10.1016/S0004-3702(98)00056-3

Castelfranchi, C. (2003). Formalising the informal? dynamic social order, bottom-up social control, and spontaneous normative relations. *Journal of Applied Logic, 1*(1–2), 47–92. doi:10.1016/S1570-8683(03)00004-1

Castronova, E. (2003). Theory of the Avatar. *CESifo Working Paper 863.* California State University at Fullerton.

Cattuto, C., Barrat, A., Baldassarri, A., Schehrd, G., & Loreto, V. (2009). Collective dynamics of social annotation. *Proceedings of the National Academy of Sciences of the United States of America, 106,* 10511–10515.

Cattuto, C., Loreto, V., & Pietronero, L. (2007). Semiotic dynamics and collaborative tagging. *Proceedings of the National Academy of Sciences of the United States of America, 104,* 1461–1464. doi:10.1073/pnas.0610487104

Cavaretta, M. (2010). Linden Lab's 'Second Life' in a Catch-22 over Virtual Property, *Information Week,* July.

Ceaparu, I., Lazar, J., Bessiere, K., Robinson, J. and Shneiderman, B. (2004) Determining Causes and Severity of End-User Frustration *International Journal of Human-Computer Interaction,* 17, 3, (2004), 333-356.

Chaharbaghi, K., & Cox, R. (2001). Problem-based learning: potential and implementation issues. *British Journal of Management, 6,* 249–256. doi:10.1111/j.1467-8551.1995. tb00098.x

Chen, C. (2004). *Information visualization: Beyond the horizon.* London: Springer.

Chodorow, A. (2010). Tracing Basis through Virtual Spaces. *Cornell Law Review, 95*(2).

Chow, C. S., & Tsitsiklis, J. N. (1991). An optimal one-way multigrid algorithm for discrete-time stochastic control. *IEEE Transactions on Automatic Control, 36*(8), 898–914. doi:10.1109/9.133184

Chung, J., & Chow, S. (2003). Promoting student learning through a student-centered problem-based learning subject curriculum. *Innovations in Education and Teaching International, 41,* 157–168. doi:10.1080/1470329042000208684

Chung, F. R. K. (1997). *Spectral graph theory.* CBMS Regional Conference Series in Mathematics, 92. Published for the Conference Board of the Mathematical Sciences, Washington, DC. Providence, RI: American Mathematical Society.

Chung, S. (2008). Real Taxation of Virtual Commerce. *Virginia Tax Review, 28*(3).

Cichosz, P. (1995). Truncating temporal differences: On the efficient implementation of TD(λ) for reinforcement learning. *Journal of Artificial Intelligence Research, 2,* 287–318.

Cichosz, P. (1996). Truncated temporal differences with function approximation: Successful examples using CMAC. *In Proceedings of the 13th European Symposium on Cybernetics and Systems Research.*

Claburn, T. (2006). Virtual Worlds Collide with Real Laws. *Information Week,* December.

Clauset, A., Newman, M. E. J., & Moore, C. (2004, August). *Finding community structure in very large networks. cond-mat/0408187,* from http://arxiv.org/abs/cond-mat/0408187 http://dx.doi.org/10.1103/PhysRevE.70.066111

Clayton, P. (2006). Conceptual Foundations of Emergence Theory. In Clayton, P., & Davies, P. (Eds.), *The re-Emergence of Emergence: The Emergentist Hypothesis from Science to Religion.* Oxford, UK: Oxford University Press.

Coase, R. H. (1995). *Essays on Economics and Economists.* Chicago: University of Chicago Press.

Coase, R. H. (1993). The Nature of The Firm. In Williamson, O. E., & Winter, S. G. (Eds.), *The Nature of the Firm: Origins, Evolution and Development.* New York: Oxford University Press.

Cohen, W.W. & Page, C.D. (1995). Learnability in Inductive Logic Programming: Methods and Results. New Generation Computing 13(1-2)

Cointet, J.-P., & Chavalarias, D. (2008). Multi-level science mapping with asymmetrical paradigmatic proximity. *Networks and Heterogeneous Media, 3*, 267–276.

Coleman, J. S. (1987). Norms as social capital. In Radnitzky, G., & Bernholz, P. (Eds.), *Economic imperialism: The economic approach applied outside the field of economics*. New York, NY: Paragon House.

Congress of the United States. (2006). *Virtual Economies Need Clarification, Not More Taxes.* Congress of the United States, Joint Economic Committee, Press Release #109-98.

Conover, A. J. (2008a). *A simulation of temporally asynchronous agent interaction dynamics.* Unpublished doctoral dissertation, Towson University, 8000 York Road, Towson MD, 21252. (Supervised by Dr. Robert Hammell II, Dr. Goran Trajkovski)

Conover, A. J. (2008b). A simulation of temporally variant agent interaction via passive examination. In S. G. Collins & G. P. Trajkovski (Eds.), *Agent-based societies: Social and cultural interactions.* Hershey, PA: IGI Global.

Conover, A. J., & Trajkovski, G. P. (2007, November 9–11). Effects of temporally asynchronous interaction on simple multi-agent behavior. In *Emergent agents and socialities: Social and organizational aspects of intelligence. technical report fs-07-04* (pp. 34–41). Menlo Park, CA: The American Association for Artificial Intelligence.

Conway, M. A. (1990). *Autobiographical Memory: An Introduction.* Buckingham: Open Univ. Press.

Conway, M. A., Wang, Q., Hanyu, K., & Haque, S. (2005). A cross-cultural investigation of autobiographical memory: On the universality and cultural variation of the reminiscence bump. *Journal of Cross-Cultural Psychology, 36*(6), 739–749. doi:10.1177/0022022105280512

Coombs, G., & Elden, M. (2004). Introduction to the special issue: problem-based learning as social inquiry - PBL and management education. *Journal of Management Education, 28*, 523–535. doi:10.1177/1052562904267540

Costa, P. T., & McCrae, R. R. (1992). *Revised NEO Personality Inventory (NEO PI-R) and NEO Five Factor Inventory. Professional Manual.* Odessa, Florida: Psychological Assessment Resources.

Cover, T., & Thomas, C. (1991). *Elements of information theory.* New York: John Wiley. doi:10.1002/0471200611

Cover, T. M., & Thomas, J. A. (2006). *Elements of Information Theory.* US: John Wiley and Sons.

Creswell, J. W. (1998). *Qualitative Inquiry and Research Design; Choosing Among Five Traditions.* Thousand Oaks, CA: Sage Publications.

Crutchfield, J. P., & Feldman, D. P. (2001). Regularities unseen, randomness observed: Levels of entropy convergence. *Santa Fe Institute Working Papers* 01-02-012.

Cvetkovic, D. M., Doob, M., & Sachs, H. (1979). *Spectra of graph theory and applications.* New York: VEB Deutscher Berlin, Academic Press.

da Silva, V. T. (2008). From the specification to the implementation of norms: an automatic approach to generate rules from norms to govern the behavior of agents. *Autonomous Agents and Multi-Agent Systems, 17*(1), 113–155. doi:10.1007/s10458-008-9039-8

Dastani, M. (2008). 2APL: a practical agent programming language. *Autonomous Agents and Multi-Agent Systems, 16*, 214–248. doi:10.1007/s10458-008-9036-y

Dautenhahn, K. (1997). I could be you: The phenomenological dimension of social understanding. *Cybernetics and Systems, 28*, 417–453. doi:10.1080/019697297126074

Dautenhahn, K. (1996). Embodiment in animals and artifacts. In *AAAI FS Embodied Cognition and Action*, pp 27-32. AAAI Press. Technical report FS-96-02.

Davies, P. (2006). The Physics of Downward Causation. In Clayton, P., & Davies, P. (Eds.), *The Re-Emergence of Emergence: The Emergentist Hypothesis from Science to Religion*. Oxford, UK: Oxford University Press.

Davis, J. H., Schoorman, D., & Donaldson, L. (1997). Towards a Stewardship Theory of Management. *Academy of Management Review, 22*(1), 20–47. doi:10.2307/259223

Davis, M. H. (2006). Empathy. In Stets, J. E., & Turner, J. H. (Eds.), *Handbook of the Sociology of Emotions* (pp. 443–466). New York: Springer. doi:10.1007/978-0-387-30715-2_20

Davis, M. H. (1996). *Empathy: A social phsychological approach.* Westview Press: A Division of Harper Collins Publishers.

Dayan, P., & Hinton, G. E. (1993). Feudal reinforcement learning. *In Proceedings of Advances in Neural Information Processing Systems.*

De Raedt, L., & Kersting, K. (2004). Probabilistic Logic Learning. *SIGKDD Explorations, 2*(2), 1–18.

De Raedt, L., & Lavrac, N. (1993). The many faces of inductive logic programming. In Proceedings of the 7th International Symposium on Methodologies for Intelligent Systems: Lecture Notes on Artificial Intelligence, Springer-Verlag.

Dede, C. (2009, January). Immersive Interfaces for Engagement and Learning. *Science, 323*(5910), 66–69. doi:10.1126/science.1167311

Deffuant, G., Neau, D., Amblard, F., & Weisbuch, G. (2001). Mixing beliefs among interacting agents. *Advances in Complex Systems, 3*, 87–98. doi:10.1142/S0219525900000078doi:10.1142/S0219525900000078

DeJong, G., & Mooney, R. (1986). Explanation-based learning: An alternative view. *Machine Learning, 1*, 145–176. doi:10.1007/BF00114116

Demil, B., & Lecocq, X. (2003). *Neither market or hierarchy or network: The emerging bazaar governance.* Université Lille/Institut d'Administration des Entreprises.

Dennett, D. C. (1987). *The intentional stance.* MIT Press.

Derényi, I., Palla, G., & Vicsek, T. (2005). CliqueClique percolation in random networks. *Physical Review Letters, 94*, 160-202. doi:10.1103/PhysRevLett.94.160202

Deville, Y., & Lau, K. (1993). Logic Program Synthesis. Journal of Logic Programming, Special Issue.

Dias, J., Ho, W.C., Vogt, T., Beeckman N., Paiva, A., & Andre, E. (2007). I Know What I Did Last Summer: Autobiographic Memory in Synthetic Characters. *Proceedings of Affective Computing and Intelligent Interaction 2007,* ACM Press.

Dietterich, T. G. (2000). Hierarchical reinforcement learning with the MAXQ value function decomposition. *Journal of Artificial Intelligence Research, 13*, 227–303.

Dignum, F., Kinny, D., & Sonenberg, L. (2002). From desires, obligations and norms to goals. *Cognitive Science Quarterly, 2*(3–4), 407–430.

Dimeas, L., & Hatziargyriou, N. D. (2004). Operation of a multi agent system for microgrid control. *IEEE Transactions on Power Systems, 20*(2), 1447–1455.

Dolsak, B., Bratko, I., & Jezernik, A. (1998). Knowledge base for finite-element mesh design learned by inductive logic programming. *AI EDAM, 12*(2), 95–106.

Dolsak, B., & Muggleton, S. (1992). The application of inductive logic programming to finite element mesh design. In Muggleton, S. (Ed.), Inductive Logic Programming, 453-472, Academic Press, London.

Domingos, P., Kok, S., Poon, H., Richardson, M., & Singla, P. (2006). Unifying Logical and Statistical AI. In Proceedings of the Twenty-First National Conference on Artificial Intelligence 2-7, Boston, MA.

Donaldson, L., & Davis, J. H. (1991). Stewardship Theory or Agency Theory: CEO Governance and Shareholder Returns. *Australian Journal of Management, 16*(1), 49–65. doi:10.1177/031289629101600103

Donath, J. (2007). Virtually trustworthy. *Science, 317*, 53. doi:10.1126/science.1142770

Donath, J. S. (1998). Identity and deception in the virtual community. In Kollock, P., & Smith, M. (Eds.), *Communities in Cyberspace*. London: Routledge.

Dörner, D. (2003). The mathematics of emotions. In F. Detje, D. Dörner & H. Schaub (Eds.), *Proceedings of the Fifth International Conference on Cognitive Modeling*, (pp. 75-79), Bamberg, Germany, Apr, 10-12 2003.

Dörner, D., & Hille, K. (1995). Artificial souls: Motivated emotional robots. *In Proceedings of the International Conference on Systems, Man and Cybernetics*, (pp. 3828-3832).

Duncan, H., & Andre, M. (2009). What's News in Tax: Sales and Use Taxation of Digital Products. *KPMG's What's News in Tax*.

Duval, A. M., & Reiner, V. (2002). Shifted simplicial complexes are Laplacian integral. *Transactions of the American Mathematical Society*, *354*(11), 4313–4344. doi:10.1090/S0002-9947-02-03082-9

Dyson, G. (2005). Turing's cathedral: A visit to Google on the occasion of the 60th anniversary of John von Neumann's proposal for a digital computer: http://www.edge.org/3rd_culture/dyson05/dyson05_index.html.

Ebel, H., Davidsen, J., & Bornholdt, S. (2002). Dynamics of social networks. *Complexity*, *8*, 24–27. doi:10.1002/cplx.10066

Ebel, H., Mielsch, L.-I., & Bornholdt, S. (2002). Scale-free topology of e-mail networks. *Physical Review E: Statistical, Nonlinear, and Soft Matter Physics*, *66*, 035103. doi:10.1103/PhysRevE.66.035103

eCIRCUS (2006). http://www.e-circus.org/. Last accessed: 30-Nov-2007.

Eguiluz, V. M., & Tessone, C. J. (2009). Critical behavior in an evolutionary ultimatum game with social structure. *Advances in Complex Systems*, *12*, 221–232. doi:10.1142/S0219525909002179

Elchardus, M., & Smits, W. (2006). The persistence of the standardized life cycle. *Time & Society*, *15*, 303–326. doi:10.1177/0961463X06066944

Ellis, G. F. R. (2006). On the Nature of Emergent Reality. In Clayton, P., & Davies, P. (Eds.), *The Re-Emergence of Emergence: The Emergentist Hypothesis from Science to Religion*. Oxford, UK: Oxford University Press.

Ellman, T. (1989, November). Explanation-based learning: A survey of programs and perspectives. *ACM Computing Surveys*, *21*(2), 163–221. doi:10.1145/66443.66445

Elster, J. (1989). Social norms and economic theory. *The Journal of Economic Perspectives*, *3*(4), 99–117.

Emmeche, C., Koppe, S., & Stjernfelt, F. (1997). Explaining Emergence: Towards an Ontology of Levels. *Journal for General Philosophy of Science*, (28): 83–119. doi:10.1023/A:1008216127933

Epstein, J. M. (2001). Learning to be thoughtless: Social norms and individual computation. *Computational Economics*, *18*(1), 9–24. doi:10.1023/A:1013810410243

Everett, M. G., & Borgatti, S. P. (1998). Analyzing Clique Overlap. *Connections*, *21*, 49–61.

Everitt, B. S. (1993). *Cluster Analysis*. London: Edward Arnold.

Fama, E. (1970). Efficient Capital Markets: A Review of Theory and Empirical Work. *The Journal of Finance*, *25*(2), 383–417. doi:10.2307/2325486

Farmer, S., & Seers, A. (2004). Time enough to work: Employee motivation and entrainment in the workplace. *Time & Society*, *13*, 213. doi:10.1177/0961463X04044574

Feng, C. (1992). Inducing temporal fault diagnostic rules from a qualitative model. In Muggleton, S. (Ed.), *Inductive Logic Programming*. London: Academic Press.

Fenn, D. J., Porter, M. A., McDonald, M., Williams, S., Johnson, N. F., & Jones, N. S. (2009). Dynamic communities in multichannel data: An application to the foreign exchange market during the 2007-2008 credit crisis. *Chaos (Woodbury, N.Y.)*, *19*, 033119. doi:10.1063/1.3184538

Fiedler, M. (1973). Algebraic connectivity of graphs. *Czechoslovak Mathematical Journal*, *23*, 298–305.

Flaherty, M., & Seipp-Williams, L. (2005). Sociotemporal rhythms in e-mail: A case study. *Time & Society*, *14*, 1. doi:10.1177/0961463X05049949

Foresight for Transport. (2001). A Foresight exercise to help forward thinking in transport and sectoral integration. European Community. Funded by the European Community under the "Competitive and Sustainable Growth" Programme: http://www.iccr-international.org/foresight/.

Fortunato, S. (2010). Community detection in graphs. *Physics Reports-Review Section of Physics Letters*, *486*(3-5), 75–174.

Fortunato, S., & Barthelemy, M. (2006, July). *Resolution limit in community detection.physics/0607100*, from http://arxiv.org/abs/physics/0607100 http://dx.doi.org/10.1073/pnas.0605965104

Fortunato, S., & Castellano, C. (2009). Community structure in graphs. In E. A. Meyers (Ed.), Encyclopedia of Complexity and System Science. Berlin: Springer. Community

Franses, P. (1998). *Time series models for business and economic forecasting*. Cambridge, UK: Cambridge University Press.

Franses, P., & Griensven, K. (1998). Forecasting exchange rates using neural networks for technical trading rules. *Studies in Nonlinear Dynamics and Econometrics*, *2*(4), 109–114.

Fraser, J. T. (1975). *Of time, passion and knowledge*. Princeton, NJ: Princeton University Press.

Fraser, J. T. (1998). *From chaos to conflict*. In Fraser, Soulsby, & Argyros.

Fraser, J. T. (1999). Appendix B, Complexity and its Measure. In *Time, conflict, and human values*. Chicago: University of Illinois Press.

Fraser, J. T. (2000). Human freedom. *KronoScope*, *2*(2), 223–247.

Fraser, J. T., Soulsby, M., & Argyros, A. (Eds.). (1998). *Time, order and chaos: The study of time IX*. Madison, CT: International Universities Press.

Freeman, P. (2008). Trade foreign currencies online. *Money*, *105*, 84–85.

Freeman, L. C. (1977). A Set of Measures of Centrality Based on Betweenness. *Sociometry*, *40*(1), 35–41. doi:10.2307/3033543

Fudenberg, D., & Levine, D. K. (1998). *The theory of learning in games*. Cambridge, MA: The MIT Press.

Gall, M. D., Gall, J. P., & Borg, W. R. (2003). *Educational research an introduction*. Boston: Pearson Education.

García-Camino, A., Rodríguez-Aguilar, J. A., Sierra, C., & Vasconcelos, W. (2006). A rule-based approach to norm-oriented programming of electronic institutions. *ACM SIGecom Exchanges*, *5*(5), 33–41. doi:10.1145/1124566.1124571

García-Camino, A., Rodríguez-Aguilar, J., & Sierra, C. (2005). Implementing norms in electronic institutions. In *Proceedings of the fourth international conference on autonomous agents* (p. 667-673). New York, NY: ACM Press.

Garcia-Martinez, R. (2000). An Integrated Approach of Learning, Planning, and Execution. *Journal of Intelligent & Robotic Systems*, *29*, 47–78. doi:10.1023/A:1008134010576

Gardner, M. (1970, Oct). Mathematical games - the fantastic combinations of John Conway's new solitaire game, Life. *Scientific American*, ▪▪▪, 120–123. doi:10.1038/scientificamerican1070-120 doi:10.1038/scientificamerican1070-120

Garriss, S., Kaminsky, M., Freedman, M. J., Karp, B., Mazières, D., & Yu, H. (2006, May). *Abstract RE: Reliable Email*. Paper presented at the Proceedings of the 3rd Symposium on Networked Systems Design and Implementation, San Jose, CA.

Gaston, M. E., & desJardins, M. (2005). Agent-organized networks for dynamic team formation. In F. Dignum, V. Dignum, S. Koenig, S. Kraus, M. P. Singh, & M. Wooldridge (Eds.), *4rd international joint conference on autonomous agents and multiagent systems (AAMAS 2005), july 25-29, 2005, utrecht, the netherlands* (pp. 230–237). ACM. Available from http://doi.acm.org/10.1145/1082473.1082508

Gençay, R. (1999). Linear, non-linear and essential foreign exchange rate prediction with simple technical trading rules. *Journal of International Economics, 47*, 91–107. doi:10.1016/S0022-1996(98)00017-8

Genesereth, M., Ginsberg, M., & Rosenschein, J. (1986). Cooperation without communications. In *Proceedings of the national conference on artificial intelligence* (p. 51-57). Philadelphia, Pennsylvania: The MIT Press.

Georgeff, M. P., & Ingrand, F. F. (1989). Decision making in an embedded reasoning system. In *Proceedings of the international joint conference on Artificial Intelligence* (pp. 972–978).

Getoor L. & Taskar B. (2007, November). Introduction to Statistical Relational Learning, MIT Press.

Ghoshal, G., Zlatic, V., Caldarelli, G., & Newman, M. E. J. (2009). Random hypergraphs and their applications. *Phys. Rew. E, 79*, 066118. doi:10.1103/PhysRevE.79.066118

Gibbs, J. P. (1981). *Norms, Deviance and social control: Conceptual matters*. New York: Elsevier.

Gibson, W. (2004). Neuromancer. In Nayar, P. (Ed.), *Virtual Worlds*. New Delhi: Sage.

Gilbert, N. (2002). *Varieties of Emergence*. Paper presented at the Social Agents: Ecology, Exchange, and Evolution Conference Chicago.

Giles, J. (2005). Internet Encyclopaedias go head to head [Electronic Version]. *Nature*. Retrieved 20 April 2007 from http://www.nature.com/news/2005/051212/full/438900a.html.

Girvan, M., & Newman, M. E. J. (2002). Community-Community structure in social and biological networks. *Proceedings of the National Academy of Sciences of the United States of America, 99*, 7821–7826. doi:10.1073/pnas.122653799

Girvan, M., & Newman, M. E. J. (2001, December). Community structure in social and biological networks. *cond-mat/0112110*, from http://arxiv.org/abs/cond-mat/0112110

Glaser, B. & Strauss, A. (1999). *The discovery of grounded theory: Strategies for qualitative research*. New York: Aldine De Gruyer.

Goertzel, B., Ikle, M., Goertzel, I. L. F., & Heljakka, A. (2008, in press). Probabilistic Logic Networks: A Comprehensive Framework for Uncertain Inference, Springer.

Gold, E. M. (1967). Language identification in the limit. *Information and Control, 10*, 447–474. doi:10.1016/S0019-9958(67)91165-5

Goldspink, C., & Kay, R. (2008). Agent Cognitive Capability and Orders of Emergence. In Trajkovski, G., & Collins, S. (Eds.), *Agent-Based Societies: Social and Cultural Interactions*.

Goldspink, C. (2008). *Towards a socio-ecological View of emergence: the reflexive turn* Paper presented at the Embracing Complexity: Advancing ecological understanding in organization EGOS Summer Workshop.

Goldspink, C., & Kay, R. (2007). *Social Emergence: Distinguishing Reflexive and Non-reflexive modes*. Paper presented at the AAAI Fall Symposium: Emergent Agents and Socialities: Social and Organizational Aspects of Intelligence.

Goldspink, C., & Kay, R. (2008). *Agent Cognitive Capabilities and Orders of Emergence: critical thresholds relevant to the simulation of social behaviours'*. Paper presented at the AISB Convention, Communication, Interaction and Social Intelligence.

Goldstein, J. (1999). Emergence as a Construct: History and Issues. *Emergence, 1*(1), 49–72. doi:10.1207/s15327000em0101_4

González, M. C., Hidalgo, C. A., & Barabási, A.-L. (2008). Understanding individual human mobility patterns. *Nature, 453*, 779–782. doi:10.1038/nature06958

Goodhew, L., & Loy, D. (2002). Momo, dogen, and the comodification of time. *KronoScope, 2*(1). doi:10.1163/15685240260186817

Gordon, G. (1995). Stable function approximation in dynamic programming. *In Proceedings of International Conference on Machine Learning.*

Granovetter, M. S. (1973). The strength of weak ties. *American Journal of Sociology, 78*, 1360–1380. doi:10.1086/225469

Granovetter, M. S. (1992). *Decision Making: Alternatives to Rational Choice Models Economic Action and Social Structure: The Problem of Embeddedness.* Newbury Park, CA: SAGE.

Grassberger, P. (1986). Toward a Quantitative Theory of Self-Generated Complexity [Springer Netherlands.]. *International Journal of Theoretical Physics, 25*, 907–938. doi:10.1007/BF00668821

Greene, B. (1999). *The elegant universe.* New York: W.W. Norton.

Grobelnik, M. (1992). MARKUS: An optimized Model inference System. Workshop on Logical Approaches to Machine Learning, Tenth European Conference on AI, Vienna, Austria.

Grone, R., Merris, R., & Sunder, V. (1990). The Laplacian spectrum of a graph. *SIAM Journal of Matrix Anaysis and Applications, 11*, 218–238. doi:10.1137/0611016

Gross, T., & Blasius, B. (2008). Adaptive Co-evolutionary Networks: A Review. *Journal of the Royal Society, Interface, 5*, 259–271. doi:10.1098/rsif.2007.1229

Guerra-Hernández, A., Fallah-Seghrouchni, A. E., & Soldano, H. (2004a). Distributed learning in intentional BDI multi-agent systems. In *Proceedings of the fifth Mexican international conference in Computer Science (ENC'04)* (pp. 225–232). Washington, DC, USA.

Guerra-Hernández, A., Fallah-Seghrouchni, A. E., & Soldano, H. (2004b). Learning in BDI multi-agent systems. In *Computational logic in multi-agent systems* (Vol. 3259, pp. 218–233). Springer Berlin / Heidelberg.

Guo, Y. (2007). *Cap optimisation for broker agent. Technical Report.* CSIRO.

Guo, Y., Li, J., & James, G. (2005). Evolutionary optimization of distributed energy resources. Advances *in Artificial Intelligence, 18th Australian Joint Conference on Artificial Intelligence.* (3809 of Springer LNCS, pp. 1086-1091).

Guo, Y., Li, R., Poulton, G., & Zeman, A. (2008). A simulator for self-adaptive energy demand management. *Second IEEE International Conference on Self-Adaptive and Self-Organizing Systems (SASO)*, Italy.

Gupta, R. (1991). The Buddhist Doctrine of Momentariness and its Presuppositions. In Prasad, H. (1991).

Habermas, J. (1976). Some Distinctions in Universal Pragmatics: A working paper. *Theory and Society, 3*(2), 12.

Hägg, S., & Ygge, F. (1995). *Agent-oriented programming in power distribution automation – an architecture, and language, and their applicability.* Licentiate thesis, Lund University.

Haggis, T. (2002). Exploring the 'black box' of process: a comparison of theoretical notions of the 'adult learner' with accounts of postgraduate learning experience. *Studies in Higher Education, 27*, 207–220. doi:10.1080/03075070220119986

Hancock, P. (2002). The time of your life: One thousand moons. *KronoScope, 2*(2). doi:10.1163/156852402320900715

Hanson, J. E., & Crutchfield, J. P. (1997). Computational mechanics of cellular automata: an example. *Physica D. Nonlinear Phenomena, 103*, 169–189. doi:10.1016/S0167-2789(96)00259-X

Harris, J. R. (1995). Where is the child's environment? A group socilization theory of development. *Psychological Review, 102*, 458–489. doi:10.1037/0033-295X.102.3.458

Hayles, N. K. (1999). *How we became posthuman.* Chicago, IL: University of Chicago Press.

Hayles, N. K. (2002). *Writing machines.* Cambridge, MA: MIT Press.

Hayles, N. K. (2005). *My mother was a computer.* Chicago, IL: University of Chicago Press.

Heimo, T., Saramäki, J., Onnela, J.-P., & Kaski K. (2007). Spectral and network methods in the analysis of correlation matrices of stock returns. *Physica A-Statistical Mechanics and its Applications 383*, 147-151.

Hemp, P. (2006). Avatar-Based Marketing. *Harvard Business Review, 84*(6), 48–57.

Herrera, M., Roberts, D. C., & Gulbahce, N. (2010). Mapping the Evolution of Scientific Fields. *PLoS ONE, 5*, e10355. doi:10.1371/journal.pone.0010355

Hidalgo, C. A., & Rodriguez-Sickert, C. (2008). The dynamics of a mobile phone network. *Physica A, 387*, 3017–3024. doi:10.1016/j.physa.2008.01.073

Hildebrand, R., Mancini, S., & Severini, S. (2008). Combinatorial laplacians and positivity under partial transpose. *Mathematical Structures in Computer Science, 18*, 205–219. doi:10.1017/S0960129508006634

Hille, K. (2007). *A theory on emotion.* http://web.unib-amberg.de/ppp/insttheopsy/dokumente/Hille_A_theory_of_emotion.pdf, 2007. Last accessed: 18-Dec-2007.

Hindriks, K. V., Boer, F. S. D., Hoek, W. V. D., & Meyer, J. J. C. (1999). Agent programming in 3APL. *Autonomous Agents and Multi-Agent Systems, 2*(4), 357–401. doi:10.1023/A:1010084620690

Hirshleifer, J. (1988). *Price Theory and Applications* (4th ed.). New York: Prentice-Hall, Inc.

Ho, W. C., Dautenhahn, K., & Nehaniv, C. L. (2008). Computational Memory Architectures for Autobiographic Agents Interacting in a Complex Virtual Environment: A Working Model. *Connection Science, 20*(1), 21–65. doi:10.1080/09540090801889469

Ho, W. C., Dias, J., Figueiredo, R., & Paiva, A. (2007a). *Agents that remember can tell stories: integrating autobiographic memory into emotional agents. Proceedings of Autonomous Agents and Multiagent Systems (AAMAS).* ACM Press.

Ho, W. C., & Watson, S. (2006). Autobiographic knowledge for believable virtual characters. *Intelligent Virtual Agents 2006 (IVA 2006)*, Springer LNAI, (pp. 383-394).

Ho, W. C., Dautenhahn, K., & Nehaniv, C. L. (2006). A study of episodic memory based learning and narrative structure for autobiographic agents. In *Proceedings of Adaptation in Artificial and Biological Systems, AISB 2006 conference, 3*, 26-29.

Ho, W. C., Watson, S., & Dautenhahn, K. (2007b). AMIA: A Knowledge Representation Model for Computational Autobiographic Agents. *Proceedings of IEEE International Conference on Development and Learning (ICDL) 2007.*

Hoffman, M. L. (1977). Sex differences in empathy and related behaviors. *Psychological Bulletin, 84*, 712–722. doi:10.1037/0033-2909.84.4.712

Hogan, R. (1969). Development of an empathy scale. *Journal of Consulting and Clinical Psychology, 33*, 306–316. doi:10.1037/h0027580

Holland, J. (1995). *Hidden order. Redwood City, CA.* Redwood City: Addison-Wesley.

Holland, J. H. (1998). *Emergence: from chaos to order.* Reading, MA: Addison Wesley.

Holme, P., Edling, Ch. R., & Liljeros, F. (2004). Structure and Time-Evolution of an Internet Dating Community. *Social Networks, 26*, 155–174. doi:10.1016/j.socnet.2004.01.007

Hopcroft, J., Khan, O., Kulis, B., & Selman, B. (2004). Tracking evolving communities in large linked networks. *Proceedings of the National Academy of Sciences of the United States of America, 101*, 5249–5253. doi:10.1073/pnas.0307750100

Hou, I. (2007). International Energy Outlook 2007. *Energy Information Administration*, http://www.eia.doe.gov/

Hu, D., Kaza, S., & Chen, H. (2009). Identifying Significant Facilitators of Dark Network Evolution. *Journal of the American Society for Information Science and Technology*, *60*, 655–665. doi:10.1002/asi.21008

Hu, Q., & Yue, W. (2007). *Markov Decision Processes with Their Applications. Advances in Mechanics and Mathematics*. New York: Springer.

Huber, M. J. (1999, May). JAM: A BDI-theoretic mobile agent architecture. In *Proceedings of the third international conference on autonomous agents, (AGENTS'99)* (p. 236-243).

HUMAINE. (2004). http://emotion-research.net/. Last accessed, 25-Nov-07.

Hume. (1978). *A treatise of human nature*. Oxford, England: Oxford University Press.

Inada, K. (1991). Time and temporality – A Buddhist approach. In Prasad, H. (1991).

Inuzuka, N., Onda, T., & Itoh, H. (2000). Learning Robot Control by Relational Concept Induction with Iteratively Collected Examples. In Wyatt, J., & Demiris, J. (Eds.), *EWLR 1999, LNAI 1812* (pp. 71–83). Springer-Verlag Berlin Heidelberg.

Jain, A. K., Murty, M. N., & Flynn, P. J. (1999). Data clustering: a review. *ACM Computing Surveys*, *31*(3), 264–323. doi:10.1145/331499.331504

James, G., Cohen, D., Dodier, R., Platt, G., & Palmer, D. (2006). A deployed multi-agent framework for distributed energy applications. *Proceedings of the Fifth international Joint Conference on Autonomous Agents and Multi-agent Systems*. AAMAS '06. New York: ACM Press, 676-678.

Janelle, D. G. (2002). Embedding time in accessibility analysis. CSISS Workshop on Accessibility in Time and Space. The Ohio State University, 22 July 2002: http://www.csiss.org/aboutus/presentations/files/janelle_etaa.pdf.

Janssen, M. A., & Ostrom, E. (2006). *Empirically Based, Agent-base models. Ecology and Society 11(2)*. Resilience Alliance.

Jappy, P., Nock, R., & Gascuel, O. (1996). Negative Robust Learnability results for Horn Clause Programs. International Conference on Machine Learning, Barri, 258-265.

Jarvis, H. (2005). Moving to London time: Household co-ordination and the infrastructure of everyday life. *Time & Society*, *14*, 1. doi:10.1177/0961463X05050302

JBoss Drools. (n.d.). Retrieved from http://jboss.org/drools.

jCiffolilli, A. (2007). Phantom Authority, self-selective recruitement and retention of members in virtual communities: The case of Wikipedia [Electronic Version]. *FirstMonday*, 8. Retrieved 20 April 2007 from http://firstmonday.org/issues/issue8_12/ciffolilli/index.html.

Jennings, N., & Wooldridge, M. (1998). *Applications of Intelligent Agents. Agent Technology: Foundations* (pp. 3–28). Applications, and Markets.

Jenny, H. (2001). *Cymatics: a study of wave phenomena and vibration*. Newmarket, NH: MACROmedia.

Jensen, M. C., & Meckling, W. H. (1976). Theory of the firm: Managerial behavior, agency costs, and ownership structure. *Journal of Financial Economics*, *3*, 305–360. doi:10.1016/0304-405X(76)90026-X

Jiménez, S., Fernández, F., & Borrajo, D. (2008). The PELA architecture: Integrating planning and learning to improve execution. In *Proceedings of the twenty-third AAAI conference on Artificial Intelligence* (AAAI'08) (pp. 1294–1299). Chicago, USA.

Johnson, N. F., Xu, C., Zhao, Z., Ducheneaut, N., Yee, N., Tita, G., & Hui, P. M. (2009). Human group formation in online guilds and offline gangs driven by a common team dynamic. *Physical Review E: Statistical, Nonlinear, and Soft Matter Physics*, *79*, 066117. doi:10.1103/PhysRevE.79.066117

Jones, C., Hesterly, W. S., & Borgatti, S. P. (1997). A General Theory of Network Governance: Exchange Conditions and Social Mechanisms. *Academy of Management Review*, 22(4), 911–945. doi:10.2307/259249

Jouffe, L. (1998). Fuzzy inference system learning by reinforcement methods. *IEEE Transactions on Systems, Man and Cybernetics. Part C, Applications and Reviews*, 28(3), 338–355. doi:10.1109/5326.704563

Kaelbling, L. P., Littman, M., & Moore, A. (1996). Reinforcement learning: A survey. *Journal of Artificial Intelligence Research*, 4, 237–285.

Kaelbling, L. P. (1993). Hierarchical learning in stochastic domains: Preliminary results. In *Proceedings of International Conference on Machine Learning*, (pp. 167-173).

Kaku, M. (1994). *Hyperspace: A scientific odyssey through parallel universes, time warps, and the tenth dimension*. New York: Oxford University Press.

Kamruzzaman, J., & Sarker, R. (2003). Comparing ANN based models with ARIMA for prediction of Forex rates. *ASOR Bulletin*, 22(2), 2–11.

Kandori, M., & Rob, R. (1995, April). Evolution of equilibria in the long run: A general theory and applications. *Journal of Economic Theory*, 65(2), 383–414. doi:10.1006/jeth.1995.1014

Kanet, J., & Barut, M. (2003). Problem-based learning for production and operations management. *Decision Sciences Journal of Innovative Education*, 1, 99–118. doi:10.1111/1540-5915.00007

Katagiri, D. (2007). *Each moment is the universe: Zen and the way of being time*. Boston: Shambala Press.

Kaufmann, W. (1973). *Relativity and cosmology*. New York: Harper and Row.

Kellert, S. (1993). *In the wake of chaos*. Chicago, IL: University of Chicago Press.

Kennedy, J., & Eberhart, R. C. (2001). *Swarm Intelligence* (1 ed.). London: Academic Press.

Kennedy, R. (2009). Law in Virtual Worlds. *Journal of Internet Law*, April.

Kietz, J.-U., & Dzeroski, S. (1994). Inductive Logic Programming and Learnability, SIGART Bulletin, Vol. 5, No. 1.

Kim, U. (2007). Analysis of Personal Email Networks using Spectral Decomposition. *International Journal of Computer Science and Network Security*, 7(4), 185–188.

Kim, H. S., & Ko, D. (2007). Culture and self-expression. In Sedikides, C., & Spencer, S. (Eds.), *Frontiers of social psychology: The self*. New York: Psychology Press.

King, R., Muggleton, S., Lewis, R., & Sternberg, M. (1992). Drug design by machine learning: The use of inductive logic programming to model the structure activity relationships of thrimethorpin analogus binding to dihydrofolate reductase. *Proceedings of the National Academy of Sciences of the United States of America*, 89(23), 11322–11326. doi:10.1073/pnas.89.23.11322

King, R. (2005). The Robot Scientist Project. In the Proceedings of the 8th International Conference on Discovery Science, Lecture Notes in Artificial Intelligence Vol. 3735.

Kirchhoff, F. (1847). Über die Auflösung der Gleichungen, auf welche man bei der Untersuchung der linearen Verteilung galvanischer Ströme geführt wird. *Annalen der Physik und Chemie*, 72, 497–508. doi:10.1002/andp.18471481202

Kiss, H. J. M., Mihalik, A., Nanasi, T., Ory, B., Spiro, Z., Soti, C., & Csermely, P. (2009). Ageing as a price of cooperation and complexity. *BioEssays*, 31, 651–664. doi:10.1002/bies.200800224

Kittur, A., Suh, B., Pendleton, B. A., & Chi, E. H. (2007). *He Says, She says: Conflict and coordination in Wikipedia*. Paper presented at the Computer/Human Interaction 2007, San Jose USA.

Klein, O. (2004). Social perception of time and high speed trains. *Time & Society*, 13, 213. doi:10.1177/0961463X04043504

Klingspor, V., Morik, K., & Rieger, A. (1996). Learning Concepts from Sensor Data of a Mobile Robot. *Machine Learning*, *23*(2/3), 305–332. doi:10.1023/A:1018245209731

Knowles, M. (1990). *The adult learner: A neglected species*. Houston, TX: Gulf Publishing.

Knudsen, S. (2004). *A Guide to Analysis of DNA Microarray Data*. Wiley-liss.

Kobrin, S. (2001). Territoriality and the Governance of CyberSpace. *Journal of International Business Studies*, *32*(4), 687–704. doi:10.1057/palgrave.jibs.8490990

Koehler, G. (2003a). Time, complex systems, and public policy: A theoretical foundation for adaptive policy making. *Nonlinear Dynamics Psychology and Life Sciences*, *7*, 1. doi:10.1023/A:1020418210366

Koehler, G. (in press). Computer simulations as hidden time-ecologies. In Vrobel, S., Rossler, O. E., & Marks-Tarlow, T. (Eds.), *Simultaneity: Temporal Structures and Observer Perspectives*. Singapore: World Scientific.

Koehler, G. (1996) *The Feigenbaum diagram: A metapattern for the social construction of time*, a paper presented at the Sixth Annual International Conference of the Society for Chaos Theory in the Psychology and the Life Science, June 25-28, 1996, University of California, Berkeley.

Koehler, G. (2001). A framework for visualizing the chronocomplexity of politically regulated time-ecologies. A paper prepared for the International Society for the Study of Time Conference, Gargonza, Italy, and for the Society for Chaos Theory in Psychology and the Life Science Conference, Madison, Wisconsin.

Koehler, G. (2003b). EU transport foresight planning: Comments on how chronocomplexity limits such strategic planning efforts. A paper presented at the Society for Chaos Theory in Psychology and Life Sciences, 12th Annual Conference, Portland State University, Portland, Oregon.

Koehler, G. (2004). Sorting out the temporal confusion of computer simulations. International Society for the Study of Time, Conference, Cambridge, England, August.

Koehler-Jones, V. (2003). The Temporal signature of small manufacturers. Unpublished draft report available from www.timestructures.com.

Kolb, D. A., & Fry, R. (1975). *Toward an applied theory of experiential learning. Theories of Group Process*. London: John Wiley.

Kolmogorov, A. N. (1965). Three approaches to the quantitative definition of information. *Problems of Information Transmission*, *1*, 1–7.

Kolodner, J. (1993). *Case-based reasoning*. San Mateo, CA: Morgan Kaufmann.

Konieczny, P. (2009). Governance, Organization, and Democracy on the Internet: The Iron Law and the Evolution of Wikipedia. *Sociological Forum*, *24*(1), 162–192. doi:10.1111/j.1573-7861.2008.01090.x

Körner, J. (1973). Coding of an information source having ambiguous alphabet and entropy of graphs. *In Proeedings of the 6th Prague Conference on Information Theory*, pp. 411-425.

Kossinets, G., & Watts, D. J. (2006). Empirical analysis of an evolving social network. *Science*, *311*, 88–90. doi:10.1126/science.1116869

Kossinets, G., & Watts, D. J. (2009). Origins of Homophily in an Evolving Social Network. *American Journal of Sociology*, *115*, 405–450. doi:10.1086/599247

Krause, P. J. (1998). Learning probabilistic networks. *The Knowledge Engineering Review*, *13*(4), 321–351. doi:10.1017/S0269888998004019

Kwinter, S. (2002). *Architectures of time*. Cambridge, Mass.: MIT Press.

Lambiotte, R., Blondel, V. D., de Kerchove, C., Huens, E., Prieur, C., Smoreda, Z., & Van Dooren, P. (2008). Geographical dispersal of mobile communication networks. *Physica A*, *387*, 5317–5325. doi:10.1016/j.physa.2008.05.014

Lambiotte, R., & Panzarasa, P. (2009). Communities, knowledge creation, and information diffusion. *Journal of Informatrics*, *3*, 180–190. doi:10.1016/j.joi.2009.03.007

Latour, B., & Woolgar, S. (1979). *Laboratory Life*. Beverly Hills: Sage.

Lavrac, N., & Dzeroski, S. (1994). *Inductive Logic Programming: Techniques and Applications*. New York: Ellis Horwood.

Lavrac, N., Dzeroski, S., & Grobelnik, M. (1991). *Learning nonrecursive definitions of relations with LINUS* (pp. 265–281). Berlin: Fifth European Working Session on Learning.

Lavrac, N., Dzeroski, S., Pirnat, V., & Krizman, V. (1993). The use of background knowledge in learning medical diagnostic rules. *Applied Artificial Intelligence*, *7*, 273–293. doi:10.1080/08839519308949989

Lawrence, W. (2002). *Dynamical cognitive science*. Boston, MA: MIT Press.

Lazaric, A., Restelli, M., & Bonarini, A. (2007). Reinforcement learning in continuous action spaces through sequential Monte Carlo methods. *In Proceeding of Neural Information Processing Systems.*

Le, C. (2007). The honeymoon's over: states crack down on the virtual world's tax-free love affair with e-commerce. *Houston Business & Tax Law Journal*, *7*(2), 395–423.

Lederman, L. (2007). *Stranger than Fiction: Taxing Virtual Worlds*. New York University Law Review, Vol. 82; Indiana Legal Studies Research Paper No. 76. Retrieved December 23, 2008 from http://ssrn.com/abstract=969984

Lee, D., Kahng, B., & Goh, K.-I. (2008). Evolution of the coauthorship network. *Journal of the Korean Physical Society*, *52*, S197–S202. doi:10.3938/jkps.52.197

Lehdonvirta, V. (2005). Virtual Economics: Applying Economics to the Study of Game Worlds. *Proceedings of the 2005 Conference on Future Play*, Lansing, MI.

Leskovec, J., Chakrabarti, D., Kleinberg, J., & Faloutsos, C. (2005). Realistic, mathematically tractable graph generation and evolution, using Kronecker multiplication. *Lecture Notes in Computer Science*, *3721*, 133–145. doi:10.1007/11564126_17

Leslie, A. M. (1994). Pretending and believing: Issues in the theory of ToMM. *Cognition*, *50*, 211–238. doi:10.1016/0010-0277(94)90029-9

Leung, K., & Bond, M. H. (1984). The impact of cultural collectivism on reward allocation. *Journal of Personality and Social Psychology*, *47*, 793–804. doi:10.1037/0022-3514.47.4.793

Lewis, D. K. (1969). *Convention: A philosophical study*. Cambridge, MA: Harvard University Press.

Li, W. (1991). On the Relationship between Complexity and Entropy for Markov Chains and Regular Languages. *Complex Systems. Complex Systems Publications*, *5*, 381–399.

Li, J., Poulton, G., James, G., Zeman, A., Wang, P., Chadwick, M., & Piraveenan, M. (2007). Performance of multi-agent coordination of distributed energy resources. *WSEAS Transactions on System and Control*, *2*(1), 52–58.

Li, J., Poulton, G., & James, G. (2007). Agent-based distributed energy management. *The 20th Australian Joint Conference on Artificial Intelligence*. Gold Coast, Queensland, Australia, 2-6 December.

Li, R., & Poulton, G. (2007). *Optimal management of multiple resource consuming devices during periods of supply restriction*. Technical Report, CSIRO, May.

Li, R., Li, J., Poulton, G., & James, G. (2008). Agent Based Optimisation Systems for Electrical Load Management. Proc. First *International Workshop on Optimisation in Multi-Agent Systems (OPTMAS), in conjunction with Seventh Conference on Autonomous Agents and Multi-Agent Systems*, 60-68, Estoril, Portugal, May.

Liljeros, F., Edling, Ch. R., Amaral, L. A. N., Stanley, H. E., & Aberg, Y. (2001). The Web of Human Sexual Contacts. *Nature*, *411*, 907–908. doi:10.1038/35082140

Lin, C.-S., & Kim, H. (1991). CMAC-based adaptive critic self-learning control. *IEEE Transactions on Neural Networks*, *2*, 530–533. doi:10.1109/72.134290

Lin, L.-J. (1992). Self-improving reactive agents based on reinforcement learning, planning and teaching. *Machine Learning, 8*, 293–321. doi:10.1007/BF00992699

Linden Research. (2005). http://www.secondlife.com/. Last accessed, 9-Nov-07.

Lindquist, J., Ma, J., van den Driessche, P., & Willeboordse, F. H. (2009). Network evolution by different rewiring schemes. *Physica D. Nonlinear Phenomena, 238*, 370–378. doi:10.1016/j.physd.2008.10.016

Liu, J., & Deng, G. (2009). Link prediction in a user-object network based on time-weighted resource allocation. *Physica A, 388*, 3643–3650. doi:10.1016/j.physa.2009.05.021

Lloyd, D. (2002). Functional fMRI and the study of human consciousness. *Journal of Cognitive Neuroscience, 14*, 818–831. doi:10.1162/089892902760191027

Lorenzo, D. (2002). Learning non-monotonic causal theories from narratives of actions, In Proceedings of The 9th International Workshop on Non-Monotonic Reasoning NMR'2002, Toulouse, France.

Lorenzo, D., & Otero, R. P. (2000). Learning to reason about actions. In Horn, W. (Ed.). Proceedings of the Fourteenth European Conference on Artificial Intelligence, IOS Press, Amsterdam.

Loyall, A. B. (1997). *Believable Agents*. PhD thesis, Carnegie Mellon University, Pittsburgh, Pennsylvania. CMU-CS-97-123.

Lu, Q., Korniss, G., & Szymanski, B. K. (2006, October 12–15). Naming games in spatially-embedded random networks and emergent phenomena in societies of agents. In *Interaction and emergent phenomena in societies of agents* (pp. 148–155). Menlo Park, CA:The American Association for Artificial Intelligence.

Luger, G. F. (2002). *Artificial Intelligence: Structure and Strategies for Complex Problem Solving*. New York: Addison-Wesley.

Luke, S., Balan, G. C., Sullivan, K., Panait, L., Cioffi-Revilla, C., Paus, S., et al. (2009). MASON Multiagent Simulation Toolkit.

Lutz, C. (1988). *Unnatural emotions*. Chicago: University of Chicago Press.

Macedo, L. Cardoso, A. (2004) *Exploration in Unknown Environments with Motivational Agents*. AAMAS 04'. July 19-23. New York.

Mahadevan, P., Krioukov, D., Fall, K., & Vahdat, A. (2006). Systematic topology analysis and generation using degree correlations. *Computer Communication Review, 36*, 135–146. doi:10.1145/1151659.1159930

Maloof, M., & Michalski, R. (2000). Selecting examples for partial memory learning. *Machine Learning, 41*, 27–52. doi:10.1023/A:1007661119649

Manin, Y. I. (1991). Mathematics as Metaphor. *Proceedings of the International Congress of Mathematicians* (pp. 1665-1671), Kyoto, Japan.

Mantegna, R. N. (1999). Hierarchical Structure in Financial Markets. *The European Physical Journal B, 11*, 63–74. doi:10.1007/s100510050929

Mantegna, R. N., & Stanley, H. E. (2000). *An Introduction to Econophysics: Correlations and Complexity in Finance*. Cambridge: Cambridge University Press.

Marcinkowski, J., & Pacholski, L. (1992). Undecidability of the Hornclanse implication problem. In Proc. 33rd Annual IEEE Symposium on Foundations of Computer Science, pages 354-362.

Markus, H. R., & Kitayama, S. (1991). Culture and the self: Implications for cognition, emotion, and motivation. *Psychological Review, 98*(2), 224–253. doi:10.1037/0033-295X.98.2.224

Marsella, S., & Gratch, J. (200)3, Modelling coping behaviour in virtual humans: Dont worry, be happy, *Autonomous Agents and Multiagent Systems (AAMAS)*, ACM Press, (pp. 313–320).

Marthi, B. (2007). Automatic shaping and decomposition of reward functions. *In Proceedings of the 24th International Conference on Machine Learning,* (pp. 601-608).

Maslow, A. (1954). *Motivation and Personality*. New York: Harper and Bros.

Matsumoto, M., & Nishimura, T. (1998). Mersenne twister: a 623-dimensionally equidistributed uniform pseudo-random number generator. *ACM Transactions on Modeling and Computer Simulation, 8*(1), 3–30. doi:10.1145/272991.272995

Maturana, H. R. & Varela, F. J. (1980), Autopoiesis and Cognition: The Realization of the Living. Boston Studies in the Philosophy of Science, 42.

McArthur, S. D. J., & Davidson, E. M. (2005). Concepts and approaches in multi-agent systems for power applications. *Proceedings of the 13th International Conference on Intelligent Systems Application to Power Systems.* Nov.

McQuiggan, S. W., & Lester, J. C. (2006). Learning empathy: a data-driven framework for modeling empathetic companion agents. *Proceedings of the fifth international joint conference on autonomous agents and multiagent systems (AAMAS 06)*, Hakodate, Japan, (pp. 961-968).

Medelyan, O., Milne, D., Legg, C., & Witten, I. H. (2009). Mining meaning from Wikipedia. *International Journal of Human-Computer Studies, 67*, 716–754. doi:10.1016/j.ijhcs.2009.05.004

Melo, F. S., Meyn, S. P., & Ribeiro, M. I. (2008). An analysis of reinforcement learning with function approximation. *In Proceedings of International Conference on Machine Learning,* (pp. 664-671).

Mendes, J. F. F., & Dorogovtsev, S. N. (2003). *Evolution of Networks: From Biological Nets to the Internet and WWW*. Oxford, UK: Oxford University Press.

Merleau-Ponty, M. (1968). *Lingis, Alphonso, trans. The visible and the invisible*. Evanston, IL: Northwestern University.

Merriam, S. B. (1998). *Qualitative research and case study applications in education*. San Francisco: Jossey-Bass.

Michon, J. (1999). Models of local time. Paper presented at the XIth International Conference of the European Society for Cognitive Psychology, Ghent, Belgium, September 1-4.

Milne, M., & McConnell, P. (2001). Problem-based learning: a pedagogy for using case materials in accounting education. *Accounting Education, 10*, 61–82.

Milo, R., Shen-Orr, S., Itzkovitz, S., & Kashtan, N., Chklovskii, & D., Alon, U. (2002). Network Motifs: Simple Building Blocks of Complex Networks. *Science, 298*, 824–827. doi:10.1126/science.298.5594.824

Mitchell, T. M. (1997). *Machine Learning*. New York: McGraw-Hill.

Mookerjee, S. (1991). The Buddhist doctrine of flux (the nature of existence). In Prasad, H. (1991).

Moore, A., Baird, L., & Kaelbling, L. P. (1999). Multivalue-functions: Efficient automatic action hierarchies for multiple goal MDPs. *In Proceedings of the International Joint Conference on Artificial Intelligence,* (pp. 1316-1323).

Moore, E. F. (1956). Gedanken-experiments on sequential machines. In Shannon, C.E. & McCarthy, J., (Ed.), Automata Studies, 129-153, Princeton University Press, Princeton, NJ.

Moran, G. (2007). *CyberSocializing. Financial Planning.* Retrieved December 23, 2008 from http://www.financialplanning.com/asset/article/528451/cybersocializing.html

Mucha, P. J., Richardson, T., Macon, K., Porter, M.-A., & Onnela, J.-P. (2010). CommunityCommunity Structure in Time-Dependent, Multiscale, and Multiplex Networks. *Science, 328*, 876–878. doi:10.1126/science.1184819

Muggleton, S., & De Raedt, L. (1994). ILP: Theory and Methods. Journal of Logic Programming, 19 and 20, 629-679.

Mukherjee, P., Sen, S., & Airiau, S. (2007, May). Norm emergence in spatially constrained interactions. In *Proceedings of aamas 2007 workshop on adaptive and learning agents (alag-07)* (pp. 79–83).

Munos, R., & Moore, A. (2002). Variable resolution discretization in optimal control. *Machine Learning, 49*(2-3), 291–323. doi:10.1023/A:1017992615625

Myerson, R. B. (1991). *Game theory: Analysis of conflict.* Cambridge, MA: Harvard University Press.

National Taxpayer Advocate. (2008). *I.R.S* (pp. 213–233). Annual Report to Congress.

Nehaniv, C. L. (1999). Narrative for artifacts: Transcending context and self. *Narrative Intelligence*, ser. AAAI Fall Symposium 1999. AAAI Press, pp. 101–104, Technical Report FS-99-01.

Nehaniv, C. L., & Dautenhahn, K. (1998). Semigroup expansions for autobiographic agents. In *Proceedings of the First Symposium on Algebra, Languages and Computation.* Osaka University, 77–84.

Nelson, K. (1993). The psychological and social origins of autobiographical memory. *Psychological Science, 4,* 7–14. doi:10.1111/j.1467-9280.1993.tb00548.x

Newman, M. E. J. (2004). Detecting community structure in networks. *The European Physical Journal B, 38,* 321–330. doi:10.1140/epjb/e2004-00124-y

Newman, M. E. J. (2006). Modularity and community structure in networks. *Proceedings of the National Academy of Sciences of the United States of America, 103*(23), 8577–8582. doi:10.1073/pnas.0601602103

Newman, M. E. J. (2002, September). *Mixing patterns in networks.* cond-mat/0209450, from http://arxiv.org/abs/cond-mat/0209450

Newman, M. E. J., & Girvan, M. (2003, August). Finding and evaluating community structure in networks. *cond-mat/0308217*, from http://arxiv.org/abs/cond-mat/0308217

Newman, M., Barabasi, A.-L., & Watts, D. J. (2006). *The Structure and Dynamics of Networks:* (1 ed.). Princeton University Press.

Ng, A. Y., Harada, D., & Russell, S. J. (1999). Policy invariance under reward transformations: Theory and application to reward shaping. *In Proceedings of the 16th International Conference on Machine Learning,* (pp. 278-287).

Nielsen, M. A., & Chuang, I. L. (2000). *Quantum computation and quantum information.* Cambridge, UK: Cambridge University Press.

Nilsson, N. (1998). *Artificial Intelligence: A New Synthesis.* San Fransico, CA: Morgan Kaufman Publishers, Inc.

Noh, J. D., Jeong, H. C., Ahn, Y. Y., & Jeong, H. (2005). Growing network model for community with group structure. *Physical Review E: Statistical, Nonlinear, and Soft Matter Physics, 71,* 036131. doi:10.1103/PhysRevE.71.036131

Nowak, M., & Sigmund, K. (2004). Evolutionary Dynamics of Biological Games. *Science, 303,* 793–799. doi:10.1126/science.1093411

Oanda Corporation. (n.d.). Retrieved from http://www.oanda.com/.

Ogston, E., Zeman, A., Prokopenko, M., & James, G. (2007). Clustering distributed energy resources for large-scale demand management, *First International Conference on Self-Adaptive and Self-Organizing Systems (SASO).*

Ohya, M., & Petz, D. (1993). *Quantum entropy and its use.* Berlin: Springer-Verlag.

Onnela, J.-P., Chakraborti, A., Kaski, K., Kertész, J., & Kanto, A. (2003). Dynamics of market correlations: Taxonomy and portfolio analysis. *Physical Review E: Statistical, Nonlinear, and Soft Matter Physics, 68,* 056110. doi:10.1103/PhysRevE.68.056110

Onnela, J.-P., Saramäki, J., Hyvonen, J., Szabó, G., Lazer, D., & Kaski, K. (2007). Structure and tie strengths in mobile communication networks. *Proceedings of the National Academy of Sciences of the United States of America, 104,* 7332–7336. doi:10.1073/pnas.0610245104

Opitz, D., & Maclin, R. (1999). Popular ensemble methods: an empirical study. *Journal of Artificial Intelligence Research*, *11*, 169–198.

Ortony, A., Clore, G., & Collins, A. (1988). *The Cognitive Structure of Emotions*. Cambridge University Press.

Packard, N. H. (1982). Measurements of Chaos in the Presence of Noise. *Phd Thesis, University of California*

Page, D. (2000). ILP: Just Do It. In Proceedings of Computational Logic 2000, Lloyd, Dahl, Kerber, Lau, Palamidissi, Pereira, Sagiv, Stuckey (Eds), Berlin: Springer, LNAI 1861, pp. 25-40.

Palla, G., Derényi, I., Farkas, I., & Vicsek, T. (2005). Uncovering the overlapping community structure of complex networks in nature and society. *Nature*, *435*, 814–818. doi:10.1038/nature03607

Palla, G., Farkas, I. J., Pollner, P., Derényi, I., & Vicsek, T. (2008). Fundamental statistical features and self-similar properties of tagged networks. *New Journal of Physics*, *10*, 123026. doi:10.1088/1367-2630/10/12/123026

Palla, G., Lovász, L., & Vicsek, T. (2010). Multifractal network generator. *Proceedings of the National Academy of Sciences of the United States of America*, *107*, 7640–7645. doi:10.1073/pnas.0912983107

Palla, G., Vicsek, T., & Barabási, A.-L. (2007). Quantifying social group evolution. *Nature*, *435*, 814–818. doi:10.1038/nature03607

Palla, G., Derényi, I., Farkas, I., & Vicsek, T. (2005). Uncovering the overlapping community structure of complex networks in nature and society. *Nature*, *435*, 814–818. doi:10.1038/nature03607

Palmonari, A., Pombeni, L., & Kirchler, E. (1992). Evolution of the self concept in adolescence and social categorization processes. *European Review of Social Psychology*, *3*, 287–308. doi:10.1080/14792779243000096

Panait, L., & Luke, S. (2005). Cooperative multi-agent learning: The state of the art. *Autonomous Agents and Multi-Agent Systems*, *11*(3), 387–434. doi:10.1007/s10458-005-2631-2

Papagiannidis, S., Bourlarkis, M., & Li, F. (2008). Making Real Money in Virtual Worlds: MMORPGs and Emerging Business Opportunities, Challenges and Ethical Implications in Metaverses. *Technological Forecasting and Social Change*, *75*, 610–622. doi:10.1016/j.techfore.2007.04.007

Parr, R., & Russell, S. (1997). Reinforcement learning with hierarchies of machines. In *Proceedings of Advances in Neural Information Processing Systems, 10*.

Parunak, H., & Van Dyke, H. (1977) "Go to the Ant": Engineering principles from natural multi-agent systems. In *Annals of Operations Research*, Special Issue on Artificial Intelligence and Management Science, 75, 69-101.

Parunak, H., Van Dyke, H., & Brueckner, S. (2001). Entropy and self-organization in multi-agent systems. Paper presented to Agents'01, May 28-June 1, 2001, Montreal Quebec, Canada.

Pasquier, P., & Chaib-draa, B. (2003). The cognitive coherence approach for agent communication pragmatics. In *Aamas* (pp. 544–551). ACM. Available from http://doi.acm.org/10.1145/860575.860662

Pavlidis, N., Tasoulis, D., Plagianakos, V., Siriopoulos, C., & Vrahatis, M. (2005). Computational intelligence methods for financial forecasting. *Lecture Series on Computer and Computational Sciences*, *1*, 1–4.

Penman, S. (2003). *Financial Statement Analysis and Security Valuation* (2nd ed.). New York: McGraw-Hill/Irwin.

Penner, L. A., Dovidio, J. F., Piliavin, J. A., & Schroeder, D. A. (2005). Prosocial behavior: Multilevel perspectives. *Annual Review of Psychology*, *56*, 365–392. doi:10.1146/annurev.psych.56.091103.070141

Phung, T., Winikoff, M., & Padgham, L. (2005). Learning within the BDI framework: An empirical analysis. In *Proceedings of the 9th international conference on knowledge-based intelligent information and engineering systems (KES'05), LNAI volume 3683* (p. 282). Melbourne, Australia: Springer Verlag.

Piaget, J. (1973). *The Child's Conception of the World*. London: Paladin.

Pike, K. L. (1954). Emic and etic standpoints for the description of behavior. In K.L. Pike (Ed.), *Language in relation to a unified theory of the structure of human behavior. Part I,* 8-28. Glendale California: Summer Institute of Linguistics.

Piskurich, G. (2002). *HPI essentials*. Alexandria, VA: American Society of Training and Development.

Platt, G. (2009). *Smart agents: an intelligent way to manage and control energy*. http://www.csiro.au/science/SmartAgents.html

Plutchik, R. (1994). *The psychology and biology of emotion*. New York: HarperCollins.

Polhill, J. G., Parker, D., Brown, D., & Grimm, V. (2008). Using the ODD Protocol for Describing Three Agent-Based Social Simulation Models of Land-Use Change. *Journal of Artificial Societies and Social Simulation, 11*(2), 3.

Pollner, P., Palla, G., & Vicsek, T. (2006). Preferential attachment of communities: The same principle, but a higher level. *Europhysics Letters, 73,* 478–484. doi:10.1209/epl/i2005-10414-6

Port, R., & Van Gelder, T. (1995). *Mind as motion: Explorations in the dynamics of cognition*. Cambridge, MA: MIT Press.

Posner, E. (2000). *Law and social norms*. Cambridge, MA: Harvard University Press.

Powers, R., & Shoham, Y. (2005). New criteria and a new algorithm for learning in multi-agent systems. In *Proceedings of NIPS*.

Prasad, H. (1991). *Essays on time in Buddhism*. Delhi: Sri Satguru Publications.

Prasad, J. Discussion of the Buddhist doctrine of momentariness and subjective idealism in the Nyaya-stras. In Prasad, H. (1991).

Premack, D. G., & Woodruff, G. (1978). Does the chimpanzee have a theory of mind? *The Behavioral and Brain Sciences, 1,* 515–526. doi:10.1017/S0140525X00076512

Prendinger, H., Becker, C., & Ishizuka, M. (2006). A study in users' physiological response to an empathic interface agent. *International Journal of Humanoid Robotics, 3*(3), 371–391. doi:10.1142/S0219843606000801

Preston, S. D., & de Waal, F. B. M. (2002). Empathy: Its ultimate and proximate bases. *The Behavioral and Brain Sciences, 25,* 1–72.

Prokopenko, M., Zeman, A., Guo, Y., & Li, R. (2007). *Hierarchy-based aggregation studies*. Technical Report, CSIRO, September.

Quinlan, R. J. (1986). Induction of decision trees. *Machine Learning, 1,* 81–106. doi:10.1007/BF00116251

Quinlan, J. (1990). Learning logical definitions from relations. *Machine Learning, 5*(3), 239–266. doi:10.1007/BF00117105

Quinlan, J. (1993). *C4.5: Programs for Machine Learning*. San Fransico, CA: Morgan Kaufmann.

Radicchi, F., Castellano, C., Cecconi, C., Loreto, V., & Parisi, D. (2004). Defining and identifying communities in networks. *Proceedings of the National Academy of Sciences of the United States of America, 101,* 2658–2663. doi:10.1073/pnas.0400054101

Randløv, J. (2001). *Solving Complex Problems with Reinforcement Learning*. PhD thesis, University of Copenhagen.

Rao, A. S., & Georgeff, M. P. (1992). An abstract architecture for rational agents. In *Proceedings of the third international conference on principles of knowledge representation and reasoning* (KR'92) (p. 439-449). San Mateo, CA, USA.

Ravasz, E., Somera, A. L., Mongru, D. A., Oltvai, Z. N., & Barabási, A.-L. (2002). Hierarchical organization of modularity in metabolic networks. *Science, 297,* 1551–1555. doi:10.1126/science.1073374

Reichenbach, H. (1956). *The direction of time*. New York, NY: Dover.

Reichenbach, H. (1958). *The philosophy of space and time*. New York, NY: Dover.

Reynolds, J. M., & Hancock, D. R. (2010). Problem-based learning in a higher education environmental biotechnology course. *Innovations in Education and Teaching International, 47*(2), 175–186. doi:10.1080/14703291003718919

Richardson, K. (1975). The Hegemony of the Physical Sciences: An Exploration in Complexity Thinking. *Futures, 37*, 615–653. doi:10.1016/j.futures.2004.11.008

Richardson, M., & Domingos, P. (2006). Markov Logic Networks. *Machine Learning, 62*, 107–136. doi:10.1007/s10994-006-5833-1

Richardson, K. A. (2002). *On the Limits of Bottom Up Computer Simulation: Towards a Non-linear Modeling Culture.* Paper presented at the 36th Hawaii International Conference on Systems Science, Hawaii.

Riedmiller, M. (2005). Neural fitted Q iteration - first experiences with a data efficient neural reinforcement learning method. In *Proceedings of the European Conference on Machine Learning,* (pp. 317-328).

Rieger, A. (1995). Data preparation for inductive learning in robotics. In Working Notes of the IJCAI Workshop on Data Engineering for Inductive Learning.

Riis, S. (2007). Graph Entropy, Network Coding and Guessing games. arXiv:0711.4175v1 [math.CO]

Rizzolatti, G., Fadiga, L., Gallese, V., & Fogassi, L. (1996). Premotor cortex and the recognition of motor actions. *Brain Research. Cognitive Brain Research, 3*(2), 131–141. doi:10.1016/0926-6410(95)00038-0

Robins, G., Snijders, T., Wang, P., Handcock, M., & Pattison, P. (2007). Recent developments in exponential random graph (p*) models for social networks. *Social Networks, 29*, 192–215. doi:10.1016/j.socnet.2006.08.003

Rodrigues, D. M. S. (2009). *Detecção de Comunidades no Sistema de Correio electrónico Unviesritário.* Lisboa: ISCTE - Instituto Superior de Ciências do Trabalho e da Empresa.

Rodrigues, D. M. S., & Louçã, J. (2009). *Mutual information to assess structural properties in dynamic networks.* Paper presented at the European Conference on Complex Systems, Warwick.

Rossi, M. A. (April, 2004). *Decoding the "Free/Open Source (F/OSS) Puzzle" - a Survey of Theretical and Empirical Contributions.* Unpublished Working paper. University of Sienna.

Rosvall, M., & Bergstrom, C. T. (2010). Mapping Change in Large Networks. *PLoS ONE, 5*, e8694. doi:10.1371/journal.pone.0008694

Rubin, D. C., Rahhal, T. A., & Poon, L. W. (1998). Things learned in early adulthood are remembered best. *Memory & Cognition, 26*(1), 3–19.

Rumelhart, D., Hinton, G., & Williams, R. (1986). Learning internal representations by error propagation. In Rumelhart, D., & McClelland, J. (Eds.), *Parallel distributed processing (Vol. 1).* Cambridge, MA: MIT Press.

Russel, S., & Norvig, P. (2002). *AI: The Modern Approach.* Pearson Education, Inc.

Salovey, P., & Mayer, J. D. (1990). Emotional Intelligence. *Imagination, Cognition and Personality, 9*, 185–211.

Sammut, C., & Banerji, R. (1986). Learning concepts by asking questions. Machine Learning: An Artificial Intelligence Aproach, II, 167-191, Morgan-Kaufmann, San Mateo, CA.

Sanger, L. (2006a). The Nupedia myth [Electronic Version]. *ZDNet.com* from http://talkback.zdnet.com/5208-10535-0.html?forumID=1&threadID=22228&messageID=422549&start=-39.

Sanger, L. (2006b). *Why Make room for experts in web 2 [Electronic Version].* Retrieved 12 April 2007 from http://www.citizendium.org/roomforexperts.html.

Sanger, L. (2007a). The Early History of Nupedia and Wikipedia: A Memoir [Electronic Version]. *Slashdot.* Retrieved 12 April 2007 from file:///C:/data/surrey/Case%20Studies/wikipedia/early%20history%20of%20nupedia%20and%20wikipedia.htm.

Sanger, L. (2007b). *Why the Citizendium Will (probably) succeed* [Electronic Version]. Retrieved 13 April 2007 from http://www.citizendium.org/whyczwillsucceed.html.

Sardina, S., de Silva, L. P., & Padgham, L. (2006). Hierarchical planning in BDI agent programming languages: A formal approach. In *Proceedings of autonomous agents and multi-agent systems (AAMAS'06)* (pp. 1001–1008). Hakodate, Japan.

Savin-Baden, M. (2000). *Problem-based learning in higher education: untold stories*. Philadelphia: SRHE and Open University Press.

Savin-Baden, M. (2010). Situating pedagogies, positions and practices in immersive worlds. *Educational Research, 52*(2), 123–133. doi:10.1080/00131881.2010.482732

Sawyer, K. (2001). Emergence in Sociology. *American Journal of Sociology, 107*(3), 551–586. doi:10.1086/338780

Sawyer, K. R. (2003). Artificial Societies: Multiagent Systems and the Micro-macro Link in Sociological Theory. *Sociological Methods & Research, 31*, 38. doi:10.1177/0049124102239079

Sawyer, K. R. (2005). *Social Emergence: Societies as Complex Systems*. Cambridge, UK: Cambridge University Press. doi:10.1017/CBO9780511734892

Schapire, R. (1990). The Strength of Weak Learnability. *Machine Learning, 5*(2), 197–227. doi:10.1007/BF00116037

Schaub, H. (1999). Die Person als Synergieeffekt. Persönlichkeit als Ergebnis der Interaktion basaler Informationsverarbeitungsprozesse. Presentation at *the 8. Herbstakademie „Selbstorganisation in Psychologie und Sozialwissenschaften"* 27.-29.9.1999 in Jena, Germany.

Schelling, T. C. (1960). *The strategy of conflict*. Havard University Press.

Schilling, R. (2006, October 12–15). A project to develop a distributed, multi-agent communication architecture using message feedback. In *Interaction and emergent phenomena in societies of agents* (pp. 96–103). Menlo Park, CA: The American Association for Artificial Intelligence.

Schlimgen, R. (2010). Virtual World, Real Taxes: A Sales and Use Tax Adventure Through Second Life Starring Dwight Schrute. *Journal of Law. Science & Technology, 11*(2), 877–899.

Schmidt-Schauss, M. (1988). Implication of clauses is undecidable. *Theoretical Computer Science, 59*, 287–296. doi:10.1016/0304-3975(88)90146-6

Scott, J. (2000). Social Network Analysis: A Handbook. London: Sage Publications. Social Network

Searle, J. R. (1969). *Speech Act: An Essay in the Philosophy of Language*. Cambridge, UK: Cambridge University Press.

Second Life News Center. (2008). *UPDATE 3 - Linden bans Second Life banks*. Retrieved August 8, 2010 from http://secondlife.reuters.com/stories/2008/01/08/breaking-linden-bans-second-life-banks/index.html

Second Life-Terms of Service. (2010). *Second Life, Terms of Service*. Retrieved July 29, 2010 from http://secondlife.com/corporate/tos.php?lang=fr-FR.

Sen, S., & Airiau, S. (2007, January). Emergence of norms through social learning. In *Proceedings of the twentieth international joint conference on artificial intelligence (ijcai'07)* (pp. 1507–1512). Menlo Park, Ca: AAAI Press.

Šešelja, B., & Tepavčević, A. (1995). Partially Ordered and Relational Valued Fuzzy Relations I. *Fuzzy Sets and Systems, 72*, 205–213. doi:10.1016/0165-0114(94)00352-8

Shamah, S. (2003). *A Foreign Exchange Primer*. West Sussex, UK: Wiley Finance.

Shannon, C. (1948). A Mathematical Theory of Communication. *Bell System Technical Journal, Bell Laboratories, 27*, 379-423, 623-656.

Shapiro, E. Y. (1983). *Algorithmic program debugging*. MIT Press.

Sherstov, A. A., & Stone, P. (2005). Function approximation via tile coding: Automating parameter choice. *In Symposium on Abstraction, Reformulation, and Approximation*, (pp. 194-205).

Shiffrin, R. M., & Börner, K. (2004). Mapping knowledge domains. *Proceedings of the National Academy of Sciences of the United States of America, 101*, 5183–5185. doi:10.1073/pnas.0307852100

Shneiderman, B. Plaisant, C. (2005) Designing the user interface. *Strategies for effective human-computer Interaction 4th edition*. University of Maryland, College Park. Addison Wesley. 2005.

Shoham, Y., & Leyton-Brown, K. (2009). *Multiagent Systems – Algorithmic, Game-theoretic, and Logical Foundations*. US: Cambridge University Press

Shortreed, S. (2006). *Learning in Spectral Clustering.*

Simon, H. (2005). Foreword. In *Callebaut, W. & Rasskin-Gutman, D. Modularity: Understanding the development and evolution of natural complex systems*. Boston: MIT Press.

Simonyi, G. (1995). Graph entropy. In L. L. W. Cook & P. Seymour (Eds.), *Combinatorial Optimization, vol 20 of DIMACS Series on Discrete Mathematics and Computer Science* (pp. 391-441).

Singh, S. P., & Sutton, R. S. (1996). Reinforcement learning with replacing eligibility traces. *Machine Learning, 22*(1-3), 123–158. doi:10.1007/BF00114726

Singh, S., & Fieldsend, J. (2001). Pattern matching and neural networks based hybrid forecasting system. *Advances in Pattern Recognition - ICAPR 2001*, pp. 72-82.

Smith, D. M. D., Onnela, J.-P., & Johnson, N. F. (2007). Accelerating networks. *New Journal of Physics, 9*, 181. doi:10.1088/1367-2630/9/6/181

Smith, G. (2005). Problem-based learning: can it improve managerial thinking. *Journal of Management Education, 29*, 357–378. doi:10.1177/1052562904269642

Smith, S. Mosier, J. (1986) Guidelines for Designing User Interface Software, Report ESD-TR-86-278, Electronic Systems Division, MITRE Corporation, Bedford, MA. Available from National Technical Information Service, Springfield, VA.

Smolin, L. (2001). *Three roads to quantum gravity*. New York, NY: Basic Books.

Sollich, P., & Krogh, A. (1996). Learning with Ensembles: How over-fitting can be useful. *Advances in Neural Information Processing Systems, 8*, 190–196.

Solomon, R. C. (1984). Getting angry: The Jamesian theory of emotion in anthropology. In Shweder, R. A., & LeVine, R. A. (Eds.), *Culture theory: Essays on mind, self, and emotion* (pp. 238–254). Cambridge: Cambridge University Press.

Šostak, A. (1997). Fuzzy categories versus categories of fuzzily structured sets: Elements of the theory of fuzzy categories. Mathematik-Arbeitspapiere. *Categorical Methods in Algebra and Topology, 48*, 407–439.

Spirin, V., & Mirny, K. A. (2003). Protein complexes and functional modules in molecular networks. *Proceedings of the National Academy of Sciences of the United States of America, 100*, 12123–12128. doi:10.1073/pnas.2032324100

Stake, R. (1995). *The art of case study research*. Thousand Oaks, CA: Sage Publications.

Stanley, E. H. (2000). Exotic Statistical Physics: Applications to Biology, Medicine, and Economics. *Physica A, 285*, 1–17. doi:10.1016/S0378-4371(00)00341-1

Stauffer, D., & Aharony, A. (1994). *Introduction To Percolation Theory* (1 ed.): CRC.

Stcherbatsky, T. The theory of instantaneous being. In Prasad, H. (1991).

Stewart, I. (2001). *Flatterland*. Cambridge: Perseus.

Stiles, W. B. (1992). *Describing Talk: A Taxonomy of Verbal Response Modes*. Thousand Oaks, CA: Sage.

Stojanov, G., Božinovski, S., & Trajkovski, G. (1997). Interactionist-Expectative View on Agency and Learning. *IMACS Journal of Mathematics and Computers in Simulation, 44*, 295–310. doi:10.1016/S0378-4754(97)00057-8

Stojanov, G., Trajkovski, G., & Božinovski, S. (1997). *The Status of Representation in Behavior Based Robotic Systems: The Problem and a Solution, Proc* (pp. 773–777). Orlando, FL: Systems, Man and Cybernetics.

Stojanov, G., & Kulakov, A. (2006). On Curiosity in Intelligent Robotic Systems. AAAI Fall Symposia, Arlington, VA, USA, October 12-15.

Stojanov, G., Stefanovski, S., & Božinovski, S. (1995), Expectancy Based Emergent Environment Models for Autonomous Agents. Proc 5th International Symposium on Automatic Control and Computer Science, Iasi, Romania.

Stone, P., Sutton, R. S., & Kuhlmann, G. (2005). Reinforcement learning for RoboCup-soccer keepaway. *Adaptive Behavior*, *13*(3), 165–188. doi:10.1177/105971230501300301

Stone, P., & Veloso, M. (2000). Layered learning. *In Proceedings of the 11th European Conference on Machine Learning.*

Stvilia, B., Twidale, M. B., Gasser, L., & Smith, L. C. (2005). *Information Quality Discussions in Wikipedia.* Illinois: Graduate School of Library and Information Science.

Summers, P. D. (1975). Program construction from examples. PhD thesis, Yale University, New Haven, CT.

Sutton, R. S. (1996). Generalization in reinforcement learning: Successful examples using sparse coarse coding. *Advances in Neural Information Processing Systems*, *8*, 1038–1044.

Sutton, R. S., & Barto, A. G. (1998). *Reinforcement Learning: An Introduction.* Cambridge, MA: MIT Press.

Sutton, R. S., Precup, D., & Singh, S. P. (1999). Between MDPs and Semi-MDPs: A framework for temporal abstraction in reinforcement learning. *Artificial Intelligence*, *112*(1-2), 181–211. doi:10.1016/S0004-3702(99)00052-1

Sutton, R. S., & Barto, A. G. (1998). *Introduction to reinforcement learning.* Cambridge, MA: MIT Press.

Sutton, R. S. (1984). Temporal credit assignment in reinforcement learning. PhD thesis, Department of Computer Science, University of Massachusetts, Amherst.

Swanson, R., & Holton, E. (1997). *Human resource development research handbook –linking research and practice.* San Francisco: Berrett-Koehler Publishers.

Swere, E., Mulvaney, D., & Sillitoe, I. (2006). A fast memory-efficient incremental decision tree algorithm in its application to mobile robot navigation. In *Proceedings of the 2006 IEEE/RSJ international conference on intelligent robots and systems* (pp. 645–650).

Swingler, K. (1994). Financial prediction: some pointers, pitfalls and common errors. *Neural Computing & Applications*, *4*(4), 192–197. doi:10.1007/BF01413817

Symons, J., Louçã, J., Morais, A., & Rodrigues, D. (2007, November 9--11, 2007). *Detecting emergence in the interplay of networks in AAAI Technical Report FS-07-04*, Arlington, Virginia.

Szepesvari, C. (2009). *Reinforcement learning algorithms for MDPs.* Technical Report TR09-13, Department of Computing Science, University of Alberta.

Taleb, N. (2007). *The Black Swan: The Impact of the Highly Improbable.* New York: Random House.

Tanahashi, K. (1985). *Moon in a dewdrop: Writings of Zen master Dogen.* San Francisco: North Point.

Tay, F., & Cao, L. (2001). Application of support vector machines in financial time series forecasting. *Omega*, *29*(4), 309–317. doi:10.1016/S0305-0483(01)00026-3

Tepavčević, A., & Trajkovski, G. (2001). L-fuzzy Lattices: An Introduction. *Fuzzy Sets and Systems*, *123*, 209–216. doi:10.1016/S0165-0114(00)00065-8

Terras, A. (1999). *Fourier analysis on finite groups and applications. London Mathematical Society Student Texts, 43.* Cambridge, UK: Cambridge University Press. doi:10.1017/CBO9780511626265

Tesauro, G. (1992). Practical issues in temporal difference learning. *Machine Learning*, *8*, 257–277. doi:10.1007/BF00992697

Therborn, G. (2002). Back to Norms! On the Scope and Dynamics of Norms and Normative Action. *Current Sociology*, *50*(6), 17. doi:10.1177/0011392102050006006

Tolman, E. C. (1932). *Purposive Behavior in Animals and Men.* New York: Appleton-Century –Crofts.

Tolman, E. C. (1948). Cognitive Maps in Rats and Men. *Psychological Review, 55*, 189–208. doi:10.1037/h0061626

Tolman, E. C., & Honzik, C. H. (1930). 'Insight' in Rats. *University of California Publications in Psychology, 4*, 215–232.

Tomasello, M. (1999). *The Cultural Origins of Human Cognition*. Harvard University Press.

Tooley, M. (1997). *Time, tense and causation*. Oxford: Clarendon Press.

Trajkovski, G., & Collins, S. (2007). (in press). Autochthony through Self-Organization:Interactivism and Emergence in a Virtual Environment. *New Ideas in Psychology*.

Trajkovski, G. (2007). *An Imitation-Based Approach to Modeling Homogenous Agent Societies*. Hershey, PA: Idea Group Publishing.

Trajkovski, G. (2002). MASIVE: A Case Study in Multiagent Systems. In Engineering, I. D., & Leaning, A. (Eds.), *Yin, H., Allison, N., Freeman, R., Keane, J., Hubbard, S* (pp. 249–254). Springer Verlag.

Trajkovski, G., & Stojanov, G. (1998). Algebraic Formalization of Environment Representation. In Tatai, G., & Gulyas, L. (Eds.), *Agents Everywhere* (pp. 59–65). Budapest: Springer.

Trajkovski, G., & Conover, A. (2007). On a Software Platform for MASIVE Simulations. In Trajkovski, G. (Ed.), *An Imitation-based approach to modeling homogenous agents societies* (pp. 136–166). Hershey: Idea Group.

Trajkovski, G. (1997), Fuzzy Relations and Fuzzy Lattices. MSc Thesis. SS Cyril and Methodius University, Skopje, Macedonia.

Trajkovski, G. (1998), An approach towards defining L-fuzzy lattices. Proc. NAFIPS'98, Pensacola Beach, FL, 221-225.

Trajkovski, G. (2003), Environment Rrepresentation in Multiagent Systems, PhD Thesis, SS Cyril and Methodius University, Skopje, Macedonia.

Trajkovski, G. Collins, S. Braman, J. Goldberg, M. (2006) *Coupling Human and Non-Human Agents.* The AAAI Fall Symposium: Interaction and Emergent Phenomena in Societies of Agents. Arlington, VA.f

Trajkovski, G., & Vincenti, G. (2005), A Fuzzy Framework for Modelling Multiagent Societies, Proc NAFIPS 2005, Ann Arbor, MI.

Triandis, H. C., & Suh, E. M. (2002). Cultural influences on personality. *Annual Review of Psychology, 53*, 133–160. doi:10.1146/annurev.psych.53.100901.135200

Tumer, K., & Wolpert, D. H. (2000). Collective intelligence and Braess' paradox. In *Proceedings of the seventeenth national conference on artificial intelligence* (p. 104-109). Menlo Park, CA: AAAI Press.

Tuyls, K., & Nowé, A. (2006). Evolutionary game theory and multi-agent reinforcement learning. *The Knowledge Engineering Review, 20*(1), 63–90. doi:10.1017/S026988890500041X

Tuyls, K., & Nowé, A. (2006, March). Evolutionary game theory and multi-agent reinforcement learning. *The Knowledge Engineering Review, 20*(1), 63–90. doi:10.1017/S026988890500041X

Tyler, V. (1995). *Metapatterns: Across space, time, and mind*. New York, NY: Columbia University Press.

Tyler, J. R., Wilkinson, D. M., & Huberman, B. A. (2003). Email as spectroscopy: automated discovery of community structure within organizations (pp. 81-96), Kluwer, B.V.

Utgoff, P. E., Berkman, N. C., & Clouse, J. A. (1997). Decision tree induction based on efficient tree restructuring. *Machine Learning, 29*(1), 5–44. doi:10.1023/A:1007413323501

Valiant, L. G. (1984). A theory of the learnable. *Communications of the ACM, 27*, 1134–1142. doi:10.1145/1968.1972

Vardi, I., & Ciccarelli, M. (2008). Overcoming problems in problem-based learning: a trial of strategies in an undergraduate unit. *Innovations in Education and Teaching International, 45*(4), 345–354. doi:10.1080/14703290802377190

Varela, F., Thompson, E., & Rosch, E. (1991). *The Embodied Mind*. Cambridge: MIT Press.

Varela, F. J. (1999). The specious present: a neurophenomenology of time consciousness. In Petitot, J., Varela, F. J., Pachoud, B., & Roy, J.-M. (Eds.), *Naturalizing Phenomenology: Issues in Contemporary Phenomenology and Cognitive Science* (pp. 266–314). Stanford: Stanford University Press.

Vazquez, F., Gonzalez-Avella, J. C., Eguiluz, V. M., & San Miguel, M. (2007). Time-scale competition leading to fragmentation and recombination transitions in the coevolution of network and states. *Physical Review E: Statistical, Nonlinear, and Soft Matter Physics, 76*, 046120. doi:10.1103/PhysRevE.76.046120

Vázquez-Salceda, J., Aldewereld, H., & Dignum, F. (2005). Norms in multiagent systems: From theory to practice. *International Journal of Computer Systems & Engineering, 20*(4), 225–236.

Vedral, V. (2001). The role of relative entropy in quantum information theory. *Reviews of Modern Physics, 74*(1), 197–234. doi:10.1103/RevModPhys.74.197

Vedres, B., & Stark, D. (2010). Structural Folds: Generative Disruption in Overlapping Groups. *American Journal of Sociology, 115*, 1150–1190. doi:10.1086/649497

Victoria, E. (1997). The Use of temporal constructs as a model for understanding perceptions of environmental hazards. Dissertation, Department of Sociology, University of Nevada, Las Vegas.

Vilela Mendes, R., Araújo, T., & Louçã, F. (2003). Reconstructing an Economic Space from a Market Metric. *Physica A, 323*, 635–650. doi:10.1016/S0378-4371(03)00014-1

Voelcke, J. (2007, November). Autonomous Vehicles Complete DARPA Urban Challenge. IEEE Spectrum.

von Luxburg, U. (2007). A Tutorial on Spectral Clustering. *Statistics and Computing, 17*(4), 395–416. doi:10.1007/s11222-007-9033-z

von Neumann, J. (1955). *Mathematical Foundations of Quantum Mechanics*. Princeton, NJ: Princeton University Press.

von Neumann, J. (1956). Probabilistic logics and the synthesis of reliable organisms from unreliable components. In S.E. McCarthy (Eds.), *Automata Studies*. Princeton: University Press.

Wang, P., González, M. C., Hidalgo, C. A., & Barabási, A.-L. (2009). Understanding the Spreading Patterns of Mobile Phone Viruses. *Science, 324*, 1071–1076. doi:10.1126/science.1167053

Warner, S. (2003). E-prints and the Open Archives Initiative. *Library Hi Tech, 21*, 151–158. doi:10.1108/07378830310479794

Wasserman, S., & Faust, K. (1994). *Social Network Analysis: Methods and Applications*. UK: Cambridge University Press.

Watkins, C., & Dayan, P. (1992). Q-learning. *Machine Learning, 8*(33), 279–292. doi:10.1007/BF00992698

Watts, D. J., Dodds, P. S., & Newman, M. E. J. (2002). Identity and search in social networks. *Science, 296*, 1302–1305. doi:10.1126/science.1070120

Watts, D. J., & Strogatz, S. H. (1998). Collective dynamics of 'small-world' networks. *Nature, 393*, 440–442. doi:10.1038/30918

Weigend, A., & Gershenfeld, N. (1993). *Time series prediction: forecasting the future and understanding the past*. Boulder, CO: Westview Press.

Weiss, G. (2000). *Multiagent systems a modern approach to distributed artificial intelligence*. Cambridge MA USA: The MIT Press.

Weka, A. P. I. (n.d.). Retrieved from http://www.cs.waikato.ac.nz/ml/weka/.

Wertheim, M. (1999). *The pearly gates: A history of space from Dante to the Internet*. New York: Norton.

Westenholz, A. (2006). Identity, time, and work. *Time & Society, 15*, 1. doi:10.1177/0961463X06061349

Wetzler, S. E., & Sweeney, J. A. (1986). Childhood amnesia: An empirical demonstration. In Rubin, D. C. (Ed.), *Autobiographical memory* (pp. 202–221). Cambridge, UK: Cambridge University Press.

White, H. C., Boorman, S. A., & Breiger, R. R. (1976). Social structure from multiple networks. I. Blockmodels of roles and positions. *American Journal of Sociology, 81*, 730–780. doi:10.1086/226141

Widrow, B., & Lehr, M. A. (1990). 30 years of adaptive neural networks: perceptron, Madaline, and backpropagation. *Proceedings of the IEEE, 78*(9), 1415–1442. doi:10.1109/5.58323

Wiewiora, E. (2003). Potential-based shaping and Q-value initialisation are equivalent. *Journal of Artificial Intelligence Research, 19*, 205–208.

Wiki Second Life. (2010). *Second Life*. Retrieved August 8, 2010 from http://wiki.secondlife.com/wiki/History_of_Second_Life

Wilensky, U. (1999). NetLogo 3.1.2 User Manual: http://ccl.northwestern.edu/netlogo/. Center for Connected Learning and Computer-Based Modeling, Northwestern University, Evanston, IL.

Williamson, O. E. (1996). *The Mechanisms of Governance*. New York: Oxford University Press.

Williamson, O. E., & Winter, S. G. (1993). *The Nature of The Firm: Origins, Evolution and Development*. New York: Oxford University Press.

Wilson, B., & Deck, C. A. (2002). The effectiveness of low price matching in mitigating the competitive pressure of low friction electronic markets. *Electronic Commerce Research, 2*(4).

Wilson, B., Rassenti, S. J., & Smith, V. L. (2003). Controlling market power and price spikes in electricity networks, demand-side bidding. *Proceedings of the National Academy of Sciences of the United States of America, 100*(5).

Winfree, A. (1980). *The geometry of biological time*. New York: Springer-Verlag.

Witten, I., & Frank, E. (2005). *Data Mining: Practical machine learning tools and techniques* (2nd ed.). San Francisco, CA: Morgan Kaufmann.

Wolpert, D. (1992). Stacked generalization. *Neural Networks, 5*(2), 241–259. doi:10.1016/S0893-6080(05)80023-1

Wooldridge, M. (2002). *An Introduction to Multiagent Systems*. Chichester: John Willey & Sons.

World Intellectual Property Organization. (n.d.). Retrieved from http://www.wipo.int/portal/index.html.en. Accessed July 28, 2010.

Wyer, R. Jr, & Srull, T. (1989). *Memory and Cognition in its Social Context*. Hillsdale, New Jersey: Lawrence Erlhaum.

Yamaguchi, H. (2004). An Analysis of Virtual Currencies in Online Games. *Social Science Research Network*. Retrieved July 29, 2010 from http://papers.ssrn.com/sol3/papers.cfm?abstract_id=544422

Yao, J., & Tan, C. (2000). A case study on using neural networks to perform technical forecasting of Forex. *Neurocomputing, 34*(1), 79–98. doi:10.1016/S0925-2312(00)00300-3

Ygge, F. (1998). *Market-oriented programming and its application to power load management*, Ph.D. Thesis. Lund University.

Yin, R. K. (2003). *Case Study Research Design and Methods*. Thousand Oaks, CA: Sage Publications.

Young, P. H. (1993, January). The evolution of conventions. *Econometrica, 61*(1), 57–84. doi:10.2307/2951778

Young, P. H. (1996). The economics of convention. *The Journal of Economic Perspectives, 10*(2), 105–122.

Young, T. (1991). Calmar Ratio: A Smoother Tool. *Futures, 20*, 40.

Young, P. T. (1936). *Motivation of behavior*. New York: John Wiley & Sons.

Young, H. P. (2008). Social norms. In Durlauf, S. N., & Blume, L. E. (Eds.), *The new palgrave dictionary of economics* (2nd ed.). London: Macmillan. doi:10.1057/9780230226203.1563

Yu, L., Lai, K., & Wang, S. (2005). Designing a hybrid AI system as a Forex trading decision support tool. *Proceedings of the 17th IEEE International Conference on Tools with Artificial Intelligence*, pp. 89-93.

Zeman, A., Prokopenko, M., Guo, Y., & Li, R. (2008). Adaptive Control of Distributed Energy Management: A Comparative Study. *Second IEEE International Conference on Self-Adaptive and Self-Organizing Systems (SASO)*, Italy.

Zheng, Y., Luo, S., & Lv, Z. (2006). Control double inverted pendulum by reinforcement learning with double CMAC network. *In The 18th International Conference on Pattern Recognition,* (pp. 639-642). IEEE Computer Society.

Zimitat, C. (2007). Capturing community of practice knowledge for student learning. *Innovations in Education and Teaching International, 44*(3), 321–330. doi:10.1080/14703290701486753

Zlatic, V., Ghoshal, G., & Caldarelli, G. (2009). Hypergraph topological quantities for tagged social networks. *Phys. Rew. E, 80*, 036118. doi:10.1103/PhysRevE.80.036118

About the Contributors

Goran Trajkovski is the founding Editor-in-chief of the *International Journal of Agent Technologies and Systems*. He is a partner and the CEO of Algoco eLearning Consulting, and the VP for Business Development for the Americas at Kreofina. He is now the Dean of the School of Computer Information Systems and the Director of Online Education at Virginia International University in Fairfax, VA, USA. In the past, he has served as faculty at different institutions, as well as the Director of Product Strategy and Development at Laureate Education, Inc., and the Chair of the Department of Information Technologies at the Education Management Corporation (EDMC)/South University, USA. In 2003, he founded the Cognitive Agency and Robotics Laboratory (CARoL) at Towson University, Towson, MD, USA. Dr. Trajkovski's research focuses on cognitive and developmental robotics, and interaction and emergent phenomena in societies of agents. He is an affiliate of the Institute for Interactivist Studies at Lehigh University, and a member of the organizing committee of the biannual Interactivist Summer Institutes. He has authored over 300 publications, including twelve books and edited volumes. He has chaired two symposia for the Association for Advancement of Artificial Intelligence. His work has been funded by NSF, the National Academies of the Sciences, and OWASP (Open Web Application Security Project). Dr Trajkovski hold a BSc in Applied Informatics, MSc in Mathematical and Computer Sciences, and PhD in Computing Sciences from the University "SS Cyril and Methodius," Skopje, Macedonia.

* * *

Stephane Airiau is a postdoc fellow at the Institute for Logic, Language, and Computation at the University of Amsterdam, Netherlands. He is working on collective decision making in combinatorial domains. He obtained his engineering degree from ENSEEIHT, Toulouse (France) in 2001, his MSc and PhD from the University of Tulsa (Oklahoma, USA) in 2007. His dissertation addresses issues of payoff distribution and fairness in coalition formation. He visited RMIT University in Melbourne where he worked on incorporating learning in BDI agents. Stéphane's interests include learning, cooperation and fairness in multiagent systems.

Rui Pedro Barbosa is a software and systems engineer currently pursuing a Ph.D. at University of Minho, Portugal. He previously worked at IBM's Silicon Valley Laboratory in San Jose, USA, and at the market maker Saen Options in Amsterdam, The Netherlands. His main field of research is applied artificial intelligence in quantitative and algorithmic trading.

Orlando Belo is an associate professor in the Department of Informatics at Minho University, Portugal. He is also a member of the Computer Science and Technology Center in the same university,

Copyright © 2011, IGI Global. Copying or distributing in print or electronic forms without written permission of IGI Global is prohibited.

working in areas like Data Warehousing Systems, OLAP, and Data Mining. His main research topics are related with data warehouse design, implementation and tuning, ETL services, and distributed multidimensional structures processing. During the last few years he was involved with several projects in the decision support systems area designing and implementing computational platforms for specific applications like fraud detection and control in telecommunication systems, data quality evaluation, and ETL systems for industrial data warehousing systems.

James Braman is a Lecturer in the Department of Computer and Information Sciences at Towson University. He currently holds a Master's Degree in Computer Science and is pursuing a Doctoral Degree in Information Technology. James also serves as a joint editor-in-chief of the (ICST) Transactions on E-Education and E-Learning. His current research focus includes: art and technology, intelligent agents, affective computing and education in virtual and immersive environments.

Samuel Collins is Associate Professor of Anthropology at Towson University. His research includes cybernetics, information society, globalization and the future, both in the United States and in South Korea. He is the author of All Tomorrow's Cultures: Anthropological Engagements with the Future and Library of Walls: The Library of Congress and the Contradictions of Information Society.

Adam J. Conover is a Lecturer in the Department of Computer and Information Sciences at Towson University in Towson, Maryland. He currently holds B.S. and M.S. degrees in Computer Science, and a D.Sc. in Applied Information Technology. Additionally, he has nearly fifteen years of professional experience in software engineering, computer programming, web development, systems integration, and technical consulting. His research topics have ranged from object-oriented software engineering to agent and swarm simulation, including the properties of emergent systems. Current academic interests have expanded to include the use of modern "scripting" languages and interactive algorithm visualization as teaching tools for introductory programming.While not engaged in teaching or research, Adam can usually be found mountain biking, studying martial arts, rock climbing, or even playing bass guitar.

Kerstin Dautenhahn received her Ph.D. degree from the Department of Biological Cybernetics at University of Bielefeld, Germany. She is Professor of Artificial Intelligence in the School of Computer Science at University of Hertfordshire where she coordinates the Adaptive Systems Research Group. She has published more than 150 research articles on social robotics, robot learning, human-robot interaction and assistive technology. Prof. Dautenhahn has edited several books and frequently organises international research workshops and conferences including hosting the AISB05 convention and general Chair of IEEE RO-MAN 2006. Currently she is a general chair of HRI08, the 3rd ACM/IEEE International Conference on Human-Robot Interaction. She is involved in several FP6 and FP7 European projects (Cogniron, Robotcub, Iromec, eCircus, LIREC, I-Talk) and is Editor in Chief of the journal Interaction Studies: Social Behaviour and Communication in Biological and Artificial Systems.

Vladimir Eidelman is a recent graduate of Columbia University in New York City with a B.S. in Computer Science and Philosophy. He intends to begin pursuing a Ph.D. in Computer Science in the fall of 2008, with research interests in machine learning and natural language processing.

Sibylle Enz is research fellow at the Institute of Theoretical Psychology at the Bamberg University where she has been involved in the EU-funded projects VICTEC and eCIRCUS. Her scientific interests centre on empathy, problem-solving in social contexts, self-presentation and evaluation. Currently, she is also working on her PhD on the role of empathy in conflicts at the workplace.

Chris Goldspink is a Director of Incept Labs. He has seventeen years experience as a consultant to industry and government in the areas of management improvement, organizational change, and public management reform. Formerly he held senior line and staff management positions with the Australian Bureau of Statistics being variously responsible for personnel and organizational development, marketing and information services and statistical analysis and output. His career has included periods in the academy, including with the International Graduate School of Management, University of South Australia and the Centre for Research in Social Simulation at the University of Surrey. He maintains an active teaching role specializing in areas including the Australian system of government, strategy, leadership, international marketing and organizational change. Chris' research interests are with the application of complex systems concepts to understanding social and organizational change. This includes an interest in the principles and practices of social simulation. He has a PhD in Social Ecology with the University of Western Sydney.

Marek Grześ is a post-doctoral research fellow in the School of Computer Science at the University of Waterloo in Canada. He received a PhD degree in computer science from the University of York in the United Kingdom, and MSc Eng degrees, also in computer science, from Białystok Technical University in Poland. His research interests focus on simulation-based dynamic optimisation, reinforcement learning, and symbolic and decision-theoretic planning. Marek Grześ is currently working on developing intelligent, assistive systems for elderly people with dementia.

Ying Guo is currently a Senior Research Scientist in the Information Engineering Laboratory of the Information and Communication Technologies Centre (ICT Centre), the Commonwealth Scientific and Industrial Research Organisation (CSIRO) of Australia. Dr. Ying Guo received the B.E. degree in 1994 and the M.E. degree in electrical engineering in 1996, both from the Northwestern Polytechnic University, China. Dr. Guo completed a Ph.D. in machine learning at the Australian National University on November 2001. Her investigations during these years cover areas in Machine learning, Complex Systems, Intelligent Sensor Networks, Multi-Agent Systems. She has developed an innovative machine learning approach to critical damage reporting in large sensor networks. She has developed an innovative machine learning approach for distributed energy management and control. She has also proposed and implemented several innovative machine learning approaches to the design of self-assembling objects from a large number of smart agents. Her current research interests include statistical machine learning theory, data mining, analysis of machine learning algorithms, and application of machine learning algorithms in different areas, including energy management and biomedical research.

Robert J. Hammell II is an Associate Professor in the Department of Computer and Information Sciences at Towson University in Towson, Maryland; he has been with the university since the fall of 2001. He teaches graduate and undergraduate courses for the Department as well as graduate courses in the Center for Applied Information Technology. In addition to his Ph.D. in computer science, he holds a masters degree in computer systems and an undergraduate business degree.Prior to joining Towson

University, Dr. Hammell served for 22 years in the U.S. Army, retiring as a Lieutenant Colonel. For the last six years of his career he served as a Senior Computer Scientist for the U.S. Army Research Laboratory, focusing on the area of tactical intelligent systems. His current research interests include applications of soft computing techniques for machine learning, decision support systems, pattern recognition, and chemical hazard prediction.

Chris Harman is currently a senior at Swarthmore College majoring in Computer Science and minoring in Engineering. His interests include emergent systems and artificial intelligence. Chris researched under Dr. Trajkovski during the summer of 2006 through the NSF-REU program. His plans for post-college life are as yet undecided. When not studying he enjoys traveling, reading, writing, snowboarding, surfing and playing lacrosse.

Wan Ching Ho received his first BSc and PhD degrees from University of Hertfordshire in year 2002 and 2005 respectively. The title of his PhD thesis is Computational Memory Architectures for Autobiographic and Narrative Virtual Agents. He is now working as a full-time postdoc research fellow in the Adaptive Systems Research Group in the same university. His research mainly focuses on developing control architectures for narrative and autobiographic virtual agents for an EU Framework 6 funded project eCircus (Education through Characters with emotional-Intelligence and Role-playing Capabilities that Understand Social interaction). Wan Ching Ho's research interests are interdisciplinary, including: applying theories from Cognitive Science and Psychology to computational agent control architectures, developing narrative and autobiographic agents for educational software and computer games. The common aim of these is to increase the agents' believability and the interactivity of the software application.

Gus Koehler is a President and cofounder of Time Structures, and an Adjunct Faculty in the School of Policy, Planning and Development, at the State Capital Center, University of Southern California. Time Structures is a consulting and research firm that focuses on temporal issues associated with technology, business, and government policy development and implementation. Dr. Koehler provides technical consultation to the California Economic Development Strategy Panel, the California Council on Science and Technology, California Space Authority, California Community Colleges, and the California Redevelopment Association. He is currently a member of the Council of Economic Advisors to the Workforce Investment Board. He has prepared public policy reports on, among other things, Nanotechnology, workforce development, California's foreign trade policy, Bioindustry and various aspects of biotechnology, small manufacturing, business networks, and California economic development. He received a Small Business Administration Vision 2000 award for his research on early-stage venture capital investment. He has written over 100 academic articles and studies, and has presented numerous papers and made speeches to various government, academic and private sector organizations. He has given testimony on many occasions to policy committees of the California State Legislature.

Daniel Kudenko is a lecturer in Computer Science at the University of York, UK. His research areas are machine learning (specifically reinforcement learning), AI for interactive entertainment, multi-agent systems and user modeling. Dr. Kudenko received a Ph.D. in machine learning in 1998 at Rutgers University, NJ. He has participated in several research projects at the University of York, Rutgers University, AT&T Laboratories, and the German Research Center for AI (DFKI) on various topics in artificial intelligence. Dr. Kudenko's work has been published in more than 70 peer-reviewed papers. He has served on multiple program committees and has been chairing a number of workshops, as well as co-edited three Springer LNCS volumes.

Andrea Kulakov is Assiatant Professor of Computer Science at the faculty of Electrical Engineering of the "SS Cyril and Methodius" University in Skopje, Macedonia, where both his BSc (1995) and PhD (2006) degrees are from. His MSc degree is in Cognitive Science and is from the New Bulgarian University, Sofia, Bulgaria (1998). He was a researcher in the project "Enactivist representations of environments in natural and artificial agents" (2001-2003), a senior researcher in the project "Modeling of learning in intelligent robots by applying the theories of dynamic systems and the interactivism" (2005-2008), both financed by the Ministry of Education and Science of the Republic of Macedonia. Currently he is also working on an EU FP6 project XPERO – Robotic learning by experimentation (2006-2009), as a principal investigator on the subcontractor side. He has more than 30 research papers presented on international conferences or published in international journals on Computer Science. His research interests include cognitive robotics, multi-robot cooperation, data-mining, and multimedia processing. In 2008 he has established an information technology company NI TEKNA – Intelligent Technologies.

Joona Laukkanen is a master student at Tampere University in Finland, currently working full time at the American University of Paris on the EU funded project XPERO: Learning by experimentation. Besides robotics and artificial intelligence his interests lie in Computer-Human Interaction, especially in new interaction techniques.

Rongxin Li is currently a Senior Research Scientist in the Information Engineering Laboratory of the Information and Communication Technologies Centre (ICT Centre), the Commonwealth Scientific and Industrial Research Organisation (CSIRO) of Australia. His background is in computer science and electrical engineering. He holds a Ph.D. degree in computer science from the Australian National University. He has conducted research in the areas of multi-objective optimisation, distributed and adaptive control, multi-agent systems, image segmentation, linear feature extraction, pattern recognition and visual perception. In each of these areas Rongxin has developed original algorithms that have been applied to a wide range of applications, including optimal energy distribution for minimising peak demand and the impact of price volatility, the management of renewable energy production and storage, automatic cancer screening, three-dimensional image-based surgery planning and radiation dosimetry estimation. His current research interests include distributed multi-objective optimisation, adaptive systems, statistical machine learning, image analysis and understanding, pattern discovery and recognition, and visual programming.

Mei Yii Lim was born in Malaysia. She did her Diploma, followed by Advanced Diploma in Computer Science at Tunku Abdul Rahman College, Malaysia from 1998 to 2002. At the same time, she pursued a BSc in Computer Science (major in Computer Science and Mathematics) from University of Campbell, North Carolina, USA and graduated in June 2002 with Summa Cum Laude. She was the winner of Wallace Ewart Prize for Computer Science and the Dwight Lamar Norwood prize for Mathematics. Later she received a MSc with distinction in Virtual Environments from University of Salford, UK in July 2004. In summer 2007, she completed a Ph.D. in Computing entitled Emotions, Behaviour and Belief Regulation in An Intelligent Guide with Attitude from Heriot-Watt University, Scotland. Currently, she is a research associate for the EU FP6 project eCircus. Her research is focused on Emotional Models, Emotional Memories, Emotional Virtual Agents, Narrative and Mobile Technologies.

Blerim Mustafa is a PhD student at the Faculty of Electrical Engineering of "SS Cyril and Methodius" University in Skopje, Macedonia, where he got his MSc degree in Computer Science in 2003.

Lin Padgham is Professor of Artificial Intelligence in the School of Computer Science and I.T. at RMIT University, Melbourne, Australia. She has a PhD from University of Linkoping, Sweden, 1989. Lin's research interests are in various aspects of commonsense reasoning with an emphasis on formal methods for knowledge representation which are coupled with computationally realisable algorithms. Lin's current research is in the area of intelligent multi-agent systems, focusing on modeling, building and understanding intelligent agents for complex application areas requiring a balance between goal directed long-term behaviour and reactive response to a dynamic environment. She has investigated various extensions to standard 'Belief Desire Intention' (BDI) reasoning, including planning, goal conflicts, and learning. Lin has been Program Chair for AAMAS 2008, is on the Editorial Board of the Journal for Autonomous Multi Agent Systems, and regularly serves on the Program Committee for major international conferences such as KR, IJCAI and ECAI.

Gergely Palla has received his PhD in 2002 at the Eötvös University, the topic of his thesis involved quantum chaos, semiclassical approximation and mesoscopic systems. From 2003 he worked in the research group at the Biological Physics Department (formerly the Biological Physics Research Group, at present the Statistical and Biological Physics Research Group). His main field of interest concerns complex networks, with a special focus on topological phase transitions, community finding (also called as network clustering), the time evolution of communities and the studies of tagged networks. During his scientific carrier he received the following prizes:Young Scientist Prize of the Hung. Acad. of Sci. (2006), Bolyai Scholarship (2008), Imre Bródi Award (2009) and Junior Prima Award (2009).

David M.S. Rodrigues was born in Viana do Castelo in the north of Portugal and has a degree in Chemical Engineering at IST, Lisbon and a MSc. in Complexity Sciences at ISCTE-IUL, Lisbon. He is presently a researcher in Complexity Sciences Doctoral Program at ISCTE-IUL and is interested in networks dynamics, synchronization phenomena, symmetry, community detection, cellular automata and emergence. He is presently member of the EU funded ASSYST (Action for the Science of complex SYstems and Socially intelligent icT – http://assystcomplexity.eu) and The Observatorium (http://theobservatorium.eu/) projects, and participated in the past in several national and European research projects (description online at www.davidrodrigues.org). He was a member of the European Conference on Complex Systems 2010 organizing committee (http://www.eccs2010.eu/) and the Chair of the Young Researchers Session at ECCS'10 satellite meeting (http://phd.eccs2010.eu). His contact email is david@sixhat.net

Jorge A. Romero has a PhD in Management Science and also holds an MBA from The University of Texas at Dallas. He has expertise in market measures of firm performance, and accounting information systems. He currently works as Assistant Professor in the Accounting Department at Towson University. Also, he has industry experience in the United States and Latin America.

Sebastian Sardina received his BSc from Universidad Nacional del Sur, Argentina, in 1997, and his MSc and PhD from the University of Toronto, Canada, in 2000 and 2005, respectively. Since 2005, Sebastian is Postdoctoral Fellow within the Artificial Intelligence Agents Group in the School of Computer Science and Information Technology at RMIT University, Melbourne, Australia. Sebastian's research interests include intelligent multi-agent systems, reasoning about action and change, Cognitive Robotics, planning, and knowledge representation and reasoning in general. Lately, he has been working most on introducing planning capabilities into BDI agents and automatically synthesizing controllers for behavior composition. Sebastian has recently co-organized workshops within the areas of agents and knowledge representation, and regularly serves on the Program Committee for major international conferences such as IJCAI, AAAI and KR.

Sandip Sen is a Professor of Computer Science in the University of Tulsa with primary research interests in multiagent systems, machine learning, and genetic algorithms. He completed his PhD in the area of intelligent, distributed scheduling from the University of Michigan in December, 1993. He has authored approximately 200 papers in workshops, conferences, and journals in several areas of artificial intelligence. In 1997 he received the prestigious CAREER award given to outstanding young faculty by the National Science Foundation. He has served on the program committees of most major national and international conferences in the field of intelligent agents including AAAI, IJCAI, ICMAS, AA, AAMAS, ICGA, etc. He was the co-chair of the Program Committee of the 5th International Conference on Autonomous Agents held in Montreal Canada in 2001. He regularly reviews papers for major AI journals and serves on the panels of the National Science Foundation for evaluating agent systems related projects. He has chaired multiple workshops and symposia on agent learning and reasoning. He has presented several tutorials on multiagent systems in association with the leading international conferences on autonomous agents and multiagent systems.

Georgi Stojanov received his master's degree in 1993 and his PhD degree in Computer Science from the Faculty of Electrical Engineering, Sts Cyril and Methodius University in Skopje, Macedonia in 1997. During his graduate studies he held posts of research and teaching assistant at the University in Skopje. He spent one year (1999-2000) as a research post-doctoral fellow in the Laboratory for Human-Computer Interaction at the University in Trieste, Italy. In 2000 he founded the Cognitive Robotics Group at the Faculty of Electrical Engineering in Skopje. In 2001 he was appointed as Associate Professor at the same faculty. He is the president and a founding member of SVEST a Macedonia based NGO dealing with the impact of modern technologies. In 2004 he was a visiting scholar at Les Archives Jean Piaget in Geneva, and visiting researcher at Université de Versailles-Saint-Quentin-en-Yvelines, Paris, France. Currently, he is teaching at the American University of Paris. In 2003 Dr Stojanov and his team completed the national project "Enactivist Environment Representation in Human and Artificial Agents". He was also the main investigator in the international project "Evolving concepts in humans inhabiting simple virtual environments – a dynamic system approach" financed by US Academies Office of Central Europe and Euroasia (2004-2005), in collaboration with Towson University, and the University of California, San Diego, USA. Dr Stojanov is in the organizing or program committees in the annual Epigenetic Robotics conference and the biannual Interactivist Summer Institute.

Tamas Vicsek is a Professor of Physics at the Biological Physics Department of Eötvös University and a head of the Statistical and Biological Physics research group of the Hungarian Academy of Sciences. Over the past 25 years he has been involved in doing computational and experimental research on fractals, pattern formation, granular materials, collective motion (bacterial colonies, tissue cells in culture, flocks, crowds, etc), and the structure and evolution of complex networks. He received his PhD degree in physics at Kossuth University and has had visiting positions at various research institutes and universities, including Emory University, Yale University and the University of Notre Dame. Tamas Vicsek is a fellow of the APS and a member of Academiae Europaea and the Hungarian Acad.Sci. He has authored/co-authored 165 papers in refereed journals, published further conference proceedings papers and book chapters and authored/edited five books about the above topics.

Giovanni Vincenti is in charge of Research and Development at Gruppo Vincenti, a family-owned company with interests across several fields. His main areas of research include Fuzzy Mediation, Information Fusion, Emotionally-Aware Agent Frameworks and Robotics. He held several positions at Towson University, including a Lecturership with the Department of Computer and Information Sciences. He also taught courses for the Center of Applied Information Technology, also at Towson University. He is the author of many publications, and the father of the concept of Fuzzy Mediation, as applied to the field of Information Fusion.

Scott Watson graduated from the University of Lincoln (UK) in 2000 with a degree in Psychology, and from the University of Hertfordshire (UK) with a MSc in Research Methodology for Psychology. He taught personality, statistics, and research methods in the School of Psychology at the University of Hertfordshire for three years. In 2005 he became a Research Assistant on the EU Framework 6 project e-CIRCUS (Education through Characters with emotional-Intelligence and Role-playing Capabilities that Understand Social interaction). He is responsible for the administration of a large-scale longitudinal evaluation of the FearNot! anti-bullying software, and analysis and publication of data from these evaluations. He is also investigating the efficacy of a computational model of autobiographic memory, developed alongside Dr. Wan Ching Ho. His professional interests are personality theory, human-computer/robot interaction, and the development of ecologically valid models of artificial intelligence. Moreover, he enjoys applying rigorous psychological principles to the HCI/HRI field.

J. Heather Welzant is the Director, Quality Assurance in the Division of Institutional Oversight and Academic Integrity for Laureate Higher Education Group (LHEG). She is responsible for creating, implementing, and sustaining quality assurance processes among all LHEG institutions to ensure maximum student learning and delivery of high quality programs. In a previous role at Laureate, Dr. Welzant was Director, Program Design for interdisciplinary products within Product Strategy and Development. In that role, she was responsible for program development for multiple institutions within the Laureate network, but primarily provided strategic oversight into the development of 36 Walden University's online General Education courses, Walden's online Interdisciplinary Doctoral Research Courses, and a B.S. in Interdisciplinary Studies. Before Laureate, she worked for the University of Phoenix Online in faculty development and as an online instructor. Dr. Welzant earned her PhD in Education with a specialization in Training and Performance Improvement from Capella University. Her area of focus was student performance improvement relevant to the learner experience in online problem-based learning courses. Dr. Welzant may be reached at heather.welzant@laureate.net.

Carsten Zoll works as a research fellow at the department for general psychology at the University of Bamberg. He studied psychology and computer science. Before joining the department for general psychology, he worked at the professorship for economic and social psychology at the Technical University of Chemnitz. In his dissertation he dealt with decision making among experts of the financial markets. His scientific work focuses on simulation of humanlike behaviour, modelling the human mind, empathy, decision making and behavioral finance. Apart from his academic career, he works as a child psychologist in both a medical office doing diagnostics and psychotherapy and for the family courthouse as an expert witness.

Index

Symbols

2D environments 133

A

active agents 19, 20
adaptive networks 72
adult learning 294
agent clustering 22
Agent Learning Framework (ALF) 134, 138
agent societies 168, 169
AIDS 2
air transport 9
algebraic connectivity 71, 75
anthropomorphic toolsets 133
artificial intelligence (AI) 118, 122, 125, 126,
    129, 130, 308
artificial spaces 153
asymptotic performance 96, 105, 108, 110,
    111, 112
ATM 267
autobiographic memory 307, 309, 310, 311,
    312, 313, 314, 315, 316, 317, 318, 319,
    320, 322, 324
automated vivification variance ratio 31
autonomous agents 1
autonomous robots 116
avatars 165

B

Bayesian tests 277
Behavioural level 313
Belief, Desire, and Intentions (BDI) agents 78,
    79, 80, 83, 87, 91, 92, 94

Belief, Desire, and Intentions (BDI)-based
    agent designs 79
Belief, Desire, and Intentions (BDI) failure
    recovery 82, 83, 89
Belief, Desire, and Intentions (BDI) program-
    mers 78, 79, 87, 91
Belief, Desire, and Intentions (BDI)-style
    agents 79, 80
Belief, Desire, and Intentions (BDI) systems
    80, 81, 86, 91
belief populations 23, 33
Big Five model 311, 313, 314, 316, 324
biology 273, 274
biotemporality 7, 8, 12
black box 293, 301, 304
bottom up learning (BUL) 85, 86, 88, 89, 90,
    91
broker agents 199, 201, 202, 203, 204, 205,
    207, 208, 209, 210, 211
brokers 213
Buddhist cosmology 1
Buddhists 1, 13, 14, 16, 17, 18

C

cap function 202, 203
case-based reasoning systems 213, 230, 241
chat rooms 154
children nodes 81
Clauset-Newman-Moore algorithm (CNM)
    275
Clique Percolation Method (CPM) 39, 40, 41,
    42, 44, 45, 46, 47
cliques 38, 40, 41, 51
closed-loop systems 209
co-authorship data records 43

Copyright © 2011, IGI Global. Copying or distributing in print or electronic forms without written permission of IGI Global is prohibited.